Lecture Notes in Artificial Intelligence   1398

Subseries of Lecture Notes in Computer Science
Edited by J. G. Carbonell and J. Siekmann

Lecture Notes in Computer Science

Edited by G. Goos, J. Hartmanis and J. van Leeuwen

Springer
Berlin
Heidelberg
New York
Barcelona
Budapest
Hong Kong
London
Milan
Paris
Santa Clara
Singapore
Tokyo

Claire Nédellec   Céline Rouveirol (Eds.)

Machine Learning: ECML-98

10th European Conference on Machine Learning
Chemnitz, Germany, April 21-23, 1998
Proceedings

Springer

Series Editors
Jaime G. Carbonell, Carnegie Mellon University, Pittsburgh, PA, USA
Jörg Siekmann, University of Saarland, Saarbrücken, Germany

Volume Editors

Claire Nédellec
Céline Rouveirol
Laboratoire de Recherche en Informatique
Unité de Recherche Associée 410 du CNRS
Bât. 490, Université Paris-Sud, F-91405 Orsay, France
E-mail: {cn,celine}@lri.fr

Cataloging-in-Publication Data applied for

Die Deutsche Bibliothek - CIP-Einheitsaufnahme

Machine learning : proceedings / ECML-98, 9th European
Conference on Machine Learning, Chemnitz, Germany, April 1998.
Claire Nédellec ; Céline Rouveirol (ed.). - Berlin ; Heidelberg ; New
York ; Barcelona ; Budapest ; Hong Kong ; London ; Milan ; Paris ;
Santa Clara ; Singapore ; Tokyo : Springer, 1998
    (Lecture notes in computer science ; Vol. 1398 : Lecture notes in
    artificial intelligence)
    ISBN 3-540-64417-2

CR Subject Classification (1991): I.2, F.2.2

ISSN 0302-9743
ISBN 3-540-64417-2 Springer-Verlag Berlin Heidelberg New York

© Springer-Verlag Berlin Heidelberg 1998
Printed in Germany

Typesetting: Camera ready by author
SPIN 10637011   06/3142 – 5 4 3 2 1 0   Printed on acid-free paper

Foreword

The Tenth European Conference on Machine Learning (ECML-98), held in Chemnitz, Germany, April 21 - 23, 1998 continues the tradition of earlier EWSL (European Working Session on Learning) and ECML conferences, being the major European scientific forum for presenting the latest advances in Machine Learning research.

The scientific program of ECML-98 consists of two invited talks by Kenneth De Jong and David D. Lewis, plenary paper presentations, and one-day workshops.

This volume contains the papers relating the invited talks and the papers presented at the conference. There are two kinds of papers: full papers (12 pages in the proceedings) and research notes (6 pages). The selection of papers was based on at least two reviews per submission. Among 100 papers submitted to ECML'98, 46 were accepted for publication and presentation (21 as full papers and 25 as research notes). The proceedings of the workshops appear as technical reports of the Department of Computer Science in Chemnitz.

We first wish to thank all the authors for submitting their papers and thus making this conference possible. We address special thanks to the members of the program committee and reviewers for their great work which contributed to the high quality of these proceedings. We wish to extend our gratitude to the invited speakers for presenting us their views on innovative fields of Machine Learning.

ECML'98 was organized by the AI Group at Chemnitz University of Technology, Dept. of Computer Science supported by FIRST Business Travel International, Chemnitz. Our gratitude goes to all members of the Organizing Committee, and all other individuals who helped in the organization of the conference. We would like to acknowledge all the sponsors of the ECML'98 for supporting this scientific event.

February 1998   Claire Nédellec
Orsay   Céline Rouveirol

Program Chairs

Claire Nédellec, Céline Rouveirol, LRI, Université Paris-Sud, France

Local Chair

Werner Dilger, Chemnitz University of Technology, Germany

Organizing Institutions

Chemnitz University of Technology, Dept. of Computer Science, AI Group
FIRST Business Travel International, Chemnitz

Organizing Committee

Werner Dilger, Andreas Ittner, Michael Schlosser, Jens Zeidler

Sponsors

Daimler-Benz AG
Chemnitz University of Technology
FIRST Business Travel International, Chemnitz
DORINT Parkhotel, Chemnitz
Parsytec, Chemnitz
City of Chemnitz
Chemnitzer Wirtschaftsförderungs- und Entwicklungsgesellschaft mbH
Prudential Systems, Knowledge Discovery and Data Mining, Chemnitz
LRI, Université Paris-Sud

Program Committee

Agnar Aamodt (Norway)
David W. Aha (USA)
Francesco Bergadano (Italy)
Ivan Bratko (Slovenia)
Pavel Brazdil (Portugal)
Walter Daelemans (Netherlands)
Luc De Raedt (Belgium)
Marco Dorigo (Belgium)
Floriana Esposito (Italy)
Terry Fogarty (UK)
Johannes Fuernkranz (Austria)
Yves Kodratoff (France)

Nada Lavrač (Slovenia)
Ramon Lopez de Mantaras (Spain)
Stan Matwin (Canada)
Katharina Morik (Germany)
G. Nakhaeizadeh (Germany)
David Page (USA)
Lorenza Saitta (Italy)
Derek Sleeman (UK)
Maarten Van Someren (Netherlands)
Paul Vitányi (Netherlands)
Stefan Wrobel (Germany)
Gerhard Widmer (Austria)

Additional Referees

Gilles Bisson
Antal van den Bosch
Andrea Bonarini
Gianluca Bontempi
Peter Brockhausen
Oliver Buechter
Rui Camacho
Pawel Cichosz
Antoine Cornuéjols
Vincent Corruble
Florence Dalche
Keith Downing
Gert Durieux
Sašo Džeroski
Stefano Ferilli
Bogdan Filipič
João Gama
Matjaz Gams
Frederic Garcia

Daniele Gunetti
Arvid Holme
Thorsten Joachims
Alipio Jorge
Hermann von Hasseln
Tamas Horvath
Jörg-Uwe Kietz
Mathias Kirsten
Volker Klingspor
Igor Kononenko
Stefan Kramer
Matjaz Kukar
Carster Lanquillon
Donato Malerba
Joel Martin
Fraser Mitchell
Marjorie Moulet
Paul Munteanu
S.M. Ndiaye

Maria Teresa Pazienza
Hervé Perdrix
Bernhard Pfahringer
Enric Plaza
Caroline Ravise
Riverson Rios
Ursula Robers
Marko Robnik Šikonja
Giancarlo Ruffo
Marc Schoenauer
Michèle Sebag
Dorian Suc
Luís Torgo
Rafal Salustowicz
Giovanni Semeraro
Gilles Venturini
Marco Wiering
Jakub Zavrel
Jieyu Zhao

Table of Contents

Invited Papers

Regular Papers

Applications of ML

Bayesian Networks

Inductive Logic Programming

Relational Learning

Instance Based Learning

Clustering

Part I

Invited Papers

Learning in Agent-Oriented Worlds

Kenneth De Jong

Computer Science Department
George Mason University
Fairfax, VA 22030
kdejong@gmu.edu

Abstract. There is an increasing level of interest in designing and implementing intelligent agents capable of surviving, performing tasks, and adapting to complex and dynamic environments. These agent-oriented worlds can range from autonomous underwater surveillance vehicles to web-based softbots, and present a variety of challenges and opportunities for machine learning. The complexity and variety of these worlds suggests the need for approaches involving learning at multiple levels and integrating more than one learning methodology.

A framework for describing such approaches has been developed and will be presented. Examples of the use of this framework to design agents using both symbolic and non-symbolic learning methods will be given, and will serve as the basis of a discussion of interesting open issues.

Naive (Bayes) at Forty: The Independence Assumption in Information Retrieval

David D. Lewis

AT&T Labs — Research
180 Park Avenue
Florham Park, NJ 07932-0971 USA
lewis@research.att.com
http://www.research.att.com/~lewis

Abstract. The naive Bayes classifier, currently experiencing a renaissance in machine learning, has long been a core technique in information retrieval. We review some of the variations of naive Bayes models used for text retrieval and classification, focusing on the distributional assumptions made about word occurrences in documents.

1 Introduction

The naive Bayes classifier, long a favorite punching bag of new classification techniques, has recently emerged as a focus of research itself in machine learning. Machine learning researchers tend to be aware of the large pattern recognition literature on naive Bayes, but may be less aware of an equally large information retrieval (IR) literature dating back almost forty years [37, 38]. In fact, naive Bayes methods, along with prototype formation methods [44, 45, 24], accounted for most applications of supervised learning to information retrieval until quite recently.

In this paper we briefly review the naive Bayes classifier and its use in information retrieval. We concentrate on the particular issues that arise in applying the model to textual data, and provide pointers to the relevant IR and computational linguistics literature. We end with a few thoughts on interesting research directions for naive Bayes at the intersection of machine learning and information retrieval.

2 The Naive Bayes Classifier

A widely used framework for classification is provided by a simple theorem of probability [10, Sec 2.1] known as *Bayes' rule*, *Bayes' theorem*, or *Bayes' formula*:

$$P(C = c_k | \mathbf{X} = \mathbf{x}) = P(C = c_k) \times \frac{P(\mathbf{X} = \mathbf{x} | C = c_k)}{P(\mathbf{x})} \tag{1}$$

where

$$P(\mathbf{X} = \mathbf{x}) = \sum_{k'=1}^{e_C} P(\mathbf{X} = \mathbf{x} | C = c_{k'}) \times P(C = c_{k'}) \tag{2}$$

We assume here that all possible events (in our case, documents) fall into exactly one of e_C classes, $(c_1, \ldots, c_k, \ldots, c_{e_C})$. C is a random variable whose values are those classes, while $\mathbf{X}$ is a vector random variable whose values are vectors of feature values $\mathbf{x} = (x_1, \ldots, x_j, \ldots, x_d)$, one vector for each document. (Except where stated, we will assume that $\mathbf{x}$ has the same length, d, for each document.) $P(C = c_k | \mathbf{X} = \mathbf{x})$ is the conditional probability that a document belongs to class c_k, given that we know it has feature vector $\mathbf{x}$. Bayes' rule specifies how this conditional probability can be computed from the conditional probabilities of seeing particular vectors of feature values for documents of each class, and the unconditional probability of seeing a document of each class.

Having made clear that c_k and $\mathbf{x}$ are values taken on by random variables C and $\mathbf{X}$ we simplify notation by omitting those random variables and instead writing Bayes' rule as:

$$P(c_k | \mathbf{x}) = P(c_k) \times \frac{P(\mathbf{x} | c_k)}{P(\mathbf{x})} \tag{3}$$

When we know the $P(c_k | \mathbf{x})$ exactly for a classification problem, classification can be done in an optimal way for a wide variety of effectiveness measures [10, 31]. For instance, the expected number of classification errors can be minimized by assigning a document with feature vector $\mathbf{x}$ to the class c_k for which $P(c_k | \mathbf{x})$ is highest.

We of course do not know the $P(c_k | \mathbf{x})$ and must estimate them from data, which is difficult to do directly. Bayes' rule suggests instead estimating $P(\mathbf{x} | c_k)$, $P(c_k)$, and $P(\mathbf{x})$, and then combining those estimates to get an estimate of $P(c_k | \mathbf{x})$. However, even estimating the $P(\mathbf{x} | c_k)$ poses problems, since there are usually an astronomical number of possible values for $\mathbf{x} = (x_1, \ldots, x_j, \ldots, x_d)$. A common strategy is to assume that the distribution of $\mathbf{x}$ conditional on c_k can be decomposed in this fashion for all c_k:

$$P(\mathbf{x} | c_k) = \prod_{j=1}^{d} P(x_j | c_k) \tag{4}$$

The assumption here is that the occurrence of a particular value of x_j is statistically independent of the occurrence of any other $x_{j'}$, given that we have a document of type c_k. The advantage of making this assumption is that we typically can model the $P(x_j | c_k)$ with relatively few parameters.

If we assume Equation 4, then Equation 3 becomes:

$$P(c_k | \mathbf{x}) = P(c_k) \times \frac{\prod_{j=1}^{d} P(x_j | c_k)}{P(\mathbf{x})} \tag{5}$$

where we now have

$$P(\mathbf{x}) = \sum_{k'=1}^{e_C} P(c_{k'}) \times \prod_{j'=1}^{d} P(x_{j'}|c_{k'}). \tag{6}$$

If we plug in estimates (indicated by carats) for the values on the right hand side, we get an estimate for $P(c_k|\mathbf{x})$:

$$\widehat{P(c_k|\mathbf{x})} = \frac{\widehat{P(c_k)} \times \prod_{j=1}^{d} \widehat{P(x_j|c_k)}}{\widehat{P(\mathbf{x})}} \tag{7}$$

This estimate can then be used for classification. If the goal of classification is to minimize number of errors, then we can assign a document with feature vector $\mathbf{x}$ to the c_k such that $\widehat{P(c_k|\mathbf{x})}$ is highest. A classifier which operates in this fashion is sometimes known as a *naive Bayes classifier*. Typically the denominator in Equation 7 is not explicitly computed for minimum-error classification, since it is the same for all c_k. Instead the maximum value of the numerator is found as used to make a classification decision.

Indeed, classification will be accurate as long as the correct class has the highest value of $\widehat{P(c_k)} \times \prod_{j=1}^{d} \widehat{P(x_j|c_k)}$, regardless of whether that is a good estimate of $P(c_k|\mathbf{x})$ (Section 6).

3 Text Representation

Before discussing the classification of documents using naive Bayes, we must say a bit about what a document is, and how it is represented. A document is typically stored as a sequence of characters, with characters representing the text of a written natural language expression.[1] Information retrieval has developed a variety of methods for transforming the character string representing a document into a form more amenable to statistical classification. These methods are analogous to, if less complex than, the feature extraction methods used in speech recognition, image processing, and related disciplines.

A wide variety of statistical, linguistic, and knowledge-based techniques, involving various amounts of machine and/or manual processing, have been used to produce representations of text for information retrieval systems ([12, Chs. 7-9], [28, Ch. 5], [29, Chs. 3-6] [46, Ch. 3], [51, Chs. 2-3]). An ongoing surprise and disappointment is that structurally simple representations produced without linguistic or domain knowledge have been as effective as any others [30, 33]. We therefore make the common assumption that the preprocessing of the document produces a bag (multiset) of *index terms* which do not themselves have internal structure. This representation is sometimes called the *bag of words* model. For the purposes of our discussion, it does not matter whether the index terms

---

[1] More generally a document may have various components (title, body, sections, etc.) which are, for the most part, pieces of text. We will concentrate here on the simplest case, where the document is a single piece of text.

are actually words, or instead character n-grams, morphemes, word stems, word n-grams, or any of a number of similar text representations.

4 The Binary Independence Model

Having reduced the richness of language to a bag of symbols, information retrieval commonly goes even farther. Suppose we have a collection of documents and associate a binary feature x_j with each of the d unique words we observe in the collection. The feature will equal 1 if the corresponding word occurs in the document, and 0 otherwise. The full document representation then is $\mathbf{x} = (x_1, \ldots, x_j, \ldots, x_d)$, where all x_j are 0 or 1.

If we make the naive Bayes assumption of conditional independence of feature values given class membership, then the conditional probability of observing feature vector $\mathbf{x}$ for a document of class c_k is given by Equation 5. However, the combination of binary features with the conditional independence assumption allows an even simpler expression for the posterior probability. Note that:

$$P(x_j|c_k) = p_{jk}^{x_j}(1 - p_{jk})^{1-x_j} \tag{8}$$

$$= \left(\frac{p_{jk}}{1 - p_{jk}}\right)^{x_j}(1 - p_{jk}) \tag{9}$$

where $p_{jk} = P(x_j = 1|c_k)$. Using this fact in combination with Equation 5 and some rearranging of terms[2] we get:

$$\log P(c_k|\mathbf{x}) = \log P(c_k) + \sum_{j=1}^{d} x_j \log \frac{p_{jk}}{1 - p_{jk}} + \sum_{j=1}^{d} \log(1 - p_{jk}) - \log P(\mathbf{x}) \tag{10}$$

for each c_k. Except for $\log P(\mathbf{x})$, this has the convenient property of being a linear function of the feature values. In many uses of naive Bayes, however, we care only which $P(c_k|\mathbf{x})$ (or $\log P(c_k|\mathbf{x})$) is largest, not their exact values. In that case, we can drop the $\log P(\mathbf{x})$, since it is the same for all c_k.

It is common in information retrieval that we have only two classes between which we wish to discriminate. In text retrieval, we want to separate those documents relevant to a user of a search engine from those not relevant. In text categorization we often need to decide only whether a document should be assigned to a particular subject category or not. In the two class case, we have $P(c_2|\mathbf{x}) = 1 - P(c_1|\mathbf{x})$, so that with some arithmetic manipulations we can replace the two functions that Equation 10 would give for the two-class case with a single function [10, Sec. 2.10]:

---

[2] See [39, Sec. 12.4.3] or [10, Sec. 2.10], though in their derivations $P(\mathbf{x})$ has already been dropped.

$$\log \frac{P(c_1|\mathbf{x})}{1 - P(c_1|\mathbf{x})} = \sum_{j=1}^{d} x_j \log \frac{p_{j1}(1 - p_{j2})}{(1 - p_{j1})p_{j2}} + \sum_{j=1}^{d} \log \frac{1 - p_{j1}}{1 - p_{j2}} + \log \frac{P(c_1)}{1 - P(c_1)}. \quad (11)$$

Equation 11 has several properties that make it particularly convenient. First, we observe that $\log \frac{P(c_1|\mathbf{x})}{1-P(c_1|\mathbf{x})}$ is monotonic with (and if necessary can be used to compute) $P(c_1|\mathbf{x})$. It therefore suffices for any purpose which we might use $P(c_1|\mathbf{x})$ for. Second, the equation is truly linear in the x_j (since $P(\mathbf{x})$ disappears completely in the two-class case), and has only $d+1$ parameters to estimate and store.

A further advantage in the context of information retrieval is that Equation 11 requires *presence weights* only. That is, if one sets the initial score of a document to be the constant term in Equation 11, the full score can be computed by adding up values involving only those words present in a document, not those absent from the document [41, 48]. Since most words do not occur in most documents, this is desirable from the standpoint of computational efficiency.

The two-class, binary feature naive Bayes model has come to be known in information retrieval as the *binary independence model*. Its use in the form of Equation 11 was promoted by Robertson and Sparck Jones in a paper [41] that did much to clarify and unify a number of related and partially ad hoc applications of naive Bayes dating back to Maron [37].

Robertson and Sparck Jones' particular interest in the binary independence model was its use in *relevance feedback* [20, 45]. In relevance feedback, a user query is given to a search engine, which produces an initial ranking of its document collection by some means. The user examines the initial top-ranked documents and gives feedback to the system on which are relevant to their interest and which are not. The search engine then applies supervised learning to these judgments to produce a formula that can be used to rerank the documents.

Robertson and Sparck Jones noted that if a system does not need to choose between c_1 and c_2, but only to rank documents in order of $P(c_1|\mathbf{x})$, then the only quantity needed from Equation 11 is:

$$\sum_{j=1}^{d} x_j \log \frac{p_{j1}(1 - p_{j2})}{(1 - p_{j1})p_{j2}}. \quad (12)$$

All other values in Equation 11 are constant across $\mathbf{x}$'s, and so can dropped. the result is still monotonic with $P(c_1|\mathbf{x})$, but does not require an estimate of the prior $P(c_1)$. Such an estimate is difficult to obtain either from users or from the small, nonrandom samples available for training in a relevance feedback context.

4.1 Weaknesses of the BIM

While the BIM has been very influential in information retrieval, it has shortcomings that mean it is now rarely used in the pure form given above. One weakness is that by considering only the presence or absence of terms, the BIM ignores information inherent in the frequencies of terms. For instance, all things being equal, we would expect that if 1 occurrence of a word is a good clue that a document belongs to a class, then 5 occurrences should be even more predictive.

A related problem concerns document length. As a document gets longer, the number of distinct words used, and thus the number of values of x_j that equal 1 in the BIM, will in general increase. Many of these word usages in very long documents will be unrelated to the core content of the document, but are treated as being of the same significance as similar occurrences in short documents. Again, all things being equal, we would expect that 1 occurrence of a good predictor in a short document is a better clue than 1 occurrence of that predictor in a long document.

Ignoring document length can have a particularly bad interaction with feature selection. It is common in IR that one class (let's say c_1) is of much lower frequency than its contrasting class (c_2). The class c_1 might be those documents relevant to a user (vs. the much larger class of nonrelevant documents), or the class of documents on a particular subject (vs. all those not on the subject). Further, it is common that most words have skewed frequencies as well, resulting in binary features that much more often take on a value of 0 than 1. In this situation, typical feature selection measures strongly prefer features correlated with c_1, so that we often have:

$$\log \frac{p_{j1}(1 - p_{j2})}{(1 - p_{j1})p_{j2}} > 0 \qquad (13)$$

for all selected features. Some feature selection measures used in IR in fact explicitly require features to have this property. When all features have this property, increasing document length can only increase the estimate $P(\widehat{c_k}|\mathbf{x})$, regardless of the actual content of the document. While a case can be made that longer documents are somewhat more likely to be of interest to any given user [43,47], the above effect is likely to be far stronger than appropriate.

5 Other Distributional Models

In this section we look at a number of variations on the naive Bayes model that attempt to address the weaknesses of the BIM.

5.1 Distributions for Integer-Valued Features

The most straightforward generalization of the BIM is to let the X_j be integer-valued random variables corresponding to *term frequencies*, that is counts of the number of occurrences of words in a document. The naive Bayes model will still assume the X_j are independently distributed, but now each is modeled by an integer-valued distribution rather than a Bernoulli one.

A variety of statistical distributions for term frequencies have been investigated, some in the context of naive Bayes classifiers and some for other purposes. The distributions investigated have mostly been Poisson mixtures [4, 26]: the Poisson itself [40], mixtures of 2, 3, or more Poissons [1, 2, 22, 23, 36], and the negative binomial (an infinite mixture of Poissons) [40]. The details of the particular models can be complex, sometimes involving latent variables that intervene between the class label and the term frequencies. Rather than attempt to survey the variations here, we refer the reader to the above references, with the suggestion that the book by Mosteller and Wallace [40] is the most clear treatment from a classification standpoint.

Despite considerable study, explicit use of Poisson mixtures for text retrieval have not proven more effective than using the BIM [35, 42]. This failure has been variously blamed on the larger number of parameters these models require estimating, the choice of estimation methods, the difficulty of accounting for document length in these models, and the poor fit of the models to actual term frequencies. In contrast, a recently proposed term weighting formula which rescales the BIM weight to in some ways approximate the behavior of a two-Poisson model has proven quite successful [43]. It should be noted, however, that most studies of Poisson mixtures (Mosteller and Wallace being an exception) have been applications to text retrieval rather than routing or categorization (where more training data is available), and/or have focused on unsupervised fitting of Poisson mixtures rather than supervised learning with a naive Bayes model.

5.2 Multinomial Models

An alternative approach to modeling term frequencies is to treat the bag of words for a length f document as resulting from f draws on a d-valued multinomial variable $\mathbf{X}$, rather than as a single draw on a vector-valued variable of length d [15]. The naive Bayes assumption then is that the draws on $\mathbf{X}$ are independent— each word of the document is generated independently from every other.

A multinomial model has the advantage that document length is accounted for very naturally in the model. The corresponding disadvantage is that it assumes independence not just between different words, but between multiple occurrences of the same word, an assumption which is strikingly violated for real data [4]. A multinomial therefore assigns extreme posterior log odds to long documents, and would presumedly be very poor for the purpose of ranking documents in a search engine. The problem is somewhat less extreme for classification tasks, where we can in some cases arrange to compare posterior log odds of classes for each document individually, without comparisons across documents. Indeed, we know of many applications of multinomial models to text categorization [3, 14, 15, 25, 32, 34] but none to text retrieval.

5.3 Non-Distributional Approaches

A variety of ad hoc approaches have been developed that more or less gracefully integrate term frequency and document length information into the BIM itself. The widely used *probabilistic indexing* approach assumes there is an ideal binary indexing of the document, for which the observed index term occurrences provide evidence [7, 13]. Retrieval or classification is based on computing (or approximating) the expected value of the posterior log odds. The expectation is taken with respect to the probabilities of various ideal indexings. While this is a plausible approach, in practice the probabilities of the ideal indexings are computed by ad hoc functions of term frequency, document length, and other quantities, making these models not truly distributional.

Another approach is to fit a distributional but nonparametric model (for instance a linear regression) to predict the probability that a given term frequency will be observed in a document of a particular length [53]. Such nonparametric approaches have been relatively rare in IR, and it appears that the sophisticated discretization and kernel based approaches investigated in machine learning have not been tried.

6 Violated Assumptions and the Success of Naive Bayes

As has often been observed, the independence assumptions on which naive Bayes classifiers are based almost never hold for natural data sets, and certainly not for textual data. This contradiction has motivated three kinds of research in both information retrieval and machine learning: 1) attempts to produce better classifiers by relaxing the independence assumption, 2) modifications of feature sets to make the independence assumption more true, and 3) attempts to explain why the independence assumption isn't really needed anyway.

Whatever its successes in machine learning, the first strategy has not met with great success in IR. While interesting research on dependence models has been done [8, 11, 21, 49, 50], these models are rarely used in practice. Even most work in the "inference net" approach to information retrieval has mostly used independence (or ad hoc) models.

Results from the second strategy are hard to judge. A variety of text representation strategies which tend to reduce independence violations have been pursued in information retrieval, including stemming, unsupervised term clustering, downcasing of text, phrase formation, and feature selection. However, these strategies have usually been pursued for reasons besides reducing feature dependence, and so there has been little attempt to correlate their actual impact on dependence with any effectiveness changes they yield. Further, the nature of this impact is more complex than might be guessed, even for very simple techniques [4]. In any case, the effectiveness improvements yielded by these strategies have been small (with the possible selection of feature selection).

IR's representative of the third strategy is Cooper [6], who points out that in the case of a two-class naive Bayes model, the usual independence assumptions (Equation 4) can be replaced by a weaker "linked dependence" assumption:

$$\frac{P(\mathbf{x}|c_1)}{P(\mathbf{x}|c_2)} = \prod_{j=1}^{d} \frac{P(x_j|c_1)}{P(x_j|c_2)} \tag{14}$$

In machine learning, considerable theoretical and experimental evidence has been developed that a training procedure based on the naive Bayes assumptions can yield an optimal classifier in a variety of situations where the assumptions are wildly violated [9].

7 Conclusion

Naive Bayes models have been remarkably successful in information retrieval. In the yearly TREC evaluations [16–19, 52], numerous variations of naive Bayes models have been used, producing some of the best results. Recent comparisons of learning methods for text categorization have been somewhat less favorable to naive Bayes models [5, 25] while still showing them to achieve respectable effectiveness. This may be because the larger amount of training data available in text categorization data sets favors algorithms which produce more complex classifiers [27], or may because the more elaborate representation and estimation tricks developed for retrieval and routing with naive Bayes have not been applied to categorization.

There are many open research questions on the application of naive Bayes in information retrieval. What is a reasonable distributional model taking into account term frequency and document length? Can we state necessary or sufficient conditions for when a naive Bayes model will produce an optimal ranking of documents? What is the optimal strategy for selecting training data for naive Bayes? And, of course, can dependence information actually be used to improve the effectiveness of naive Bayes classifiers? These and other questions will provide great interest for both machine learning and information retrieval in the years to come.

References

1. Abraham Bookstein and Don Kraft. Operations research applied to document indexing and retrieval decisions. *Journal of the Association for Computing Machinery*, 24(3):418–427, 1977.
2. Abraham Bookstein and Don R. Swanson. A decision theoretic foundation for indexing. *Journal of the American Society for Information Science*, pages 45–50, January-February 1975.
3. Soumen Chakrabarti, Byron Dom, Rakesh Agrawal, and Prabhakar Raghavan. Using taxonomy, discriminants, and signatures for navigating in text databases. In Matthias Jarke, Michael Carey, Klaus R. Dittrich, Fred Lochovsky, Pericles Loucopoulos, and Manfred A. Jeusfeld, editors, *Proceedings of the 23rd VLDB Conference*, pages 446–455, 1997.
4. Kenneth Ward Church. One term or two? In Edward A. Fox, Peter Ingwersen, and Raya Fidel, editors, *SIGIR '95: Proceedings of the 18th Annual International ACM SIGIR Conference on Research and Development in Information Retrieval*, pages 310–318, New York, 1995. Association for Computing Machinery.
5. William W. Cohen and Yoram Singer. Context-sensitive learning methods for text categorization. In *SIGIR '96: Proceedings of the 19th Annual International ACM*

SIGIR Conference on Research and Development in Information Retrieval, pages 307–315, 1996.

6. W. S. Cooper. Some inconsistencies and misidentified modeling assumptions in probabilistic information retrieval. *ACM Transactions on Information Systems*, 13(1):100–111, January 1995.

7. W. B. Croft. Experiments with representation in a document retrieval system. *Information Technology: Research and Development*, 2:1–21, 1983.

8. W. Bruce Croft. Boolean queries and term dependencies in probabilistic retrieval models. *Journal of the American Society for Information Science*, 37(2):71–77, 1986.

9. Pedro Domingos and Michael Pazzani. On the optimality of the simple bayesian classifier under zero-one loss. *Machine Learning*, 29(2/3):103–130, November 1997.

10. Richard O. Duda and Peter E. Hart. *Pattern Classification and Scene Analysis*. Wiley-Interscience, New York, 1973.

11. B. Del Favero and R. Fung. Bayesian inference with node aggregation for information retrieval. In D. K. Harman, editor, *The Second Text Retrieval Conference (TREC-2)*, pages 151–162, Gaithersburg, MD, March 1994. U. S. Dept. of Commerce, National Institute of Standards and Technology. NIST Special Publication 500-215.

12. William B. Frakes and Ricardo Baeza-Yates, editors. *Information Retrieval: Data Structures and Algorithms*. Prentice Hall, Englewood Cliffs, NJ, 1992.

13. Norbert Fuhr. Models for retrieval with probabilistic indexing. *Information Processing and Management*, 25(1):55–72, 1989.

14. William A. Gale, Kenneth W. Church, and David Yarowsky. A method for disambiguating word senses in a large corpus. *Computers and the Humanities*, 26:415–439, 1993.

15. Louise Guthrie, Elbert Walker, and Joe Guthrie. Document classification by machine: Theory and practice. In *COLING 94: The 15th International Conference on Computational Linguistics. Proceedings, Vol. II.*, pages 1059–1063, 1994.

16. D. K. Harman, editor. *The First Text REtrieval Conference (TREC-1)*, Gaithersburg, MD 20899, 1993. National Institute of Standards and Technology. Special Publication 500-207.

17. D. K. Harman, editor. *The Second Text REtrieval Conference (TREC-2)*, Gaithersburg, MD 20899, 1994. National Institute of Standards and Technology. Special Publication 500-215.

18. D. K. Harman, editor. *Overview of the Third Text REtrieval Conference (TREC-3)*, Gaithersburg, MD 20899-0001, 1995. National Institute of Standards and Technology. Special Publication 500-225.

19. D. K. Harman, editor. *The Fourth Text REtrieval Conference (TREC-3)*, Gaithersburg, MD 20899-0001, 1996. National Institute of Standards and Technology. Special Publication 500-236.

20. Donna Harman. Relevance feedback and other query modification techniques. In William B. Frakes and Ricardo Baeza-Yates, editors, *Information Retrieval: Data Structures and Algorithms*, pages 241–263. Prentice Hall, Englewood Cliffs, NJ, 1992.

21. D. J. Harper and C. J. van Rijsbergen. An evaluation of feedback in document retrieval using co-occurrence data. *Journal of Documentation*, 34:189–216, 1978.

22. Stephen P. Harter. A probabilistic approach to automatic keyword indexing. Part I. On the distribution of specialty words in a technical literature. *Journal of the American Society for Information Science*, pages 197–206, July-August 1975.

23. Stephen P. Harter. A probabilistic approach to automatic keyword indexing. Part II. An algorithm for probabilistic indexing. *Journal of the American Society for Information Science*, pages 280–289, September-October 1975.

24. David J. Ittner, David D. Lewis, and David D. Ahn. Text categorization of low quality images. In *Symposium on Document Analysis and Information Retrieval*, pages 301–315, Las Vegas, NV, 1995. ISRI; Univ. of Nevada, Las Vegas.

25. Thorsten Joachims. Text categorization with support vector machines: Learning with many relevant features. LS-8 Report 23, University of Dortmund, Computer Science Dept., Dortmund, Germany, 27 November 1997.

26. S. Katz. Distribution of content words and phrases in text and language modelling. *Natural Language Engineering*, 2(1):15–59, March 1996.

27. Ron Kohavi. Scaling up the accuracy of Naive-Bayes classifiers: a decision-tree hybrid. In *Proceedings of the Second International Conference on Knowledge Discovery and Data Mining*, pages 202–207, 1996.

28. Robert R. Korfhage. *Information Storage and Retrieval*. John Wiley, New York, 1997.

29. Gerald Kowalski. *Information Retrieval Systems: Theory and Implementation*. Kluwer, Boston, 1997.

30. David D. Lewis. Text representation for intelligent text retrieval: A classification-oriented view. In Paul S. Jacobs, editor, *Text-Based Intelligent Systems*, pages 179–197. Lawrence Erlbaum, Hillsdale, NJ, 1992.

31. David D. Lewis. Evaluating and optimizing autonomous text classification systems. In Edward A. Fox, Peter Ingwersen, and Raya Fidel, editors, *SIGIR '95: Proceedings of the 18th Annual International ACM SIGIR Conference on Research and Development in Information Retrieval*, pages 246–254, New York, 1995. Association for Computing Machinery.

32. David D. Lewis and William A. Gale. A sequential algorithm for training text classifiers. In W. Bruce Croft and C. J. van Rijsbergen, editors, *SIGIR 94: Proceedings of the Seventeenth Annual International ACM-SIGIR Conference on Research and Development in Information Retrieval*, pages 3–12, London, 1994. Springer-Verlag.

33. David D. Lewis and Karen Sparck Jones. Natural language processing for information retrieval. *Communications of the ACM*, 39(1):92–101, January 1996.

34. Hang Li and Kenji Yamanishi. Document classification using a finite mixture model, 1997.

35. Robert M. Losee. Parameter estimation for probabilistic document-retrieval models. *Journal of the American Society for Information Science*, 39(1):8–16, 1988.

36. E. L. Margulis. Modelling documents with multiple Poisson distributions. *Information Processing and Management*, 29:215–227, 1993.

37. M. E. Maron. Automatic indexing: An experimental inquiry. *Journal of the Association for Computing Machinery*, 8:404–417, 1961.

38. M. E. Maron and J. L. Kuhns. On relevance, probabilistic indexing, and information retrieval. *Journal of the Association for Computing Machinery*, 7(3):216–244, July 1960.

39. Marvin Minsky and Seymour Papert. *Perceptrons: An Introduction to Computational Geometry (Expanded Edition)*. The MIT Press, Cambridge, MA, 1988.

40. Frederick Mosteller and David L. Wallace. *Applied Bayesian and Classical Inference*. Springer-Verlag, New York, 2nd edition, 1984.

41. S. E. Robertson and K. Sparck Jones. Relevance weighting of search terms. *Journal of the American Society for Information Science*, pages 129–146, May-June 1976.

42. S. E. Robertson, C. J. van Rijsbergen, and M. F. Porter. Probabilistic models of indexing and searching. In R. N. Oddy, S. E. Robertson, C. J. van Rijsbergen, and P. W. Williams, editors, *Information Research and Retrieval*, chapter 4, pages 35–56. Butterworths, 1981.

43. S. E. Robertson and S. Walker. Some simple effective approximations to the 2-poisson model for probabilistic weighted retrieval. In W. Bruce Croft and C. J. van Rijsbergen, editors, *SIGIR 94: Proceedings of the Seventeenth Annual International ACM-SIGIR Conference on Research and Development in Information Retrieval*, pages 232–241, London, 1994. Springer-Verlag.

44. J. J. Rocchio, Jr. Relevance feedback in information retrieval. In Gerard Salton, editor, *The SMART Retrieval System: Experiments in Automatic Document Processing*, pages 313–323. Prentice-Hall, Inc., Englewood Cliffs, New Jersey, 1971.

45. Gerard Salton and Chris Buckley. Improving retrieval performance by relevance feedback. *Journal of the American Society for Information Science*, 41(4):288–297, 1990.

46. Gerard Salton and Michael J. McGill. *Introduction to Modern Information Retrieval*. McGraw-Hill Book Company, New York, 1983.

47. Amit Singhal, Chris Buckley, and Mandar Mitra. Pivoted document length normalization. In *SIGIR '96: Proceedings of the 19th Annual International ACM SIGIR Conference on Research and Development in Information Retrieval*, pages 21–29, 1996.

48. Karen Sparck Jones. Search term relevance weighting given little relevance information. *Journal of Documentation*, 35(1):30–48, March 1979.

49. Howard R. Turtle and W. Bruce Croft. Evaluation of an inference network-based retrieval model. *ACM Transactions on Information Systems*, 9(3):187–222, July 1991.

50. C. J. van Rijsbergen. A theoretical basis for the use of co-occurrence data in information retrieval. *Journal of Documentation*, 33(2):106–119, June 1977.

51. C. J. van Rijsbergen. *Information Retrieval*. Butterworths, London, second edition, 1979.

52. E. M. Voorhees and D. K. Harman, editors. *Information Technology: The Fifth Text REtrieval Conference (TREC-5)*, Gaithersburg, MD 20899-0001, 1997. National Institute of Standards and Technology. Special Publication 500-238.

53. Clement T. Yu and Hirotaka Mizuno. Two learning schemes in information retrieval. In *Eleventh International Conference on Research & Development in Information Retrieval*, pages 201–215, 1998.

Part II

Regular Papers

Learning Verbal Transitivity
Using LogLinear Models*

Nuno Miguel Marques (nmm@di.fct.unl.pt)**[1], Gabriel Pereira Lopes
(gpl@di.fct.unl.pt)[1], and Carlos Agra Coelho (coelho@isa.utl.pt)[2]

[1] Dep. Informática - FCT/UNL
[2] Dep. Matemática - ISA/UTL

Abstract. In this paper we show how loglinear models can be used to
cluster verbs based on their subcategorization preferences. We describe
how the information about the phrases or clauses a verb goes with can
be computationally learned from an automatically tagged corpus with
9,333,555 words. We will use loglinear modeling to describe the relation
between the acquired counts for the part-of-speech tags co-occurring with
the verbs on predetermined positions. Based on these results an unsupervised clustering algorithm will be proposed.

Keywords: Subcategorization Learning from Corpora, Loglinear Modeling, Clustering, Natural Language Processing.

1 Introduction

Every word in every language has preferences about the phrases it may combine with. The set of syntactic restrictions a word imposes on its arguments
(the phrases or clauses that follow that word) is called word syntactic subcategorization. This paper describes work done in order to automatically extract
Portuguese verbal subcategorization from an automatically tagged Portuguese
corpus ([ML96]) with $9,333,555$ words.

Brent [Bre93] proposed an approach where each subcategorization frame
could be extracted by using a small set of highly specific and discriminating
morpho-syntactic cues (ex. pronoun *me*). A probabilistic filter, based on a binomial assumption about the presence or absence of each cue, was used to determine if each cue co-occurs with a verb by chance, or, otherwise, if it signals a
given subcategorization frame. Only highly accurate, but extremely rare, cues
were used. More recently, Manning [Man93] and Briscoe and Carroll [BC97] replaced Brent's cues by using a part-of-speech tagger and a grammar (a simple
finite state grammar by Manning and a wide coverage partial parser by Briscoe
and Carroll). In order to overcome problems due to verbs with unusual patterns

---

* Work supported by JNICT Projects CORPUS (PLUS/C/LIN/805/93) and DIXIT
  (2/2.1/TIT/1670/95)
** Work supported by PhD scholarship JNICT-PRAXIS XXI/BD/2909/94

Ushioda et all. [UEGW96] present an extension to the previous work. Some verbs were manually assigned their correct subcategorization frames. Based on this manually assigned information and on the counts acquired by using regular expression grammar rules, loglinear supervised statistical learning [Fra96] was used to correct the assigned subcategorization classes.

In this paper it will be shown how the independence loglinear model ([Agr90]) can be successfully used for clustering verbs with the same subcategorization behavior. In next section loglinear independence model will be introduced. Later, some experiments will be described in order to pave the ground for introducing a novel clustering algorithm based on loglinear modeling. According to an evaluation presented in [MLC98] this algorithm seems to accurately distinguish between sets of verbs with the same subcategorization behavior.

2 Modeling Transitivity

The Independence Loglinear Model We trained a neural network based part-of-speech tagger [ML96] using a 5000 word manually tagged corpus. This trained part-of-speech tagger was used for automatically tagging text from LUSA corpus with $9, 333, 555$ words. Then we counted the number of times each part of speech occurred with each verb in the tagged corpus taking into account positional information, i.e. we counted each tag in positions ranging from -5 (five words to the left of our verb) up to +5 (five words to the right of our verb). For the purposes of this paper we will only use global frequencies of articles in position 1 (just after the verb) and nouns in position 2 (that is the total count of *verb, any tag, noun*). Obtained counts are shown in the left part of table 1.

Tables such as this one are usually called contingency tables. We will try to model the relationship between a row variable X (associated to different verbs) and a column variable Y (associated to the part-of-speech co-occurring with the row verb). We assume an independent Poisson model for the frequencies in that table, since our tagger works on a word by word basis, taking only one word as contextual information. In that sense it is different from other known taggers where the best tagging is chosen according to a Viterbi searching procedure over an Hidden Markov Model. So we think the independent Poisson sample assumption still holds. When the two variables we are modeling are independent, we can use the independence model [Agr90] :

$$logE_{ij} = \lambda + \lambda_i^X + \lambda_j^Y \qquad (i = 1, ..., I; j = 1, ..., J).$$

where $logE_{ij}$ is the logarithm of the expected frequency of cell (i, j) and equals the sum of a constant λ with a row parameter λ_i^X and a column parameter λ_j^Y.

Maximum likelihood techniques have been developed for estimating expected frequencies for loglinear models. The GLIM package (Numerical Algorithms Group 1986, [Hea88]) was used to fit our parameters. GLIM uses the Newton-Raphson method for ML model fitting.

The main advantage of this approach over previous ones is that we have a way to measure if our data is really independent. This is done by comparing the estimated values with the real ones. GLIM presents us with the likelihood-ratio statistics:

$$G^2 = 2\sum_{i=1}^{I}\sum_{j=1}^{J} O_{ij} \log(\tfrac{O_{ij}}{E_{ij}})$$

where O_{ij} are the observed frequencies for cell (i,j). When a model holds, this statistic has a large-sample chi-squared distribution with $(I-1)(J-1)$ degrees of freedom[Agr90].

Verbal Behavior By using loglinear models we are able to analyze the interactions among several part-of-speech tags (either for the same verb, or for two or more different verbs). By not rejecting the independence assumption we are both saying that the row ordering is irrelevant, and that the pattern of evolution of the values in each row, that is the part-of-speech information, may be used to help estimating the values in other rows. This way, by joining several verbs together we are also clustering verbs with similar part-of-speech preferences, and probably with the same subcategorization behavior.

Without loss of generality, we performed a first study on noun phrase subcategorization. Since, the most common noun phrase pattern is built by an article followed by a noun, we have built contingency tables that describe positions 1 and 2 for articles (Art_1) and nouns (N_2)[1], respectively. Then we selected as transitive verbs Portuguese verbs *abandonar* (*to abandon*), *integrar* (*to integrate*), *prometer* (*to promise*), *provocar* (*to provoke*). Verb *cair* (*to fall*), was used as a negative example (as an intransitive verb). Acting like this we aimed at having a clear perspective about how good were the used tags and their position for modeling noun phrase subcategorization. We have compared the column variable $X = < Art_1, N_2 >$ with the row variable Y containing the verbs under study. Left part of table 1 presents the observed frequencies for these verbs. Right part of table 1 presents, in the lower diagonal matrix, the scaled deviance returned by the independence model for the verb pairs we have experimented. The upper diagonal matrix displays the scaled deviance for groups containing more than two verbs. Subscripts give the number of degrees of freedom for each model. If a significance rate of 95% is used, then all models marked with a '*' should be rejected.

Results obtained, as we will see ahead, seem to confirm that the pair $< article_1 - noun_2 >$, relates verbs with the same transitive behavior. Indeed, by comparing all the possible pairs of transitive verbs, only to the pair (*to provoke,to integrate*) does not fit a loglinear independence model. After analysis of our data, we have found that indeed this verb has a different pattern. Although it subcategorizes a noun phrase, the structure of this noun phrase is different from the usual. In the case of the verb *to provoke*, articles are immediately followed by possessive pronouns, more frequently than in the other cases. This

---

[1] We will assume that subscripts in the tag names are referring to the tag position to the right (or left, if the index is negative) of the verb.

	Art_1	N_2		abandon	integrate	promise	provoke	fall
to abandon	374	272	abandon	-	2.5291_2		6.9401_3	$*20.095_3$
to integrate	494	332	integrate	$0,54717_1$	-			
to provoke	425	364	promise	$1,1304_1$	$2,4288_1$	-		
to promise	94	82	provoke	$2,3387_1$	$*5,8095_1$	$0,012064_1$	-	$*22,612_4$
to fall	29	54	fall	$*15,673_1$	$*18.901_1$	$*7.8144_1$	$*10.882_1$	-

Table 1. The left table displays observed frequencies for articles and nouns in positions +1 and +2, respectively. The studied verbs are represented in column 1. The right table displays the residuals for fitted loglinear models at the 95% significance level. Subscripts represent degrees of freedom

led us to conclude that in terms of the noun phrases it accepts, this verb selects a different syntactic pattern. Currently used subcategorization methodologies ([Bre93], [Man93], [BC97],[UEGW96]) aren't able to distinguish this peculiar preference from the other preferences. We also noticed that verb *cair* (to fall) doesn't fit with any other considered verb. This is the intended behavior since none of the other verbs is also intransitive.

We seem to have found a good way to measure the degree of association between verbs, taken either individually or in group. These observations led us to propose a methodology, described in the next section, for automatically finding verbs with similar subcategorization patterns.

3   A Clustering Algorithm

If we have a group of verbs $\vec{v_1}$ and a candidate verb v_2, by modeling the contingency table $X =< Art_1, N_2 >$, $Y =< \vec{v_1}, v_2 >$, we will be able to decide if verb v_2 has the same transitive behavior as the group of verbs $\vec{v_1}$. We have used this property to build the following, very simple, clustering algorithm:

1. We start with a list of N verbs $V =< v_1, ..., v_N >$, occurring in a Corpus C, having for each verb v_i their frequency vector X_i (e.g. $X_i =< freq(Art_1), freq(N_2) >_i$).
2. Verbs in V are sorted by decreasing order of the sum of their feature values (e.g. $freq(Art_1)_i + freq(N_2)_i$).
3. set List-of-clusters equal to a single cluster containing a single verb, the most frequent verb.
4. For each v_i in V do
   (a) Join v_i to the group $\vec{v_j}$ in $List - of - clusters$ where the independence model best explains the contingency table for $Y \times X$ (e.g. the table $Y =< \vec{v_j}, v_i >$, $X =< Art_1, N_2 >$).
   (b) If v_i doesn't fit with any of the models in $List - of - clusters$ add a new cluster to the list containing v_i.

Verbs are analyzed by order of frequency, this allows us to use first the most informative verbs to define our seed clusters. In the end, we will get K verb clusters, and K loglinear, independent models. This means that we are able to calculate expected frequencies of modeled tags and positions for every verb in a cluster within a certain confidence interval.

We want groups of verbs to be homogeneous in what concerns the distributions of frequencies of article at position 1 and noun at position 2. In order to accomplish this goal, in each step, verbs were added to the cluster only if a loglinear model of independence still fits to the table where this verb was added. The verb *to provoke* illustrates a possible problem with this approach. If we have a verb (such as *to provoke*), that individually doesn't fit with some verbs in a low deviance accepted cluster (such as the cluster of verbs *to abandon*, *to integrate* and *to promise*), and add it to that cluster, then, an independence model can be fitted with the new set of verbs. A possible solution to this could involve taking into account the increase in scaled deviance. Adding the verb *to provoke* to the previously referred cluster shouldn't be allowed since it results in an increase in the scaled deviance (4.411) that is greater than the 95th chi-square percentile for the number of degrees of freedom added, 1, that is 3.841455. This change could result in an undesired higher number of clusters for our algorithm, and it was not implemented in current version.

Generalization of the proposed algorithm has been experimented [MLC98] but due to space restrictions, we can not fully describe those experiments in this paper. However we will explain our main claims. There are part-of-speech tags that can be used for flagging out the presence of certain subcategorization frames. We could use infinitive verb tag for concluding about the existence of an infinitive clause; article tag for a noun phrase; preposition tag for prepositional phrases and subordinated conjunction tag for subordinated clauses.

As we are also interested on the evaluation of our clustering algorithm, in order to have a rough estimate of how well our method is performing, we extracted a list of verbs from our corpus and tagged them as transitive or intransitive, according to Porto Editora's Portuguese dictionary classification. Clusters have been defined as transitive or intransitive based on the classification in the dictionary of the most frequent verb in that cluster. Until now we have found that the best results are achieved when we use a tag that signals the presence of the phrase we want to detect and its complement (the frequency of the verb minus the frequency of the tag). Using a sample of 81 Portuguese verbs, obtained results (over our corpus), have 96.64% precision and 99.17% recall for noun phrases, if evaluated on a corpus where the precision baseline (tagging all verbs as transitive) is 91.35%[2]. Evaluation on prepositional phrases headed by Portuguese preposition *a* (*to*) achieved 92.38% precision and 100.0% recall, for a 52,86% precision baseline. We discuss these results in detail elsewhere ([MLC98]).

---

[2] As usual, precision is the percentage of correctly tagged verbs (correctly tagged verbs/total verbs) and recall is the percentage of tagged verbs that were correctly tagged (correctly tagged verbs/total of verbs tagged).

4   Conclusions

In our work we have found that the linguistic restrictions imposed by a word on its arguments are more informative than we could expect. Ushioda et alia and Briscoe and Carroll ([BC97], [UEGW96]) report that several subcategorization frames are recognized for each verb and different ranks are assigned to those frames. Yet we have found that even for a simple subcategorization frame, such as the noun phrase direct object for verbs, several types of distinct verbal preferences were observed *inside* the subcategorization frame. If we ever wanted to uncover this kind of phenomena, we should never use a limited predefined set of pattern preferences. By expressing subcategorization as model parameters for contingency tables we can really learn from data.

In the described methodology, no grammar knowledge was required by the system. Correlations were found between words taking into account occurrence frequencies of the distinct part-of-speech tags following analyzed verbs. It is now a task on grammar development the use of the provided lexical subcategorization information, by incorporating it in the lexicon and by adapting existing grammar rules in order to use this quantified lexical information. This approach has the advantage of not committing the extraction process with a particular grammar formalism. The data provided by our analysis once it is incorporated in a lexicon can increase efficiency at several parsing levels.

References

[Agr90]   Alan Agresti. *Categorical Data Analysis*. John Wiley and Sons, 1990.

[BC97]   Ted Briscoe and John Carroll. Automatic extraction of subcategorization from corpora. In *Proceedings of the 5th Conference on Applied Natural Language Processing (ANLP'97)*, 1997.

[Bre93]   Michael R. Brent. From grammar to lexicon: Unsupervised learning of lexical syntax. *Computacional Linguistics*, 19(2):245–262, 1993.

[Fra96]   Alexander Franz. *Automatic Ambiguity Resolution in Natural Language Processing*, volume 1171 of *Lecture Notes in Artificial Intelligence*. Springer, 1996.

[Hea88]   M. J. R. Healy. *GLIM: An Introduction*. Clarendon Press, Oxford, 1988.

[Man93]   Cristopher Manning. Automatic acquisition of a large subcategorization dictionary from corpora. In *Proceedings of the 31st Annual Meeting of ACL*, pages 235–242, 1993.

[ML96]   Nuno C. Marques and José Gabriel Lopes. A neural network approach to part-of-speech tagging. In *Proceedings of the Second Workshop on Computational Processing of Written and Spoken Portuguese*, pages 1–9, Curitiba, Brazil, October 21-22 1996.

[MLC98]   Nuno Miguel Cavalheiro Marques, Gabriel Pereira Lopes, and Carlos Agra Coelho. Using loglinear clustering for subcategorization identification. In *Coling-ACL, submitted paper*, Available at http:\\www-ssdi.di.fct.unl.pt\ ~nmm, 1998.

[UEGW96] Akira Ushioda, David Evans, Ted Gibson, and Alex Waibel. Estimation of verb subcategorization frame frequencies based on syntactic and multidimensional statistical analysis. In Harry Bunt and Masaru Tomita, editors, *Recent Advances in Parsing Technology*. Kluwer Academic Publishers, 1996.

Part–of–Speech Tagging Using Decision Trees*

Lluís Màrquez and Horacio Rodríguez

Dep. Llenguatges i Sistemes Informàtics. Universitat Politècnica de Catalunya
c/ Jordi Girona 1–3. Barcelona 08034, Catalonia
{lmarquez,horacio}@lsi.upc.es

Abstract. We have applied inductive learning of statistical decision trees to the Natural Language Processing (NLP) task of morphosyntactic disambiguation (Part Of Speech Tagging). Previous work showed that the acquired language models are independent enough to be easily incorporated, as a statistical core of rules, in any flexible tagger. They are also complete enough to be directly used as sets of POS disambiguation rules. We have implemented a quite simple and fast tagger that has been tested and evaluated on the Wall Street Journal (WSJ) corpus with a remarkable accuracy. In this paper we basically address the problem of tagging when only small training material is available, which is crucial in any process of constructing, from scratch, an annotated corpus. We show that quite high accuracy can be achieved with our system in this situation. In addition we also face the problem of dealing with *unknown* words under the same conditions of lacking training examples. In this case some comparative results and comments about close related work are reported.

1 Introduction and State of the Art

POS Tagging is a very well known NLP problem which consists of assigning to each word of a text the proper morphosyntactic tag in its context of appearance. Figure 1 shows the correct part of speech assignment to the words of a sentence, together with the list of valid labels for each word taken in isolation[1]. The base of POS tagging is that being most words ambiguous regarding their POS, they can be almost completely disambiguated taking into account an adequate context.

Starting with the pioneer tagger TAGGIT (Greene & Rubin 71), used for an initial tagging of the Brown Corpus (BC), a lot of efforts have been devoted to improve the quality of the tagging process in terms of accuracy and efficiency. Existing taggers can be classified into three main groups according to the kind of knowledge they use: linguistic, statistic and machine–learning family. Of course

* This research has been partially funded by the Spanish Research Department (CI-CYT's ITEM project TIC96–1243–C03–02), by the EU Commission (EuroWordNet LE4003) and by the Catalan Research Department (CIRIT's quality research group 1995SGR 00566).

[1] All tags appearing in the paper are from the Penn Treebank tag set. They are described in figure 2. For a complete description see for instance (Marcus et al.93).

The_DT first_JJ time_NN he_PRP was_VBD shot_VBN in_IN the_DT hand_NN
as_IN he_PRP chased_VBD the_DT robbers_NNS outside_RB ._.

first	time	shot	in	hand	as	chased	outside
JJ	NN	NN	IN	NN	IN	JJ	IN
RB	VB	VBD	RB	VB	RB	VBD	JJ
		VBN	RP			VBN	NN
							RB

Fig. 1. A sentence and its POS ambiguity

DT: Determiner	RB: Adverb	VBD: Verb, past tense
IN: Preposition	RP: Particle	VBN: Verb, past participle
JJ: Adjective	TO: *to*	
NN: Noun, singular	VB: Verb, base form	

Fig. 2. A subset of the Penn Treebank tag set

some taggers are difficult to classify into these classes and hybrid approaches
must be considered.

Within the linguistic approach most systems codify the involved knowledge
as a set of rules (or constraints) manually written by linguists (usually around a
thousand rules). The work of the TOSCA group (Oostdijk 91) and more recently
the development of Constraint Grammars (Karlsson et al. 95) can be considered
the most important in this direction.

The most extended approach nowadays is the statistical family (obviously
due to the limited amount of human effort involved). Basically it consists of
building a statistical model of the language and using this model to disambiguate a word sequence. There are different approaches in the estimation of
the parameters of the model, i.e. the lexical and transition probabilities. The
form of the model and the way of determining the sequence to be modeled
can be approached too in several ways. Many systems reduce the model to
unigrams, bi-grams, tri-grams, or to a combination of them. Hidden Markov
Models have been widely used too. The seminal work in this direction is the
CLAWS system (Garside et al. 87), which was the probabilistic version of TAG-
GIT. (Church 88), (DeRose 88) or (Cutting et al. 92) are notable examples of
statistic taggers. (Merialdo 94) presents an excellent overview.

Other works that can be placed in this class are those of (Schmid 94a) which
performs energy-function optimization using neural nets and (Rosenfeld 94)
which has applied a Maximum Entropy Approach to POS tagging. A comparison
between linguistic and statistic taggers can be found in (Samuelsson & Voutilainen 97).

Although the statistic approach involves some kind of learning, either supervised or unsupervised, of the parameters of the model from a training corpus, we
place in the machine-learning family only those systems that include more sophisticated information than a n-gram model. (Brill 92) and (Brill 95) automat-

ically learn a set of transformation rules which best repair the errors commited by a most–likely–tag tagger, (Samuelsson et al. 96) acquires Constraint Grammar rules from tagged corpora and (Daelemans et al. 96) or the work presented here learn decision trees from tagged corpora.

An example of hybrid approach is (Padró 97) that applies relaxation techniques over a set of constraints involving statistical, linguistic and machine–learning obtained information.

The accuracy reported by most statistic taggers overcomes 96–97% while Constraint Grammars overcome 99% allowing a residual ambiguity of 1.026 tags per word. Taking these figures into account one may think that POS tagging is a solved and closed problem being this accuracy perfectly acceptable for most NLP systems. So why wasting time in designing yet another tagger? What does an increasing of 0.3% in accuracy really mean? We think that there are several reasons for thinking that there is still work to do in the field of automatic POS tagging.

Common sentences in running texts have an average lenght of around 30 words. If we admit an error rate of 3–4% then it follows that, on average, each sentence contains one error. Since POS tagging is a very basic task in most NLP understanding systems, starting with an error in each sentence could be a severe drawback, specially considering that the propagation of this errors could grow more than linearly. Other NLP tasks that are very sensitive to POS disambiguation errors can be found in the domain of Word Sense Disambiguation (Wilks and Stevenson 97) and Information Retrieval (Krovetz 97).

Another issue refers to the need of adapting and tuning taggers that have acquired (or learned) their parameters from an specific corpus onto another one trying to minimizing the cost of transportation. No serious attempts have been performed to test the reported accuracy of taggers (usually measured against reference corpora as Wall Street Journal corpus –WSJ– or BC) on different, perhaps domain-specific, corpora.

Finally, some specific problems must be addressed when applying taggers to other languages than English. Beside the problems derived from the richer morphology of the particular language, there is a more general problem consisting of the lack of large, manually annotated corpora for training.

Although a *bootstrapping* approach can be carried out, using a low-accurate tagger, for producing annotated text that could be used then for learning a more accurate model, the results of such approach are dubious. So there is a real need for methods achieving high accuracy, both on known and unknown words, learning from small high-quality corpora.

In this direction, we are involved in a project for tagging Spanish and Catalan corpora (over 5M words) with limited linguistic resources, that is, departing from a manually tagged core of a size not greater than 50000 words.

For the sake of comparability the experiments reported here are performed over a reference corpus of English. However we fairly believe that qualitative results could be extrapolated to Spanish or Catalan.

The paper is organized as follows: In section 2 we describe the domain of application, in section 3 we describe the language model acquisition and the tagger implementation and in section 4 we describe the whole set of experiments together with a comparative analysis of the obtained results. Finally, the main conclusions and an overview of the future work can be found in section 5.

2   Domain of Application

Choosing, from a set of possible tags, the proper syntactic tag for a word in a particular context can be seen as a problem of classification. In this case, classes are identified with the tags. Decision trees, recently used in several NLP basic tasks, such as tagging and parsing (Schmid 94b), (McCarthy & Lehnert 95), (Daelemans et al. 96), (Magerman 96), are suitable for performing this task.

Ambiguity classes

It is possible to group all the words appearing in the corpus according to the set of their possible tags (i.e. *adjective–noun, adjective–noun–verb, adverb–preposition,* etc.). We will call this sets *ambiguity classes.* It is obvious that there exists an inclusion relation between these classes (i.e. all the words that can be *adjective, noun* and *verb,* can be, in particular, *adjective* and *noun*), so the whole set of ambiguity classes is viewed as a taxonomy with a DAG structure. In this way we split the general POS tagging problem into one classification problem for each ambiguity class.

Description of the corpus

We have used a portion of $1,170$ Kwords of the WSJ, tagged according to the Penn Treebank tag set, to train and test the system. The tag set contains 45 different tags[2]. About 36.5% of the words in the corpus are ambiguous, with an ambiguity ratio of 2.44 tags/word over the ambiguous words, 1.52 overall. The corpus contains 243 different ambiguity classes, but they are not all equally important. In fact, only the 40 most frequent ambiguity classes cover 83.95% of the occurrences in the corpus, while the 194 most frequent cover almost all of them (>99.50%).

The training corpus has been used also to create a word form lexicon with the associated lexical probabilities for each word. These probabilities are simply estimated by counting the number of times each word appears in the corpus with each different tag.

Statistical decision trees

We identify some particular features in our domain, comparing with common

---

[2] The size of tag sets differ greatly from one domain to another. Depending on the contents, complexity and level of annotation they are moving from 30–40 to several hundreds of different tags. Of course, these differences have important effects in the performance rates reported by different systems and imply difficulties when comparing them. See (Krenn & Samuelsson 96) for a more detailed discussion.

classification domains in Machine Learning field. Firstly, there is a so high number of training examples: up to 60000 examples for a single tree. Secondly, there is quite significant noise in the training/test data: WSJ corpus contains about 2–3% of mistagged words.

The main consequence of the above characteristics, together with the fact that simple context conditions cannot explain all ambiguities (Karlsson et al. 95)), is that it is not possible to obtain trees for completely classify the training examples. Instead, we aspire to obtain more adjusted probability distributions of the words over their possible tags, conditioned to the particular contexts of appearance. So we will use *Statistical* decision trees, instead of common decision trees, for representing this information.

3 Brief Description of the Tree-Based Tagger

3.1 Language Model Acquisition

The algorithm we used for constructing the statistical decision trees is a non–incremental supervised learning–from–examples algorithm of the TDIDT (Top Down Induction of Decision Trees) family. It constructs the trees in a top–down way, guided by the distributional information of the examples (Quinlan 93).

Training Set

For each class of POS ambiguity the initial example set is built by selecting from the training corpus all the occurrences of the words belonging to this ambiguity class. For most of the experiments reported in section 4, the set of attributes that describe each example consists of the part–of–speech tags of the neighbour words, and the information about the word itself: orthography and the proper tag in its context. The window considered is 3 words to the left and 2 to the right. The following are two real examples from the training set for the words that can be preposition and adverb at the same time (IN-RB class).

```
VB DT NN <"as",IN> DT JJ
NN IN NN <"once",RB> VBN TO
```

Attributes with many values (for instance the *word–form* and other attributes used when dealing with unknown words) are treated by dynamically adjusting the number of values to the N most frequent and joining the rest in a new *default* value. The maximum number of values is fixed to 45 (the number of different tags) in order to have homogeneous attributes.

Attribute Selection Function

After testing several attribute selection functions, with no significant differences between them, we used an attribute selection function due to López de Mántaras (López de Mántaras 91), belonging to the information–based family, which showed a slightly higher stability than the others. Roughly speaking, it defines a distance measure between partitions and selects for branching the attribute that generates the closest partition to the *correct partition*, namely the one that joins together all the examples of the same class.

Branching Strategy

Usual TDIDT algorithms consider a branch for each value of the selected attribute. However other solutions are possible. For instance, some systems perform a previous recasting of the attributes in order to have binary–valued attributes (Magerman 96). The motivation could be efficiency (dealing only with binary trees has certain advantages), and avoiding excessive data fragmentation (when there is a large number of values). Although this transformation of attributes is always possible, the resulting attributes lose their intuition and direct interpretation, and explode in number. We have chosen a mixed approach which consists of splitting for all values and afterwards joining the resulting subsets into groups for which we have not enough statistical evidence of being different distributions. This statistical evidence is tested with a χ^2 test at a 5% level of significance, with a previous smoothing of data in order to avoid zero probabilities.

Pruning the Tree

In order to decrease the effect of *over-fitting*, we have implemented a post pruning technique. In a first step the tree is completely expanded and afterwards is pruned following a minimal cost–complexity criterion (Breiman et al. 84), using a comparatively small fresh part of the training set. The alternative of smoothing the conditional probability distributions of the leaves using fresh corpus (Magerman 96) has been left out because we also wanted to reduce the size of the trees. Experimental tests have shown that in our domain the pruning process reduces tree sizes up to 50% and improves their accuracy in a 2–5%.

3.2 Tagging Algorithm

We have implemented a *reductionistic* tagger in the sense of constraint grammars (Karlsson et al. 95). In a initial step a word-form frequency dictionary constructed from the training corpus provides each input word with all possible tags with their associated lexical probability. After that, an iterative process reduces the ambiguity (discarding low probable tags) at each step until a certain stopping criterion is satisfied. The whole process is represented in figure 3.

More particularly, at each step and for each ambiguous word the work to be done is: 1) Classify the word using the corresponding decision tree[3]. 2) Use the resulting probability distribution to update the probability distribution of the word[4]. 3) Discard the tags with *almost* zero probability, that is, those with probabilities lower than a certain *discard boundary* parameter.

After the stopping criterion is satisfied some words could still remain ambiguous. Then there are two possibilities: 1) Choose the most-likely tag for each

---

[3] Ambiguity of the context during classification may generate multiple answers for the questions of the nodes. In this case, all the paths are followed and the result is taken as a weighted average of the results of all possible paths.

[4] The updating of the probabilities is done by simply multiplying previous probabilities per new evidences.

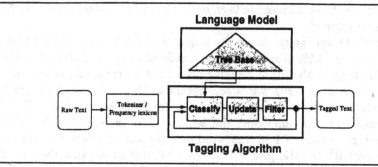

Fig. 3. The tagging process

still ambiguous word to completely disambiguate the text. 2) Accept the residual ambiguity (perhaps for treating it in successive stages).

Note that a unique iteration forcing the complete disambiguation is equivalent to use directly the trees as classifiers and results in a very efficient tagger, while performing several steps reduces progressively the efficiency but takes advantage of the statistical nature of the trees.

Another important point is to determine an appropriate stopping criterion. First experiments seem to indicate than the performance increases up to a unique maximum and then softly decreases as the number of iterations increases. For the experiments reported in section 4, the number of iterations was fixed to 3.

4 Experiments

We report here the results of four experiments. The first two summarize the work done for testing the system when all the training material is available. These two experiments were reported in previous papers (Màrquez & Rodríguez 95), (Màrquez & Rodríguez 97), (Màrquez & Padró 97). Third and fourth experiments are devoted to the testing of the tagger when using small training sets. We treat separately the cases of dealing either with known or unknown words. In both cases we give comparative results with similar work by (Daelemans et al. 96).

4.1 First Experiment

We divided the WSJ corpus in two parts: 1, 120 Kw were used as a training/pruning set, and 50 Kw as a fresh test set. We used a lexicon derived from training corpus, containing all possible tags for each word, as well as their lexical probabilities. The noise in the lexicon was filtered by manually checking the lexicon entries for the most frequent 200 words in order to eliminate the tags due to errors in the training set. Note that the 200 most frequent words in the corpus represent over half of it. For the words in the test corpus not appearing in the train set, we stored all possible tags, but no lexical probability (i.e. assuming uniform distribution)[5].

From the 243 ambiguity classes the acquisition algorithm learned a base of 194 trees covering 99.5% of the ambiguous words and requiring about 500 Kb of storage. The tagging algorithm, running on a SUN UltraSparc2, processed the test set at a speed of >300 words/sec, obtaining the following global results: when forcing a complete disambiguation the resulting accuracy was 97.29%, while accepting residual ambiguity the accuracy rate increased up to 98.22%, with an ambiguity ratio of 1.08 tags/word over the ambiguous words and 1.026 tags/word overall[6]. In (Màrquez & Rodríguez 97) it is shown that these results are, at least, as good as the results of a number of the non linguistically motivated state–of–the–art taggers.

4.2 Second Experiment

Another test of the appropriateness of the tree model was done in a previous experiment with another tagger. The group of the 44 most representative trees (covering 83.95% of the examples) were translated into a set of weighted context constraints and used to feed a relaxation–labelling–based tagger, together with bi/tri–gram information. The usual way of expressing trees as a set of rules was used to construct the context constraints. For instance the two following constraints, extracted from a real tree branch for the IN-RB (preposition–adverb) ambiguity class,

```
-5.81 <["as" "As"],IN> ([RB]) ([IN]);
 2.366 <["as" "As"],RB> ([RB]) ([IN]);
```

express the compatibility (either positive or negative) of the word–tag pair in angle brackets with the given context. The compatibility value for each constraint is calculated as the *mutual information* (Cover & Thomas 91) between the tag and the context.

Reported results, 97.09% accuracy when using the tree model alone and 97.39% when combining with a trigram model, showed that the addition of the automatically acquired context constraints led to an improvement in the accuracy of the tagger[7].

4.3 Small Training Sets

We present in figure 4 the performance achieved by our tagger with increasing sizes of the training corpus. Results in accuracy are taken over all words. The same figure includes most-likely results, which can be seen as a lower bound.

---

[5] That is, we assumed a morphological analyzer that provides all possible tags for unknown words.

[6] In other words, 2.75% of the words remained ambiguous, retaining only 2 tags for over 96% of them.

[7] Overcoming the bi/tri-gram models and properly cooperating with them and with a small set of linguistically motivated hand-written constraints.

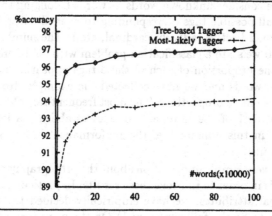

Fig. 4. Performance of the tagger related to the training set size

Following the intuition, we see that performance grows as the training set size grows. The maximum is at 97.29%, as reported in the first experiment. For the case of our interest we can see that using only 50000 training examples, the accuracy rate is 95.69%. This figure has been calculated as the average of the results obtained by repeating the experiment ten times on completely different training material. This mean value has a confidence interval of ±0.17%, at a 95% confidence rate.

We think this result is quite accurate. In order to corroborate this statement we can compare our result on a training set of 100K examples (an accuracy of 96.16%) with the figures reported in (Daelemans et al. 96) for the IGTree[8] system (96.0%). So our results can be considered, at least, as good as theirs.

4.4 Unknown Words

Unknown words are those words not present in the lexicon[9]. In the previous experiments we have not considered the possibility of unknown words. Instead we have assumed a morphological analyzer providing the set of possible tags with a uniform probability distribution. However, there exist several approaches to deal with real unknown words. On the one hand one can assume that unknown words may potentially take any tag, excluding those tags corresponding to closed categories (preposition, determiner, etc.), and try to the disambiguate between them. On the other hand, other approaches includes a pre-process that tries to guess the set of candidate tags for each unknown word to feed the tagger with this information. See (Padró 97) for a detailed explanation of the methods.

---

[8] IGTree system is a Memory-Based POS tagger which uses a tree representation of the training set of examples. The main difference from our solution is that, in IGTree, the order of application of attributes is predetermined in the construction of the trees.

[9] That is, in our case, the words not present in the training corpus.

In our case we consider unknown words as words belonging to the ambiguity class containing all possible tags corresponding to opened categories (i.e. noun, proper noun, verb, adjective, adverb, cardinal, etc.). The number of candidate tags sum to 20, so we state a classification problem with 20 different classes. We have estimated the proportion of each of these tags appearing naturally in the WSJ as unknown words and we have collected the examples from the training corpus according to these proportions. The most frequent tag, NNP (proper noun), represents almost 30% of the sample. This fact establishes a lower bound for accuracy of 30% in this domain (i.e. the performance that a *most–likely–tag* tagger would obtain).

We have used very simple information about the orthography and the context of unknown words in order to improve these results. In particular, from an initial set of 17 potential attributes, we have empirically decided the most relevant, which turned out to be the following ten: 1) On the word form: the first letter, the last three letters, and four binary-valued attributes more, accounting for capitalization, whether the word is a multi-word or not, and for the existence of some numeric characters in the word. 2) On the context: just the preceding and the following POS tags.

Table 1 shows the generalization performance of the trees learned from training sets of increasing sizes up to 50000 words. In order to compare these figures again with the results of IGTree, we have implemented IGTree algorithms and we have tested its performance exactly under the same condition as ours. These results are also shown in table 1.

#exs.		Tree–based Tagger	IGTree
2000	accuracy	77.53%	70.364%
	#nodes	224	627
5000	accuracy	80.90%	76.33%
	#nodes	520	1438
10000	accuracy	83.300%	79.18%
	#nodes	1112	2664
20000	accuracy	85.82%	82.30%
	#nodes	1644	4783
30000	accuracy	87.32%	85.11%
	#nodes	2476	6477
40000	accuracy	88.00%	86.78%
	#nodes	2735	8086
50000	accuracy	88.12%	87.145%
	#nodes	4056	9554

Table 1. Generalization performance of the trees for unknown words

Note that our system produces better quality trees than those of IGTree. We measure this quality in terms of generalization performance (how well these trees fit new examples) and size (number of nodes). Of course, this conclusion has to be taken in the domain of small training sets. Using big corpora for training might improve performance significantly. For instance, (Daelemans et al. 96) report an accuracy rate of 90.6% on unknown words when training with 2 million words of the WSJ.

5 Conclusions and Future Work

We have applied a classical supervised algorithm of the machine learning field, in order to automatically acquire a language model for POS tagging based on statistical decision trees. This learning algorithm uses more complex contextual information than usual n–gram models and it can easily accept other kinds of information. We have used this model for developing a fast and simple tagger tested on the WSJ corpus with a remarkable accuracy. In addition we have shown the independence of the acquired language model from the particular tagging algorithm, by translating the trees into a set of context constraints to feed a flexible relaxation–labelling–based tagger. Results obtained with this tagger are fairly good. Finally, we have tested the appropriateness of our system when dealing with small training corpora, as a previous step for applying the tagger to the Spanish and Catalan. We have obtained encouraging results both in tagging known and unknown words.

However, further work is still to be done in several directions. Referring to the language model learning algorithm, we are interested in testing more informed attribute selection functions, considering more complex questions in the nodes and finding a good smoothing procedure for dealing with very small ambiguity classes. See (Màrquez & Rodríguez 97) for a first approach.

About the information that this algorithm uses, we want to explore the inclusion of more morphological and semantic information, as well as more complex context features, such as non–limited distance or barrier rules in the style of (Samuelsson et al. 96).

Regarding the current work, we are beginning to apply our tagger to Spanish and Catalan languages. In this direction we are interested in testing our system —alone and in cooperation with other taggers, as (Padró 97)— in order to verify the hypothesis stated in this paper.

We conclude saying that we have done first attempts in using the same techniques to tackle another classification problem in NLP area, namely Word Sense Disambiguation (WSD). We believe, as other authors do, that we can take profit of treating both problems jointly.

References

Breiman, L., Friedman, J.H., Olshen, R.A. and Stone, C.J.: *Classification and Regression Trees*. Wadsworth International Group, Belmont, California, 1984.

Brill, E.: *A Simple Rule–Based Part–of–Speech Tagger*. In Proceedings of the 3rd ACL Conference on Applied Natural Language Processing, 1992.

Brill, E.: *Unsupervised Learning of Disambiguation Rules for Part–of–speech Tagging*. Proceedings of 3rd Workshop on Very Large Corpora, Massachusetts, 1995.

Church, K.W.: *S Stochastic Parts Program and Noun Phrase Parser for Unrestricted Text*. In proc. of 2nd Conference on Applied Natural Language Processing, 1988.

Cover, T.M. and Thomas, J.A. (Editors): *Elements of Information Theory*. John Wiley & Sons, 1991.

Cutting, D., Kupiec, J., Pederson, J. and Sibun, P.: *A Practical Part–of–Speech Tagger*. In proc. of 3rd Conference on Applied Natural Language Processing, 1992.

DeRose, S.J.: *Grammatical Category Disambiguation by Statistical Optimization*. Computational Linguistics 14(1), pp. 31–39.

Daelemans, W., Zavrel, J., Berck, P. and Gillis, S.: *MTB: A Memory-Based Part-of-Speech Tagger Generator*. Proc. of 4th Workshop on Very Large Corpora, 1996.

Garside, R., Leech, G. and Sampson, G.: *The Computational Analysis of English*. London and New York: Longman, 1987.

Greene, B.B., and Rubin, G.M.: *Automatic Grammatical Tagging of English*. Technical Report, Department of Linguistics, Brown University, 1971.

Karlsson, F., Voutilainen, A., Heikkilä, J. and Anttila, A.: *Constraint Grammar. A Language-Independent System for Parsing Unrestricted Text*. Mouton de Gruyter, Berlin, New York, 1995.

Krenn, B. and Samuelsson, C.: *The Linguist's Guide to Statistics. Don't Panic*. Universität des Saarlandes. Saarbrücken. Germany. WWW: http://coli.uni-sb.de

Krovetz, R.: *Homonymy and Polysemy in Information Retrieval*. In Proceedings of the 35th Annual Meeting of the Association for Computational Linguistics, ACL '97.

López de Mántaras, R.: *A Distance-Based Attribute Selection Measure for Decision Tree Induction*. Machine Learning, Kluwer Academic, 1991.

Magerman, M.: *Learning Grammatical Structure Using Statistical Decision-Trees*. In proc. of the 3rd International Colloquium on Grammatical Inference, ICGI '96.

Marcus, M.P., Marcinkiewicz, M.A. and Santorini, B.: *Building a Large Annotated Corpus of English: The Penn Treebank*. Computational Linguistics, v.19, n.2, 1993.

Màrquez, L. and Rodríguez, H.: *Towards Learning a Constraint Grammar from Annotated Corpora Using Decision Trees*. ESPRIT BRA-7315, WP #15, 1995.

Màrquez, L. and Padró, L.: *A Flexible POS Tagger Using an Automatically Acquired Language Model*. In Proceedings of the 35th Annual Meeting of the Association for Computational Linguistics, ACL '97.

Màrquez, L. and Rodríguez, H.: *Automatically Acquiring a Language Model for POS Tagging Using Decision Trees*. In Proceedings of the Second Conference on Recent Advances in Natural Language Processing, RANLP '97.

McCarthy, J.F. and Lehnert, W.G.: *Using Decision Trees for Coreference Resolution*. Proceedings of 14th IJCAI, 1995.

Merialdo, B.: *Tagging English Text with a Probabilistic Model*. Computational Linguistics 20(2), pp. 155-171.

Oostdijk, N.: *Corpus Linguistic and the automatic analysis of English*. Rodopi, Amsterdam, 1991.

Padró, L.: *A Hybrid Environment for Syntax-Semantic Tagging*. PhD Thesis, Dep. Llenguatges i Sistemes Informàtics, Universitat Politecnica de Catalunya, 1998.

Quinlan, J.R.: *C4.5: Programs for Machine Learning*. San Mateo, CA. Morgan Kaufmann, 1993.

Rosenfeld, R.: *Adaptive Statistical Language Modeling: A Maximum Entropy Approach*. PhD Thesis. School of Computer Science, Carnegie Mellon University, 1994.

Samuelsson, C., Tapanainen, P. and Voutilainen, A.: *Inducing Constraint Grammars*. Proceedings of the 3rd International Colloquium on Grammatical Inference, 1996.

Samuelsson, C. and Voutilainen, A.: *Comparing a Linguistic and a Stochastic Tagger*. In Proceedings of the 35th Annual Meeting of the ACL, 1997.

Schmid, H.: *Part-of-speech tagging with neural networks*. Proceedings of 15th International Conference on Computational Linguistics, COLING '94.

Schmid, H.: *Probabilistic Part-of-Speech Tagging Using Decision Trees*. In Proceedings of the Conference on New Methods in Language Processing, Manchester, UK, 1994.

Wilks, Y. and Stevenson, M.: *Combining Independent Knowledge Sources for Word Sense Disambiguation*. In Proceedings of the Second Conference on Recent Advances in Natural Language Processing, RANLP '97.

Inference of Finite Automata: Reducing the Search Space with an Ordering of Pairs of States

François Coste and Jacques Nicolas

IRISA- INRIA
Campus de Beaulieu, F-35042 Cedex, France

Abstract. We investigate the set of all minimal deterministic finite automata accepting a given set of words and rejecting another given set of words. We present several criteria to order the exploration of the corresponding search space. Three criteria are shown to have a very good behavior with respect to the pruning they imply in the search space. Best results have been obtained for the prefix ordering. We have also worked on a new dynamic ordering based on an entropy computation.

keywords :grammatical inference, DFA, constraints, search tree, entropy.

1 Introduction : regular grammar inference

Regular Grammar Inference is an important inductive inference issue with applications in language processing, pattern recognition and genomics. It is defined as the process of learning a regular language from examples of words of this language and words that do not belong to the language. More precisely, we are looking in this paper for all minimal deterministic finite automata accepting a given set of words and rejecting another given set of words. Formally, we are concerned with the following DFA learning problem:

Given a set of positive sentences I_+ and a set of negative sentences I_-, find the set BS_d (Border Set, Dupont& al. 1994, of deterministic automata) of all automata A verifying :

1. A is a deterministic finite state automata ;
2. I_+ is structurally complete for A (i. e. there exists an acceptance of I_+ such that every transition of A is exercised and every final state of A is used as an accepting state);
3. $L(A)$, the language accepted by A, does not contain any string of I_- ;
4. $L(A)$ is a most general language
   (i.e. no other solution A' is such that $L(A) \subseteq L(A')$).

The natural generality relation between languages is inclusion, corresponding to inclusion between sets of accepted words. In case of a representation of languages with automata, a weaker generality relation is known: the set of finite automata may be partially ordered with a derivation relation, corresponding to the merging of states in the automata:

Definition 1. (Derived automata A/π) Given an automata $A = (Q, \Sigma, \delta, q_0, F)$ and a partition $\pi = (B_0, B_1, \ldots, B_r)$ of the set of states Q, the derived or quotient automaton $A/\pi = (\pi, \Sigma, \Delta, B_0, R)$ is defined as follows:

- initial sate : $q_0 \in B_0$;
- final states : $R = \{B_i \in \pi, \exists q \in B_i \, tq \, q \in F\}$;
- transition function : $B_j \in \Delta(B_i, a)$ iff $\exists q \in B_i, q' \in B_j$ such that $q' \in \delta(q, a)$.

The set of all automata derived from A is a lattice denoted $Lat(A)$.

In our case, learning may be reduced to a search in the lattice $Lat(PTA(I_+))$ (Dupont& al. 1994), where $PTA(I_+)$ is a most specific automaton specified by I_+, the *prefix tree acceptor*. $PTA(I_+)$ accepts every word of I_+ and no other.

A number of algorithms have been proposed to explore this lattice. Almost all of them are looking for one particular solution. The main algorithms search a solution in the lattice proceeding either with a greedy state merging approach (Trakhenbrot & Barzdin 1973, RPNI Oncina & Garcia 1992, Lang 1992), a beam search strategy (BRIG), or with an optimization method (GIG). Few authors have studied the characterization of the set of all solutions. Ensuring a complete search presents however many advantages : it allows to design an incremental approach, to be more robust with respect to noise in the training set and to select useful training words. Miclet has proposed a heuristic algorithm. An incremental approach using membership queries has been proposed by Parekh and Honavar. Preliminary studies have also been tried in the context free case by Vanlehn and Ball and by Giordano.

In Coste & Nicolas 1997b, we have proposed a compact representation of the set of all solutions, based on a *constraints system*. This constraints system specifies the set F_{Nok} of couples of states that cannot be merged. We have given an efficient algorithm to build the minimal elements of BS_d, reducing the problem to the *coloring of the graph of constraints*. Pairs of states may be considered as binary attributes taking value $=$ or $\neq$, depending on whether states are merged or not. In these experiments, we have seen that the efficiency of the search is very sensitive to the order in which attributes are considered.

In algorithms such as RPNI (Oncina & Garcia 1992) or the algorithm of Lang (Lang 1992), the states to be merged are chosen in a breadth-first predetermined order (prefix order): a state is ordered with respect to the word leading to this state. A recent study (Lang 1997) shows that better results can be obtained by considering candidate merges in order of the amount of evidence supporting them, as claimed by De la Higuera, Oncina and Vidal . Basically, Lang proposes to merge states with most matching labels in the suffix trees associated with the candidate states. In the following we note Rlb the order resulting from this criterion.

We propose to study the influence of these orders on the search space while looking for all solutions. It is thus interesting to try new criteria for the selection of attributes. Using the same idea of dynamically computing the evidence of a merge we have developed an entropy based criterion. We present the search tree and this criterion in the next section. Experiments comparing orders are reported in the last section.

2 Ordering the choices of state mergings

2.1 The search space as a search tree

We have seen that the search space is a set of partitions and that there is one operation, namely merging two blocks in a partition, to move from one node to another more general one in the search space.

An alternative representation of this space consider each pair of states to be an attribute with two possible values : = if states have to be merged and $\neq$ if states differ in the target automaton. At each node of the search tree, one may associate a set of automata (corresponding to an incompletely specified, current automaton) all of them derived from the PTA, where all merges along the path from the root to the given node have been made, all states that cannot be merged along this path are indeed different, and all consequences of these choices have been drawn (i.e. propagation of constraints has been done).

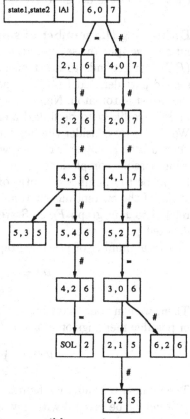

We give a search tree of sample 1 of language 2, for a random selection of attributes.

It is possible to obtain a complete search tree if one follows every possible choice along the branches of this tree, until either a single solution or a failure is discovered. In this way, heuristics of every known algorithm searching a single solution may be used for the selection of attributes in this tree and thus these algorithms may be extended naturally to the search of all solutions. This is possible because, unlike other algorithms, we explicitly and dynamically manage the F_{Nok} set of incompatible mergings.

The question is then to find the most efficient heuristic with respect to this new goal, and this is not a trivial task since a given algorithm may well find very quickly a first solution, taking advantage of a property of this solution, and then be laborious in finding the other ones, that do not respect this property.

2.2 The search tree as a decision tree

We have so far presented the search space as an ordered set of choices of pairs of states. Another way to look at it is that the search tree is a kind of decision tree, the leaves of this tree being labeled either success, failure or incomplete, depending on whether the corresponding automata are either correct, rejected or incompletely specified.

Given this framework, reducing the amount of search to be done is equivalent to finding the smallest tree where all leaves contain either a single solution automaton or lead to a failure. Following the TDIDT methodology (Quinlan 1986), we have tried various criteria in order to select the best attribute at each node.

However, one has to keep in mind that this is an analogy and not the usual framework, since we do not know how many solutions or failures are below a given node. All we can do is to estimate this number. Defining this estimate for each node in the decision tree is the purpose of the next part of this section.

Estimating the number of solutions In order to estimate the number of solutions, we split the set of states into two parts. The first part, *the pseudo-clique* (*PC*), corresponds to a set of candidates such that every other state (in the second part denoted $\overline{PC}$) is supposed to be merged with one of them to obtain the target automaton. Name "pseudo-clique" refers to graph F_{Nok}, where states in PC are likely to be linked and form a clique (or a densest 'almost' clique). We then only consider the bipartite subgraph of F_{Nok} between PC and $\overline{PC}$.

Once a pseudo-clique is chosen, we estimate the number of solutions by considering possible completions of this subgraph (each one specifying an automaton). Let m be the number of states of the target automaton, $|A|$ be the number of states of the current automaton, $degree(x)$ denotes the number of states of PC related to x in graph F_{Nok}. States of PC are denoted p_i and states of $\overline{PC}$ are denoted q_i.

The total number of possible graphs *tot* is:

$$tot = \prod_{1 \leq i \leq |A|-m} 2^{(m-degree(q_i))}$$

Then, we can roughly estimate the number of solution graphs p as the number of possible mergings of states in $\overline{PC}$ with states in PC.

$$p = \prod_{1 \leq i \leq |A|-m} (m - degree(q_i))$$

The number of failure configurations n is the number of graphs where a state of $\overline{PC}$ cannot be merged with any state of PC.

$$n = \sum_{1 \leq i \leq |A|-m} \left(\prod_{1 \leq j < i} (2^{m-degree(q_j)} - 1) \right) \cdot \prod_{i < j \leq |A|-m} 2^{m-degree(q_j)}$$

Therefore, the number i of incomplete configurations is

$$i = tot - (p + n)$$

Then the estimated entropy of a given node is

$$I = -\frac{p}{tot}log_2(\frac{p}{tot}) - \frac{n}{tot}log_2(\frac{n}{tot}) - \frac{i}{tot}log_2(\frac{i}{tot})$$

Finally, averaging entropies of the *left* and *right* edges of a given node, we propose to choose the attribute (i.e. the pair of states) minimizing E:

$$E = tot_{left}I_{left} + tot_{right}I_{right}$$

3 Experimentation

3.1 Setting

We have used a benchmark described in Dupont 1996 for a first validation of ideas developed in this paper. Target automata are small (< 6 states) but structurally complex. For instance, L_{11} is the language accepting an even number of a and an odd number of b.

For each language, 20 training samples have been drawn. The size of these sets of words is less than or equal to 50. The size of words varies from 1 to 40.

We have used four orderings while building a complete search tree of the solutions: Random order r (20 trials have been made for each training set); Prefix order p; Entropy-based order e and Rlb order R (Lang 1997). In each case, pseudo-cliques have been computed and used to detect failure nodes.

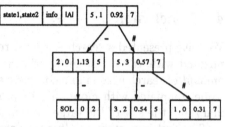

(if a clique of size greater than m is detected, it means that the corresponding automaton is not minimal, and the search may be pruned). As an illustration, we give the search tree of sample 1 of language 2 for the entropy criterion.

3.2 Results

Lang.	#s/#t	#sol	APTA	#FN	#nr	#np	#ne	#nR
L1	1/1	1	3.2	0	2.5	2.0	2.0	2.0
L2	2/2	1	25.3	43.0	10.3	2.9	3.0	3.1
L3	4/7	1.75	180.9	998.2	4325.6	13.7	16.1	52.9
L4	3/5	8.5	102.2	192.2	3297.2	58.7	71.6	268.8
L5	4/8	2.1	65.1	217.8	30836.7	32.3	48.5	73.1
L6	3/6	2.45	40.7	108.5	9842.9	19.3	18.7	73.4
L7	4/7	4.75	85.2	545	27291.4	92.6	119.9	405.5
L8	2/2	1.25	19.0	43.0	3.6	2.7	2.7	3.1
L9	4/7	1.65	60.8	357.9	114.7	5.8	7.0	7.1
L10	5/6	2.4	81.2	431.7	97.5	15.7	10.4	16.7
L11	4/8	2.85	64.8	214.85	37035.1	27.0	55.6	74.2
L12	3/3	1.5	37.6	120.2	8.6	4.4	4.1	4.2
L13	2/4	1.25	32.4	70.7	475.8	5.8	5.6	5.6
L14	3/4	1.4	37.6	100.5	30.1	5.5	6.2	6.4
L15	4/6	2.1	70.7	353.3	35.6	8.9	9.1	9.2

#s/#t characterizes the size of target automata in terms of number of states and transitions, #sol is the mean number of minimal automata in BS_d. #FN is the mean size of F_{Nok} at the root node. #nr, #np, #ne, #nR are the mean number of nodes of the tree for respectively a random, a prefix, an entropy, and a Rlb selection.

Results first show how important is the choice of a good ordering for the reduction of the search space. A random selection of nodes may increase the size of the tree by several orders of magnitude, with respect to best criteria. Second, results are in favor of the prefix order. The refined Rlb order is not only not necessary but give worse results in almost every case. The entropy order behaves well but seems to be not as efficient as the prefix order. We have to temperate these observations with two important remarks : our benchmark contains target automata of small size and furthermore, each learning sample admits a very low number of solutions. A second remark is that it remains a full range of possible variations to improve the calculation and use of the entropy criterion that we have not checked.

4 Conclusion

We have presented a search space for regular grammatical inference and experimented with various ordering criteria allowing a substantial reduction of the amount of search needed in a complete strategy. The benchmark needs of course to be completed with more difficult problems, increasing the size of the vocabulary and the size of the target automaton.

The first important result is that ordering the choices of pairs of states to be merged remains a key issue when considering the "all solutions" search problem. The simple prefix order seems to be a good candidate for this search. We have studied a new entropy based criterion that behaves well either but is more costly. We expect it to be interesting in large search spaces with a great number of solutions. Finally, splitting the set of states of an automaton into two parts, based on the number of impossible mergings between them, and taking advantage of this partition to further prune the search space has contributed to very small search trees in our experiment. This point has to be emphasized since algorithms inferring automata usually consider possible mergings but not impossible ones.

References

Coste, F. and Nicolas, J. : Regular Inference as a Graph Coloring Problem. Workshop on Grammar Inference, Automata Induction, and Language Acquisition (ICML' 97), Nashville, TN.

Dupont, P.; Miclet, L.; and E.Vidal. What is the search space of the regular inference ? *ICGI'94, Grammatical inference and Applications* 25–37. Springer Verlag.

Dupont, P. *Utilisation et apprentissage de modèles de langages pour la reconnaissance de la parole continue.* Ph.D. Dissertation, Ecole Nationale Supérieure des Télécommunications.

Lang, K. Random DFA's can be Approximately Learned from Sparse Uniform Examples. In *proceedings of the fifth annual ACM Workshop on Computational Learning Theory* 45–52, July 1992.

Lang, K. Merge Order count NECI Tech Report, Sept26, 1997

Oncina, J., and Garcia, P. Inferring regular languages in polynomial update time. *Pattern Recognition and Image Analysis* 49 – 61.

Quinlan, J.R. Induction of decision trees. *Machine Learning* (1):81–106.

Trakhenbrot, B. and Barzdin, Y., Finite Automata : Behavior and Synthesis *Amsterdam, North Holland Pub. Comp,*

Automatic Acquisition of Lexical Knowledge from Sparse and Noisy Data

René Schneider

Daimler-Benz AG, Institute of Information Technology,
Department of Speech and Language Understanding, Ulm, Germany
`rene.schneider@dbag.ulm.DaimlerBenz.COM`

Abstract. Optical character recognition (OCR) still garbles a considerable amount of information reduction and noise on texts so that many documents are unsuitable for information extraction systems. This paper introduces a statistical method for bootstrapping a lexicon from a very small number of "noisy ," domain-specific texts. This method determines regularity in grammatical forms and also reoccuring ungrammatical forms from the input text. Through a combination of frequency lists and Levenshtein matrices, a language independent, robust core lexicon is constructed that supports the analysis of "noisy texts," too.

1 Motivation

The growth of electronically transmissible and freely available texts that has taken place in recent years has not lead to a reduction of paperbound text. Therefore, the development of optical character recognition (OCR) systems and the improvement of their efficiency is still a major task in the area of document processing. [1] But anyway, even with high quality scanners a 100% recognition rate remains the ideal case. Besides the mistakes caused by OCR, a considerable number of documents include typographical or grammatical mistakes (misspellings, wrong inflection or word order, etc.). Therefore new methodologies should be invented that enable NLP-Systems to learn automatically from very small and grammatically incorrect corpora.

Statistical learning algorithms are usually applied to processing large corpora, but in real life, huge samples are hard to find for commercial and industrial applications. In our case, the corpora consists of a small sample of short letters requesting annual business reports from a company.

2 Information Theoretical Background

2.1 Syntactic vs. Pragmatic Information

Traditionally [4], information was computed as the negative sum of the probabilities of certain events. In other words: the less frequent the event was, the higher its information value was. In the case of natural languages this means for example that the word *the* has a very low value of information compared to very specific and less frequent words like e.g. *benign*. But what happens if the information is transmitted through a noisy channel? In this case the number of seldom and arbitrary sequences grows dramatically, e.g. sequences like *7O)ankyouverynouchhoadvance* (caused by the use of multifont) or even *+ -; p*mj -pL* (as a consequence of dirt specks).

In these cases Shannon and Weaver's measure of syntactic information is no longer applicable. A solution has to be found, regarding the other two dimensions of information, namely semantic and pragmatic information. Both are very hard to measure, due to their subjective nature and even semantic information presumes a noiseless channel. Therefore Weizsäcker [5] introduced the concept of *pragmatic information* that deals with the *where*, the *when*, and the *how* of information. In this way, information can only be computed after it has taken place and with respect to a given situation. Basically, pragmatic information consists of the complementary parts of *novelty* and *confirmation* . Novelty means that at a certain point in time an event occurs for the first time. But even when the information itself is new for us, generally we are able to make predictions about the speaker, the location, etc. The event includes at least something already known, quantified as confirmation. In other words, information exchange is only possible when sender and receiver have a common semantic basis. To give an

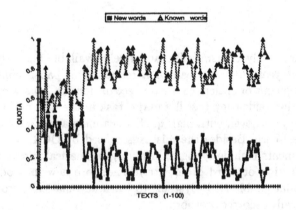

Fig. 1. Firstness and confirmation of word forms

example of the difference of novelty and confirmation, natural languages have a very high amount of novelty but require on the other hand constant confirmation, whereas artificial languages (e.g. machine code) constitute of nothing but confirmation and do not allow any kind of firstness or novelty.

2.2 Evaluation

Every text (or text body) of the training corpus can be seen as a closed unit and all the texts can be brought into a random order required to create a temporal structure. To better understand the concepts of novelty and confirmation, the relative amounts of unknown and verified words were computed. As can be seen in Figure 1, the number of new words is very high at the beginning and rapidly decreases to a more or less constant value. The curve of confirmed words shows the opposite effect. After a very low number of texts, generally 80 % of the information is confirmed, i.e. the words appeared already in one of the former texts. These 80 % cover generally the functional words such as articles, conjunctions etc. and of course the domain–specific information. The residual 20 % consist of text–relevant information, unimportant and less interesting information, misspellings, and — in OCR–texts — noisy information. The curve's oscillation is caused by factors such as text size and the OCR quality of the different texts.

A linguistic interpretation of the different qualities of the words with a high confirmation value (see 3.1, Unordered lexicon entries) shows that they are usually correct and not inflected. These results lead to the following assumptions: 1. The more often a word is confirmed in a noisy corpora, the higher is its probability of being a graphically *correct* word form. 2. If these words can be altered in their morphology, words with a high frequency are *stems* or *lemmata*.

3 Acquisition of Lexical Knowledge

3.1 Frequency Lists

Since the introduction of Zipf's law [6] one of the most simplest, but nevertheless powerful methods of finding statistical regularities is to build a frequency list (see Table 1) or rank-frequency distribution. Due to the small size of the corpora and especially the large number of "noisy" words, which enlarge increadibly the number of single-occurence words (or hapax legomena), the conditions for a proof of Zipf's law are not adequate. As already pointed out in 2.2, correct and

rank	freq	word(s)	rank	freq	word(s)	rank	freq	word(s)
1	210	to	11	109	I, we	21	49	copy
2	209	the	12	105	annual	22	47	could
3	205	your	13	89	report	23	44	on
4	201	of	14	85	be	24	42	company
5	169	you	15	81	send	25	41	information, mailing
6	164	and	16	71	our	26	40	are, this
7	145	in	17	69	if	27	39	list, with
8	121	for	18	62	reports	28	38	thank
9	120	would	19	60	please, as, us	29	30	latest, address
10	111	a	20	54	is me	30	29	any

Table 1. Rank-Frequency List (first 30 ranks)

stem forms and here especially words with a domain specific meaning appear on the higher ranks. So frequency can be taken as a decisive characteristic to find the lemma for a number of correct or incorrect variants. The remaining problem is to find a way to subsume the variants under the more frequent stems and to measure the similarity between words in order to find the necessarily derivable and possible modalities of a stem. The following section shows a simple but efficient solution for this problem.

3.2 Levenshtein Distance

The most frequent problems caused by OCR (e.g. Merging, Splitting or Replacement of characters; incorrect word boundary recognition) can be captured using a method based on the Levenshtein distance that can also be used to determine lexical similarity [3]. Two words (with the same or different lengths) are compared with each other in a distance matrix, which measures the least effort of transforming one word into the other. Least effort means the lowest number of insertions, deletions, or replacements (as a combination of deletion and insertion). The effort is normalized to the length of the longest word to obtain a ratio-scaled value. Table 2 shows the unordered lexicon entries for the word form *rbport* with all similar words that were found in the corpus, having Levenshtein distance lower than 1.0. Against all expectations and as already proved in sec-

word	variants	distance	freq	variants	distance	freq	variants	distance	freq
	report	0.333	89	xport	0.666	1	importance	0.8	1
	reports	0.428	62	sports	0.714	1	portfolios	0.777	1
rbport	roports	0.428	1	cort	0.666	1	opportunity	0.818	3
freq = 1	ofreports	0.555	1	fjeport	0.714	1	north	0.833	1
	reporting	0.555	2	portfolio	0.777	1	opportunities	0.846	2
	reporting"	0.6	1	important	0.777	1			

Table 2. Unordered lexicon entry

tion 2.2 the number of correct forms and "deflected" forms is always higher than those of *typical* OCR-mistakes. In fact it must be asked, whether typical OCR mistakes exist at all due to the different types of reasons for these mistakes and the multitude of effects they may have.

3.3 The Core Lexicon

The lexicon that consists so far of all unordered lexicon entries (s. Tab. 2) has very low structure and consists of entries for all types and word forms having a certain similarity to them. No differentiation concerning lemmata and variants is done. To reduce the number of entries and to bring some order to the lexicon, the results of the frequency lists and Levensthein distances $d_{(s/v)}$ are combined as follows.

The algorithm processes successively through the frequency list, starting with the most frequent word and finishing with the last hapax legomenon. Each word that can be found in the frequency list is considered as the top of a new lexicon entry or lemma. Afterwards, the algorithm looks for the word forms in the lexicon, that are similar to this word, assigns them as variants in the new entry and recursively looks for all variants of the previously assigned variants. Each one of these variants can no longer be regarded as top of another entry and consequently is taken out of the frequency lists, that simultaneously shrinks more and more. The variants frequency is added to that of the lemma. The effects of the algorithm depend a lot on an *a priori* specified threshold value for the Levenshtein distances. In our tests, good results are achieved with a value of 0.45 for direct similarity and 0.7 for indirect similarity, meaning the newly computed distance of variants of a variant to a given lemma.

The result of this process is a core lexicon that consists of a) high frequent synsemantica or function words having no variants, b) high frequent, domain specific autosemantica or content words and most of their occuring variants, c) middle and low frequency words and their variants, and d) one single entry for all the remaining hapax legomena having no similarity to one of the preceding words lower than 0.45, in order of their summarized frequencies. Hence, the number of entries in the core lexicon is at about one third of the total number of types. Table 3 shows some of the domain significant entries for the English corpus. As follows, many of the wrongly analyzed combinations of *your annual*

stem	variants	$d_{(s/v)}$	freq	stem	variants	$d_{(s/v)}$	freq	stem	variants	$d_{(s/v)}$	freq
your			205	annual			105	report			89
	yours	0.2	1		"annual	0.142	2		reports	0.142	62
	youuor	0.2	1		iannual	0.142	1		reprt	0.166	2
	ofyour	0.333	2		annuai	0.333	4		repo	0.333	1
	z&your	0.333	1		annuad	0.333	1		rbport	0.333	1
	yours.	0.428	1		annua#	0.333	1		ofreports	0.333	1
					semiannual	0.4	1		reporting	0.333	2
					yourannual	0.4	1		reporting"	0.4	1
									roports	0.428	1
									fjeport	0.428	1
Σ	5		211	7			116	9			161

Table 3. Lexicon entries: *your, annual, report*

report that lead to a rejection of the text, now can be transformed into their correct forms. This increases the number of documents that can be analyzed by the system considerably.

A comparision of the core lexicon with common frequency analyses [2] for correct texts shows that even with a very small text sample the resulting information for linguistically allowed alterations or lemmatizations of a lexical base form are achieved, at least in restricted domains. Additional information is achieved with the subsumption of linguistically incorrect variants. Thus, the core lexicon docs not only bear the basic lexical knowledge that is needed for a "robust lemmatization" of a given text but furthermore enables the "cleaning" of documents from noisy sequences as can be seen in Fig. 2: 1. The words in normal print are identified as a lemma already existing. 2. The words in italic are identified as a variant of a lemma already existing and is lemmatized (italic print). 3. The word is neither a lemma nor a confirmed variant and is compared with the base entries (bold print). 4. The words (in parenthesis) are not recognized as similar to one of the core lexicon's entries.

Our collecon of buslness roports and accOunts is an important and well-used resource for staff and students of our Business Sc oo and we feel that as many companies as possible should be represented. We shouid therefore be very grateful if ou could send .us a copy of all reports since 199-2 and re-add our name to your maiing list to recieve them in future.	our **collection** of *business report* and **accounts** is an important and (**wellused**) *resources* for staff and students of (our) business sc (oo) and we feel that as many *company* as possible should be **present** . we **should** therefore be very grateful if ou **would** send (.us) a copy of all *report* since **1992** and (re-add) our name to your **maiing** list to *receive* them in future .

Fig. 2. Robust Lemmatisation of an unknown Text

4 Conclusions

The paper reflects a quantitative approach to language independent lexical acquisition considering the sparseness and noisiness of certain text corpora. Word forms are aligned automatically to their lemmata with a set of very small, but domain specific texts. First results show that the core lexicon that is learned during the training process can be used to "clean" documents from noisy sequences. It builds the basis for the processing of new documents, dynamically enlarging with each new text. Meanwhile the learning process continues and converts into a rather symbolic approach with the determined lemmata as patterns. Each new variant is assigned to the corresponding lemma.

References

1. T. Bayer, U. Bohnacker, and I. Renz. Information extraction from paper documents. In H. Bunke and P.S.P. Wang, editors, *Handbook on Optical Character Recognition and Document Image Analysis*, pages 653–677. World Scientific Publishing Company, 1997.
2. W.N. Francis and H. Kučera. *Frequency Analysis of English Usage*. Houghton Mifflin, Boston, 1982.
3. J. Nerbonne, W. Heeringa, E. van den Hout, P. van der Kooi, S. Otten and W. van de Vis. Phonetic distance between dutch dialects. In Durieux, G., Daelemans, W., and Gillis, S., editors, *Proceedings of Computational Linguistics in the Netherlands*, pages 185–202, Antwerp, Centre for Dutch Language and Speech (UIA), 1996.
4. C.E. Shannon. A mathematical theory of communication. *The Bell Systems Technical Journal*, 27:623–656, 1948.
5. E. von Weizsäcker. Erstmaligkeit und Bestätigung als Komponenten der pragmatischen Information. In E. von Weizsäcker, editor, *Offene Systeme I*, pages 83–113. Klett, Stuttgart, 1974.
6. G.K. Zipf. *The Psycho-Biology of Language*. Houghton Mifflin, Boston, 1935.

A Normalization Method for Contextual Data: Experience from a Large-Scale Application

Sylvain Létourneau[1], Stan Matwin[2], and Fazel Famili[1]

[1] Integrated Reasoning Group,
National Research Council of Canada, Ottawa
{sletour, fazel}@ai.iit.nrc.ca
[2] School of Information Technology and Engineering,
University of Ottawa, Canada
stan@site.uottawa.ca

Abstract. This paper describes a pre-processing technique to normalize contextually-dependent data before applying Machine Learning algorithms. Unlike many previous methods, our approach to normalization does not assume that the learning task is a classification task. We propose a data pre-processing algorithm which modifies the relevant attributes so that the effects of the contextual attributes on the relevant attributes are cancelled. These effects are modeled using a novel approach, based on the analysis of variance of the contextual attributes. The method is applied on a massive data repository in the area of aircraft maintenance.

Keywords: Learning in contextual domains, attribute normalization, data-mining.

1 Introduction

In this paper, we address the problem of learning models from contextual data, i.e. data acquired from a system operating in a dynamic environment. We assume that the contextual data contains information on both the environment and the system under study. A wide variety of real world industrial applications generate such contextual data. The information on the environment is typically represented by a limited set of *contextual attributes* such as humidity, temperature, and pressure while the domain specific information is described by a set of *relevant attributes* such as start-time and exhaust gas temperature. What we need is a learning approach that will learn appropriate models while taking into account the effects of the contextual attributes on the relevant attributes.

The pre-processing domain independent method proposed here is a form of feature selection/extraction approach in which we normalize the relevant attributes with respect to the contextual attributes. In this manner their influence will be taken into account by a one-time transformation of the values of performance attributes, which will remove the dependency. The output of our pre-processing method is a new set of relevant attributes that are available for learning. The models obtained from the new normalized attributes will be more general than the ones obtained without normalization, since they are independent from the variations in the contextual attributes.

The paper describes our approach for handling contextual data as well as results obtained from experiments with a large volume of commercial aircraft engine data. The data consists of automatically acquired sensor measurements from the auxiliary power units (APU) of 34 Airbus A320 over the last two years along with all repairs done on these aircraft engines. The end goal of the project is to discover patterns from these data that can be used to predict component failures.

One of the advantages of our application was the existence of manufacturer's normalization formulas which come from statistical experiments with real engines operating in a controlled environment. For the purpose of evaluation, we have cast the prediction of an engine component failure as a classification task. We have ran a standard inductive learner on this task using non-normalized data, normalized data with manufacturer's formulas, and normalized data obtained with our approach. We have compared the results with respect to the standard accuracy. We have also compared the results of learning from different datasets with respect to the numbers of false positives, as this type of errors is critically important in our application.

The problems related to context-sensitive applications are fairly new to the machine learning community. Turney & Halasz [4] describe a project in which contextual normalization is applied to the diagnosis of engine faults. The normalization in that work is performed by a transformation based on the average and standard deviations of the contextual parameters.

Related to dynamic environments, Taylor & Nakhaeizadeh [3] describe in general the state of the art in learning in dynamically changing domains. They list a number of directions for further research, leading to the the development of robust, scalable systems for dynamic environments. Our work belongs to two of the three fundamental subproblems raised by them: drift/change detection, adaptation/classifier update, characterization and/or explanation of change.

The paper is organized as follows. Section 2 describes the normalization approach. Section 3 describes the data used for validation as well as the results. Section 4 consists of discussion and conclusion. This is a report on the work in progress. A longer version of this paper [2] is available.

2 The normalization approach

The normalization approach proposed here is a pre-processing technique that transforms the contextual sensitive data in order to cancel the effects of the contextual attributes. As usual a fixed set of attributes is used to represent the data. The attributes are divided in two categories: the performance attributes $p_1, \ldots, p_m$ and the contextual attributes $c_1, \ldots, c_k$. Contextual attributes can be numeric or symbolic while performance attributes have to be numeric. The output of the normalization process is a set of normalized performance attributes $p'_1, \ldots, p'_m$ that are no longer affected by the variations in $c_1, \ldots, c_k$.

The normalization approach is composed of two steps: the *contextual analysis* and the *normalization*. In the contextual analysis, we model the effects of each contextual attribute on the performance attributes. During the normalization step, we use the output of the contextual analysis to cancel the effects of the contextual attributes. These two steps may need to be repeated more than once to completely cancel the effects of contexts. Figure 1 presents the global algorithm of the proposed approach. The following sections describe the contextual analysis and the normalization processes.

Algorithm RemoveContextEffects
Input: A dataset in which each of the N instances is described by a set of
attributes $\{p_1, \ldots, p_m, c_1, \ldots, c_k\}$, where p_i and c_i are the
performance and contextual attributes, respectively.
Output: A normalized set of performance attributes $\{p'_1, \ldots, p'_m\}$

$\{CM_1, \ldots, CM_k\}$ = ContextualAnalysis($\{p_1, \ldots, p_m, c_1, \ldots, c_k\}$);
While $\exists$ a cluster name $\neq 1$ in $\{CM_1, \ldots, CM_k\}$ do begin
$\quad \{p'_1, \ldots, p'_m\}$ = Normalize($\{p_1, \ldots, p_m, c_1, \ldots, c_k\}$, $\{CM_1, \ldots, CM_k\}$);
$\quad \{CM_1, \ldots, CM_k\}$ = ContextualAnalysis($\{p'_1, \ldots, p'_m, c_1, \ldots, c_k\}$);
end;
return the new set of performance values $\{p'_1, \ldots, p'_m\}$;

Fig. 1. Remove Contextual Effects Algorithm

2.1 Contextual Analysis

The aim of the contextual analysis is to model the effects of the contextual attributes on the performance attributes. We perform this step using the analysis of variance framework. The contextual attributes are analyzed independently. The procedure is as follows. We first partition each c_i into a set of intervals. A unique label is assigned to each interval. Secondly, we map c_i to c'_i by replacing each value by its corresponding interval label. Finally, we cluster this set of intervals for each of the m performance attributes. Figure 2 summarizes this procedure. As output, the contextual analysis returns a set of k contextual matrices $CM_1, \ldots, CM_k$, where each CM_i describes the clustering of the performance attributes $p_1, \ldots, p_m$ according to c_i.

Partitioning a contextual attribute into a set of intervals The first step is to partition each c_i into interval cells that are appropriate for ANOVA. The performance attributes are not used during the partitionning step. The number of intervals created may differ from one contextual attribute to another. A sligthly different approach is used for numerical and symbolic attributes. When c_i is symbolic, an interval is defined for each observed outcome (i.e. each interval corresponds to a value). When c_i is numeric, the intervals are built in such a way that i) the intervals are approximately of equal size, and ii) each interval has a minimum of 50 elements. We introduce these conditions due to their impact on

Algorithm ContextualAnalysis

Input: A dataset as described in Algorithm RemoveContextEffects.

Output: A set of k matrices $CM_1,\ldots,CM_k$ describing the contextual effects of each c_i.

For $i:=1$ to k do begin

    Partition c_i in a set of r intervals labeled $1,\ldots,r$;

    Record definition of intervals in first two columns of CM_i;

    For $j:=1$ to N do $c_i'[j] :=$ IntervalLabelOf($c_i[j]$);

    For $j:=1$ to m do begin

        $V :=$ ClusterIntervals(p_j, c_i') ;

        Record vector V in column $2 + j$ of CM_i;

    end;

end;

return $CM_1,\ldots,CM_k$;

Fig. 2. Contextual Analysis Algorithm

the results of the ANOVA. The set of intervals for c_i are lablelled from $1,\ldots,r_i$. We then create c_i' by mapping each value of c_i to its corresponding interval label.

Cluster the intervals: Use of ANOVA The attribute c_i' is now used to find clusters of intervals that model the effects of c_i on each p_j. We use the ANOVA approach as a basis for the search for these clusters. The ANOVA is a remarkably robust and efficient technique to handle large volume of data.

As shown in Figure 2, the procedure that clusters the intervals is repeated for each pair of c_i and p_j. The procedure starts by performing an ANOVA to test whether c_i' has an overall effect on p_j. If there is no effect then it assigns all intervals to a unique cluster (i.e. cluster #1). If there is an effect then the procedure performs pairwise mean comparisons (with a t test equivalent to the Fisher's protected LSD test). If means of p_j over intervals l and m are different (at a level of 0.05) then it assigns intervals l and m to two different clusters, otherwise it assigns these intervals to the same cluster. As output, the procedure returns a 1 by r_i vector V that describes the clustering obtained for the intervals of c_i.

2.2 Normalization

The normalization step leads to a new set of performance attributes $\{p_1',\ldots,p_m'\}$ for which the effects described in $CM_1,\ldots,CM_k$ are reduced. The normalization algorithm is summarized in Figure 3. The basic idea is very simple: we normalize each performance value $p_j[i]$ ($j = 1,\ldots,m$ and $i = 1,\ldots,N$) by adding to it a *context penalty number*, denoted by δ. δ is defined as the difference between the expected value of $p_j[i]$ (noted β) and the overall mean of p_j (noted $\bar{p}_j$). β combines the effects of the contextual attributes by averaging the $\bar{p}_{j,clu_l}$ for $l = 1,\ldots,k$, where $\bar{p}_{j,clu_l}$ denotes the mean of p_j in cluster clu_l. In the current version of the algorithm, we consider all attributes as equally important during the computation of β. However, we think that a faster convergence rate could be obtained by the use of a weighting average that would take into account the relative importance of each contextual attribute on p_j. The information contained in the CM_i seems to have some potential to weigh the contextual attributes, but this issue hasn't been investigated yet.

Algorithm Normalize

Input: i) A dataset as described in Algorithm RemoveContextEffects.

    ii) A set of k matrices $CM_1,\ldots,CM_k$ generated by ContextAnalysis.

Output: A (partially) normalized set of performance attributes $\{p'_1,\ldots,p'_m\}$.

For $i:=1$ to N do begin

    For $j:=1$ to m do begin

        Determine context status C for the value $p_j[i]$;

        Compute β, the expected value of p_j given C;

        $\delta := \beta - \overline{p}_j$ { δ is the *contextpenaltynumber* and $\overline{p}_j$ is the mean of p_j. }

        $p'_j[i] := p_j[i] + \delta$;

    end;

end;

return the new set of performance values $\{p'_1,\ldots,p'_m\}$;

Fig. 3. Normalization Algorithm

3 Experimental results

The data used in our exprimentation comes from the Auxiliary Power Unit engines of a fleet of Airbus A-320. The dataset consists of 31059 cases of 23 attributes (2 symbolic, 19 numeric, and 2 for date and time of the event).The task was to develop classifiers to predict starter motor failures. Domain experts have identified three performance attributes for the starter problem: *STA*, *EGP*, and *NPA*. These attributes are all affected by variations in the environment (pressure, temperature, altitude, etc.) We used our normalization approach to normalize these performance attributes according to the remaining 18 contextual attributes (2 symbolic and 16 numeric). As usual in diagnosis problem, early predictions would have been appreciated, but the client insisted on the fact that false alarms (i.e. prediction of a problem when there is no problem) should be avoided as much as possible. To address these issues, we have selected four targets for prediction: 45 days, 30 days, 15 days, and 10 days. For each of these targets, we have developed four classifiers by respectively using: 1) the initial 21 attributes, 2) the three initial performance attributes before normalization, 3) the three normalized attributes obtained using formulas provided by the manufacturer of the APUs, and 4) the three normalized attributes obtained from our approach. Table 1 presents the average accuracies and average number of false alarms (obtained from two-fold cross-validation experiments) of the classifiers developped.

Attributes used	Task 45 days		Task 30 days		Task 15 days		Task 10 days	
	Acc	F.Alarm	Acc	F.Alarm	Acc	F.Alarm	Acc	F.Alarm
21 APU att.	94.9	141.5	96.0	131.0	97.8	74.5	98.6	31.5
3 init. perf. att.	94.3	81.5	96.1	80.0	97.9	57.0	98.6	27.5
3 Manuf. norm. att.	94.2	144.0	96.2	78.0	98.0	51.0	98.5	40.0
3 new norm. att.	94.3	85.0	96.0	61.0	98.0	47.5	98.5	35.0

Table 1. Accuracies and number of false alarms (false positive errors) for the runs for the different tasks

Since the four target tasks use different data, one should only compare results within one column. Comparing just the accuracies for different classifiers is not of great help for two reasons: i) the accuracies of the classifiers in each task are very close, and ii) no classifier consistently outperformed the others over the four learning tasks. The inadequacy of simple accuracies for this problem can be explained by the fact that our data sets are imbalanced[1]. In terms of number of false alarms, values obtained from our approach performed very well. In two cases (30 and 15 days), they have lead to the minimum number of false alarms. In the other two cases (45 and 10 days), the numbers of false alarms with the new values were close to the minimum number obtained. It is also interesting to note that the classifier obtained with values from our approach generates fewer false alarms than the one obtained with the manufacturer's formulas in all four tasks.

4 Discussion and conclusion

It is important to note that the approach presented in this paper is less sensitive than ANOVA regarding the violation of the following assumptions: i) normality of the data, ii) equal variances for the different groups, and iii) independent error components. In fact, the only impact of a violation of these assumptions will be on the convergence rate. When these assumptions do not hold, we are likely to increase the number of errors during pairwise mean comparisons which will results in non-optimal normalization in each iteration of the approach. As a consequence, the overall process will be slower.

In this paper, we describe a pre-processing method that cancels the effects of contextual attributes. This method includes two algorithms: one for contextual analysis and the other for normalization. Evaluating our approach, we have developed classifiers for prediction tasks. Results showed that the number of false alarms would be substantially lower when we used our normalized attributes instead of using the ones obtained from manufacturer-supplied formulas.

We believe that our approach has a lot of potential for performing advanced data analysis in context sensitive domains where the class attribute is not known ahead of time. The approach could be applied for timely prediction of failures that in most cases is very expensive to deal with. Finally, our approach can also be used for dimensionality reduction so that data analysis is performed more precisely.

Acknowledgments The authors would like to thank Air Canada for providing the data and the very useful feedback on this research. The first author is partially supported by the Natural Sciences and Engineering Research Council of Canada.

References

1. Kubat, M., Holte, R. C., Matwin, S.: Machine Learning for the Detection of Oil Spills in Satellite radar Images Machine Learning Journal, Special Issue on Applications of ML. (1998) to appear.
2. Letourneau, S., Matwin, S., Famili, F.: A Normalization Method for Contextual Data: Experience From A Large- Scale Application. TR-98-02, www.csi.uottawa.ca/~stan/public_html/techrep/TR-98-02.ps.
3. Taylor, C., Nakhaeizadeh, G.: Learning in Dynamically Changing Domains: Theory Revision and Context Dependence Issues. Proceedings of ECML-97. (1997) 353-360.
4. Turney, P, Halasz, M: Contextual Normalization Applied to Aircraft Gas Turbine Engine Diagnosis. Journal of Applied Intelligence **3** (1993) 109-129

Learning to Classify X-Ray Images Using Relational Learning

Claude Sammut[1] and Tatjana Zrimec[1,2]

[1] School of Computer Science and Engineering, University of New South Wales,
Sydney 2052, Australia
[2] Faculty of Computer and Information Science, University of Ljubljana,
Tržaška 25, 1001 Ljubljana, Slovenia

Abstract: Image understanding often requires extensive background knowledge. The problem addressed in this paper is such knowledge can be acquired. We discuss how relational machine learning methods can be used to automatically build rules for classifying types of blood vessels. We introduce a new learning system that can make use of background knowledge coded as arbitrarily complex Prolog programs to construct concept descriptions, particularly those needed to classify features in an image.

1   Introduction

Model-based image processing is the application of knowledge about objects expected in a scene to the recognition of those objects if they appear in an image. In medical image understanding (Zrimec & Sammut 1997; Robinson *et al* 1993), expert radiologists bring a wealth of experience to bear on the problem of interpreting x-ray images. Much of the knowledge needed for such a task can be obtained from text books. However, each radiologist accumulates a large amount of personal experience in understanding the contents of an x-ray image. The challenge for an automated image understanding system is how such experience can be gathered by a program. In this paper, we argue that a relational learning system can acquire such knowledge. However, the program itself must also be capable of using extensive background knowledge.

We introduce a new learning system that extends Cohen's (1996) work on refinement rules. This system, which is part of the *iProlog* machine learning environment (Sammut 1997), can take advantage of background knowledge encoded as arbitrarily complex Prolog programs. As we shall see, this is particularly useful in constructing some of the high-level relations needed to synthesise programs capable of recognising different types of blood vessels.

A further problem for learning in this domain is that while the examples are quite complex, there are only a few of them. This is due to the difficulty of obtaining x-ray images that have been fully interpreted and labelled by an expert. Because of the small sample size, we employ a specific-to-general search based on Plotkin's (1971) relative least general generalisation (RLGG). However, we severely limit the number of literals in the RLGG in a manner related to those described by Page and Frisch (1992).

X-ray image

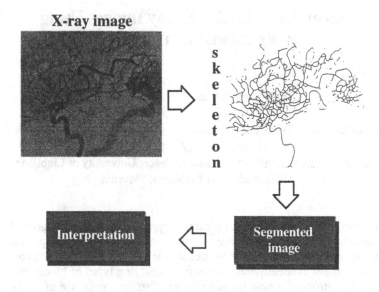

Fig.1. The image interpretation process

In the following section, we briefly describe the image processing required to obtain the input to the learning program. We then introduce the mechanisms for generating clausal descriptions of the examples and the generalisation mechanism. We conclude with a discussion of the current status of the work and future directions.

2 Interpreting X-ray Images

Figure 1 outlines the process of interpretating x-ray angiograms of a patient's cerebral vasculature. X-rays are normally taken from several standard views of the patient's brain. An image passes through the following preprocessing stages.

1. The grey-scale x-ray image is thresholded to obtain a black-and-white image.
2. The black-and-white image is *skeletonised* to reduce thick vessels to lines only a single pixel wide.
3. The skeleton is traced to join pixels into segments of blood vessels.
4. The segmented skeleton is used to guide further processing of the grey-scale image to obtain diameters and intensity values of each blood vessel segment.

In practice, this process is iterative. Different levels of thresholding reveal more detail and also more noise. The method used here is to first apply aggressive thresholding, obtaining only the most prominent blood vessels. Gradually, the threshold is decreased to admit more detail. The blood vessels recognised in the previous pass can be used to guide further recognition. For the purposes of this paper, we will only consider a single pass with a high threshold to obtain a relatively simple set of segments.

The output of the tracing program is a set of Prolog facts that will be input to the learning program. For example, the following clauses:

```
blood_vessel(mb1, 1, 'ICA').
segment(1, mb1, n, 40, 130, [2]).
segment(2, mb1, w, 40, 144, [3]).
segment(3, mb1, nw, 35, 135, [4, 5]).
segment(4, mb1, n, 40, 50, [6, 7]).
segment(6, mb1, ne, 20, 170, [8, 9]).
segment(5, mb1b1, e, 10, 100, []).
segment(7, mb1b2, w, 5, 125, []).
segment(8, mb1b3, e, 18, 90, []).
segment(9, mb1b4, n, 15, 100, []).
```

describe a blood vessel *mb1*, of type *ICA* (Internal Carotid Artery) which starts with segment number 1. Each segment is described by an atom with the following arguments: the segment's segment number, the identifier of the blood vessel to which the segment belongs, the direction of the segment (north, north-east, east, south-east, *etc*), the diameter of the segment the grey-level intensity of the segment and finally, a list of segments that branch from the end of this segment. A segment's boundaries are where there is a branch or a bend in the blood vessel.

Suppose we wish to train the learning program to recognise different types of blood vessels. What kinds regularities would we expect the program to discover from examples of, say, the Internal Carotid Artery? One may be that the diameter reaches its maximum somewhere near the middle segment and this always corresponds to the intensity at its lowest value. Another may be that the final segment always ends pointing north-east. And another is that the internal carotid artery always has branches leading to two other arteries before it bifurcates into two more arteries, one of which goes north and the other east. The learning system must invoke background knowledge to obtain a useful set of predicates for such descriptions. In the following section, we describe how we make use of background knowledge.

3   Refinement Rules and Generalisation

Cohen (1996) introduced refinement rules as a method for constructing new literals to add to clauses during a general-to-specific search. A restricted second order theorem prover was is to interpret these rules. However, this theorem prover is limited to a simple function-free language. The system described in this paper is a component of *iProlog* (Sammut 1997). This is an ISO compatible Prolog interpreter with a variety of machine learning tools embedded as built-in predicates. Since the full power of Prolog is available, the refinement rules we implement can invoke arbitrary Prolog programs.

Two types of refinement rule must be defined. A *head rule* has the form:

$$\langle A, Pre, Post \rangle$$

where A is a positive literal, *Pre* is a conjunction of literals and *Post* is a set of positive literals. A *body rule* has the form:

$$\langle \leftarrow B, Pre, Post \rangle$$

where B is a positive literal and *Pre* and *Post* are as above.

There must only be one head rule to that A should be used to create the head of the clause being learned, provided that the condition *Pre* is satisfied. After A has been constructed, the literals in *Post*, are asserted into Prolog's database. There may be any number of body rules to generate literals for the body of the clause under construction. Literals in the precondition of these rules may invoke any Prolog program.

Suppose we wish to create a saturated clause (Rouveirol & Puget 1990; Sammut 1986) based on the example of blood vessel *mb1*, shown in the previous section. The left-hand side of the following rule is the template for the head literal.

```
blood_vessel(VesselName, StartingSegment, VesselType)
    where
            true
    asserting
            seg_list(VesselName, [StartingSegment]).
```

The *where* part of the rule is the precondition and the *asserting* part is the post-condition. Refinement rules are invoked in a forward chaining manner. The head rule matches the predicate blood_vessel(mb1, 1, 'ICA'). Since there are no preconditions, the head of the new clause is created and the predicate seg_list(mb1, [1]) is asserted into the database. This enables the following body rule to construct literals for the segments of the blood vessel:

```
(:- segment(SegId, VesselName, Dirn, Diam, Inten, SegList))
    where
            seg_list(VesselName, S),
            member(SegId, S)
    asserting
            seg_list(VesselName, SegList),
            diameter(VesselName, SegId, Diameter),
            intensity(VesselName, SegId, Intensity).
```

For each match of the template and for each solution to the preconditions, a new segment literal is created and the corresponding post-conditions are asserted. After execution of this rule, the clause is:

```
blood_vessel(mb1, 1, 'ICA') :-
            segment(1, mb1, n, 40, 130, [2]),
            segment(2, mb1, w, 40, 144, [3]),
            segment(3, mb1, nw, 35, 135, [4, 5]),
            segment(4, mb1, n, 40, 50, [6, 7]),
            segment(6, mb1, ne, 20, 170, [8, 9]).
```

We next include a rule that constructs a '>' relation on the diameters and intensities of the blood vessel segments.

```
(:- X > Y)
    where
            measurement(M), M(V, S1, X), M(V, S2, Y).

measurement(distance).
measurement(intensity).
```

A second order extension to Prolog permits the principal functor of a predicate to be a variable provided that at run time, the variable is bound to a valid predicate symbol. Without the precondition above, it would be possible to have comparisons where one argument is a diameter and another is an intensity or between numbers belonging to different blood vessels. We can now see that the assertions in the *segment* rule provide type information used by the X > Y rule. Execution of this rule would add literals of the form X > Y for all pairs of diameters and intensities of segments in *mb1*.

A more sophisticated piece of background knowledge is required if we wish to include in the concept description which segment has, say, the maximum diameter. This is a little tricky because the refinement rule must scan all of the segments to find the maximum value. We now see the power of Prolog being used to construct a new literal. First, we require a predicate that can find the maximum value of a measurement. We use the second order extension to make this predicate generic for different types.

```
max(M, V, S, X) :-
    findall(M(V, S, N), M(V, S, N), L),
    max(L, M(V, S, X)).

max([X], X) :- !.
max([M(V, SA, A)|B], M(V, S, X)) :-
    max(B, M(V, SY, Y)),
    (A > Y -> S = SA, X = A; S = SY, X = Y).
```

This can be read as: the maximum value of measurement *M* in blood vessel, *V*, occurs in segment, *S*, and has value, *N*. The predicate can be invoked from the body rule:

```
(:- max(M, V, S, N))
    where
            measurement(M),
            blood_vessel(V, _, _),
            max(M, V, S, N).
```

A corresponding rule can defined for the minimum value. After execution of these rules, the following literals are added to the clause:

```
            max(diameter, mb1, 1, 40)
            max(diameter, mb1, 2, 40)
            max(diameter, mb1, 4, 40)
            max(intensity, mb1, 6, 170)
            min(diameter, mb1, 6, 20)
            min(intensity, mb1, 4, 50)
```

The segment of interest is number 4 since it has the maximum diameter and minimum intensity.

Once a clause has been saturated, we need a generalisation mechanism. We mentioned earlier that while the examples in this domain can give rise to quite complex descriptions, only small data sets are available. Typically, general-to-specific search methods require a reasonably large sample for their statistics to be accurate. For this reason, we have chosen to experiment with a specific-to-general search based on Plotkin's (1971) relative least general generalisation (RLGG). The first step is to use saturation, as described in the previous section, to build clauses which are then passed to an LGG algorithm for generalisation. However, a pure LGG generates far too many irrelevant literals. Therefore, we follow an approach similar in spirit to the constrained atoms of Page and Frisch (1992). Since the refinement rules impose restrictions on the form of literals that can be generated through saturation, it is reasonable to apply the same restrictions to literals constructed by generalisation. Thus, we modify Plotkin's LGG algorithm to filter literals so that whenever an LGG of two literals is found, it is tested against the refinement rules. If no refinement rule is satisfied, the LGG is rejected. As a result, the RLGG's do not grow to impractical sizes.

4 Discussion

The current status of this project is that the programming of the image processing and machine learning software has been completed. Initial testing on sample x-ray images is has begun, but full-scale trials are yet to be conducted. There are several novel aspects to this work:

- We have modified Cohen's refinement rule approach to permit the introduction of complex background knowledge through Prolog programs.
- We have used the refinement rules, together with a method for tagging literals to constrain the size of RLGG's.
- We have applied this approach to the problem of model-based image interpretation, particularly for x-ray images.

We believe that studying methods for making effective use of intentional background knowledge is important for the development of ILP. It's greatest advantage over propositional learning methods is the possibility of employing background knowledge to construct concept descriptions that are beyond the capabilities of other kinds of learning systems.

References

Cohen, W. (1996). Learning to classify English text with ILP methods. In L. D. Raedt (Eds.), *Advances in Logic programming*. (pp. 124-143). IOS Press.

Page, C. D., & Frisch, A. M. (1992). Generalization and Learnability: A study of constrained atoms. In S. Muggleton (Eds.), *Inductive Logic Programming*. (pp. 29-61). Academic Press.

Plotkin, G. D. (1971). A further note on inductive generalization. In B. Meltzer & D. Michie (Eds.), *Machine Intelligence 6*. New York: Elsevier.

Robinson, G.P., Colchester , A.C.F., Griffin, L.D. (1993) Model Based Recognition of Anatomical Objects from Medical Images. In *Information Processing in Medical Imaging*, 13th International Conference, IPMI'93, Arizona, USA, (pp. 197–211).

Rouveirol, C., & Puget, J.-F. (1990). Beyond Inversion of Resolution. In *Proceedings of the Seventh International Conference on Machine Learning*, Morgan Kaufmann.

Sammut, C. A., & Banerji, R. B. (1986). Learning Concepts by Asking Questions. In R. S. Michalski Carbonell, J.G. and Mitchell, T.M. (Eds.), *Machine Learning: An Artificial Intelligence Approach, Vol 2*. (pp. 167-192). Los Altos, California: Morgan Kaufmann.

Sammut, C. (1997). Using background knowledge to build multistrategy learners. *Machine Learning*, **27**, 241-257.

Zrimec, T. and Sammut, C.A., (1997). A Medical Image Understanding System, *Engineering applications of Artificial Intelligence*, February, **10** (1), 31-39.

ILP Experiments in Detecting Traffic Problems

Sašo Džeroski[1], Nico Jacobs[2], Martin Molina[3], Carlos Moure[3]

[1] J. Stefan Institute, Jamova 39, SI-1000 Ljubljana, Slovenia
[2] K.U.Leuven, Celestijnenlaan 200A, B-3001 Heverlee, Belgium
[3] Universidad Politecnica de Madrid, E-28660 Boadilla del Monte, Madrid, Spain

Abstract. Expert systems for decision support have recently been successfully introduced in road transport management. These systems include knowledge on traffic problem detection and alleviation. The paper describes experiments in automated acquisition of knowledge on traffic problem detection. The task is to detect road sections where a problem has occured (critical sections) from sensor data. It is necessary to use inductive logic programming (ILP) for this purpose as relational background knowledge on the road network is essential. Preliminary results show that ILP can be used to successfully learn to detect traffic problems.

1 Introduction

Expert systems for decision support have recently been successfully introduced in road transport management. Some of the proposals in this direction are TRYS [4], KITS [3] and ARTIST [6]. From a general perspective, the goal of a real time traffic expert system for decision support is to advise traffic management center operators by proposing control actions to eliminate or reduce problems according to the global state of traffic. To asses the global state of traffic, the system periodically receives readings from sensors on the road, which measure magnitudes such as speed (Km/h), flow (veh/h) and occupancy (percentage of time that the sensor is occupied by vehicles), as well as information about the current state of control devices, such as traffic signals at intersections, traffic signals at sideway on-ramps, CMS (Changeable Message Signs), etc. The system interprets sensor data, detects the presence of a problem, gives the possible cause and proposes recommendations about how to solve or reduce it.

The usual approach to building traffic expert systems is to use knowledge based architectures that support the strategies of reasoning followed by operators. This approach requires to develop knowledge bases using symbolic representations (such as rules, frames, or constraints) that include specific domain knowledge of transport management corresponding to the city for which the system is developed. Among other things, knowledge on detecting specific traffic problems is necessary.

On the other hand, traffic management centers have databases that include basic information about different traffic scenarios, such as congestions at certain locations caused by lack of capacity due to accidents or excess of demand (rush hours). This data, collected from sensors on the road, can be used to either generate or improve the knowledge base for problem (incident) detection of the expert system. The paper explores the possibility to use inductive learning techniques (such as ILP-inductive logic programming) to generate knowledge on traffic problem detection from from historical data that contains parameters recorded by sensors.

The learning experiments described in this paper take place within the context of the traffic management expert system TRYS [4], developed for the cities of Madrid and Barcelona. The system uses knowledge distributed in a collection of knowledge bases that use different representations and address specific tasks (such as data abstraction, incident detection, problem diagnosis, prediction of behaviour, and recommendation of control actions). The knowledge for incident (traffic problem) detection has been formulated by domain experts in a first-order frame-based representation. Therefore, ILP is a suitable tool for learning to detect traffic problems in this context.

Overall, two kinds of input are available to the learning process. The first type is background knowledge on the road network, which is present in and used by the TRYS system. An object oriented representation is used to capture the different types of road sections, the relations among them, and the placement of sensors on individual road sections. The second type is sensor readings on three basic quantities describing traffic behaviour: speed, flow and occupancy. Both types of input will be described in more detail in Section 2. The goal of the learning process is to identify critical sections (where problems have occured) by using sensor readings and road geometry. Technically speaking, a critical section is a section of the road which constrains the road capacity the most, e.g., because an accident has occured just after this section in the immediate past. In the paper, the term accident critical section refers to such a section and not to a section where accidents occur frequently.

Let us note at this point that in practice real sensor data are available. However, we have used simulated data in our experiments for three reasons. The first is that real sensor data were not immediately available because of management reasons. The second is missing sensor data from broken sensors (which amounts to approximately 20% of the sensors). Finally, using a simulator makes it possible to easily generate a wide range of different traffic problems (including accidents that should not be artificially produced in the real world).

We used AIMSUN (Advanced Interactive Microscopic Simulator for Urban and Non-Urban Networks) [1], a software tool able to reproduce the real traffic conditions of any urban network on a computer. AIMSUN follows a microscopic simulation approach. It means that the behaviour of each individual vehicle in the network is continuously modelled throughout the simulation time period it remains inside the system (i.e. the traffic network), according to several vehicle behaviour models. A model of the urban-ring of the city of Barcelona was developed using this simulator. This model includes exactly the same variables that the real information system records using sensors and was calibrated using information from the real system. Using this model, a collection of examples (including accidents and congestions due to rush hours) were produced for the learning experiments presented in the paper.

2 Road network and sensor data

In TRYS [4], the road network is represented in an object oriented fashion. The basic object in the road network representation is the section. A section refers to a cross-section of the road and typically has an array of sensors associated to it. There exist several types of sections, such as off-ramp, on-ramp or highway. Relations between sections, such as previous and next, are included in the TRYS knowledge base. The complexity of road structures makes it possible for a section to have more than two previous or next sections.

A link describes a logical group of sections. For instance, the section just before and just after an off-ramp, together with the off-ramp itself, form an off-ramp-link. There are about ten different types of links. TRYS also uses other concepts like nodes, problem areas and measurement points, but these were not used in our experiments.

The information about sections and links is static. Each section is of a certain type and is associated to a number of sensors (as many sensors as there are lanes at that cross-section of the road) and each link is of a certain type and links a predefined set of sections. These relationships can therefore be considered background knowledge for the learning process.

Sensors provide us with a continuous stream of information, sending five readings each minute that refer to the last minute and each of the four minutes preceding it. Typically, flow (number of cars that passed the sensor in the last minute) and occupancy (the pro mille of time the sensor is occupied) are measured. Some sensors (which are actually double sensors) also measure the average speed of the cars that passed the sensor during the last minute. The measurements of sensors related to a single section are aggregated: flow is summed across lanes, while occupancy and velocity are averaged across lanes. Saturation is a derived quantity defined as the ratio between the flow and the capacity of a section: the latter depends on the number of lanes and is part of the background knowledge.

The TRYS system stores its information in two formats: in CONCEL format, which is a frame-based format, and in Prolog format. The Prolog format is object-oriented and consists mainly of facts about the predicates `instance` and `value`. For simplicity reasons, we transform these facts in the following fashion: facts of the form `instance(Instance,Class)` are translated to facts of the form `Class(Instance)` and facts of the form `value(Instance,Attribute,Value)` are translated to facts of the form `Attribute(Instance, Value)`. For example, the fact `instance(salida_a_rambla_Prim,off_ramp)` is transformed to `off_ramp(salida_a_rambla_Prim)`.

3 An experiment with CLAUDIEN

In a preliminary experiment, nine accidents and two congestions at two different off-ramp links were simulated. In addition to the data transformation described above, the values for speed, saturation and occupancy were discretized according to expert provided thresholds that are in use in TRYS. One of the reasons for discretizing was the small number of examples used.

The static information about sections and links was used as background knowledge. Examples consisted of facts specifying the speed, occupancy and saturation for all sections in the relevant problem area at one moment in time. Each example also contained exactly one fact of the form accidentat(X) or congestionat(X), where X is the critical section. The task was to find rules that identify critical sections by using sensor values and road geometry.

The ILP system CLAUDIEN [5] was used in this experiment for two reasons. First, the small number of examples dictates the use of a strong declarative bias (which is provided by CLAUDIEN) in order to obtain reasonable rules. Second, CLAUDIEN generates all valid rules, providing some redundancy that might be useful in the light of missing sensor information which will occur in real world data.

Three rules cover all 9 accident examples. The first says there is an accident at critical section X, which is the previous section of off-ramp link Y (enlace de salida) with next section O and ramp section R, if the speed (velocidad) at X is not high (alta), the speed at O is high and the saturation on R is low (baja). The predicate names originating from the TRYS-system are in Spanish.

```
accidentat(X) :-
  seccion(X), seccion_anterior(Y,X), seccion_posterior(Y,O),
  enlace_de_salida(Y), velocidad(X,VX), not VX = alta,
  velocidad(O,VO), VO = alta,
  seccion_en_rampa(Y,R), saturacion(R,SR), SR = baja.
```

There were also two examples of congestion at an off-ramp and two rules rules covered both examples. The first of these says there is a congestion at the ramp section X (seccion en rampa) of the off-ramp link Y (enlace de salida) when the occupancy of X is not low. All five rules describe sensible conditions that were already known to the domain experts. This indicated that ILP might be useful in this domain, and encouraged us to undertake further experiments.

4 Experiments with TILDE

An extended dataset containing 66 examples of congestion and 62 examples of accidents on different locations (off-ramp, on-ramp and highway sections) was generated using the simulator. The aim of the experiments with the extended dataset was to understand which measurements and road geometry predicates are relevant to the learning task at hand. Given this aim and the larger set of simulations, the task was formulated as a classification task.

Each section at a particular moment of time was treated as an example, classified into one of three classes: an accident critical section, a congestion critical section or a non critical section. In this way we obtained a dataset consisting of 5952 examples. Facts on sensor values (which were not discretized) were moved to the background knowledge, which also included facts on road geometry. Predicates that allow access to sections before and after a given section, as well as predicates that calculate the speed-, saturation- and occupancy-gain (also in percentages) between sections were added to the background knowledge.

The TILDE system [2] — based on top down induction of logical decision trees — was used for experiments with this dataset for a number of reasons. First, TILDE addresses classification problems in a first-order setting. Second, it allows for a very weak language bias that easily handles a variety of situations (unlike our preliminary experiment where all critical sections were on an off-ramp). Third, it can deal with real-valued sensor measurements directly, performing discretization itself. Finally, TILDE is very efficient, an important aspect for our problem where we have background knowledge of size approx. 1 MB and 5952 examples.

Two experiments were performed. In the first experiment TILDE had to build a classifier for all three classes, while in the second experiment it was only given critical sections and had to build a classifier that distinguishes between the two types of critical sections. In both experiments a 6-fold cross-validation was performed.

The first experiment gave some encouraging results: 80% of the congestion critical sections were classified correctly and only 39 out of the 5824 non critical sections were classified incorrectly. None of the congestion critical sections were classified as accident or vice versa. The results for accident critical sections were much worse: only 38 out of the 62 examples (61%) were classified correctly. Why accidents are harder to classify than congestions needs to be investigated. A potential problem is also the extremely skewed class distribution (only 128 of almost 6000 examples are critical sections).

When we take a look at the predicates used, we see that the trees very rarely refer to previous sections, but often refer to sections downstream (the use of the gain-predicates is not considered as a reference to the previous section). Regarding the predicates related to sensor measurements, speed (used 60 times), occupancy gain (57) and saturation (54) seem to be important concepts, whereas the gain and percentage gain predicates seem to be less important.

As expected, the second task of predicting the class of a given critical section is much simpler that the first: 96.9% of the congestions and 96.7% of the accidents were classified correctly. Moreover, the decision tree was built very fast (about 3 seconds, compared to the 4 hours it took in the first experiment). Surprisingly, very few predicates were used: saturation, occupancy and the type of section were used in most trees, whereas a reference to the next section appears in only one of the six trees. One of the decision trees states that a section is accident critical if its saturation is below 42.75, otherwise it is congestion critical unless of type highway (when it is again accident critical).

5 Discussion

We have presented a novel application domain for inductive logic programming, namely the domain of detecting traffic problems. The task addressed was to learn rules that identify critical road sections due to accidents or congestions. Background knowledge on road geometry is available, requiring the use of ILP for this task. While simulated data were used for our experiments, it should be noted that the simulator is very realistic and has been calibrated using real-world data.

In a preliminary experiment with CLAUDIEN interesting (but already known) rules were found, encouraging further experiments. A larger set of examples generated using the simulator was supplied to TILDE. The trees generated indicate that sections downstream provide important information on whether the section at hand is a critical one, as well as the predicates providing the values of speed, occupancy gain and saturation.

Much work remains to be done. High on the priority list is the task of learning to distinguish between non critical and any type of critical section. A difficulty that has to be taken into account is the skewed class distribution. Distinguishing among different types of critical sections seems to be an easier task as indicated by our second experiment with TILDE.

Exploring the use of other ILP systems and other biases (background knowledge predicates) will also receive considerable attention. A practical issue of utmost importance is the issue of using real sensor data instead of simulated data. Missing sensor values are a problem that has to be dealt with here and redundant rules will have to be built for this purpose.

Other issues to be addressed include mapping the induced problem detection rules into a frame-based representation with which experts are familiar and using the time series of sensor values instead of the current values only. The domain of traffic control also holds other challenges for machine learning techniques. Detecting traffic problems is only one step of the traffic management process: suggesting actions to alleviate the problems is the natural next step. Since examples of operator actions in response to detected problems exist, there is hope that the problem of suggesting appropriate actions for alleviating traffic problems can also be addressed using machine learning and inductive logic programming.

Acknowledgements Nico Jacobs is financed by a specialisation grant of the Flemish Institute for supporting scientific-technological research in the industry (IWT). This work was supported by the ESPRIT IV Project 20237 ILP2.

References

1. Barcelo, J., Ferrer J.L., and Montero, L. (1989). *AIMSUN: Advanced Interactive Microscopic Simulator for Urban Networks. Vol I: System Description, and Vol II: User's Manual.* Departamento de Estadistica e Investigacion Operativa, Facultad de Informatica, Universidad Politecnica de Cataluna, Barcelona, Spain.
2. Blockeel, H., and De Raedt, L. (1997). Lookahead and discretization in ILP. In *Proc. 7th Intl. Workshop on Inductive Logic Programming*, pages 77–84, Springer, Berlin.
3. Cuena, J., Ambrosino, G., and Boero M. (1992) A general knowledge-based architecture for traffic control: The KITS approach. In *Proc. Intl. Conf. on Artificial Intelligence Applications in Transportation Engineering*. San Buenaventura, CA.
4. Cuena, J., Hernandez, J., and Molina, M. (1995). Knowledge-based models for adaptive traffic management systems. *Transportation Research: Part C*, 3(5): 311-337.
5. De Raedt, L., and Dehaspe, L. (1997). Clausal discovery. *Machine Learning*, 26: 99–146.
6. Deeter, D.L., and Ritchie, S.G. (1993). A prototype real-time expert system for surface street traffic management and control. In *Proc. 3rd Intl. Conf. on Applications of Advanced Technologies in Transportation Engineering*, Seattle, WA.

Simulating Children Learning and Explaining Elementary Heat Transfer Phenomena: A Multistrategy System at Work

Filippo Neri

Università di Torino
Dipartimento di Informatica
Corso Svizzera 185
10149 Torino (Italy)
neri@di.unito.it

Keywords: cognitive modelling, multistrategy learning, conceptual change, causality

Abstract

The multistrategy learning system WHY is used as a testbed for investigating a computational cognitive model of conceptual change in children learning elementary physics[1]. Goal of the simulation is to support the cognitive scientist's investigation of learning in humans.

The student's mental model is manually inferred by the cognitive scientist, and by interacting with WHY, from a sequence of interviews collected along a period of eleven teaching sessions. The hypothesized cognitive models are based on a theory of conceptual change, derived from psychology results and educational experiences, which accounts for the evolution of the student's knowledge over a learning period.

The multistrategy learning system WHY, able to handle domain knowledge (including a causal model of the domain), has been chosen as tool for the *interactive* simulation of the cognitive models evolution. The system is able to model both the answers and the causal explanations given by the children. An example of modelisation of an observed conceptual change is provided.

1 Introduction

People acquire, in their lifetime, models of the world that they use to interpret data, to explain phenomena and to make predictions. These models usually evolve when new information is gathered, and their evolution can be described as a particular aspect of learning, called *conceptual change* [Tiberghien, 1989, 1994; Vosniadou & Brewer, 1994; Caravita & Halldén,1994; Chi et al., 1994; Vosniadou, 1994]. The issue of conceptual change has been addressed from a variety of perspectives, but, even though quite a large body of experimental findings has been collected, still no single definition of conceptual change is universally accepted [White,1994]. Conceptual

---

[1] This work has been performed within the project "Learning in Humans and Machines", supported by the European Science Foundation

change has been mainly studied in the context of learning Mathematics or Physics [Forbus & Gentner, 1986; diSessa, 1993; Vosniadou, 1994; Chi et al., 1994].

Goal of our research is to help the cognitive scientist in developing a **computational model** of the student. In turn, this could also produce a deeper understanding of how and when conceptual change happens thus allowing to fully automatize the model evolution process. Instead, we are not currently concerned with the task of providing the cognitive scientist with some machine-generated student's model to be tested with time consuming psychological experiments.

Models of conceptual change proposed in Cognitive Science have a **descriptive** nature: they describe mental models or knowledge states, but do not provide an account for the actual mechanisms of transition from a knowledge state to another.

Rumelhart and Norman [1977] have categorized the type of transitions occurring as *Accretion, Tuning* and *Restructuration*, which are reminiscent of Piaget's *Assimilation, Accomodation*, and *Self-Regulation*. Accretion involves addition of new information to existing theories, and presents no problem when the new information does not contradict previous knowledge. When the new information is inconsistent with previous theories, tuning or restructuration may occur. However, when a contradiction emerges, also *failures in learning* may happen, taking the form of *inert knowledge* or *misconceptions*.

Computational model of human learning have been studied in [Sleeman et al., 1990; Baffes & Mooney, 1996; Sage & Langley, 1983; Newell, 1990; Schmidt & Ling, 1996; Shultz et al., 1994]. However, two aspects are overlooked in these models: the first is the strict *interconnection* between the *heuristic knowledge* in a specific domain (substantially the one modelled in the Machine Learning systems) and pre-existing *deeper knowledge structures* or theories [Murphy & Medin, 1985; Vosniadou, 1994, 1995; Tiberghien, 1994; Chi et al. 1994]. The second aspect is the importance of *explanation*. Human learning is, to a great extent, a search for explanations; then, any model of human learning should provide an explanatory framework, allowing not only answers to questions to be predicted, but also reasons put forward in support of those answers to be formulated. Consequently, along the paper, we consider student's learning in the sense of EBL [Mitchell, Keller & Kedar-Cabelli; 1986]. That is the capability to explain previously unknown phenomena and, also, the ability to change the explanation level for the observed phenomena.

The main novelty of our approach is in the *differentiation* between the *pragmatic knowledge* a student uses to answer questions and/or to interpret experimental results, and an *explanatory framework*, which the student uses to "make sense" of what he/she observes or is taught. A central hypothesis of the approach is that explanation corresponds to *causal* attribution. This hypothesis derives from a number of previous studies (for instance, [diSessa, 1993; Tiberghien, 1994]), and from the direct observation that children, even young ones, spontaneously use verbal constructs suggesting causality. The learning/teaching context we want to model envisages the task of acquiring basic concept in Physics, specifically *Heat* and *Temperature* concepts by middle school students. The specific learning context is: a group of secondary school students (12-13 years old, 6-5th grades), were exposed to a Physics course, outside normal teaching, consisting of 11 sessions, once a week, including experimentation, questions, discussions and explicit teaching. Content of the course were basic concepts and qualitative relations in the domain of *heat transfer* in everyday life situations.

As computational modelling tool it has been selected the multistrategy learning system WHY [Saitta, Botta & Neri, 1993; Giordana et al., 1997], which learns and revises a knowledge base for classification problems using domain knowledge and examples. The domain knowledge consists of a *causal model* C of the domain, stating the relationships among basic phenomena, and a body of *phenomenological theory*, describing the links between abstract concepts and their possible manifestations in the world. The causal model provides explanations in terms of causal chains among events, originating from "first" causes.

The evolution of our modelling approach together with a critical discussion can be found in [Saitta, Neri and al., 1995; Neri, Saitta and Tiberghien, 1997a; Saitta, Neri and Tiberghien, 1997].

For sake of completeness, we note that WHY can automatically make changes from one model to the following by using automatic induction as in [Sleeman et al., 1990; Baffes & Mooney, 1996]. But, this is not the primary goal of our research. In fact, we want to help the cognitive scientist in developing what she believe to be the evolution of the student's model. The long term goal of our research, instead, may be the (fully) automatization of the learning process. In order to accomplish this long term goal, we discuss some temptative computational definitions of the different kinds of conceptual change that have been observed during the psychological experiments.

The last important point to be kept present while reading this work, is that we are going to study a model that capture the "functionality" of the student's understanding and answering to problems. Instead, we are not making any claim about the (unlikely) cognitive validity of the described model.

2 The Modelling Tool WHY

In this section a brief description of the functionalities of the learning system WHY is given. WHY learns and revises a knowledge base for classification problems using domain knowledge and examples. The domain knowledge consists of a *causal model* C of the domain, stating the relationships among basic phenomena[2], and a body of *phenomenological theory*, describing the links between abstract concepts and their possible manifestations in the world.

The causal model C provides explanations in terms of causal chains among events, originating from "first" causes. The phenomenological theory P contains the semantics of the vocabulary terms, structural information about the objects in the domain, ontologies, taxonomies, domain-independent background knowledge (such as symmetry, spatial and temporal relations); finally, P contains a set of rules aimed at describing the manifestations of abstractly defined concepts in terms of properties, objects and events in the specific domain of application.

The causal model C is represented as a directed, labelled graph. Three kinds of nodes occur in the graphs: *causal* nodes, corresponding to processes or states related by cause-effect relations, *constraint* nodes, attached to edges and representing conditions which must be verified in order to instantiate the corresponding cause-

---

[2]   In general, C may contain any "deep" model of the domain, not necessarily a causal one.

effect relation, and *context* nodes, associated to causal nodes, representing contextual conditions to be added to the cause in order to obtain the effect.

The goal of WHY is to build up or revise a knowledge base **KB** of heuristic classification rules. A causal explanation (justification) of any **KB** revision is automatically provided.

It is important to clarify the relations between the causal model C and the heuristic knowledge base **KB**. The causal model could be used directly to obtain classifications. However, causal reasoning is slow, and the rules in **KB** act as shortcuts, compiled from C. On the other hand, the fact that the rules are justified by C (being derived from it according to the method described in [Saitta, Botta & Neri, 1993]) guarantees their validity and correctness (with respect to that of C) and also allows for explanations of the given classification in terms of the deep knowledge. On the other hand, **KB** and C may not be related at all, for instance in the case that **KB** is not derived from C but is directly "taught" by a teacher or acquired by the learner on a pure inductive basis. In this case, **KB** will give unjustified classifications (correct or not), for which no explanation exists with respect to C. Exploiting these different types of relations between **KB** and C, all the learning models emerged in the experimentation can be modelled. In the interplay between **KB** and C, the knowledge in **P** supplies the links between the general principles stated in C and the concrete experiments. The content of **P** contributes, as well, to enrich the modelling of students' misconceptions and conceptual change. Actually, it is in **P**, for instance, that ontological shift occurs.

3   The Modelling Methodology

As WHY learns knowledge for classification tasks, and provide explanations thereof, the task considered in this paper has to be mapped accordingly. We have chosen to follow the individual evolution of three students over two years (6th and 5th grades), because our goal was not to verify general hypotheses about learning, but rather to show how conceptual change in an individual can actually be modelled with WHY. In this paper we will show how the model can be built up and used through a specific example: the knowledge evolution of the student "David" with respect to learning in the 6th grade.

Before outlining the methodology used, we will briefly describe the material available from the David's history:

T_0 = <u>Before teaching</u>

Answers to Questionnaires Q_1 and Q_2 and their explanations. Answers to the initial Interview I_0 and their explanations. (An example of the type of questions is reported in Appendix A)

T_i $(1 \leq 1 \leq 11)$ = <u>During teaching</u>

Answers to questions, predictions of outcomes from practical manipulations, and given explanations during the i-th teaching session.

T_f = <u>After teaching</u>

New answers to Questionnaires Q_1 and Q_2 and their explanations. Answers to the final Interview I_f and their explanations.

T_t = <u>Post test</u>

Answers to a test Interview I_t and their explanations, six months after the end of teaching.

In order to use WHY to model David, each practical experiment is represented as an example, consisting of two parts: a description of the experimental setting and a question. The experimental setting corresponds to the description of the example, whereas the possible answers to the question are considered as alternative classes. Then, the process of predicting the outcome of an experiment is mapped onto the problem of predicting the correct answer. An examples of this mapping is given in Appendix A.

In the current experimentation, the various knowledge bodies **C**, **P** and **KB** have been manually constructed and encoded by the experimenters. WHY relies on a sophisticated algorithm for uncovering errors or incompleteness in its knowledge that can be triggered when one of WHY's explanations (answers) does not match the student's ones. This provides useful information to the educational/cognitive scientist in discovering where her hypothesized student's model is incorrect.

4 An Instance of Observed Conceptual Change

Due to space bound we cannot fully described our modelling methodology. So we only give an idea of the formalism used **to represent the evolution** of part of the **knowledge of David** (a student). Moreover, we also sketch how **David's conceptual change** can be pointed out by comparing its knowledge before and after teaching.

In this section, we will compare two knowledge state of David represented as two WHY's causal models. A causal model consists in an oriented graph where causal relationships among the domain's abstract phenomena are represented.

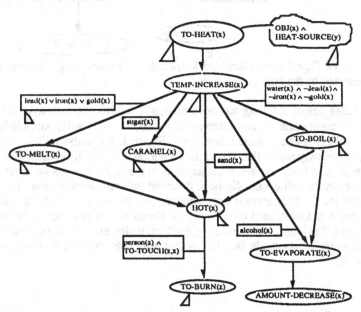

Figure 1 – Part of the causal model C_0, hypothesized to represent David's knowledge before teaching. Elliptic nodes contains the domain relevant phenomena. Arrows represent causal relationships among them. Rectangle and clouds represent accessory conditions.

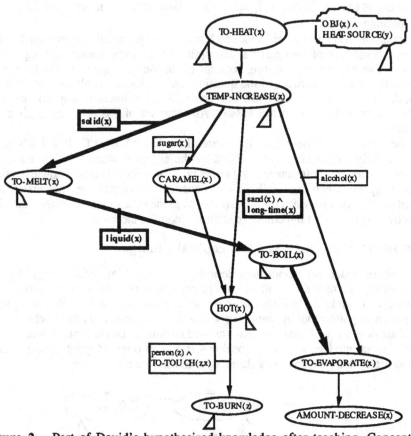

Figure 2 – Part of David's hypothesized knowledge after teaching. Conceptual change is represented by the bold causal path.

David's knowledge before teaching has been manually inferred on the basis of his initial answers to questionnaires and interviews. Part of David's initial knowledge, represented as a WHY's causal model, appears in Figure 1. By analysing the causal model (network), we may notice that David uses a notion of material causality linked to the "substance" of a body; in fact, what happens to the body depends on what "it is". For instance, water will eventually boil, if heated, whereas lead or iron or gold will melt; for this reason, they become hot. Similarly, sugar becomes "caramel" and, again, it becomes hot. Questioned on the subject, David shows evidence to believe that "boiling" and "melting" are alternative (and mutually exclusive) behaviours, exhibited by different substance. In fact, he say that iron, gold and lead shall not boil, *because they melt*.

By linking the behaviour of the bodies, with respect to heating, to specific substances, David is then unable to answer questions about materials that he does not about: for instance, he answers "I don't know" to questions about the possibility of diamond, salt and aluminium to become liquid or gaseous.

After the teaching course, during which David has seen several other experiments, involving different materials, he is able to fill the final questionnaires and the final interview in such a way that we may infer that his deep knowledge of the world is changed, under various respect. In the following, we will just illustrate one of the changes, which can be considered as a **conceptual change**. In Figure 2, David's hypothesized knowledge after the cycle of lesson is reported. Two changes can be noticed. The first one is that David is able to consider the importance of time in determining the final state of a material. At the beginning, in fact, he simply said that the sand would become hot, when heated. Now, he is able to understand that the effect of heating takes time to happens, suggesting the idea of a "process". This finding is confirmed by the fact that now David says that, in order for the water to start boiling, "at least a quarter of an hour is necessary".

However, the most important change, with respect to the goal of the teaching course, is that David seems less committed to a material causality for determining behaviours. In fact, he is able to generalize, from "iron", "lead", "gold" and "ice", that any "solid" may become liquid is sufficiently heated. Moreover, "to boil" and "to melt" are no more mutually exclusive behaviours, but they are possibly in sequence, as it should be. David's causality shows a shift of the "cause" from the "substance" to some underlying process, which, on the other hand, he is not yet capable of pinning down.

The actual transition from the two states of knowledge could be sketched as follows. During the lessons, David performs manipulation in which a number of different substances undergo a change of state: he observes ice transformed into water, water into ice and water into vapor, as well as lead and salt to melt. Then, he keeps adding to his causal network additional links, corresponding to the new observed substance. Observing commonalties (also helped by the teacher) he notices that all the substance that melt are solid and that vapors derive from liquids. Technically, the constraints on the edges of the causal net are generalized from specific substances to "solid" or "liquid", respectively and, then, all these edges collapse into a single one.

5 Tentative Computational Definition of Conceptual Change

In order to make possible the future automatization of the learning process, we associate, as described in the following, each type of observed change to the application of one or more WHY's revision operators.

Accretion

Learning by accretion *increases coverage,* in the sense that more experimental situations can be handled (independently of their correct interpretation/prediction). A rule is applicable to a situation when all the conditions specified by the rule's antecedent are defined, i.e. they have a "true" or "false" value. Accretion, then, affects both the *phenomenological theory* or the *heuristic knowledge base,* by adding to any of them a new rule. Accretion may also consists of addition of a property to an ontological node. In our approach, accretion is not considered conceptual change in a strict sense. Accretion can be implemented with the "adding rules" operator.

A typical situation in which accretion occurs is when a student memorizes, without explanation, a piece of information taught by the teacher. This information can be added, as a rule, to the student's knowledge, without checking for compatibility with previous knowledge. The rule can be accessed, on the basis of recency, for giving a correct answer for a while, until it is forgotten, or other pieces of knowledge, incorrect but supported by the student's deep beliefs, gain higher priority.

Tuning

Tuning *increases the number of correct predictions or explanations*, but does not modify the deep explanatory framework. It may affect the *heuristic knowledge base* or the *phenomenological theory*, by changing the preconditions in some rule or by adding new rules. Tuning may also involve the *causal model*, but only with addition/deletion in the constraint and context nodes (causal nodes and links between them cannot be changed). Tuning can be implemented with the operators that generalize or specialize rule antecedents, or add and delete rules. Also tuning is not considered here a conceptual change in a strict sense.

Restructuration

Restructuration affects the explanatory framework. It involves the *causal model*, via addition/deletion of causal nodes, or modification of causal links, and the *ontologies* of the domain, via addition/deletion of nodes or changing a node from one ontology to another. Restructuration is considered conceptual change.

As it can be seen, we have given a stricter definition of conceptual change than in some approaches (for instance, [Vosniadou, 1994, 1995]), but larger than in others (for instance, [Chi et al., 1994]).

6 Conclusion

We discussed a way of interpreting learning in relation with teaching in the domain of physics. Our analysis is based on a type of knowledge processing which can be a relevant frame of reference from the points of view of both personal knowledge of a learner and "official" knowledge, such as that of Physics. Our framework allows us to establish an independence between analysis of the learner's acquisition and of Physics knowledge. Thus, it is possible to take into account the *coherence of the learner per se* , even if it is incompatible with Physics. The structuring of the analysis in terms of causal theory, phenomenological knowledge and field of applicability allows the learner's knowledge and Physics knowledge to be compared. This independence and this comparison are essential to the characterisation of different types of learning.

Moreover, WHY's articulated knowledge representation allows most of phenomena observed in children learning elementary physics to be modelled, notably their explanation in terms of simple causality, and the interdependence of "surface" heuristic knowledge and deep beliefs.

Appendix A.   Representing Questionnaires in WHY

In this appendix we will show, through an example, how questions are translated into a first order logic ground formula to become training instances for WHY. The questions in the interview are expressed in natural language and describe experiments, whose outcome the student is supposed to explain, guided by the teacher. The experimental material is actually provided during the interview, and the student is allowed to freely manipulate it. The student is supposed to answer verbally.

Question: "Two saucepans A and B, with thermometers inside, are put on two gas stoves g_a and g_b, which are equal (denoted by the predicate "same-feature"). A contains a smaller amount (a) of water than B does (b). The initial temperature of the system is 20 ºC. After a short time interval, the thermometer in A indicates 50 ºC.
1) Will the thermometer h_b in B indicate the same, a greater or a lower temperature than that h_a in A?
2) Please, explain your answer"
To answer the question is modelled as a classification problem, in which there are three classes

    {GREATER-THERMOM-READING(h_b,h_a,t_2),

    SAME-THERMOM-READING(h_b,h_a,t_2),

    LOWER-THERMOM-READING(h_b,h_a,t_2)},

among which David has to choose. Then, he is confronted with the actual outcome of the manipulation (In this case he answered correctly).

person(David) ∧ saucepan(A) ∧ saucepan(B) ∧
∧ same-features(A,B) ∧ water(a) ∧ water(b) ∧ thermometer(h_a) ∧ thermometer(h_b) ∧
same-features(h_a ,h_b) ∧ gas-stove(g_a) ∧
∧ gas-stove(g_b) ∧ same-features(g_a,g_b) ∧ ignited(g_a) ∧
∧ ignited(g_b) ∧ on(A,g_a) ∧ on(B,g_b) ∧ person(Tournesol) ∧
∧ person(Tintin) ∧ person(Haddock)
∧ to-put-inside(Tournesol,a,A) ∧ amount(a,small) ∧
∧ to-put-inside(Tournesol,b,B) ∧ to-put-inside(Tournesol,h_a,A) ∧
∧ to-put-inside(Tournesol,h_b,B) ∧ amount(b,large) ∧
∧ temp(a, 20,initial) ∧ temp(b, 20,initial) ∧ not-boiling(a,initial) ∧
∧ not-boiling(b,initial) ∧ time-elapsed(a,short) ∧
∧ time-elapsed(b,short) ∧ time-elapsed(g_a,short) ∧
∧ time-elapsed(g_b,short) ∧ thermom-reading(h_a,50,final)

References

Baffes P. T. and Mooney R. J. (1996). "A Novel Application of Theory Refinement to Student Modelling". *Proc. of Thirteenth National Conference on Artificial Intelligence* (Portland, OR), pp. 403-408.

Caravita S. and Halldén O. (1994). "Re-framing the Problem of Conceptual Change". *Learning and Instruction, 4,* 89-111.

Chi M. T. H., Slotta J. D. and de Leeuw N. (1994). "From Things to Processes: A Theory of Conceptual Change for Learning Science Concepts". *Learning and Instruction, 4,* 27-43.

diSessa A. (1993). "Toward an Epistemology of Physics". *Cognition and Instruction, 10,* 105-225.

Forbus K.D. and Gentner D. (1986). "Learning Physical Domains: Toward a Theoretical Framework". In R. Michalski, J. Carbonell & T. Mitchell (Eds.),

Machine Learning: An Artificial Intelligence Approach, Vol. II, Morgan Kaufmann, Los Altos, CA, pp. 311-348.

Giordana A. and Neri F., Saitta L. and Botta M. (1997). "Integrating Multiple Learning Strategies in First Order Logics". *Machine Learning* , **27**, 209–240.

Mitchell T., Keller R., Kedar-Cabelli S. (1986). "Explanation Based Generalization", *Machine Learning, 1*, 47-80.

Murphy L.G. and Medin D.L. (1985). "The Role of Theories in Conceptual Coherence". *Psychological Review, 92*, 289-316.

Neri F., Saitta L. and Tiberghien A. (1997a). "Modelling Physical Knowledge Acquisition in Children with Machine Learning". Proc. of *19th Annual Conference of the Cognitive Science Society*, Stanford (CA), Morgan Kaufmann, pp. 566–571.

Newell A. (1990). *Unified Theories of Cognition*, Harvard University Press, Cambridge, MA.

Rumelhart D. E. and Norman D. A. (1977). "Accretion, Tuning and Restructuring: Three modes of Learning", in Cotton J. W. and Klatzky R. L. (Eds.), *Semantic Factors in Cognition* , Erlbaum (Hillsdale, NJ).

Sage S. and Langley P. (1983). "Modeling Cognitive Development on the Balance Scale Task". *Proc. 8th Int. Joint Conf. on Artificial Intelligence* (Karlsruhe, Germany), pp. 94-96.

Saitta L., Botta M., Neri F. (1993). "Multistrategy Learning and Theory Revision". *Machine Learning, 11*, 153-172.

Saitta L., Neri F. and al. (1995). "Knowledge Representation Changes in Humans and Machines". In P. Reimann and H. Spada (Eds.), *Learning in Humans and Machines: Towards an Interdisciplinary Learning Science*, Elsevier (Oxford), pp. 109-128.

Saitta L., Neri F. and Tiberghien A. (1997). "World Model Construction in Children during Physics Learning". Proc. of *International Symposium on Methodologies for Intelligent Systems '97 (ISMIS 97)*, Lecture Notes in Artificial Intelligence series, Springer Verlag (Berlin, Germany), in press.

Schmidt W.C. and Ling C.X. (1996). "A Decision-Tree Model of Balance Scale Development". *Machine Learning, 24*, 203-230.

Shultz T.R., Mareschal D. and Schmidt W. (1994). "Modeling Cognitive Developemnt on Balance Scale Phenomena". *Machine Learning, 16*, 57-86.

Sleeman D., Hirsh H., Ellery I. and Kim I. (1990). "Extending Domain Theories: two case Studies in Student Modeling". *Machine Learning, 5*, 11-37.

Tiberghien A. (1989). "Learning and Teaching at Middle School Level of Concepts and Phenomena in Physics. The Case of Temperature". In H. Mandl, E. de Corte, N. Bennett and H.F. Friedrich (Eds.), *Learning and Instruction. European Research in an International Context, Volume 2.1*, Pergamon Press, Oxford, UK, pp. 631-648.

Tiberghien A. (1994). "Modelling as a Basis for Analysing Teaching-Learning Situations". *Learning and Instruction, 4*, 71-87.

Vosniadou S. (1994). "Capturing and Modeling the Process of Conceptual Change". *Learning and Instruction, 4*, 45-69.

Vosniadou S. and Brewer W.F. (1994). "Mental Models of the Day/Night Cycle". *Cognitive Science, 18*, 123-183.

White R. T. (1994). "Commentary Conceptual and Conceptional Change". *Learning and Instruction, 4*, 117-121.

Bayes Optimal Instance-Based Learning

Petri Kontkanen, Petri Myllymäki, Tomi Silander, and Henry Tirri

Complex Systems Computation Group (CoSCo)
P.O.Box 26, Department of Computer Science
FIN-00014 University of Helsinki, Finland

Abstract. In this paper we present a probabilistic formalization of the instance-based learning approach. In our Bayesian framework, moving from the construction of an explicit hypothesis to a data-driven instance-based learning approach, is equivalent to averaging over all the (possibly infinitely many) individual models. The general Bayesian instance-based learning framework described in this paper can be applied with any set of assumptions defining a parametric model family, and to any discrete prediction task where the number of simultaneously predicted attributes is small, which includes for example all classification tasks prevalent in the machine learning literature. To illustrate the use of the suggested general framework in practice, we show how the approach can be implemented in the special case with the strong independence assumptions underlying the so called Naive Bayes classifier. The resulting Bayesian instance-based classifier is validated empirically with public domain data sets and the results are compared to the performance of the traditional Naive Bayes classifier. The results suggest that the Bayesian instance-based learning approach yields better results than the traditional Naive Bayes classifier, especially in cases where the amount of the training data is small.

1 Introduction

Machine learning research aims at constructing automated methods for deducing useful information from sample data. In principle the work can be divided into two main subareas of research. In the first research area, the goal is to find useful high-level knowledge representations from the data through exploratory data analysis (this *descriptive* aspect is very related to the research performed in the field of *data mining* [10]). In the second research area, the goal is to predict the outcome of some future event by using the data given. In this paper, we are motivated purely by this latter, *predictive* aspect of machine learning.

The standard approach to machine learning can be viewed as a three phase modeling process. Initially, the models to be considered are restricted to some limited set of models, the *model family*. Examples of common model families include the set of feedforward neural network models, the set of Bayesian networks, or the set of decision trees. In the second phase, some specific *model class*, i.e., a skeleton or a template structure for a model without fixing any parameter values, is selected from the chosen model family. In the third phase, the parameter values for the selected model class are estimated from the sample data. The resulting full model (model structure + parameter values) can then be used for making predictions. Bayesian probability theory provides a unifying theoretically solid framework for choosing a proper model family, model class, and parameter instantiation during all the three phases of the machine learning process, as discussed for example in [14, 20].

In contrast to the traditional (*eager*) approach described above, in the *instance-based* (also known as the *memory-based* or the *case-based*) approach [29, 24, 1, 4], the learning algorithms base their predictions directly on the sample data, without producing any specific models of the problem domain. This type of machine learning is often referred to as *lazy learning*, since the algorithms defer all the essential computation until the prediction phase [2].

For making predictions, instance-based learning algorithms typically use a distance function (e.g., Euclidean distance) for determining the most relevant data items for the prediction task in question. Some simple function, such as majority voting in classification problems, is then used for determining the prediction from the most relevant data items. It has been shown in various studies (see e.g., [23] for references) that this type of an approach in some cases produces quite accurate predictions, when compared to alternative machine learning methods. The method suffers, however, from several drawbacks when applied in practice (see, e.g., the discussion in [32]). Most importantly, the performance of instance-based learning algorithms seems to be highly sensitive to the selection of distance function to be used as demonstrated in recent work reported in [34, 13, 5].

In [32, 31, 26, 25] we proposed a Bayesian framework for instance-based learning based on probability theory and the finite mixture model family [9, 33]. The approach suggested in those studies can be seen as a "partially lazy" approach [2], i.e., a hybrid between the traditional machine learning and the instance-based learning approach, which is based solely on the given data. The studies were based on the probabilistic viewpoint, where the given data vectors are transformed into local distributions, which can be seen as sample points in a distribution space. Thus the predictive distributions required for making predictions could then be computed by using the instance-based learning approach in the distribution space, i.e., by introducing a probabilistic "distance metric". Somewhat similar frameworks have been suggested in [16, 30, 11, 12].

The goal of this paper is to present a novel alternative probabilistic formalization of the *purely lazy learning approach*. The framework suggested here extends our earlier results by presenting a Bayesian approach for making (discrete) predictions directly from data, *without the transformation step between the original sample space and the distribution space*. Intuitively this new approach is based on the following notion: if we wish to make predictions by using only the sample data given, avoiding the notion of individual models, from the Bayesian point of view we can take this as a requirement for averaging over all the possible models.

In the Bayesian framework, prediction can be viewed as a missing data problem, where the criterion for filling in the missing data (for making the predictions) is the integral over all the possible models. Intuitively, the joint probability distribution produced by a (possibly infinite) mixture of individual models reflects the true (unknown) problem domain distribution better than any single model, thus it should also produce more accurate predictions. In fact, it is known that this type of integrated predictions are optimal from the Bayesian point of view, given a fixed model family. To avoid terminological confusion it should be observed that any type of learning is with respect to some model family. In traditional instance-based learning approaches the model family is implicitly induced by the combination of the distance function and the domain of the data, also in the cases where the distance function is allowed to vary locally.

At first glance the Bayes optimal instance-based learning framework may seem to be a computationally infeasible approach — after all, the integration (summation) may go over an infinite number of models. Nevertheless, it turns out that for some simple model families the integral over all the model instantiations, i.e., the so called *evidence* or the *marginal likelihood* [6], can in fact be solved analytically, and calculated with modest computational effort. An example of such a model family is the family of Bayesian networks (see e.g. [7, 15]), where the model family is determined by defining a set of independence relations between the problem domain variables. For more complex model families including those with latent variables, there exist several computationally feasible methods for approximating the evidence integral — see e.g., the discussion in [19].

It should be emphasized that we make no claims about having invented the idea of making predictions by marginalizing over all the (possibly infinitely many) models, which is a known technique in the Bayesian community. *The main goal of this paper is to point out how the Bayesian formalism can be used for developing a theoretically solid framework for instance-based learning.* A formalization of this Bayesian instance-based learning approach is given in Section 2. As an illustrative example of our general approach, we demonstrate in Section 3 how the Bayesian instance-based learning approach can be applied with a set of strong independence assumptions underlying a simple Bayesian network model structure, the naive Bayes classifier. Section 4 shows the results of an empirical comparison between the Bayesian instance-based learning approach presented here, and the traditional approach, based on a single maximum a posteriori model, in this special case. The tests were performed by using publicly available real-world classification datasets.

2 Bayesian Instance-Based Learning

Let D denote a random sample of N i.i.d. (independent and identically distributed) data vectors $d_1, \ldots, d_N$. For simplicity, we assume here that the data is coded by using only discrete, i.e., finite-valued, attributes $X_1, \ldots, X_m$, although the Bayesian approach described can be extended to continuous attributes as well. More precisely, we regard each attribute X_i as a random variable with possible values from the set $\{x_{i1}, \ldots, x_{in_i}\}$. Consequently, each data vector d is represented as a value assignment of the form $(X_1 = x_1, \ldots, X_m = x_m)$, where $x_i \in \{x_{i1}, \ldots, x_{in_i}\}$.

In the following, let $\mathcal{M}$ denote a *model family*, a set of models each determining some probability distribution on the problem domain. Examples of model families include the set of feedforward neural network models, the set of Bayesian networks, and the set of decision trees. For notational convenience, it is often useful to partition the models within a model family $\mathcal{M}$ to some number of subsets, *model classes*, where all the models within a model class share the same parametric form (the same number of parameters). Consequently, the model classes usually correspond to some specific model structure. Examples of such structures are the topology of a feedforward neural network, a Bayesian network, or a decision tree. A *model* Θ is here defined as a parameter instantiation within some model class M, fully determining a probability distribution in the data vector space. Consequently, a single model is defined by fixing the parameters attached to a given model structure, e.g., by fixing the weights of a neural network architecture or the decision rules of a decision tree.

In traditional (eager) machine learning, the model family, model class, and the model parameters must all be fixed in order to produce a single model for making predictions. Bayesian probability theory provides a theoretically solid framework for these tasks, as demonstrated, e.g., in [21] in the neural network model family case, and in [32] in the finite mixture model family case. In the Bayesian approach, the model parameters to be used within a model class M are taken to be the *maximum a posteriori (MAP)* values $\hat{\Theta}$ of the parameters,

$$\hat{\Theta} = \arg\max_{\Theta} P(\Theta \mid D, M, \mathcal{M}).$$

Similarly, the model class to be used is the class with the maximal posterior probability,

$$\hat{M} = \arg\max_{M} P(M \mid D, \mathcal{M}).$$

Nevertheless, as

$$P(M \mid D, \mathcal{M}) = \frac{P(D \mid M, \mathcal{M})P(M \mid \mathcal{M})}{P(D \mid \mathcal{M})},$$

it is sufficient to find the model class M maximizing $P(D \mid M, \mathcal{M})$, the *evidence* or *marginal likelihood* of the data,

$$P(D \mid M, \mathcal{M}) = \int P(D \mid \Theta, M, \mathcal{M})P(\Theta \mid M, \mathcal{M})d\Theta, \tag{1}$$

assuming that all the model classes are equally probable a priori.

In principle, the model family can be chosen by maximizing a similar posterior probability $P(\mathcal{M} \mid D)$ over all model families $\mathcal{M}$,

$$P(\mathcal{M} \mid D) = \sum_{k} P(\mathcal{M}, M_k \mid D).$$

Nevertheless, computing the model family posterior probability for all the possible model families is obviously intractable in practice. Instead, some individual model family, determined by a set of assumptions made about the problem domain, is normally fixed in advance. The assumptions are based on some prior knowledge, or just on practitioner's personal preferences.

Having fixed the model family $\mathcal{M}$, model class $\hat{M}$, and the model parameters $\hat{\Theta}$, the Bayes optimal predictive distribution for a new *test vector* d is the conditional distribution

$$P(d \mid D, \hat{\Theta}, \hat{M}, \mathcal{M}) = \frac{P(d, D \mid \hat{\Theta}, \hat{M}, \mathcal{M})}{P(D \mid \hat{\Theta}, \hat{M}, \mathcal{M})}. \tag{2}$$

As the probability $P(D \mid \hat{\Theta}, \hat{M}, \mathcal{M})$ can be regarded as a constant with respect to the test vector d, for predictive purposes it is sufficient to be able to compute the joint probability distribution $P(d, D \mid \hat{\Theta}, \hat{M}, \mathcal{M})$. In the sequel, we call distribution (2) the *MAP predictive distribution*.

In instance-based lazy learning approach, on the other hand, we wish to base our predictions directly on the data D, without having to determine individual models Θ. In the Bayesian framework, we can express this by marginalizing out the individual models — in other words, instead of computing the MAP predictive distribution (2), we wish to compute

$$P(d \mid D, \hat{M}, \mathcal{M}) = \int P(d \mid D, \Theta, \hat{M}, \mathcal{M}) P(\Theta \mid D, \hat{M}, \mathcal{M}) d\Theta. \tag{3}$$

Furthermore, if the model class M is not to be fixed, we need to sum over different model classes within the chosen model family, yielding

$$P(d \mid D, \mathcal{M}) = \sum_k P(d \mid D, M_k, \mathcal{M}) P(M_k \mid D, \mathcal{M}). \tag{4}$$

In the sequel, by *Bayesian instance-based learning (BIBL)* we mean the approach based on formulas (4) and (3).

Note that formula (4) offers a formal motivation for the idea of *model averaging* (see, e.g., [22, 3] and the references therein), i.e., for combining multiple predictors for increasing the prediction accuracy: the individual predictions $P(d \mid D, M_k, \mathcal{M})$ produced by different predictors M_k (for example, model classes determined by different decision tree structures), are combined by summing the individual predictions weighted by the model class probabilities $P(M_k \mid D, \mathcal{M})$. As a matter of fact, from the probability theory point of view the Bayesian instance-based learning predictive distribution (4) produces optimally accurate predictions within the chosen model family. In [17, 18], we described how the recently published new coding scheme by Rissanen [28] for representing the stochastic complexity measure [27] offers an alternative definition for an optimal predictive distribution. This definition can be justified by information theoretic arguments, but this approach will not be addressed in this paper.

3 Bayesian IBL with the Naive Bayes Assumptions

For notational simplicity, in the sequel we drop the variable names, and denote a value assignment $(X_1 = x_1, \ldots, X_{m-1} = x_{m-1})$ by writing $(x_1, \ldots, x_{m-1})$. In addition, instead of explicitly stating for each specific model the corresponding model class M and model family $\mathcal{M}$, we use $P(\cdot \mid \Theta)$ for denoting $P(\cdot \mid \Theta, M, \mathcal{M})$.

The MAP predictive distribution distribution (2), and the BIBL predictive distribution (4) can be used for solving various predictive inference problems. As an example, let us consider the standard classification problem, where the goal is to predict the value of the *class variable*, denoted here by X_m, given the values of other variables $X_1, \ldots, X_{m-1}$. In the MAP case (using a given MAP model $\hat{\Theta}$), we need to find a classification x_m (value assignment for variable X_m) maximizing the conditional probability

$$P(x_m \mid x_1, \ldots, x_{m-1}, D, \hat{\Theta}) \propto P(x_m, x_1, \ldots, x_{m-1} \mid D, \hat{\Theta}) = P(d \mid D, \hat{\Theta}), \quad (5)$$

denoting $d = (x_m, x_1, \ldots, x_{m-1})$. Consequently, the resulting conditional probability is a predictive distribution of the form (2). Equivalently, in the BIBL case we wish to compute

$$P(x_m \mid x_1, \ldots, x_{m-1}, D, \mathcal{M}) \propto P(x_m, x_1, \ldots, x_{m-1} \mid D, \mathcal{M}), \quad (6)$$

which corresponds to formula (4).

As an illustrative example of the Bayesian instance-based learning approach, in the following let us consider the model family determined by the set of independence assumptions underlying behind the well-known Naive Bayes classifier. In this case, the variables $X_1, \ldots, X_{m-1}$ are assumed to be independent given the value of the class variable X_m. It follows that the joint probability distribution for a data vector d can be written as

$$P(d \mid \Theta) = P(x_1, \ldots, x_m \mid \Theta) = P(x_m) \prod_{i=1}^{m-1} P(x_i \mid x_m).$$

Consequently, in the Naive Bayes model family, a single predictive distribution can be uniquely determined by fixing the values of the model parameters $\Theta = (\alpha, \Phi)$, where

$$\alpha = (\alpha_1, \ldots, \alpha_K) \text{ and } \Phi = (\Phi_{11}, \ldots, \Phi_{1m}, \ldots, \Phi_{K1}, \ldots, \Phi_{Km}),$$

$K \ (= n_m)$ is the number of possible values for the class variable X_m, and

$$\alpha_k = P(X_m = x_{mk}), \Phi_{ki} = (\phi_{ki1}, \ldots, \phi_{kin_i}),$$

where $\phi_{kil} = P(X_i = x_{il} \mid X_m = x_{mk})$.

In the following we assume that $\alpha_k > 0$ and $\phi_{kil} > 0$ for all k, i, and l. Furthermore, both the class variable distribution $P(X_m)$ and the intra-class conditional distributions $P(X_i \mid X_m = x_{mk})$ are multinomial, i.e., $X_m \sim \text{Multi}(1; \alpha_1, \ldots, \alpha_K)$, and $X_{i|k} \sim \text{Multi}(1; \phi_{ki1}, \ldots, \phi_{kin_i})$. Since the family of Dirichlet densities is *conjugate* (see e.g., [8]) to the family of multinomials, i.e., the functional form of parameter distribution is invariant in the prior-to-posterior transformation, we assume that the prior distributions of the parameters are from this family. More precisely, let $(\alpha_1, \ldots, \alpha_K) \sim \text{Di}(\mu_1, \ldots, \mu_K)$, and $(\phi_{ki1}, \ldots, \phi_{kin_i}) \sim \text{Di}(\sigma_{ki1}, \ldots, \sigma_{kin_i})$, where $\{\mu_k, \sigma_{kil} \mid k = 1, \ldots, K; i = 1, \ldots, m; l = 1, \ldots, n_i\}$ are the *hyperparameters* of the corresponding distributions. Assuming that the parameter vectors α and Φ_{ki} are independent, the joint prior distribution of all the parameters Θ is

$$\text{Di}(\mu_1, \ldots, \mu_K) \prod_{k=1}^{K} \prod_{i=1}^{m-1} \text{Di}(\sigma_{ki1}, \ldots, \sigma_{kin_i}).$$

Having now defined the prior distribution, the predictive distributions (2) and (4) can be written more explicitly. Let $d[k] = (X_m = x_{mk}, q)$ denote a data vector where the values of variables $X_1, \ldots, X_{m-1}$ correspond to the given query q, and the value of the class variable X_m is set to x_{mk}. The MAP predictive distribution (2) needed for computing the predictive distribution (5) for $d[k]$ is in the Naive Bayes case

$$P(d[k] \mid D, \hat{\Theta}) \stackrel{\text{i.i.d.}}{=} P(d[k] \mid \hat{\Theta}) = \hat{\alpha}_k \prod_{i=1}^{m} \hat{\phi}_{kix_i}, \text{ where} \qquad (7)$$

$$\hat{\alpha}_k = \frac{h_k + \mu_k - 1}{N + \sum_{k'=1}^{K} \mu_{k'} - K}, \quad \hat{\phi}_{kil} = \frac{f_{kil} + \sigma_{kil} - 1}{h_k + \sum_{l=1}^{n_i} \sigma_{kil} - n_i},$$

and h_k and f_{kil} are the *sufficient statistics* of the training data D: h_k is the number of data vectors in D where $X_m = x_{mk}$, and f_{kil} is the number of data vectors where $X_m = x_{mk}$ and $X_i = x_{il}$. If we assume a uniform prior distribution for the parameters, we get $\hat{\alpha}_k = h_k/N$, $\hat{\phi}_{kil} = f_{kil}/h_k$, which produces the standard maximum likelihood Naive Bayes classifier with the parameters set according to the relative frequencies of different variable values.

The above analysis gives us the Bayesian maximum posterior probability answer to the question of how to determine the parameters of the Naive Bayes classifier. We now turn our focus on the BIBL case. First it should be noted that the formal assumptions listed above can be expressed by, e.g., using a simple two-level tree-structured Bayesian network, where the class variable corresponds to the root of the tree, and the other variables form the leaves. This means that the Naive Bayes assumptions determine a single model class M, so there is no need to sum over the model classes in (4), and hence the predictive distribution (4) reduces to (3). Producing this predictive distribution corresponds to the case where instead of using a single set of parameters for the Naive Bayes classifier, as in the MAP predictive distribution (7), we sum over all the (infinitely many) parameter alternatives for the Naive Bayes classifier. As shown in [7, 15, 19], with the assumptions listed above the marginal likelihood (1) of the data can be computed by

84

$$P(D \mid M) = \frac{\Gamma\left(\sum_{k=1}^{K} \mu_k\right)}{\Gamma\left(N + \sum_{k=1}^{K} \mu_k\right)} \prod_{k=1}^{K} \frac{\Gamma(h_k + \mu_k)}{\Gamma(\mu_k)}$$

$$\cdot \prod_{k=1}^{K} \prod_{i=1}^{m-1} \left(\frac{\Gamma(\sum_{l=1}^{n_i} \sigma_{kil})}{\Gamma(h_k + \sum_{l=1}^{n_i} \sigma_{kil})} \prod_{l=1}^{n_i} \frac{\Gamma(f_{kil} + \sigma_{kil})}{\Gamma(\sigma_{kil})} \right), \quad (8)$$

where $\Gamma(\cdot)$ denotes the gamma function, a generalization of the common factorial function. By using this result it is relative easy to see that the predictive distribution (4) can in this case be written as

$$P(d[k] \mid D, M) = \int P(d[k] \mid \Theta, D, M) P(\Theta \mid D, M) d\Theta = \bar{\alpha}_k \prod_{i=1}^{m} \bar{\phi}_{kix_i}, \quad (9)$$

where the parameters α_k and ϕ_{kix_i} are set to their expected (*not* maximum probability) values:

$$\bar{\alpha}_k = \frac{h_k + \mu_k}{N + \sum_{k'=1}^{K} \mu_{k'}}, \quad \bar{\phi}_{kil} = \frac{f_{kil} + \sigma_{kil}}{h_k + \sum_{l=1}^{n_i} \sigma_{kil}}.$$

Consequently, in this special case the BIBL approach leads to the somewhat surprising result that if one wishes to sum over all the possible Naive Bayes classifiers (summing over all the infinitely many parameter settings), the resulting predictive distribution is the same as the one obtained by using a single Naive Bayes classifier where the parameters are set to their expected values! Hence the time and space complexity requirements of the BIBL approach are in this case exactly the same as with the standard Naive Bayes classifier. Nevertheless, it is important to realize that this phenomenon is not true in general, and only caused by the specific independence assumptions made above — with other sets of assumptions the BIBL approach would not necessarily lead to a predictive distribution that can be obtained by using a single model.

4 Empirical Results

To validate the Bayesian instance-based learning approach described in the previous sections, we performed a series of experiments with a set of public domain classification datasets from the UCI repository[1]. Each classification query was classified by using both the single MAP Naive Bayes model with uniform priors (MLNB) given by formula (7), and the Bayesian IBL approach with the Naive Bayes assumptions (BIBL) defined in (9), again with uniform priors. Description of the datasets used, and the results obtained can be found in Table 1. The results are averages over 100 independent crossvalidation runs, and the number of

---

[1] http://www.ics.uci.edu/~mlearn/

folds used was the same as in [23]. By the 0/1-score we mean the relative number of the correct classifications made, while the log-score is obtained by computing minus the logarithm of the probability given to the correct class (thus the smaller the score, the better the result).

Table 1. The datasets used in the experiments, and the averages of the corresponding crossvalidated classification accuracies obtained.

| | | | | CV | 0/1-SCORE | | | | LOG-SCORE | | | |
| | | | | | 100% data | | 10% data | | 100% data | | 10% data | |
Dataset	N	m	K	folds	MLNB	BIBL	MLNB	BIBL	MLNB	BIBL	MLNB	BIBL
Australian	690	15	2	10	**85.0**	84.9	76.2	**83.0**	0.7	**0.5**	9.5	**0.5**
Breast cancer	286	10	2	11	71.7	**72.3**	62.3	**69.4**	2.5	**0.6**	16.1	**0.8**
Diabetes	768	9	2	12	**75.7**	**75.7**	70.4	**72.4**	0.6	**0.5**	8.1	**0.6**
Glass	214	10	6	7	**66.9**	66.4	38.5	**50.5**	7.5	**1.0**	17.2	**1.6**
Heart disease	270	14	2	9	83.4	**84.1**	70.1	**80.0**	1.2	**0.4**	14.1	**0.5**
Hepatitis	150	20	2	5	**84.1**	81.5	63.1	**78.6**	4.2	**0.7**	3.4	**0.7**
Iris	150	5	3	5	93.4	**94.4**	77.5	**94.1**	1.9	**0.1**	2.9	**0.2**
Lymphography	148	19	4	5	78.9	**84.3**	39.3	**72.2**	5.7	**0.4**	6.8	**0.7**
Primary tumor	339	18	21	10	45.7	**48.8**	20.9	**32.2**	18.5	**2.0**	38.8	**3.0**

To see how the methods rely on the size of the data set available for training, we repeated the 100 independent crossvalidation runs, but used at each stage of the crossvalidation cycle only a (randomly selected) subset of the data in the training folds for classifying the data in the test fold. In Table 1 we list the results obtained when only $F = 10\%$ of the training data was used at each stage. Figure 1 illustrates the typical behavior of the averages of the crossvalidated scores as a function of F.

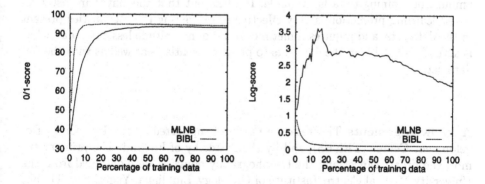

Fig. 1. Average crossvalidated 0/1-scores (left) and log-scores (right) in the Iris dataset case as a function of the percentage of the training data used.

The results show that first of all, although the model family used for the experiments was determined by the strong independence assumptions underlying the structurally simple naive Bayes model, the results are quite competitive when compared to the results obtained by using much more elaborate model families (see, e.g., the results collected in [23]). Secondly, we can see that when full datasets are used, in the 0/1-score sense the difference between the performance of the BIBL classifier and the MLNB classifier is not very large, whereas in the log-score sense the BIBL approach produces consistently better results. The experiments with restricted training data sets show that the BIBL approach is very effective in extracting regularities present in the data, and it clearly outperforms the standard single model approach in cases with very small amounts of data, both in the 0/1-score and in the log-score sense. This is due to the fact that BIBL is much more "conservative" than the single model MLNB. For small samples it is well known that the traditional MLNB classifier is too dependent on the observed data and does not take into account that future data *may* turn out to be different. A more detailed discussion on this topic can be found in [17, 18].

5 Conclusion

In this paper we proposed a Bayesian framework for defining the instance-based learning approach. The framework is based on the observation that moving from a model based learning approach, such as decision tree learning, to an instance-based learning approach that relies solely on data, is in probabilistic terms equivalent to averaging over all the (possibly infinitely many) models. We presented the formalization of the general framework, and illustrated how the approach can be implemented in the special case with a set of strong independence assumptions.

Our experiments with public domain classification data sets indicate that the Bayesian instance-based approach outperforms the (eager) use of a single model from the respective model class, especially in cases where only a small amount of training data is available. It turns out that the Bayesian instance-based learning prediction is very effective in extracting the regularities present in the data sets, and requires sometimes order of magnitude less data than what is actually available in the data sets to predict essentially as well as with the full data set.

Acknowledgements This research has been supported by the Technology Development Center (TEKES), and by the Academy of Finland. The primary tumor, the breast cancer and the lymphography domains were obtained from the University Medical Centre, Institute of Oncology, Ljubljana, Yugoslavia. Thanks go to M. Zwitter and M. Soklič for providing the data.

References

1. D. Aha. *A Study of Instance-Based Algorithms for Supervised Learning Tasks: Mathematical, Empirical, an Psychological Observations.* PhD thesis, University of California, Irvine, 1990.

2. D. Aha, editor. *Lazy Learning.* Kluwer Academic Publishers, Dordrecht, 1997. Reprinted from Artificial Intelligence Review, 11:1–5.

3. K. Ali and M. Pazzani. Error reduction through learning multiple descriptions. *Machine Learning*, 24(3):173–202, September 1997.

4. C. Atkeson. Memory based approaches to approximating continuous functions. In M. Casdagli and S. Eubank, editors, *Nonlinear Modeling and Forecasting. Proceedings Volume XII in the Santa Fe Institute Studies in the Sciences of Complexity.* Addison Wesley, New York, NY, 1992.

5. C. Atkeson, A. Moore, and S. Schaal. Locally weighted learning. In Aha [2], pages 11–73.

6. J.O. Berger. *Statistical Decision Theory and Bayesian Analysis.* Springer-Verlag, New York, 1985.

7. G. Cooper and E. Herskovits. A Bayesian method for the induction of probabilistic networks from data. *Machine Learning*, 9:309–347, 1992.

8. M.H. DeGroot. *Optimal statistical decisions.* McGraw-Hill, 1970.

9. B.S. Everitt and D.J. Hand. *Finite Mixture Distributions.* Chapman and Hall, London, 1981.

10. U. Fayyad, G. Piatetsky-Shapiro, P. Smyth, and R. Uthurusamy, editors. *Advances in Knowledge Discovery and Data Mining.* MIT Press, Cambridge, MA, 1996.

11. D. Fisher. Noise-tolerant conceptual clustering. In *Proceedings of the International Joint Conference on Artificial Intelligence*, pages 825–830, Detroit, Michigan, 1989.

12. D. Fisher and D. Talbert. Inference using probabilistic concept trees. In *Proceedings of the Sixth International Workshop on Artificial Intelligence and Statistics*, pages 191–202, Ft. Lauderdale, Florida, January 1997.

13. J.H. Friedman. Flexible metric nearest neighbor classification. Unpublished manuscript. Available by anonymous ftp from Stanford Research Institute (Menlo Park, CA) at playfair.stanford.edu., 1994.

14. A. Gelman, J. Carlin, H. Stern, and D. Rubin. *Bayesian Data Analysis.* Chapman & Hall, 1995.

15. D. Heckerman, D. Geiger, and D.M. Chickering. Learning Bayesian networks: The combination of knowledge and statistical data. *Machine Learning*, 20(3):197–243, September 1995.

16. S. Kasif, S. Salzberg, D. Waltz, J. Rachlin, and D. Aha. Towards a better understanding of memory-based reasoning systems. In *Proceedings of the Eleventh International Machine Learning Conference*, pages 242–250, New Brunswick, NJ, 1994. Morgan Kaufmann Publishers.

17. P. Kontkanen, P. Myllymäki, T. Silander, H. Tirri, and P. Grünwald. Comparing predictive inference methods for discrete domains. In *Proceedings of the Sixth International Workshop on Artificial Intelligence and Statistics*, pages 311–318, Ft. Lauderdale, Florida, January 1997. Also: NeuroCOLT Technical Report NC-TR-97-004.

18. P. Kontkanen, P. Myllymäki, T. Silander, H. Tirri, and P. Grünwald. On predictive distributions and Bayesian networks. In W. Daelemans, P. Flach, and A. van den Bosch, editors, *Proceedings of the Seventh Belgian-Dutch Conference on Machine Learning (BeNeLearn'97)*, pages 59–68, Tilburg, the Netherlands, October 1997.

19. P. Kontkanen, P. Myllymäki, and H. Tirri. Comparing Bayesian model class selection criteria by discrete finite mixtures. In D. Dowe, K. Korb, and J. Oliver, editors, *Information, Statistics and Induction in Science*, pages 364–374, Proceedings of the ISIS'96 Conference, Melbourne, Australia, August 1996. World Scientific, Singapore.

20. P. Kontkanen, P. Myllymäki, and H. Tirri. Experimenting with the Cheeseman-Stutz evidence approximation for predictive modeling and data mining. In D. Dankel, editor, *Proceedings of the Tenth International FLAIRS Conference*, pages 204–211, Daytona Beach, Florida, May 1997.

21. D. Mackay. *Bayesian Methods for Adaptive Models*. PhD thesis, California Institute of Technology, 1992.

22. D. Madigan, A. Raftery, C. Volinsky, and J. Hoeting. Bayesian model averaging. In *AAAI Workshop on Integrating Multiple Learned Models*, 1996.

23. D. Michie, D.J. Spiegelhalter, and C.C. Taylor, editors. *Machine Learning, Neural and Statistical Classification*. Ellis Horwood, London, 1994.

24. A. Moore. Acquisition of dynamic control knowledge for a robotic manipulator. In *Seventh International Machine Learning Workshop*. Morgan Kaufmann, 1990.

25. P. Myllymäki and H. Tirri. Bayesian case-based reasoning with neural networks. In *Proceedings of the IEEE International Conference on Neural Networks*, volume 1, pages 422–427, San Francisco, March 1993. IEEE, Piscataway, NJ.

26. P. Myllymäki and H. Tirri. Massively parallel case-based reasoning with probabilistic similarity metrics. In S. Wess, K.-D. Althoff, and M Richter, editors, *Topics in Case-Based Reasoning*, volume 837 of *Lecture Notes in Artificial Intelligence*, pages 144–154. Springer-Verlag, 1994.

27. J. Rissanen. *Stochastic Complexity in Statistical Inquiry*. World Scientific Publishing Company, New Jersey, 1989.

28. J. Rissanen. Fisher information and stochastic complexity. *IEEE Transactions on Information Theory*, 42(1):40–47, January 1996.

29. C. Stanfill and D. Waltz. Toward memory-based reasoning. *Communications of the ACM*, 29(12):1213–1228, 1986.

30. K. Ting and R. Cameron-Jones. Exploring a framework for instance based learning and Naive Bayes classifiers. In *Proceedings of the Seventh Australian Joint Conference on Artificial Intelligence*, pages 100–107, 1994.

31. H. Tirri, P. Kontkanen, and P. Myllymäki. A Bayesian framework for case-based reasoning. In I. Smith and B. Faltings, editors, *Advances in Case-Based Reasoning*, volume 1168 of *Lecture Notes in Artificial Intelligence*, pages 413–427. Springer-Verlag, Berlin Heidelberg, November 1996.

32. H. Tirri, P. Kontkanen, and P. Myllymäki. Probabilistic instance-based learning. In L. Saitta, editor, *Machine Learning: Proceedings of the Thirteenth International Conference*, pages 507–515. Morgan Kaufmann Publishers, 1996.

33. D.M. Titterington, A.F.M. Smith, and U.E. Makov. *Statistical Analysis of Finite Mixture Distributions*. John Wiley & Sons, New York, 1985.

34. D. Wettschereck, D. Aha, and T. Mohri. A review and empirical evaluation of feature-weighting methods for a class of lazy learning algorithms. In Aha [2], pages 273–314.

Bayesian and Information-Theoretic Priors for Bayesian Network Parameters

Petri Kontkanen[1], Petri Myllymäki[1], Tomi Silander[1], Henry Tirri[1], and
Peter Grünwald[2]

[1] Complex Systems Computation Group (CoSCo)
P.O.Box 26, Department of Computer Science
FIN-00014 University of Helsinki, Finland
[2] CWI, Department of Algorithms and Architectures
P.O. Box 94079, NL-1090 GB Amsterdam, The Netherlands

Abstract. We consider Bayesian and information-theoretic approaches for determining non-informative prior distributions in a parametric model family. The information-theoretic approaches are based on the recently modified definition of *stochastic complexity* by Rissanen, and on the Minimum Message Length (MML) approach by Wallace. The Bayesian alternatives include the uniform prior, and the equivalent sample size priors. In order to be able to empirically compare the different approaches in practice, the methods are instantiated for a model family of practical importance, the family of Bayesian networks.

1 Introduction

Given some sample data, our goal is to learn about the regularities in the problem domain so that we can arrive at a "good" predictive distribution $\mathcal{P}$ that can be used to predict well. In the following we restrict the search for such a $\mathcal{P}$ to a class $\mathcal{M}$ of probabilistic models, which all share the same parametric form. All the approaches considered here depend on a prior distribution $P(\Theta)$ over all the models (parameter instantiations) Θ in the class $\mathcal{M}$. In this paper we study different alternatives for choosing $P(\Theta)$ in an *non-informative setting*, where no "data independent" prior knowledge about the problem domain is available.

The statistical literature contains many proposals for "optimal" non-informative prior distributions. While all of these satisfy some optimality criterion, in practice they give rise to different predictions. The main purpose of this paper is to compute several different "optimal" prior distributions P for a model class of practical importance, the class of Bayesian networks (see, e.g., [5]). In particular, we will compare priors which are in accordance with the Bayesian interpretation of probability, to priors motivated by information-theoretic considerations: a prior based on Rissanen's *Minimum Description Length (MDL)* principle [10], and a prior based on Wallace & Boulton's *Minimum Message Length (MML) principle* [15]. Though MDL and MML are similar in spirit, we will see that they do not lead to the same prior distribution.

In Section 2 we introduce the general setting of the problem by discussing and motivating the priors we will use. In Section 3 the priors and predictive distributions are instantiated for the special case where the models are defined by a Bayesian network structure with a particular arbitrary, but fixed, topology. For some of the priors, this instantiation has been presented in [4, 6]. The contribution of this section is to derive explicit formulas for the MDL and MML priors for the case of Bayesian networks, which involves computing the (expected) Fisher information matrix for Bayesian networks. For comparing the predictive distributions presented in this paper, we have run an extensive series of tests on real world data, but due to space constrains the results of the tests are presented elsewhere [8].

2 Predictive Distributions and Their Priors

We model the problem domain by a set X of m discrete random variables, $X = \{X_1, \ldots, X_m\}$, where a random variable X_i can take on any of the values in the set $\mathbf{X}_i = \{x_{i1}, \ldots, x_{in_i}\}$. A *data instantiation* $d = (x_1, \ldots, x_m)$ is a vector in which all the variables X_i have been assigned a value: by $X = d$ we mean that $X_1 = x_1, \ldots, X_m = x_m$, where $x_i \in \mathbf{X}_i$. A *random sample* $D = (d_1, \ldots, d_N)$ is a set of N i.i.d. (independent and identically distributed) data instantiations, where each d_j is assumed to be sampled from the joint distribution of the variables in X.

Given a random sample D, we are interested in the question of how to define the *predictive distribution* $\mathcal{P}(d|D)$ for a given vector d. We investigate several candidates for $\mathcal{P}(d|D)$, relative to a parametric family $\mathcal{M}$ of probabilistic models: each model $\Theta \in \mathcal{M}$ defines a probability $P(d|\Theta)$ for each data instantiation d, and, under the i.i.d. assumption, a probability $P(D|\Theta)$ (the *likelihood*) for each dataset D. Given the likelihood, and a prior distribution $P(\Theta)$ for all $\Theta \in \mathcal{M}$, we can arrive at a posterior distribution for the models:

$$P(\Theta|D) \propto P(D|\Theta)P(\Theta). \tag{1}$$

The *MAP (maximum a posteriori probability)* predictive distribution is given by

$$\mathcal{P}_{\text{MAP}}(d \mid D, \Phi) = P(d \mid D, \hat{\Theta}_\Phi(D)) \overset{\text{i.i.d.}}{=} P(d \mid \hat{\Theta}_\Phi(D)), \tag{2}$$

where Φ denotes the (hyper)parameters used for defining the prior distribution $P(\Theta)$, and $\hat{\Theta}(D)$ is the MAP model maximizing the posterior (1).

A more sophisticated approach is to average (integrate) over all the models $\Theta \in \mathcal{M}$, which produces the *evidence* or *marginal likelihood* predictive distribution

$$\mathcal{P}_{\text{Ev}}(d|D, \Phi) = \int P(d|D, \Theta, \Phi)P(\Theta|D, \Phi)d\Theta \overset{\text{i.i.d.}}{=} \int P(d|\Theta)P(\Theta|D, \Phi)d\Theta. \tag{3}$$

Both the MAP predictive distribution and the evidence predictive distribution are defined by using the posterior $P(\Theta|D)$, which depends on the prior $P(\Theta)$. We now consider different alternatives for determining the prior distribution.

The Uniform Prior The conceptually simplest non-informative prior is the *uniform prior*, in which case the prior distribution $P(\Theta)$ is a constant. One can see from (1) that in this case the MAP predictive distribution becomes the *Maximum Likelihood (ML) model* of classical statistics, i.e., the model $\tilde{\Theta}$ maximizing the data likelihood $P(D|\Theta)$.

Equivalent Sample Size Priors In the Bayesian philosophy the prior probability of a model Θ can be regarded as a prior (initial) *degree of belief* in the model Θ. Given a sufficiently regular model class $\mathcal{M}$, we can construct *Equivalent Sample Size (ESS)* priors Φ for $\mathcal{M}$ so that the following property holds for all d and all D of any size:

$$P(d \mid D, \Phi) = P(d \mid \tilde{\Theta}(D \cup D')), \tag{4}$$

where $\tilde{\Theta}$ is the maximum likelihood model (see above) for the training data D plus some additional "virtual data" D'. This virtual data D' depends only on the prior Φ, i.e., for each dataset D' of any size there is exactly one prior $\Phi_{D'}$ that corresponds to it. Hence using P in combination with Φ is always equivalent to predicting using the model that renders the training data D plus the extra data D' in the most likely manner. We can now interpret D' as *a priori data* that governs how strongly we let our predictions be influenced by the actual sample D (see [5]).

An MDL Prior Intuitively speaking, the *Minimum Description Length (MDL) Principle* [10–12] states that the more we are able to compress a set of data, the more we have learned about it, and the better we will be able to predict future data. *Stochastic complexity* of a data set D relative to a class of models $\mathcal{M}$ is defined as the code length of D when it is encoded using the shortest code obtainable with the help of the class $\mathcal{M}$. Here by the "shortest code" one means the code that gives as short as possible a code length to *all* possible data sets D. It follows from the Kraft Inequality (see for example [11]) that the stochastic complexity S can be written as $S = -\log \mathcal{P}_{SC}$ where $\mathcal{P}_{SC}$ is some probability distribution.

There are several reasons why $S = -\log \mathcal{P}_{EV}(D) = \int P(D|\Theta)\pi(\Theta)d\Theta$ is a good candidate for defining the stochastic complexity explicitly [11]. Recently, however, Rissanen [12] has shown that there exists a code that is itself not dependent on any prior distribution of parameters, and which yields even shorter codelengths than the code with lengths $-\log \mathcal{P}_{EV}(D)$, except for the special case where a particular prior $\pi(\Theta) \propto |I(\Theta)|^{1/2}$, the so-called *Jeffrey's prior* [2,3], is used for $\mathcal{P}_{EV}(D)$. Here $|I(\Theta)|$ denotes the determinant of the *Fisher information matrix* $I(\Theta)$ as defined in [2]. In this case it can be shown [12] that under suitable technical conditions, $\mathcal{P}_{EV}$ and $\mathcal{P}_{SC}$ asymptotically coincide:

$$-\log \mathcal{P}_{SC}(D) = -\log \mathcal{P}_{EV}(D) + o(1), \tag{5}$$

which means that from the MDL point of view, the optimal predictive distribution is obtained by using $\mathcal{P}_{EV}$ with Jeffrey's prior.

An MML Prior *Minimum Message Length (MML) Inference* [14, 15] is based on a similar philosophy to the *MDL* principle, but there are also some subtle differences which cause the actual formulas used in MDL and MML estimation to differ considerably (see [1] for a detailed discussion on this subject). For our purposes, it is sufficient to note the following two differences: first, in MML modeling the predictive distribution $P(d|\Theta_{\text{MML}}(D))$ is defined by using a single "MML-optimal" model, whereas $\mathcal{P}_{\text{SC}}$ as defined above uses an integral over all the models in the given class. Second, although both employ priors, the priors used in MDL serve only as a technical tool for computing an approximation to $\mathcal{P}_{\text{SC}}$ (which itself does not depend on any prior), while MML adopts a Bayesian philosophy regarding priors, and assumes the user to provide a *subjective prior* $P(\Theta)$ to reflect his/her prior beliefs. Omitting all mathematical details (which can be found in [15]), the MML-optimal model $\Theta_{\text{MML}}(D)$ is defined by

$$\Theta_{\text{MML}}(D) = \arg \max_{\Theta \in \mathcal{M}} \frac{P(D|\Theta)P(\Theta)}{|I(\Theta)|^{1/2}}, \tag{6}$$

where $|I(\Theta)|$ is the determinant of the Fisher information matrix. We now see that $\Theta_{\text{MML}}(D)$ for prior $P(\Theta)$ is equal to the MAP-model $\hat{\Theta}(D)$ for prior $P'(\Theta) \propto P(\Theta)/\pi(\Theta)$. Interestingly, while the formula for the MDL predictive distribution involves *multiplying* $P(D|\Theta)$ by Jeffrey's prior, the formula for the MML predictive distribution involves *dividing* $P(D|\Theta)$ by Jeffrey's prior.

3 Priors for Bayesian Networks

A Bayesian (belief) network [9, 13] is a representation of a probability distribution over a set of discrete variables, consisting of an acyclic directed graph, where the nodes correspond to domain variables $X_1, \ldots, X_m$. Each network topology defines a set of independence assumptions which allow the joint probability distribution for a data vector d to be written as a product of simple conditional probabilities,

$$P(d) = P(X_1 = x_1, \ldots, X_m = x_m) = \prod_{i=1}^{m} P(X_i = x_i | \text{pa}_i = q_i), \tag{7}$$

where q_i denotes a configuration of (the values of) the parents of variable X_i. Consequently, in the Bayesian network model family, a distribution $P(d \mid \Theta)$ is uniquely determined by fixing the values of the parameters $\Theta = (\theta^1, \ldots, \theta^m)$, where $\theta^i = (\theta^i_{11}, \ldots, \theta^i_{1n_i}, \ldots, \theta^i_{c_i 1}, \ldots, \theta^i_{c_i n_i})$, n_i is the number of values of X_i, c_i is the number of configurations of pa_i, and $\theta^i_{q_i x_i} := P(X_i = x_i \mid \text{pa}_i = q_i)$.

In the following all the conditional distributions of the variables, given their parents, are assumed to be multinomial, i.e., $X_{i|q_i} \sim \text{Multi}(1; \theta^i_{q_i 1}, \ldots, \theta^i_{q_i n_i})$. Since the family of Dirichlet distributions is *conjugate* (see e.g. [2]) to the family of multinomials, it would be convenient if we could assume that the prior distributions of the parameters are from this family. More precisely, this would mean that $(\theta^i_{q_i1},\dots,\theta^i_{q_in_i}) \sim \mathrm{Di}(\mu^i_{q_i1},\dots,\mu^i_{q_in_i})$, where $(\mu^i_{q_i1},\dots,\mu^i_{q_in_i})$ are the hyperparameters of the corresponding distributions. From the definition of Dirichlet distributions [2], it is relatively easy to see that both the uniform prior and the ESS priors are Dirichlet distributions (see, e.g., [6]). For the subclass of Bayesian Networks used in our experiments reported in [8], Jeffrey's prior is of the Dirichlet form too. Moreover, we have seen in the previous section that the priors we need for the MML predictive distributions are arrived at by dividing the user's subjective prior by Jeffrey's prior. If the subjective prior is Dirichlet, it is easy to see that the resulting prior is of the Dirichlet form too. Consequently, all the priors used here are Dirichlet, which allows us to derive explicit expressions for $\mathcal{R}_{\mathrm{MAP}}$ and $\mathcal{R}_{\mathrm{BV}}$, as shown in [4,6]. The computation of the ESS priors for Bayesian Networks can be found in [5]. In the following we show how to compute the Jeffrey's prior $\pi(\Theta)$ for Bayesian networks, which is required for determining the MDL and MML priors discussed above.

Let $I(\cdot)$ denote the indicator function, i.e., $I(a,b) = 1$ if $a = b$ and 0 otherwise. We write d_{ji} for the i-th entry of data instantiation d_j; q_{ji} stands for the configuration of the parent variables of X_i in d_j. For computing the Fisher information matrix $I(\Theta)$, let us consider the element $[I(\Theta)]_{r,s}$ where (r,s) is the entry corresponding to $\theta^{i_1}_{q_{i_1}l_1}$ and $\theta^{i_2}_{q_{i_2}l_2}$. By deriving an explicit expression for $\log P(X|\Theta)$ one can show that if either the variable indices i_1,i_2 or the parent configurations q_{i_1}, q_{i_2} are different, then $[I(\Theta)]_{r,s} = 0$. If $q_{i_1} = q_{i_2}$ and $i_1 = i_2$, one obtains after some calculations:

$$[I(\Theta)]_{r,s} = \mathrm{E}_\Theta\left[\frac{-\partial^2 \log P(d_j|\Theta)}{\partial(\theta^i_{q_il})^2}\right] = \frac{P(\mathrm{pa}_i = q_i|\Theta)}{\theta^i_{q_in_i}} + I(l_1,l_2)\frac{P(\mathrm{pa}_i = q_i|\Theta)}{\theta^i_{q_il_1}}.$$

We now have an expression for each element of $I(\Theta)$, which gives us

$$\pi(\Theta) \propto \sqrt{|I(\Theta)|} = \prod_{i=1}^{m}\prod_{q_i=1}^{c_i}(N \cdot P^i_{q_i})^{\frac{n_i-1}{2}}\prod_{l=1}^{n_i}(\theta^i_{q_il})^{-\frac{1}{2}}$$

$$\propto \prod_{i=1}^{m}\prod_{q_i=1}^{c_i}(P^i_{q_i})^{\frac{n_i-1}{2}}\prod_{l=1}^{n_i}(\theta^i_{q_il})^{-\frac{1}{2}}.$$

Details of the derivation of this result can be found in [7].

4 Conclusion

In this paper we have discussed various Bayesian and information-theoretic approaches for determining non-informative prior distributions in a parametric model family: Minimum Description Length (MDL) prior, Minimum Message Length (MML) prior, uniform prior, and equivalent sample size priors. To be able to study the relevance of the various approaches in practice, we instantiated the methods for the family of Bayesian networks. Our empirical results reported in [8] show that while in the case of large training samples all methods give very good results, some of them perform close to optimal already when only a very small amount of training data is available. The results suggest that if the size of the training data is small, it would be a good idea to use either the evidence-based approach (with any prior), or the MAP approach with the ESS priors.

Acknowledgments This research has been supported by the ESPRIT Working Group on Neural and Computational Learning (NeuroCOLT), the Technology Development Center (TEKES), and the Academy of Finland.

References

1. R.A. Baxter and J.O. Oliver. MDL and MML: Similarities and differences. Technical Report 207, Department of Computer Science, Monash University, 1994.
2. J.O. Berger. *Statistical Decision Theory and Bayesian Analysis*. Springer-Verlag, New York, 1985.
3. B.S. Clarke and A.R. Barron. Jeffrey's prior is asymptotically least favorable under entropy risk. *Journal of Statistical Planning and Inference*, 41:37–60, 1994.
4. G. Cooper and E. Herskovits. A Bayesian method for the induction of probabilistic networks from data. *Machine Learning*, 9:309–347, 1992.
5. D. Heckerman. A tutorial on learning with Bayesian networks. Technical Report MSR-TR-95-06, Microsoft Research, Advanced Technology Division, One Microsoft Way, Redmond, WA 98052, 1996.
6. D. Heckerman, D. Geiger, and D.M. Chickering. Learning Bayesian networks: The combination of knowledge and statistical data. *Machine Learning*, 20(3):197–243, September 1995.
7. P. Kontkanen, P. Myllymäki, T. Silander, H. Tirri, and P. Grünwald. On predictive distributions and Bayesian networks. Technical Report NC-TR-97-032, ESPRIT Working Group on Neural and Computational Learning (NeuroCOLT), 1997.
8. P. Kontkanen, P. Myllymäki, T. Silander, H. Tirri, and P. Grünwald. A comparison of non-informative priors for Bayesian networks. Technical Report NC-TR-98-002, ESPRIT Working Group on Neural and Computational Learning (NeuroCOLT), 1998.
9. J. Pearl. *Probabilistic Reasoning in Intelligent Systems: Networks of Plausible Inference*. Morgan Kaufmann Publishers, San Mateo, CA, 1988.
10. J. Rissanen. Stochastic complexity. *Journal of the Royal Statistical Society*, 49(3):223–239 and 252–265, 1987.
11. J. Rissanen. *Stochastic Complexity in Statistical Inquiry*. World Scientific Publishing Company, New Jersey, 1989.
12. J. Rissanen. Fisher information and stochastic complexity. *IEEE Transactions on Information Theory*, 42(1):40–47, January 1996.
13. R.D. Shachter. Probabilistic inference and influence diagrams. *Operations Research*, 36(4):589–604, July-August 1988.
14. C.S. Wallace and D.M Boulton. An information measure for classification. *Computer Journal*, 11:185–194, 1968.
15. C.S. Wallace and P.R. Freeman. Estimation and inference by compact coding. *Journal of the Royal Statistical Society*, 49(3):240–265, 1987.

Feature Subset Selection in Text-Learning

Dunja Mladenić

Department for Intelligent Systems, J.Stefan Institute,
Jamova 39, 1100 Ljubljana, Slovenia
Phone: (+38)(61) 1773 272, Fax: (+38)(61) 1258-158
E-mail: Dunja.Mladenic@ijs.si
http://www-ai.ijs.si/DunjaMladenic

Abstract. This paper describes several known and some new methods
for feature subset selection on large text data. Experimental comparison
given on real-world data collected from Web users shows that characteristics of the problem domain and machine learning algorithm should
be considered when feature scoring measure is selected. Our problem
domain consists of hyperlinks given in a form of small-documents represented with word vectors. In our learning experiments naive Bayesian
classifier was used on text data. The best performance was achieved by
the feature selection methods based on the feature scoring measure called
Odds ratio that is known from information retrieval.

1   Introduction

In propositional learning problem domain is given by a set of examples, where
each example is described with a class value and a vector of feature values.
Features used to describe examples are not necessary all relevant and beneficial
for the inductive learning and may reduce quality of induced model. Additionally,
a high number of features may slow down the induction process while giving
similar results as obtained with much smaller feature subset.

Section 2 describes approach commonly used for feature subset selection in
learning on text data (text-learning). In Section 4 we experimentally compare
different feature scoring measures on real-world data collected from Web users.
Section 3 describes our problem domain and naive Bayesian classifier for text
that we used in experiments. Discussion is given in Section 5.

2   Feature subset selection approaches

Different methods have been developed and used for feature subset selection
in statistics, pattern recognition and machine learning, using different search
strategies and evaluation functions. John et al. [4] pointed out the difference
between the two main approaches used in machine learning to feature subset
selection: filtering approach where the feature subset is selected independent of
the learning method and wrapper approach where the feature subset is selected
using the same learning algorithm that will be used for learning on domain
represented with the selected feature subset.

The usual way of learning on text defines a feature for each word that occurred in training documents. This can easily result with several tens of thousands of features. Most methods for feature subset selection that are used information retrieval and text-learning (eg. [1], [3], [11]) are very simple compared to the methods developed in machine learning. Basically, some scoring measure that is used on a single feature is selected, a score is assigned to each feature independently, features are sorted according to the assigned score and a predefined number of the best features is taken to form the solution feature subset. Scoring of individual features can be performed using some of the measure used in machine learning for feature selection during the learning process, for example, *Information gain* used in decision tree induction. In information retrieval a commonly used feature scoring is by *Odds ratio* [12], where the problem is to rank out documents according to their relevance for the positive class value C_1 using occurrence of different words as features.

$$OddsRatio(F) = \log \frac{odds(W|C_1)}{odds(W|C_2)} = \log \frac{P(W|C_1)(1 - P(W|C_2))}{(1 - P(W|C_1))P(W|C_2)}$$

Where $P(W|C_i)$ is the conditional probability of word W occurring given the i-th class value. We handle singularities as proposed in [13]. Notice that Odds ratio is not averaged over all feature values, like Information gain, but only the value recording that word occurred is considered. We experimented also with three measures inspired by the original Odds ratio formula: $FreqOddsRatio(A) = Freq(W) \times OddsRatio(W)$, $FreqLogP(A) = Freq(W) \times \log \frac{P(W|C_1)}{P(W|C_2)}$, $ExpP(A) = e^{P(W|C_1) - P(W|C_2)}$. In our experimental comparison, we also include a very simple measure reported to work well in text classification domains [14] that scores each word by $Freq(W)$ frequency of word W. As a baseline measure we used Random score assignment.

In some text-classification experiments some other measures similar to Information gain are used like expected *Cross entropy*, *Keyword checker* and *Mutual information* used in [6], [5], [14] respectively. These are not included in our experiments, since Information gain they are based on performed worst on our data than Odds ratio (see Section 4 for more details).

3 Domain description

Machine learning problem is here defined as predicting clicked hyperlinks from the set of Web documents visited by the user. This is performed on-line while user is sitting behind some Web browser and waiting for the requested document. Our prototype system called Personal WebWatcher [10] uses text-learning on this problem, learning separate model for each user and highlighting hyperlinks on the requested Web documents. All hyperlinks from the visited documents are used as machine learning examples. Each is assigned one of the two class values: positive (user clicked on the hyperlink) or negative. We use machine learning to model the function $User_{HL} : HyperLink \rightarrow \{pos, neg\}$. Our hope is that this function is also some approximation of interesting hyperlinks (user clicked on hyperlinks that she/he is interested in and skipped all other hyperlinks, that is of course not always true!). We represented each hyperlink as a small document containing underlined words, words in a window around them and words in all the headings above the hyperlink. Our documents are represented as word vectors (using so called bag-of-words representation commonly used in information retrieval) and learning was performed using Naive (simple) Bayesian classifier the same way as in [3] or [10]. For each word position in the document, a feature is defined having a word as its value [9].

Our experiments are performed on data collected for users participating in the HOMENET project [2]. Results for two users are described in Section 4 with the data characteristics are given in Table 1. For each user approximately 4000 different words occurred in documents resulting here with 4000 features.

Domain (user id.)	Positive class probability	Number of examples	data entropy
usr150101	0.104	2 528	0.480
usr150211	0.044	2 221	0.259

Table 1. Domain description for data collected from two HomeNet users. It can be seen that we are dealing with unbalanced class distribution, since 10 % or less examples are positive, all other are negative.

4 Experiments

We used hold-out testing with 10 repetitions using 30% randomly selected examples as testing examples and reported average value and standard error. Feature selection and learning was performed on training examples only. For each data set we observed the influence of the number of the best features selected for learning (vector size) to the system performance. Since we have unbalanced class distribution (see Table 1), Classification accuracy can give misleading results. For such domains more appropriate measure is Information score [7] or Geometric mean of accuracy [8]. In the experimental results presented in Figure 1 Classification accuracy and Information score are used to estimate model quality. For both domains the highest Classification accuracy and the highest Information score are achieved by the measures based on Odds ratio: $ExpP, FreqLogP, OddsRatio$ (see Table 2 and Figure 1). For these measures the best vector size is approximately between 60 and 200 best features. This means that the selected feature subset includes just 2% - 5% of all features. The similar reduction (up to 90%) in the number of features used in text-learning was observed in [14]. The other three measures ($InfGain, Freq, FreqOddsRatio$) for most vector sizes achieved worst results than $Random$. Closer look to words sorted by Information gain showed that most best words are characteristic for negative class value (their probability for positive documents is 0). This means that in classification a new positive hyperlink is represented with a word vector almost full of zeros, since it contains very few of the selected best words. In our experiments we didn't remove any common or frequent words. That resulted with html-tags and other common words to be the most frequent, contributing to the poor performance of the Frequency measure *Freq* (the lowest line on the all four graphs). Our explanation for bad results achieved by the combination of Frequency and Odds ratio *FreqOddsRatio* is that the value of Frequency is standing out in this combination. Odds ratio has most values between 1 and 20, Frequency between 1 and 1000 and their combination between 10 and 1000. In case of the combination of Frequency with logarithm of probability quotient *FreqLogP*, the logarithmic part is standing out and measure achieves better results.

Scoring measure	Accuracy					Information score				
best features	10	100	200	500	1000	10	100	200	500	1000
user150101										
ExpP	94.35	94.49	94.52	94.49	94.19	0.037	0.042	0.043	0.038	0.021
FreqLogP	94.32	94.49	94.52	94.50	94.18	0.036	0.041	0.042	0.037	0.019
OddsRatio	94.08	94.27	94.04	93.68	93.26	0.030	0.036	0.027	0.016	-0.002
InfGain	94.24	92.62	92.27	92.16	92.09	0.011	-0.064	-0.073	-0.074	-0.071
FreqOddsRatio	92.44	92.35	92.33	92.15	91.87	0.048	-0.045	-0.044	-0.047	-0.06
Freq	91.72	90.85	90.75	90.73	91.74	0.264	-0.242	-0.227	-0.210	-0.197
Random	93.39	93.37	93.37	93.23	92.73	0.005	-0.012	-0.020	-0.035	-0.059
user150211										
ExpP	96.61	96.63	96.60	96.42	95.97	0	0.001	-0.003	-0.014	-0.039
FreqLogP	96.60	96.62	96.56	96.41	95.97	-0.001	0	-0.005	-0.017	-0.042
OddsRatio	96.61	96.64	96.51	96.22	95.76	0.002	0.005	-0.008	-0.027	-0.055
InfGain	94.31	94.01	93.66	93.29	93.09	-0.226	-0.294	-0.320	-0.334	-0.337
FreqOddsRatio	95.76	95.52	95.43	95.25	94.86	0.130	-0.136	-0.138	-0.145	-0.16
Freq	94.49	92.60	92.05	91.74	91.62	-0.374	-0.40	-0.420	-0.428	-0.427
Random	96.57	996.46	96.38	96.18	95.77	0.003	-0.015	-0.035	-0.066	-0.103

Table 2. Subset of classification results plotted in Figure 1 for two domains.

5 Discussion

We experimentally compared seven attribute scoring measures on our data: Information gain used in most machine learning experiments on text data (eg. [3], [11], [14]), four variants of Odds ratio as the most promising for our problem, Frequency and Random that we used as a baseline measure.

The results of experiments suggest that in feature subset selection for text-learning the best 2 % to 5 % of features should be selected. This finding is not in contradiction with the results reported on other text-learning problem domains eg. [11], [14]. The experimental results further suggest that for our problem domain, where one class value is the target class value, features should be scored using some measure based on Odds ratio. In our problem, we would like to identify as many positive examples as possible and we don't really care about identifying negative examples. The prior probability of positive class value is rather low (0.1 or lower). Naive Bayesian formula that we used in learning, considers only words that occurred in document. When we use rapid feature reduction, many examples are represented with word vectors almost full of zeros that are

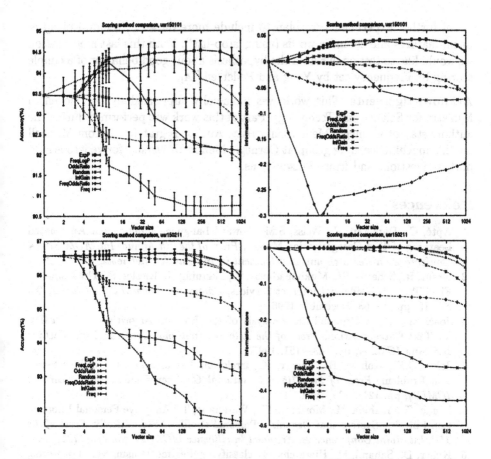

Fig. 1. Influence of vector size to Classification accuracy and Information score on data for HomeNet usr150101 (upper) and usr150211 (lower). Notice that curve names are sorted according to the values at the end (vector size=1000).

classified mostly according to the prior probability. This means that in order to identify positive documents $P(`pos'|D) > P(`neg'|D)$, we have to select features that will raise the probability of positive class value. This is possible only if $P(W_j|`pos') > P(W_j|`neg')$ holds with sufficient difference for sufficient number of the product members used in naive Bayesian formula. Thus, we based our new feature scoring measures ($FreqLogP$, $ExpP$) on that condition.

Experimental results pointed out the need to consider problem domain and machine learning algorithm characteristics when selecting a feature scoring measure. This is especially important for such simple feature subset selection approach as used in text-learning, where the solution quality is traded for time complexity. The feature subset found in this way is an approximation that assumes feature independence. The same false assumption is used by naive Bayesian classifier that was used is our experiments.

In further experiments we plan to include more datasets, removal of infrequent features and common words (using 'stop-list'). With this last modification we would like to test on our data the hypothesis about good behavior of a simple scoring by Frequency set by Yang and Pedersen [14].

Acknowledgements This work was financially supported by the Slovenian Ministry for Science and Technology. Part of this work was performed during the authors stay at Carnegie Mellon University. Author is grateful to Tom Mitchell and his machine learning group at Carnegie Mellon University for generous support, suggestions and fruitful discussions.

References

1. Apté, C., Damerau, F., Weiss, S.M., Toward Language Independent Automated Learning of Text Categorization Models, *Proc. of the 7th Annual Int. ACM-SIGIR Conference on Research and Development in Information Retrieval*, 1994.
2. Kraut, R., Scherlis, W., Mukhopadhyay, T., Manning, J., Kiesler, S., The HomeNet Field Trial of Residential Internet Services, *Communications of the ACM* Vol. 39, No. 12, pp.55—63, December 1996.
3. Joachims, T., A Probabilistic Analysis of the Rocchio Algorithm with TFIDF for Text Categorization, *Proc. of the 14th International Conference on Machine Learning ICML97*, pp. 143—151, 1997.
4. John, G.H., Kohavi, R., Pfleger, K., Irrelevant Features and the Subset Selection Problem, *Proc. of the 11th International Conference on Machine Learning ICML94*, pp. 121—129, 1994.
5. Kindo, T., Yoshida, H., Morimoto, T., Watanabe, T., Adaptive Personal Information Filtering System that Organizes Personal Profiles Automatically, *Proc. of the 15th Int. Joint Conference on Artificial Intelligence IJCAI-97*, pp. 716—721, 1997.
6. Koller, D., Sahami, M., Hierarchically classifying documents using very few words, *Proc. of the 14th International Conference on Machine Learning ICML97*, pp. 170—178, 1997.
7. Kononenko, I. and Bratko, I., Information-Based Evaluation Criterion for Classifier's Performance, *Machine Learning 6*, Kluwer Academic Publishers, 1991.
8. Kubat, M., Holte, R., Matwing, S., Learning When Negative Examples Abound, *9th European Conference on Machine Learning ECML97*, pp. 146—153, 1997.
9. Mitchell, T.M., Machine Learning, The McGraw-Hill Companies, Inc., 1997.
10. Mladenić, D., Personal WebWatcher: Implementation and Design, *Technical Report IJS-DP-7472*, October, 1996. http://www-ai.ijs.si/DunjaMladenic/papers/PWW/
11. Pazzani, M., Billsus, D., Learning and Revising User Profiles: The Identification of Interesting Web Sites, *Machine Learning 27*, Kluwer Academic Publishers, pp. 313—331, 1997.
12. van Rijsbergen, C.J,. Harper, D.J., Porter, M.F., The selection of good search terms, *Information Processing & Management*, 17, pp.77—91, 1981.
13. Shaw Jr, W.M., Term-relevance computations and perfect retrieval performance, *Information Processing & Management*, 31(4), pp.491—498, 1995.
14. Yang, Y., Pedersen, J.O., A Comparative Study on Feature Selection in Text Categorization, *Proc. of the 14th International Conference on Machine Learning ICML97*, pp. 412—420, 1997.

A Monotonic Measure for Optimal Feature Selection

Huan Liu[1] and Hiroshi Motoda[2] and Manoranjan Dash[3]

[1] Dept of Info Sys & Comp Sci, National University of Singapore, Singapore 119260.
[2] Division of Intelligent Sys Sci, Osaka University, Ibaraki, Osaka 567, Japan.
[3] BioInformatics Centre, National University of Singapore, Singapore 119074.
{liuh, manoranj}@iscs.nus.edu.sg motoda@sanken.osaka-u.ac.jp

Abstract. Feature selection is a problem of choosing a subset of relevant features. In general, only exhaustive search can bring about the optimal subset. With a monotonic measure, exhaustive search can be avoided without sacrificing optimality. Unfortunately, most error- or distance-based measures are not monotonic. A new measure is employed in this work that is monotonic and fast to compute. The search for relevant features according to this measure is guaranteed to be complete but not exhaustive. Experiments are conducted for verification.

1 Introduction

The basic problem of classification is to classify a given pattern (example) to one of m known classes. A pattern of features presumably contains enough information to distinguish among the classes. When a classification problem is defined by features, the number of features (N) can be quite large. A classifier may encounter problems to learn something meaningful because the required amounts of data ($\mathcal{N}$, or the number of patterns) increase exponentially in proportion with N. The task of feature selection is to determine which features to select in order to achieve maximum performance with the minimum measurement effort [2]. Reducing features directly alleviates the measurement effort. Performance of a classifier can be its predictive accuracy, i.e., *1 - error rate*.

As was mentioned in [2], if the goal is to minimize the error rate, and the measurement cost for all the features is equal, then the most appealing function to evaluate the potency of a feature to differentiate between the classes is the Bayes Classifier. Due to the inductive nature of classification problems, no full distribution of data can be obtained. Extensive research effort was devoted to the investigation of other functions (mostly based on distance and information measures, or simply on classifiers) for feature evaluation. If there exist N features, to find an optimal subset of features without knowing how many features are relevant, it requires to explore all the 2^N subsets. When N is large, this exhaustive approach is out of the question. Therefore, various feature selection methods have been designed to avoid exhaustive search while still aiming at the optimal subset. Examples are Branch & Bound [7], Focus [1], Relief [4], Wrapper methods [3], and LVF [5].

The feature selection problem can be viewed as a search problem [9]. The search process starts with either an empty set or a full set. For the former, it expands the search space by adding one feature at a time (Sequential Forward Selection) [1]; for the latter, it expands the search space by deleting one feature at a time (Sequential Backward Selection) [7]. As we shall see, a good alternative to exhaustive search is Branch & Bound like algorithms if there exists a monotonic function of evaluating features. Assuming we have subsets $\{S_0, S_1, ..., S_n\}$, we have a measure U that evaluates each subset S_i. The monotonicity condition requires that:

$$S_0 \supset S_1 \supset ... \supset S_n \Rightarrow U(S_0) \leq U(S_1) \leq ... \leq U(S_n).$$

In this case, the search can be complete but not exhaustive. In other words, the optimal subset is guaranteed. Many distance and information based measures have been shown to be non-monotonic [9]. Many researchers pointed out that the only remaining alternative is to use the error rate of a classifier as the measure. Among many classifiers, however, only the Bayes Classifier satisfies this monotonicity condition [1] because other classifiers adopt some assumptions and employ certain heuristics [9,2,3]. Another disadvantage of using the error rate as a measure in the wrapper models of feature selection is it is slow to compute. For example, to construct a decision tree, it would take at least $O(\mathcal{N} \log \mathcal{N})$. We present here a measure that is monotonic as well as fast to compute ($O(\mathcal{N})$) in search of optimal subsets.

2   A Non-exhaustive yet Complete Search Algorithm

For two subsets of features, S_i and S_j, one is preferred to the other based on a measure U of feature-set evaluation. S_i and S_j are indifferent if $U(S_i) = U(S_j)$ and $\#(S_i) = \#(S_j)$ where $\#$ is the cardinality; S_i is preferred to S_j if $U(S_i) = U(S_j)$ but $\#(S_i) < \#(S_j)$, or if $U(S_i) < U(S_j)$ and $\#(S_i) \leq \#(S_j)$. As we know, the condition for Branch & Bound to work optimally is that U is monotonic.

In this work, U is an *inconsistency rate* over the data set given S_i. The inconsistency rate is calculated as follows: (1) two patterns are considered inconsistent if they match all but their class labels, for example, patterns (0 1 1) and (0 1 0) match with respective to the first two attributes, but are different in the last attribute (class label); (2) the inconsistency count is the number of all the matching patterns minus the largest number of patterns of different class labels: for example, there are n matching patterns, among them, c_1 patterns belong to $label_1$, c_2 to $label_2$, and c_3 to $label_3$ where $c_1 + c_2 + c_3 = n$. If c_3 is the largest among the three, the inconsistency count is $(n - c_3)$; and (3) the inconsistency rate is the sum of all the inconsistency counts divided by the total number of patterns ($\mathcal{N}$). By employing a hashing mechanism, we can compute the inconsistency rate approximately with a time complexity of $O(\mathcal{N})$.

---

[1] But it requires the full distribution of the data.

A proof outline is given to show that this inconsistency rate measure is monotonic, i.e., if $S_i \subset S_j$, then $U(S_i) \geq U(S_j)$. Since $S_i \subset S_j$, the discriminating power of S_i can be no greater than that of S_j. It's known that the discriminating power is reversely proportional to the inconsistency rate. Hence, the inconsistency rate of S_i is greater than or equal to that of S_j, or $U(S_i) \geq U(S_j)$. The monotonicity of the measure can also be proved as follows. Consider three simplest cases of $S_k (= S_j - S_i)$ without loss of generality: (i) features in S_k are irrelevant, (ii) features in S_k redundant, and (iii) features in S_k relevant. If features in S_k are irrelevant, based on the definition of irrelevancy, these extra features do not change the inconsistency rate of S_j since S_j is $S_i \cup S_k$, so $U(S_j) = U(S_i)$. Likewise for case (ii) based on the definition of redundancy. If features in S_k are relevant, that means S_i does not have as many relevant features as S_j. Obviously, $U(S_i) \geq U(S_j)$ in the case of $S_i \subset S_j$. It is clear that the above results remain true for cases that S_k contains irrelevant, redundant as well as relevant features.

ABB is a Branch & Bound algorithm with its bound set to the inconsistency rate δ of the data set with the full set of features. It starts with the full set of features S^0, removes one feature from S_j^{l-1} in turn to generate subsets S_j^l where l is the current level and j specifies different subsets at the lth level. If $U(S_j^l) > U(S_j^{l-1})$, S_j^l stops growing (the branch is pruned), otherwise, it grows to level $l + 1$, in other words, one more feature will be removed. In short, ABB seeks the smallest S_j whose inconsistency rate is δ. S is the full feature set and D the data set.

```
δ = inConCal(S, D);
ABB (S, D) {
    /* subset generation */
    For all feature f in S {
        S₁ = S - f; /* remove one feature at a time */
        enQueue(Q, S₁);} /* add at the end */
    while notEmpty(Q) {
        S₂ = deQueue(Q); /* remove at the start */
        if (S₂ is legitimate ∧ inConCal(S₂, D) ≤ δ)
            /* recursion */
            ABB (S₂, D); }}
```

Function inConCal() calculates the consistency rate of data given a feature subset. Care has to be taken in implementing the algorithm such that (1) no duplicate subset will be generated via proper enumeration; and (2) no child node of a pruned node will be generated by ensuring that the Hamming distance between a new subset at the current level and any pruned subset at the parent level is greater than 1^2 (this is the legitimacy test in ABB).

It is not required anymore to specify the size of a desired subset, M, or a bound for the measure as normally required by Branch & Bound. Thus, its name

---

[2] A full set of N attributes entails an N-bit binary array in which ith value 1 means ith attribute is chosen to include in the subset.

ABB. At the end of search, we just need to report the legitimate subsets with the smallest cardinality as the optimal subsets.

An example.

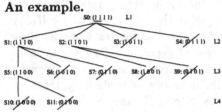

Refer to the figure: there are four features, assuming only the first two are relevant. The root $S_0 = (1\ 1\ 1\ 1)$ of the search tree is a binary array with four '1's. Following ABB, we expand the root to four child nodes by turning one of the four '1's into '0' (L2). All four are legitimate: $S_1 = (1\ 1\ 1\ 0)$, S_2

$= (1\ 1\ 0\ 1)$, $S_3 = (1\ 0\ 1\ 1)$, and S_4 $= (0\ 1\ 1\ 1)$. Since one of the relevant features is missing, $U(S_3)$ and $U(S_4)$ will be greater than $U(S_0)$ where U is the inconsistency rate on the given data. Hence, the branches rooted by S_3 and S_4 are pruned and will not grow further. Only when a new node passes the legitimacy test will its inconsistency rate be calculated. Doing so improves the efficiency of ABB because $\mathcal{N}$ (number of patterns) is normally much larger than N (number of attributes). The rest of the nodes are generated and tested in the same spirit.

3 Empirical Study

The objectives of this empirical study are to verify: 1. ABB indeed finds optimal subsets for various data sets, and 2. features selected are good for various learning algorithms. We select two groups of data sets: one with known relevant features and the other with unknown relevant features as shown in Table 1. All data sets are from [6] except for Corral [3]. For the first group of 5 data sets we compare the subsets selected by ABB with the known. For the second group we compare the outputs of ABB with that of Focus, a popular method in literature that guarantees optimal subsets. For the second objective we choose two different learning algorithms: a decision tree method (C4.5 [8]) and a standard back-propagation neural network (SNNS [10]). Two thirds of the data is used for selecting features by ABB and Focus. The other one third is the testing data for SNNS. We run 10-fold cross validation with C4.5 on the whole data. Results showed that ABB indeed finds optimal subsets as validated by Focus and *a priori* knowledge. Focus does breadth first search starting from the empty set and stops after reaching the first consistent subset. In fact, the subset found by Focus can be just one of the solutions of ABB.

While running ABB and Focus, we found an interesting fact that *"ABB and Focus complement each other with respect to time taken to reach optimal subset"*. To verify this, we collected the number of subsets evaluated by ABB and Focus in Table 1. ABB and Focus adopt different search directions. So, if the size of the optimal subset is not small, choose ABB, otherwise, choose Focus. To take advantage of both algorithms one may run both simultaneously till any one of the two algorithms stops.

Data set	D_{Tr}	D_{To}	C	N	M	ALL #	ABB #	Focus #
CorrAL	32	64	2	6	4	64	14	42
Monk1	124	432	2	6	3	64	12	24
Monk2	169	432	2	6	6	64	7	63
Monk3	122	432	2	6	3	64	19	35
Par3+	341	512	2	9	3	512	265	46
WBC	463	699	2	9	4	2^9	188	145
LED-7	400	600	10	7	5	2^7	9	99
Letter	5980	8968	26	16	9	2^{16}	1971	42,634
LYM	100	148	4	18	6	2^{18}	82,156	23,167
Vote	300	435	2	16	8	2^{16}	301	39,967
KrVsKp	2131	3196	2	36	29	2^{36}	4367	$> 2^{28}$

Table 1. D_{Tr} - training set, D_{To} - total set, C - no. of classes, N - no. of original features; M - no. of selected features, All # - no. of all possible subsets, ABB # - no. of subsets evaluated by ABB, Focus # - no. of by Focus.

Based on the subsets found for each data set, we obtain the results shown in Table 2. In general, C4.5 (10-fold cross validation) gave better or equally good accuracy after feature selection. But the results for tree size are interesting, some showing larger tree sizes after feature selection as pointed out by $\leftarrow$ in Table 2 Researchers noticed that smallest trees do not necessarily give the best predictive accuracy. What is observed here is that better accuracy may not mean a smaller tree size. We also noticed that "after" feature selection, in most cases, C4.5 used all features selected by ABB, which indicates that features selected by ABB are relevant in decision tree induction. However, C4.5 did choose features not selected by ABB in the "before" setting, e.g., in the case of CorrAL data.

To run the neural network classifier, we fixed the learning rate as 0.1, the momentum as 0.5, one hidden layer, the number of hidden units as half of the original input units for all data sets. We found a proper number of CYCLES for each data set by observing a sustained trend of no decrease of error (MSE) in a trial run. Later, with these parameters, two runs of SNNS were made on data sets with and without feature selection via ABB respectively. This experiment is very simplistic and designed to get some rough idea about the effect of selected features to a neural network classifier. In most cases, their error rates drop. Error rates for Letter are dubiously high. Due to the complication of parameter setting, more sophisticated experiments are being planned.

4 Conclusion

We demonstrated that the inconsistency rate is a monotonic measure and it is fast to compute. With such a measure, Branch & Bound is a good deterministic algorithm (the search is not exhaustive, yet complete), The new method ABB is simple to implement and guarantees optimal subsets of features. The empirical

Data set	C4.5						NN		
	Tree Size		Error Rate %		CYCLES	#HU	Error Rate %		
	Before	After	Before	After				Before	After
CorrAL	14.6	13.0	6.0	0.0	1000	3		4.55	**9.09**
Monk1	43.0	41.0	0.7	0.0	1000	3		50.68	37.84
Monk2	16.3	16.3	21.1	21.1	1000	3		29.73	29.73
Monk3	19.0	19.0	1.1	1.1	1000	3		12.16	0.0
Par3+3+3	13.0	**15.0**	17.2	0.0	← 1000	5		59.09	9.09
WBC	38.0	36.0	6.6	6.0	1000	5		8.05	6.78
LED-7	19.0	19.0	0.0	0.0	1000	4		0.0	0.0
Letter	6660.0	6113.0	28.1	27.9	15000	8		75.5	61.42
LYM	26.9	**29.6**	21.8	21.0	← 7000	9		25.0	**29.17**
Vote	16.0	**19.0**	2.8	2.3	← 4000	8		6.67	4.0
KrVsKp	54.8	**64.8**	0.52	**0.83**	← 8000	18		2.07	1.50

Table 2. Results of C4.5 (10-fold cross validation) and Back-propagation neural network. #HU - number of hidden units.

study suggests that (1) ABB removes irrelevant, redundant, and/or correlated features even with the presence of noise (as in Monk3 with 5% noise); and (2) the performance of a classifier with the features selected by ABB also improves. Another finding from this study is Focus and ABB complement each other due to their opposite search directions.

References

1. H. Almuallim and T.G. Dietterich. Learning with many irrelevant features. In *Proceedings of AAAI*, 1991.
2. M. Ben-Bassat. Pattern recognition and reduction of dimensionality. In P. R. Krishnaiah and L. N. Kanal, editors, *Handbook of statistics-II*, pages 773–791. North Holland, 1982.
3. G.H. John, R. Kohavi, and K. Pfleger. Irrelevant feature and the subset selection problem. In *Proceedings of ICML*, pages 121–129. Morgan Kaufmann, 1994.
4. K. Kira and L.A. Rendell. The feature selection problem: Traditional methods and a new algorithm. In *Proceedings of AAAI*, pages 129–134. 1992.
5. H. Liu and R. Setiono. A probabilistic approach to feature selection - a filter solution. In *Proceedings of ICML*, pages 319–327. Morgan Kaufmann, 1996.
6. C.J. Merz and P.M. Murphy. UCI repository of machine learning databases. http://www.ics.uci.edu/~mlearn/MLRepository.html . Irvine, CA: University of California, Department of Information and Computer Science, 1996.
7. P.M. Narendra and K. Fukunaga. A branch and bound algorithm for feature subset selection. *IEEE Trans. on Computer*, C-26(9):917–922, September 1977.
8. J.R. Quinlan. *C4.5: Programs for Machine Learning*. Morgan Kaufmann, 1993.
9. W. Siedlecki and J Sklansky. On automatic feature selection. *International Journal of Pattern Recognition and Artificial Intelligence*, 2:197–220, 1988.
10. A. Zell and et al. Stuttgart neural network simulator (SNNS), user manual, version 4.1. ftp.informatik.uni-stuttgart.de/pub/SNNS, 1995.

Inducing Models of Human Control Skills

Rui Camacho[1]

LIACC
Rua do Campo Alegre, 823
4150 PORTO
Portugal
Fax: (+351) 2 600 3654

FEUP
Rua dos Bragas
4099 PORTO CODEX
Portugal
Fax: (+351) 2 319 280

e-mail: rcamacho@fe.up.pt
www : http://www.ncc.up.pt/~tau

key words: behavioural cloning, decision trees, cognitive modeling

Abstract. A new model of human control skills is proposed and empirically evaluated. It is called the incremental correction model and is more adequate for reverse engineering human control skills than any other previously proposed models. The experimental results show a considerable increase in robustness of the controllers that use the new model. The new model also attenuates the problem of unbalanced classes, noticed already in previous experiments. By means of Parameterised Decision Trees, propositional learners are still usable within the new model's framework.

1 Introduction

The problem addressed by the reported investigation concerns the reverse engineering of human control skills, also known as behavioural cloning. The problem specification attends the following restrictions. Machine Learning (ML) algorithms are to be used to induce the controllers. The controllers constructed by the ML algorithm, using performance data, should be induced automatically, intelligible to human understanding and should replicate the robustness features of the human subject being modeled.

An automatic process of reverse engineering human control skills offers a useful process of fast construction of controllers, specially in tasks where traditional Control Theory is not applicable. As pointed out by [10] it is also a very useful tool for training student pilots, particularly with regard to determining the aptitude of a candidate at an early stage of training. Hamm 92 ([7]) refers that Westland Helicopters Ltd uses helicopter engineering simulations, controlled by pilot models, for rotor loads and performance prediction studies. Because a human pilot is not included in the control loop, it is not necessary for the helicopter simulation to run in real time — performance models may be run faster than real time for chart data production, and complex models may be run at less than real time, in cheap workstations, for applications such as rotor load prediction studies. Urbančič *et al*([11]) describe the application of the reverse engineer methodology to the control of a crane in loading/unloading ships in a harbor.

The problem of reverse engineering human control skills encounters several challenges. Since a real-time control strategy can not be articulated by the human subject, the model and its parameters must be conjectured and experimentally evaluated. The datasets that result from the behavioural traces have a set of features that make them "hard" for ML algorithms. The dataset is usually of large proportions, consisting of thousands of examples, and most of the attributes are real valued. The data is, usually, very noisy due to the fact that humans do not provide ideal control actions. There is also a natural unbalance in the dataset classes. Most of the time the system is near an equilibrium state and therefore, most of the time the controls do not change. Less often there are strong deviations from the desirable situation and the control values have to be changed substantially.

The controllers synthesised by Sammut *et al.*([10]) and [9][5][1] have the following limitations. They are not robust and the same controller is not adequate to fly different flight plans. The Decision Trees that constitute the controllers are very large (thousands of nodes). The model and ML tool parameters are hand tuned.

The reported work overcomes the mentioned limitations by proposing a new cognitive model for human control skills that include the use of goals. The new model has an underlying control strategy based on a sequence of adaptive control actions. Each control action, apart from the first of the sequence, corrects the previous action after its effects on the controlled system have been perceived. The experimental results show that the new model produces a significant improvement in the controllers robustness and a significant reduction in the complexity of the trees that code the controllers. The use of goals in the model allows the same controller to be used with different task plans. The use of a *wrapper* ([8]) facilitates the tuning of the model and the ML tool parameters.

The new framework prompts the improvements in the methodology for reverse engineering human control skills described in the next section.

The structure of the rest of the paper is as follows. In Section 2 the methodology for reverse engineering human control skills is described. Section 3 surveys the models of Human Control Skills and describes the new model in more detail. In Section 4 the evaluation of the model's performance is presented. The experiments description and the results obtained are reported in Section 5. The last section draws the conclusions.

2 Methodology

The methodology for reverse engineering human control skills, as described in [10], consists in the following steps.

(1) Characterisation of the system being controlled as a set of state and control variables, representatives of the system status and decisions made by the human controller. (2) Definition of a task plan as a temporal sequence of stages. (3) Execution of the control task by the human controller according to the task plan. While performing the control task the system's state and control variables are recorded at regular intervals (the behavioural traces). (4) Pre-processing of the trace files to produce the ML tool datasets. (5) Induction of the decision trees using the ML tool. One tree for each control variable and for each stage. (6) Post-processing procedure by assembling all parts into an artificial controller. Apart from the induced code for determining the value of each control variable, there is a hand-coded part that is responsible for switching the set of trees whenever there is a stage change in the task plan. The artificial controller replaces the human subject in the control cycle.

In the pre-processing procedure the data undergoes a series of filtering operations. The first filter splits the trace data into stages. A dataset is then created for each control variable and for each stage.

Each dataset is then subject to another filter that transforms samples into ML cases. In each sample, the value of the control variable is associated with the state variables and the other control variables of a sample recorded some time before. That time lag accounts for the human perceive-act delay. The control variable of the data set constitutes the class and the state, and the other control variables constitute the attributes.

When the synthesised controller is run as an auto-pilot the perceive-act delay used in the pre-processing procedure is introduced in the control cycle.

The proposed improvement in the methodology, [4], covers two aspects. First, the usage of goals. Second, the use of a wrapper to facilitate the controller's construction process by tuning the ML and model's parameters.

The two kinds of goals, *Achievable goals* and *Homeostatic goals*, used in the models are imported from the work on AI planning by [6]. *Achievable goals* have a well-defined set of start and final states in the state space; arriving at anyone of the final state marks the achievement and termination of such a goal. These goals are the most common type in AI systems. *Homeostatic goals* are achieved continuously. They do not terminate when the system is in one of the final states; when changes occur, and the state has changed, activity to re-achieve the final state is re-initiated.

A set of basic operations should be defined[1] using the two kinds of goals defined above. During a basic operation the homeostatic and achievable goals remain constant. The task plan is then defined as a sequence of basic operations. In the flight domain, for example, the basic operations are a straight and level flight, a levelled left turn, a climb right turn etc. In a levelled turn, for example, the homeostatic goals are the bank angle, the altitude and the climb rate and the achievable goal is the final heading. A flight plan is a sequence of straight climb, levelled left turn, levelled right turn, etc.

---

[1] as already suggested in [10] but not possible within the models used so far.

3 Models of Human Control Skills

The model of the artificial controller used in the experiments of [10], [9] and [11] has a two-level hierarchy of control: a high level module and a low-level one. The high-level module is hand coded and its only role, so far, is to sequence the stages of the task plan. Within the new model, the high-level module is also responsible for establishing the context for the low-level module. It switches the low-level modules according to the stage of the task plan. The context is further specified by defining the goal values for the new stage. The low-level module has been implemented as a set of decision trees, one for each aircraft control and for each stage. At each stage only the trees constructed for that stage are active. This module is the only one induced from the behavioural traces and will be referred as the "model" from now on. In this section two types of models are considered and compared: the "Goals" model; and the "Incremental Correction" model.

3.1 The "Goals" Model

As can be seen in Figure 1 the Goals model extends the earlier model used in [10] and [9]. In the "Goals" model each control value is not only determined by the state and other control variables of the system, but also by the set of goal values defined for each stage of the control task as given by the equation:

control value(t+1) = f(state variables, goals, other control variables)

This model uses the goal values to compute features that represent deviations from the goal values and also their temporal derivatives.

To use goals in a model within a ML propositional setting, a new computational model is required. As the new computational model is an extension of Decision Trees, it is called *Parameterised Decision Trees*.

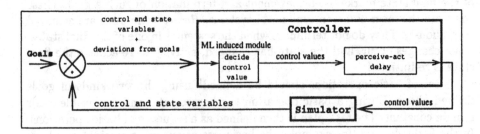

Fig. 1. "Goals Model".

A Decision Tree may be defined as a function from the space of attributes to the class space. A Parameterised Decision Tree is a function from the space of attributes and goals to the class space. The only difference between Decision

Trees and Parameterised Decision Trees is in non-leaf nodes in which a continuous homeostatic attribute[2] is used in a test. In such a node the difference between the attribute value and the corresponding goal value is computed before the comparison with the threshold is performed.

The Decision Tree construction algorithm is unchanged and therefore, any decision tree tool may be extended in this fashion. There is no loss in construction efficiency. What is required is a pre- and post-processing procedure. For details see [2].

A controller induced within the Goals model framework acts as a mapping from a situation (or range of situations) to a control device position (a value). This model, therefore requires that the control device position has to be memorise for each situation or range of situations. Which humans most certainly do not do.

3.2   The Incremental Correction Model

In order to understand the proposed control model consider the two situations illustrative of human real-time control skills. As a first illustrative situation consider a driver going in a car along a straight road and a second car going in front of him. Both cars drive at constant speed. Suddenly the car going ahead of him reduces considerably its speed. Perceiving the reduction in the distance between the two cars, the driver presses the break pedal. The amount of force applied is more or less, depending on the driver's initial judgment of the circumstances (distance reduction between the cars, speed differences, etc). After pressing the break pedal, the driver waits for the effect of the breaking to be perceivable and reevaluates the situation (distance between the cars, speed difference, etc). If the pressing was not sufficient the force is increased. If, on the other hand the speed reduction was excessive, the pressure is reduced. The driver repeats this procedure, of (re)evaluating the situation, adjusting the break pedal pressure and waiting for the effects of the previous action taken. The process stops when the situation is considered acceptable.

As a second illustrative situation consider an aircraft pilot flying straight and levelled when suddenly comes across an air sink. Perceiving the sudden loss in altitude the pilot undergoes a sequence of correction actions where each move of the control column corrects the previous move after its effects have been perceived. The sequence is stopped only when goal altitude is recovered.

Key aspects of the illustrative situations just described, and of general human real-time control, are as follows. There is a acceptable situation in which the controlled system is most of the time. The acceptable situation is characterised by a very small or non existing deviation from the homeostatic goal values. An acceptable situation requires no control change. Action is taken whenever the goal variables values deviate from the goal value. There is a reasonable "wild guess" to make the first correction, specially if the deviation is large. After the

---

[2] an attribute for which a homeostatic goal as been defined.

first change, a sequence of (re)evaluation, corrections and waiting for the effects of the correction to become perceivable takes place until the acceptability of the situation is restored. The amount of waiting time involved in real-time control is usually very small. The control strategy is adaptive, in the sense that the direction and magnitude of the correction is directly affected by the previous change. If the previous change produces a too small reduction in the deviation then the direction of the next change is maintained and the amount of change increased. On the other hand, if the deviation is reduced too much or an overshooting is expected, then the direction is changed in the next cycle.

The equations to compute the control values within the IC model are:

$$control(t+1) = \begin{cases} control(t), & sit.\ ok \\ control(t) + \Delta(state\ vars, goals, other\ controls), & sit.\ not\ ok \end{cases}$$

As shown in Figure 2, the IC model has a module to determine if the situation requires a change in the controls, the Coarse Decision module. If a change in the controls is required (*sit. not ok*), then another module computes the values of the increment/decrement of the control variables, the Refined Decision module. Whenever a change in a control is made the controller uses a waiting time for the effects of control change to become perceivable. The IC model inherits the goals and the perceive-act delay from the Goals model.

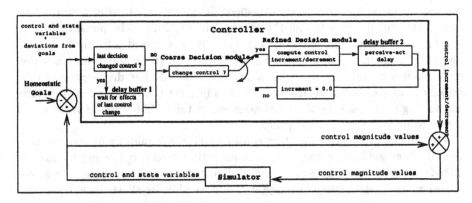

Fig. 2. *Incremental Correction* Model evaluated by the current experiments.

Both modules, Coarse Decision and Refined Decision, in Figure 2, are ML induced from the behavioural traces of the human subject as explained in Section 5. The Coarse Decision module implements the *action/noaction* decision making. The Refined Decision module determines the increment control value to apply whenever a control value has to be changed. The buffers 1 and 2, in the same figure, implement the "wait for effects" delay and the "perceive-act" delay respectively.

4 Performance Evaluation

Reverse engineering human control skills may serve two aims. The first one concerns the construction of an accurate model of the human control skills on the given task. The second one concerns the automatic construction of a robust controller independently of being a good representative of the human behaviour. The first purpose will pay more attention to induction time measurements and to some tree statistics, whereas the second purpose will considers simulation time measurements as the crucial ones.

Evaluation of Accuracy of the IC model

The following error measures give an indication on how close the model is to the original system, the human controller.

The predictive power of the induced trees is estimated by measuring the Error Rate, the Mean Absolute Error (MAE), and the Root Mean Square Error (RMSE) on an independent test set. The Error Rate measures the percentage of errors made on the test set giving equal weight to each individual error. The MAE and RMSE are defined as

$$MAE = \frac{\sum_{i=1}^{N} |cls'_i - cls_i|}{N} \qquad RMSE = \sqrt{\frac{\sum_{i=1}^{N} (cls'_i - cls_i)^2}{N}}$$

where cls_i is the actual class and cls'_i is the predicted value. Since the Coarse Decision module of the IC model outputs an action/no action decision, that is, a non numerical decision, only the Error Rate is used in this case.

The tree statistics that are gathered serve the purpose of estimating the interestingness of the tree as a cognitive model. One of the most desirable features of the constructed model is its intelligibility. To estimate such feature the tree size is measured.

Flight simulation performance measurements

The *robustness* of the controllers is estimated by the number of successful missions within the total used. A mission is successful if there is no crash between the initial and final points.

The flight *smoothness* is evaluated using a deviation measure associated with each of the three homeostatic attributes. For each homeostatic attribute the Mean Absolute Deviation (MAD) is measured using the definition

$$MAD = \frac{\sum_{i=1}^{N} |att_i - goal|}{N}$$

Associated with each homeostatic goal there is a maximum acceptable deviation for that variable values. The frontier of the n-dimensional region containing the maximum acceptable values for the homeostatic variables is called the security envelope. All missions flown by the human subject that produce the behavioural traces were flown within the security envelope. The boundary for the altitude deviation is 100 ft, for the climb rate is 1000 ft/min and for the bank angle is 3°. The performance is evaluated by measuring the flight time percentage spent outside the envelope.

5 Experimental Settings

The control task chosen for the experimental evaluation of the models consists in the control of a simulation of an F-16 aircraft performing a levelled left turn. A levelled turn is a nontrivial manoeuvre requiring a close coordination among the controls. The experiments were carried out using ACM 2.4 public domain flight simulator running on a HP Apollo *Series* 735 workstation. The author played the role of the human pilot necessary for this study. A detailed description of the empirical evaluation of the models can be found in [3] and [4].

The data used in the experiments are traces of 90 levelled left turn missions performed by the author. Aircraft state and control variables were sampled every 0.1 second. For the levelled left turn the achievable goal is the final heading. The homeostatic goals are the bank angle, the altitude and the climb rate. For each mission the achievable and homeostatic goals (except climb rate) were randomly generated from a range of admissible values. In all missions and at all times the aircraft was kept within the security envelope. The missions were flown by instruments only, the landscape was not rendered, reducing the possibility of the pilot to use features not measured (sampled) by the aircraft instruments. For a more detailed description of the experiments refer to [4] and [3]

The 90 missions are split into two halves, one for constructing the model and the other to estimate the predictive accuracy of the constructed model. The 90 missions contain approximately 481 000 samples.

Following the methodology described in Section 2, the construction and test of the model is performed in three steps. In step one the pre-processing procedure converts the traces of the 90 missions into C4.5 data format. The data from the two sets of missions, training and testing, are always kept separate. The second step, using the *wrapper*, constructs the control trees by calling C4.5 and converts them into a Parameterised Decision Tree in C code. The control variables used in the experiments are the ailerons and the elevators control, which are enough to perform the levelled turn. One tree is constructed for each. The C code of both trees is joined to the rest of the controller code and linked to the simulator. In the third step, the model replaces the human pilot in the control loop of the simulator. The values for each control variables are obtained by interpreting the corresponding tree. The auto-pilot then "flies" all the 90 missions flight plans and the flight simulation performance measurements are made.

The *wrapper* algorithm, used in the second step, tunes the model's delays and the C4.5 *m*, *cf* and *gain/gain ratio*. The wrapper's search is described in detail in [4] and exploits the simplex method. The function to minimise is estimated by a 5-fold cross validation procedure. In the construction of the Goals model the wrapper's guiding function is the RMSE. In the IC model the wrapper's function for the Coarse Decision module is the Error Rate and the RMSE for Refined Decision module. The perceive-act delay values used are 0.5s, 1.0s, 1.5s and 2.0s. The values used for the "wait for effect" delay, in the IC model, are 0.0s, 0.5, and 1.0s.

The attributes used in the construction of the controller's ailerons trees were: bank angle; bank angle derivative; bank angle acceleration; pitch; pitch rate; and the Δelevators(t). The attributes used in the construction of the controller's elevators trees were: altitude deviation; climb rate; climb rate derivative; bank angle; bank angle derivative; climb rate acceleration; and the Δailerons(t).

For the IC model all samples are initially considered. The target definitions to learn within the IC model are: "change the control or not" and if the previous decision is favorable to change the control then the next decision is "what is the increment/decrement value to use". However the samples with no change in the control value largely outnumber the samples with "events" (the ratio is 36:1). The unbalance of such a data set is critical. The adopted procedure is as follows. In the first decision (action/no action) consider all the "event" as belonging to the same class (action) and all non-event samples as the other class (noaction). Build a data set with two classes equally represented by sampling from the noaction cases a number of cases equal to the action cases. The tree constructed with such dataset is then used to filter the "events" and produce the dataset for the Refined Decision module. In such a filtering procedure an event case is retained if it is predicted as action by the tree of the Coarse Decision module, otherwise is discarded. In the dataset of the Refined Decision module the increment of the control variable is restored as the class value.

6 Results and Discussion

Model	crashes		altitude (ft)		climb rate (ft/min)		bank angle (°)	
	train set	test set	train set	test set	train set	test set	train set	test set
Goals	19	15	1806	1970	1664	1814	8	8
IC	0	0	36	34	95	94	0.5	0.5
Human	0	0	21		194		0.70	

Table 1. Flight simulation results. The results for altitude, climb rate and bank angle represent the average of the MADs. The average is computed using the successful missions and weighted with flight time.

The flight simulation performance of the two models together with the human subject performance are shown in Table 1. The entries for the altitude, climb rate and bank angle measurements in the table represent the average of the MADs. The average is computed using the successful missions and are weighted with the flying times. The flight simulation results for the Goals model controller show a considerable lack in robustness since only 26 missions were successful in the training set conditions and only 30 on the test set conditions. On the other hand, the IC model controller successfully flew the same 90 missions exhibiting therefore a better degree of robustness. The smoothness measure of the Goals model controller (MAD) also indicate that most of the time the aircraft is considerably far from the acceptable situation. For example, the average magnitude of the altitude is 1806 ft which is eighteen times more than the altitude boundary of the security envelope that was never surpassed by the human controller. The smoothness results indicate that the IC model controller largely outperforms, the Goals model controller. The results of Table 1 also show that the IC model controller outperformed the human controller in two of the three measures (climb rate and bank angle).

partition	p1	p2	p3	p4	p5
altitude (ft)	35(14)	73(68)	85(57)	27(10)	39(7)
climb rate (ft/min)	94(11)	83(9)	117(16)	102(13)	82(18)
bank angle (°)	0.5(0.1)	0.6(0.1)	0.5(0.1)	1.4(1.4)	0.5(0.1)

Table 2. Flight simulation MAD. p_i represent a different partition on the train/test set missions. The values are the mean and standard deviation over the 90 missions.

In order to gather more support for the claim that the IC model is better than the Goals model, four more controllers were constructed using different partitions of the 90 missions. The results of the all five IC model controllers are shown in Table 2. The entries in the table represent the mean and standard deviation over the 90 missions weighted by flying time. Each column in that table represents a different partition of the train/test set missions. All the controllers successfully flew the 90 missions and all of them largely outperform the Goals model controller. The results of all the five controllers are better than the original human controller in two of the three measures (climb rate and bank angle).

Model		ailerons				elevators		
	t. size	Err Rate	RMSE	MAE	t. size	Err Rate	RMSE	MAE
Goals	255	74.7	4.8e-4		3173	84.2	5.0e-3	
IC Coarse Dec.	83	38.6	-	-	65	42.4	-	-
Refined Dec.	663	-	4.0e-4		143	-	2.1e-3	

Table 3. Independent test set results. *t. size* stands for tree size. *Coarse Dec.* stands for Coarse Decision module. *Refined Dec.* stands for Refined Decision module.

The evaluation of the trees that constitute the controllers was done on an independent test set, and the results are shown in Table 3. With the exception of the ailerons of the Refined Decision module, the size of the trees of the IC model controller are much smaller than the corresponding tree size of the Goals model controller and of previous reverse engineering experiments [1]. The error rates of the IC model are nearly half the values found with the Goals model trees. The RMSE of the IC model trees are also smaller than the Goals model ones. The RMSE associated with the elevators trees is less than half the corresponding value of the Goals model.

We observe that the pruning facility of the ML tool may discard cases with class values that are used in exceptional situations (few examples in the data set), but are essential to recover from those exceptional situations. To measure how pruning parameters discard some classes less represented in the data and their relative importance the number of classes in the final tree is measured as well as the range of the classes that are used in the tree. The results are depicted in Table 4 and are taken from the elevators dataset of Goals model. The two levels of decision adopted in the IC model attenuates this pruning effect.

m	range	n. classes	tree size
1	[0.012:0.078] (100%)	61 (100%)	10717
5	[0.012:0.057] (68%)	42 (69%)	2563
50	[0.015:0.051] (55%)	23 (38%)	199
500	[0.017:0.027] (15%)	6 (10%)	21

Table 4. Decrease in range and number of classes as C4.5's m parameter increases.

7 Conclusions

The use of goals and attributes that measure deviations from the defined goals is a significant improvement in the models. It makes possible to use data from different task plans when constructing the controllers and it allows the use of the same controller in different circumstances.

The main contribution of the IC model is a substantial increase in robustness of the new controllers. The flight simulation performance values are very close to the human subject performance on the same missions.

The trees constructed within the new model exhibit a smaller size than the ones from previous experiments in reverse engineering human control skills. Intelligibility of the models is an essential point in the success criteria and the small tree sizes are a good step towards their comprehensibility.

The new model avoids the "situation-control value" indexing mechanism underlying the previous models. The referred indexing mechanism would require a controller to have a memory of control positions for each situation(s), which is not realistic.

The main open problem found in the current investigation concerns the lack of correlation between the measures made on the independent test set and the flight simulation measures. If such a correlation can not be established there will be no guarantee that the set of the best trees, found by the wrapper, will produce a good controller. Automatisation of the controller construction process depends on such a correlation.

Acknowledgments

Thanks are due to Pavel Brazdil for valuable comments on this work. I thank also to Universidade do Porto and JNICT for the financial support during the PhD. Thanks are also due to Programa PRAXIS and FEDER and to the Programa de Financiamento Plurianual de Unidades de I&D da JNICT.

References

1. R. Camacho. Laboratory note: On robustness tests of induced auto-pilots from single flight plan missions, Sept. 1994. Available from: http://www.ncc.up.pt/~tau.
2. R. Camacho. Laboratory note: Learning to turn: decision-trees to perform a levelled turn, Sept. 1995. Available from: http://www.ncc.up.pt/~tau.
3. R. Camacho. Laboratory note. an incremental correction model for reverse engineering human control skills, Oct. 1997. Available from: http://www.ncc.up.pt/~tau.
4. R. Camacho. Laboratory note. learning to turn: Parameterised decision trees to perform a levelled turn, June 1997. Available from: http://www.ncc.up.pt/~tau.
5. R. Camacho and D. Michie. Behavioural cloning: a correction. *AI Magazine*, 16(2):92, Summer 1995.
6. A. A. Covrigaru and R. K. Lindsay. Deterministic autonomous systems. *AI Magazine*, 12(3):110–117, fall 1991.
7. J. C. Hamm. The use of pilot models in dynamic performance and rotor load prediction studies. In *Proceedings of the Eighteenth European Rotorcraft Forum*, pages 15–18, Avignon, France, September 1992. Association Aeronautique et Astronautique de France.
8. H. G. John, R. Kohavi, and K. Pfleger. Irrelevant features and the subset selection problem. In *Machine Learning: Proceedings of the Eleventh International Conference*, pages 121 – 129, Rutgers Univ., New Jersey, July 1994. eds. William Cohen and Haym Hirsh.
9. D. Michie and R. Camacho. Building symbolic representations of intuitive real-time skills from performance data. In *Machine Intelligence 13*, pages 385–418. Oxford University Press, Oxford, United Kingdom, 1994. eds. K. Furukawa, D. Michie and S. Muggleton.
10. C. Sammut, S. Hurst, D. Kedzier, and D. Michie. Learning to fly. In *Proceedings of the Ninth International Workshop of Machine Learning 92*, pages 385–393, Aberdeen, U.K., July 1992.
11. T. Urbančič and I. Bratko. Reconstructing human skill with machine learning. In *The Eleventh European Conference on Artificial Intelligence*, pages 498 – 502, Amsterdam, Netherlands, 1994.

God Doesn't Always Shave with Occam's Razor – Learning When and How to Prune

Hilan Bensusan

School of Cognitive and Computing Sciences
University of Sussex
Falmer, Brighton
BN1 9QH
UK
phone:+44 1273 678524
fax:+44 1273 671320
email:hilanb@cogs.susx.ac.uk

God doesn't always shave with Occam's razor. Malcom Dixon, quoted in
New Scientist 23/4/94 p.51.

Abstract. The work shows how a meta-learning technique can be successfully applied to decide when to prune, how much pruning is appropriate and what the best pruning technique is for a given learning task.

1 Introduction: the simplicity issue

'All truth is simple' - is that not a compound lie? Friedrich Nietzsche
Pruning decision trees sometimes prevents overfitting and compensates for the presence of noise in the training set. Often, however, it oversimplifies the trees missing most of their predictive potential. This work makes the assumption that similar problems are likely to require similar pruning patterns and proposes a meta-learning approach to select among various pruning alternatives.

Simplicity has always been seen as somehow connected with successful inductions. Among the many possible rationales for the Occam's principle - everything else being equal, prefer the simplest hypotheses -, one that is solely based on inductive considerations (and not, for example, on the assumption that the world is simple) is the one that claims that simpler hypotheses enjoy greater prior probability. This idea has inspired the minimal encoding principles that explore the balance between simplicity and consistency as an Occam consequence of the balance between prior and posterior probabilities. These principles have been taken farther than the Occam's razor for they consider that even when everything else is not equal, simplicity still matters. In the context of decision tree induction, the Occam's principle is often used to justify a preference for simpler trees. Apart from general theoretical challenges to this idea, recent experimental work has called into question the general use of a simplicity soft bias [6, 8]. There were various theoretical attempts to establish conditions under which simpler hypotheses are better (see for example [4]). This work provides an experimental approach to the appropriateness of simplicity biases.

2 The meta-learning system

THE ENTRENCHER system learns to choose the best learning bias for a learning task among the ones provided in a bias pool [1]. Therefore, it performs a kind of meta-learning. It contrasts with other methods (see [2]) because it uses induction on training problem descriptions. THE ENTRENCHER uses the decision tree generated from the training set and related information to describe a learning task. THE ENTRENCHER then performs a supervised meta-learning on a set of classified problems divided into training and test sets. The system acts as follows:

1. Applies all the learners in the bias pool to the training problems and tests their performance;
2. Classifies the problems in terms of the best performing bias;
3. Applies a meta-learning procedure to the classified training set of problems, generating a bias classifier;

The performance of the system is tested by assessing the average accuracy achieved by the bias classifier in a set of test problems [2] The system then comprises the following components:

A baseline learner generates consistent hypotheses that are the working representations of the problems.

A problem descriptor generates values for the descriptor vector.

A bias pool manager classifies the training problems by accuracy and simplicity [3].

A meta-learner generates a bias classifier.

THE ENTRENCHER uses a decision tree baseline learner – similar to a non-pruning C4.5 [7]. The descriptor vector consists of the following real-valued descriptors: Tree nodes per attribute, tree nodes per instance, the average strength of support of each tree leaf, difference in goodness-as-a-splitting-point between the attributes, maximum depth of the tree, number of repeated nodes, shape of the tree, number of leaves divided by tree shape, balance of the tree, number of subtrees with more than two (possibly internal) nodes repeated in the tree. The shape of the tree by the probability of arriving at each leaf given a randomly chosen path from the root to the leaf. This probability $p(N_i)$ of arriving at node N_i among the m sibling nodes from the ancestor N_A is given by $p(N_i) = p(N_A)/m$. The shape is then measured from the probability of the leaves $p(L_j)$, given a tree with x leaves, by $-\sum_{j=0}^{x} p(L_j) \log_2(p(L_j))$. Balance is measured as follows. Given all the possible values V_i for $p(L_j)$, calculate $G(V_i)$ as $G(V_i) = n * V_i$ where n is the number of times V_i occurs in the set of all the leaves of the tree. The balance is then measured by sum $\sum_{j=0}^{x} G(V_j) \log_2(G(V_j))$ for all the x possible values for $p(L_j)$.

---

[1] The system is a development of the one described in [1].

[2] Notice that the meta-learner misclassifications might have different impact on the overall system performance.

[3] Notice that the meta-learning system itself assumes a simplicity bias. A meta-learner, as any learner, requires biases.

3 Experiments with pruning strategies

*Learning builds daily accumulation, but the practice of pruning builds
daily simplification.*D'après Lao Tzu

THE ENTRENCHER system can be applied to a simplicity bias pool to produce a learned bias classifier that can decide between different pruning options.
Different pruning strategies have been proposed [4]. Quinlan's C4.5 system popu-
larised error-based pruning. A major alternative to the error-based approach is
the cost-complexity pruning approach that has been adopted by some decision
tree learning systems including Quinlan's own ID3.

The cost-complexity pruning technique considered here, as Quinlan's error-
based strategy, admits of different levels of pruning according to the different
values of the acceptable cost threshold. Pruned trees are generated by replacing
subtrees by a leaf labeled by the majority class that covers all but exception
($E_{majority}$) cases of the subtree coverage ($X_{subtree}$), whenever the cost of the
subtree is greater than the acceptable cost threshold. Let $D_{subtree}$ be the depth
of a subtree, D_{tree} the depth of the whole tree and $S_{subtree}$ the size in terms
of the number of nodes of the subtree. Cost is then defined as $Cost_{subtree} = \frac{((D_{tree}-D_{subtree}+1)^2)*S_{subtree}}{E_{majority}/X_{subtree}}$. Pruning proceeds from the leaves to the root of the
tree.

The experiments reported in this paper involve learning tasks from an artificial domain consisting of MONK-like problems [3]. Given the original 6 attributes
of the MONK problems, there are $2^4 32$ possible classifications. For the current
experiments, 100 classifications were randomly chosen and 10 problems, composed by training and a test sets of 50 instances, were constructed for each
classification. The meta-learning system was trained on an increasing number
of problems and then tested on different test sets of problems randomly drawn
from the 1000 existing problems. The performances were compared to the best
possible pruning option available for each problem and with the fixed different
pruning options. In the graphs that report the experiments, the X-axis represents the training set sizes and the Y-axis the accuracy in the test sets of 50
problems. Each point represents the average of 10 runs under a fixed training
set size.

3.1 Learning when to prune

*It is clear that there are no grounds for believing that the simplest course
of events will really happen.* Ludwig Wittgenstein

For each pruning strategy considered, a first question to ask is when pruning
will enhance performance. In the first experiment, the meta-learning system is
applied to decide between pruning with confidence level of 25%, C4.5's default
value, and leaving the original C4.5 tree unpruned. In another experiment, the
appropriateness of cost-complexity pruning has been considered. Here the meta-
learner decides between pruning with a fixed acceptable cost threshold of 150

---

[4] Refer to [5] for overview and an comparison.

and leaving the original tree unpruned. Fig. 1 shows the result. The two bottom lines represent pruning and no pruning. In the case of cost-complexity, unpruned trees have the worse performance all along whereas in the error based pruning case, the bottommost line is the performance of pruned trees. In both cases the top line is the best pruning option for each problem and the second line approaching it is the performance of THE ENTRENCHER.

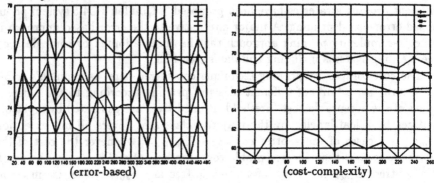

(error-based)   (cost-complexity)

Fig. 1. Learning when to prune

3.2 Learning how much to prune

...as simple as possible but not simpler. Albert Einstein

Another question is how much simplicity is good enough. Fig. 2 plots the performance of the meta-learning system when selecting between different confidence levels for error-based pruning (0, 25, 50, 75). Fig. 3 plots the curves for selecting the amount of cost-complexity pruning that the 50 test problems require by considering different acceptable cost thresholds (50, 150, 250).

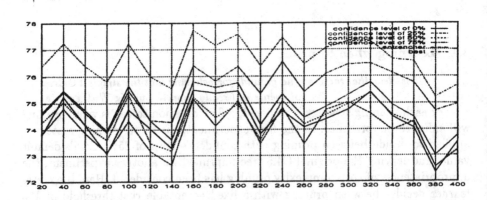

Fig. 2. Learning how much error-based pruning is required

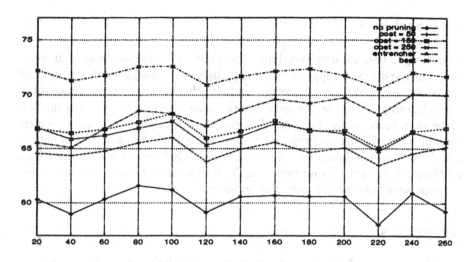

Fig. 3. Learning how much cost-complexity pruning is required

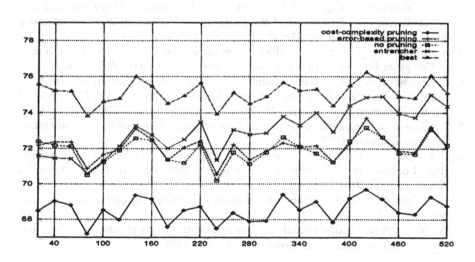

Fig. 4. Learning how to prune

3.3 Learning how to prune

> *One thing at least is certain [...], that the simple injunction "Simplify" is*
> *inadequate, if only because it is ambiguous.* Mario Bunge

A third question concerns simplicity is related to the choice between different pruning strategies. An informed choice between C4.5 trees with no pruning, cost-complexity pruning with acceptable cost threshold of 150 and error-based pruning with confidence level of 25% can be provided by the use of THE ENTRENCHER, as Fig. 4 reports.

4 Conclusion

Since simplicity is not a universal bias, the question is: How do we find out when, how much and how to apply it? The experiments in this paper show that THE ENTRENCHER allows for a successful (inductively) informed choice between different learning options as the system performance curves tend towards the best curve as training set size increases. It is therefore possible to learn about the appropriateness of different simplicity biases. Whitehead once said *seek simplicity and distrust it*. We should understand that since God doesn't always shave with an Occam razor and Occam razors don't come with user's manuals, we are left to grope with nothing but induction to aid us.

References

1. H. Bensusan and P. Williams. Learning to learn boolean tasks by decision tree descriptors. In M. V. Someren and G. Widmer, editors, *Poster Papers - 9th European Conference on Machine Learning*, pages 1–11. 1997.
2. P. Brazdil, J. Gama, and B. Henery. Characterizing the applicability of classification algorithms using Meta-Level Learning. In Francesco Bergadano and Luc de Raedt, editors, *Proceedings of the European Conference on Machine Learning*, volume 784 of *LNAI*, pages 83–102, Berlin, April 1994. Springer.
3. S. Thrun et al. The monk's problems. Technical Report CMU-CS-91-197, School of Computer Science, Carnegie-Mellon University., Pittsburgh, PA - USA, 1991.
4. D. Gamberger and N. Lavrac. Conditions for Occam's Razor applicability and noise elimination. In Marteen van Someren and Gerhard Widmer, editors, *Proceedings of the 9th European Conference on Machine Learning*, pages 108–123. Springer, 1997.
5. J. Mingers. An empirical comparison of pruning methods for decision tree induction. *Machine Learning*, 4:227–243, 1989.
6. P. Murphy and M. Pazzani. Exploring the decision forest: An emprical imvestigation of occam's razor in decision tree induction. *Journal of Artificial Intelligence Research*, 1:257–275, 1994.
7. J. R. Quinlan. *C4.5: Programs for Machine Learning*. Morgan Kaufmann, San Mateo, CA, USA, 1993.
8. G. Webb. Further experimental evidence against the utility of occam's razor. *Journal of Artificial Intelligence Research*, 4:397–417, 1996.

Error Estimators for Pruning Regression Trees

Luís Torgo

LIACC - FEP
R. Campo Alegre, 823, 2° - 4150 PORTO - PORTUGAL
Phone : (+351) 2 607 8830   Fax : (+351) 2 600 3654
email : ltorgo@ncc.up.pt   URL : http://www.ncc.up.pt/~ltorgo

Abstract. This paper presents a comparative study of several methods for estimating the true error of tree-structured regression models. We evaluate these methods in the context of regression tree pruning. The study is focused on problems where large samples of data are available. We present two novel variants of existent estimation methods. We evaluate several methods that follow different approaches to the estimation problem, and perform experimental evaluation in twelve domains. The goal of this evaluation is to characterise the performance of the methods in the task of selecting the best possible tree among the alternative trees considered during pruning. The results of the comparison show that certain estimators lead to very bad decisions in some domains. Our proposed variant of the holdout method obtained the best results in the experimental comparisons.

1 Introduction

This paper describes an experimental comparison of several alternative methods for obtaining *reliable* error estimates of tree-based regression models. These methods are evaluated in the context of pruning regression trees which is considered one of the key issues for obtaining accurate and simple trees (Breiman *et al.*,1984). Our comparative study has a particular emphasis on large samples of data.

The standard procedure for post-pruning regression trees consists of growing an overly large tree and then generating a sequence of pruned trees from which the final solution is selected. This selection phase is guided by reliable estimates of the "true" error of the pruned trees. Several methodologies exist to obtain unbiased estimates of an unknown parameter based on samples of an unknown population. *Resampling* techniques obtain the estimates using separate samples "independent" of the data used to grow the models. Examples of this technique are Cross Validation or the Holdout methods used in CART (Breiman *et al.* 1984). Other approaches use certain sampling properties of the distribution of the parameter being estimated, to "correct" to the estimates obtained with the training sample. C4.5 (Quinlan, 1993) for instance, uses a binomial correction to the distribution of the error rate. Bayesian methods combine prior knowledge of the parameter with the observed value to obtain a posterior estimate of the target parameter. *M*-estimates (Cestnik, 1990) are an example of such techniques and have been used in the context of pruning regression trees (Karalic and Cestnik, 1991).

2   The Estimation Methods

Breiman *et al.* (1984) described the pruning task as a three steps process :
- Generate a set of "interesting" candidate pruned trees.
- Obtain reliable estimates of the error of these trees.
- Choose one of these trees according to these estimates.

The key issue of this pruning process is how to obtain reliable estimates of the error. We require that the estimates perform a correct ranking of the candidate trees. This ensures the selection of the best possible tree from the set of candidate pruned trees. This tree selection problem is completely independent from the techniques used to obtain the trees. As it was mentioned by Weiss & Indurkhya (1994) error estimation is the sole basis of tree selection. In our study we compare several alternative estimation methods in 12 problems, where large samples of data were available.

We have chosen the *Holdout* as the "representative" of resampling methods due to our emphasis on large samples. Methods like *N*-fold cross validation (Stone, 1974), or bootstrap (Efron, 1979) do not provide significant advantages in terms of the accuracy of the estimates in large data sets (Breiman *et al.*,1984). The use of the holdout in the context of regression trees can be described as follows. Given a sample of cases we randomly divide this sample in a training and a pruning set (the holdout). The tree is grown without seeing the pruning cases. A set of pruned trees is obtained and the holdout is used to obtain reliable estimates of their error. Based on these estimates the final tree model is selected. A major decision when using this method concerns the proportion of data that should be used for obtaining the estimates. Ideally one wants to have a pruning set as large as possible to ensure good estimates. However, this may lead to a shortage of cases for growing the tree, which will most probably have an adverse effect on the overall accuracy of the obtained regression model. In our experiments we have tried several set-ups for this proportion. The best results were obtained using the following method for deciding the size of the holdout :

$$\#\{PruningSet\} = \min(0.3 \times \#\{AvailableData\}, 1000)$$

This method can be seen as a 30% holdout limited to a maximum of 1000 cases. Empirical evidence is the sole justification for our proposal. We have observed that 1000 cases was sufficient to ensure accurate estimates without removing too many cases for learning. We intend to look for a theoretical justification of these results.

In our comparative study we have also included *m*-estimators (Cestnik, 1990). This bayesian method estimates a population parameter by a combination between prior and observed knowledge. Due to the difficulty of obtaining priors for the variance of the target variable[1], the usual approach consists of taking the estimate on

---

[1] Which is necessary for obtaining the error of regression trees.

the entire training sample as the prior estimate. The m-estimate of the variance based on a sample of size n (for instance in a leaf of the tree), given that the size of all data set is N, uses the m-estimate of the mean and is given by

$$m-\text{Est}(\mu_Y) = \frac{1}{n+m} \sum_{i=1}^{n} y_i + \frac{m}{N(n+m)} \sum_{i=1}^{N} y_i$$

$$m-\text{Est}(\sigma_Y^2) = \frac{1}{n+m} \sum_{i=1}^{n} y_i^2 + \frac{m}{N(n+m)} \sum_{i=1}^{N} y_i^2 - (m-\text{Est}(\mu))^2 \qquad (1)$$

Several values for the m parameter were tried in the context of our experimental comparisons. The best results were obtained with the value 2.

Least squares regression trees use an error criterion that relies on the estimates of variance in the leaves of the trees (Breiman et al., 1984). Statistics textbooks tell us that the sampling distribution of the variance follows a χ^2 distribution. According to the properties of this distribution a $100 \times (1-\alpha)\%$ confidence interval for the population variance based on a sample of size n, is given by

$$\left(s_Y \sqrt{\frac{n-1}{\chi_{\alpha/2}^2}}, s_Y \sqrt{\frac{n-1}{\chi_{(1-\alpha/2)}^2}} \right) \qquad (2)$$

where s_Y is the sample variance (in our case obtained on each tree leaf).

Behind this formulation there is a strong assumption on the normality of the distribution of the variable Y. In most real-world domains we can not guarantee *a priori* that this assumption holds. If it does not, this may lead to unreliably narrow intervals for the location of the true population parameter. However, we should recall that in the context of our work we are not particularly interested in the precision of the estimates, but in guaranteeing that the estimate provides a correct ranking of the candidate pruned trees. Being so, we have decided to use this method, adopting a kind of heuristic (and pessimistic) estimate of the variance by choosing the highest value of the interval given by Equation 2 as the estimate.

3 The Experiments

In our experiments we have used 12 data sets whose main characteristics are described in Table 1. Each data set was randomly divided in a large independent test set and a training pool. Using this training pool we have randomly obtained samples of increasing size. For each size we have grown a large regression tree and obtained a set of pruned trees. Each of the estimation methods was then used to select one of these trees and the accuracy of these choices was evaluated on the independent test set. Using this test set we have also observed what would be the best possible selection.

Table 1. The used Data Sets showing the number of cases used.

Data Set	Training Pool;Test Set	Data Set	Training Pool;Test Set
Abalone	3133;1044	Kinematics	4500;3692
Pole	5000;4065	Fried1	30000;5000
Elevators	8752;7847	Census16H	17000;5784
Ailerons	7154;6596	Census8L	17000;5784
CompActiv.	4500;3692	2Dplanes	20000;5000
CompActiv(s)	4500;3692	Mv1	20000;5000

We have calculated the percentage accuracy loss of the tree selected by each method when compared to the best possible choice. This enables the characterization of each method in correctly ranking the pruned trees for different training sample sizes. This experiment was repeated with several variants of the estimation methods. Table 2 shows the average loss in accuracy of the three most promising set-ups. These set-ups were : 30% of the data for pruning limited to a maximum of 1000 cases in the holdout method; the value 2 for the m parameter for m-estimates; and confidence level of 97.5% for χ^2. The results were divided in two groups : medium size training samples and large samples.

Table 2. Average percentage accuracy losses for different error estimation methods.

	Medium Sizes (500-2500 cases)			Large Sizes (> 2500 cases)		
	Holdout	m-est.	χ^2	Holdout	m-est.	χ^2
Abalone	4.8	16.4	12.1	6.6	6.7	5.4
2Planes	0.1	9.8	0	0.0	0.0	0.0
Pole	0.5	0.5	1.9	0.2	0.6	0.2
Elevators	5.4	16.3	15.7	2.8	3.3	3.6
Ailerons	0.8	2.1	2.1	0.8	1.0	1.4
Mv1	0	5.9	0	0.0	0.2	0.0
Fried1	2.4	6.1	2.5	0.5	9.3	0.3
CompAct	0.0	0.1	0	0.0	0.2	0.0
CompAct(s)	0	0.9	0	0.0	0.0	0.0
Census16H	3.8	5.9	4.9	2.0	3.7	3.3
Census8L	1.8	3.4	3.2	1.6	2.0	1.9
Kinematics	2.7	6.0	9.5	1.1	5.5	8.8
Averages	1.9	6.1	4.3	1.3	2.7	2.1

The holdout method has a clear advantage if we look at the results over all domains. In effect, this method usually performs better than the other ones in all domains. The χ^2 method seems to have a slight advantage over m-estimates. However, sometimes there are large differences on particular data sets. For instance, m-estimates perform quite badly in *Fried1* even with large samples. This confirms that the pruning stage is a key issue for inducing regression trees, as it can strongly determine the accuracy of the learned models. The holdout method has less extreme losses over all domains, while the other two do sometimes lead to quite poor tree selections. In summary, these experiments indicate that the holdout method is the best method for selecting among a set of pruned trees. However, a question arises whether the trees selected by the holdout are more accurate than the others. In effect, the use of the holdout method implies that less data is used for learning the trees. It is the goal of our second set of experiments to check if the better performance of the holdout in the ranking task is sufficient to overcome the loss of data for training.

The second set of experiments compares the trees selected by each method both in terms of accuracy in the test set as well as in terms of size. Table 3 shows these results for samples with 2500 cases and all training pool (winners are underlined).

Table 3. Comparison between the trees selected by the different estimation methods.

| | Mean Squared Error | | | | | | Tree Size (n. leaves) | | | | | |
| | Medium | | | Large | | | Medium | | | Large | | |
	Hld.	m	χ^2	Hld.	m	χ^2	Hld.	m	χ^2	Hld.	M	χ^2
Abalone	6.86	7.57	7.484	6.843	6.873	6.909	99	206	194	113	221	237
2Planes	1.631	1.679	1.679	1.671	1.671	1.671	20	18	18	18	18	18
Pole	161.24	154.35	154.35	119.76	103.50	102.42	33	32	32	61	49	55
Elevators	36.76	24.06	24.06	15.93	16.12	16.03	48	154	157	188	441	428
Ailerons	0.06	0.06	0.06	0.05	0.05	0.05	75	161	186	263	305	435
Mv1	7.54	7.48	7.48	7.30	7.21	7.21	10	10	10	10	10	10
Fried1	7.30	7.06	6.24	3.60	4.00	3.56	91	96	229	931	628	989
CompAct	26.95	28.14	28.14	29.90	29.93	29.93	6	5	5	5	5	5
CompAct(s)	32.21	32.87	32.87	33.76	32.28	32.29	7	8	8	7	7	7
Census16H	2.2E9	2.1E9	2.1E9	1.6E9	1.9E9	1.9E9	56	114	118	392	733	736
Census8L	1.8E9	1.5E9	1.5E9	1.3E9	1.4E9	1.4E9	58	115	72	584	717	676
Kinematics	0.04	0.05	0.05	0.04	0.04	0.05	65	204	346	323	335	620

This table shows that the performance of the holdout in terms of accuracy is similar to the other methods. This confirms that sometimes having a separate set of data may have an adverse effect on the "quality" of the learned trees. However, the trees selected by the holdout method are generally much smaller than the trees selected by the other two methods. To assert the statistical significance of the differences in accuracy we have conducted paired t-test comparisons using the large test sets. Table 4 presents these results.

Table 4. Number of statistically significant of wins.

| | Holdout | | m-estimates | | χ^2 | | TOTAL WINS | |
	medium	Large	medium	large	Medium	large	Medium	large
Holdout	-	-	3 (5)	1 (8)	3 (5)	0 (7)	6(10)	1(15)
m-estimates	1 (7)	1 (4)	-	-	2 (3)	1 (2)	3(9)	2(6)
χ^2	2 (7)	2 (5)	1 (4)	2 (6)	-	-	3(11)	4(11)
TOTAL LOSSES	3(14)	3 (9)	4 (9)	3(14)	5 (8)	1 (9)		

Each cell of the table contains two numbers. The first is the number of statistically significant wins (99% confidence) of the tree selected by the method in the respective line over the method in the column. The number in parenthesis is the total number of wins (with and without statistical significance). For instance the table indicates that trees selected by m-estimates outperformed the trees chosen by holdout 7 times but only once with statistical significance (for medium samples).

The results of this table show that things are more or less leveled-up between the holdout method and χ^2 when it comes to statistical significance of accuracy differences. However, we should recall that holdout trees are generally smaller. M-estimates, on the contrary, do not bring any advantage over the other two methods.

4   Conclusions

Post-pruning of tree-based models is considered a key step for obtaining accurate and simple trees. We have presented a comparative study of error estimation methods in the context of regression tree pruning. Our study focused on large samples of data.

We have introduced two new error estimation methods : one variant of the well-known holdout method and the other, the pessimistic approach to the statistical estimation of the variance. We have compared these with m-estimators.

The main conclusions of this study can be summarised as follows. With respect to the problem of selecting the best possible tree from a sequence of pruned trees the best method appears to be our proposed variant of the holdout method. Comparing the trees in terms of accuracy on a large independent test set it appears that there is no statistically significant advantage of the holdout method over the χ^2 method. In our comparisons m-estimates appears to be the worst estimation method among the three tried out. If we take into account both accuracy and tree size the conclusion is that our proposed holdout variant is the best possible choice for guiding the tree selection stage of pruning in large data sets.

Acknowledgements: I would like to thank PRAXIS XXI and FEDER for their financial support. Thanks also to my colleagues and my supervisor Pavel Brazdil.

References

Breiman,L. , Friedman,J., Olshen,R. and Stone,C. (1984) : *Classification and Regression Trees*, Wadsworth Int. Group, Belmont, California, USA, 1984.

Cestnik,B. (1990) : Estimating probabilities : A crucial task in Machine Learning. In Proc. of the 9th European Conference on Artificial Intelligence (ECAI-90), Pitman Publishers.

Efron,B. (1979): Bootstrap methods: Another look at the jackknife. *Annals Statistics*,7:1-26.

Karalic,A., Cestnik,B. (1991) : The bayesian approach to tree-structured regression. In proceedings of the ITI-91.

Quinlan,J.R. (1993) : *C4.5: programs for machine learning*. Morgan Kaufmann, 1993.

Stone, M. (1974) : Cross-validatory choice and assessment of statistical predictions, *Journal of the Royal Statistical Society*. B 36, 111-147, 1974.

Weiss,S., Indurkhya,N. (1994) : Decision Tree Pruning : Biased or Optimal ?. In Proceedings of the AAAI-94.

Pruning Decision Trees
with Misclassification Costs

Jeffrey P. Bradford[1] Clayton Kunz[2]
Ron Kohavi[2] Cliff Brunk[2] Carla E. Brodley[1]

[1] School of Electrical Engineering
Purdue University

[2] Data Mining and Visualization
Silicon Graphics, Inc.
2011 N. Shoreline Blvd.

West Lafayette, IN 47907
{jbradfor,brodley}@ecn.purdue.edu

Mountain View, CA 94043
{clayk,ronnyk,brunk}@engr.sgi.com

Abstract. We describe an experimental study of pruning methods for decision tree classifiers when the goal is minimizing *loss* rather than *error*. In addition to two common methods for error minimization, CART's cost-complexity pruning and C4.5's error-based pruning, we study the extension of cost-complexity pruning to loss and one pruning variant based on the Laplace correction. We perform an empirical comparison of these methods and evaluate them with respect to loss. We found that applying the Laplace correction to estimate the probability distributions at the leaves was beneficial to all pruning methods. Unlike in error minimization, and somewhat surprisingly, performing no pruning led to results that were on par with other methods in terms of the evaluation criteria. The main advantage of pruning was in the reduction of the decision tree size, sometimes by a factor of ten. While no method dominated others on all datasets, even for the same domain different pruning mechanisms are better for different loss matrices.

1 Pruning Decision Trees

Decision trees are a widely used symbolic modeling technique for classification tasks in machine learning. The most common approach to constructing decision tree classifiers is to grow a full tree and prune it back. Pruning is desirable because the tree that is grown may overfit the data by inferring more structure than is justified by the training set. Specifically, if there are no conflicting instances, the training set error of a fully built tree is zero, while the true error is likely to be larger. To combat this overfitting problem, the tree is pruned back with the goal of identifying the tree with the lowest error rate on previously unobserved instances, breaking ties in favor of smaller trees (Breiman, Friedman, Olshen & Stone 1984, Quinlan 1993). Several pruning methods have been introduced in the literature, including cost-complexity pruning, reduced error pruning, pessimistic pruning, error-based pruning, penalty pruning, and MDL pruning. Historically, most pruning algorithms have been developed to minimize the expected *error rate* of the decision tree, assuming that classification errors have the same unit cost.

Our objective in this paper is different than the above-mentioned studies. Instead of pruning to minimize *error*, we aim to study pruning algorithms with the goal of minimizing *loss*. In many practical applications one has a *loss matrix* associated with classification errors (Turney 1997), and pruning should be performed with respect to the loss matrix. Pruning for loss minimization can lead to different pruning behavior than does pruning for error minimization. In this paper, we investigate the behavior of several pruning algorithms. In addition to the two most common methods for error minimization, cost-complexity pruning (Breiman et al. 1984) and error-based pruning (Quinlan 1993), we study the extension of cost-complexity pruning to loss and a pruning variant based on the Laplace correction (Good 1965, Cestnik 1990). We perform an empirical comparison of these methods and evaluate them with respect to loss under two different matrices. We found that even for the same domain, different pruning mechanisms are better for different loss matrices. In addition, we found that adjusting the probability distributions at the leaves using the Laplace correction was beneficial to all methods.

2 The Pruning Algorithms and Evaluation Criteria

Most pruning algorithms perform a post-order traversal of the tree, replacing a subtree by a single leaf node when the estimated error of the leaf replacing the subtree is lower than that of the subtree. The crux of the problem is to find an *honest* estimate of error (Breiman et al. 1984), which is defined as one that is not overly optimistic for a tree that was built to minimize errors in the first place. The resubstitution error (error rate on the training set) does not provide a suitable estimate because a leaf-node replacing a subtree will never have fewer errors on the training set than the subtree. Two commonly used pruning algorithms for error minimization are C4.5's error-based pruning (Quinlan 1993) and CART's cost-complexity pruning (Breiman et al. 1984).

We attempted to extend several error-based pruning to loss-based pruning. In some cases the extensions are obvious, but C4.5's error-based pruning based on confidence intervals does not extend easily. The naive idea of computing a confidence interval for each probability and computing the losses based on the upper bound of the interval for each class yields a distribution that does not add to one. Experimental results we made on some variants (e.g. normalizing the probabilities) did not perform well. Instead, we decided to use a Laplace-based pruning method.

The Laplace-based pruning method we introduce here has a similar motivation to C4.5's error-based pruning. The Laplace correction method biases the probability towards a uniform distribution. Specifically, if a node has m instances, c of which are from a given class, in a k-class problem, the probability assigned to the class is $(c+1)/(m+k)$ (Good 1965, Cestnik 1990). The Laplace correction makes the distribution at the leaves more uniform and less extreme. Given a node, we can compute the expected loss using the loss matrix. The expected loss of a subtree is the sum of expected loss of the leaves.

The cost-complexity-pruning (CCP) algorithm used in CART penalizes the estimated error based on the subtree size. Specifically, the error estimate assigned to a subtree is the resubstitution error plus a factor α times the subtree size. An efficient search algorithm can be used to compute all the distinct α values that change the tree size and the parameter is chosen to minimize the error on a holdout sample or using cross-validation. Once the optimal value of α is found, the entire training set is used to grow the tree and it is pruned using this optimal value. In our experiments, we have used the holdout method, holding back 20% of the training set to estimate the best α parameter.

Cost complexity pruning extends naturally to loss matrices. Instead of estimating the error of a subtree, we estimate its loss (or cost), using the resubstitution loss and penalizing by the size of the tree times the α factor as in error-based CCP.

3 A Comparison of Pruning Algorithms

Our goal in designing these experiments was to understand which pruning methods work well when the decision tree classifier is evaluated on loss given a loss matrix. The basic decision tree growing algorithm is implemented in $\mathcal{MLC}$++ (Kohavi, Sommerfield & Dougherty 1996) and called MC4 ($\mathcal{MLC}$++ C4.5). It is a Top-Down Decision Tree induction algorithm very similar to C4.5. The algorithm grows the decision tree following the standard methodology of choosing the best attribute according to the gain-ratio evaluation criterion and stopping when a node has two or fewer instances. The trees are pruned using the following pruning algorithms:

eb-fr Error-based pruning (C4.5) with probabilities estimated using frequency counts.

eb-lc Error-based pruning with probabilities estimated using the Laplace correction.

np-lc No-pruning with probabilities estimated using the Laplace correction.

lp Laplace-based pruning with probabilities estimated using the Laplace correction.

ccp-lc Cost-complexity pruning based on loss with probabilities estimated using the Laplace correction.

The leaves of the trees are labeled with the class that minimizes expected loss based on the probability estimates at each leaf. In our initial experiments, the Laplace correction outperformed frequency counts in all variants. Therefore, excluding the basic method of error-based-pruning, all other pruning methods were run with the Laplace correction.

Ten datasets were chosen from the UCI repository (Merz & Murphy 1997): adult (salary classification based on census bureau data), breast cancer diagnosis, chess, crx (credit), german (credit), pima diabetes, road (dirt), satellite images, shuttle, and vehicle. In choosing the datasets, we decided on the following desiderata:

1. Datasets should be two-class to make the evaluation easier. This desideratum was hard to satisfy and we resorted to converting several multi-class problems into two-class problems by choosing the least prevalent class as the goal class.
2. Datasets should not have too many unknowns. To avoid another factor in this evaluation, we removed all instances with unknown values from the files.
3. The standard error of the estimated loss should be small. This was very important because with loss matrices the standard deviations of the estimates can be large. We therefore decided to require at least 500 instances and train on only 25% of the data, leaving the remaining instances for testing.

We wanted to test the following hypotheses:

1. The Laplace correction for estimating probabilities at the leaves leads to lower loss than frequency counts.
2. Considering the loss matrix during pruning leads to lower loss than pruning based on errors.

For all datasets we trained on 25% of the data and tested on 75% of the data, repeating the process 10 times. We compared performance of the pruning algorithms on two different loss matrices, which respectively set a loss of 10 and 100 for misclassifying the less frequent of the two classes. This was done to simulate real-world scenarios in which the less frequent class is the important class. Experiments were also done with the losses reversed, with similar conclusions to those shown below.

The results are displayed as graphs showing the average loss for the ten files as bars using the scale on the left, and the average relative loss as X-symbols with the scale on the right. The relative losses are computed as the ratio between the loss of the pruning method and eb-fr, our baseline method. These ratios are then averaged across the ten datasets to create summary graphs. In cases for which the losses are small, the ratio is a better indicator of performance. The average losses and average relative losses for the two loss matrices are shown in Figure 1. The following observations can be made:

1. Error-based pruning with frequency counts performs the worst.
2. The Laplace-based pruning (lp) performs the best on the 10 to 1 loss matrix and is comparable to the best on the 100 to 1 loss matrix.
3. No-pruning (np-lc) performs surprisingly well on both loss matrices!
4. Cost-complexity pruning (ccp-lc) is slightly inferior to no-pruning, but better than error-based pruning (eb) on the 100 to 1 loss matrix.
5. Tree sizes were radically different. The average tree sizes for the 10 to 1 loss matrix are: ccp(47), eb(118), lp(382), and np(670). Cost-complexity pruning was by far the smallest, confirming the observation by Oates & Jensen (1997) for error minimization.

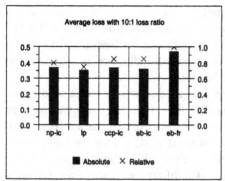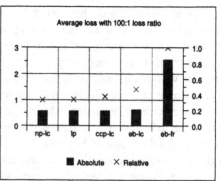

Fig. 1. Average absolute and relative losses for the different algorithms and for a 10 to 1 loss matrix (left) and a 100 to 1 matrix (right).

Our hypothesis that the Laplace correction for estimating probabilities at the leaves outperforms frequency counts was confirmed. It was also confirmed for the np and ccp pruning methods when they were run with frequency counts (results not shown). Interestingly, no-pruning performed *very* well, suggesting that when we have loss matrices and when tree size is not important, pruning need not be done if the Laplace correction is used. This result differs from error minimization, where pruning was consistently shown to help.

Pruning based on loss matrices performed better than pruning based on error for frequency counts for all methods. This result (for frequency counts) has been observed previously for reduced error/cost pruning (Draper, Brodley & Utgoff 1994). When the Laplace correction was used, pruning with loss matrices performed better than error-based pruning (eb-lc) for the 100:1 (ccp-lc, lp) but there was no significant difference for the 10:1 loss matrix.

For each pruning method, applying the Laplace correction improved performance on average. Only in a few cases did the Laplace correction lead to a higher distribution MSE (mean-squared-error) than frequency counts. The distribution MSE was similar for all the Laplace correction algorithms. The main difference between the pruning algorithms was in the tree size. The average tree sizes were ccp(27), eb(118), lp(280), and np(670).)

4 Conclusions

Of the two steps in inducing a decision tree—growing and pruning—we concentrated only on the latter stage. We view this as a good first step to study before studying different growing techniques as was done in Pazzani, Merz, Murphy, Ali, Hume & Brunk (1994).

We extended cost-complexity pruning to loss and introduced a new method that can be used with loss matrices, Laplace-pruning. Laplace-pruning was the best pruning method with the 10 to 1 loss matrix and tied for best pruning with no-pruning with the Laplace correction for the 100 to 1 loss matrix.

Our study revealed that using the Laplace correction at the leaves is extremely beneficial and aids all pruning methods used. We also found that for the datasets tested, pruning did not help much in reducing the loss, but did lead to smaller trees. Cost-complexity pruning was especially effective at reducing the tree size without significantly increasing the loss.

No single pruning algorithm dominated over all datasets in terms of loss, but more interestingly, even for a fixed domain, different pruning algorithms were better for different loss matrices. In the long version of this paper (Bradford, Kunz, Kohavi, Brunk & Brodley 1998) we showed ROC curves for different algorithms, including another pruning method. These differences, however, were not major. Given the fact that there was little difference in loss even for algorithms that did not use the loss matrix during tree pruning stage, we conclude that it will usually suffice to induce a single probability tree and use it with different loss matrices.

References

Bradford, J. P., Kunz, C., Kohavi, R., Brunk, C. & Brodley, C. E. (1998), Pruning decision trees with misclassification costs (long).
http://robotics.stanford.edu/~ronnyk/prune-long.ps.gz.

Breiman, L., Friedman, J. H., Olshen, R. A. & Stone, C. J. (1984), *Classification and Regression Trees*, Wadsworth International Group.

Cestnik, B. (1990), Estimating probabilities: A crucial task in machine learning, *in* L. C. Aiello, ed., 'Proceedings of the ninth European Conference on Artificial Intelligence', pp. 147–149.

Draper, B. A., Brodley, C. E. & Utgoff, P. E. (1994), 'Goal-directed classification using linear machine decision trees', *IEEE Transactions on Pattern Analysis and Machine Intelligence* 16(9), 888–893.

Good, I. J. (1965), *The Estimation of Probabilities: An Essay on Modern Bayesian Methods*, M.I.T. Press.

Kohavi, R., Sommerfield, D. & Dougherty, J. (1996), Data mining using $\mathcal{MLC}$++: A machine learning library in C++, *in* 'Tools with Artificial Intelligence', IEEE Computer Society Press, pp. 234–245.
http://www.sgi.com/Technology/mlc.

Merz, C. J. & Murphy, P. M. (1997), UCI repository of machine learning databases.
http://www.ics.uci.edu/~mlearn/MLRepository.html.

Oates, T. & Jensen, D. (1997), The effects of training set size on decision tree complexity, *in* D. Fisher, ed., 'Machine Learning: Proceedings of the Fourteenth International Conference', Morgan Kaufmann, pp. 254–262.

Pazzani, M., Merz, C., Murphy, P., Ali, K., Hume, T. & Brunk, C. (1994), Reducing misclassification costs, *in* 'Machine Learning: Proceedings of the Eleventh International Conference', Morgan Kaufmann.

Quinlan, J. R. (1993), *C4.5: Programs for Machine Learning*, Morgan Kaufmann, San Mateo, California.

Turney, P. (1997), Cost-sensitive learning.
http://ai.iit.nrc.ca/bibliographies/cost-sensitive.html.

Text Categorization with Support Vector Machines: Learning with Many Relevant Features

Thorsten Joachims

Universität Dortmund
Informatik LS8, Baroper Str. 301
44221 Dortmund, Germany

Abstract. This paper explores the use of Support Vector Machines (SVMs) for learning text classifiers from examples. It analyzes the particular properties of learning with text data and identifies why SVMs are appropriate for this task. Empirical results support the theoretical findings. SVMs achieve substantial improvements over the currently best performing methods and behave robustly over a variety of different learning tasks. Furthermore, they are fully automatic, eliminating the need for manual parameter tuning.

1 Introduction

With the rapid growth of online information, text categorization has become one of the key techniques for handling and organizing text data. Text categorization techniques are used to classify news stories, to find interesting information on the WWW, and to guide a user's search through hypertext. Since building text classifiers by hand is difficult and time-consuming, it is advantageous to learn classifiers from examples.

In this paper I will explore and identify the benefits of *Support Vector Machines (SVMs)* for text categorization. SVMs are a new learning method introduced by V. Vapnik et al. [9] [1]. They are well-founded in terms of computational learning theory and very open to theoretical understanding and analysis.

After reviewing the standard feature vector representation of text, I will identify the particular properties of text in this representation in section 4. I will argue that SVMs are very well suited for learning in this setting. The empirical results in section 5 will support this claim. Compared to state-of-the-art methods, SVMs show substantial performance gains. Moreover, in contrast to conventional text classification methods SVMs will prove to be very robust, eliminating the need for expensive parameter tuning.

2 Text Categorization

The goal of text categorization is the classification of documents into a fixed number of predefined categories. Each document can be in multiple, exactly one, or no category at all. Using machine learning, the objective is to learn classifiers from examples which perform the category assignments automatically. This is a supervised learning problem. Since categories may overlap, each category is treated as a separate binary classification problem.

The first step in text categorization is to transform documents, which typically are strings of characters, into a representation suitable for the learning algorithm and the classification task. Information Retrieval research suggests that word stems work well as representation units and that their ordering in a document is of minor importance for many tasks. This leads to an attribute-value representation of text. Each distinct word[1] w_i corresponds to a feature, with the number of times word w_i occurs in the document as its value. To avoid unnecessarily large feature vectors, words are considered as features only if they occur in the training data at least 3 times and if they are not "stop-words" (like "and", "or", etc.).

This representation scheme leads to very high-dimensional feature spaces containing 10000 dimensions and more. Many have noted the need for feature selection to make the use of conventional learning methods possible, to improve generalization accuracy, and to avoid "overfitting". Following the recommendation of [11], the *information gain* criterion will be used in this paper to select a subset of features.

Finally, from IR it is known that scaling the dimensions of the feature vector with their *inverse document frequency (IDF)* [8] improves performance. Here the "tfc" variant is used. To abstract from different document lengths, each document feature vector is normalized to unit length.

3 Support Vector Machines

Support vector machines are based on the *Structural Risk Minimization* principle [9] from computational learning theory. The idea of structural risk minimization is to find a hypothesis h for which we can guarantee the lowest true error. The true error of h is the probability that h will make an error on an unseen and randomly selected test example. An upper bound can be used to connect the true error of a hypothesis h with the error of h on the training set and the complexity of H (measured by VC-Dimension), the hypothesis space containing h [9]. Support vector machines find the hypothesis h which (approximately) minimizes this bound on the true error by effectively and efficiently controlling the VC-Dimension of H.

SVMs are very **universal learners**. In their basic form, SVMs learn linear threshold function. Nevertheless, by a simple "plug-in" of an appropriate kernel function, they can be used to learn polynomial classifiers, radial basic function (RBF) networks, and three-layer sigmoid neural nets.

One remarkable property of SVMs is that their ability to learn can be **independent of the dimensionality of the feature space**. SVMs measure the complexity of hypotheses based on the margin with which they separate the

---

[1] The terms "word" and "word stem" will be used synonymously in the following.

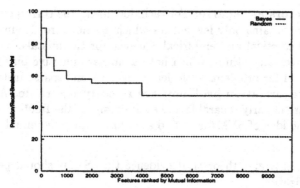

Fig. 1. Learning without using the "best" features.

data, not the number of features. This means that we can generalize even in the presence of very many features, if our data is separable with a wide margin using functions from the hypothesis space.

The same margin argument also suggest a heuristic for **selecting good parameter settings** for the learner (like the kernel width in an RBF network) [9]. The best parameter setting is the one which produces the hypothesis with the lowest VC-Dimension. This allows fully automatic parameter tuning without expensive cross-validation.

4   Why Should SVMs Work Well for Text Categorization?

To find out what methods are promising for learning text classifiers, we should find out more about the properties of text.

High dimensional input space: When learning text classifiers, one has to deal with very many (more than 10000) features. Since SVMs use overfitting protection, which does not necessarily depend on the number of features, they have the potential to handle these large feature spaces.

Few irrelevant features: One way to avoid these high dimensional input spaces is to assume that most of the features are irrelevant. Feature selection tries to determine these irrelevant features. Unfortunately, in text categorization there are only very few irrelevant features. Figure 1 shows the results of an experiment on the Reuters "acq" category (see section 5). All features are ranked according to their (binary) information gain. Then a naive Bayes classifier [2] is trained using only those features ranked 1-200, 201-500, 501-1000, 1001-2000, 2001-4000, 4001-9962. The results in figure 1 show that even features ranked lowest still contain considerable information and are somewhat relevant. A classifier using only those "worst" features has a performance much better than random. Since it seems unlikely that all those features are completely redundant, this leads to the conjecture that a good classifier should combine many features (learn a "dense" concept) and that aggressive feature selection may result in a loss of information.

Document vectors are sparse: For each document, the corresponding document vector contains only few entries which are not zero. Kivinen et al. [4] give both theoretical and empirical evidence for the mistake bound model that "additive" algorithms, which have a similar inductive bias like SVMs, are well suited for problems with dense concepts and sparse instances.

Most text categorization problems are linearly separable: All Ohsumed categories are linearly separable and so are many of the Reuters (see section 5) tasks. The idea of SVMs is to find such linear (or polynomial, RBF, etc.) separators.

These arguments give theoretical evidence that SVMs should perform well for text categorization.

5 Experiments

The following experiments compare the performance of SVMs using polynomial and RBF kernels with four conventional learning methods commonly used for text categorization. Each method represents a different machine learning approach: density estimation using a naive Bayes classifier [2], the Rocchio algorithm [7] as the most popular learning method from information retrieval, a distance weighted k-nearest neighbor classifier [5][10], and the C4.5 decision tree/rule learner [6]. SVM training is carried out with the SVM^{light2} package. The SVM^{light} package will be described in a forthcoming paper.

Test Collections: The empirical evaluation is done on two test collection. The first one is the "ModApte" split of the Reuters-21578 dataset compiled by David Lewis. The "ModApte" split leads to a corpus of 9603 training documents and 3299 test documents. Of the 135 potential topic categories only those 90 are used for which there is at least one training and one test example. After preprocessing, the training corpus contains 9962 distinct terms.

The second test collection is taken from the Ohsumed corpus compiled by William Hersh. From the 50216 documents in 1991 which have abstracts, the first 10000 are used for training and the second 10000 are used for testing. The classification task considered here is to assign the documents to one or multiple categories of the 23 MeSH "diseases" categories. A document belongs to a category if it is indexed with at least one indexing term from that category. After preprocessing, the training corpus contains 15561 distinct terms.

Results: Figure 2 shows the results on the Reuters corpus. The *Precision/Recall-Breakeven Point* (see e. g. [3]) is used as a measure of performance and *microaveraging* [10][3] is applied to get a single performance value over all binary classification tasks. To make sure that the results for the conventional methods are not biased by an inappropriate choice of parameters, all four methods were run after selecting the 500 best, 1000 best, 2000 best, 5000 best, (10000 best,) or all features using information gain. At each number of features the values $\beta \in \{0, 0.1, 0.25, 0.5, 1.0\}$ for the Rocchio algorithm and $k \in \{1, 15, 30, 45, 60\}$

---

[2] http://www-ai.informatik.uni-dortmund.de/thorsten/svm_light.html

	Bayes	Rocchio	C4.5	k-NN	SVM (poly) degree $d =$					SVM (rbf) width $\gamma =$			
					1	2	3	4	5	0.6	0.8	1.0	1.2
earn	95.9	96.1	96.1	97.3	98.2	98.4	**98.5**	98.4	98.3	**98.5**	98.5	98.4	98.3
acq	91.5	92.1	85.3	92.0	92.6	94.6	**95.2**	95.2	95.3	95.0	95.3	95.3	**95.4**
money-fx	62.9	67.6	69.4	78.2	66.9	72.5	75.4	74.9	**76.2**	74.0	75.4	**76.3**	75.9
grain	72.5	79.5	89.1	82.2	91.3	93.1	**92.4**	91.3	89.9	**93.1**	91.9	91.9	90.6
crude	81.0	81.5	75.5	85.7	86.0	87.3	88.6	**88.9**	87.8	**88.9**	89.0	88.9	88.2
trade	50.0	77.4	59.2	77.4	69.2	75.5	76.6	77.3	**77.1**	76.9	78.0	**77.8**	76.8
interest	58.0	72.5	49.1	74.0	69.8	63.3	67.9	73.1	**76.2**	74.4	75.0	**76.2**	76.1
ship	78.7	83.1	80.9	79.2	82.0	85.4	86.0	**86.5**	86.0	**85.4**	86.5	87.6	87.1
wheat	60.6	79.4	85.5	76.6	83.1	84.5	85.2	**85.9**	83.8	**85.2**	85.9	85.9	85.9
corn	47.3	62.2	87.7	77.9	86.0	86.5	85.3	**85.7**	83.9	**85.1**	85.7	85.7	84.5
microavg.	**72.0**	**79.9**	79.4	82.3	84.2	85.1	85.9	86.2	85.9	86.4	86.5	86.3	86.2
					combined: **86.0**					combined: **86.4**			

Fig. 2. Precision/recall-breakeven point on the ten most frequent Reuters categories and microaveraged performance over all Reuters categories. k-NN, Rocchio, and C4.5 achieve highest performance at 1000 features (with $k = 30$ for k-NN and $\beta = 1.0$ for Rocchio). Naive Bayes performs best using all features.

for the k-NN classifier were tried. The results for the parameters with the best performance on the test set are reported.

On the Reuters data the k-NN classifier performs best among the conventional methods (see figure 2). This replicates the findings of [10]. Compared to the conventional methods all SVMs perform better independent of the choice of parameters. Even for complex hypotheses spaces, like polynomials of degree 5, no overfitting occurs despite using all 9962 features. The numbers printed in bold in figure 2 mark the parameter setting with the lowest VCdim estimate as described in section 3. The results show that this strategy is well-suited to pick a good parameter setting automatically and achieves a microaverage of 86.0 for the polynomial SVM and 86.4 for the RBF SVM. With this parameter selection strategy, the RBF support vector machine is better than k-NN on 63 of the 90 categories (19 ties), which is a significant improvement according to the binomial sign test.

The results for the Ohsumed collection are similar. Again k-NN is the best conventional method with a microaveraged precision/recall-breakeven point of 59.1. C4.5 fails on this task (50.0) and heavy overfitting is observed when using more than 500 features. Naive Bayes achieves a performance of 57.0 and Rocchio reaches 56.6. Again, with 65.9 (polynomial SVM) and 66.0 (RBF SVM) the SVMs perform substantially better than all conventional methods. The RBF SVM outperforms k-NN on all 23 categories, which is again a significant improvement.

Comparing training time, SVMs are roughly comparable to C4.5, but they are more expensive than naive Bayes, Rocchio, and k-NN. Nevertheless, current research is likely to improve efficiency of SVM-type quadratic programming problems. SVMs are faster than k-NN at classification time. More details can found in [3].

6 Conclusions

This paper introduces support vector machines for text categorization. It provides both theoretical and empirical evidence that SVMs are very well suited for text categorization. The theoretical analysis concludes that SVMs acknowledge the particular properties of text: (a) high dimensional feature spaces, (b) few irrelevant features (dense concept vector), and (c) sparse instance vectors.

The experimental results show that SVMs consistently achieve good performance on text categorization tasks, outperforming existing methods substantially and significantly. With their ability to generalize well in high dimensional feature spaces, SVMs eliminate the need for feature selection, making the application of text categorization considerably easier. Another advantage of SVMs over the conventional methods is their robustness. SVMs show good performance in all experiments, avoiding catastrophic failure, as observed with the conventional methods on some tasks. Furthermore, SVMs do not require any parameter tuning, since they can find good parameter settings automatically. All this makes SVMs a very promising and easy-to-use method for learning text classifiers from examples.

References

1. C. Cortes and V. Vapnik. Support-vector networks. *Machine Learning*, 20:273–297, November 1995.
2. T. Joachims. A probabilistic analysis of the rocchio algorithm with tfidf for text categorization. In *International Conference on Machine Learning (ICML)*, 1997.
3. T. Joachims. Text categorization with support vector machines: Learning with many relevant features. Technical Report 23, Universität Dortmund, LS VIII, 1997.
4. J. Kivinen, M. Warmuth, and P. Auer. The perceptron algorithm vs. winnow: Linear vs. logarithmic mistake bounds when few input variables are relevant. In *Conference on Computational Learning Theory*, 1995.
5. T. Mitchell. *Machine Learning*. McGraw-Hill, 1997.
6. J. R. Quinlan. *C4.5: Programs for Machine Learning*. Morgan Kaufmann, 1993.
7. J. Rocchio. Relevance feedback in information retrieval. In G. Salton, editor, *The SMART Retrieval System: Experiments in Automatic Document Processing*, pages 313–323. Prentice-Hall Inc., 1971.
8. G. Salton and C. Buckley. Term weighting approaches in automatic text retrieval. *Information Processing and Management*, 24(5):513–523, 1988.
9. Vladimir N. Vapnik. *The Nature of Statistical Learning Theory*. Springer, New York, 1995.
10. Y. Yang. An evaluation of statistical approaches to text categorization. Technical Report CMU-CS-97-127, Carnegie Mellon University, April 1997.
11. Y. Yang and J. Pedersen. A comparative study on feature selection in text categorization. In *International Conference on Machine Learning (ICML)*, 1997.

A Short Note About the Application of Polynomial Kernels with Fractional Degree in Support Vector Learning

Rolf Rossius, Gérard Zenker, Andreas Ittner, and Werner Dilger

Department of Computer Science
Artificial Intelligence Group
Chemnitz University of Technology
D-09107 Chemnitz
{ros,gze,ait,wdi}@informatik.tu-chemnitz.de
http://www.tu-chemnitz.de/informatik/HomePages/KI/

Abstract. In the mid 90's a fundamental new Machine Learning approach was developed by V. N. Vapnik: The Support Vector Machine (SVM). This new method can be regarded as a very promising approach and is getting more and more attention in the fields where neural networks and decision tree methods are applied. Whilst neural networks may be considered (correctly or not) to be well understood and are in wide use, Support Vector Learning has some rough edges in theoretical details and its inherent numerical tasks prevent it from being easily applied in practice. This paper picks up a new aspect - the use of fractional degrees on polynomial kernels in the SVM - discovered in the course of an implementation of the algorithm. Fractional degrees on polynomial kernels broaden the capabilities of the SVM and offer the possibility to deal with feature spaces of infinite dimension. We introduce a method to simplify the quadratic programming problem, as the core of the SVM.

1 Introduction

Well known representatives of classification and prediction methods in the field of Machine Learning are neural networks and methods for generation different kinds of decision trees. An innovative and still relatively unknown learning approach is the Support Vector Machine (SVM) developed by V. N. Vapnik in the mid 90's. Support Vector Learning [IRZ98] is not just another approach to learning techniques, rather it can be regarded as a fundamental new philosophy in the area of Machine Learning.

The underlying principle of the SVM is the principle of the *Structural Risk Minimization* (SRM) [Vap95]. In contrast to a pure minimization of the empirical risk the SRM is based on the "idea of the simplicity" and unifies *Empirical Risk Minimization* and the problem of *Model Selection*. The searched binary classifier for the problem

$$(x_1, y_1), \ldots, (x_l, y_l), \ x_i \in \mathbf{R}^n, \ y_i \in \{+1, -1\} \ ,$$

has to be a function from the set

$$\{f_\alpha : \alpha \in \Gamma\}, \; f_\alpha : \mathbf{R}^n \to \{+1, -1\}, \; x \mapsto y \,,$$

and should reflect the real inherent essence of the given learning problem. This essence can be regarded as the simplest (in some sense) separation of the feature space. Here simplicity will be formalized by means of the *VC dimension*, i. e. a measure of the considered set of feasible functions, e. g. the family of separating hyperplanes. The SRM is enforced by controlled bounding of the VC dimensions of the set $\{f_\alpha\}$ and ensures the excellent generalization ability of the SVM. The underlying theory of the SRM will not be explained in detail in this paper. We refer to [Vap95] which covers the SRM and the application in the SVM.

The separating hyperplane is characterized by $\langle \omega, x \rangle + b = 0$. The distance between the hyperplane and the examples should be maximized, i. e. one has to solve a problem of mathematical programming. For the non-separable case slack variables $\xi_i \geq 0$ are introduced, which leads to:

$$\begin{cases} \frac{1}{2}\langle \omega, \omega \rangle + C \sum_{i=1}^l \xi_i \to \min \\ y_i \left[\langle \omega, x_i \rangle + b \right] \geq 1 - \xi_i & \forall i = 1, \ldots, l \\ \xi_i \geq 0 & \forall i = 1, \ldots, l \,, \end{cases} \quad (1)$$

where the capacity parameter $C > 0$ controls the interrelationship between the accuracy of the classifier on the learning set and its ability of generalization, i. e. the accuracy on an unseen test set.

The vector ω, as the solution of (1), determines the optimal hyperplane. It can be expressed as a linear combination of a possibly small subset of the whole learning data:

$$\omega = \sum_{i=1}^l \alpha_i y_i x_i = \sum_{SV} \alpha_i y_i x_i \,. \quad (2)$$

Support Vectors are such vectors x_i, which satisfy $y_i \left[\langle \omega, x_i \rangle + b \right] = 1$, i. e. which have a nonzero α_i and effectively contribute to the description of the separating hyperplane. Hence in (2) one can reduce ω to a linear combination of support vectors. Less formally these support vectors can be viewed as the examples on the frontline guarding the own class against the examples of the other one and are essential for the concept to be learned.

Considering (2) one has to solve the following optimization problem:

$$\begin{cases} \Lambda^T \mathbf{1} - \frac{1}{2}\Lambda^T A\Lambda \to \max \\ 0 \leq \Lambda \leq C\mathbf{1} \\ \Lambda^T Y = 0 \end{cases} \quad (3)$$

with $\Lambda = (\alpha_1, \ldots, \alpha_l), \mathbf{1} = (1, \ldots, 1)$, and $Y = (y_1, \ldots, y_l)$. The HESSE matrix A consists of the elements $A_{ij} = y_i y_j \langle x_i, x_j \rangle$ for $i, j = 1, \ldots, l$ [CV95].

However in the general case the linear separation in the original feature space will not provide a sufficient classifier. Therefore the original feature space is expanded to a very high dimensional image space by (e.g.):

$$\Phi : \mathbf{R}^n \to \mathbf{R}^N, n \ll N, \Phi(x) = (1, \gamma_1 x_1, \ldots, \gamma_n x_n, \gamma_{n+1} x_1^2, \gamma_{n+2} x_1 x_2, \ldots, \gamma_k x_n^d),$$

and in this space the linear separation is performed. An inverse transformation back into $\mathbf{R}^n$ results in a non-linear separation in the original space of the task supplied features:

$$f(x) = \langle \omega, \Phi(x) \rangle + b .$$

It is not necessary to expand the feature space explicitly. One way to do the mapping implicitly is to use kernels $K(u, v)$ (respectively dot products). In this context the fundamental interrelation is:

$$K(u, v) = \langle \Phi(u), \Phi(v) \rangle.$$

The symmetric function $K(u, v)$ may be a dot product for the high dimensional image space, if the eigenvalues are positive. One rather simple type of such kernels is representable as

$$K(u, v) = (\langle u, v \rangle + 1)^d , \quad d = 1, 2, \ldots \tag{4}$$

with degree d as an integer. Another choice may be $K(u, v) = e^{-\frac{\|u-v\|}{\sigma}}$. A generalized kind of the kernel (4) will be examined in this paper.

2 Polynomial Kernels with Fractional Degree

Interestingly a fixed chosen kernel $K(u, v)$ induces not only exactly one transformation but a manifold of such mappings Φ. Even the dimensionality of the image space $\mathbf{R}^N$ is not determined. From (4) for $d = 2$ and $n = 2$ one gets:

$$\Phi(u) = (1, \sqrt{2}u_1, \sqrt{2}u_2, u_1^2, \sqrt{2}u_1 u_2, u_2^2), \quad u = (u_1, u_2)$$

as well as

$$\Phi(u) = (1, u_1, u_1, u_2, u_2, u_1^2, u_1 u_2, u_2 u_1, u_2^2)$$

and infinite number of others.

Therefore a question arises: Choosing a kernel $K(u, v)$ – which is the space of smallest dimension for an image of Φ? The answer for $d \in N$ is $\binom{n+d}{d}$ (or equivalently $\binom{n+d}{n}$). While selecting an appropriate kernel K via the exponent d, there are huge discontinuities in the dimensionalities of the corresponding image spaces. The approximation and generalization capacity may be controlled by bounding the norm of the separating hyperplane, but another tuning parameter will still be there: the dimensionality (cf. Table 1).

Using a fractional exponent in the kernel (4) we encounter an interesting property: the dot product $\langle u, v \rangle$ may be less than -1 and we have a negative

$n \setminus d$	1	2	3	4	5	6	7
2	2	6	10	15	21	28	36
16	16	153	969	4.8×10^3	2.0×10^4	7.5×10^4	2.5×10^5
256	256	3.3×10^4	2.9×10^6	1.9×10^8	9.7×10^9	4.2×10^{11}	1.6×10^{13}

Table 1. Dimension of image space for polynomial kernel with exponent d and n original features. The dimension of the image space (where the linear separation takes place) grows quite rapidly – an explicit computation in this space would be impossible. But as mentioned before, this is fortunately not required. Rather the value itself should guide the user to a conjecture about the separating abilities of the associated hyperplane.

base to raise. [1] Hence the HESSE Matrix A will not be real valued and therefore symmetric ($A^T = A$) anymore, but in fact contain complex entries. Nevertheless, A has the property of hermiticity ($A^T = \overline{A}$). This allows for a new formulation of (3). Because

$$A^T A \Lambda = \Lambda^T A^T \Lambda = \Lambda^T \frac{1}{2} \left(A + A^T \right) \Lambda = \Lambda^T \frac{1}{2} \left(A + \overline{A} \right) \Lambda = \Lambda^T \mathrm{Re}\,(A)\, \Lambda$$

we equivalently solve

$$\begin{cases} \Lambda^T \mathbf{1} - \frac{1}{2} \Lambda^T \mathrm{Re}\,(A)\, \Lambda \to \max \\ \mathbf{0} \leq \Lambda \leq C\mathbf{1} \\ \Lambda^T Y = 0 \end{cases} \tag{5}$$

instead, and get rid of the complex entries. ($\mathrm{Re}(A)$ denotes the real part.)

Exposing the kernel for arbitrary exponents d we get according to TAYLOR:

$$(\langle u, v \rangle + 1)^d = 1 + d\langle u, v \rangle + \frac{d\,(d-1)}{2!}\langle u, v \rangle^2 + \frac{d\,(d-1)\,(d-2)}{3!}\langle u, v \rangle^3$$
$$+ \frac{d\,(d-1)\,(d-2)\,(d-3)}{4!}\langle u, v \rangle^4 + \dots$$

Non-integer exponents do not terminate the series like the integer ones, but the influence of high-order terms decreases nevertheless. In contrast to kernels with an integer exponent there are no mappings Φ corresponding to such a fractional exponent kernel which have an image space of finite dimension.

Fractional degrees allow a more continuous range of concepts. The resulting separating hyperplanes smoothly change the shapes with the exponent d. This will be of importance especially for domains dealing with feature spaces which already cover tens, hundreds or more dimensions (e.g. recognition of graphical images), where a lower degree of a polynomial kernel is preferred. A simple artificial problem in a two dimensional feature space is presented in Figure 1. [Fri93]

---

[1] One could imagine this in the original space: The representing vectors u and v of both participating examples form a sufficient obtuse angle.

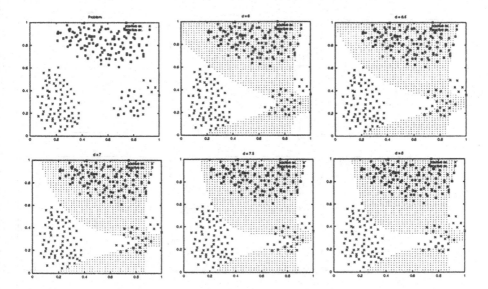

Fig. 1. Continuous variation of exponent d. 226 examples, class distribution 93/133, 90 % used to generate the separation. Two properties of the problem are significant: low dimensionality of the original feature space, difficultly crossed arrangement of examples in the lower right area. As expected, a somewhat higher exponent of the polynomial kernel is necessary for the approximation of the concept.

3 The "1/2 Trick"

Realizing the SVM as a whole, the solution of the quadratic optimization problem (quadratic programming, QP) – actually a series of such, with different parameters – constitutes the real amount of work. Generally the QP task is for the most part determined by the calculation of function values, gradients (or its estimations). It makes more difficulties here because of the (potential) large HESSE matrix and its nonsparsity.

We tackle this by choosing a kernel of the type $(\langle u, v \rangle + 1)^d$ with $d = m + \frac{1}{2}$ and $m \in \mathbb{N}$. The corresponding entry in the resulting HESSE matrix ($\mathrm{Re}(A)$ in (5)) will vanish for negative $(\langle u, v \rangle + 1)$.

The SVM algorithm selects a separating hyperplane according to a criterion of sufficient values on the training examples as well as the minimization of the norm of the hyperplane. Unfortunately, Φ is nonlinear – the resulting shape of the function and thus the border between the predicted areas of both classes varies with uniform translations of the examples in the feature space. For instance the resulting separation lines for different centered sets of the well known XOR problem are depicted in Figure 2. A second degree kernel is used.

Despite of the non-invariance against the uniform translation of the examples in the feature space, one could center the set into the origin of the co-ordinate system to obtain a sufficient obtuse angle between a large number of pairs of examples. This will result in a sparser HESSE matrix for the QP task. Up to 50 % of the entries may be zeroed by means of this smart approach.

148

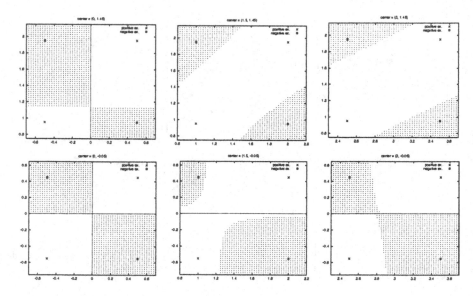

Fig. 2. Noninvariance of separation with respect to translation. $\left(x - \frac{1}{2}, y - \frac{1}{2}\right)$, $\left(x + \frac{1}{2}, y + \frac{1}{2}\right)$ are members of one class, while the two other examples $\left(x - \frac{1}{2}, y + \frac{1}{2}\right)$, $\left(x + \frac{1}{2}, y - \frac{1}{2}\right)$ belong to a second class. The four points are centered on (x, y).

4 Summary

The Support Vector algorithm shows some promising properties but needs some refinement especially on the level of practical realization to soften the enormous effort to find the "simplest" explanation for a learning problem. Polynomial kernels with fractional degrees provide a broader range of concepts as well as a way to reduce the numerical effort to be spent in the QP.

The algorithm works well with a feature space of "similar" features. Is is often preferred to do a componentwise transformation to normalize the data in front of the number crunching task of the SVM itself. For specific domains this could be done in the kernel function.

References

[CV95] C. Cortes and V. N. Vapnik. Support-vector networks. *Machine Learning*, 20:273–297, 1995.
[Fri93] B. Fritzke. Growing cell structures – a self-organizing network for unsupervised and supervised learning. Technical Report 93-026, International Computer Science Institute, Berkeley, California, 1993.
[IRZ98] A. Ittner, R. Rossius, and G. Zenker. Support Vector Learning. Technical Report CSR-98, Chemnitz University of Technology, Chemnitz, Germany, 1998.
[Vap95] V. N. Vapnik. *The Nature of Statistical Learning Theory*. Springer-Verlag, 1995.

Classification Learning Using All Rules

Murlikrishna Viswanathan and Geoffrey I. Webb

School of Computing and Mathematics
Deakin University, Geelong, Vic, Australia, 3217

Abstract. The covering algorithm has been ubiquitous in the induction of classification rules. This approach to machine learning uses heuristic search that seeks to find a minimum number of rules that adequately explain the data. However, recent research has provided evidence that learning redundant classifiers can increase predictive accuracy. Learning all possible classifiers seems to be a plausible ultimate form of this notion of redundant classifiers. This paper presents an algorithm that in effect learns all classifiers. Preliminary investigation by Webb (1996b) suggested that a heuristic covering algorithm in general learns classification rules with higher predictive accuracy than those learned by this new approach. In this paper we present an extensive empirical comparison between the learning-all-rules algorithm and three varied established approaches to inductive learning, namely, a covering algorithm, an instance-based learner and a decision tree learner. Empirical evaluation provides strong evidence in support of learning-all-rules as a plausible approach to inductive learning.

1 Introduction

The heuristic covering algorithm (as typified by Michalski, 1984; Clark and Niblett, 1989; Muggleton and Feng, 1990; and Quinlan, 1990) has been the predominant approach to learning classification rules. A basic characteristic of inductive learning is the use of search. In this context machine learning is often regarded as a search for generalizations and specializations of concepts. The covering algorithm seeks to develop a minimal set of rules that adequately explains the training data.

In contrast, recent research (Ali, Brunk, and Pazzani, 1994; Breiman, 1996; Dietterich and Bakiri, 1994; Domingos, 1995; Kwok and Carter, 1990; Nock and Olivier, 1995; Oliver and Hand, 1995; Schapire, 1990; Webb, 1996a; Wogulis and Langley, 1989) has provided increasing evidence in support of learning redundant classifiers. While most of this research has occurred in the context of learning decision trees rather than the classification rules with which the current research is concerned, there is no reason to believe that the results do not generalise to this latter context. Webb (1996b) presented a system that in effect infers and employs all possible classification rules, and after preliminary investigation concluded that a heuristic covering algorithm in general provided higher predictive accuracy. In this paper we present results of extensive empirical comparison of the learning-all-rules approach against a heuristic covering algorithm, a benchmark instance-based learner and a benchmark decision tree based learning algorithm. We find that the learning-all-rules approach in general gives superior performance over the traditional covering algorithm and has equivalent performance levels to the decision tree and instance based learners.

2 The Covering Approach

The covering technique for the induction of classifiers from examples has been a popular generic approach among machine learning systems that infer classification rules. The covering strategy forms a set of rules by inferring the rules one at a time. At each step it searches for a rule that covers many positive examples and few or no negative examples. The covered examples are then removed and the algorithm starts again on the remainder. This heuristic approach to learning a set of rules seeks to infer a minimal number of rules.

Although the covering algorithm has been a commonly used technique, it is subject to several well known weaknesses. The foremost among these is the application of hill climbing search. This search technique has well known limitations, including the problems of local maxima, plateaus and ridges. These can prevent it from reaching an optimal solution. Another problem with heuristic search is that it is often difficult to determine whether the search technique has introduced additional implicit biases that evade proper identification. Such implicit biases could have a profound effect on experimental results. There is also a growing body of evidence that learning a minimal set of rules is in general sub-optimal with respect to predictive accuracy. Empirical evidence from recent research (Ali, Brunk, and Pazzani, 1994; Breiman, 1996; Dietterich and Bakiri, 1994; Domingos, 1995; Kwok and Carter, 1990; Nock and Olivier, 1995; Oliver and Hand, 1995; Schapire, 1990; Webb, 1996a; Wogulis and Langley, 1989) has shown that learning classifiers that contain elements in addition to the bare minimum needed, can improve predictive accuracy.

3 Induction of All Rules

Webb's (1996b) new technique learning-all-rules, in effect learns all possible rules defined by the rule-description language. The number of possible rules for a given domain or learning task may be infinite. As a result it is infeasible to develop explicit representations for all possible rules. However, explicit representations of all rules are not necessary in order to apply all possible rules. Webb (1996b) adopts an approach whereby explicit rules are only developed when an example is classified by the algorithm. Then, only the single rule that determines the class to be assigned to the unclassified item is explicitly represented. Thus, in this technique the training set is retained until actually classifying an instance. When an example is classified those rules relevant to that instance will be inferred from the training set. This can be viewed as a lazy learning (Aha, 1997) approach to learning classification rules. However, learning-all-rules differs from most lazy learners that construct temporary classifiers (such as lazy decision trees, Friedman, Kohavi, and Yun, 1996) by performing complete search, instead of heuristic search, for the best classifier with respect to the target object.

3.1 The Learning-All-Rules Algorithm

Every inductive machine learning system necessarily embodies some search technique in its quest for hypotheses. OPUS (Webb, 1993; Webb, 1995) is a search algorithm that provides efficient complete search to select individual classification rules from a search space of all possible non-disjunctive rules. OPUS takes as input a training set t, an evaluation function e, and a set of specialisation operators o, and outputs a set of operators from o which generate a classifier that maximises e with respect to t.

The evaluation function e specifies the inductive bias. The max consistent and Laplace accuracy estimate metrics of empirical support were used in this research. The max consistent metric favours rules that cover the most positive examples and no negative examples while the Laplace metric allows for a trade-off between the coverage of positive and negative examples. Given that N is the number of negative training examples covered, P the number of positive examples and C the number of classes from the training data, the max consistent empirical support value for a rule equals $-N$, if $N > 0$, else P and the Laplace empirical support for a rule equals $(P + 1)/(P + N + C)$.

The OPUS algorithm is not presented here, as the search algorithm employed is not significant to the research, so long as that algorithm performs complete search.

An abstract specification of the learning-all-rules algorithm is presented as follows. Let,

T : set of training examples.

instance : an unclassified object to be classified.

OPUS(T,instance, E) : function that takes as its inputs the training set T, an example to be classified *instance*, and an inductive bias function E and returns a rule that covers instance, and has maximal support for the inductive bias function E with respect to the training set T.

X → C : a classification rule.

$$X \to C = OPUS(T, instance, E)$$
assign class C to *instance*

The OPUS algorithm performs complete search in contrast to heuristic search. Hence, the rules it generates are always optimal with respect to the preference function.

3.2 Advantages

The learning-all-rules approach embodies a number of major advantages in comparison to the traditional covering technique.

As opposed to the covering approach, learning and employing all rules involves no search heuristics. The representation language for expressing rules used by the system determines the set of rules generated. The exclusion of heuristics from the inference process eliminates the limitations of the heuristic search.

The learning-all-rules approach employs OPUS (Webb, 1995), an admissible search algorithm which guarantees to find the nominated target as opposed to heuristic search algorithms that cannot guarantee to find the designated targets. Regarding the introduction of implicit biases discussed in the previous section, admissible search assures that the search technique is not introducing confounding unidentified implicit biases into the experimental evaluation.

For any inductive learning strategy that seeks to develop a minimal set of rules there will be a number of possible sets of rules based on the data but only one of them may be selected. According to Webb (1995) this introduces an element of uncertainty which may affect the quality of the induced classifiers. This uncertainty is eliminated in the learning all rules approach which in effect learns and employs all rules.

Exemplar-based methods have been popular in data mining due to their strong approximation properties in determining the similarity between instances (Fayyad, Piatetsky-Shapiro, Smyth, and Uthurusamy, 1996). The learning-all-rules approach offers specific advantages to data mining. Primarily the use of admissible search to explore the space of all possible rules enables a wider exploration of the instance space, which can be valuable in some data mining contexts. Learning-all-rules also offers computational advantages when the number of cases to be classified by a single classifier is low. This is because only those portions of the search space pertaining to the cases to be classified need to be explored. This may be of particular value in applications where new training examples are continually becoming available, leading to frequent updating of the inferred classifier. One of the main limitations with instance-based methods is the need to define a priori distance metric to compute similarity between instances. Often the interdependencies between attributes and the diverse measurement units of attribute values make this a formidable task. The learning-all-rules algorithm uses the inferred rules to define similarity between instances, thus eliminating the need to define an a priori distance metric.

4 Evaluation with a Covering Algorithm

The covering algorithm used is a reimplementation of CN2 (Clark and Niblett, 1989) using unordered rules and the Laplacian error estimate evaluation function (Clark and Boswell, 1991). In order to minimise possible confounds in the experimental comparision, the covering algorithm uses OPUS to provide complete search in place of the heuristic search algorithm employed in the original

CN2 algorithm. If the original heuristic search were employed, it would not be possible to determine to what extent differences between the system could be attributed to the difference between complete and heuristic search, and to what extent they were due to differences between learning all rules and the use of a covering algorithm.

An abstract specification of the covering algorithm, COV, is presented as follows. Let,

T : set of training examples.

instance : an unclassified object to be classified.

OPUS(T,class,E) : function that takes as its inputs the training set T, a class *class*, and an inductive bias function E and returns a rule for the class that has maximal support for the inductive bias function E with respect to the training set T.

$ruleset = \emptyset$
For *class* = each class in turn
    examples = the training examples
    while *examples* contains objects belonging to *class*
        rule = $OPUS(examples, class, E)$
        if no rule found
            remove from *examples* all objects of class *class*
        otherwise
            remove from *examples* all objects of class *class* covered by *rule*
            add *rule* to *ruleset*

Note that whereas in learning-all-rules the OPUS algorithm is used to search for a rule for any class that covers a specific case, in COV it is used to search for any rule of a specific class, in both cases seeking the rule that maximises the preference function.

5 Evaluation with Instance Based Learning

Instance-based learning (IBL) is the most widely employed form of lazy learning. Instance-based learning algorithms are an offspring of nearest neighbour (NN) algorithms and k-nearest neighbour algorithms (k-NN) (Fix and Hodges, 1952). As opposed to most other supervised learning methods, instance-based learners do not construct explicit abstractions such as decision trees or rules (Aha, Kibler, and Albert, 1991). In typical instance-based learning systems the training data (either in its entirety or a selected subset thereof) is retained for use in classification. A new example is classified by finding the nearest stored example from the training data based on some similarity function/metric, and assigning its class to the new example. Basically the performance of an instance-based learner depends critically on the metric used to compute the similarity between the instances (Domingos, 1995).

The similarities between the learning-all-rules approach and instance-based learning suggested an empirical evaluation of their relative performances. The learning-all-rules approach shares certain features with instance-based learners. First, in both approaches the entire training set or a subset is retained and referenced during classification. Webb (1996b) suggests that the learning-all-rules approach could be considered to be a form of qualitative instance-based learning whereby the selected rule is used to define a similarity metric for classification in place of the use of a distance metric.

This paper includes in the comparative evaluation with the learning-all-rules approach the IB1 instance-based learning algorithm implemented by Aha (1990). IB1 is an adaptation of the k-nearest neighbour algorithm that retains all the training instances for classification. Three successors to IB1—IB2, IB3, and IB4—were also evaluated, but in general provided worse results than IB1, and hence results are not presented herein. IB2 is an edited nearest neighbour algorithm that retains only the misclassified instances. Since the instance selection method stores noisy instances and uses them for classification this algorithm is susceptible to noise in the data. The IB3 algorithm is an adaptation of IB2 and is similar in retaining the misclassified instances but in addition keeps a classification record for each instance and removes some of the stored instances that are believed to be noisy using a significance test. Finally IB4 includes the complete functionality of IB3 in addition to an attribute weight learning capability.

6 Experimental Evaluation

As mentioned above, the primary objective of this paper is to present an extensive empirical comparison between the learning-all-rules and other learning methods. Webb's (1996b) preliminary empirical evaluation led him to conclude that the covering algorithm enjoyed a statistically significant general advantage (in terms of predictive accuracy) over learning-all-rules. However, there was a flaw in the statistic analysis underlying this conclusion. Webb used a Friedman rank test comparing the number of times each approach outperformed the other. Experiments were conducted using 100 runs over 16 different domains. The Friedman rank test analysis was performed over all resulting 1600 comparisons. However, the results for each domain are not independent of one another, and hence the analysis is invalid. Such an analysis could be applied to a single domain to determine whether there was a significant difference within that domain, but should only be applied to a single result for each domain (such as the mean accuracy across all 100 runs) if it is to be used to evaluate the significance of an general advantage across domains. On extending the initial evaluation by incorporating additional data domains and analyzing mean performance on each domain, it is found that the covering algorithm outperforms learning-all-rules for

9 domains while learning-all-rules outperforms the covering algorithm for 22 domains. This does not support the claim of a general advantage for the covering algorithm.

Webb's (1996b) results also suggested that the learning-all-rules algorithm performed better with the max-consistent metric while the covering algorithm performed optimally with Laplace metric. Therefore the learning-all-rules algorithm employing the max consistent metric along with the covering algorithm employing the Laplace metric; C4.5 (Quinlan, 1993), the decision tree learner and the instance-based learner were applied to a representative collection of 33 datasets from the UCI Machine Learning Repository (Merz and Murphy, 1997) that were considerably diverse in size, number and type of attributes and number of classes.

It would also have been interesting to compare learning-all-rules with some further lazy learning algorithms, but did not have access to implementations of these systems for this purpose. This remains an interesting subject for future research.

6.1 Discretization of Continuous-Valued Attributes

Due to the limitation of the current implementation of the OPUS search algorithm to searching for categorical attribute-value rules, all the data domains that contained continuous values for the attributes had to be discretized. The discretization system provided by Ting (1995) employs Fayyad and Irani's (1993) discretisation method that considers all possible cut-points (i.e., all values in the training set) and selects the cut-point that gives the highest information gain. The method is recursively applied to the subsets of the previous split until the stopping criterion is met. The stopping criterion is based on the minimum description length principle, MDLP (Rissanen, 1989).

Note that C4.5 was applied to the discretized version of the data even though it has the capacity to perform its own discretization. This was done in order to minimize the number of possible confounding factors in the comparison. After all, in theory, the learning-all-rules approach could be applied to continuous valued data. The only reason that it was not is our lack of access to a search algorithm capable of performing complete search through such data.

6.2 Description of Experiment

The final experiment included the following steps.

- Each data set containing continuous attributes was discretized.
- Each data set was randomly divided into training (80%) and evaluation (20%) sets 100 times and for each pair of training and evaluation sets so formed all learning methods which included the covering algorithm with the Laplace metric (COV), learning-all-rules (LAR) with the max consistent metric, IB1 and C4.5 were applied to the training set and the predictive accuracy of the resulting classifiers was evaluated on the evaluation set.

All systems were run with their default settings in all experiments.

6.3 Analysis of Results

The mean predictive accuracy achieved by each treatment on each domain is presented in Table 1. In order to analyze these raw figures, Table 2 outlines the win/loss ratio. As can be seen, learning-all-rules with the max consistent metric achieves a higher mean predictive accuracy than the covering algorithm in 22 out of 33 domains. Learning-all-rules also outperforms the instance-based learner. Learning-all-rules achieves higher predictive accuracy than IB1 in 19 of the 33 domains. In comparison to the pruned version of C4.5, learning-all-rules achieves higher predictive accuracy in 11 of the 33 domains.

A multiple comparisons test was performed in order to compare each combination of pairs of treatments. The test was used in evaluating the statistical significance of the observed differences between the different learning methods. This test indicates the learning methods whose rankings significantly differ and also the direction of the difference. In the Table 3, '>' indicates that the treatment for the row has obtained a higher rank (at the 0.05 level) more often than the treatment for the column. '<' indicates that the treatment for the row has obtained a lower rank significantly (at the 0.05 level) more often than the treatment for the column. Finally, '=' indicates no overall significant difference in ranking. In the light of this experiment the table suggested that:

- Learning all rules with the max consistent metric was ranked significantly higher than the covering algorithm. In contrast to Webb's (1996b) earlier erroneous conclusions, this supports the existence of a general advantage to learning-all-rules over the covering algorithm.
- There was no significant difference between the general rankings of learning-all-rules with the max consistent metric and C4.5 or IB1. This suggests that these algorithms perform at similar levels.

7 Conclusions

The empirical analysis conducted so far has clearly and significantly yielded evidence against Webb's (1996b) hypotheses on the superior performance of the covering algorithm. The comparison with a benchmark decision tree learner and an instance based learning system suggests that the learning-all-rules algorithm is a plausible alternative to state-of-the-art heuristic inductive learning systems. In domains where constant acquisition of novel training examples results in frequent updating of the inferred classifier, a classifier will only be used to classify a small number of cases each time. In such domains, the learning-all-rules approach, owing to its use of lazy learning, enjoys a computational advantage over conventional machine learning. Therefore in such a context if a suitable metric is not available to support reliable instance-based learning, learning-all-rules provides an attractive alternative.

Table 1. Mean Predictive Accuracy for each Treatment and Domain

DOMAIN	LAR	COV	C4.5-U	C4.5-P	IB1
Australian	84.79	79.88	82.63	85.63	81
AutoS	71.75	68.87	75.95	73.85	73.33
Cleveland	80.91	74.01	74.39	76.57	76.38
Credit screening	84.97	80.81	82.89	86.01	81.01
Diabetes	73.02	70.98	72.33	74.85	69.64
Echocardiogram	67.60	65.80	73.8	74.53	69.33
Glass	65.88	62.44	67.11	67.25	69.32
Heart	80.46	76.01	75.81	77.14	78.22
Hepatitis	80.61	82.77	77.90	81.80	81.47
Horse-colic	85.41	80.05	83.67	86.58	82.47
Hungarian	81.90	78.20	79.87	79.63	70.83
Hypothyroid	97.82	98.17	98.79	98.82	97.91
Ionosphere	91.15	89.14	88.84	89.25	86.53
Iris	93.93	90.53	93.26	93.20	93.23
Pima-diabetes	72.08	69.71	71.83	73.93	69.42
Satimage	79.01	74.83	79.29	80.98	85.54
Segment	90.91	91.17	94.42	94.08	95.11
Shuttle	99.64	99.75	99.77	99.74	99.76
Vehicle	63.38	60.25	68.23	68.86	68.48
Slovenian breast cancer	69.08	69.17	66.65	71.03	66.77
Winconscin breast cancer	95.49	91.67	93.58	94.58	95.62
House-votes-84	94.25	92.43	94.42	94.94	92.70
KR-vs-KP	96.90	97.79	99.29	99.35	95.67
Lymphography	80.93	76.56	74.99	77.13	79.26
Monk1	100	100	93.70	96.71	84.02
Monk2	81.14	80.74	61.33	64.34	87.87
Monk3	97.37	97.73	98.61	98.89	82.75
MP11	98.62	98.61	87.05	86.45	85.17
Mushroom	100	100	100	100	100
Promoters	60.59	68.68	76.77	76.45	77.27
Primary tumor	39.52	35.01	39.52	39.63	36.85
Soybean-large	59.53	76.41	79.58	79.45	76.48
tic-tac-toe	96.50	96.49	83.77	83.05	96.15

Acknowledgments

Thanks to Zijian Zheng for helpful comments and suggestions on previous drafts of this paper. We are grateful to Kai Ming Ting for providing the discretization system and to David Aha for providing the IB family of instance-based learning systems.

158

Table 2. General Performance Summary

Learning-all-rules **Verses**	Won	Lost	Tied
C4.5-Unpruned	18	13	2
C4.5-Pruned	11	21	1
Cover	22	9	2
IB1	19	13	1

Table 3. Multiple Comparisons Test

Method	LAR	COV	C4.5-U	C4.5-P	IB1
LAR	na	>	=	=	=
COV	<	na	<	<	<
C4.5-U	=	>	na	<	=
C4.5-P	=	>	>	na	>
IB1	=	>	=	<	na

References

Aha, D.W. (1990). *A Study of Instance-Based Algorithms for Supervised Learning Tasks*. PhD Thesis, Department of Information and Computer Science, University of California, Irvine, Technical Report 90-42.

Aha, D. W. (1997). Editorial on Lazy Learning. *Artificial Intelligence Review*, **11**: 7-10.

Aha, D. W., Kibler, D., and Albert, M. (1991). Instance-based learning algorithms. *Machine Learning*, **6**: 37-66.

Ali, K., Brunk, C., and Pazzani, M. (1994). On learning multiple descriptions of a concept. In *Proceedings of Tools with Artificial Intelligence*. New Orleans, LA.

Breiman, L. (1996) Bagging predictors. *Machine Learning*, **24**: 123-140.

Clark, Peter and Niblett, T. (1989). The CN2 induction algorithm. *Machine Learning*, **3**: 261-284.

Clark, P. and Boswell, R. (1991). Rule induction with CN2: Some recent improvements. In *Proceedings of the Fifth European Working Session on Learning*, pp. 151-163.

Dietterich, T. G. and Bakiri, G. (1994). Solving multiclass learning problems via error-correcting output codes. *Journal of Artificial Intelligence Research*, **2**: 263-286.

Domingos, P. (1995). Rule induction and instance-based learning: A unified approach. In *Proceedings of the 13th International Joint COnference on Artificial Intelligence*, Montreal, Morgan Kaufmann, pp. 226-1232.

Fix, E. and J.L. Hodges (1952). *Discriminatory analysis - Nonparametric discrimination: Consistency properties*. From Project 21-49-004, Report Number 4, USAF School of Aviation Medicine, Randolph Field, Texas, pp. 261-279.

Fayyad, U.M. and Irani, K.B. (1993). Multi-interval discretization of continuous-valued attributes for classification learning. In *Proceedings of the Thirteenth International Joint Conference on Artificial Intelligence*, pp. 1022-1027, Morgan Kaufmann publishers.

Fayyad, U.M., Piatetsky-Shapiro, G., Smyth, P., and Uthurusamy, R. (1996). *Advances in knowledge discovery and data mining*. MIT Press, Menlo Park, Ca.

Friedman, J. H., Kohavi, R., and Yun, Y. (1996). Lazy decision trees. In *Proceedings of the Thirteenth National Conference on Artificial Intelligence*. AAAI Press, Portland, OR, pp. 717-724.

Kwok, S. W. and Carter, C. (1990). Multiple decision trees. In Shachter, R. D. and Levitt, T. S. and Kanal, L. N. and Lemmer, J. F. (Eds.) *Uncertainty in Artificial Intelligence 4*. North Holland, Amsterdam, pp. 327-335.

Michalski, R. S. (1984) A theory and methodology of inductive learning. In Michalski, R. S. and Carbonell, J. G. and Mitchell, T. M. (Eds.) *Machine Learning: An Artificial Intelligence Approach*. Springer-Verlag, Berlin, pp. 83-129.

Merz, C.J., and Murphy, P.M. (1997). UCI Repository of machine learning databases [http://www.ics.uci.edu/ mlearn/MLRepository.html]. Irvine, CA: University of California, Department of Information and Computer Science.

Muggleton, Stephen and Feng, C. (1990). Efficient induction of logic programs. In *Proceedings of the First Conference on Algorithmic Learning Theory*, Tokyo.

Nock, R. and Olivier G. (1995). On learning decision committees. In *Proceedings of the Twelfth International Conference on Machine Learning*, pp. 413-420, Taho City, Ca. Morgan Kaufmann publishers.

Oliver, J. J. and Hand, D. J. (1995). On pruning and averaging decision trees. In *Proceedings of the Twelfth International Conference on Machine Learning*, Morgan Kaufmann, Taho City, Ca., pp. 430-437.

Quinlan, J.R. (1990) Learning logical definitions from relations. *Machine Learning*, 5: 239-266.

Quinlan, J.R. (1993). *C4.5: Programs for Machine Learning*. Morgan Kaufmann, San Mateo, CA.

Rissanen, J. (1989). *Stochastic Complexity in Statistical Inquiry*. World Scientific, Singapore.

Schapire, R. E. (1990). The strength of weak learnability. *Machine Learning*, 5: 197-227.

Ting K. M., (1995). *Common Issues in Instance-based and Naive Bayesian Classifiers*. PhD thesis, Basser Dept of Computer Science, University of Sydney.

Webb, G. I. (1993). Systematic search for categorical attribute-value data-driven machine learning. In *AI'93 - Proceedings of the Sixth Australian Joint Conference on Artificial Intelligence*, World Scientific, Melbourne, pp. 342-347.

Webb, G. l.(1995). OPUS: An efficient admissible algorithm for unordered search. *Journal of Artificial Intelligence Research*, 3: 431 -465.

Webb, G. I. (1996a). Further experimental evidence against the utility of Occam's razor. *Journal of Artificial Intelligence Research*, 4: 397-417.

Webb, G. I. (1996b). A heuristic covering algorithm has higher predictive accuracy than learning all rules. In *Proceedings of Information, Statistics and Induction in Science*, Melbourne, pp. 20-30.

Wogulis, J. and Langley, P. (1989). Improving efficiency by learning intermediate concepts. In *Proceedings of the Eleventh International Joint Conference on Artificial Intelligence*, Morgan Kaufmann, San Mateo, CA, pp. 657-662.

Improved Pairwise Coupling Classification with Correcting Classifiers

Miguel Moreira and Eddy Mayoraz *

IDIAP—Dalle Molle Institute of Perceptual Artificial Intelligence
P.O. Box 592, 1920 Martigny, Switzerland
{miguel,mayoraz}@idiap.ch

Abstract. The benefits obtained from the decomposition of a classification task involving several classes, into a set of smaller classification
problems involving two classes only, usually called dichotomies, have
been exposed in various occasions. Among the multiple ways of applying
the referred decomposition, Pairwise Coupling is one of the best known.
Its principle is to separate a pair of classes in each binary subproblem,
ignoring the remaining ones, resulting in a decomposition scheme containing as much subproblems as the number of possible pairs of classes
in the original task. Pairwise Coupling decomposition has so far been
used in different applications. In this paper, various ways of recombin-
ing the outputs of all the classifiers solving the existing subproblems are
explored, and an important handicap of its intrinsic nature is exposed,
which consists in the use, for the classification, of impertinent information. A solution for this problem is suggested and it is shown how it can
significantly improve the classification accuracy. In addition, a powerful
decomposition scheme derived from the proposed correcting procedure
is presented.
Keywords: Classification, decomposition into binary subproblems, pairwise coupling.

1 Introduction

The goal in automated learning consists in finding an approximation $\hat{F}$ of an
unknown function F defined from an *input space* Ω onto an *output space* Σ,
given a *training set*: $T = \{(x^p, F(x^p))\}_{p=1}^P \subset \Omega \times \Sigma$. When the output space
is discrete and unordered, a *classification* problem is presented and the function
$F : \Omega \to \{1, \ldots, K\}$ defines a K-partition of the input space into sets $F^{-1}(k)$
called *classes* and denoted ω_k.

The collection of learning algorithms available to solve classification problems originate in different domains such as: statistics (e.g. Bayesian classifiers,
see [8]), logic (e.g.logical analysis of data [4, 1]), neural networks (e.g. perceptron
algorithm [16], backpropagation [19]), artificial intelligence (e.g. decision trees [2,

* The authors are thankful to Prof. Alain Hertz for the valuable discussions that
greatly contributed to the present work. The support of the Swiss National Science
Foundation under grant FN 21-46974.96 is also gratefully acknowledged.

14]). Among these, only those capable of handling multiclass problems are applied, in general, to solve problems where the number of classes exceeds two.

It is possible, however, to apply Boolean methods (i.e. those that can handle only two-class problems) to learn tasks where $K \gg 2$. In fact, different reasons motivate the decomposition of a large scale problem into smaller subproblems dealing with only two classes. On the one hand, some algorithms do not scale up nicely with the size of the training set. Others are not suited to handle a large number of classes. On the other hand, even when using an approach which can deal with large scale problems, an adequate decomposition of the classification problem into subproblems can be favorable to the overall computational complexity as well as to the generalization ability of the global classifier [17, 3, 20].

The use of a *decomposition scheme* allows the transformation of a K-partition $F : \Omega \rightarrow \{1, \ldots, K\}$, into a series of L bipartitions, $f_1, \ldots, f_L$. A *reconstruction method* is coupled with each decomposition scheme to make the fusion of the answers of all the L classifiers for a particular input in order to select one of the K classes. Among the simplest decomposition schemes frequently used, there is the *one-per-class* (OPC) and the *pairwise coupling* (PWC). A K-partition is decomposed by the former method into K bipartitions, each separating one class from all the others. The latter requires $\frac{1}{2}K(K-1)$ 2-class problems, one for each pair of classes, the bipartition for the pair (i, j) focusing on the separation of class ω_i from class ω_j and ignoring all other data. This paper concentrates on these two decomposition schemes, which are quite intuitive. A more sophisticated scheme is proposed in [7, 5, 10]; in ECOC, redundancy is explored in the decomposition as a way of increasing the error-correcting capability of the reconstruction. This method has served as base for other developments in the same framework. The authors in [11] present a similar scheme where the error-correcting component is kept, but the decomposition is made a posteriori, so that the grouping of classes in the sub-problems respects the class distribution in the input space. As another example, Shapire [18] combines ECOC with Boosting.

2 Decomposition

The decomposition scheme specifies the target function $f_l : \Omega \rightarrow \{-1, +1\}$ for subproblem l. To be valid, $\boldsymbol{f} = (f_1, \ldots, f_L)^\top$ should allow reconstruction, *i.e.* there should not be two pairs $(\boldsymbol{x}, k), (\boldsymbol{y}, k') \in T$, with $k \neq k'$ and $\boldsymbol{f}(\boldsymbol{x}) = \boldsymbol{f}(\boldsymbol{y})$. If no additional information is available, typically, all data of a same class will be associated to the same value by f_l. Therefore, the overall decomposition scheme can be specified by a *decomposition matrix* $\boldsymbol{D} \in \{+1, -1, 0\}^{L \times K}$ such that

$$D_{lk} = \begin{cases} +1 \text{ if class } \omega_k \text{ is associated with } +1 \text{ by } f_l \\ -1 \text{ if class } \omega_k \text{ is associated with } -1 \text{ by } f_l \\ 0 \text{ if class } \omega_k \text{ does not belong to the task of } f_l \ . \end{cases}$$

The validity of the decomposition scheme is expressed by the constraint that for every two columns of $\boldsymbol{D}$, there is at least one row for which the coefficients in the two columns are $+1$ and -1.

The subproblem l will be trained using all the information available, *i.e.* the training sample T_l used to learn f_l is the set of all the pairs (x, D_{lk}) such that $D_{lk} \neq 0$ and $(x, k) \in T$.

As illustration, the decomposition of the one-per-class and pairwise coupling schemes, for $K = 4$, are given by the decomposition matrices of Fig. 1 (a) and (b).

$$
\begin{pmatrix}
+1 & -1 & -1 & -1 \\
-1 & +1 & -1 & -1 \\
-1 & -1 & +1 & -1 \\
-1 & -1 & -1 & +1
\end{pmatrix}
\qquad
\begin{pmatrix}
+1 & -1 & 0 & 0 \\
+1 & 0 & -1 & 0 \\
+1 & 0 & 0 & -1 \\
0 & +1 & -1 & 0 \\
0 & +1 & 0 & -1 \\
0 & 0 & +1 & -1
\end{pmatrix}
$$

$$(a)$$

$$(b)$$

Fig. 1. Classical decomposition matrices D. Each row corresponds to one dichotomy and each column to one class. (a) illustrates the decomposition matrix of the one-per-class scheme; the matrix in (b) corresponds to the pairwise coupling scheme

3 Pairwise Coupling Reconstruction

In PWC, when an input vector x is to be classified, it is presented to all the classifiers, each providing a partial answer that concerns the two involved classes. Considering these answers as votes, a natural approach for the global classification consists in selecting the class that wins more votes. Assuming that the classifier discriminating between class ω_i (as positive) and class ω_j (as negative) computes an estimate $\hat{p}_{ij}$ of the probability

$$p_{ij} = P(x \in \omega_i \mid x , x \in \omega_i \cup \omega_j) , \qquad (1)$$

then, the classification is determined by

$$\arg \max_{1 \leq i \leq K} \sum_{j \neq i} [\![\hat{p}_{ij} > 0.5]\!] . \qquad (2)$$

The operator $[\![.]\!]$ is defined as:

$$[\![\eta]\!] = \begin{cases} 1 \text{ if } \eta \text{ is true,} \\ 0 \text{ otherwise} \end{cases}$$

This combination considers the outputs of the classifiers as binary decisions. A different reconstruction approach consists in taking into consideration the fact that the outputs $\hat{p}_{ij}$ of the classifiers represent probabilities. Then, these values can be used to calculate approximations $\hat{p}_i$ of the a posteriori probabilities

$$p_i = P(x \in \omega_i \mid x) .$$

Considering a square matrix $\hat{P}$ with the value $\hat{p}_{ij}$ in position $(i,j)_{i,j=1,\ldots,K,\ i\neq j}$ and with $\hat{p}_{ji} = 1 - \hat{p}_{ij}$, the values of the $\hat{p}_i$'s can be obtained from

$$\hat{p}_i = \frac{2}{K(K-1)} \sum_{j\neq i} \hat{p}_{ij} , \tag{3}$$

and the classification can then be given by

$$\arg \max_{1\leq i\leq K} \hat{p}_i. \tag{4}$$

This procedure will hereafter be called *soft reconstruction*, as opposed to the voting procedure (2), referred to as *rough reconstruction*. The formulation given in (3) and (4) can be generalized to incorporate the two kinds of reconstruction:

$$\arg \max_{1\leq i\leq K} \hat{p}_i \ , \ \hat{p}_i = \frac{2}{K(K-1)} \sum_{j\neq i} \sigma(\hat{p}_{ij}) ,$$

where σ takes the form of a threshold function at 0.5 for the rough reconstruction and the identity function for the soft reconstruction. Note that whenever σ is symmetric on $[0,1]$, i.e. $\sigma(1-x) = 1-\sigma(x)$, then the p_i's sum to 1 and can thus be considered as probability estimates.

The two schemes presented explore the available information differently and about this a remark can be made. The following example follows from an observation made in [9]. Consider the matrix P with the $\hat{p}_{ij}$'s for a particular input vector x in a problem with three classes:

$$\begin{pmatrix} - & 0.6 & 0.6 \\ 0.4 & - & 0.9 \\ 0.4 & 0.1 & - \end{pmatrix} \tag{5}$$

It can be verified that x is classified as class ω_1 by a rough reconstruction, while a soft reconstruction will classify it as class ω_2. Given that these two functions may produce different outputs, some experiments were made to compare their performance. In addition, alternative forms for the function σ have been proposed and also experimented. The reconstruction schemes are summarized and labeled from PWC1 to PWC5 in Fig. 2.

The schemes PWC1 and PWC2 are the threshold and linear combinations, while the sigmoidal function used in PWC3 is a compromise between the two. PWC4 is a semi-threshold function where the linear behavior of the first half range aims at recovering negative information that is close to the threshold and that might be caused by poor classifier performance. By negative information it is meant here the probability values below 0.5, which correspond to a negative

$$\sigma(x) = \begin{cases} 1 \text{ if } x \geq 0.5 \\ 0 \text{ otherwise} \end{cases} \quad \text{(PWC1)} \qquad \sigma(x) = x \qquad \text{(PWC2)}$$

$$\sigma(x) = \frac{1}{1+e^{-12\,(x-0.5)}} \quad \text{(PWC3)} \qquad \sigma(x) = \begin{cases} 1 \text{ if } x \geq 0.5 \\ x \text{ otherwise} \end{cases} \quad \text{(PWC4)}$$

$$\sigma(x) = \begin{cases} x \text{ if } x \geq 0.5 \\ 0 \text{ otherwise} \end{cases} \quad \text{(PWC5)}$$

Fig. 2. The function σ used in the reconstruction schemes PWC1 to PWC5. The plots of these functions are presented in Fig. 3.

vote in the case of a threshold function. PWC5 uses a concept similar to the previous scheme, but in this case negative information is given full meaning while positive information is given increasing importance with increasing distance from the threshold. Fig. 3 contains the plots of the different forms of σ.

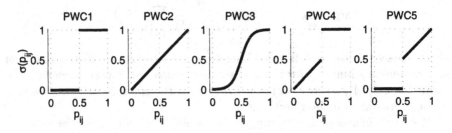

Fig. 3. The different forms of the function σ as defined in Fig. 2.

In [13], a different way of approximating the class probabilities is proposed. Given

$$p_{ij} = \frac{p_i}{p_i + p_j}$$

and considering that for all i,

$$\sum_{j \neq i} (p_i + p_j) - (K-2)\, p_i = 1\ ,$$

then the following expression can be derived:

$$p_i = \frac{1}{\sum_{j \neq i} \frac{1}{p_{ij}} - (K-2)} \quad \text{(PWC6)}\ .$$

This scheme has been included in the experiments and is labeled PWC6.

The results of the experiments are presented in Fig. 4. The learning algorithm used to implement the classifiers is the decision tree algorithm C4.5 [15]. For each of the five databases from [12] that have been used in the tests, 20 runs with 3-folding were executed. The *3-fold cross-validated paired t test* [6] was applied to check for significant differences between the average error rates, with a confidence level of 0.95.

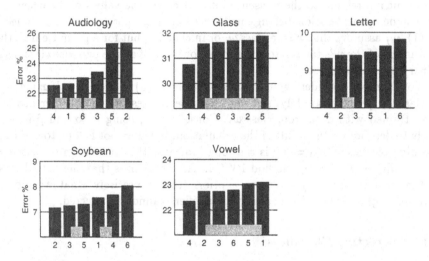

Fig. 4. Comparison between different PWC reconstruction methods. Numerical values are presented in Table 1. Bars connected by the same light-coloured horizontal strip represent values that do not differ significantly (0.95).

Table 1. Comparison between different PWC reconstruction methods. The values represent the average percentage of misclassification on the test set (and respective standard deviations).

Method	audiology	glass	letter	soybean	vowel
PWC1	22.64±4.2	30.75±4.6	9.64±0.4	7.56±1.5	23.09±2.2
PWC2	25.33±4.3	31.71±4.8	9.39±0.4	7.16±1.4	22.73±2.4
PWC3	23.42±4.1	31.69±4.6	9.39±0.4	7.24±1.4	22.73±2.4
PWC4	22.51±4.2	31.57±4.4	9.31±0.4	7.68±1.5	22.34±2.4
PWC5	25.31±4.3	31.88±4.9	9.48±0.4	7.30±1.5	23.04±2.2
PWC6	23.04±4.3	31.62±4.5	9.82±0.4	8.04±1.4	22.79±2.3

The major outcome of Fig. 4 is that the results are quite regular, with none of the proposed reconstruction schemes performing significantly better than the others. This means that although the methods differ in behavior at a local level, they perform similarly globally, and thus there is no reason to give preference to any of them.

4 Improvement of the PWC Decomposition Scheme

A closer analysis of the PWC decomposition scheme reveals an important problem, which is related to the nonsense introduced by the values of $\hat{p}_{ij}$ when the item under consideration belongs neither to class ω_i nor to class ω_j. Indeed, by (1), p_{ij} assumes that x is in class ω_i or in class ω_j, but for a given item x, the estimation of the p_i's takes into account the outputs of all the pairwise classifiers, either significant or not.

For example, consider again the 3-class problem (5) in Section 3. If x belongs to class ω_1, p_{23} is absolutely irrelevant because the respective classifier has not been trained with data from class ω_1. Consequently, using it to find $\hat{p}$ is very likely to deteriorate the result of the calculation. If x does not belong to class ω_1, the high coefficient $p_{23} = 0.9$ is a strong indicator that x belongs to class ω_2, which will be selected by method PWC2. The problem is that the actual class of the item is obviously unknown a priori (this is precisely what we aim at determining) and thus the meaningful classifiers cannot be selected.

4.1 Correcting Classifiers

A procedure to overcome the referred problem is proposed here, which consists of, for each pairwise classifier separating class i from class j and with output $\hat{p}_{ij}$, training an additional classifier separating classes i and j from all the other classes, producing output $\hat{q}_{ij}$. The decomposition matrix notation is used in Fig. 5 to illustrate the case of four classes. The $\hat{q}_{ij}$'s provide an estimate that item x belongs to class i or class j, and it can be included in (3), which becomes:

$$\hat{p}_i = \frac{2}{K(K-1)} \sum_{j \neq i} \hat{p}_{ij} \cdot \hat{q}_{ij} \ .$$

The use of the correcting classifiers should cause the irrelevant $\hat{p}_{ij}$'s to loose significance and allow the quality of the estimation of the $\hat{p}_i$'s to be improved. This scheme is labeled PWC-CC.

In the correcting scheme proposed, each value $\hat{q}_{ij}$ is in fact an estimate of $p_i + p_j$, which suggests a different approach for its calculation. In the OPC scheme referred in Sect. 1, the classifier of each subproblem provides directly an estimate $\hat{p}_i$. So, OPC can be used to perform the PWC correction task, by using the provided values of $\hat{p}_i$, that will be referred to as q_i, for all $i = 1,...,K$, to find the $\hat{q}_{ij}$'s. The great advantage of this combination is that the total number of classifiers is $\frac{1}{2}K(K+1)$, which is lower than $K(K-1)$ in PWC-CC, when $K > 3$. The label for the combination with OPC as correcting scheme is PWC-OPC.

Experiments were made to compare the performance of the corrected schemes with the standard ones. The same algorithm (C4.5), the same databases, and the

$$
\begin{pmatrix}
+1 & -1 & 0 & 0 \\
+1 & 0 & -1 & 0 \\
+1 & 0 & 0 & -1 \\
0 & +1 & -1 & 0 \\
0 & +1 & 0 & -1 \\
0 & 0 & +1 & -1
\end{pmatrix}
\qquad
\begin{pmatrix}
+1 & +1 & -1 & -1 \\
+1 & -1 & +1 & -1 \\
+1 & -1 & -1 & +1 \\
-1 & +1 & +1 & -1 \\
-1 & +1 & -1 & +1 \\
-1 & -1 & +1 & +1
\end{pmatrix}
$$

$\qquad\quad$ (a) Regular PWC matrix $\qquad\qquad$ (b) Additional classifiers

Fig. 5. Decomposition matrices for the PWC-CC corrected scheme. (a) contains the standard PWC subproblems; the matrix in (b) corresponds to the correcting classifiers.

same statistical test used in the experiments reported in Fig. 4 were used here. The standard PWC reconstruction scheme used is PWC2. Figure 6 contains the results; the performance obtained by C4.5 applied regularly as a multiclass algorithm is included for comparison.

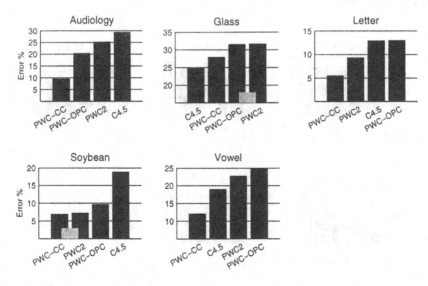

Fig. 6. Comparison between standard and corrected PWC. Numerical values are presented in Table 2. Bars connected by the same light-coloured horizontal strip represent values that do not differ significantly (0.95).

Two important conclusions may be drawn from the experiments: 1) The correcting classifiers in PWC-CC introduce a significant correcting effect and improve the performance of PWC2 remarkably. 2) The performance of the PWC-

168

OPC combination is worse than that of PWC-CC. For most of the databases, it even performs worse than PWC2.

4.2 Analysis of the Correcting Schemes Proposed

In order to investigate the cause of such a substantial difference between the performances of PWC-CC and PWC-OPC, experiments were made to compare the correcting component of each of the two combinations. Indeed, the set of additional classifiers used in PWC-CC can be used as a decomposition scheme by itself, as depicted in Fig. 5 (b), since it respects the constraint defined in Sect. 2. Its label is CC, by derivation. Given that the output of each classifier f_l is in $[0,1]$ and that the decomposition matrix D is defined as in Fig. 5 (b) with values in $\{-1,+1\}$, the reconstruction in CC is made by:

$$\arg\max_k \sum_l (2f_l - 1)D_{lk} .$$

OPC is, as known, a decomposition scheme also. Figure 7 contains the results of the comparison; the performance of PWC2, PWC-CC, and C4.5 multiclass are included for reference. The same procedure was followed as in the experiments described previously.

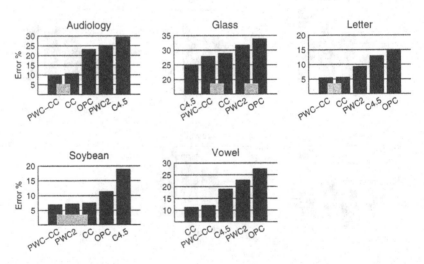

Fig. 7. Comparison between the CC and the OPC correcting schemes when used as decomposition schemes. Numerical values are presented in Table 2. Bars connected by the same light-coloured horizontal strip represent values that do not differ significantly (0.95).

From Fig. 7, it arises that the scheme CC has by itself a level of accuracy comparable to the combination PWC-CC, while OPC has a very poor performance. A logical explanation for this difference between the two schemes is their

Table 2. Comparison between the various decomposition schemes discussed in this paper. The values represent the average percentage of misclassification on the test set (and respective standard deviations).

Method	audiology	glass	letter	soybean	vowel
C4.5	29.35±1.9	24.72±1.6	12.90±0.2	18.84±0.8	18.93±0.8
PWC2	25.11±4.1	31.69±4.8	9.31±0.4	7.15±1.4	22.68±2.4
PWC-CC	9.59±3.1	27.89±4.8	5.49±0.3	6.85±1.4	12.00±1.9
PWC-OPC	20.26±4.1	31.55±5.3	12.97±0.4	9.62±1.9	24.83±2.4
CC	10.62±2.6	28.87±4.4	5.54±0.3	7.40±1.4	11.24±1.9
OPC	23.06±3.5	33.80±5.5	15.04±0.4	11.26±2.0	27.49±2.4

class separability. The class separability Δ of a decomposition scheme is defined as the minimal distance $d_{\rm cl}$ between every pair of columns (classes) in its decomposition matrix, and it has a major influence on the error recovering capability of the scheme. The distance measure $d_{\rm cl}$ between classes is defined as:

$$d_{\rm cl}(i, j) = |\{l \; : \; D_{li} \cdot D_{lj} = -1\}|.$$

For CC, $\Delta = 2(K-2)$, while $\Delta = 1$ in OPC. Considering that the reconstruction method adopted in OPC is the selection of the class associated with the classifier with the highest output, then, a single defective answer of any of the classifiers is likely to produce a misclassification. The reconstruction in CC allows, on the contrary, to recover from errors in the classifiers. In general, the error correcting capability of a decomposition scheme, when using a rough reconstruction, is at least

$$\left\lfloor \frac{\Delta - 1}{2} \right\rfloor .$$

As $\Delta = 2(K-2)$, CC allows the correction of at least $K-3$ errors.

The reasoning exposed above is not sufficient to explain the better performance of PWC-CC against PWC-OPC, because the correcting classifiers are not used directly in the reconstruction as normal classifiers, and thus they do not raise the class separability. The required explanation is, however, closely related to the one used to justify the difference between the correcting schemes alone and it also has to do with error-recovering capability. When OPC is used as correcting scheme, each output q_i will be used in the estimation of $K-1$ of the $\frac{1}{2} K(K-1)$ values of $\hat{q}_{ij}$. So, when one of the correcting classifiers makes a mistake, it will be propagated along part of the correcting scheme and subvert the global combination. In CC, each $\hat{q}_{ij}$ value is calculated by a single, different correcting classifier, which makes the global combination more tolerable to errors from the classifiers and thus more robust.

It can be concluded from Fig. 7 that the CC scheme may be preferred to standard PWC, with the disadvantage of having to train each classifier with all the data. This has the virtue, however, of eliminating the problem of the incompetent classifiers. Another interesting result is that CC is able to attain by itself the same level of performance as the combination PWC-CC in which it takes part. This result is in accordance with the theory behind the ECOC method, where the redundancy associated with a good class separation allows the reconstruction to be more robust, due to its error-correcting ability.

5 Conclusions

Decomposition by pairwise coupling is one of the existing techniques allowing a classification problem with several classes to be solved by a set of binary classifiers. It has been so far used in different applications, despite the fact that it suffers from the problem of using irrelevant information. That problem has been addressed here, and the proposed correcting procedure has been shown to be able to avoid the use of such information and to improve the performance of the decomposition scheme. Although that improvement is achieved at the cost of having twice as many subproblems as in standard PWC, with the additional fact that in the case of the correcting classifiers the whole training data is used to train each of them, it is also true that this task can be easily distributed, where in an ultimate solution all the classifiers can be trained and used in parallel.

As a side result, CC has been found to be a good decomposition scheme by itself. It is not affected by the problem of the incompetent classifiers and it can be favorably used as a replacement to standard PWC. The disadvantage is that all the data is used for the training of each classifier, which is negative from a point of view of training time.

Finally, it has been shown that the technique of decomposing by one-per-class has poor accuracy due to its high sensitivity to classifier performance.

References

1. E. Boros, P. L. Hammer, Toshihide Ibaraki, A. Kogan, E. Mayoraz, and I. Muchnik. An implementation of logical analysis of data. RRR 22-96, RUTCOR–Rutgers University's Center For Operations Research, http://rutcor.rutgers.edu:80/~rrr/, Submitted, July 1996.
2. L. Breiman, J. Olshen, and C. Stone. *Classification and Regression Trees.* Wadsworth International Group, 1984.
3. Pierre J. Castellano, Stefan Slomka, and Sridha Sridharan. Telephone based speaker recognition using multiplt binary classifier and Gaussian mixture models. In *ICASSP*, volume 2, pages 1075–1078. IEEE Computer Society Press, 1997.
4. Yves Crama, Peter L. Hammer, and Toshihide Ibaraki. Cause-effect relationships and partially defined boolean functions. *Annals of Operations Research*, 16:299–326, 1988.
5. Thomas G. Dietterich and Ghulum Bakiri. Solving multiclass learning problems via error-correcting output codes. *Journal of Artificial Intelligence Research*, 2:263–286, 1995.
6. Thomas G. Dietterich. Statistical tests for comparing supervised classification learning algorithms. OR 97331, Department of Computer Science, Oregon State University,, 1996.

7. T. G. Dietterich and G. Bakiri. Error-correcting output codes : A general method for improving multiclass inductive learning programs. In *Proceedings of AAAI-91*, pages 572–577. AAAI Press / MIT Press, 1991.

8. R. O. Duda and P. E. Hart. *Pattern Classification and Scene Analysis.* John Wiley & Sons, New York, 1973.

9. Trevor Hastie and Robert Tibshirani. Classification by pairwise coupling. Technical report, Stanford University and University of Toronto, 1996. ftp://utstat.toronto.edu/pub/tibs/coupling.ps, to appear in the Proceedings of NIPS*97.

10. E. B. Kong and T. G. Dietterich. Error-correcting output coding corrects bias and variance. In *The XII International Conference on Machine Learning*, pages 313–321, San Francisco, CA, 1995. Morgan Kaufmann.

11. Eddy Mayoraz and Miguel Moreira. On the decomposition of polychotomies into dichotomies. In Douglas H. Fisher, editor, *The Fourteenth International Conference on Machine Learning*, pages 219–226, 1997.

12. C.J. Merz and P.M. Murphy. UCI repository of machine learning databases. Irvine, CA: University of California, Department of Information and Computer Sciences, http://www.ics.uci.edu/~mlearn/MLRepository.html, 1996.

13. David Price, Stefan Knerr, Leon Personnaz, and Gerard Dreyfus. Pairwise neural network classifiers with probabilistic outputs. In G. Tesauro, D. Touretzky, and T. Leen, editors, *Advances in Neural Information Processing Systems 7 (NIPS*94)*, volume 7, pages 1109–1116. The MIT Press, 1995.

14. J. R. Quinlan. Induction of decision trees. *Machine Learning*, 1:81–106, 1986.

15. J. R. Quinlan. *C4.5 Programs for Machine Learning.* Morgan Kaufmann, 1993.

16. F. Rosenblatt. The perceptron: a probabilistic model for information storage and organization in the brain. *Psychological Review*, 63:386–408, 1958.

17. Laszlo Rudasi and Stephen A. Zahorian. Text-independent talker indentification with neural networks. In *ICASSP*, volume 1, pages 389–392, 1991.

18. Robert E. Shapire. Using output codes to boost multiclass learning problems. In Douglas H. Fisher, editor, *The Fourteenth International Conference on Machine Learning*, pages 313–321, 1997.

19. P. Werbos. *Beyond Regression: New Tools for Prediction and Analysis in the Behavioral Sciences.* PhD thesis, Harvard University, 1974.

20. Stephen A. Zahorian, Peter Silsbee, and Xihong Wang. Phone classification with segmental features and a binary-pair partitioned neural network classifier. In *ICASSP*, volume 2, pages 1011–1014. IEEE Computer Society Press, 1997.

Experiments on Solving Multiclass Learning Problems by n^2-classifier

Jacek Jelonek and Jerzy Stefanowski

Institute of Computing Science, Poznan University of Technology,
Piotrowo 3A, 60-965 Poznan, Poland
jacek.jelonek@cs.put.poznan.pl
jerzy.stefanowski@cs.put.poznan.pl

Abstract. The paper presents an experimental study of solving multiclass learning problems by a method called n^2-classifier. This approach is based on training $(n^2 - n)/2$ binary classifiers - one for each pair of classes. Final decision is obtained by a weighted majority voting rule. The aim of the computational experiment is to examine the influence of the choice of a learning algorithm on a classification performance of the n^2-classifier. Three different algorithms are considered: decision trees, neural networks and instance based learning algorithm.

1 Introduction

In this paper, we focus our attention on using multiple classifiers to solve *multiclass learning problems*. The multiclass learning problem involves finding a classification system that maps descriptions of training examples into a discrete set of n decision classes ($n > 2$). Although the standard way to solve multiclass learning problems includes the direct use of the multiclass learning algorithm such as, e.g. algorithm for inducing decision trees, neural network, or instance-based algorithm, there exist more specialized methods dedicated to this problem. As it is discussed in literature such approaches, e.g., one-per-class method, distributed output codes classification schemes, error-correcting techniques (ECOC) can outperform the direct use of the single multiclass learning algorithms (see, e.g. [3, 4, 8, 10]).

We consider another model which we called the n^2-classifier. It is inspired by the concept of multiple classification models [3]. The n^2-classifier is composed of $(n^2 - n)/2$ base binary classifiers. Each base classifier is specialized to discriminate respective pair of decision classes. A new example is classified by applying its description to all base classifiers. Then, their predictions are aggregated to a final classification decision using a weighted majority voting rule.

This approach is quite similar to the concept of *pairwise coupling* classification which was independently introduced in [5, 6]. Our n^2-classifier approach differs, however, from the above concept by using another combination rule. It takes into account the information about a class that is indicated by majority of base classifiers. Additionally, the voting scheme is adjusted by the credibility of the base classifiers, which are calculated during learning phase of classification.

As it has been indicated in [5, 6, 7] such integration of binary classifiers performs usually better than the respective, single multiclass classification model. One of the important aspects of constructing the homogenous n^2-classifier is the choice of learning algorithms to be used by base classifiers. We think that the expected improvement of classification accuracy may depend on both the particular problem and used proper base classifier.

Therefore, the main research aim of the following study is to perform an evaluation of the homogeneous n^2-classifier constructed by various base classifiers. Several known learning algorithms may be employed. However, we think that algorithms with inherent capability of reducing the influence of irrelevant features could be more appropriate in this approach than algorithms in which all features are treated as equally important. According to this hypothesis we decided to compare usefulness of three different learning algorithms, i.e. decision trees, neural networks and instance based learning.

2 The n^2-classifier

The n^2-classifier belong to the group of multiple classification models adopted to solve multiclass learning problems. The main principle of the n^2-classifier is the discrimination of each pair of the classes: $(i,j); i,j \in [1..n] i \neq j$, by an independent binary classifier C_{ij}. The classifier C_{ij} produces a binary classification indicating whether a new example $\mathbf{x}$ belongs to class i or to class j. Let $C_{ij}(\mathbf{x})$ denotes the classification of an example $\mathbf{x}$ by the base classifier C_{ij}. We assume that $C_{ij}(\mathbf{x}) = 1$ means that example $\mathbf{x}$ is classified by C_{ij} to class i, otherwise $(C_{ij}(\mathbf{x})= 0)$ $\mathbf{x}$ is classified to class j. Based on definition: $C_{ij}(\mathbf{x}) = 1 - C_{ji}(\mathbf{x})$.

For a new example $\mathbf{x}$, a final classification is obtained by an aggregation of the base classifiers predictions - $C_{ij}(\mathbf{x})$. The simplest aggregation is based on finding a class that wins the most pairwise comparisons. The classification performance of base classifiers is usually diverse because they are trained on different pairs of classes. So, it is necessary to estimate their credibility. In this study we assume that with each classifier C_{ij} we associate a credibility coefficient P_{ij} defined in following way:

$$P_{ij} = \frac{v_i}{v_i + e_j}$$

where e_j is a number of misclassified examples from class j, and v_i is a number of correctly classified examples from class i. The computation of the credibility coefficients is performed during the learning phase of constructing the n^2-classifier (i.e. done on the training examples). Final classification decision is determined by a weighted majority voting rule, which indicates to choose such a decision class i for which the following formula returns the maximum value:

$$\sum_{j=1,i\neq j}^{n} P_{ij} \cdot C_{ij}(\mathbf{x})$$

The introduced definition of the n^2-classifier is general and therefore any base learning algorithm can be employed in this framework.

3 Computational experiments

We performed learning decision trees using our own implementation based on a Quinlan's ID3 algorithm. This implementation contains some of the modifications introduced in the Assistant system [2], i.e. binarization and prepruning of decision trees. Artificial neural networks were implemented as typical feed forward multi-layer networks. The instance based learning algorithm is a typical approach based on k nearest neighbor principle [1]. We implemented a non-incremental version of IBL1, where all training examples are stored.

Table 1. Data sets used in the experiments

No.	Data set	Number of examples	Number of classes	Number of attributes
1.	Automobile	159*	6	25
2.	Cooc	700	14	22
3.	Ecoli	336	8	7
4.	Glass	214	6	9
5.	Hist	700	14	17
6.	Meta-data	528	5*	20
7.	Primary Tumor	339	21	17
8.	Soybean-large	542*	14*	35
9.	Vowel	990	11	10
10.	Yeast	1484	10	8

All computation experiments have been performed on the typical benchmark data sets. Some characteristics of the employed multiclass data sets are summarized in Table 1. The most of them are coming from the Machine Learning Repository at the University of California at Irvine [9]. The Cooc and Hist data sets come from our previous experiments and concern the recognition of tumors of the central nervous system on the basis of features extracted from microscopic images. Some of the studied data sets have been slightly modified - what is indicated in Table 1 by asterisks. First modifications concern the choice of decision attributes for two problems, i.e. for Automobile data set we have used the first ("symboling") attributes, and the Meta-data set is characterized by continuos decision attribute which has been discretized using thresholds: 6, 13, 20 and 50, thus giving five classes. Then, for Automobil and Soybean-large data sets we removed examples or attributes containing too many missing values. In the case of the Meta-data and the Primary Tumor, missing values have been replaced by the most frequent values. The classification accuracy was estimated by stratified version of 10-fold cross-validation technique, i.e. the training examples were partitioned into 10 equal-sized blocks with similar class distributions as in the original set.

Table 2. Performance of n^2-classifier based on decision tree (n^2_{DT}) and single decision tree (DT)

No.	Name of data set	Accuracy of DT (%)	Accuracy of n^2_{DT} (%)	Improvement n^2 vs DT (%)
1.	Automobile	85.5 ± 1.9	87.0 ± 1.9	1.5* ± 1.8
2.	Cooc	54.0 ± 2.0	59.0 ± 1.7	5.0 ± 1.0
3.	Ecoli	79.7 ± 0.8	81.0 ± 1.7	1.3 ± 0.7
4.	Glass	70.7 ± 2.1	74.0 ± 1.1	3.3 ± 1.8
5.	Hist	71.3 ± 2.3	73.0 ± 1.8	1.7 ± 1.7
6.	Meta-data	47.2 ± 1.4	49.8 ± 1.4	2.6 ± 1.3
7.	Primary Tumor	40.2 ± 1.5	45.1 ± 1.2	4.9 ± 1.5
8.	Soybean-large	91.9 ± 0.7	92.4 ± 0.5	0.5* ± 0.7
9.	Vowel	81.1 ± 1.1	83.7 ± 0.5	2.6 ± 0.7
10.	Yeast	49.1 ± 2.1	52.8 ± 1.8	3.7 ± 2.2

Table 3. Performance of n^2-classifier based on neural network (n^2_{ANN}) and single artificial neural network (ANN)

No.	Name of data set	Accuracy of ANN (%)	Accuracy of n^2_{ANN} (%)	Improvement n^2 vs ANN (%)
1.	Automobile	52.6 ± 2.0	58.1 ± 2.3	5.5 ± 1.1
2.	Cooc	56.0 ± 1.9	65.3 ± 0.7	9.3 ± 1.4
3.	Ecoli	81.7 ± 1.7	83.0 ± 1.6	1.3* ± 2.0
4.	Glass	62.7 ± 2.0	62.8 ± 0.8	0.1* ± 1.6
5.	Hist	65.7 ± 3.0	83.3 ± 1.4	17.6 ± 2.0
6.	Meta-data	50.5 ± 1.6	47.2 ± 1.5	-3.3 ± 1.2
7.	Primary Tumor	38.2 ± 1.5	43.4 ± 1.2	5.2 ± 1.5
8.	Soybean-large	90.1 ± 0.8	92.9 ± 0.7	2.8 ± 0.7
9.	Vowel	59.7 ± 2.4	86.1 ± 1.0	26.4 ± 2.3
10.	Yeast	53.1 ± 1.4	59.0 ± 0.9	5.9 ± 1.0

Table 4. Performance of n^2-classifier based on IBL algorithm (n^2_{IBL}) and single instance based learning algorithm (IBL)

No.	Name of data set	Accuracy of IBL (%)	Accuracy of n^2_{IBL} (%)	Improvement n^2 vs IBL (%)
1.	Automobile	77.7 ± 0.9	76.7 ± 1.0	-1.0 ± 0.2
2.	Cooc	68.4 ± 0.6	68.3 ± 0.6	-0.1 ± 0.1
3.	Ecoli	81.3 ± 0.5	81.3 ± 0.4	0.0* ± 0.2
4.	Glass	68.8 ± 0.8	68.5 ± 1.0	-0.3* ± 0.5
5.	Hist	89.3 ± 0.5	89.3 ± 0.5	0.0 N/A
6.	Meta-data	40.6 ± 1.6	42.1 ± 1.6	1.5 ± 0.6
7.	Primary Tumor	33.4 ± 1.2	36.2 ± 1.5	2.8 ± 1.2
8.	Soybean-large	89.9 ± 0.4	89.9 ± 0.4	0.0 N/A
9.	Vowel	98.9 ± 0.2	98.9 ± 0.2	0.0 N/A
10.	Yeast	52.8 ± 0.7	53.3 ± 0.7	0.5 ± 0.2

The validation technique was repeated 10 times for each data set. For each average accuracy we calculated the standard deviation. The improvement of n^2-classifier is expressed as the difference of average accuracy of the appropriate classifiers with a confidence interval. It was calculated based on a t-test for paired differences of means, with confidence level 0.95. An asterisk indicates that the difference of the accuracy is not statistically significant.

First, we evaluated the classification performance of the n^2-classifier based on decision trees. We also compared it to the single multiclass decision tree (DT). All decision tree classifiers were trained in a unpruned manner. The results of the experiment are presented in Table 2.

Then, we tested the performance of the n^2-classifier employing artificial neural networks. We systematically checked various topologies of networks depending on the particular data, e.g. for data sets with smaller number of input features (ecoli, glass, vowel, yeast) we tested the following number of neurons in input and hidden layers: 8, 10, 12, 14. Moreover with each combination of these topologies we tested various number of epoch: 50, 100, 150, 250. It means that for each learning problem we systematically looked through 64 combinations to find the best learning parameters. The results of the experiments with n^2-classifier and single classification model (ANN) for neural networks are presented in Table 3.

As the third classification model, we examined instance based learning algorithm. The computation results are presented in Table 4 in an identical way as in previous tables.

4 Conclusions

Let us summarize the results obtained for the particular learning algorithms. In a case of applying the decision tree as a base classifier we can observe that in 8 of all (10) problems the integration of decision trees into the n^2-classifier results in significantly better classification accuracy than the direct use of multiclass single decision tree. For two remaining problems the improvement is indistinguishable. The highest improvement is observed for Cooc data set - 5.0%. Similarly for neural networks the results show that the n^2-classifier performs generally better than single multiclass approach. The increase of classification accuracy is noticed in 9 of 10 data sets. Moreover, the improvements are relatively higher than for decision trees. Particularly high increase is observed for Vowel data - 26.3%. On contrary using IBL usually does not result in better classification ability of the n^2-classifier. The increase exists only for 3 data sets. For the remaining ones the results are similar, while for two data sets the classification ability slightly decreases for the n^2-classifier.

The obtained results showed clearly that the classification performance of the introduced n^2-classifier is generally better than the accuracy of single classifier approach for two considered base learning algorithms, i.e. decision trees and neural networks. Let us also notice that experimental results presented in [5, 6] also indicate that coupling strategy improves the classification accuracy although the relative performance of different approaches depends on the problem.

177

In our case study, we can summarize that the neural network seems to be the best model for the n^2-classifier. The decision trees are the second model according to the improvement of the classification accuracy. On the other hand the use of instance based learning algorithm is not so encouraging. Its the worst performance could result from the fact that IBL treats all features as equally important while two former approaches have inherent capability of reducing the irrelevant features what may help with defining proper subspace of features for efficient solving two-class problem.

There exist several on-going research problems that could be investigated in the future within the n^2-classifier framework. For instance, one can analyze the problem using the architecture of heterogeneous base classifiers or verify an idea of using n^2-classifier in constructive induction problems.

Acknowledgements

The computational experiments have been partially carried out at the Poznan Supercomputing and Networking Center affiliated to the Institute of Bioorganic Chemistry at the Polish Academy of Sciences. Research on this paper was supported by the grant KBN no. 8T11C 013 13 and CRIT 2 - Esprit Project no. 20288.

References

1. Aha D.W., Kibler E., Albert M.K.: Instance-based learning algorithms. Machine Learning, 6, (1991) 37-66.
2. Cestnik, B., Kononenko, I., Bratko, I.: Assistant 86, a knowledge elicitation tool for sophisticated users. In Bratko I., Lavrac N. (eds.) Progress in Machine Learning, Sigma Press, Wilmshow, (1987) 31-45.
3. Chan, P.K., Stolfo, S.J.: Experiments on multistrategy learning by meta- learning. In Proceedings of the Second International Conference on Information and Knowledge Management, (1993) 314-323.
4. Dietterich, T.G., Bakiri, G.: Solving muliclass learning problems via error- correcting output codes. Journal of Artificial Intelligence Research, 2, (1995) 263-286.
5. Friedman, J.H.: Another approach to polychotomous classification, Technical Report, Stanford University, 1996.
6. Hastie, T., Tibshirani R.: Classification by pairwise coupling, Proc. NIPS97.
7. Jelonek, J., Stefanowski J.: Using n^2-classifier to solve multiclass learning problems. Technical Report, Poznan University of Techonology 1997.
8. Mayoraz, E., Moreira, M.: On the decomposition of polychotomies into dichotomies, Proc. 14th Int. Conf. Machine Learning, July 1997, 219-226.
9. Murphy, P.M., Aha, D.W.: Repository of Machine Learning. University of California at Irvine. [URL: http://www.ics.uci.edu/ mlearn/MLRepositoru.html].
10. Schapire, R.E. Using output codes to boost multiclass learning problems. In Proceedings of the 14th International Machine Learning Conference (1997).

Combining Classifiers by Constructive Induction

João Gama

LIACC, FEP - University of Porto
Rua Campo Alegre, 823
4150 Porto, Portugal
Phone: (+351) 2 678830 Fax: (+351) 2 6003654
Email: jgama@ncc.up.pt
WWW: http://www.up.pt/liacc/ML

Abstract. Using multiple classifiers for increasing learning accuracy is an active research area. In this paper we present a new general method for merging classifiers. The basic idea of Cascade Generalization is to sequentially run the set of classifiers, at each step performing an extension of the original data set by adding new attributes. The new attributes are derived from the probability class distribution given by a base classifier. This constructive step extends the representational language for the high level classifiers, relaxing their bias. Cascade Generalization produces a single but structured model for the data that combines the *model class* representation of the base classifiers. We have performed an empirical evaluation of Cascade composition of three well known classifiers: *Naive Bayes, Linear Discriminant*, and *C4.5*. Composite models show an increase of performance, sometimes impressive, when compared with the corresponding single models, with significant statistical confidence levels.

1 Introduction

Given a learning task which algorithm should we use? Previous empirical studies have shown that there is no overall better algorithm. The ability of a chosen algorithm to induce a good generalization depends on how appropriate the class model underlying the algorithm is for the given task. An algorithm class model is the representation language it uses to express a generalization of the examples. The representation language for a standard decision tree is the DNF formalism that splits the instance space by axis-parallel hyper-planes, while the representation language for a linear discriminant function is a set of linear functions that split the instance space by oblique hyper-planes.

In statistics, Henery[12] refers Rescaling as a method used when some classes are over-predicted leading to a bias. Rescaling consists on applying the algorithms in sequence, the output of an algorithm being used as input to another algorithm. The aim would be to use the estimated probabilities $W_i = P(C_i|X)$ derived from a learning algorithm, as input to a second learning algorithm the purpose of which is to produce an unbiased estimate $Q(C_i|W)$ of the conditional probability for class C_i.

Since different learning algorithms employ different knowledge representations and search heuristics, different search spaces are explored and diverse results are obtained. The problem of finding the appropriate bias for a given task is an active research area. We can consider two main lines: on one side methods that select the most appropriate algorithm for the given task, for example Schaffer's selection by Cross-Validation, and on the other side, methods that combine predictions of different algorithms, for example Stacked Generalization [21].

The work that we present here follows the second research line. Instead of looking for methods that fit the data using a single representation language, we present a family of algorithms, under the generic name of Cascade Generalization, whose search space contains models that use different representation languages. Cascade generalization performs an iterative composition of classifiers. At each iteration a classifier is generated. The input space is extended by the addition of new attributes. Those new attributes are obtained in the form of a probability class distribution given, for each example, by the generated base classifier. The language of the final classifier is the language used by the high level generalizer. But it uses terms that are expressions from the language of low level classifiers. In this sense, Cascade Generalization generates a unified theory from the base theories. The experimental work shows that this methodology usually improves the accuracy with significant statistical levels.

The next section of the paper presents the framework of cascade generalization. In section 3, we present an illustrative example. In section 4 we review previous work in the area of multiple models. In section 5, we perform an empirical study using UCI data sets. The last section presents an analysis of the results and concludes the paper.

2 Cascade Generalization

Consider a learning set $D = (\mathbf{x_n}, Y_n)$ $n = 1, ..., N$, where $\mathbf{x_n} = [x_1, ..., x_m]$ is a multidimensional input vector, and Y_n is the output variable. Since the focus of this paper is on classification problems, Y_n takes values from a set of pre defined values, that is $Y_n \in Cl_1, ..., Cl_c$, where c is the number of classes. A classifier $\Im$ is a function that is applied to the training set in order to construct a predictor $\Im(\mathbf{x}, D)$ of y values. This is the traditional framework for classification tasks. Nevertheless, our framework requires that the predictor $\Im(\mathbf{x}, D)$ outputs a vector of conditional probability distribution $[p1, ..., pc]$, where p_i represents the probability that the example $\mathbf{x}$ belongs to class i, this is $P(y = Cl_i | \mathbf{x})$. The class that is assigned to the example $\mathbf{x}$, is that one that maximizes this last expression.

Most of the commonly used classifiers, such as *Naive Bayes* and *Discriminant*, classify each example in this way. Other classifiers, for example *C4.5*, have a different strategy for classifying an example, but it requires small changes in order to obtain a probability class distribution.

We define a constructive operator $\Phi(D', \Im(\mathbf{x}, D))$. This operator has two input parameters: a data set D' and a classifier $\Im(\mathbf{x}, D)$. The classifier $\Im$ generates a theory from the training data D. For each example $\mathbf{x} \in D'$, the generated theory outputs a probability class distribution. The operator Φ concatenates both the input vector $\mathbf{x}$ with the output probability class distribution. The output of $\Phi(D', \Im(\mathbf{x}, D))$ is a new data set D". The cardinality of D" is equal to the cardinality of D' (they have the same number of examples). Each example in $\mathbf{x} \in D''$ has an equivalent example in D', but augmented with c new attributes. The new attributes are the elements of the vector of probability class distribution obtained when applying classifier $\Im(\mathbf{x}, D)$ to the example $\mathbf{x}$.

Cascade generalization is a sequential composition of classifiers, that at each generalization level applies the Φ operator. Given a training set L, a test set T, and two classifiers $\Im_1$, and $\Im_2$, Cascade generalization proceeds as follows: Using classifier $\Im_1$, generates the $Level_1$ data:

$$Level_1 train = \Phi(L, \Im_1(\mathbf{x}, L))$$
$$Level_1 test = \Phi(T, \Im_1(\mathbf{x}, L))$$

Classifier $\Im_2$ learns on $Level_1$ training data and classifies the $Level_1$ test data:

$$\Im_2(\mathbf{x}, Level_1 train) \text{ for each } \mathbf{x} \in Level_1 test$$

Those steps perform the basic sequence of a cascade generalization of classifier $\Im_2$ after classifier $\Im_1$. We represent the basic sequence by the symbol ∇. The previous composition could be shortly represented by:

$$\Im_2 \nabla \Im_1 = \Im_2(\mathbf{x}, \Phi(L, \Im_1(\mathbf{x}', L))) \text{ for each } \mathbf{x}' \in \Phi(T, \Im_1(\mathbf{x}'', L))$$

This is the simplest formulation of *Cascade Generalization*. Some possible extensions include the composition of n classifiers, and the parallel composition of classifiers.

A composition of n classifiers is represented by:

$$\Im_n \nabla \Im_{n-1} \nabla \Im_{n-2} ... \nabla \Im_1$$

In this case, Cascade Generalization generates n-1 levels of data. The high level theory, is that one given by the $\Im_n$ classifier.

A variant of cascade generalization, which include several algorithms in parallel, could be represented in this formalism:

$$\Im_{n+1} \nabla [\Im_1, ..., \Im_n] = \Im_{n+1}(\mathbf{x}, \Phi(L, [\Im_1(\mathbf{x}', L), ..., \Im_n(\mathbf{x}', L)]))$$
$$\text{for each } \mathbf{x} \in \Phi(T, [\Im_1(\mathbf{x}', L), ..., \Im_n(\mathbf{x}', L)])$$

The algorithms $\Im_1, ..., \Im_n$ run in parallel. The operator $\Phi(L, [\Im_1(\mathbf{x}', L), ..., \Im_n(\mathbf{x}', L)])$ returns a new data set L'. L' contains the same number of examples of L. Each example on L' contains $n * c$ new attributes, where c is the number of classes. Each algorithm in the set $[\Im_1, ..., \Im_n]$ contributes with c new attributes.

3   An Illustrative Example

In this example we will consider the UCI data set *Monks-2* [20]. The *Monk's problems* are an artificial robot domain, well known in the Machine Learning community. The robots are described by six different attributes and classified into one of two classes. We have chosen the *Monks-2 problem* because it is known that this is a difficult task for systems that learn decision trees in an attribute-value logic formalism. The decision rule for the problem is: **"The robot is O.K. if exactly two of the six attributes have their** *first* **value"**. This problem is similar to *parity* problems. It combines different attributes in a way which makes it complicated to describe in DNF or CNF using the given attributes only.

Using ten fold Cross Validation, the error rate of *C4.5* is 32.9%, and of *Naive Bayes* is 49.5%. The composite model C4.5 after *Naive Bayes*, *C4.5∇NaiveBayes*, operates as follows: the *Level₁* data was generated, using the *Naive Bayes* as the classifier. C4.5 was used for the *Level₁* data. The composition *C4.5∇NaiveBayes*, obtains an error rate of 17.8%, which is substantially lower than the error rates of both *C4.5* and *Naive Bayes*. None of the algorithms in isolation can capture the underlying structure of the data. In this case, Cascade was able to achieve a notable increase of performance. Figure 1 presents one of the trees generated by *C4.5∇NaiveBayes*.

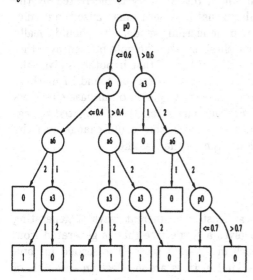

Fig. 1. Tree generated by C4.5 ∇Bayes

The tree contains a mixture of the original attributes (a3, a6) and the new attributes constructed by *Naive Bayes* (*p0*). At the root of the tree, appears the attribute *p0*. This attribute is the conditional probability $p(Class = False|\mathbf{x})$ given by the *Naive Bayes*. The classification rule used by *Naive Bayes* is: choose the $Class_i$ that maximizes $p(Class_i|\mathbf{x})$. The decision tree generated by C4.5 uses the constructed attributes given by Naive Bayes, but redefining different decision surfaces. Because this is a two class problem, the Bayes rule uses *p0* with threshold 0.5, while the decision tree chose the threshold at 0.6. Those decision nodes are a kind of function given by the Bayes strategy.

For example, the attribute *p0* can be seen as a function that computes $p(Class = False|\mathbf{x})$ using the Bayes theorem. The decision tree performs a sequence of tests based on the conditional probabilities given by the Bayes theorem. In a certain sense, this decision tree combines both representation languages: Bayes and Trees. The constructive step performed by *Cascade*, inserts new axis that incorporates new knowledge provided by the Naive Bayes. It is this new knowledge that allows the significant increase of performance verified with the Decision Tree, despite the limitations of Naive Bayes to fit complex spaces. It is this kind of synergies between classifiers that Cascade Generalization explores.

4 Related Work

We can analyze previous work on the area of multiple models through two dimensions. One dimension is related to the different methods used for combining classifications. The other dimension is related to the methods used for generating different models.

4.1 Combining Classifications

Combining classifications usually occurs at classification time. We can consider two main lines of research. One group includes methods where all base classifiers are consulted in order to classify a query example, the other, methods that characterize the area of expertise of the base classifiers and for a query point only ask the opinion of the experts. Voting is the most common method used to combine classifiers. As pointed in Ali[1], this strategy is motivated by the Bayesian learning theory which stipulates that in order to maximize the predictive accuracy, instead of using just a single learning model, one should ideally use all hypotheses (models) in the hypothesis space. The vote of each hypothesis should be weighted by the posterior probability of that hypothesis given the training data. Several variants of the voting method can be found in machine learning literature: from uniform voting where the opinion of all base classifiers contributes to the final classification with the same strength, to weighted voting, where each base classifier has a weight associated, that could change over the time, and strengthens the classification given by the classifier.

4.2 Generating Different Models

Buntine's Ph.D. thesis [5], refers to at least two different ways of generating multiple classifiers. The first one, involves a single tree that is generated from the training set and then pruned back in different ways. The second method is referred to as Option Trees. These kind of trees are in effect an ensemble of trees. Each decision node contains not only a univariate test, but also stores information about other promising tests. When using an Option Tree as a classifier the different options are consulted and the final classification is given by voting. He shows that, if the goal is to obtain an increase of performance, the second method out performs the first, basically, due to the fact that it produces different syntactic models. Breiman[2] proposes Bagging, that produces replications of the training set by sampling with replacement. Each replication of the training set has the same size as the original data, but some examples don't appear in it, while others may appear more than once. From each replication of the training set a classifier is generated. All classifiers are used in order to classify each example on the test set, usually using a uniform vote scheme.

The Boosting algorithm from Freund and Schapire [9] maintains a weight for each example in the training set that reflects its importance. Adjusting the weights causes the learner to focus on different examples leading to different classifiers. Boosting is an iterative algorithm. At each iteration the weights are adjusted in order to reflect the performance of the corresponding classifier. The weight of the misclassified examples is increased. The final classifier aggregates the learned classifier at each iteration by weighted voting. The weight of each classifier is a function of its accuracy.

Wolpert [21] proposes Stacked Generalization, a technique that uses learning in two levels. A learning algorithm is used to determine how the outputs of the base classifiers should be combined. The original data set constitutes the level zero data. All the base classifiers run at this level. The level one data are the outputs of the base classifiers. Another learning process occurs using as input the level one data and as output the final classification. This is a more sophisticated technique of cross validation that could reduce the error due to the bias.

Brodley[4] presents MCS, a hybrid algorithm that combines in a single tree, nodes that are univariate tests, multivariate tests generated by linear machines, and instance based learners. At each node MCS uses a set of If-Then rules in order to perform a hill-climbing search for the best hypothesis space and search bias for the given partition of the dataset. The set of rules incorporates knowledge from expert domains. Gama[10, 11] presents *Ltree*, also a hybrid algorithm that combines a decision tree with a linear discriminant by means of constructive induction.

Chan and Stolfo[6] presents two schemes for classifier combination: *arbiter* and *combiner*. Both schemes are based on meta learning, where a meta-classifier is generated from a training data, built based on the predictions of the base classifiers. An arbiter is also a classifier and is used in order to arbitrate among predictions generated by the different base classifiers. Later[7], extended this framework using *arbiters/combiners* in an hierarchical fashion generating *arbiter/combiner* binary trees.

4.3 Discussion

Reported results relative to Boosting or Bagging are quite impressive. Using 10 iterations (that is generating 10 classifiers) Quinlan[16] reports reductions of the error rate between 10% and 19%. Quinlan argues that these techniques are mainly applicable for unstable classifiers. Both techniques requires that the learning system should not be stable, in order to obtain different classifiers when there are small changes in the training set.

Under an analysis of bias-variance decomposition of the error of a classifier[13], the reduction of the error observed when using Boosting or Bagging is mainly due to the reduction in the *variance*. Ali[1] refers to that *"the number of training examples needed by Boosting increases as a function of the accuracy of the learned model. Boosting could not be used to learn many models on the modest training set sizes used in this paper.".*

Wolpert[21] says that successful implementations of Stacked Generalization is a *"black art"*, for classification tasks and the conditions under which Stacked works are still unknown. Recently, Ting[18] have shown that successful stacked generalization requires to use output class distributions rather than class predictions. In their experiments, only the MLR algorithm (a linear discriminant) was suitable for level-1 generalizer.

Tumer[19] presents analytical results that showed that the combined error rate depends on the error rate of individual classifiers and the correlation among them. This was confirmed in the empirical study presented in [1].

The main point of Cascade Generalization is its ability to merge different models. As such, we get a single model whose components are terms of the base model's language. The bias restriction imposed by using single model classes is relaxed in the directions given by the base classifiers. Cascade Generalization gives a single structured model for the data, and this is a strong advantage over the methods that combine classifiers by voting. Another advantage of Cascade Generalization is related to the use of probability class distributions. Usual learning algorithms produced by the Machine Learning community uses categories when classifying examples. Combining classifiers by means of categorical classes looses the strength of the classifier in its prediction. The use of probability class distributions allows us to explore that information.

5 Experiments

5.1 The Algorithms

Ali [1] and Tumer[19] among other authors, suggest as a method that allows us to reduce the correlation errors, the use of "radically different types of classifiers". This was the criterion that we have used in order to select the algorithms for the experimental work. We use three classifiers: a *Naive Bayes*, a *Linear Discriminant*, and a *Decision Tree*.

Naive Bayes The Bayes approach in order to classify a new example E, is the use of Bayes theorem in order to compute the probability of each class C_i, given the example. The chosen class is the one that maximizes: $p(C_i|E) = p(C_i)p(E|C_i)/p(E)$. If the attributes are independent, $p(E|Ci)$ can be decomposed into the product $p(v_1|C_i) * ... * p(v_k|C_i)$. Domingos [8] show that this procedure has a surprisingly good performance in a wide variety of domains, including many where there are clear dependencies between attributes. The required probabilities are computed from the training set. In the case of nominal attributes we use counts. Continuous attributes were discretized. The number of bins that we use is a function of the number of different values observed on the training set: $k = min(10; nr. different values)$. This heuristic was used in [8] and elsewhere with good overall results. Missing values were treated as another possible value for the attribute, both on the training and test data. *Naive*

185

Bayes uses all the attributes in order to classify a query point. Langley [14] refers that *Naive Bayes* relies on an important assumption: that the variability of the dataset can be summarized by a single probabilistic description, and that these is sufficient to distinguish between classes. From an analysis of *Bias-Variance*, this implies that *Naive Bayes* uses a reduced set of models to fit the data. The result is low variance, but if the data cannot be adequately represented by the set of models, we obtain a large bias.

Linear Discriminant A linear discriminant function is a linear composition of the attributes where the sum of the squared differences between class means is maximal relative to the internal class variance. It is assumed that the attribute vectors for examples of class C_i are independent and follow a certain probability distribution with probability density function f_i. A new point with attribute vector $\mathbf{x}$ is then assigned to that class for which the probability density function $f_i(\mathbf{x})$ is maximal. This means that the points for each class are distributed in a cluster centered at μ_i. The boundary separating two classes is a hyper-plane and it passes through the mid point of the two centers. If there are only two classes one hyper-plane is needed to separate the classes. In the general case of q classes, $q - 1$ hyper-planes are needed to separate the classes. By applying the linear discriminant procedure described below, we get $q_{node} - 1$ hyper-planes. The equation of each hyper-plane is given by[12]:

$$H_i = \alpha_i + \sum_j \beta_{ij} * x_j \text{ where } \alpha_i = -\tfrac{1}{2}\mu_i^T S^{-1} \mu_i \text{ and } \beta_i = S^{-1}\mu_i$$

We use a Singular Value Decomposition (SVD) in order to compute S^{-1}. SVD is numerically stable and is a tool for detecting sources of collinearity. This last aspect is used as a method for reducing the features used at each linear combination. *Discrim* uses all, or almost all, the attributes in order to classify a query point. Breiman,[3] refers that from an analysis of Bias-Variance, Linear Discriminant is a stable classifier although it can fit a small number of models. It achieves their stability by having a limited set of models to fit the data. The result is low variance, but if the data cannot be adequately represented by the set of models, then the result is a large bias.

Decision Tree We have used *C4.5* (release 8) [17]. This is a well known decision tree generator and widely used by the Machine Learning community. In order to obtain a probability class distribution, we need to modify C4.5. C4.5 stores a distribution of the examples that fall at each leaf. From this distribution and using m-estimates [15] we obtain a probability class distribution at each leaf. A *Decision tree* uses only a subset of the available attributes, in order to classify a query point. Breiman [3] among other researchers, note that Decision Trees are unstable classifiers. Small variations on the training set could cause large changes in the resulting predictors. These classifiers have high variance but they can fit any kind of data: the bias of a decision tree is low.

---
[1] In all the experiments reported m was set to 0.5.

5.2 The Datasets

We have chosen 17 data sets from the UCI repository. All of them are well known and previously used in other comparative studies. In order to evaluate the proposed methodology we performed a 10 fold Cross Validation (CV) on the chosen datasets. Datasets were permuted once before the CV procedure. All algorithms where used with the default settings. In each iteration of CV, all algorithms were trained on the same training partition of the data. Classifiers were also evaluated on the same test partition of the data. Comparisons between algorithms were performed using *t-paired tests* with significant level set at 95%.

Table 1 presents data sets characteristics and the error rate and standard deviation of each base classifier. Relative to each algorithm, + (-) sign in the first column means that the error rate of this algorithm is significantly better (worse) than C4.5. These results provide an evidence, once more, that no single algorithm is better overall.

Dataset	Class	Examples	Types		Bayes		Discrim	C4.5
Australian	2	690	7 N 6 Cont		13.8 ±3.5		14.1 ±6	15.3 ±6.3
Balance	3	625	4 Cont	-	28.8 ±6.3	+	13.3 ±4.4	22.3 ±5.3
Breast	2	699	9 Cont		2.4 ±1.9	+	4.1 ±6	6.1 ±6.1
Diabetes	2	768	8 Cont		25.7 ±5.5	+	22.7 ±5	24.8 ±6.6
German	2	1000	24 Cont		27.7 ±4.4	+	24.0 ±6.2	29.1 ±3.7
Glass	6	213	9 Cont	-	41.8 ±12	-	41.3 ±11	32.3 ±9.6
Heart	2	270	6 N 7 Cont	+	16.7 ±5		16.7 ±3.6	19.9 ±7.2
Ionosphere	2	351	33 Cont		9.1 ±6.3	-	13.4 ±5.4	9.1 ±5.8
Iris	3	150	4 Cont		6.0 ±4.9		2.0 ±3.2	4.7 ±4.5
Monks-1	2	432	6 Nom	-	25.0 ±3.9	-	33.3 ±11.3	2.3 ±4.4
Monks-2	2	432	6 Nom	-	49.6 ±9.0		34.0 ±5.9	32.9 ±5.9
Monks-3	2	432	6 Nom	-	2.8 ±2.4	-	22.5 ±8.7	0.0 ±0.0
Satimage	6	6435	36 Cont	-	18.8 ±1.5	-	16.1 ±1.5	13.9 ±1.3
Segment	7	2310	18 Cont	-	9.5 ±2.1	-	8.3 ±2.5	3.3 ±1.3
Vehicle	4	846	18 Cont	-	41.4 ±3.9	+	22.2 ±5.1	28.8 ±3.9
Waveform	3	2581	21 Cont	+	18.8 ±1.5	+	15.3 ±2	24.0 ±2.2
Wine	3	178	13 Cont		2.8 ±4		1.7 ±3.8	6.7 ±8.2
Average of Error rates					20.1		17.9	16.2

Table 1. Data Characteristics and Results of Base Classifiers

5.3 Cascade Generalization

We have run all the possible two level combinations of base classifiers. Table 2(a) presents the results of using C4.5 at the top level. Each column corresponds to a Cascade Generalization combination. For each combination, the significance of *t test* is presented comparing the composite model with the individual components, in the same order that they appear on the header.

The trend on these results is a clear improvement over the base classifiers. We never observe an error rate degradation of a composite model in relation to the individual components. Using C4.5 as the high level classifier the performance is improved with a significant statistical level of 95%, 22 times over one of the components, and it degraded 5 times. Using *Naive Bayes* at the top, there

Dataset			C4.5∇Bayes	C4.5∇C4.5			C4.5∇Disc	C4∇Dis∇Bay		Stacked Gen
Australian			14.3 ±3.1	15.2 ±6.2			14.8 ±6.1	13.6 ±6		14.3 ±5
Balance	+	+	6.1 ±2.8	22.1 ±5.2	+	+	5.4 ±2.0	6.6 ±2	+	12.5 ±5
Breast(W)			2.8 ±1.7	5.6 ±4.8	+		4.1 ±6.0	2.7 ±2		2.4 ±2
Diabetes			25.2 ±6.9	24.4 ±6.9			24.2 ±5.8	24.8 ±9		22.4 ±6
German	+	+	24.9 ±4.4	29.1 ±3.7			26.2 ±6.0	28.4 ±4	-	25.0 ±5
Glass			38.1 ±9.6	32.3 ±12.0			36.1 ±10.9	37.6 ±12		34.3 ±12
Heart	-		21.1 ±4.9	20.0 ±7.2			17.8 ±5.5	17.0 ±5		16.3 ±8
Iono	-		13.1 ±6.6	8.9 ±5.8	-		13.1 ±5.1	10.6 ±6		10.6 ±6
Iris			6.7 ±5.4	4.7 ±4.5			3.4 ±3.4	3.3 ±4		4.0 ±3
Monks-1		+	1.6 ±3.1	2.3 ±4.4		+	2.3 ±4.4	1.4 ±3		2.3 ±4
Monks-2	+	+	17.9 ±9.9	32.9 ±5.9			32.9 ±5.9	16.7 ±9	+	32.9 ±6
Monks-3		+	0.4 ±0.9	0.0 ±0.0		+	0.0 ±0.0	0.2 ±1	+	2.1 ±2
Satimage	+	+	13.0 ±1.4	13.7 ±1.3	+	+	12.4 ±1.5	13.0 ±1		13.5 ±1
Segment		+	4.0 ±0.8	3.2 ±1.4		+	3.4 ±1.5	3.0 ±1		3.4 ±1
Vehicle		+	27.4 ±5.9	28.2 ±4.3	-		28.2 ±4.3	22.1 ±3	+	29.2 ±4
Waveform	+		17.2 ±2.3	24.4 ±2.0	+		16.6 ±1.4	16.9 ±2		16.5 ±2
Wine			3.9 ±4.6	6.7 ±8.2			2.2 ±3.9	3.4 ±4		2.8 ±4
Mean			13.9	16.1			14.3	13.0		14.4

Table 2. (a) Results of Cascade Generalization. (b)Comparison with Stacked

are 21 cases against 9. Using *Discrim* at the top, there are 22 cases against 7. In same cases, there is a significant increase of performance when compared to all the components. For example, the composition $C4.5 \nabla Naive\ Bayes$ improves, with statistical significance, both components on 4 datasets, $C4.5 \nabla Discrim$ and *Naive Bayes* $\nabla Discrim$ on 2 datasets, and $Discrim \nabla C4.5$ on 1 dataset. The most promising combinations are $C4.5 \nabla Discrim$ and $C4.5 \nabla Naive\ Bayes$. The new attributes built by *Discrim* or *Naive Bayes* set relations between attributes, that are outside the scope of DNF algorithms like $C4.5$. Those new attributes systematically appears at the root of the composite models. A particular successful application of *Cascade* is on *Balance* dataset.

In another experiment, we have compared C4∇Discrim∇Bayes against *Stacked Generalization*, which was reimplemented following the method of Ting[18]. In this scheme *Discrim* is the $level_1$ algorithm. C4.5 and Bayes are the $level_0$ algorithms. The attributes of the $level_1$ data are the conditional probabilities $P(C_i|\mathbf{x})$, given by the $level_0$ classifiers. The $level_1$ data is built using a (internal) 5 fold stratified cross validation. On those datasets, C4∇Discrim∇Bayes performs significantly better on 4 datasets and worst on one. *Cascade* competes well with Stacked method, with the advantage that it doesn't use the *internal cross validation*.

5.4 How Far from the Best?

Error rates are not comparable between datasets. Although the *t paired tests* procedure is commonly used for determining whether two means are statistically different, this procedure only permits to compare two algorithms. We are interested in comparisons which involve several algorithms. As such, for each dataset we identify the classifier with lowest error rate. Call it E_{low}. Denote the error rate of $algorithm_i$ on the given dataset as E_{alg_i}. Now we compute the *Error margin* as

C4∇Dis	C4∇Bay	SG	C4∇C4	C4	Bay∇C4	Dis∇Bay	Disc	Bay∇Dis	Dis∇C4	Dis∇Dis	Bay∇Bay	Bayes
1.8	1.9	2.5	4.8	4.9	5.5	5.9	7.0	7.1	7.1	7.5	8.3	8.9

Table 3. Average of Distances to Best

the standard deviation of a Bernoulli distribution: $E_m = \sqrt{E_{low} * (1 - E_{low})/N}$ where N is the number of examples in the test set. For each algorithm in comparison, we compute the distance to the best algorithm in terms of E_m. That is, low value of $Distance_i$, means that the $algorithm_i$ has an error rate similar to the best algorithm, whilst high value means that the performance of $algorithm_i$ is far from that of the best algorithm. The goal of this analysis is to compare algorithm performance across datasets. E_m is a criterion that can give insights about the difficulty of the problem. Table 3 summarizes the averages of distances of all models.

6   Conclusions

This work presents a new methodology for classifier combination. The basic idea of Cascade Generalization consists on a reformulation of the input space by means of insertion of new attributes. The new attributes are obtained by applying a base classifier. The number of new attributes is equal to the number of classes, and for each example, they are computed as the conditional probability of the example belonging to $class_i$ given by the base classifier. The new attributes are terms, or functions, in the representational language of the base classifier. This constructive step acts as a way of extending the description language bias of the high level classifiers.

There are two main points that differentiate Cascade Generalization from other previous methods on multiple models. The first one is related with its ability in merging different models. We get a single model whose components are terms of the base model's language. The bias restrictions imposed by using single model classes are relaxed in the directions given by the base classifiers. This aspect is explored by combinations like C4.5∇*Discrim* or C4.5∇*Naive Bayes*. The new attributes built by *Discrim* or *Naive Bayes* set relations between attributes, that are outside the scope of DNF algorithms like *C4.5*. Those new attributes systematically appears at the root of the composite models.

Cascade Generalization gives a single structured model for the data, and in this way is more adapted to capture insights about problem structure. The second point is related to the use of probability class distributions. The use of probability class distributions allows us to exploit the information about the strength of the classifier. This is very useful information, especially when combining predictions of classifiers. We have shown that this methodology can improve the accuracy of the base classifiers, preserving the ability to provide a single and structured model for the data.

Acknowledgments: Gratitude is expressed to the support given by the FEDER and PRAXIS XXI projects and the Plurianual support attributed to LIACC. Also to P.Brazdil and the anonymous reviewers for useful comments.

References

1. Ali, K. and Pazzani, M. (1996) "Error reduction through Learning Multiple Descriptions", in *Machine Learning, Vol. 24, No. 1* Kluwer Academic Publishers
2. Breiman,L. (1996) "Bagging predictors", in *Machine Learning, 24* Kluwer Academic Publishers
3. Breiman,L. (1996) "Bias, Variance, and Arcing Classifiers", Technical Report 460, Statistics Department, University of California
4. Brodley, C. (1995) "Recursive Automatic Bias Selection for Classifier Construction", in *Machine Learning, 20*, 1995, Kluwer Academic Publishers
5. Buntine, W. (1990) "A theory of Learning Classification Rules", Phd Thesis, University of Sydney
6. Chan P. and Stolfo S., (1995) "A Comparative Evaluation of Voting and Meta-learning on Partitioned Data", in *Machine Learning Proc of 12th International Conference*, Ed. L.Saitta
7. Chan P. and Stolfo S. (1995) "Learning Arbiter and Combiner Trees from Partitioned Data for Scaling Machine Learning", KDD 95
8. Domingos P. and Pazzani M. (1996) "Beyond Independence: Conditions for the Optimality of the Simple Bayesian Classifier", in *Machine Learning Proc. of 12th International Conference*, Ed. L.Saitta
9. Freund, Y. and Schapire, R (1996) "Experiments with a new boosting algorithm", in *Machine Learning Proc of 13th International Conference*, Ed. L. Saitta
10. Gama, J, (1997) "Probabilistic Linear Tree", in *Machine Learning Proc. of the 14th International Conference* Ed. D.Fisher
11. Gama,J. (1997) "Oblique Linear Tree", in *Advances in Intelligent Data Analysis - Reasoning about Data'*, Ed. X.Liu, P.Cohen, M.Berthold, Springer Verlag LNCS
12. Henery R. (1997) "Combining Classification Procedures" in *Machine Learning and Statistics. The Interface.* Ed. Nakhaeizadeh, C. Taylor, John Wiley & Sons, Inc.
13. Kohavi, R and Wolpert, D. (1996) "Bias plus Variance Decomposition for zero-one loss function", in *Machine Learning Proc of 13th International Conference*, Ed. Lorenza Saitta
14. Langley P. (1993) "Induction of recursive Bayesian Classifiers", in *Machine Learning: ECML-93* Ed. P.Brazdil, LNAI n667, Springer Verlag
15. Mitchell T. (1997) *Machine Learning*, MacGraw-Hill Companies, Inc.
16. Quinlan R., (1996) "Bagging, Boosting and C4.5", *Procs. 13th American Association for Artificial Intelligence*, AAAI Press
17. Quinlan, R. (1993) *C4.5: Programs for Machine Learning*, Morgan Kaufmann Publishers, Inc.
18. Ting K.M. and Witten I.H. (1997) "Stacked Generalization: when does it work ?", in *Procs. International Joint Conference on Artificial Intelligence*
19. Tumer K. and Ghosh J. (1995) "Classifier combining: analytical results and implications", in *Proceedings of Workshop in Induction of Multiple Learning Models*
20. Thrun S., et all, (1991) *The Monk's problems: A performance Comparison of different Learning Algorithms*, CMU-CS-91-197
21. Wolpert D. (1992) "Stacked Generalization", *Neural Networks Vol.5*, Pergamon Press

Boosting Trees for Cost-Sensitive Classifications

Kai Ming Ting[1] and Zijian Zheng[2]

[1] Department of Computer Science, University of Waikato, Hamilton, New Zealand.
[2] School of Computing and Mathematics, Deakin University, Vic 3217, Australia.

Abstract. This paper explores two boosting techniques for cost-sensitive tree classifications in the situation where misclassification costs change very often. Ideally, one would like to have only one induction, and use the induced model for different misclassification costs. Thus, it demands robustness of the induced model against cost changes. Combining multiple trees gives robust predictions against this change. We demonstrate that the two boosting techniques are a good solution in different aspects under this situation.

1 Introduction

Most research on classifier learning has focused on minimum error classification. It aims to minimize the number of incorrect predictions or classifications made by classifiers. This kind of learning method ignores the differences between different types of incorrect prediction. It is very common in real world applications that different types of incorrect prediction cost differently. The cost of incorrect predictions is more important than the number of incorrect predictions in many real world domains such as in medical and financial areas. For example, in medical diagnosis, diagnosing someone as healthy when one has a life-threatening disease is usually considered to be more serious (thus higher cost) than another type of error—of diagnosing someone as ill when one is in fact healthy. Nevertheless, very little attention has been paid to cost-sensitive classification where the objective is to minimize the total cost of incorrect predictions or the number of high cost errors.

Moreover, in some cost-sensitive classification situations, misclassification costs may change very often. For example, in bank loan decision making, managers in different branches may assign different costs to the same type of incorrect decision. In addition, the costs may change from time to time even within the same branch. To the best knowledge of the authors, this situation has not been investigated. In this paper, we explore cost-sensitive classification techniques to handle this type of situation, and focus on decision tree learning in this study.

The most straightforward and simple approach to this problem is to alter the prediction selection process during classification, without modifying the classifier learning process. This can be done for a decision tree learning algorithm, such as C4.5 (Quinlan, 1993), in the following fashion. During the classification stage, an example to be classified is assigned the class with the minimum expected misclassification cost (Michie, Spiegelhalter, & Taylor, 1994) at the leaf to which the example is traced down, rather than the class with the maximum weight.

Because no modification to the tree induction process is required, the same tree can be re-used when the misclassification costs change. C4.5c is the variant of C4.5 modified in this manner and it is used as the base line of this research.

Intuitively, combining multiple models shall give more robust predictions than a single model under the situation where misclassification costs change very often. Boosting has been shown to be an effective method of combining multiple models in order to enhance the predictive accuracy of a single model (Quinlan, 1996; Schapire, Freund, Bartlett, & Lee, 1997). Thus, it is natural to think that boosting might also reduce the misclassification costs of C4.5c. In this paper, we explore two techniques of boosting C4.5c. The first technique is ordinary boosting combined with the minimum expected cost criterion. The second technique is a variant of ordinary boosting which utilizes the misclassification cost information during the induction of decision trees. We call the first method *Boosting*, and the second *Cost-Boosting*. We conduct empirical evaluation to assess the performance of Boosting and Cost-Boosting under the situation.

The next section describes the procedures used in Boosting and Cost-Boosting. Section 3 reports experiments with C4.5c, Boosting, and Cost-Boosting. We summarize our findings in the final section.

2   Boosting and Cost-Boosting

Here, Boosting is implemented by maintaining a weight for each training example (Quinlan, 1996) rather than drawing a succession of independent bootstrap samples from the original examples. Boosting induces multiple individual classifiers in sequential trials. At the end of each trial, the vector of weights is adjusted to reflect its importance for the next induction trial. This adjustment effectively increases the weights of misclassified examples. These weights cause the learner to concentrate on different instances in each trial and so lead to different classifiers. Finally, the individual trees are combined through voting to form a composite classifier. The Boosting procedure is shown as follows. Note that the weight adjustment formula in step (iii) below are from a new version of boosting (Schapire, Freund, Bartlett, & Lee, 1997).

Boosting procedure: Given a training set T containing N examples, $w_k(n)$ denotes the weight of the nth example at the kth trial, where $w_1(n) = 1/N$ for every n. In each trial $k = 1, \ldots, K$, the following steps are carried out.

(i) A decision tree T_k is constructed by using C4.5 from the training set under the weight distribution w_k.

(ii) T is classified using the decision tree T_k. Let $d(n) = 1$ if the nth example in T is classified incorrectly; $d(n) = 0$ otherwise. The error rate of this tree, ϵ_k, is defined as

$$\epsilon_k = \sum_n w_k(n)d(n). \tag{1}$$

If $\epsilon_k \geq 0.5$ or $\epsilon_k = 0$, then all $w_k(n)$ is set equal and perturbed with uniform noise and re-normalized, and carry on the process from step (i).

(iii) The weight vector $w_{(k+1)}$ for the next trial is created from w_k as follows:

$$w_{(k+1)}(n) = w_k(n) \frac{exp(-\alpha_k(-1)^{d(n)})}{z_k}, \tag{2}$$

where the normalizing term z_k and α_k are defined as

$$z_k = 2\sqrt{(1 - \epsilon_k)\epsilon_k}, \qquad \alpha_k = \tfrac{1}{2}ln((1 - \epsilon_k)/\epsilon_k). \tag{3}$$

After K trials, the decision trees $T_1, \ldots, T_K$ are combined to form a single composite classifier. Given an example, the final classification of the composite classifier relies on the votes of all the individual trees. The vote of the tree T_k is worth α_k units. Since we use the expected misclassification cost to select the predicted class, the voting is not simply summing up the vote of every individual tree. Instead, the following computation is performed.

Let $t_k(x)$ be the leaf of the tree T_k where the example x falls into, and $W_i(t_k(x))$ be the total weight of class i examples in $t_k(x)$. The expected misclassification cost for class j with respect to the example x and the composite classifier consisting of trees $T_1, \ldots, T_K$ is given by:

$$EC_j(x) \propto \sum_i^I \sum_k^K \alpha_k W_i(t_k(x))cost(i, j), \tag{4}$$

where $cost(i, j)$ is the misclassification cost of classifying a class i example as class j; and I is the total number of classes.

To classify a new example x, $EC_j(x)$ is computed for every class. The example x is assigned to class j with the smallest value for $EC_j(x)$. That is, $EC_j(x) < EC_{j'}(x)$ for all $j' \neq j$.

From the description above, it can be seen that Boosting only utilizes the misclassification cost information during classification through Equation (4). Its classifier induction process does not employ the cost information. This allows a single Boosting induction to be used for different misclassification costs.

One can modify the Boosting procedure so that the weights of misclassified examples are updated according to the costs associated with these misclassifications. Thus, each subsequent tree is cost-sensitive. Based on this idea, Boosting is modified to create a variant: **Cost-Boosting**. Cost-Boosting uses the same procedure as Boosting except the weight adjustment process in step (iii). We assume a unity condition $cost(i, j) \geq 1, \forall i \neq j$ (see details in the next section); and the weight adjustment is re-defined as follows.

$$w_{(k+1)}(n) = \frac{w'_{(k+1)}(n)}{\sum_n w'_{(k+1)}(n)}, \tag{5}$$

$$w'_{(k+1)}(n) = \begin{cases} cost(actual(n), predicted(n)), & \text{if } actual(n) \neq predicted(n); \\ Nw_k(n), & \text{otherwise.} \end{cases} \tag{6}$$

Because all trees (except the first one) are cost-sensitive, Cost-Boosting needs to perform induction every time the misclassification costs change.

During the classification stage, Cost-Boosting also uses Equation (4) for selecting the class with the minimum expected cost except that each individual tree in Cost-Boosting is worth 1 unit for voting, that is, $\alpha_k = 1$.

As Boosting and Cost-Boosting, the base line algorithm C4.5c also employs the same formulae for selecting the class, in which $K = 1$ and $\alpha_k = 1$.

Note that the first tree in both Boosting and Cost-Boosting is exactly the same as that produced by C4.5c.

3   Experiments

In this section, we empirically evaluate Boosting and Cost-Boosting by comparing with C4.5c. Twenty natural domains from the UCI machine learning repository (Merz & Murphy, 1997) are used in the experiments. This test suite covers a wide variety of different domains with respect to dataset size, the number of classes, the number of attributes, and types of attributes.

The misclassification cost information is provided in the form of a cost matrix of size $I \times I$, where I is the number of classes in a domain. The off-diagonal entries contain the costs of misclassifications, while the entries on the diagonal contain the cost of correct classifications which are equal to zero.

Since no datasets from real-world domains where misclassification costs often change are available to us, we simulate this type of situation by artificially generating cost matrices. A cost matrix for each domain is randomly generated for each experimental run. In each matrix, the costs in the off-diagonal entries are any randomly generated integer between 1 and 10. In two-class domains, one of the two off-diagonal entries must be 1 and the other more than 1. In multi-class domains, at least one of the entries is 1. The only reason using this *unity condition* is to allow us to measure the number of high cost errors.

One 10-fold cross-validation is carried out in each domain, except in the Waveform domain where 10 pairs of training set of size 300 and test set of size 5000 are randomly generated. In each fold, we conduct 10 runs on the same training and test sets using 10 randomly generated cost matrices to simulate the cost changing situation. In each run, the same cost matrix is employed in training and testing. All reported results are averaged over 100 runs.

We use two measures to evaluate the performance of the algorithms employed for cost-sensitive classification. The first measure is the *total cost of misclassifications* made by a classifier on a test set (i.e., $\sum_m cost(actual(m), predicted(m))$). The second measure is the *number of high cost errors*. It is the number of misclassifications associated with costs higher than 1 made by a classifier on a test set. Note that the lowest misclassification cost is 1 in a normalized cost matrix. A good cost-sensitive classifier should have low total misclassification cost, or small number of high cost errors, or both.

The parameter K controlling the number of classifiers generated in both Boosting and Cost-Boosting is set at 10 for the experiments. It is interesting to see the performance improvement that can be gained by a single order of magnitude increase in computation. All C4.5c parameters have their default values, and only pruned trees are used.

Table 1. Comparison of C4.5c, Boosting and Cost-Boosting

Datasets	C4.5c		Boosting vs C4.5c		Cost-Boosting vs C4.5c		Cost-Boosting vs Boosting	
	cost	#hce	cost ratio	#hce ratio	cost ratio	#hce ratio	cost ratio	#hce ratio
Echocardiogram	7.9	0.82	.82	.16	.81	.32	.99	2.00
Hepatitis	7.5	0.93	.71	.13	.68	.42	.96	3.25
Heart	19.6	2.67	.64	.13	.62	.31	.97	2.40
Horse	17.0	1.62	1.08	.04	.93	.74	.86	20.00
Credit	24.5	2.88	1.15	.26	.81	.59	.70	2.25
Breast-W	12.8	1.85	.66	.21	.51	.36	.78	1.76
Diabetes	39.0	3.75	.92	.22	.84	.43	.92	1.98
Hypothyroid	8.4	1.20	1.42	.47	.90	.78	.63	1.65
Euthyroid	21.2	3.00	1.26	.42	.89	.73	.70	1.74
Coding	1277.9	139.68	.70	.07	.67	.13	.95	1.91
Lymphography	14.9	2.52	.95	1.17	.89	1.10	.94	.94
Glass	38.1	6.41	.67	.82	.69	.84	1.03	1.03
Waveform	7330.9	1189.75	.61	.72	.60	.70	.99	.98
Soybean	29.6	5.21	.90	.99	.72	.89	.80	.90
Annealing	30.0	5.52	.86	.97	.82	.98	.95	1.01
Vowel	103.8	17.27	.56	.73	.60	.81	1.07	1.10
Splice	96.7	15.38	1.05	1.19	.83	.94	.79	.79
Abalone	691.8	118.70	.81	.92	.77	.87	.95	.94
Nettalk(s)	475.7	82.42	.79	.93	.75	.87	.95	.95
Satellite	466.9	77.84	.67	.85	.64	.79	.96	.93
Mean			.86	.57	.75	.68	.89	2.43

Table 1 shows the misclassification costs and the number of high cost errors of C4.5c, and the ratios for the pair-wise comparison among C4.5c, Boosting, and Cost-Boosting are presented in the last three columns. A ratio of less than 1 for Boosting vs C4.5c, for example, represents an improvement due to Boosting. The mean ratios over 20 domains are shown in the last row.

Boosting reduces the misclassification costs of C4.5c in 15 out of the 20 domains, and increases the misclassification costs of C4.5c in the other 5 domains. On average, Boosting achieves 14% reduction over C4.5c in terms of the misclassification costs. Cost-Boosting further reduces the misclassification costs of C4.5c. Cost-Boosting obtains lower costs than C4.5c in all 20 domains. The average reduction is 25%. Compared with Boosting, Cost-Boosting has lower costs in 18 domains, and higher costs in only 2 domains. On average, Cost-Boosting achieves 11% lower misclassification costs than Boosting. These results clearly show the advantage of Boosting over C4.5c, and the advantage of Cost-Boosting over both C4.5c and Boosting in terms of misclassification costs.

In terms of the number of high cost errors, Boosting improves C4.5c dramatically. It achieves 43% reduction over C4.5c on average. In comparison to C4.5c, Cost-Boosting achieves the average reduction of 32%. Comparing Cost-Boosting directly to Boosting, the former has the number of high cost errors 2.43 times larger than the latter. Note that one single domain, Horse, makes a significant contribution to this increase. In this domain, Boosting has 0.06 high cost errors, while Cost-Boosting has 1.20 high cost errors. This gives a ratio of 20.00 for Cost-Boosting vs Boosting.

Due to lack of space, results of investigations on some related issues, such as the effect of K, are not reported here. They can be found in the full report (Ting & Zheng (1998) at [http://www.cs.waikato.ac.nz/cs/Pub/Staff/kaiming.html]).

4 Summary

This paper has explored two techniques for dealing with cost-sensitive decision tree classification in the situation where misclassification costs change very often. One is Boosting—the ordinary boosting with the minimum expected cost criterion. It makes use of the cost information during classification stage by using the minimum expected cost criterion to select the predicted class.

Another technique is Cost-Boosting, a variant of Boosting, designed specifically for cost-sensitive classification in this paper. This technique takes the advantage of the available misclassification cost information during training, which makes the boosting procedure more sensitive to the cost of misclassification. However, this advantage comes at a price of extra computation—Cost-Boosting needs to create new classifiers every time misclassification costs change.

Experimental results show that both Boosting and Cost-Boosting can significantly reduce the misclassification cost and the number of high cost errors of a single decision tree under the frequent cost change situation—combining multiple trees in Boosting and Cost-Boosting gives more robust predictions against cost changes. In terms of misclassification cost, Cost-Boosting is a better choice than Boosting. When the aim is to minimize the number of high cost errors, we strongly recommend to use Boosting.

References

Merz, C.J. & P.M. Murphy (1997), *UCI Repository of machine learning databases* [http://www.ics.uci.edu/~mlearn/MLRepository.html]. Irvine, CA: University of California, Department of Information and Computer Science.

Michie, D., D.J. Spiegelhalter, & C.C. Taylor (1994), *Machine Learning, Neural and Statistical Classification*, Ellis Horwood Limited.

Pazzani, M., C. Merz, P. Murphy, K. Ali, T. Hume, & C. Brunk (1994), Reducing misclassification costs, in *Proceedings of the Eleventh International Conference on Machine Learning*, pp. 217-225, Morgan Kaufmann.

Quinlan, J.R. (1993), *C4.5: Program for machine learning*, Morgan Kaufmann.

Quinlan, J.R. (1996), Bagging, boosting, and C4.5, in *Proceedings of the 13th National Conference on Artificial Intelligence*, pp. 725-730, AAAI Press.

Schapire, R.E., Y. Freund, P. Bartlett, & W.S. Lee (1997), Boosting the margin: A new explanation for the effectiveness of voting methods, in *Proceedings of the Fourteenth International Conference on Machine Learning*, pp. 322-330.

Ting, K.M. & Z. Zheng (1998), Boosting Trees for Cost-Sensitive Classifications, *Working Paper 1/98*, Dept. of Computer Science, University of Waikato.

Naive Bayesian Classifier Committees

Zijian Zheng

School of Computing and Mathematics
Deakin University, Geelong, Victoria 3217, Australia
Email: zijian@deakin.edu.au

Abstract. The naive Bayesian classifier provides a very simple yet surprisingly accurate technique for machine learning. Some researchers have examined extensions to the naive Bayesian classifier that seek to further improve the accuracy. For example, a naive Bayesian tree approach generates a decision tree with one naive Bayesian classifier at each leaf. Another example is a constructive Bayesian classifier that eliminates attributes and constructs new attributes using Cartesian products of existing attributes. This paper proposes a simple, but effective approach for the same purpose. It generates a naive Bayesian classifier committee for a given classification task. Each member of the committee is a naive Bayesian classifier based on a subset of all the attributes available for the task. During the classification stage, the committee members vote to predict classes. Experiments across a wide variety of natural domains show that this method significantly increases the prediction accuracy of the naive Bayesian classifier on average. It performs better than the two approaches mentioned above in terms of higher prediction accuracy.

1 Introduction

Naive Bayesian classifier learning is based on Bayes' theorem and an attribute independence assumption (Duda and Hart 1973; Kononenko 1990; Langley and Sage 1994). Given training examples described using a vector of attribute values together with a known class for each example, the naive Bayesian classifier predicts the class of a new example $V = < v_1, v_2, \cdots, v_n >$ as the one with the highest probability of C_i given V:

$$P(C_i|V) = \frac{P(C_i) \prod_j P(v_j|C_i)}{P(V)}. \tag{1}$$

This learning technique is simple and fast. It has been shown that in many domains the prediction accuracy of the naive Bayesian classifier compares surprisingly well with that of other more complex learning algorithms such as decision tree learning, rule learning, and instance-based learning algorithms (Cestnik, Kononenko, and Bratko 1987; Langley, Iba, and Thompson 1992; Domingos and Pazzani 1996). In addition, naive Bayesian classifier learning is robust to noise and irrelevant attributes. Some experts report that the learned theories are easy to understand (Kononenko 1993). However, when the strong attribute independence assumption is violated, which is very common, the performance of the naive Bayesian classifier can be poor.

A few techniques have been developed to improve the performance of the naive Bayesian classifier. Two examples are the constructive Bayesian classifier (BSEJ) (Pazzani 1996), and the naive Bayesian tree (NBTREE) approach (Kohavi 1996). It has been shown that it is possible to improve the naive Bayesian classifier, although Domingos and Pazzani (1996) argue that the naive Bayesian classifier is still in fact optimal when the independence assumption is violated so long as the ranks of the conditional probabilities of classes given an example are correct. The extent to which the above approaches improve upon the performance of the naive Bayesian classifier suggests that these ranks are in practice incorrect in a substantial number of cases.

Most existing techniques for improving the performance of the naive Bayesian classifier require complex induction processes. For example, NBTREE adopts a hybrid model of decision trees and naive Bayesian classifiers. Each leaf of such a tree contains a naive Bayesian classifier. BSEJ employs a wrapper model (John, Kohavi, and Pfleger 1994) with the leave-1-out cross-validation estimation to find the best Cartesian product attributes from existing nominal attributes for the naive Bayesian classifier (Pazzani 1996). It also considers deleting existing attributes. This paper proposes a simple method to improve naive Bayesian classifier learning. It is called the naive Bayesian classifier committee (NBC).

The idea of NBC is inspired by recent promising theoretical and empirical research results in boosting (Freund and Schapire 1996a, 1996b; Quinlan 1996; Schapire, Freund, Bartlett, and Lee 1997). Boosting induces multiple individual classifiers in sequential trials. At the end of each trial, instance weights are adjusted to reflect the importance of each training example for the next induction trial. The objective of the adjustment is to increase the weights of misclassified training examples. Change of instance weights causes the learner to concentrate on different training examples in different trials,[1] thus resulting in different classifiers. Finally, the individual classifiers are combined through voting to form a composite classifier. Quinlan (1996) shows that boosting can significantly increase the prediction accuracy of decision tree learning.

We implemented a boosting algorithm for naive Bayesian classifier using a similar method to that for boosting decision trees (Quinlan 1996). Although the algorithm achieves higher accuracy than the naive Bayesian classifier in some domains, the overall accuracy improvement over the naive Bayesian classifier in a large set of natural domains is very marginal. The reason might be that boosting implicitly requires the instability of the boosted learning systems (Quinlan 1996). Naive Bayesian classifier learning is more stable than decision tree learning. A small change to the training set will have little impact on a naive Bayesian classifier. On the other hand, naive Bayesian classifier learning is not stable in the sense that a small change to the attribute set could lead to very different classifiers. Moreover, due to the attribute independence assumption, a naive Bayesian classifier built on an attribute subset might perform better than a

---

[1] This can be implemented by either changing the weights of training examples directly if the learner can handle it, or drawing a succession of independent bootstrap samples from the original training set.

naive Bayesian classifier created using all attributes (Langley and Sage 1994). Therefore, generating naive Bayesian classifier committees could be an approach to improving the performance of the naive Bayesian classifier. In the committee, each member is a naive Bayesian classifier built using a subset of attributes. The final class prediction is made through committee voting.

2 The NBC Algorithm

Table 1 details the naive Bayesian classifier committee learning algorithm, NBC. The idea is to generate a set of naive Bayesian classifiers in sequential trials to form a committee. Each naive Bayesian classifier is based on a different subset of attributes. All committee members make the final decision through voting when classifying examples. The estimated performance of a naive Bayesian classifier is used to guide the formation of the attribute subset for creating the naive Bayesian classifier in the following trial.

Leave-1-out cross-validation is used to estimate the error rates of naive Bayesian classifiers, since the leave-1-out cross-validation error rate is a better estimate than the resubstitution error rate (Breiman, Friedman, Olshen, and Stone 1984). In addition, for a naive Bayesian classifier, the operations of removing and adding an example are very easy and efficient. At the beginning, NBC builds a naive Bayesian classifier (called NB_{base}) using all attributes. Its leave-1-out cross-validation error rate is used as the reference for performance comparison when generating the committee.

To decide how to choose a subset of attributes for building a naive Bayesian classifier in a trial, NBC maintains a probability vector P with one element for each attribute. Each trial starts from sampling an attribute subset from the set of all attributes using P. The attribute a has the probability $P[a]$ of being selected. Given a learning task, we usually do not know which attributes can be used to built a good naive Bayesian classifier. NBC just initialises each $P[a]$ with 0.5. The idea is to let each attribute has 50% probability of being chosen at the beginning. Therefore, the subset contains about a half of all attributes.

After the attribute subset is created, NBC does not need to do any calculation to build the naive Bayesian classifier using this attribute subset, since all necessary probabilities and conditional probabilities are already available from the generation of the naive Bayesian classifier based on all attributes. The naive Bayesian classifier resulted from each trial only needs to maintain its attribute subset. However, to decide whether this naive Bayesian classifier is accepted as a committee member, it is evaluated using leave-1-out cross-validation on the training set. If its error rate ϵ_t is lower than the error rate of NB_{base}, $\epsilon_{NB_{base}}$, it is accepted. Otherwise, it is discarded.

At the end of each trial, $P[a]$ for each attribute in the subset of the current trial t is modified by multiplying the value $1/\beta_t$ which is defined in Equation 2. Note that $\beta_t < 1$, if $\epsilon_t < \epsilon_{NB_{base}}$; and $\beta_t > 1$, if $\epsilon_t > \epsilon_{NB_{base}}$. The objective of this modification is that the probabilities that the attributes used in this trial will be selected in the next trial should be increased, if the naive Bayesian classifier built

Table 1. The naive Bayesian classifier committee learning algorithm

---

$NBC(Att, D_{training}, T)$
  $INPUT$: Att: a set of attributes,
        $D_{training}$: a set of training examples described
              using Att and classes,
        T: the number of trials for generating the committee
              with the number of attributes, N, as its default value.
  $OUTPUT$: a naive Bayesian committee.

Build a naive Bayesian classifier using Att and $D_{training}$, called NB_{base}
$\epsilon_{NB_{base}}$ = Leave-1-out-Evaluation($NB_{base}, D_{training}$)
Add NB_{base} into $Committee$ as the first member which uses all attributes,
    that is, $NB_0 = NB_{base}$
$MaxT = 10 \times T$
Initialise $P[a] = 0.5$ for each attribute a in Att
$l = 1$
$t = 1$
$WHILE$ ($t <= T$ and $l <= MaxT$)
{ Att_{subset} = Sample attributes from Att based on P
        NB_{temp} = Build a naive Bayesian classifier using Att_{subset}
        ϵ_t =Leave-1-out-Evaluation($NB_{temp}, D_{training}$)
        $\alpha_t = (\epsilon_t - \epsilon_{NB_{base}} + 1)/2$
        $\beta_t = \alpha_t/(1 - \alpha_t)$
        FOR each attribute a in Att_{subset}
              $P[a] = P[a]/\beta_t$
        Normalise P such that $\sum_{a=1}^{N} P[a] = 0.5N$
        IF ($\beta_t < 1$)
        { $NB_t = NB_{temp}$
            $t = t + 1$
        }
        $l = l + 1$
}
$T = t - 1$
$RETURN$ the naive Bayesian committee containing $NB_t, t = 0, 1, \cdots, T$

---

in this trial performs better than NB_{base}. They should be decreased otherwise. After the modification, the probabilities of all attributes are normalised such that their sum is equal to 0.5 times the number of all attributes. This makes the attribute subset in the following trial also contain about a half of all attributes.

$$\beta_t = \alpha_t/(1 - \alpha_t), \quad \text{where } \alpha_t = (\epsilon_t - \epsilon_{NB_{base}} + 1)/2 \qquad (2)$$

NBC generates T naive Bayesian classifiers using different attribute subsets and put them into the committee. T is equal to the number of all attributes by default. To make NBC efficient in practice, NBC is set to carry out at most

$10 \times T$ trials, even if too many naive Bayesian classifiers which have higher error rates than NB_{base} are created. In this situation, the committee may contain less than T naive Bayesian classifiers. To avoid the extreme situation where no naive Bayesian classifier better than NB_{base} is created in any trial, NBC includes NB_{base} in the committee. Therefore, the committee always has at least one member at the end. It usually contains $T + 1$ naive Bayesian classifiers.

To classify a new example, each naive Bayesian classifier in the committee is invoked to produce the probability that this example belongs to each possible class. For each class, the probabilities provided by all committee members are summed up. The class with the largest summed probability wins the vote, and is used as the predicted class for this example. Ties are broken randomly.

3 Experiments

In this section, we use experiments in natural domains to study the performance of the naive Bayesian classifier committee learning algorithm by comparing with a naive Bayesian classifier learning algorithm, NB. Note that classifiers generated by NB are identical to the naive Bayesian classifiers created on all attributes in NBC. The performance measure used here is the error rate on the test set (unseen cases). In addition, the computational requirement of NBC is addressed.

3.1 Experimental Domains and Methods

Twenty-nine natural domains are used in the experiments. They include all the domains used by Domingos and Pazzani (1996) for studying the naive Bayesian classifier. These twenty-nine domains cover a wide variety of different domains and all are available from the UCI machine learning repository (Merz and Murphy 1997).

In each domain, two stratified 10-fold cross-validations (10-CV) (Breiman *et al.* 1984; Kohavi 1995) are performed for each algorithm. A 10-CV is carried out by randomly splitting the data set into 10 subsets that have similar size and class distribution. For each subset in turn, an algorithm is run using the examples in the remaining nine subsets as a training set and tested on the unseen examples in the hold-out subset. All the algorithms are run with their default option settings on the same training and test set partitions in every domain. An error rate reported in this paper is an average of the 20 trials for an algorithm.

Since the current implementations of the NBC and NB algorithms can only deal with nominal attributes, continuous attributes are discretized as a pre-process in the experiments. An entropy-based discretization method (Fayyad and Irani 1993; Ting 1994) is used. For each pair of training set and test set, the test set is discretized by using cut points found from the training set.

3.2 Experimental Results

Table 2 shows error rates of NBC and NB. In the column headed "NBC", bold-face font indicates that the error rate of NBC is lower than that of NB at a

Table 2. Comparison of the error rates (%) of NBC and NB

Domain	NB	NBC	NBC / NB	NBC − NB
Annealing	2.78	2.73	.98	-0.05
Audiology	23.19	**17.89**	.77	-5.30
Breast (W)	2.65	2.72	1.03	0.07
Chess (KR-KP)	12.20	**6.07**	.50	-6.13
Credit (Aust)	13.98	13.91	.99	-0.07
Echocardiogram	28.95	30.49	1.05	1.54
Glass	30.91	31.59	1.02	0.68
Heart (C)	16.82	17.32	1.03	0.50
Hepatitis	14.19	14.50	1.02	0.31
Horse colic	20.79	**16.58**	.80	-4.21
House votes 84	9.75	**7.69**	.79	-2.06
Hypothyroid	1.69	**1.50**	.89	-0.19
Iris	6.33	5.33	.84	-1.00
Labor	9.00	8.00	.89	-1.00
LED-24	34.25	**30.00**	.88	-4.25
Liver disorders	35.08	34.48	.98	-0.60
Lung cancer	47.08	50.83	1.08	3.75
Lymphography	16.12	17.88	1.11	1.76
Pima	25.20	24.42	.97	-0.78
Postoperative	33.89	30.55	.90	-3.34
Primary tumor	50.91	52.66	1.03	1.75
Promoters	9.27	8.54	.92	-0.73
Solar flare	19.44	**16.34**	.84	-3.10
Sonar	23.55	24.55	1.04	1.00
Soybean	9.16	8.65	.94	-0.51
Splice junction	4.38	**3.94**	.90	-0.44
Tic-Tac-Toe	30.64	29.70	.97	-0.94
Wine	2.22	2.22	1.00	0.00
Zoology	5.45	4.00	.73	-1.45
average	18.62	17.76	.93	-0.85
w/t/l				20/1/9
significance level				.0436

significance level better than 0.05 using a two-tailed pairwise t-test (Chatfield 1978) on the results of the 20 trials in a domain. The error rate ratios and differences of NBC and NB are also included in the table. A ratio less than 1.00 or a difference less than 0.00 means that NBC has lower error rate than NB. The line headed "w/t/l" shows the "won-tied-lost" record in the 29 domains, that is, the number of domains in which NBC has lower, the same, and higher error rates than NB.

From Table 2, the significant advantage of NBC over NB in terms of lower error rate can be clearly seen. On average over the 29 domains, NBC reduces the error rate of NB by 7%. The one-tailed pairwise sign test (Chatfield 1978) on the error rates of NBC and NB in the 29 domains shows that NBC is more accurate than NB at a significance level of 0.0436 (see the last line of the table). In 8 out of these 29 domains, NBC achieves significantly lower error rates than NB. NBC does not obtain any significantly higher error rates than NB in all of these domains. If ignoring the differences between NBC and NB that are not significant (only considering the significant differences), the one-tailed pairwise sign test shows that NBC is significantly more accurate than NB at a level of 0.0039 in these domains.

Since the class prediction of NBC relies on the voting of the naive Bayesian classifier committee, it is interesting to know the effect of the committee size on the performance of NBC. Figure 1 depicts the error rate of NBC as a function of T in the Chess (KR-KP) and Splice junction domains, the two largest domains in the test suite. For each value of T, the same experimental method described above is used except that T uses the given value instead of the default one. The error rates of NB, as a reference, are also given in the figure. Since T has nothing to do with NB, the error rates of NB are always the same when T changes.

We can see, from Figure 1, that NBC always has significantly lower error rates than NB in the Chess (KR-KP) domain as T changes. NBC has significantly lower error rates than NB for most values of T in the Splice junction domain. Only when T is equal to 20 (the first point), does NBC has the same error rate as NB in this domain. In the Chess (KR-KP) domain, NBC achieves the lowest error rate when T is 40. This value is close to the number of attributes of this domain, which is 36. In the Splice junction domain, NBC has the lowest error rate at the point 180. It is 3 times the number of attributes of this domain, which is 60. However, the error rate of NBC for T with the value 60 is not significantly higher than this lowest error rate. Therefore, using the number of attributes as the default value of T is reasonable, although it might not be optimum in some domains.

3.3 Computational Requirement

NBC is slower than NB. However, the extra cost of NBC for generating each committee member is creating an attribute subset and performing a leave-1-out cross-validation evaluation. Therefore, NBC's time complexity is $O(m \cdot n \cdot T)$,[2] while NB's time complexity is $O(m \cdot n)$, where m is the size of the training set, n is the number of attributes. Since T is equal to n by default, NBC's time complexity is $O(m \cdot n^2)$. Note that n is usually much smaller than m.

Figure 2 shows the execution time of NBC (including both learning and classification stages) as a function of T in the Chess (KR-KP) and Splice junction domains. The time is measured using CPU second on a SUN SPARCstation 5. The experimental method is exactly the same as that for drawing the learning curves above. These two curves indicate that the computational requirement of NBC is linear in T.

---

[2] The time complexity of NBC is $O(m \cdot n + T \cdot (n + m \cdot n)) = O(m \cdot n \cdot T)$.

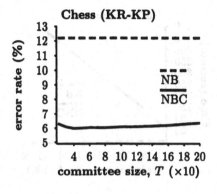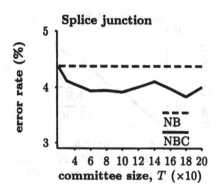

Fig. 1. Effect of T on the performance of NBC

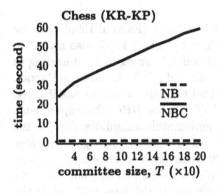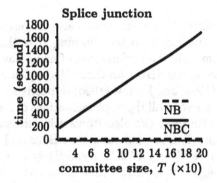

Fig. 2. Computational requirement of NBC as a function of T

Figure 3 depicts the execution time of NBC (including both learning and classification stages) as a function of training set size in the Chess (KR-KP) and Splice junction domains. T uses its default value (the number of attributes) in this experiment. Each point of a learning curve is an average value over 20 trials. For each trial, the training set used at every point is a randomly selected subset of the training set used in the corresponding trial of the two 10-fold cross-validations on the entire dataset of the domain. In each trial, the training set at a point is a proper subset of the training set at the next adjacent point. The test set at every point of a trial is the same as the test set used in the corresponding trial of the two 10-fold cross-validations.

This figure clearly shows that the computational requirement of NBC is linear in training set size, although the time for NBC increases faster than that for NB as the training set size increases.

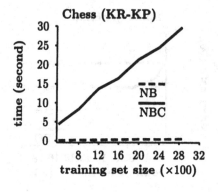
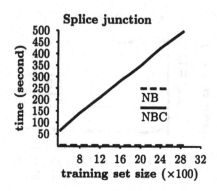

Fig. 3. Computational requirement of NBC as a function of training set size

4 Discussion

Since the constructive naive Bayesian classifier BSEJ (Pazzani 1996) and the
naive Bayesian tree learning algorithm NBTREE (Kohavi 1996) also intend to
improve the performance of naive Bayesian classifier learning, it is interesting to
compare NBC with them. We implemented BSEJ and NBTREE based on Pazzani
(1996) and Kohavi (1996) respectively. Note that the naive Bayesian classifier NB
is used in all the implementations of BSEJ, NBTREE, and NBC. Our experiments
with these two algorithms using the same experimental method described in the
previous section show that BSEJ and NBTREE achieve the average error rates
18.10% and 17.90% respectively in these 29 domains. The one-tailed pairwise
sign test indicates that neither the error rate reduction of BSEJ nor the error
rate reduction of NBTREE over NB is significant at the level 0.05, while the
error rate reduction of NBC over NB is significant. It has been found that both
BSEJ and NBTREE obtain significantly higher error rates than NB in two out of
the 29 domains. The average error rates of BSEJ and NBTREE are 2% and 1%
higher than that of NBC in the 29 domains respectively. These results suggest
that NBC performs better than the constructive naive Bayesian classifier and
the naive Bayesian tree learning method in terms of lower error rate.

During the classification stage, for each example to be classified, NBC sums
up the class distributions produced by all committee members. The class with
the highest summed probability is used as the predicted class of the example. An
alternative method is the majority vote. Instead of the class distribution, each
committee member provides a predicted class for a given example. Then, NBC
classifies the example as the class with the support from the largest number
of committee members. With this voting technique, the average error rate of
NBC over the 29 domains is 17.75%, very close to the error rate of the method
described in Section 2.

Another issue is voting weights for classification. NBC does not use weights
for committee voting. In other words, the vote of each committee member in

NBC is worth 1 unit. One might think that weighted voting may further improve the performance of NBC. Unfortunately, although this issue is worthy of further investigation, our preliminary exploration has not found any appropriate weighting method that can reduce the error rate of the current NBC on average. For example, NBC with $\log(1/\beta_t)$ as the weight of the naive Bayesian classifier generated in trail t obtains an average error rate of 17.80% in the 29 domains. It is slightly higher than the error rate of NBC without voting weights, although the difference is not significant. It remains an open question whether an appropriate weighting method can be designed to significantly reduce the average error rate of NBC.

5 Related Work

From the point of view of improving the performance of naive Bayesian classifier learning, the work related to NBC includes the constructive Bayesian classifier (BSEJ) (Pazzani 1996) and the naive Bayesian tree (NBTREE) approach (Kohavi 1996) mentioned in the introduction section, as well as the semi-naive Bayesian classifier (Kononenko 1991) and the attribute deletion technique (Langley and Sage 1994). Kononenko's semi-naive Bayesian classifier performs exhaustive search to iteratively join pairs of attribute values (Kononenko 1991). The aim is to optimise the tradeoff between the "non-naivety" and the reliability of estimates of probabilities. Langley and Sage (1994) have shown that attribute deletion can improve the performance of the naive Bayesian classifier when attributes are inter-dependent, especially when some attributes are redundant.

The investigation of the naive Bayesian classifier committee learning method is motivated by recent research on boosting (Freund and Schapire 1996a, 1996b; Quinlan 1996; Schapire et al. 1997). Another related approach is bagging (Breiman 1996; Quinlan 1996). Bagging builds a set of classifiers with each using a separately sampled training set (with replacement) of the same size from the original training set. Final classification is also through voting among all of these classifiers. Both boosting and bagging generate different classifiers by deriving different training sets from the original one, while NBC creates different classifiers by deriving different attribute subsets. Boosting and bagging have been applied on weak learning algorithms with great success, such as decision tree learning (Quinlan 1996). No published research has been seen so far on applying boosting or classifier committee techniques to naive Bayesian classifier learning. No effort has been made to explore approaches to generating, as a composite classifier, a set of classifiers using different attribute subsets.

When generating a naive Bayesian classifier as a committee member, NBC chooses an attribute subset based on the probability distribution of all attributes that are resulted from the performance of naive Bayesian classifiers created in the previous trials. Attribute subset selection has been studied for a while for classification learning (e.g. Almuallim and Dietterich (1992), Kira and Rendell (1992), John et al. (1994), and Langley (1994)). However, all of these existing methods choose an attribute subset to build a single classifier, while NBC generates a set of classifiers with each based a different attribute subset.

6 Conclusions and Future Work

This paper presented a method of generating naive Bayesian classifier committees by building individual naive Bayesian classifiers using different attribute subsets in sequential trials. During classification stage, the committees make the class prediction through voting. In the current implementation of the NBC algorithm, no weights are used for voting. Appropriate weighting techniques may further improve the performance of NBC. NBC chooses about a half of attributes, to create a naive Bayesian classifier, using the probability distribution of all attributes, which is built up based on the performance of naive Bayesian classifiers generated previously. Other approaches to attribute subset selection for this purpose are worth exploring.

The experimental study in a wide variety of natural domains shows that the naive Bayesian classifier committee learning can significantly increase the prediction accuracy of naive Bayesian classifier learning on average. It performs better, on average, than the naive Bayesian tree learning and the constructive naive Bayesian classifier learning in the set of domains under investigation.

Acknowledgements

The author is grateful to Geoffrey Webb for his helpful comments on this research and earlier drafts of the paper. Many thanks to Kai Ming Ting for supplying the discretization program.

References

Almuallim, H. and Dietterich, T.G.: Efficient algorithms for identifying relevant features. *Proceedings of the 9th Canadian Conference on Artificial Intelligence*. Vancouver, BC: Morgan Kaufmann (1992) 38-45.

Breiman, L., Friedman, J.H., Olshen, R.A., and Stone, C.J.: *Classification And Regression Trees*. Belmont, CA: Wadsworth (1984).

Breiman, L.: Bagging predictors. *Machine Learning*. **24** (1996) 123-140.

Cestnik, B., Kononenko, I., and Bratko, I.: ASSISTANT 86: A knowledge-elicitation tool for sophisticated users. In I. Bratko & N. Lavrač (Eds.), *Progress in Machine Learning – Proceedings of the 2nd European Working Session on Learning (EWSL87)*. Wilmslow, UK: Sigma Press (1987) 31-45.

Chatfield, C.: *Statistics for Technology: A Course in Applied Statistics*. London: Chapman and Hall (1978).

Domingos, P. and Pazzani, M.: Beyond independence: Conditions for the optimality of the simple Bayesian classifier. *Proceedings of the 13th International Conference on Machine Learning*. San Francisco, CA: Morgan Kaufmann (1996) 105-112.

Duda, R.O. and Hart, P.E.: *Pattern Classification and Scene Analysis*. New York: John Wiley (1973).

Fayyad, U.M. and Irani, K.B.: Multi-interval discretization of continuous-valued attributes for classification learning. *Proceedings of the 13th International Joint Conference on Artificial Intelligence.* Morgan Kaufmann (1993) 1022-1027.

Freund, Y. and Schapire, R.E.: A decision-theoretic generalization of on-line learning and an application to boosting. Unpublished manuscript, available from the authors' home pages ("http://www.research.att.com/{~yoav,~schapire}") (1996a).

Freund, Y. and Schapire, R.E.: Experiments with a new boosting algorithm. *Proceedings of the 13th International Conference on Machine Learning.* Morgan Kaufmann (1996b) 148-156.

John, G.H., Kohavi, R., and Pfleger, K.: Irrelevant features and the subset selection problem. *Proceedings of the 11th International Conference on Machine Learning.* San Francisco, CA: Morgan Kaufmann (1994) 121-129.

Kira, K. and Rendell, L.A.: The feature selection problem: Traditional methods and a new algorithm. *Proceedings of the 10th National Conference on Artificial Intelligence.* Menlo Park, CA: AAAI Press/Cambridge, MA: MIT Press (1992) 129-134.

Kohavi, R.: A study of cross-validation and bootstrap for accuracy estimation and model selection. *Proceedings of the 14th International Joint Conference on Artificial Intelligence.* San Mateo, CA: Morgan Kaufmann (1995) 1137-1143.

Kohavi, R.: Scaling up the accuracy of naive-Bayes classifiers: A decision-tree hybrid. *Proceedings of the 2nd International Conference on Knowledge Discovery and Data Mining.* Menlo Park, CA: The AAAI Press (1996) 202-207.

Kononenko, I.: Comparison of inductive and naive Bayesian learning approaches to automatic knowledge acquisition. In B. Wielinga *et al.* (Eds.), *Current Trends in Knowledge Acquisition.* Amsterdam: IOS Press (1990).

Kononenko, I.: Semi-naive Bayesian classifier. *Proceedings of European Conference on Artificial Intelligence* (1991) 206-219.

Langley, P., Iba, W.F., and Thompson, K.: An analysis of Bayesian classifiers. *Proceedings of the 10th National Conference on Artificial Intelligence.* Menlo Park, CA: The AAAI Press (1992) 223-228.

Langley, P.: Selection of relevant features in machine learning. *Proceeding of the AAAI Fall Symposium on Relevance,* New Orleans, LA: The AAAI Press (1994).

Langley, P. and Sage, S.: Induction of selective Bayesian classifiers. *Proceedings of the 10th Conference on Uncertainty in Artificial Intelligence.* Seattle, WA: Morgan Kaufmann (1994) 339-406.

Merz, C.J. and Murphy, P.M.: UCI Repository of Machine Learning Databases [http://www.ics.uci.edu/~mlearn/MLRepository.html]. Irvine, CA: University of California, Department of Information and Computer Science (1997).

Pazzani, M.J.: Constructive induction of Cartesian product attributes. *Proceedings of the Conference, ISIS'96: Information, Statistics and Induction in Science.* Singapore: World Scientific (1996) 66-77.

Quinlan, J.R.: Bagging, boosting, and C4.5. *Proceedings of the 13th National Conference on Artificial Intelligence,* Menlo Park: The AAAI Press (1996) 725-730.

Schapire, R.E., Freund, Y., Bartlett, P., and Lee W.S.: Boosting the margin: A new explanation for the effectiveness of voting methods. *Proceedings of the 11th International Conference on Machine Learning.* Morgan Kaufmann (1997) 322-330.

Ting, K.M.: Discretization of continuous-valued attributes and instance-based learning (Technical Report 491). Sydney, Australia: University of Sydney, Basser Department of Computer Science (1994).

Batch Classifications with Discrete Finite Mixtures

Petri Kontkanen, Petri Myllymäki, Tomi Silander, and Henry Tirri

Complex Systems Computation Group (CoSCo)
P.O.Box 26, Department of Computer Science
FIN-00014 University of Helsinki, Finland

Abstract. In this paper we study batch classification problems where multiple predictions are made simultaneously, in contrast to the standard independent classification case, where the predictions are made independently one at a time. The main contribution of this paper is to demonstrate how the standard EM algorithm for finite mixture models can be modified for the batch classification case. In the empirical part of the paper, the results obtained by the batch classification approach are compared to those obtained by independent predictions.

1 Introduction

In the standard classification approach, the model used to classify data is first constructed by using the available training data, and each classification problem is then solved independently with the produced model. In this paper, we extend this classification problem by allowing multiple predictions (classifications) to be made at the same time. In this *batch classification* case, all the classification problems are given simultaneously, and instead of dealing with a single vector to be classified, the task is to find a correct classification for a set of vectors.

The batch classification problem can be regarded as a missing data problem, where the missing data consists of the correct classifications of *query vectors*, the vectors to be classified. Intuitively, one could expect the batch classification to produce better results than independent classifications, since in the batch case the data available for making predictions consists not only of the original training data, but also of the set of all the query vectors. A closer look reveals, however, that the amount of missing data has also increased, making the missing data estimation problem more difficult. Therefore it is interesting to investigate the trade-off between the advantage of using the increased information available in the query batch, and the disadvantage of increased complexity in the search process. Similar work has been reported in [2], where the unclassified vectors were used as background knowledge for a conceptual-clustering algorithm.

In order to study this problem, we use the probabilistic model family of finite mixtures [3, 7], where the problem domain probability distribution is approximated as a finite, weighted sum of simple component distributions. The standard way to fix a finite mixture model is to estimate the values of the latent clustering variable via the *Expectation Maximization (EM)* algorithm [1] (see, e.g., [5]), and then to choose the *maximum a posteriori probability (MAP)* parameter values.

The contribution of this paper is to demonstrate how the standard EM algorithm for finite mixtures is modified for the batch classification case, so that it can be used for estimating both the missing classification data, and the missing latent variable data at the same time. In other words, the same algorithm used normally for constructing the models from training data, is in our approach used also for making predictions. In the empirical part of the paper, we compare the results obtained by using the batch classification with the modified EM algorithm to the results obtained by the standard approach, where each query vector is classified independently.

2 Discrete finite mixtures

In the following, the problem domain is modeled by using m discrete random variables $X_1, \ldots, X_m$ (continuous variables are assumed to be discretized by quantization). A *data instantiation* d is a vector in which all the variables X_i have been assigned a value, $d = (X_1 = x_1, \ldots, X_m = x_m)$, where $x_i \in \{x_{i1}, \ldots, x_{in_i}\}$. A *random sample* $D = (d_1, \ldots, d_N)$ is a set of N i.i.d. data instantiations, where each d_j is sampled from the joint distribution of the variables $X_1, \ldots, X_m$.

In the discrete variable case, the *finite mixture* [3,7] distribution for a data instantiation d can be written as

$$P(d) = \sum_{k=1}^{K} \left(P(Y = y_k) \prod_{i=1}^{m} P(X_i = x_i | Y = y_k) \right).$$

where Y denotes a latent *clustering random variable*, the values of which are not given in the data D, K is the number of possible values of Y, and the variables $X_1, \ldots, X_m$ are assumed to be independent, given the value of the clustering variable Y.

In the following, we assume both the cluster distribution $P(Y)$ and the intra-class conditional distributions $P(X_i | Y = y_k)$ to be multinomial. Thus a finite mixture model can be defined by first fixing K, the model class (the number of the mixing distributions), and then by determining the values of the model parameters $\Theta = (\alpha, \Phi), \Theta \in \Omega$, where $\alpha = (\alpha_1, \ldots, \alpha_K)$ and $\Phi = (\Phi_{11}, \ldots, \Phi_{1m}, \ldots, \Phi_{K1}, \ldots, \Phi_{Km})$, with the denotations $\alpha_k = P(Y = y_k)$, and $\Phi_{ki} = (\phi_{ki1}, \ldots, \phi_{kin_i})$, where $\phi_{kil} = P(X_i = x_{il} | Y = y_k)$.

3 Batch classifications with the EM algorithm

In this paper we consider prediction problems where the goal is to correctly classify a set of L *test vectors* $q_1, \ldots, q_L$ by using the given training data D. In the following, let X_m denote the class variable, the values of which are to be estimated, in which case all the test vectors q_j are of the form

$$q_j = (X_1 = x_1, \ldots, X_{m-1} = x_{m-1}).$$

The standard Bayesian procedure for solving this problem is to first to construct the *maximum a posterior probability (MAP)* model $\hat{\Theta}_D$ with respect to the given data D, and then to classify the test cases independently by using the model constructed. In the Bayesian framework for a single test vector q_j this is done by determining the following *predictive distribution* for all the possible values x_m of the class variable X_m:

$$P(x_m \mid q_j, \hat{\Theta}_D) \propto P(q_j, x_m \mid \hat{\Theta}_D) = \sum_{k=1}^{K} P(q_j, x_m, z_j = k \mid \hat{\Theta}_D), \qquad (1)$$

where the value of variable z_j denotes the value of the clustering variable Y corresponding to the test case q_j.

Unfortunately, determining the MAP parameter values $\hat{\Theta}_D$ exactly is not possible in practice because of the missing data imposed by the latent variable Y. However, the *Expectation Maximization (EM)* algorithm [1] is an iterative algorithm that can be used for finding an approximation of the MAP model. The EM algorithm can also be understood as an unsupervised clustering algorithm, where the estimated values of the latent variable determine the (probabilistic) clusters. In the E-step of the algorithm the conditional expected values of the sufficient statistics of the complete data (D, Z) are needed, in our case the expected values of the parameters h_k and f_{kil}, where $h_k = \sum_{j=1}^{N} z_{jk}$ is the number of instantiations in cluster k, and $f_{kil} = \sum_{j=1}^{N} z_{jk} v_{jil}$ is the number of instantiations in cluster k with variable X_i having value x_{il}. Here the indicator variable z_{jk} has value 1 if d_j is sampled from $P(\cdot|Y = y_k)$, and the indicator variable v_{jil} has value 1 if $d_{ji} = x_{il}$.

The expectations of the sufficient statistics at the time step t of the EM algorithm are computed by setting $\bar{h}_k = E[h_k \mid D, \Theta^{(t)}] = \sum_{j=1}^{N} w_{jk}$, and $\bar{f}_{kil} = E[f_{kil} \mid D, \Theta^{(t)}] = \sum_{j=1}^{N} w_{jk} v_{jil}$, where

$$w_{jk} = E[Z_{jk} \mid D, \Theta^{(t)}] = \frac{\alpha_k^{(t)} \prod_{i=1}^{m} \prod_{l=1}^{n_i} \left(\phi_{kil}^{(t)}\right)^{v_{jil}}}{\sum_{k'=1}^{K} \left(\alpha_{k'}^{(t)} \prod_{i=1}^{m} \prod_{l=1}^{n_i} \left(\phi_{k'il}^{(t)}\right)^{v_{jil}}\right)}.$$

In the batch classification case, the predictive distribution can be written as

$$P(c_1, \dots, c_L, q_1, \dots, q_L \mid \hat{\Theta}_{D,Q}) = \prod_{j=1}^{L} P(q_j, c_j \mid \hat{\Theta}_{D,Q}), \qquad (2)$$

where $c = (c_1, \dots, c_L)$ denotes a vector consisting of classifications of all the test vectors $Q = (q_1, \dots, q_L)$. Consequently, the test vectors can be classified independently also in the batch classification case, *but the MAP model $\hat{\Theta}$ must in this case be estimated by using the joint database (D, Q), not the original data D alone.* In addition to this, the missing data consists not only of the cluster indicators z_{jk}, but also of the classifications of the test vectors, $c_1, \dots, c_L$. By conditioning the class indicator variables $C_1, \dots, C_L$ with the cluster indicator variables, we get $\bar{c}_{jlk} = P(C_j = l \mid Z_{jk} = 1, q_j, \Theta^{(t)}) = \phi^{(t)}_{kml}$, where as before, m denotes the index of the class variable. The last equality follows from the fact that the attributes are assumed to be independent, given the value of the clustering variable Y.

Because of the absence of the values of the class variable X_m, the expectations of the cluster indicators corresponding to the test cases must be calculated differently than with the standard EM. The modified formulas for computing these expectations are given by

$$w_{jk} = E[Z_{jk} \mid D, \Theta^t] = \frac{\alpha_k^{(t)} \prod_{i=1}^{m-1} \prod_{l=1}^{n_i} \left(\phi_{kil}^{(t)}\right)^{v_{jil}}}{\sum_{k'=1}^{K} \left(\alpha_{k'}^{(t)} \prod_{i=1}^{m-1} \prod_{l=1}^{n_i} \left(\phi_{k'il}^{(t)}\right)^{v_{jil}}\right)}. \tag{3}$$

In addition, the expectations of the parameters f_{kml} must now be calculated by using $\bar{f}_{kml} = \sum_{j=1}^{L} w_{jk} \bar{c}_{jlk}$. Detailed derivation of these formulas is similar to the derivations used in [5], but technically somewhat involved and omitted here.

In the M-step, the parameter values are updated in such a way that the obtained expected posterior is maximized (for the update formulas, see e.g. [5]).

4 Empirical results

To validate the batch classification approach described in the previous section, we performed a series of experiments with a set of public domain classification datasets from the UCI repository[1]. For simplicity, in our experiments we used the uniform prior (Dirichlet with all the hyperparameters set to 1) for both the independent (IC) and batch classification (BC). In the independent classification case each classification query was classified one at a time by using the MAP prediction defined by formula (1), where the approximation found by the EM algorithm was taken as the MAP model $\hat{\Theta}$. In the batch classification case, the predictive distribution (2) was used instead, the difference being that the MAP model was estimated from the joint database (D, Q) by using the EM algorithm as described in Section 3. Description of the datasets used, and the crossvalidated classification results obtained can be found in Table 1. The results are averages over 100 independent crossvalidation runs, and the number of folds used was the same as in [6].

The results show that the batch classification approach does not demonstrate significant improvement over independent predictions. The reasons for this are twofold. Firstly, as discussed before, it seems likely that the increase in the amount of missing data makes the search for good local maxima in the enlarged search space much more difficult, so the theoretical advantage of using the query information is in this case nullified by the increase in the complexity of the search problem. Secondly, if the training data is already sufficient to model the joint distribution well, the auxiliary information in the query batch Q (sampled from the same distribution) cannot improve the predictions significantly.

---

[1] http://www.ics.uci.edu/~mlearn/

Table 1. The datasets used in the experiments and the corresponding crossvalidated classification accuracies obtained.

Dataset	Size	Attrs	Classes	IC	BC
Lymphography	148	19	4	73.0	73.3
Hepatitis	150	20	2	79.5	79.6
Heart disease	270	14	2	81.9	81.9
Primary tumor	339	18	21	41.5	41.8
Australian	690	15	2	81.3	80.6
Diabetes	768	9	2	68.6	68.6

In order to test the latter hypothesis we performed a second set of experiments to see how the methods perform when the training sets D are not sufficient for building very good models, and small with respect to the size of the query batch Q. In these experiments we sampled small training sets randomly from the datasets, and used the rest of the data as the test set. For each case, classification was done by using both IC and BC methods. The average classification success rate was then plotted as a function of the size of the training set. In Fig. 1 a typical behavior can be seen. Each data point corresponds to an average of 100 independent tests.

Fig. 1. Average classification success rate as a function of the size of the training set in the Heart Disease data set case.

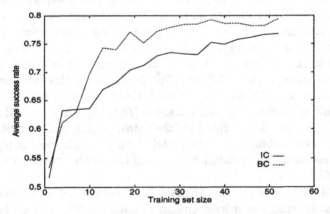

In these tests the results show a clear difference in the performance. The batch approach is more efficient in extracting regularities present in the data, and outperforms the standard IC approach in cases with very small amounts of data. When the size of the training set is increased, we can see IC "catching up" as the amount of training data becomes more sufficient for constructing a good model for the joint distribution. It seems probable that this saturation effect is the cause for the indifference in the results in the first set of experiments, since in crossvalidation the amount of training data is usually quite high, e.g., in 10-fold

213

crossvalidation 90% of all the data available. This observation seems even more plausible as it is known that for many of the UCI data sets a rather small sample of the actual training data is enough for building a good predictive model (see the discussion in [4]).

5 Conclusion

We have studied the batch classification problem where multiple predictions can be made simultaneously, instead of performing the classifications independently one at a time. We demonstrated how the standard EM algorithm for finite mixtures can be modified for estimating both the missing latent variable data, and the classification data at the same time. In this unifying approach EM can be used both for model construction from training data and for making predictions. The empirical results with public domain classification datasets indicate that the batch approach may outperform the standard independent classification approach in cases with small sample sizes, where the extra information in the query batch can improve the model constructed.

Acknowledgements This research has been supported by the Technology Development Center (TEKES), and by the Academy of Finland. The primary tumor and the lymphography domains were obtained from the University Medical Centre, Institute of Oncology, Ljubljana, Yugoslavia. Thanks go to M. Zwitter and M. Soklič for providing the data.

References

1. A.P. Dempster, N.M. Laird, and D.B. Rubin. Maximum likelihood from incomplete data via the EM algorithm. *Journal of the Royal Statistical Society, Series B*, 39(1):1–38, 1977.
2. W. Emde. Inductive learning of characteristic concept descriptions from small sets of classified examples. In F. Bergadano and L. De Raedt, editors, *Proceedings of the 7th European Conference on Machine Learning (ECML94)*, pages 103–121, 1994.
3. B.S. Everitt and D.J. Hand. *Finite Mixture Distributions*. Chapman and Hall, London, 1981.
4. P. Kontkanen, P. Myllymäki, T. Silander, H. Tirri, and P. Grünwald. Comparing predictive inference methods for discrete domains. In *Proceedings of the Sixth International Workshop on Artificial Intelligence and Statistics*, pages 311–318, Ft. Lauderdale, Florida, January 1997. Also: NeuroCOLT Technical Report NC-TR-97-004.
5. P. Kontkanen, P. Myllymäki, and H. Tirri. Constructing Bayesian finite mixture models by the EM algorithm. Technical Report NC-TR-97-003, ESPRIT Working Group 8556: Neural and Computational Learning (NeuroCOLT), 1996.
6. H. Tirri, P. Kontkanen, and P. Myllymäki. Probabilistic instance-based learning. In L. Saitta, editor, *Machine Learning: Proceedings of the Thirteenth International Conference*, pages 507–515. Morgan Kaufmann Publishers, 1996.
7. D.M. Titterington, A.F.M. Smith, and U.E. Makov. *Statistical Analysis of Finite Mixture Distributions*. John Wiley & Sons, New York, 1985.

Induction of Recursive Program Schemes

Ute Schmid & Fritz Wysotzki

Department of Computer Science
Technical University Berlin
email: schmid,wysotzki@cs.tu-berlin.de

Abstract. In this paper we present an approach to the induction of recursive structures from examples which is based on the notion of recursive program schemes. We separate induction from examples in two stages: (1) constructing initial programs from examples and (2) folding initial programs to recursive program schemes. By this separation, the induction of recursive program schemes can be reduced to a pattern-matching problem which can be handled by a generic algorithm. Construction of initial programs is performed with an approach to universal planning. "Background knowledge" is given in the form of operators and their conditions of application. Furthermore synthesizing recursive program schemes instead of programs in a predefined programming language enables us to combine program synthesis and analogical reasoning. A recursive program scheme represents the class of structural identical programs and can be assigned different semantics by interpretation. We believe that our approach mimicks in some way the problem solving and learning behavior of a (novice) human programmer and that our approach integrates theoretical ideas and empirical results of learning by doing and learning by analogy from cognitive science in a unique framework.

Keywords: Inductive Program Synthesis, Planning and Learning, Analogy, Cognitive Modelling

1 Introduction

Building recursive definitions from examples is an old topic in automatic program construction [3]. Such techniques can be exploited in different fields as automatic theorem proving or generation of (robot) action sequences. There was a lot of interest on inductive approaches to the synthesis of recursive programs during the seventies and eighties in the context of functional (LISP) programming which is now revived in inductive logic programming (ILP; [9]). The general idea of inductive program synthesis is to generalize over the structures of a set of (positive) examples with a kind of unsupervised learning algorithm.

We propose an approach to inductive program synthesis which differs from the LISP-based methods and from ILP in two aspects: Firstly, we take a more abstract view on programs, that is, we describe programs as elements of a term algebra and we infer recursive program schemes (RPSs; cf. [6,7]) instead of LISP functions or PROLOG clauses. Secondly, we separate the problem of program synthesis from examples in two distinct processes: we deal with the construction of "Summers"-like initial programs from examples [18, 20] with methods of "universal planning" [17, 21] and use the initial programs as input to our program synthesis algorithm.

We believe that our approach mimicks certain aspects of human (novice) programmers (cf. [2]). Building initial programs from examples by planning can be viewed as constructing the minimal sequence of operations by which the example input can be transformed into the desired output (i.e. goal state) by using only primitive functions (i.e. predefined operators). Combining different simulation traces in one planning tree can be viewed as integrating experience with different inital states of a problem (i.e. examples) into a single structure which is composed of conditional expressions. This process corresponds roughly to compilation/chunking of rules in cognitive models of skill acquisition (cf. [1]). Using the planning tree (initial program) as input to program synthesis describes a second stage of learning, generalization over recursive enumerable problem spaces. This stage of skill acquisition sketches the learning of a specific problem solving strategy. Using RPSs rather than a programming language enables us to model a third stage of learning, generalization over classes of programs, by abstracting from the concrete semantics of the symbols contained in an RPS.

Let's illustrate this idea with an example: A novice programmer or our system is confronted with the problem to write a program to sum the elements of a list of natural numbers. In a first step he/it constructs sequential solution sequences for example lists of length zero, one, two and three:

1. *if empty(l) then 0,*
2. *if empty (tail(l)) then head(l),*
3. *if empty(tail(tail(l))) then plus(head(l), head(tail(l))),*
4. *if empty(tail(tail(tail(l)))) than plus(head(l), plus(head(tail(l)), head(tail(tail(l)))))).*

These traces (describing cases mutually excluding each other) are integrated in a kind of universal plan representing the initial program:

```
if empty(l) then 0
  else if empty(tail(l)) then head(l)
    else if empty(tail(tail(l))) then plus(head(l), head(tail(l)))
      else if empty(tail(tail(tail(l))))
        then plus (head(l), plus(head(tail(l)), head(tail(tail(l))))).
```

The experience with lists up to length three provides the basis for generalization to lists of arbitrary length n, that is for inferring an RPS: *sumlist(l) = if empty(l) then 0 else plus(head(l), sumlist(tail(l)))*. The infered RPS is stored in memory and can be used to solve structural identical problems with different semantics by analogical reasoning, for example *sum(x) = if eq0(x) then 0 else plus(succ(x), sum(pred(x)))*.

In this paper - in contrast to other work on inductive program synthesis - we do not focus on the usual list or number problems (as the programs given above) but we will concentrate on blockworld problems (cf. [13]). Thereby we hope to bridge the gap between planning and inductive programming. Especially, our approach could help to overcome the complexity problems in universal planning [10] by restricting planning to problems of small complexity and using inductive program synthesis to scale up. In section 4.2 will be shown, that using block-world problems (and interpreting them as RPSs) does not restrict the class of recursive programs which can be inferred to this domain. For most list or number problems there are structural equivalent blockworld problems. A blockworld problem corresponding to the linear structure of the examples given above is for example to clear a given block x in a tower: *clearblock(x,s)* = *if cleartop(x) then s else puttable(topof(x), clearblock(topof(x),s))*, where s is a situation variable.

In the following we will first describe work which is related to our approach. Afterwards we will introduce the concept of recursive program schemes and describe our induction algorithm together with examples of synthetizised structures. Than we will shortly illustrate our use of planning and analogical reasoning in inductive program syntheses. The paper finishes with a conclusion and plans for further work.

2 Related Work

Our approach has its background in the work on synthesis of functional programs (esp. [11,18]). That the methodologies introduced in the seventies are apt to handle the benchmarks for recursive program synthesis given by ILP was shown on the example of the BMW algorithm [4,11].

The original idea of inferring RPSs rather than LISP functions and of separating the generation of initial programs from program synthesis was presented in [20] and [21]. In contrast to most work in ILP (cf. [9]), we use only a small number of positive examples (also of interest now in ILP; cf. [14]). By restricting the synthesis task to generalizing over initial programs we have no need of regarding background knowledge, that is, our work is similar to the generalization-to-n approaches in grammatical inference (cf. [5]). That is, by splitting program synthesis in construction of initial programs (where domain specific background knowledge is used) and folding initial programs to RPSs we can reduce the synthesis algorithm to pattern-matching which can be performed with a generic algorithm.

Our main interest is not to present theoretical results on inductive synthesis of recursive structures but to make these ideas useful in the context of planning and problem solving. While [13] presented a formal approach to deductive reasoning in planning, we want to introduce inductive program synthesis as an alternative approach to learning in the domain of plan construction as for example employed in PRODIGY (cf. [19]). Finally, we believe, that our approach integrates ideas and empirical findings in the area of skill acquistion as introduced in cognitive science (cf. [1]). The notion of RPSs enables us to model the acquisition of problem solving schemes and their use in analogical reasoning in a unified way (see [16]).

3 Recursive Program Schemes (RPSs)

The theoretical framework for induction of RPSs was presented in [6], which we use as background for our approach. In the following we give some basic definitions before introducing the concept of an RPS.

Definition 1 (Term Algebra) *Let V be a set of variables and F a set of function symbols with $F^i \subseteq F$ as set of function symbols with arity i and $\Omega \in F$ as symbol for "undefined". Then $M(V, F)$ is the set of all welldefined terms:*
1. *$v \in V$ and $c \in F^0$ (constant symbols) are terms.*
2. *if $t_1 \ldots t_n$ are terms and $f \in F^n$ is a function symbol of arity n then $f(t_1 \ldots t_n)$ is a term.*

Definition 2 (Extended Term Algebra) *Let $\Phi = \{G_1, \ldots G_n\}$ be a set of function variables with arity $G_i = k_i$. Then we call $M(V, F \cup \Phi)$ the extended term algebra.*

Definition 3 (Partial Order over M) *The term algebra can be extended to include infinite terms by defining a partial order over it. Ω is the bottom element and we define $t < t'$ if t' can be generated from t by replacing Ω in t by a term $\neq \Omega$ (but which may contain the symbol Ω). Every ordered subset $A \subseteq M$ has an upper limit $Sup(A)$ which can be infinite.*

Definition 4 (McCarthy-Conditional) *The McCarthy-Conditional $g(x, y, z)$ is a function of arity three which can be interpreted as conditional expression (if x then y else z).*

Definition 5 (Recursive Program Scheme) *An RPS is a pair $< \Sigma, t >$ with $\Sigma =< G_i(v_1 \ldots v_n) = t_i \mid i = 1 \ldots n >$ is a system of equations ("subroutines") and $t \in M$ is the "main program".*

If G_i is contained in t_i, the equation defines a recursive function.

To illustrate the notion of an RPS we give an example. We define the extended term algebra as $M(\{x, s\}, \{\Omega, cleartop^1, topof^1, puttable^2\} \cup \{clearblock^2\})$. We define Σ as $clearblock(x, s) = g(cleartop(x), s, puttable(topof(x), clearblock(topof(x), s)))$ and $t = clearblock(x, s)$. That is, our Σ consists of a single equation. Note that the lefthand side of the equation corresponds to the head of a function, the righthand side to the body. We have terms in M with $\Omega < g(cleartop(x), s, puttable(topof(x), \Omega)) < g(cleartop(x), s, puttable(topof(x), g(clearblock(topof(x), s, puttable(topof(topof(x)), \Omega)))) < \ldots$.

In a similar way as in eval-apply interpreters, a system of equations (functions) can be solved, by replacing the name of a user-defined function (i.e. a function variable) by its body:

Definition 6 (Rewrite Rule) *An expression can be transformed by the rewrite rule Θ in the following way:*
1. *$\Theta(x) = x$ if $x \in V \cup F^0$*
2. *$\Theta(f(t_1 \ldots t_k)) = f(\Theta(t_1) \ldots \Theta(t_k))$*
3. *$\Theta(G(t_1 \ldots t_k)) = \theta(G)_{[\Theta(t_1)/v_1 \ldots \Theta(t_k)/v_k]}$.*
   That is, the head of G is replaced by its body $\theta(G)$ where all variables v_i are substituted by the rewritten terms t_i with which G was "called". Note, that with an expression $[t/v]$ we denote the substitution of a variable v by a term t (often written as $v \leftarrow t$).

We can use the rewrite rule given above to expand an RPS to a certain length l. A sequence of expansions from $l = 0, 1, 2 \ldots$ is called Kleene-sequence:

Definition 7 (Kleene-Sequence) *Let $G_i = t_i \in \Sigma$ be a recursive equation. We can define a sequence $\mathcal{G}_i^l$ for $l = 0, 1, 2 \ldots$ by: $\mathcal{G}_i^0 = \Omega$, $\mathcal{G}_i^l = \Theta(t_i) = t_i[\mathcal{G}_1^{l-1}/G_1 \ldots \mathcal{G}_n^{l-1}/G_n]$. That is, an expansion of length l can be constructed by substituting function calls G_i in t by expansions $\mathcal{G}_i^{l-1}$.*

For the example given above we can expand $clearblock(x, s)$ by

$$\mathcal{G}^0 = \Omega$$
$$\mathcal{G}^1 = g(cleartop(x), s, puttable(topof(x), \Omega))$$
$$\mathcal{G}^2 = g(cleartop(x), s, puttable(topof(x),$$
$$\qquad g(cleartop(topof(x)), s, puttable(topof(topof(x)), \Omega))))$$

$$\cdots$$
$$\mathcal{G}^l = g(cleartop(x), s, puttable(topof(x), \mathcal{G}^{l-1}_{[topof(x)/x]})).$$

For the Kleene-sequence it can be shown that $\mathcal{G}^{l-1} < \mathcal{G}^l$ and that $Sup(\mathcal{G}^l)$ is the least fixpoint of Σ (see fixpoint semantics; cf. [8, App. B]).

Up to now we only have regarded the syntactical aspects of RPSs. To calculate a value for an RPS (i.e. to compute a result), the symbols of the RPS have to be interpreted by functions and values have to be assigned to the variables:

Definition 8 (Interpretation and Valuation)
- *Interpretation I of an RPS: Function and constant symbols in the RPS are interpreted by functions and constants of a domain model with corresponding arity (and possibly types).*
- *Valuation β of variables: Each variable occuring in the (head of the) RPS has to be assigned a value (corresponding to variable type).*
- *In the following we will regard untyped structures only.*

4 Synthesis of RPSs from Initial Progams

4.1 An Algorithm for Induction of RPSs

Our approach to inductive synthesis of RPSs is based on the idea of the Kleene-sequence given above. That is, we reverse the process of expanding an RPS as proposed originally by [20]. We regard a given initial program as element of some Kleene-sequence which we try to identify and than fold the initial program to an RPS. Note, that our approach currently is restricted to infer a *single* recursive equation.

Definition 9 (Induction of a (linear) RPS) *Let $G \in M$ be an initial program. Then G can be folded into an RPS if G can be segmented in a sequence $\mathcal{G}^0 = \Omega$, $\mathcal{G}^l = tr(\mathcal{G}^{l-1}_{[t/v]}/m)$, where t is a vector of terms by which the vector v of variables in tr is replaced and where m is the place in term tr where the substitution by $\mathcal{G}^{l-1}$ is performed.*
If the complete initial program G can be described equations $\mathcal{G}^l$, that is if $G = \mathcal{G}^{l^*}$ for some l^*, we assume, that we can generalize $\mathcal{G}^{l^*}$ to an infinite sequence. That is, we extrapolate the RPS $\mathcal{G} = tr(\mathcal{G}_{[t/v]}/m)$.

Let's go back to our *clearblock*-example for illustrating this idea: Input into the synthesis algorithm may be the following initial program, defined for one up to three-block towers:

$G = g(cleartop(x), s, puttable(topof(x),$

$\quad g(cleartop(topof(x)), s, puttable(topof(topof(x)),$

$\quad g(cleartop(topof(topof(x))), s, puttable(topof(topof(topof(x))),$

$\quad \Omega)))))).$

We can segment G into $\mathcal{G}^0$, $\mathcal{G}^1$, $\mathcal{G}^2$ as shown in section 3 and in $\mathcal{G}^3 = G$. G can be folded by induction into an RPS according to definition 9:

$$\mathcal{G} = g(cleartop(x), s, puttable(topof(b), \mathcal{G}_{[topof(x)/x]})).$$

This RPS generalizes the experience with clearing the bottom block of towers consisting of one up to three blocks to towers of arbitrary height.

The definition given above covers all structures with a single recursive call only, that is tail recursion and linear recursion (see figure 2). To deal with structures with more than one recursion point and with tree recursion (see section 4.2), the definition can be extended:

Definition 10 (Induction of an RPS) *Let $G \in M$ be a initial program. Then G can be folded into an RPS if G can be segmented in a sequence $\mathcal{G}^0 = \Omega$, $\mathcal{G}^l = tr(\mathcal{G}^{l-1}_{[t_1/v]}/m_1 \ldots \mathcal{G}^{l-1}_{[t_n/v]}/m_n)$ with m_i as positions in tr where the substitution by $\mathcal{G}^{l-1}$ is performed. If l is sufficiently high, we can extrapolate the RPS*

$$\mathcal{G} = tr(\mathcal{G}_{[t_1/v]}/m_1 \ldots \mathcal{G}_{[t_n/v]}/m_n).$$

An operational method for performing the induction of an RPS is given in algorithm 1. To find an RPS according to the definition above, we have to construct hypothetical segmentations of an initial program G and check the current hypothesis tr by matching it with subexpressions of G. For a given tr we than have to determine substitutions σ which hold for G. Our aim is to find the simplest hypothesis to fold the initial program G into an RPS. Therefore we enumerate the hypotheses in the order given in algorithm 1.

Algorithm 1 (Induction of an RPS)
– **Find structure tr:**
   For all the following hypotheses tr of the recursive structure of G, the hypothesis holds if G can be segmented into subexpressions which are unifyable with tr
   1. Assume tr starts at the root node, consists of a single conditional expression and of one recursion point only
   2. If this assumption fails: enlarge the number of conditional expressions contained in tr (from two up to half of the number of occurences of the symbol g in G)
   3. If these assumptions fail: assume a constant initial part in G and move the starting point for looking for tr from the root to another occurence of g (from the second position of g in G up to $n - 2$ if n is the number of occurences of g in G)

4. If these assumptions fail: assume that there exists more than one recursion point in G and start with assuming two recursion points and enlarge the hypothesis up to half of the number of occurences of g in G

- **Find substitutions σ_i:**

  1. If the hypothesis consists of a single recursion point, generate a hypothesis for σ by unifying tr with that subexpression of G at which tr occurs for the second time
  2. If the hypothesis consists of more than one recursion point, generate separate hypotheses σ_i for each recursion point by unifying tr with that subexpression t_i of G where tr ouccures the i-th time.

The expansion of tr is restricted by the number of conditional expressions of which an initial program G is composed. For example, we restrict the number of conditional expressions in tr to half the number of conditional expressions contained in G. Otherwise, we would construct a hypothesis which could not be validated for the given G. An illustration of algorithm 1 with the *clearblock*-problem is given in figure 1. The procedure can be made more intuitive if we represent G as a tree.

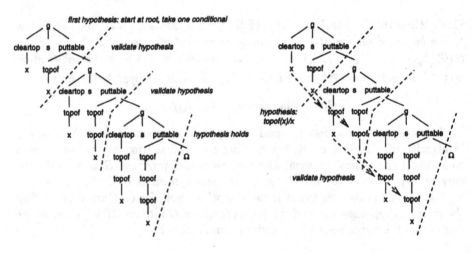

Fig. 1. Illustration of algorithm 1

Algorithm 1 was implemented and tested for a variety of recursive structures. The recursive structure tr can be composed of one ore more conditional expression and the possibility of a constant part in G not contained in the recursive structure is included in the algorithm. Up to now we are only dealing with cases, where the substitutions of variables are independent from each other. The separation of "find structure" and "find substitution" is introduced because we are planning to extend our substitution algorithm to cases of dependent variables. This extension is needed to deal with problems like the sorting of lists, where a counter j is substituted in relation to a counter i (i.e. we have a "nested loop").

4.2 Performance of the Algorithm

We will give some examples to illustrate the performance of algorithm 1. The structures given in figure 2 are initial programs for the well known recursive functions *last* (fig. 2a, tail recursive), *member* (fig. 2b, tail recursive with two conditional expressions), *addlist* (fig. 2c, linear recursive, similar to *clearblock*) and the function *myadd* (fig. 2d), which has a constant part not included in the recursive structure.

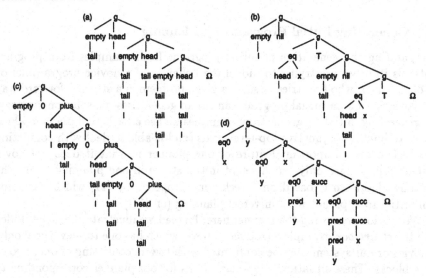

Fig. 2. Examples for recursive structures: tail recursion (a), tail recursion with two conditionals (b), linear recursion (c) and tail recursion with constant initial part (d)

Function *last* can be folded by the first hypothesis algorithm 1 generates. Function *member* can be folded by the second hypothesis, that *tr* consists of two conditional expression: $\mathcal{G} = g(empty(l), nil, g(eq(head(l), x), T, \mathcal{G}_{[tail(l)/l]}))$. Function *addlist* can be folded by the first hypothesis again, similar to the *clearblock*-problem given above. Function *myadd* can be folded after the hypotheses for *tr* starting at the root and consisting of one or two conditional expressions have failed by starting for a recursive structure in G at the second conditional expression. The RPS can be constructed by concatenating the constant part $g(eq0(x), y, \Omega)$ with $\mathcal{G} = g(eq0(y), x, \mathcal{G}_{[succ(x)/x, pred(y)/y]})$. (Note that the initial programs for *member* and *myadd* have to be expanded one level deeper to validate the hypothesis for σ).

We presented only cases for structures growing in the *else*-part of a conditional expression (i.e. right-recursive structures). But our algorithm can also deal with left-recursive cases and with structures with more than one recursion point as well. For example we can synthesize the function *maxlist* which consists of two tail recursions:

$$\mathcal{G} = g(empty(l), x, g(greater(head(l), x), \mathcal{G}_{[tail(l)/l, head(l)/x]}, \mathcal{G}_{[tail(l)/l]}))$$

and the tree recursive function for calculating *fibonacci*-numbers:

$$\mathcal{G} = g(eq0(x), 1, g(eq1(x), 1, plus(\mathcal{G}_{[pred(x)/x]}, \mathcal{G}_{[pred(pred(x))/x]}))).$$

5 Integrating Planning, Program Synthesis and Analogical Problem Solving

The algorithm for induction of RPSs is the core of the system IPAL which is implemented in a first prototype in LISP. In IPAL we realize our idea of combining inductive program synthesis with planning and analogical problem solving. We give a short description of both aspects in the following.

5.1 Generating Initial Programs by Planning

In separating the generation of initial programs from examples from program synthesis itself we are trying to model the behavior of a novice programmer or problem solver, who first tries to solve a given problem in a straight-forward way (i.e. constructing an initial program) and than generalizes his solution strategy. For generating initial programs from examples we use a backward-planner which is able to handle conjunctive top-level goals (and is able to deal with conflicting goals). The most important feature of our planner is, that it does not cover a single initial state only but a set of initial states in one planning trial. The planning algorithm is based on a technique proposed by [21] which has some similarities to approaches to universal planning (cf. [17]).

We are not presenting the planner here. Instead we illustrate the general idea with the *clearblock*-example introduced above, which has one top-level goal only. A novice or our system may be confronted with towers consisting of one, two or three blocks. These situations are initial states for our planner corresponding to the input part of examples in program synthesis. The initial states are described by conjunctions of predicates. Three possible initial states for the *clearblock*-problem are given in figure 3.

The system has to solve the problem to clear the base of the tower, i.e. block C. The goal state, which corresponds to the output part of examples in program synthesis, is represented by a single predicate: *cleartop(C)*. Note that our planner can deal also with conjunctions of goals as for example $on(A, B), on(B, C)$. The novice or our system has knowledge about operations and their conditions of application, corresponding to the background knowledge used in ILP approaches. This knowledge is represented as production rules with ADD and DEL lists for specifying the semantic of an operation. The operation needed to achieve the goal to clear a block is *on(x,y), cleartop(x) → puttable(x); ADD cleartop(y) DEL on(x,y)*.

Our planner builds a tree starting with the goal as root node. A left branch is introduced for the case that the goal is already fulfilled and a right branch for the case that it is not. The right branch is labelled with that operation which is given at the righthand side of a production rule containing the desired predicate in the ADD-list. Predicates given in the condition part of this rule and not occuring in the DEL-list are introduced as new subgoals. That is, our planner works with a backward chaining algorithm. Variables occuring in the goal predicate are used to instantiate the selected production rules. If there remain unbound variables these are instantiated by a lookup in the set of initial states.

In our example we start with *cleartop(C)* as the root. In the left successor, no subgoal is left. Here we terminate with a leaf *s* which represents a situation variable. In the right branch we introduce the operator *puttable(x)*. Variable *y* in the production rule is instantiated with *C* and we find situations s_1 and s_2 in our set of initial states so that *on(x, C)* can be unified with *on(B, C)* and variable *x* in the production rule is instantiated accordingly. A new subgoal, *cleartop(B)* is introduced as right successor-node. The resulting plan is given in figure 3.

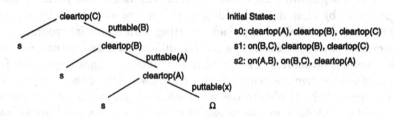

Fig. 3. Plan for dealing with the clearblock-problem

The plan can be reformulated with help of the background knowledge $on(x, y) \equiv topof(y) = x$. Thereby we gain the initial program which is than used in program synthesis.

5.2 Programming by Analogy

If an RPS was succesfully generated from an initial tree, we store it in memory. These RPSs enlarge the set of predefined functions available to IPAL and they can be used for analogical programming. Analogical programming can be seen as a special case of analogical problem solving which is described by four subprocesses in cognitive science literature [15]: (1) Retrieval of an example problem already solved which is structural similar to the current problem; (2) mapping the structures of example and goal problem; (3) adapt the example solution to the goal problem; and (4) generalize over the structure of example and goal problem.

In the case of our programming problems, we assume, that a programmer/the system has already constructed an initial program and now wants to fold it to an RPS. The RPSs stored in memory can be expanded to initial programs of a given depth by the rewrite rule given in definition 6. We compare (map) the current initial program for which the RPS is unknown with initial programs expanded from RPSs stored in memory. Comparision of initial programs is done by a transformation algorithm: The current initial tree is tried to be made identical to an initial tree belonging to an RPS expanded from memory by substitution, deletion and insertion of nodes (i.e. symbols contained in the initial program term). This method is implemented as a special version of the tree-to-tree distance algorithm proposed by [12]. If the transformation can be performed by unique subsitutions of symbols only, the structures of the example and goal tree are isomorphic. The new RPS can than be gained by subsituting symbols of the example RPS according to the mapping function. We can show that this is less expensive than performing inductive program synthesis if the memory is effectively organized.

Currently we are employing this method of analogical problem solving for iso-morphic structures only. But we are working on an extension to non-isomorphic cases, modifying example RPSs by deletion and insertion rules.

6 Conclusions and Future Research

We believe that segmenting inductive program synthesis in two parts - building initial programs by planning and folding initial programs to RPSs by a generic algorithm - may be a fruitful approach. Starting with an initial program as in-put makes program synthesis itself a not too difficult task and we can deal with complex recursive structures. The problem of inductive program synthesis from examples of course remains with all its well known difficulties. We only shift the greater part of the burden to the subproblem of generating initial programs from examples. But here we see possibilities to overcome some limitations in employing planning methodologies using heuristic techniques proposed in arti-ficial intelligence. Additionally we look at our approach as a potential model for human skill acquisition in the domain of problem solving. We can describe skill acquisition by three levels of generalization, all reported in cognitive science literature: the chuncking of rules in learning by doing (i.e. building initial pro-grams), descriptive generalization of the problem solving experience to a more general problem solving strategy (i.e. inductive program synthesis) and making use of already solved problems in analogical reasoning (i.e. giving an RPS a new semantic by interpreting the operation symbols w.r.t. another domain model).

Currently we can synthesize a variety of recursive structures from initial programs but our approach is restricted to independend variables, that is, we can not deal with nested loops. Our next goal therefore is, to extend the synthesis algorithm to finding dependencies in variable substitution. That is, we have to extend the "find subsitution" part of our algorithm from simple unification to a second cycle of induction. Another restriction to our approach is, that initial programs can be generated only for problems with finite data structures and primitive operations which can be defined by production rules, as blocksworld or Tower of Hanoi problems. While we are able to fold given initial programs representing numerical or list problems to RPSs, we are not able to construct initial programs from examples for these domains. To overcome this limitation we have to expand our planning algorithm from applying user-defined production rules only to making use of the operational semantics of already built-in functions of a given programming language (as *plus* or *tail*) and predicates (as *eq0* or *empty*). That is, we have to integrate the eval-apply interpreter of a functional language (as for example LISP) in plan construction. Last but not least, our approach can be extended to use not only predefined functions but making use of already inferred RPSs which makes it possible to infer complex recursive programs containing subprograms.

Acknowledgements

We thank a number of students participating in our students projects for supporting the implementation of the IPAL system, especially: Mark Müller and Martin Mühlpfordt.

References

1. J.R. Anderson. Knowledge compilation: A general learning mechanism. In R.S. Michalski, J.G. Carbonell, and T.M. Mitchell, editors, *Machine Learning - An AI Approach*, volume 2, pages 289–310. Tioga, 1986.
2. J.R. Anderson, P. Pirolli, and R. Farrell. Learning to program recursive functions. In M.T.H. Chi, R. Glaser, and M.J. Farr, editors, *The Nature of Expertise*, pages 153–183. Lawrence Erlbaum, 1988.
3. A. W. Biermann, G. Guiho, and Y. Kodratoff, editors. *Automatic Program Construction Techniques*. Collier Macmillan, 1984.
4. G. Le Blanc. BMWk revisited: Generalization and formalization of an algorithm for detecting recursive relations in term sequences. In F. Bergadano and L. de Raedt, editors, *Machine Learning, Proc. of ECML-94*, pages 183–197, 1994.
5. W. W. Cohen. Desiderata for generaization-to-n algorithms. In *Int. Workshop AII '92, Dagstuhl Castle, Germany*, volume LNAI 642, pages 140–150. Springer, 1992.
6. B. Courcelle and M. Nivat. The algebraic semantics of recursive program schemes. In Winkowski, editor, *Math. Foundations of Computer Science*, volume 64 of *LNCS*, pages 16–30. Springer, 1978.
7. J. Engelfriet. *Simple Program Schemes and Formal Languages*. Springer, 1974.
8. A.J. Field and P.G. Harrison. *Functional Progamming*. Addison-Wesley, 1988.
9. P. Flener and S. Yilmaz. Inductive synthesis of recursive logic programs: Achievements and prospects. to appear.
10. M. Ginsberg. Universal planning: An (almost) universally bad idea. *AI Magazine*, 10(4):40–44, 1989.
11. J. P. Jouannaud and Y. Kodratoff. Characterization of a class of functions synthesized from examples by a summers like method using a 'B.M.W.' matching technique. In *IJCAI*, pages 440–447, 1979.
12. S. Lu. A tree-to-tree distance and its application to cluster analysis. *IEEE Transactions on Pattern Analysis and Machine Intelligence*, PAMI-1(2):219–224, 1979.
13. Z. Manna and R. Waldinger. How to clear a block: a theory of plans. *Journal of Automated Reasoning*, 3(4):343–378, 1987.
14. S. Muggleton. Learning from positive data. In S. Muggleton, editor, *Proc. of the 6th Int. Workshop on Inductive Logic Programming*, pages 225–244. Stockholm University, Royal Institute of Technology, 1996.
15. L. R. Novick and K. J. Holyoak. Mathematical problem solving by analogy. *Journal of Experimental Psychology: Learning, Memory, and Cognition*, 14:510–520, 1991.
16. U. Schmid and F. Wysotzki. Skill acquisition can be regarded as program synthesis. In U. Schmid, J. Krems, and F. Wysotzki, editors, *Proc. of the First European Workshop on Cognitive Modelling (TU Berlin)*, pages 39–45, 1996.
17. M.J. Schoppers. Universal plans for reactive robots in unpredictable environments. In *IJCAI '87*, pages 1039–1046, 1987.
18. P. D. Summers. A methodology for LISP program construction from examples. *Journal ACM*, 24(1):162–175, 1977.
19. M. Veloso, J. Carbonell, M. A. Pérez, D. Borrajo, E. Fink, and J. Blythe. Integrating planning and learning: The prodigy architecture. *J. of Experimental and Theoretical AI*, 7(1):81–120, 1995.
20. F. Wysotzki. Representation and induction of infinite concepts and recursive action sequences. In *Proc. of the 8th IJCAI, Karlsruhe*, 1983.
21. F. Wysotzki. Program synthesis by hierarchical planning. In P. Jorrand and V. Sgurev, editors, *Artificial Intelligence: Methodology, Systems, Applications*, pages 3–11. Elsevier Science, Amsterdam, 1987.

Predicate Invention and Learning from Positive Examples Only

Henrik Boström

Dept. of Computer and Systems Sciences
Stockholm University
Electrum 230, 164 40 Kista, Sweden
henke@dsv.su.se
Tel: +46-8-16 16 16
Fax: +46-8-703 90 25

Abstract. Previous bias shift approaches to predicate invention are not applicable to learning from positive examples only, if a complete hypothesis can be found in the given language, as negative examples are required to determine whether new predicates should be invented or not. One approach to this problem is presented, MERLIN 2.0, which is a successor of a system in which predicate invention is guided by sequences of input clauses in SLD-refutations of positive and negative examples w.r.t. an overly general theory. In contrast to its predecessor which searches for the minimal finite-state automaton that can generate all positive and no negative sequences, MERLIN 2.0 uses a technique for inducing Hidden Markov Models from positive sequences only. This enables the system to invent new predicates without being triggered by negative examples. Another advantage of using this induction technique is that it allows for incremental learning. Experimental results are presented comparing MERLIN 2.0 with the positive only learning framework of Progol 4.2 and comparing the original induction technique with a new version that produces deterministic Hidden Markov Models. The results show that predicate invention may indeed be both necessary and possible when learning from positive examples only as well as it can be beneficial to keep the induced model deterministic.

1 Introduction

Bias shift approaches to predicate invention (e.g. [15, 6, 8, 1, 16]) introduce new predicates whenever the learning method fails to produce a consistent hypothesis in the given language [13]. This means that as long as it is possible to formulate a complete hypothesis in the given language (i.e. such that all positive examples are covered), negative examples are necessary for detecting inconsistency, and thus for inventing new predicates[1].

---

[1] Other approaches to predicate invention according to [13] fall outside the scope of this work. These are *reformulation approaches*, which uses predicate invention for optimising a theory w.r.t. size or compression, and *transformation approaches*, which base their decision on introducing new predicates on the operationality or efficiency of the induced hypothesis.

In this work we present one approach to this problem, the system MERLIN 2.0^2. The system is a successor of MERLIN 1.0 [5], which uses an overly general theory to find SLD-refutations[3] of positive and negative examples, and then searches for the minimal finite-state automaton that can generate all sequences of input clauses in the SLD-refutations of the positive examples and none of the sequences in the SLD-refutations of the negative examples. For example, assume that we are given the following overly general theory T:

(c1) p([]).
(c2) p([a|L]):- p(L).
(c3) p([b|L]):- p(L).

together with the positive examples $E^+ = \{$p([a,a,a,b,b]),p([a,a,b,b,b,b])$\}$ and the negative examples $E^- = \{$p([a]), p([a,b,a])$\}$. The corresponding positive sequences are $\{c2c2c2c3c3c1, c2c2c3c3c3c3c1\}$ and the negative sequences are $\{c2c1, c2c3c2c1\}$. The minimal automaton found by MERLIN 1.0 that is consistent with these sequences are:

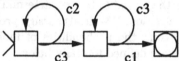

This automaton is used together with the overly general hypothesis to construct the folllowing hypothesis:

p([a|A]) :- p(A).
p([b|A]) :- p_1(A).
p_1([]).
p_1([b|A]) :- p_1(A).

Note that without the invention of a new predicate (in this case p_1), it is not possible to formulate the hypothesis that the argument of p should be a list in which all a's are followed by one or more b's.

Clearly, if MERLIN 1.0 is given positive examples only, there is nothing that prevents the system from reducing the automaton to a one-state automaton that accepts all strings consisting of symbols that appear in the positive sequences. In the above example, this would result in a hypothesis identical to the overly general theory. In order to overcome this problem, MERLIN 2.0 uses a technique for inducing Hidden Markov Models from positive sequences only [14], that instead of minimising the size of the resulting automaton maximises the posterior probability. This enables MERLIN 2.0 to invent new predicates without being triggered by negative examples. In the next section, we present the technique for inducing Hidden Markov Models as well as a new extension which makes the induced Hidden Markov Model deterministic. In section three it is shown how

---

[2] The system can be obtained from http://www.dsv.su.se/ML/MERLIN.html
[3] Familiarity with logic programming terminology is assumed [9].

this technique is incorporated in MERLIN 2.0. In section four, we present experimental results comparing the system with positive only learning in Progol 4.2 [10, 11] as well as comparing the deterministic and non-deterministic versions of the technique for induction of Hidden Markov Models. Finally, in section five we give concluding remarks and point out directions for future research.

2 Induction of Hidden Markov Models

We first give a definition of Hidden Markov Models adopted from [14] and then briefly present the technique for inducing Hidden Markov Models that was introduced in [14].

2.1 Hidden Markov Models

Hidden Markov Models (HMMs) can be viewed as a stochastic generalisation of the non-deterministic finite automata (NFAs) [7]. As NFAs, HMMs accept (or generate) strings over the alphabet by non-deterministic walks between the initial and final states. In addition, HMMs also assign probabilities to the strings they generate, computed from the probabilities of individual transitions and emissions. These concepts are defined formally below.

Definition 1. A Hidden Markov Model is a quintuple $HMM = (Q, \Sigma, q_I, q_F, P)$ where Q is a set of states, Σ is an output alphabet, q_I is the initial state, q_F is the final state and P is a set of probability parameters, consisting of *transition probabilities* $p(q \to q')$ specifying the probability that state q' follows q, for all $q, q' \in Q$ and *emission probabilities* $p(q \uparrow \sigma)$ specifying the probability that symbol σ is emitted while in state q for all $q \in Q$ and $\sigma \in \Sigma$. It is assumed that $p(q \to q_I) = p(q_F \to q) = 0$ for all $q \in Q$ and $p(q_I \uparrow \sigma) = p(q_F \uparrow \sigma) = 0$ for all $\sigma \in \Sigma$.

Definition 2. An HMM is said to generate a string $x = \sigma_1 \sigma_2 \cdots \sigma_l \in \Sigma^*$ if and only if there is a state sequence, or *path*, $q_I q_1 q_2 \cdots q_l q_F \in Q^*$ with non-zero probability, such that q_t outputs σ_t with non-zero probability for $t = 1, \dots, l$. The *probability of a path* is the product of all transition and emission probabilities along it.

Definition 3. The *structure* or *topology* of an HMM consists of its states Q, its outputs Σ, a subset of its transitions $q \to q'$ with $p(q \to q') = 0$ and a subset of its emissions with $p(q \uparrow \sigma) = 0$.

Definition 4. The *conditional probability* $P(x|M)$ of a string $x = \sigma_1 \cdots \sigma_l$ given an HMM M is computed as the sum of the probabilities of all paths that generate x:

$$P(x|M) = \sum_{q_1 \cdots q_l \in Q^l} p(q_I \to q_1)p(q_1 \uparrow \sigma_1)p(q_1 \to q_2) \dots p(q_l \uparrow \sigma_l)p(q_l \to q_F)$$

2.2 Induction of Hidden Markov Models

Traditional HMM estimation is based on the Baum-Welch algorithm [3], which assumes a certain topology and adjusts the parameters so as to maximise the model likelihood on the given samples. However, as we are primarily interested in finding the topology, and not the parameters, the technique in [14] is more appropriate than the former, as it in contrast to the former can be used for finding the HMM with maximimal posterior probability of the structure[4]. We first introduce the concept of posterior probability of an HMM structure according to [14] and then present their Best-first merging algorithm for finding an HMM with maximal posterior probability. Finally, we present an extension to the algorithm that forces the induced HMM to be deterministic.

Posterior probability for HMM structures We assume that there exists a distribution $P(M)$ independent of the data that assigns each model M an *a priori* probability, i.e. a bias. A model M can be decomposed into its structure part M_S and its parameter part θ_M, and the prior $P(M)$ can therefore be written as:

$$P(M) = P(M_S)P(\theta_M|M_S) \tag{1}$$

Given some data X, the problem is to find a model structure that maximises the posterior probability $P(M_S|X)$. Bayes' Law expresses the posterior as:

$$P(M_S|X) = \frac{P(M_S)P(X|M_S)}{P(X)} \tag{2}$$

Since the data X is fixed, this amounts to finding a model that maximises $P(M_S)P(X|M_S)$. Using the *Dirichlet distribution* as a parameter prior and a description length prior for the structure together with *the Viterbi approximation*[5] and the assumption that the Viterbi paths do not change as θ_M varies, the expression to be maximised, $P(M_S)P(X|M_S)$, can now be written:

$$\prod_{q \in Q} (|Q| + 1)^{-n_t(q)} (|\Sigma| + 1)^{-n_e(q)} F(t_{q_1}, \ldots, t_{q_{n_t(q)}}) F(e_{q_1}, \ldots, t_{q_{n_e(q)}}) \tag{3}$$

where t_{q_i} and e_{q_i} are the total counts of transitions and emissions, called *Viterbi counts*, occurring along the Viterbi paths associated with the samples in X and the n-dimensional function $F(t_1, \ldots, t_n)$ is defined as:

$$F(t_1, \ldots, t_n) = \frac{B(t_1 + 1/n, \ldots, t_n + 1/n)}{B(1/n, \ldots, 1/n)} \tag{4}$$

---

[4] The Baum-Welch algorithm can in principle also be used for finding a structure, as it may set some parameters to zero, but it requires that the maximal number of states is known and also that initial values are chosen for the model parameters, a choice of which the outcome of the algorithm is highly dependent.

[5] All paths except the most likely one, called the *Viterbi path*, are assumed to have zero probability.

where $B(\alpha_1, \ldots, \alpha_n)$ is the n-dimensional Beta function:

$$B(\alpha_1, \ldots, \alpha_n) = \frac{\Gamma(\alpha_1) \cdots \Gamma(\alpha_n)}{\Gamma(\alpha_1 + \cdots + \alpha_n)} \qquad (5)$$

Best-first merging Below we present the incremental version of the Best-first merging algorithm in [14]. It takes as input a sequence of samples, incorporates them one by one into the current model and after each incorporation uses Hill-Climbing (with look-ahead) to find a new current model with maximal posterior probability by merging states. After all samples are processed, the current model is returned. Since the calculation of the posterior probability uses Viterbi counts, rather than transition and emission probabilities, such are kept by the algorithm.

The incorporation of a new sample $x = \sigma_1 \cdots \sigma_l$ into an existing model M results in that a set of new states $q_1, \ldots, q_l$ are added to Q and that the Viterbi counts for the transitions $q_I \rightarrow q_1$, $q_i \rightarrow q_i + 1$, $1 \leq i \leq l - 1$, and $q_l \rightarrow q_F$ and the emissions $q_i \uparrow \sigma_i$, $1 \leq i \leq l$, are set to one. When merging two states, the corresponding Viterbi counts are added and recorded as the counts for the new state.

---

function Best-first merging($x_1 \cdots x_n$, *LookAhead*)
  $M :=$ the empty model
  for $i := 1$ to n **do**
    Incorporate x_i into M, $L := $ *LookAhead* and $B := M$
    repeat
      Let C be the set of models obtained from merging two states in B
      Let $B \in C$ be the model with maximal posterior probability $P(B|X)$
      if $P(B|X) > P(M|X)$ **then** $M := B$, $L := $ *LookAhead* **else** $L := L - 1$
    until $L = 0$ or $C = \emptyset$
  return M

Example After having incorporated one sample $x_1 = c2c2c2c3c3c3c1$ into the empty model, the resulting model is as follows:

One of the models with highest posterior probability obtained from merging two states is obtained by merging the last two states that emit c3. However, the posterior probability of this model is less than the initial model, but if look-ahead is allowed, the merging of the two states emitting c3 in this model gives a model with higher posterior probability than the initial one. The merging process continues with the above model, eventually reaching the following model (using one-step look-ahead):[6]

Inducing Determistic HMMs Whenever a new sample is to be incorporated into the current model, a large part (or even all) of it may in fact already be accepted by the model, requiring little (or no) factual alterations to the model. The Best-first merging algorithm, however, generates a completely new sub-model for each sample and relies on the merging process to eventually incorporate the sample in the best way. In many cases, this is not only inefficient but may also mislead the Hill-Climbing search, as the chances of making the wrong choices increases with the number of states. The above approach can be viewed as being maximally pessimistic regarding the use of the current model for generating the new sample.

One could also consider a maximally optimistic version, which incorporates the sample into the existing model as far as possible. Assuming this means incorporating the longest prefix of the sample for which there is a path in the current model, this can be done efficiently by keeping the model *deterministic*, i.e. no state may have transitions leading to two different states that emit the same symbol. When incorporating a new sample, determinism is kept by aligning the sample as far as possible with the current model[7], introducing new states and transitions only for the suffix of the sample for which there is no path in the current model. When having merged two states, determinism can be kept by checking whether the new state has transitions leading to two different states that emit the same symbol, and if so, merging these two states. In section 4, we empirically compare the pessimistic with the optimistic approach.

3   MERLIN 2.0

Having induced an HMM that shows what sequences of input clauses are allowed in SLD-refutations of a given theory, MERLIN 2.0 produces a new theory that allows only those sequences that are allowed by both the original theory and the induced HMM. This is done by first converting the HMM into an NFA and by representing the set of sequences allowed by the given theory as a context-free grammar, and then deriving the intersection of the NFA and the first grammar. Finally, the intersection is used to produce the resulting hypothesis.

3.1   Converting an HMM into an NFA

The construction of an NFA from the structure of an HMM can be done in two ways: for each state, either the transitions leading from the state or the

---

[6] It should be noted that the term $P(X|M_S)$ prevents the HMM to be further reduced as the conditional probability of the sample would decrease.

[7] This includes updating the Viterbi counts.

transitions leading to the state are labeled with the symbols emitted by the state. We have chosen the latter option, since it avoids introducing transitions labeled with the empty string. Furthermore, all states with transitions leading to the final state in the HMM will become final states in the NFA.

Example The final HMM in the last example is converted into the following NFA:

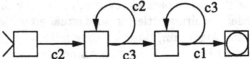

3.2 Representing the Theory as a Context-Free Grammar

The set of possible sequences of input clauses in SLD-refutations of any instance of a goal G for a given program P can be represented by a context-free grammar, referred to as a *proof grammar*, (S, R), where S is the start symbol and R is a set of rules, where each rule is on the form $L \to C R_1 \ldots R_n$, where $n \geq 0$, $L, R_1 \ldots R_n$ are non-terminal symbols and C is a terminal symbol. Below, we show how to produce such a grammar by an example (for algorithmic details see [5]).

Example Given the goal {:- p(L)} together with the program in section 1, the above procedure produces the following proof grammar $(p/1, R)$, where R is the following set of rules:

$p/1 \to c1$
$p/1 \to c2\ p/1$
$p/1 \to c3\ p/1$

3.3 Deriving the Intersection

The intersection of a context-free language and a regular language is a context-free language [2]. In [5], a derivation of the algorithm in [2] is presented, which finds a context-free grammar that represents the intersection of a proof grammar and an NFA.

Example Given the NFA and the proof grammar in the previous examples, the following rules are produced by the procedure mentioned above, together with the start symbol $(p/1, q_0, \epsilon)$[8]:

---

[8] *Dead rules* have been removed.

$$(p/1, q_0, \epsilon) \rightarrow c2\ (p/1, q_1, \epsilon)$$
$$(p/1, q_1, \epsilon) \rightarrow c2\ (p/1, q_1, \epsilon)$$
$$(p/1, q_1, \epsilon) \rightarrow c3\ (p/1, q_4, \epsilon)$$
$$(p/1, q_4, \epsilon) \rightarrow c1$$
$$(p/1, q_4, \epsilon) \rightarrow c3\ (p/1, q_4, \epsilon)$$

3.4 Producing the Final Program

Having derived the intersection of the learned automaton and the original proof grammar, MERLIN 2.0 produces the final hypothesis in the form of a logic program, in which there is one clause for each rule in the intersection, and where each predicate symbol corresponds to a non-terminal symbol. This is achieved using the procedure presented in [5].

Example Given the context-free grammar in the previous example, together with the predicate symbol $p/1$, the above procedure produces the following program:

```
p([a|A]) :- p_1(A).
p_1([a|A]) :- p_1(A).
p_1([b|A]) :- p_2(A).
p_2([]).
p_2([b|A]) :- p_2(A).
```

4 Empirical Evaluation

In this section we present an empirical evaluation of the performance of MERLIN 2.0 both with the original Best-first merging algorithm and with the extension that forces the algorithm to produce deterministic HMMs[9]. MERLIN 2.0 is also compared to Progol 4.2, which is able to learn from positive examples only, but not to invent new predicates[10]. We first present the theories and example sets that were used in the experiments and then the experimental results.

---

[9] The lookahead was set to 5 for the non-deterministic version and to 1 for the deterministic version. Following [14], a logarithmic version of Bayes' law was used in the implementation including a global prior weight λ, giving $\lambda\ log\ P(M_S) + log\ P(X|M_S)$ as the quantity to be maximised. λ was set to 0.30 for the non-deterministic version and to 0.25 for the deterministic version. Furthermore, both versions first work in an incremental phase, in which states may only be merged if they have identical emissions and then in a second, non-incremental phase, in which all states may be merged.

[10] The default parameter settings were used in Progol except for the *posonly* parameter which was set to ON and the variable depth parameter (i) and the maximum clause length (c), which were set to 7.

4.1 Domains

The first theory that was investigated is the following:

(c1) nn(0).
(c2) nn(s(X)):- nn(X).

The entire set of examples consisted of the first 40 natural numbers, where the instances were classified as positive if they were odd, and negative otherwise (i.e. 50% positive examples). A correct definition of the odd numbers can be found without inventing new predicates, which means that Progol at least in theory is able to find it.

The second theory that was investigated is the same as presented in section 1, and the set of positive examples consisted of instances of p(L) where L contained up to 7 elements representing the regular expression $a^+b^+a^+$. A set of negative examples was generated by randomly replacing one of the elements in each positive example with the other constant, such that the new instance did not belong to the set of positive examples. The total number of examples in this set is 70 (of which 50% are positive). It should be noted that a correct hypothesis can not be produced for this domain without predicate invention.

The third theory extends the previous with one additional recursive clause, allowing the constant c to appear in the lists. The set of positive examples consisted of instances of p(L) where L contained up to 33 elements representing the regular expression $ac^*a \cup bc^*b$ (this target was also used in [14]). The set of negative examples were generated in the same way as for the previous domain, resulting in a set of 128 examples in total (of which 50% are positive).

The fourth theory and example set that were investigated were taken from [5], where the target predicate turing(M) represents a sequence of movements of a Turing machine, where each move is on the form $(Read, Write, Move)$ and the positive examples correspond to movements of a Turing machine performing addition. The total number of examples for this domain was 72 (of which 50% were positive).

4.2 Experimental Results

Each set of positive examples and each set of negative examples were randomly split into two halves. One half of the positive examples together with one half of the negative examples were used for testing. Subsets of the other half of positive examples were used for training, and the number of examples in these sets were varied, where a larger set always included a smaller. The same training and test sets were used for all three techniques. Each experiment was iterated 50 times and the mean accuracy on the test examples is presented below.

In Figure 1, the results from the odd number domain are presented. In this domain, the deterministic version of MERLIN 2.0 clearly outperforms the two other techniques, which produce overly general hypotheses (the mean number of clauses produced by Progol is 1.0 for all training sizes).

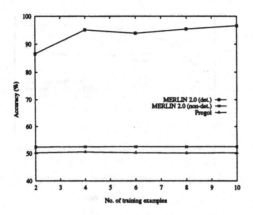

Fig. 1. Accuracy for the odd number domain.

In Figure 2, Figure 3 and Figure 4, the results from the $a^+b^+a^+$, $ac^*a \cup bc^*b$ and the Turing machine domains are presented. As for the previous domain, Progol produces overly general hypotheses in all three domains. That Progol would not perform well in these domains was expected as predicate invention is necessary for obtaining correct hypotheses. The deterministic version of MER-LIN 2.0 outperforms the non-deterministic version in the first two of the three domains, due to that the non-deterministic version in the first case produces overly specific hypotheses and in the second case overly general hypotheses. In the last domain, the deterministic version suffers from producing overly specific hypotheses.

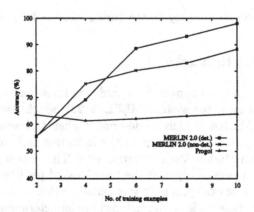

Fig. 2. Accuracy for the $a^+b^+a^+$ domain.

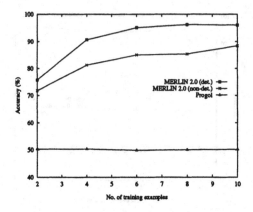

Fig. 3. Accuracy for the $ac^*a \cup bc^*b$ domain.

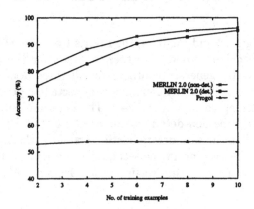

Fig. 4. Accuracy for the Turing machine domain.

5 Concluding Remarks

We have presented a novel approach to predicate invention when learning from positive examples only, the system MERLIN 2.0, which uses a technique for inducing Hidden Markov Models to determine when to invent new predicates. We have also proposed an extension to the induction technique, which makes the induced Hidden Markov Model deterministic. The system and the extension has been evaluated empirically, and the usefulness of predicate invention when learning from positive examples only was demonstrated as well as it was shown that it can be beneficial to keep the induced model deterministic.

There are a number of possible directions for future research. One is to experiment with the approach using other techniques for inducing finite-state automata from positive examples only (e.g. [4]). Another direction is to investigate extensions to the technique for inducing Hidden Markov Models, including techniques for finding a good global prior weight, using other search techniques than Hill-climbing and allowing negative examples. A third direction is to actually use the parameters which are set by the induction algorithm in order to induce stochastic logic programs [12].

Acknowledgements This work has been supported by the European Community ESPRIT Long Term Research Project no. 20237 *Inductive Logic Programming II* and the Swedish Research Council for Engineering Sciences (TFR).

References

1. Bain M. and Muggleton S., "Non-Monotonic Learning", in Muggleton S. (ed.), *Inductive Logic Programming*, Academic Press (1992) 145–161
2. Bar-Hillel Y., Perles M. and Shamir E., "On formal properties of simple phrase structure grammars", *Zeitschrift für Phonetik, Sprachwissenschaft und Kommunikationsforschung*, 14, 1, Akademie Verlag, Berlin (1961) 143–172
3. Baum L., Petrie T, Soules G. and Weiss N., "A maximization technique occurring in the statistical analysis of probabilistic functions in Markov chains", *The Annals of Mathematical Statistics* 41 (1970) 164–171
4. Biermann A. W. and Feldman J. A.," On the Synthesis of Finite-State Machines from Samples of Their Behavior", *IEEE Transactions on Computers* 21 (1972) 592–597
5. Boström H., "Theory-Guided Induction of Logic Programs by Inference of Regular Languages", *Proc. of the 13th International Conference on Machine Learning*, Morgan Kaufmann (1996) 46–53
6. Kijsirikul B., Numao M. and Shimura M., "Discrimination-based constructive induction of logic programs", *Proceedings of the 10th National Conference on Artificial Intelligence*, Morgan Kaufmann (1992) 44–49
7. Lewis H. R. and Papadimitriou C. H., *Elements of the Theory of Computation*, Prentice-Hall (1981)
8. Lapointe S., Ling, C. and Matwin S., "Constructive Inductive Logic Programming", *Proceedings of the 13th International Joint Conference on Artificial Intelligence*, Morgan Kaufmann (1993) 1030–1036
9. Lloyd J. W., *Foundations of Logic Programming*, (2nd edition), Springer-Verlag (1987)
10. Muggleton S., "Inverse entailment and Progol", *New Generation Computing* 13 (1995) 245–286
11. Muggleton S., "Learning from positive data", *Proc. of the Sixth International Workshop on Inductive Logic Programming* (1996)
12. Muggleton S., "Stochastic Logic Programs", *Advances in Inductive Logic Programming* (Ed. L. De Raedt), IOS Press (1996) 254–264
13. Stahl I., "Predicate Invention in Inductive Logic Programming", *Advances in Inductive Logic Programming* (Ed. L. De Raedt), IOS Press (1996) 34–47
14. Stolcke A. and Omohundro S., "Best-first Model Merging for Hidden Markov Model Induction", TR-94-003, International Computer Science Institute, Berkeley, CA (1994)
15. Wirth R. and O'Rorke P., "Constraints on Predicate Invention", *Proceedings of the 8th International Workshop on Machine Learning* , Morgan Kaufmann (1991) 457–461
16. Wrobel S., "Concept Formation During Interactive Theory Revision", *Machine Learning Journal* 14 (1994) 169–192

An Inductive Logic Programming Framework to Learn a Concept from Ambiguous Examples

Dominique BOUTHINON[1,2]   Henry SOLDANO[1,2]
[1] Atelier de BioInformatique (ABI)
[2] Laboratoire d'Informatique Paris Nord (LIPN)

Atelier de BioInformatique 12, rue Cuvier 75005 PARIS (FRANCE)
email : Dominique.Bouthinon@snv.jussieu.fr
phone : (33) 01 44 24 65 82
fax   : (33) 01 44 27 63 12

Abstract. We address a learning problem with the following peculiarity : we search for characteristic features common to a learning set of objects related to a target concept. In particular we approach the cases where descriptions of objects are ambiguous : they represent several incompatible realities. Ambiguity arises because each description only contains indirect information from which assumptions can be derived about the object. We suppose here that a set of constraints allows the identification of "coherent" sub-descriptions inside each object.

We formally study this problem, using an Inductive Logic Programming framework close to characteristic induction from interpretations. In particular, we exhibit conditions which allow a pruned search of the space of concepts. Additionally we propose a method in which a set of hypothetical examples is explicitly calculated for each object prior to learning. The method is used with promising results to search for secondary substructures common to a set of RNA sequences.

1. Introduction

A problem of molecular biology is in the origin of this study, namely the one of finding a secondary substructure common to a set of RNA sequences[2,3]. A major feature of this problem is that, as often, learning consists in searching for a characteristic description related to the target-concept, but only an ambiguous representation of each object is known. More precisely when considering the whole description of an object there are several, and possibly a great number, of incompatible realities. This occurs either because various realities exist (in Diettrich [6] the object is a molecule which has various, alternative, 3-D conformations), either because, as the observation is indirect, a unique reality is dissimulated among a set of possibilities. The RNA problem mentioned above corresponds to this later case. But let us take a simpler example : the object is a scene figuring a stoplight, the description, due to a color-blind person is the following: "*Stoplight(s), Red(s), Green(s), Car(v), Run(v,s)*". The difficulty is that the observation is imperfect (because the witness is color-blind) and indirect (as run(s) is an interpretation rather than a direct perception). There are two incompatible realities depending whether the stoplight were either Red or Green. In the former case the object should be described as "*Stoplight(s), Red(s),Car(v), run(v,s)*", in the latter case "*Stoplight(s), Green(s), Car(v)*". Suppose now that this color-blind person builds up a set of such ambiguous observations related to a target concept (for instance the responsibility of a driver in a car crash), each observation containing a single positive instance. The learning problem would be to find a characteristic description, belonging to the hypothesis space, i.e. a most specific hypothesis that explains all positive instances. Note that in the ordinary case an incoherent statement as "Red(s), Green(s)" could be generated but would be rejected since it could not recognize any positive instance. It is not the case when considering ambiguous observations. Then, how to avoid such hypothesis? What we propose here is to use integrity constraints, as for instance " *Stoplight(s) and Red(s) and Green(s)*, is incoherent ". We state that part of an observation is "coherent" if it satisfies all the constraints, and that an hypothesis is coherent if it does not recognize any incoherent *sub-observation* (a part of any observation).

The constraints allows the identification, within an observation, of the largest coherent sub-observations, i.e. the possible realities on which induction should be performed. We have here the inductive view of the idea of « extension » as used in non-monotonic reasoning [5,17]. For now on we will refer to a learning problem with ambiguous examples and integrity constraints as *a class A problem*.

The framework described in section 2 relies on logic programming, with a closed-world assumption (within a sub-observation anything which is not stated nor can be deduced is false) together with negation by failure when expressing constraints. In section 3 we show that such ambiguities within examples result in several difficulties about completeness and consistency when searching a space of concepts and studying properties allowing for an efficient reduction of the search space. Then we propose a general method to perform concept learning in which we first build and select, the set of largest coherent sub-observations for each example. Section 4 addresses the RNA secondary structure problem mentioned at the beginning of the paper. We describe the application of our method to this problem and discuss some encouraging results. We conclude by discussing related work, in particular the work on the «multiple instance problem » as described by Dietterich [6,10].

2. Class A problems

A class A problem formally consists in learning from a set O of observations, and, given a domain theory T, a set H of characteristic representations of a target concept. Each observation o contains one example e(o) of the target concept. Our framework is embedded in Inductive Logic Programming [7,11,12], and from now on, H, O, and T will be logic programs without functional terms. We allow the use of a negation by failure operator, **not**, within the body of clauses belonging to the domain theory T.

An observation o is represented as a conjunction of ground atoms: $o = a_1 \wedge a_2 \wedge a_m$. The example e(o) hidden inside o is a particular sub-observation, i.e. a part of o. The definitions of the concepts in H are searched inside a space of hypothesis. Any hypothesis h of this space is represented as a conjunction of single clauses (ground or not) ($h = b_1 \wedge b_2 \wedge ...b_n$).

The domain theory T contains a set C of constraints together with a set B of definite clauses describing background knowledge about constraints. Each constraint is a goal, i.e. a negative clause $\leftarrow d_1 \wedge d_2 \wedge ...d_u$ where d_i is a (possibly negative) literal. The idea here is that $d_1 \wedge d_2 \wedge ...d_u$ represents an incoherent statement :

Definition 1 a sub-observation o is incoherent iff o violates a constraint $c = $ «$\leftarrow d_1 \wedge d_2 \wedge ...d_u$ » i.e. iff the goal $\leftarrow d_1 \wedge d_2 \wedge ...d_u$ succeeds within the logical program $o \wedge B$.

Generally observations are incoherent and examples, by definition, are not.

As defined the constraints in a class A problem are close to integrity constraints as presented by De Raedt [14] and used in various works [18-21,26].

Hereafter we exemplify our framework using an « arch problem » similar to the famous problem due to Winston [25]. Arches are hidden inside the observations, as could happen if each arch were represented by a picture suffering from unexpected superposition

Example 1

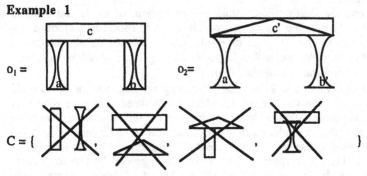

The domain theory T contains :

- the following constraints:

$c_1 = \leftarrow column(X) \wedge pillar(Y)$ (there cannot be columns and pillar in the same arch)
$c_2 = \leftarrow lintel(X) \wedge triangle(Y)$ (there cannot be lintels and triangles in the same arch)
$c_3 = \leftarrow$ **incompatibility** (this constraints is defined thanks to the background
knowledge)

- The background knowledge
B = {incompatibility   ← pillar(X) ∧ triangle(Y) ∧ sustains(X,Y),
    incompatibility ← column(X) ∧ lintel(Y) ∧ sustains(X,Y)}
(there is an incompatibility when a pillar sustains a triangle, or when a column sustains a lintel)

$\{o_1, o_2\}$ is the set of observations :

$o_1 = column(a) \wedge pillar(a) \wedge column(b) \wedge pillar(b) \wedge$ **lintel(c)** $\wedge$ **sustains(a,c)**
$\wedge$ **sustains(b,c)**.
$o_2 =$ **column(a')** $\wedge$ **column(b')** $\wedge$ **lintel(c')** $\wedge$ triangle(c') $\wedge$ **sustains(a',c')** $\wedge$
sustains(b',c').

Within the observations the conjunction of italic atoms and the conjunction of bold atoms represent incoherent sub-observations (not all ones) which violate the constraints printed with the corresponding typographic style. For instance o_1 violates c_1 and c_3 since there are pillars and columns within o_1, i.e. the goal $= \leftarrow column(X) \wedge pillar(Y)$ succeeds within the logic program $o_1 \wedge B$ with the answer-substitutions {X/a, X/b}, and there is an incompatibility due to the fact that a column (a or b) sustains a lintel (c), i.e. the goal <- incompatibility succeeds within $o_1 \wedge B$.

The observations o_1 and o_2 each contains an example corresponding to an (unidentified) coherent sub-observation:

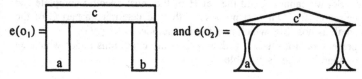

$$e(o_1) = \qquad \text{and } e(o_2) =$$

End example 1

A class A problem is then represented by the pair $(O, T = B \cup C)$. The purpose is then to build *the set H of most specific hypothesis that "cover" all the examples* (completeness).

We state that an hypothesis **h** is complete relatively to the set O of observations, if and only if **h** theta-subsume [4,9,13] each example within O. In the same way, the hypothesis **h** is *more general* than the hypothesis **g** (denoted as **h** ≤ **g**) whenever **h** theta-subsumes **g**.

Definition 2 An hypothesis h is complete ⇔ ∀ o ∈ O, ∃θ such that hθ ⊆ e(o) (denoted as h ≤ e(o)).
Here, for sake of clarity, the domain theory is not used to check completeness. However there would be no conceptual difficulties in using generalized subsumption as proposed by Buntime [4].

However as examples are hidden within observations, completeness checking is difficult : an hypothesis **h** can cover an observation and still not cover the embedded example. Constraints are then used to ensure that a part of such absurd (relatively to the domain theory) hypothesis are not selected. Hereafter we define the incoherence of an hypothesis relative to the set of constraints :

Definition 3 An hypothesis h is incoherent iff there exists a substitution λ such that hλ corresponds to some incoherent sub-observation (∃λ ∃o ∈ O, hλ ⊆ o and hλ incoherent) .

Example 2
let us go back to example 1. The sub-observation $o' = column(b) \wedge lintel(c) \wedge$ sustains(b,c) included in o_1 is incoherent. As a consequence the hypothesis $h = column(X) \wedge lintel(Y) \wedge$ sustains(X,Y) is incoherent because when $\lambda = \{X/b, Y/c\}$, we have o' =hλ.
End example 2

The set H we search is then the set of most specific hypothesis both complete and coherent. Notice that, whenever there is no ambiguity, i.e. the examples are exactly the observations, then observations have to be coherent. However incoherence still could eliminate hypothesis that can be unified with an incoherent part of some example (the whole example being coherent). As we will see an interesting case (hereafter referred to as "monotonicity") is the one in which whenever a sub-observation is coherent no part of it can be incoherent.

3. Solving a class A problem

As stated above direct use of completeness ($\forall o \in O, h \leq e(o)$) is in this case prohibited since $e(o)$ is unknown. So, we cannot build the set H of the most specific complete and coherent hypothesis we search for. Our first purpose is then to determine a part G of the hypothesis space, as small as possible, which necessarily includes H ($H \subseteq G$).
In what follows we present such a set G together with some conditions under which an efficient pruning of the search space is possible.

3.1 Bounding the set of solutions

We determine hereafter a set L of hypothesis which is a lower bound of H. Later we will discuss to what extent searching for L is interesting when solving class A problems. The first step consists in weakening completeness in order to have a computable criteria.

Definition 4 An hypothesis g is stated as O-complete if and only if g theta-subsumes each observation ($\forall o \in O, g \leq o$).

A O-complete and coherent hypothesis is said to be O-*valid*, or, in short, *valid*. The set G of valid hypothesis includes H since any complete hypothesis necessarily is O-complete ($\forall o \in O, h \leq e(o) \Rightarrow h \leq o$).
Let us denote as L the set of the most specific valid hypothesis. Let h be an hypothesis belonging to H, then there exists at least one hypothesis in L which is more specific than h (consequently no hypothesis of L can be strictly more general than h). So L is a lower bound of H within the set of valid hypothesis. Of course when the examples are exactly the observations, then there is no ambiguity and so L = H. However an interesting case is the one in which we assume that H is included in L. We will give some rationale for such an assumption in section 3.3 and argue that this assumption holds when considering the real-world problem presented in 4.
Hereafter we consider top-down methods to search for G. As G is bounded by L these methods also apply when only searching for L. The starting point is the (always valid) null hypothesis .

3.2 Pruning the top-down search

An O-complete but incoherent hypothesis happen to be specialized in a valid hypothesis 1) by grounding variables within **h,** 2) by adding atoms to **h**. Generally speaking **h** is specialized in **h'** = h$\pi \wedge$ **b** where π is a substitution and **b** a conjunction of atoms.

Example 3

Let us consider the following class A problem (O, T= B $\cup$ C) :
O ={o} with o = **true(a,3)** $\wedge$ **implies(a,b)** $\wedge$ **true(b,5)** $\wedge$ *true(c,7)*.
C = {$\leftarrow$ *true(c,X)*, $\leftarrow$ **true(X,U)** $\wedge$ **implies(X,Y)** $\wedge$ **not true(Y,V)**}.
B = $\varnothing$.
1) The hypothesis **h** = *true(X,U)* is incoherent as h can be unified to the incoherent sub-observation *true(c,7)*. However the hypothesis **h'** = true(a,U), more specific than h (by grounding X) is coherent.
2) The hypothesis **g** = **true(X,U)** $\wedge$ **implies(X,Y)** is incoherent as g and the sub-observation o' = **true(a,3)** $\wedge$ **implies(a,b)** are unifiable (o' is incoherent as the goal $\leftarrow$ **true(X,U)** $\wedge$ **implies(X,Y)** $\wedge$ **not true(Y,V)** succeeds in (o' $\wedge$ B)). Here again the

hypothesis g' = true(X,U) ∧ implies(X,Y) ∧ true(Y,V), more specific than g (by adding true(Y,V)), is coherent.
End example 3

The situation shown in the example 3 prohibits any pruning relying on validity. We study hereafter the cases in which such situations cannot occur and so pruning becomes possible. For that purpose we use the framework of Torre and Rouveirol [23, 24] who states that a property P is « private », relatively to a relation R whenever for any pair (h_1,h_2), $\{h_1 R h_2$ and $\neg P(h_1)\}$ implies $\neg P(h_2)$. In our case, asserting that validity is private relatively to the subsumption relation, means that any hypothesis that is not valid will not have valid specializations. We exhibit hereafter two conditions which are sufficient to insure that validity is private relatively to subsumption. Notice that example-1/2 satisfies both condition when example-3 satisfies none of them.

The first condition,'*incoherence discrimination*', is denoted as D(O,T).

Definition 5 D(O,T) is true whenever for any observation, two sub-observations which are identical except for constant names, are either both coherent or both incoherent.

The second condition '*incoherence monotony*' is denoted as M(O,T) :

Definition 6 M(O,T) is true whenever any sub-observation including an incoherent sub-observation also is incoherent.

Considering example 3, D(O,T) does not hold since o contains the sub-observation *true(a,3)* which is coherent and also contains *true(c,7)* which is incoherent. M(O,T) neither holds since the sub-observation **true(a,3) ∧ implies(a,b)** ∧ true(b,5) is coherent and includes the incoherent sub-observation **true(a,3) ∧ implies(a,b)**. Here falsity of M(O,T) is related to negative literals appearing in constraints.
So D(O,T) appears to limit the ambiguity tolerated within an observation when M(O,T) restricts the expressiveness of constraints.
The following property states that D(O,T) and M(O,T) are sufficient to insure that validity is private relatively to subsumption (proofs of properties are given in appendix) :

Property 1 If M(O,T) and D(O,T) both hold then whenever an hypothesis h is not valid, none of its specializations h' are valid.

Now suppose that M(O,T) and D(O,T) both hold. Then, when considering top-down search of the hypothesis space, specialization of an hypothesis can be safely stopped whenever it is not O-complete or it is incoherent.

3.3 Prior construction of hypothetical examples

M(O,T) together with D(O,T) suggest a top-down search starting from the null hypothesis (always valid) and maintaining at each step a set of valid hypothesis.
A natural idea when dealing for a class A problem is to associate to each observation o the set E(o) *of hypothetical examples* i.e. the largest coherent sub-observations of o. One can observe that each hypothetical example represents a coherent and not ambiguous part of the

data associated with a given observation. In our framework, using hypothetical examples has several advantages. First, a given incoherent sub-observation causes incoherence of many hypothesis (by way of substitutions) and so prior computation of largest coherent sub-observations avoid unnecessary calculations. Second, some class A problems are naturally expressed as « multiple instances » problems, as we will see in section 4. Third, reformulating ambiguity in terms of alternatives results in a different view of class A problems. Note that as examples are supposed to be coherent, e(o) is included in at last one hypothetical example.

First we give two properties that relate incoherence monotony and incoherence discrimination to hypothetical examples.

Property 2 If M(O,T) holds then a sub-observation o' of a given observation o is coherent if and only if it is included in at least one hypothetical example of o.

Property 3 if M(O,T) and D(O,T) both hold then an hypothesis h is valid if and only if h theta subsumes at least one hypothetical example of each observation o

Now a general way to solve a class A problems requires two steps:
1) Build the set E(o) corresponding to each observation o. This is performed by classical branch and bound methods whose bound part is based on the integrity constraints.
2) Build the set G of valid hypothesis. This is performed by classical Top-Down methods using property 3.

During step 2 it is possible, whenever we assume that H is included in the lower bound L of G, to only retain hypothesis belonging to L. This means that no hypothesis more specific than any hypothesis h belonging to H (h is a most specific complete and coherent hypothesis) can subsume at least one hypothetical example of each observation. Whenever possible, sorting G (or L) using a problem dependent preference criterion helps in selecting most « plausible » hypotheses.

Example 4

M(O,T) and D(O,T) both hold when considering example-1. We also suppose that we have at our disposal the two sets $E(o_1)$ and $E(o_2)$ of hypothetical examples respectively related to o_1 and o_2 Furthermore a top-down search starting from the null hypothesis and using $E(o_1)$ and $E(o_2)$ has selected a set G of valid hypothesis, the following set L containing the most specific ones $(L \subseteq G)$:

---

[1] the dashed line means that the shape of considered element the arch is not known.

$(h_1 = column(X) \wedge column(Y) \wedge lintel(Z)$
$h_2 = column(X) \wedge lintel(Z) \wedge sustains(Y,Z)$
$h_3 = lintel(Z) \quad \wedge sustains(X,Z) \wedge sustains(Y,Z)$)

In this case, the solution set H only contains one most specific hypothesis h that covers the two examples e(o1) and e(o2) (h = sustains(X,Z) $\wedge$ sustains(Y,Z) representing

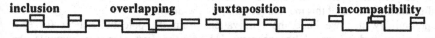

On can note that h is valid and complete but does not belong to the set L of the most specific valid and O-complete hypothesis. This shows that an important final ambiguity remains since H must be searched in G. Thus a plausibility criterion must be applied on G to select one (of few) preferred hypothesis.

End example 4

4. Application

The theoretical study we have presented is inspired in a biomolecular problem concerning the prediction of the secondary structure common to a set of RNA molecules. A RNA is a molecule made of a *sequence* of nucleotides, that is folded in such a way that some nucleotides are paired (two paired nucleotides constitute a *base-pairing*), in several places named *helices*. The helices of a RNA determinate its *secondary structure* which is determinant to the biological function of the molecule. It is very hard, often impossible, to experimentally identify RNAs secondary structures. Therefore, one has to compute all potential helices of each RNA sequence using theoretical methods. These potential helices constitute an indirect and ambiguous view of the secondary structure of a RNA: indeed some helices are incompatible among each other, thus the actual secondary structure is one of the (numerous) sets of compatibles helices. Hence, predicting the secondary structure common to a set of RNA molecules is a class A problem: for each RNA the set of all potential helices is an observation, the hypothetical examples are the largest sets of compatible helices, and the example is one particular set of compatible helices. The domain theory of the problem only contains the single compatibility constraint between helices.

Two helices can have one of the following four structural relations (an helix is represented by the following scheme ⌐===⌐___⌐===⌐)

inclusion   overlapping   juxtaposition   incompatibility

We are only interested by the structural shape of the secondary structures, so an observation describing all the structural relationships between potential helices of a RNA will contain a conjunction of atoms written from the four binary predicates « juxtaposition », « overlapping », « inclusion », « incompatibility ». The single constraint is represented by the goal ← *incompatible(X,Y)*.

246

Therefore any *completely defined sub-observation* (i.e. a sub-observation describing all the relationships between helices it mentions) that does not contain the atom « incompatible » represents a potential secondary structure since the goal ← *incompatible(X,Y)* fails in this context.

Example 5

Let the 5 potential helixes of a RNA sequence s, with the following structural relations (one can observe that the helices **c** and **d** are incompatible) be:

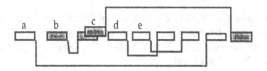

The hypothetical examples contain, respectively, all the relations of the helixes {a,b,c,e} and {a,b,d,e}.Let the observation describing the relationships between the helices of s be :
inclusion(a,b) ∧ overlapping(a,c) ∧ inclusion(a,d) ∧ inclusion(a,e) ∧
incompatible(b,c) ∧ juxtaposition(b,d) ∧ juxtaposition(b,e) ∧
inclusion(c,d) ∧ inclusion(c,e) ∧ overlapping(d,e).
Let the constraint be ← *incompatible(X,Y)*, and the knowledge associated with the domain be empty (B = ∅), then each sub-observation containing the atom *incompatible* is incoherent. One observes that the sub-observation *inclusion(a,b) ∧ inclusion(a,c)* which is formally coherent is not completely defined due to the absence of the relationship « incompatible(b,c) » (the sub-observation inclusion(a,b) ∧ inclusion(a,c) ∧ incompatible(b,c) is completely defined and incoherent).

End example 5

In this problem, we will only consider the completely defined sub-observations reducing the space of the hypothesis to the ones unifiable with such sub-observations (all the properties described in the theoretical part remaining true).
The solution set H contains only one hypothesis **h** representing the actual secondary substructure common to all RNAs. Moreover we will suppose that H is included in the set L containing the most specific valid hypothesis (any valid hypothesis represents a structure that is potentially present in all RNAs), which means that **h** is one of the largest (most specific) potential common substructures.
This problem satisfies the conditions D(O,T) and M(O,T), thus we have designed a new method of prediction using the scheme of resolution presented in part 3. We expose hereafter the main ideas of this method (cf. [2,3] for the details) :
In a preliminary step we build the observations from the potential helices (of each sequence) identified by an ad hoc program [1]. At the first step we compute the hypothetical examples E(o) of each observation o, that represent the secondary structures potentially present in the RNA associated with o, through a branch and bound algorithm using the constraint of compatibility. Because of the cardinality of E(o) we only keep the 200 potential structures with best energies in each observation (remark that this criterion cannot be use to directly search for the common secondary structure).
At the second step, a top-down ad hoc method is used to build the set containing the largest potential secondary structures common to all RNAs, i.e. the sets L of the valid

hypothesis that are maximally specific. We have shown that thanks to a new way of encoding secondary structures, building L is equivalent to searching for the longest prefixes in a dictionary, where each entry of the dictionary represents a potential structure. This is done with an algorithm derived from KMR [8,22], that we have adapted.

At the third step we sort L with a plausibility measure that consists in comparing for each candidate structure represented by a single hypothesis h of L, the number of RNA sequences covered by h with the number of previously built random sequences also covered by h.

This new method presents interesting features because it does not require the prior alignment of the sequences[2] and allows taking into account all theoretical shapes of secondary structures. The first results are promising : we applied the method to several sets of sequences (about 200 in a set), each sequence containing one transfer RNA (tRNA) and non relevant data. We were able to discover the tRNA structure in all the sets.

5. Conclusion

As stated above a major feature of class A problems is the ambiguity of examples which are considered as hidden in observations. More precisely the part of the observation outside each example is not only useless (not related to a target concept) but does not correspond to the reality.

As a consequence inside an observation we may find incoherent parts resulting either from uncertainties as for instance "heavy(x) and light(x)" or from misunderstandings as « dead(x) and smiling(x) ». Then background knowledge has to include constraints to prevent considering such incoherent parts. We have seen above that ambiguity together with incoherence modify the statement of the classical "learning a characteristic concept description" problem, and that, when certain properties are satisfied, a convenient strategy consists in first building the sets of hypothetical examples related to each observation.

Class A problems are close to the «multiple instance problem» as described by Diettrich, but differ from it in two main points. First, in class A problems we have to compute hypothetical examples, Diettrich assumes direct access to « multiple » instances. Diettrich assumes that there are various realities : in this problem a molecule has several conformations, some of which are related to the target-concept, and these conformations are not mixed up, but correspond to different descriptions. Second, Diettrich uses counter-examples to constraint the search of discriminant features, in our framework this search is more difficult because we do not have such knowledge.

We are now working on extending the class A framework with negative observations (each containing a negative example), and generalized subsumption. Moreover we are studying links between our framework and *characteristic induction from interpretations* [15,16].

Acknowledgments
We thanks Alain Viari and Marc Champesme for their contribution to this work, and Eduardo Rocha for his help in carefully reading this manuscript.

Appendix

Proof of property 1 :

---

[2]Aligning two RNA sequences is equivalent to establish a map between the sets containing the positions of their nucleotides.

h incoherent $\Rightarrow \exists o \subsetneq O, \exists \sigma$ such that $h\sigma \subseteq o$ and $h\sigma$ incoherent. Let us suppose that **h'** is valid (consequently O-complete and coherent). $h \leq h' \Rightarrow h' = h\pi \wedge b$, where π is a substitution and **b** a conjunction of atoms. **h'** O-complete $\Rightarrow \exists \theta$ such that $(h\pi \wedge b)\theta \subseteq o$ $\Rightarrow h\pi\theta \subseteq o$. D(O,T) and $h\sigma \subseteq o$ and $h\pi\theta \subseteq o$ and $h\sigma$ incoherent $\Rightarrow h\pi\theta$ incoherent (Definition 5). $h\pi\theta$ incoherent and $h\pi\theta \subseteq (h\pi \wedge b)\theta \subseteq o \Rightarrow (h\pi \wedge b)\theta$ incoherent (Definition 6), thus **h'** is incoherent (consequently not valid) ◊

Proof of property 2 :
"$\Rightarrow$" : **o'** being coherent either **o'** is maximal (thus $o' \in E(o)$), either $\exists e \in E(o)$ such that $o' \subset e$.
"$\Leftarrow$" : Let $o' \subseteq e$. Because **e** is coherent (by definition) the property M(O,T) entails that **o'** is coherent (otherwise **e** should not) ◊

Proof of property 3 :
"$\Rightarrow$" : **h** O-complete entails $\forall o \in O, h \leq o \Rightarrow \exists \theta$ such that $h\theta \subseteq o$. As **h** is coherent the property 2 entails that $\exists e \in E(o)$ such that $h\theta \subseteq e$, so $h \leq e$.
"$\Leftarrow$" : Let $\forall o \in O \; \exists e \in E(o)$ such that $h \leq e$ be. We want to proof that a) $h \leq o$ and b) **h** is coherent :
a) $\exists e \in E(o)$ such that $h \leq e \Rightarrow \exists \theta \; h\theta \subseteq e$, as $e \subseteq o$ we can derive $h\theta \subseteq e \subseteq o$, what entails $h \leq o$.
b) if **h** is incoherent then $\exists o \in O$ and $\exists \theta'$ such that $h\theta' \subseteq o$ and $h\theta'$ is incoherent. According to a) $\exists \theta$ such that $h\theta \subseteq e \subseteq o$, and $h\theta$ is coherent (property 2). Thus $h\theta'$ is incoherent and $h\theta$ is coherent what contradicts the property D(O, T), thus $h\theta'$ (consequently **h**) is not incoherent ◊

References

1. B. Billoud, M. Kontic and A. Viari, Palingol: a declarative programming language to describe nucleic acids' secondary structures and to scan sequence databases, *Nucleic Acids Research*, vol 24, n° 8, pp. 1395-1403, 1996.
2. D. Bouthinon, Apprentissage à Partir d'Exemples Ambigus : Etude Théorique and Application à la Découverte de Structures Communes à un Ensemble de Séquences d'ARN, doctorat de l'université Paris XIII-Institut Galilée, 1996.
3. D. Bouthinon, H. Soldano and B. Billoud, Apprentissage d'un concept commun à un ensemble d'objets dont la description est hypothétique : application à la découverte de structures secondaires d'ARN, *Journées Francophones d'Apprentissage*, Sètes (France), pp. 206-220, 1996.
4. W. Buntime, Generalized subsumption and its applications to induction and redundancy, *Artificial Intelligence*, pp. 149-176, 1988.
5. D. MacDermott and J. Doyle, Non-monotonic logic I, *Artificial Intelligence*, vol. 13, n° 1-2, pp.41-72, 1980.
6. T.G. Dietterich, R.H. Lathrop and T. Lozano-Perez, Solving the Multiple-Instance Problem with Axis-Parallel Rectangles, *Artificial Intelligence*, vol 89(1-2), pp. 31-71, 1997.
7. P.A. Flach, A Framework for Inductive Logic Programming, *Inductive Logic Programming*, 1992.

8. R.M. Karp, R.E. Miller and A.L. Rosenberg, Rapid identification of repeated patterns in strings, trees and arrays, *Proc. 4th Annu. ACM Symp. Theory of Computing*, pp. 125-136, 1972.

9. J.U. Kietz and M. Lübbe, An efficient subsumption algorithm for inductive logic programming, *Machine Learning*, pp. 130-138, 1994.

10. R. Lindsay, B. Buchanan, E. Feigenbaum and J. Lederberg, Applications of artificial intelligence to organic chemistry : The Dendra projects, New-York McGraw-Hill., 1980.

11. S. Muggleton, Inductive Logic Programming, *Inductive Logic Programming*, 1992.

12. S. Muggleton and C. Feng, Efficient induction of logic programs, *Inductive Logic Programming*, 1992.

13. S.H. Nienhuys-Cheng and R.D. Wolf, The subsumption theorem in inductive logic programming : facts and fallacies, *International Workshop on Inductive Logic Programming*, Leuven, 1995.

14. L. De Raedt and M. Bruynooghe, Belief updating from integrity constraints and queries, *Artificial Intelligence*, vol 53, pp. 291-307, 1992.

15. L. De Raedt, Logical settings for concept-learning, *Artificial Intelligence*, 95 187-201 (1997).

16. L. De Raedt and L. Dehaspe, Clausal Discovery, *Machine Learning*, 26, 99-146 (1997).

17. R. Reiter, A logic for default reasoning, *Artificial Intelligence*, vol. 13, n° 1-2, pp. 81-131, 1980.

18. M. Sebag, A constraint-based induction algorithm in FOL, *Machine Learning*, pp. 275-283, 1994.

19. M. Sebag and C. Rouveirol, Induction of maximally general clauses consistent with integrity constraints, *Inductive logic programming*, 1994.

20. M. Sebag and C. Rouveirol, Constraint inductive logic programming, *Advances in inductive logic programming*, 1995.

21. M. Sebag, C. Rouveirol and J.F. Puget, Inductive Logic Programming + Stochastic Bias = Polynomial Approximate Learning, Multi Strategy Learning, J. Wrete & R.S. Michalski, MIT Press, 1996.

22. H. Soldano, A. Viari and M. Champesme, Searching for flexible repeated patterns using a non transitive similarity relation, *Pattern Recognition Letters*, vol 16, pp. 233-245, 1995.

23. F. Torre and C. Rouveirol, Opérateurs naturels en programmation logique inductive, JICAA' 97, Roscoff 20-22 Mai 1997, pp. 53-64, 1997.

24. F. Torre and C. Rouveirol, Natural ideal operators in inductive logic programming, *Proceeding of the ninth European Conference on Machine Learning* pp. 274-289, Springer-Verlag, 1997.

25. P.H. Winston, Learning structural descriptions from examples, *The psychology of computer vision*, P.H. Winston, MacGraw-Hill, 1975.

26. S. Wrobel, First order theory refinement, Advances in inductive logic programming, L. De Raedt, IOS press, 1996.

First-Order Learning for Web Mining*

Mark Craven, Seán Slattery and Kamal Nigam

School of Computer Science, Carnegie Mellon University
Pittsburgh, PA 15213-3891, USA
e-mail: ⟨firstname⟩.⟨lastname⟩@cs.cmu.edu

Abstract. We present compelling evidence that the World Wide Web is
a domain in which applications can benefit from using first-order learning
methods, since the graph structure inherent in hypertext naturally lends
itself to a relational representation. We demonstrate strong advantages
for two applications – learning classifiers for Web pages, and learning
rules to discover relations among pages.

1 Introduction

In recent years, there has been a large body of research centered around the
topic of learning first-order representations. Although these representations can
succinctly represent a much larger class of concepts than propositional representations, to date there have been only a few problem domains in which first-order
representations have demonstrated a decided advantage over propositional representations. The graph-like structure provided by pages on the World Wide Web
is one domain that seems natural for first-order representation, yet has not been
previously studied in this context. Cohen [1] has used first-order methods for
text classification, but the focus was on finding relations between words rather
than between documents. The lower half of Figure 1 illustrates the notion of the
Web as a directed graph where pages correspond to the nodes in the graph and
hyperlinks correspond to edges. Using this representation, we address two types
of learning tasks: *learning definitions of page classes*, and *learning definitions of
relations between pages*. In contrast to related efforts on similar Web tasks, our
work focuses on learning concepts which represent relational generalizations of
the inherent graph structure.

Our work on these two learning tasks has been conducted as part of a larger
effort aimed at developing methods for automatically constructing knowledge
bases by extracting information from the Web [2]. Given an ontology defining
classes and relations of interest, such as that shown in the top half of Figure 1,
along with training examples consisting of labeled Web pages, the system learns
a set of information extractors for the classes and relations in the ontology, and
then populates a knowledge base by exploring the Web. The task of recognizing
class instances can be framed as a page-classification task. For example, we can

---

* This research was supported in part by the Darpa HPKB program under contract
F30602-97-1-0215.

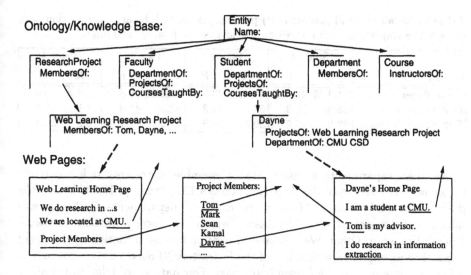

Fig. 1. The top part of the figure shows part of an ontology that defines page classes and relations between pages. The bottom part shows the Web represented as a directed graph, which forms examples of the classes and relations in the ontology.

extract instances of the Faculty class by learning to recognize the home pages of faculty members. Similarly, we can identify relations that exist among objects by recognizing prototypical patterns of hyperlink connectivity among pages. Consider the lower half of Figure 1, which shows an example of an instance of the MembersOfProject relation: Dayne is a member of the Web Learning project.

The applicability of these two learning tasks (learning page classes and learning page relations) extends beyond the setting of building knowledge bases from the Web. A variety of applications, including information filtering systems and browsing assistants, have used trainable page classifiers. As an example of learning relations among pages, consider the task of automatically extracting job listings by starting from company Web sites and finding the "employment opportunities" page. This task can be framed as one of learning a concept definition that specifies search-control rules for navigating the Web. In general, there are many potential applications of such search-control rules for finding a particular Web resource from a given class of starting points.

2 Learning First-Order Definitions of Page Classes

This section presents four classification problems and reports that a first-order learner can perform better than a more traditional document classifier which ignores document relationships. We first present two classification algorithms, a conventional text learning algorithm (Naive Bayes) which ignores document relationships, and a first-order learner (FOIL) which can use such information. More complete details of the data set, algorithms and experiments can be found elsewhere [2].

Table 1. Recall (R) and precision (P) percentages on each binary classification task using Naive Bayes, FOIL with words only, and FOIL with words and links.

method	Student R	Student P	Course R	Course P	Faculty R	Faculty P	Project R	Project P
Naive Bayes	51.4 %	42.6 %	46.4 %	28.2 %	23.0 %	16.8 %	1.3 %	3.6 %
FOIL (words)	25.3	50.3	34.5	44.3	43.3	48.4	6.1	10.0
FOIL (words & links)	73.0	70.2	39.5	53.8	58.2	61.2	10.2	21.3

For these experiments, we use a data set assembled for our research in extracting knowledge bases from the Web. It contains 4,127 pages and 10,945 hyperlinks drawn from the Web sites of four computer science departments. Each page was labeled as belonging to one of the classes Department, Faculty, Student, Research-Project, Course, or Other. We also labeled relation instances consisting of pairs of pages. For example, each instance of the InstructorsOfCourse relation consists of a Course home page and a Person home page. Our data set of relation instances comprises 251 InstructorsOfCourse instances, 392 MembersOfProject instances, and 748 DepartmentOfPerson instances.

As a representative conventional text classifier, we use the Naive Bayes classifier [4]. To classify a document with n words $(w_1, w_2, \ldots, w_n)$ into one of a set of classes C we simply calculate:

$$\arg \max_{c_j \in C} \Pr(c_j) \prod_{i=1}^{n} \Pr(w_i | c_j) \quad \text{where} \quad \Pr(w_i | c_j) = \frac{N(w_i, c_j) + 1}{N(c_j) + T} .$$

$N(w_i, c_j)$ is the number of times word w_i appears in training set examples from class c_j, $N(c_j)$ is the total number of words in the training set for class c_j and T is the total number of unique words in the corpus.

We use version 4.2 of Quinlan's FOIL [5] system for learning first-order clauses, and two types of background relations to describe the data:
• has_word(Page) : This set of relations indicates that *word* occurs on Page. To reduce the number of predicates, standard text categorization techniques were used, leaving between 500 and 800 word predicates per training set.
• link_to(Page, Page) : This relation represents hyperlinks between web pages in our corpus. The first argument is the page on which the link occurs, and the second is the page to which it is linked.

Using leave-one-university-out cross validation we build and test binary classifiers for four classes. We assess the classifiers using recall (R) and precision (P) defined as:

$$R = \frac{\text{\# correct positive examples}}{\text{\# of positive examples}} , P = \frac{\text{\# correct positive examples}}{\text{\# of positive predictions}} .$$

To test the value of a first-order representation, we run FOIL using two different sets of background relations, one which has only the word predicates (words) and one which has both the word and link predicates (words & links). Table 1

Table 2. Some rules induced by FOIL with good test set performance. Also shown are the number of positive and negative test set examples covered by each rule.

student_page(A) :- link_to(B,A), has_*michael*(B), has_*graduat*(B),   151 ⊕ 27 ⊖
                  has_*richard*(B), not(has_*depart*(B)).

course_page(A) :- has_*instructor*(A), not(has_*good*(A)), link_to(A,B),   31 ⊕ 3 ⊖
                not(link_to(B,_1)), has_*assign*(B).

faculty_page(A) :- has_*professor*(A), has_*ph*(A), link_to(B,A), has_*faculti*(B). 18 ⊕ 3 ⊖

shows the precision and recall results averaged over the four test sets. Using descriptions of the words and links, FOIL outperformed the other methods on these binary classification tasks. The power of using a relational description is evident from the difference in performance between the two FOIL runs.

Table 2 shows three of the rules induced by FOIL with high test-set accuracy. After analyzing the results, we found that the B variable in the sample student_page rule binds to directory pages of graduate students (the literals test for common names and the stemmed version of the word *graduate*). In effect, the rule states that A is a student home page if it is linked to by a directory page of graduate students. On average, FOIL using words and links induced 20 clauses for Student, 19 clauses for Course, 12 for Faculty and 7 for ResearchProject.

The results of this experiment lead us to believe that first-order representations and algorithms are well suited to Web page classification tasks. They use hyperlink information easily and can outperform traditional text-classification approaches which have no means to use such information effectively.

3 Learning First-Order Definitions of Page Relations

In this section, we discuss the task of learning to recognize relations of interest that exist among pages. An assumption underlying our approach is that relations among pages are represented by *hyperlink paths* in the Web. Thus, the learning task is to characterize the prototypical paths of the target relations. We learn definitions for the following target relations from the ontology shown in Figure 1: department_of_person(Page, Page), instructors_of_course(Page, Page), and members_of_project(Page, Page). In addition to the positive instances for these relations, our training sets include approximately 300,000 negative examples.

The problem representation we use consists of the following background relations:

- *class*(Page) : For each *class* from the previous section, the corresponding relation lists the pages that represent instances of *class*. These instances are determined using actual classes for pages in the training set and predicted classes for pages in the test set.
- link_to(Hyperlink, Page, Page) : This relation represents the hyperlinks that interconnect the pages in the data set.
- has_*word*(Hyperlink) : This set of relations indicates the words that are found in the anchor (i.e., underlined) text of each hyperlink. The vocabulary for this

Table 3. Recall (R) and precision (P) results for the relation learning tasks. The symbols ◇ and ⋆ precede each result that is uniformly superior (i.e. better than on all four test sets) to the same measure for FOIL, and m-estimate FOIL, respectively.

method	DepartmentOfPerson		InstructorsOfCourse		MembersOfProject	
	R	P	R	P	R	P
FOIL	26.9%	97.1%	53.8%	84.9%	32.1%	80.8%
FOIL w/m-estimates	26.9	97.1	59.8	89.3	◇ 44.9	83.8
PATH-MCP	◇⋆ 78.5	98.0	◇⋆ 64.9	89.1	◇⋆ 49.7	82.6

set of relations includes about 350 words for each training set.

- all_words_capitalized(Hyperlink) : The instances of this relation are hyperlinks in which the words in the anchor text all start with a capital letter.
- has_alphanumeric_word(Hyperlink) : The instances of this relation are hyperlinks which contain a word with both alphabetic and numeric characters.
- has_neighborhood_word(Hyperlink) : This set of relations indicates the words that are found in the "neighborhood" of each hyperlink. A neighborhood is the paragraph, list item, table entry, title or heading in which a hyperlink is contained. The vocabulary for this set includes 200 words.

The algorithm we use for learning page relations augments FOIL's hill-climbing search with a deterministic variant of Richards and Mooney's *relational pathfinding* method [6]. The basic idea underlying this method is that a relational problem domain can be thought of as a graph in which the nodes are the domain's constants and the edges correspond to relations which hold among constants. The algorithm tries to find a small number of prototypical paths in this graph that connect the arguments of the target relation. Richards and Mooney's algorithm is nondeterministic in that it randomly selects an uncovered positive instance to use as a seed. We have developed a deterministic variant (PATH-MCP) that finds the *most common path* among the uncovered positive instances. Once such a path is found, an initial clause is formed from the relations that constitute the path, and the clause is further refined by a hill-climbing search. Like Džeroski and Bratko's m-FOIL [3], PATH-MCP uses m-estimates of a clause's error to guide its construction. We have found that this evaluation function results in fewer, more general clauses than FOIL's information gain measure.

We evaluate our approach using the same four-fold cross-validation methodology we used in Section 2. Table 3 shows precision and recall results for learning the three target relations using basic FOIL, FOIL with m-estimates, and PATH-MCP. The results in this table indicate several interesting conclusions. First, all of the methods are able to learn accurate (i.e., high-precision) rules for all three tasks. The primary differences are in terms of coverage. A second interesting result is that the PATH-MCP method achieves higher levels of recall than the non-pathfinding methods. This result is due to the fact that both versions of FOIL fail to learn any clauses describing paths of more than one hyperlink, whereas PATH-MCP is able to learn clauses characterizing multiple-hyperlink paths.

Table 4. Two of the clauses learned by PATH-MCP. Also shown are the number of positive and negative test-set examples covered by each clause.

department_of_person(A,B) :- person(A), department(B), link_to(C,A,D),   371 ⊕ 4 ⊖
                            link_to(E,D,F), link_to(G,F,B),
                            has_neighborhood_*james*(E).
members_of_project(A,B) :- research_project(A), person(B), link_to(C,A,D), 18 ⊕ 0 ⊖
                            link_to(E,D,B), has_neighborhood_*people*(C).

Finally, Table 4 shows two of the interesting clauses learned by PATH-MCP. Both of them describe relations represented by multiple hyperlinks, and the DepartmentOfPerson clause is similar to the Student clause shown in Section 2 in that it has learned to exploit directory pages of people (referenced by the variable E) in order to find the people associated with a given department. On average, PATH-MCP learned 3 clauses for the DepartmentOfPerson relation, 7 clauses for InstructorsOfCourse, and 5 clauses for MembersOfProject.

4 Conclusions

We have presented experiments in two real-world learning problems that involve mining information from the Web, an interesting testbed for first-order learning. Our experiments in learning page classifiers show that, in some cases, first-order learning algorithms learn definitions that have higher accuracy than commonly used statistical text classifiers. When learning definitions of page relations, we demonstrate that first-order learning algorithms can learn accurate, non-trivial definitions that necessarily involve a relational representation.

Finally, we note that although the background relations used in our experiments represent the graph structure of hypertext, we could also use first-order representations that describe the internal layout of Web pages. In future work, we plan to investigate the value of learning with this additional relational structure.

References

1. W. W. Cohen. Learning to classify English text with ILP methods. In L. De Raedt, editor, *Advances in Inductive Logic Programming*. IOS Press, 1995.
2. M. Craven, D. DiPasquo, D. Freitag, A. McCallum, T. Mitchell, K. Nigam, and S. Slattery. Learning to extract symbolic knowledge from the World Wide Web. Technical report, Department of Computer Science, Carnegie Mellon Univ., 1998.
3. S. Džeroski and I. Bratko. Handling noise in inductive logic programming. In S.II. Muggleton and K. Furukawa, editors, *Proc. of the 2nd International Workshop on Inductive Logic Programming*.
4. T. Mitchell. *Machine Learning*. McGraw Hill, 1997.
5. J. R. Quinlan and R. M. Cameron-Jones. FOIL: A midterm report. In *Proc. of the European Conf. on Machine Learning*, pages 3–20, Vienna, Austria, 1993.
6. B. Richards and R. Mooney. Learning relations by pathfinding. In *Proc. of the 10th Nat. Conf. on Artificial Intelligence*, pages 50–55, San Jose, CA, 1992. AAAI Press.

Explanation-Based Generalization in Game Playing: Quantitative Results

Stefan Schrödl

Institut für Informatik
Albert-Ludwigs-Universität
Am Flughafen 17, D-79110 Freiburg, Germany
e-mail: schroedl@informatik.uni-freiburg.de

Abstract. *Game playing* has attracted researchers in Artificial Intelligence ever since its beginnings. By comparison with human reasoning, learning by operationalization of general knowledge, as formalized by the *Explanation-Based Generalization (EBG)* paradigm, appears to be highly plausible in this domain. Nevertheless, none of the previously published approaches is (provably) sufficient for the target concept, and at the same time applicable to arbitrary game states.
We trace this paradox back to the lack of the expressive means of *Negation as Failure* in traditional EBG, and constructively support our claim by applying the respective extension proposed in [Schr96] to the chess endgame king-rook vs. king-knight.
Methodically, endgames are well-suited for quantitative evaluation and allow to obtain more rigorous results concerning the effects of learning than in other domains. This is due to the fact that the entire problem space is known (and can be generated) in advance.
We present the main results of a large-scale empirical study. The issues of training complexity, speedup for recognition and classification, as well as the question of optimal reasoning under time constraints are analyzed.

Keywords: Explanation-Based Learning, applications

1 Introduction

Explanation-Based Generalization (EBG) is a speedup learning technique which tries to re-organize existing knowledge, guided by a given "typical" problem instance, such that similar instances can be solved more efficiently in the future. A general, domain-independent algorithm was early developed in the context of logic programming [KCMcC87]: Initially, a *domain theory D* (set of facts and rules) is already available which includes a correct and complete definition of the *target concept* (a distinguished atom Q). However, D may be overly general and cumbersome for its intended use by the *performance element* (such as a Prolog system). Thus, the primary aim is to re-formulate D in a more practical form as specified by an *operationality criterion* which defines a list of predicate symbols allowed to occur in the derived rule. In order to cover a frequent usage pattern a *training example* is employed, i.e., a set of facts E such that an instance $Q\sigma$ of Q is logically implied by $D \cup E$. The *explanation* is identified with the respective *proof*; it is generalized (e.g., by pruning the proof tree at operational atoms) and transformed into a new rule C, which is a logical consequence of D and generalizes E (i.e., $E \cup \{C\} \models \exists(Q\sigma)$ holds).

By means of C, similar instances whose proof structure differs only in operational features can subsequently be recognized more efficiently than using D alone. By changing the inference strategy such that C is always tried before resorting to D (in a Prolog system, it simply suffices to add C at the beginning), it is hoped to improve also the overall performance. However, since in general C is not complete, nothing can be deleted in return. Hence, an additional computational overhead is inevitably imposed for cases where C cannot be successfully applied, particularly for all negative examples. If training instances are not well-chosen, and if numerous rules are learned, the overall efficiency can even degrade; this undesirable effect has been termed the *utility problem* [Mi90].

Numerous factors are involved in a quantitative analysis of the effects of EBG, including specific characteristics of the performance element, and the statistical distribution of the target concept. In order to be predictive, similarly as in PAC-learning, the assumption is made that the distribution of past examples does not significantly differ from that of future ones. Since a mathematical model soon becomes too complicated, the common approach is to address the problem of efficiency empirically [Kel88, Mi90].

Game Playing. We consider two-player, perfect information (the game state is totally accessible to both players), zero-sum (what is good for one player is bad for his opponent) games. The value of an arbitrary legal state (e.g. 1, 0, and -1 for won, drawn, and lost, respectively) can be determined by exploring the respective *game tree* until all its *terminal states* are reached, whose values are fixed by the rules. Search procedures such as *minimax* or *alpha-beta* then back them up by maximizing resp. minimizing the values of successor states on every other level. In the equivalent *negmax* formulation, both players try to maximize their "subjective" evaluation with equal absolute, but opposite sign. Since exhaustive search is mostly intractable, the usual solution is to cut off the game tree at a predefined depth threshold and to propagate a *heuristic evaluation function* instead of the true value.

EBG in Game Playing: Previous Approaches. Game playing has attracted researchers in Artificial Intelligence ever since its beginnings: problems, though well-structured and concisely described, are computationally expensive due to combinatorial complexity; despite this fact, human reasoning is considerably efficient and still unmatched for some games such as Go.

All relevant knowledge (i.e., the rules of the game) can be described in a concise and exact way. Nevertheless, a novice has to become acquainted with typical situations and strategies in order to achieve an acceptable quality of play. Although, in principle, such patterns could be invented from scratch by only reflecting on the rules, it is much easier to inspect examples from actual (commented) matches and to extract the general principles behind them. Indeed, this is the prevalent style of chess textbooks. For example, once we have detected and memorized the pattern of a pinning (e.g., by search applied to Fig. 2 (a)), we are able to recall it immediately in new situations (as in Fig. 2 (b)), thereby saving computation time. Thus, by comparison with human behavior, exploiting the potential of speedup learning by knowledge operationalization, as formalized by the EBG paradigm, appears to be highly plausible.

In fact, several publications address the issue of Explanation-Based Learning in the domain of two-player games ([FlaDi86, Min84, Ta89, YSUB90] is an incomplete but representative list). In brief, the approach taken in most cases is to represent states and move operators in a STRIPS-like fashion [FiNi71], to use *goal regression* [Wa75] to propagate (winning or losing) conditions along the edges of the game tree back to the root, and to finally conjoin all conditions obtained in this way from different edges. Two main inherent problems are associated with this view. First, the STRIPS-language (essentially consisting of conjunctions of atoms without function symbols) turns out to be too restricted for more complex rules, as e.g. for the variable-length moves of the rook in chess; this results in descriptions which are awkward and not well-suited for generalization. Secondly, in order to be correct, a learned condition has to take into account all the legal moves which could be available at its application time, not only those ones occurring in the training example. Predicting them in advance is a difficult task. Consequently, to the best of our knowledge, all previously reported approaches suffer from significant weaknesses. Minton's Constraint-Based Generalization [Min84], which was implemented for tic-tac-toe, go-moku, and chess, is restricted to certain types of states, where a tactical strategy exists that confronts the losing player at each point with two independent threats which cannot be blocked simultaneously Tadepalli's *Lazy Explanation-Based Learning* [Ta89] intently sacrifices soundness by considering only a single line of play; derived rules may be subsequently refined at the time their use leads to a fault. Generally, the paradox that EBG is not directly applicable, although a complete axiomatization of the domain theory can be provided, was termed the *intractable theory problem.*

2 Overcoming the Difficulties by the Use of Extended EBG for Negation as Failure

The outlined difficulties seem to contradict the fact that a *universal* EBG procedure was already known [KCMcC87]. However, this traditional technique requires the domain theory to be represented as a set of pure *Horn clauses*, whose bodies consist of conjunctions of atoms. We argue that a declarative and natural logical description of game playing concepts requires the expressive means of *negation* (Of course, this is a practical, knowledge engineering requirement, as definite programs are already Turing-equivalent). Informally, excluding draws for simplicity, a game state is won (for the current player) if some legal move exists leading to a successor state that can *not* be won (by the opponent). Thus, a straightforward negmax implementation is along the lines of the clause $win(X)$ $\leftarrow$ $move(X, Y)$, $\sim win(Y)$. The more detailed version *negMaxAtLeast* of Fig. 1 holds if the game tree with root *State*, where it is *Player*'s turn to move, truncated at the level of N plies, has a value which is greater than or equals *Bound*. The equivalent minimax formulation depends on negation in a similar way.

negMaxAtLeast($State$, $Player$, N, $Value$) ←
  (terminalState($State$, $Player$); $N = 0$),
  value($State$, $Player$, $Value1$),
  $Value1 >= Value$.
negMaxAtLeast($State$, $Player$, N, $Value$) ←
  ~terminalState($State$, $Player$),
  $N > 0$, $N1$ is $N - 1$,
  opponent($Player$, $Opponent$),
  $Value1$ is $-Value$,
  legalMove($State$, $State1$, $Player$),
  ~negMaxGreater($State1$, $Opponent$, $N1$, $Value1$).

Fig. 1. Testing the negmax value of a game state. We assume $negMaxGreater/4$ to be analogously defined by replacing ">=" by ">" in the first clause and recursively calling $negMaxAtLeast$ in the second one.

The need for negation has partly been obscured by the alternative use of non-logical *set predicates* (such as Prolog's *findall* or *setof*), which can also be found in most Prolog textbooks (Note that set predicates can likewise be implemented in a declarative way using negation, but not via Horn programs alone due to their monotonicity). While their use is justified when efficiency is the primary concern, the lack of a logical semantics excludes them from a general treatment in EBG.

Since negation lies beyond the scope of traditional EBG, its use in game playing was seriously restricted, as revealed by previous approaches. As it shall be demonstrated below, it is now possible to overcome this limitation on the basis of an extension of traditional EBG to the rule of *Negation as Failure*, which was proposed in [Schr96]. Herein, the Clark completion [Cla78] is adopted as a declarative semantics of SLDNF-resolution. Roughly speaking, in contrast to the case of success, explaining failures involves taking into account all possible proof alternatives. Therefore, the main idea of the described method is to generalize the usual concept of *proof trees* (i.e., *AND-trees*) to so-called *AND/OR/NOT-trees*. By this means, success and failure become exactly dual cases. We implemented a Prolog-meta-interpreter which builds, in parallel to the usual derivation, the corresponding AND/OR/NOT-tree by successively replacing atoms by their completed definitions. Operational atoms, as well as those atoms which are not selected anywhere in the derivation, are pruned. The constructed AND/OR/NOT-tree can be interpreted as a first-order expression, which is finally converted into a normal program using a set of simple equivalence transformations. Related ideas how to explain failures can be found in [SiPu88] and [Pu94].

3 The Chess Endgame King-Rook vs. King-Knight

In general, endgames lend themself readily to quantitative evaluation. The complexity of problem instances can be clearly defined and controlled (namely, by the search depth). In contrast to other domains where it might be difficult to estimate the population of future instances, here the entire problem space is a priori known: it can be completely generated, e.g. through retrograde analysis (as we did in this case, too). This allows us to assess the distribution of positive as well as of negative examples for the target concepts, which is crucial for the prediction of accuracy and efficiency of derived programs. We subsequently keep to the hypothesis that all legal positions are equally likely.

Our testbed was the chess endgame king and rook against king and knight (*krkn*, for short). This choice was inspired by Quinlan's studies with ID3 decision trees [Qu83]. Though not too complex for extensive evaluation, this application exhibits non-trivial features (such as the variable-length moves of the rook).

Suppose w.l.o.g. the rook is white. Consistent with [Qu83], we define black to have immediately lost if he is either checkmate, or if the black knight has been captured and he cannot retaliate by capturing the white rook. A *State* is *won in at most N plies* (for odd N) for a *Player* if it follows from this termination condition by a negmax tree of depth at most N; then *negMaxAtLeast(State, Player, N, 1)* of Fig. 1 holds. Call it *won-N-ply* if additionally it is not won in less than N plies. For even N, *lost-N-ply* is defined analogously (in this case, ~*negMaxGreater(State, black, N, −1)* holds). Fig. 2 shows two won-3-ply positions.

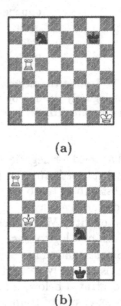

(a)

(b)

Fig. 2. Won-3-ply positions

Out of the approximately 15 million possible ways of placing the four pieces on the board, about 75% are legal black-to-move positions and approximately 64% are legal white-to-move positions (the difference arises because, for instance, the white king cannot be in check in a black-to-move position). Table 1 lists, for some concepts Q (won-N-ply resp. lost-N-ply), the ratio h_Q of positive instances with respect to all legal (white-to-move resp. black-to-move) positions.

3.1 Implementation

In the negmax procedure of Fig. 1, the predicates *legalMove/3*, *terminalState/2*, and *value/3* encapsulate the entire game-specific knowledge. For our purposes, we used a slightly simplified chess theory which borrows from that of Flann and Dietterich [FlaDi89]. A state is described using the predicate *on/3*; e.g., *on(state1, (8,1), [king,white])* holds in Fig. 2 (a). In [FlaDi89] a state consists of sixty-four assertions which list empty squares by a special dummy "piece"; however, this can be simplified by using negation, since we can now define a square to be empty "by default" unless proven otherwise. Predicate *connected/3* specifies adjacent squares together with their direction. Move generation dis-

Table 1. (Notation explained in the text)

depth	concept Q	$h_Q[\%]$	Δt_Q $[\%]$	$\bar{\epsilon}_Q$ $[\%]$	$t^{rel}_{Q,min}$ $[\%]$	t^{rel}_Q $[\%]$	$\epsilon_Q(t+\Delta t)/\epsilon_Q(t)$ $[\%]$
1	won-1-ply	24.54	5.54	18.0	85.6	102 – 123	83.2
2	lost-2-ply	3.495	2.15	56.4	94.9	97 – 119	80.5
3	won-3-ply	6.032	0.87	79.0	95.9	104 – 119	78.4
4	lost-4-ply	0.951	0.39	89.0	98.6	99 – 116	76.8
5	won-5-ply	3.449	0.19	91.3	97.0	102 – 107	63.7

tinguishes between *singleStep* pieces such as king and knight, and *slidingPieces* such as the rook. For each type, the set of move vectors (*legalDirection*) is provided. For the latter class, it has to be checked whether all intermediate squares between the source and the destination are empty. In order for the generalization to cover moves of arbitrary length, not just the length occurring in the example, this property was expressed using two predicates *between/3* and *openline/4*. States derived by move sequences are represented as in situation calculus, with appropriate regression and frame axioms provided.

3.2 Experimental Setting

Let D_{op} denote the definitions of operational predicates, and let D be the negmax procedure of Fig. 1, together with our chess program except for D_{op}. The only relation that changes across training instances is *on/3*; four such assertions determine a *krkn* board position, which are always given in the order white king/white rook/black king/black knight.

Our *operationality criterion* $\mathcal{OP}$ consists of the predicates *on/3*, *connected/3*, *openline/4*, *between/3*, *opponent/2*, *singleStepPiece/1*, *slidingPiece/1*, *legalDirection/2*, as well as of some general arithmetic built-ins.

The chosen target concepts Q were won-N-ply, for $N \in \{1,3,5\}$, and lost-N-ply, for $N \in \{2,4\}$. Our available hardware resources did not allow a comprehensive study beyond this depth. The algorithms proposed in [Schr96] are able to deduce a common generalization for multiple training examples by merging several AND/OR/NOT-trees into one. For each such target concept Q, a sequence of programs $C_1^Q, C_2^Q \ldots$ is derived from a corresponding sequence of successively larger training sets $\mathcal{E}_1^Q, \mathcal{E}_2^Q, \ldots$, where $\mathcal{E}_{i+1}^Q$ is obtained from $\mathcal{E}_i^Q$ by adding a randomly drawn board configuration E_i^Q which is a positive instance of Q, and which is not yet covered by the previous program C_{i-1}^Q (i.e., the eight coordinates are repeatedly created by a random number generator according to a uniform distribution until these two properties are satisfied). $E_1^{won-3-ply}$ is depicted in Fig. 2 (a). The proof for Q is always carried out under the Prolog selection rule, applying the basic negmax procedure of Fig. 1 without any heuristics.

We measured Prolog's execution time using the SICSTUS profiling package; by counting the number of calls, backtracks, choice-points, etc., artificial units are calculated in a machine-independent way [GoKe87].

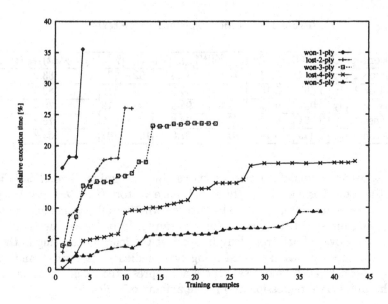

Fig. 3. Utility for positive instances

4 Results

4.1 Speedup for Recognition

First, consider the mere recognition task, where the existence of a solution is known in advance. Each C_i^Q is tested on a random sample of 1000 board positions $\tilde{E}_j^Q$ which are positive instances of Q and do not occur in the training set. We determine the average execution time $t_Q^+(C_i^Q)$ for the attempt to prove Q from $C_i^Q \cup D_{op} \cup \tilde{E}_j^Q$, over all j. The *relative execution time* is obtained by dividing it by the respective figure $t_Q^+(D)$ for the original domain theory. E.g., D needed 124378633 units to process a won-3-ply test set in this way, compared to 4844826 units using the program $C_1^{\text{won}-3-\text{ply}}$ derived for the first training example; hence, the respective relative execution time amounts to 3.9%. Fig. 3 plots these values for each program C_i^Q in dependence of the size i of the training set.

For a fixed concept Q, $t_Q^+(C_i^Q)$ grows approximately linear (with slightly decreasing slope) with i. A better speedup can be achieved for greater search depth. The values Δt_Q, defined as the average of $(t_Q^+(C_{i+1}^Q) - t_Q^+(C_i^Q))/t_Q^+(D)$ over all examples, can be found in the fourth column of Table 1.

Since no move sorting is applied, the arrangement of clauses within the program strongly influences the order of exploration, and hence on execution time. In Fig. 2 (a) only the rook takes an active part in white's winning strategy; thus, if its position is asserted first unlike our standard order, execution time for the original domain theory is reduced from 134982 to 100676 units. The derived program $C_1^{\text{won}-3-\text{ply}}$, however, is almost indifferent to this permutation (4610 compared to 4618 units). As also a closer look at the generated code reveals, its search for moves of the winning side is already restricted to the subset of rook moves (more precisely: moves of sliding pieces). We might state that selectivity is the very source of performance gain.

As a very coarse-grained model, assume that a program derived for one training example uniformly considers, on each level of the game tree, only a constant fraction p of the moves taken into account by D. Then we should expect the relative execution time to grow proportionally to p^d, where d is the search depth of the target concept. A corresponding least square fit for the fourth column of Table 1 yields a value of $p = 43\%$.

4.2 Training Complexity

Generally, an algorithm for learning from examples is called efficient if it is capable of producing approximations with tolerable error using only moderate computational resources, essentially time. Since the generalization effort of EBG is proportional to that of proof construction, we may focus on the number of training examples needed to achieve a given accuracy threshold.

Recall that the error of EBG is biased: positive instances may be taken for negative ones, but not vice versa. Therefore, we measure the generality of a derived program C_i^Q by means of a new test set of 1000 randomly drawn positive instances of Q. For each of them, an attempt is made to prove Q using C_i^Q. The number of failures, divided by 1000, yields the ratio $\epsilon(C_i^Q)$ of misclassifications. E.g, the program $C_1^{\text{won}-3-\text{ply}}$ deduced for Fig. 2 (a) on 1000 randomly drawn won-3-ply states succeeded in 186 cases, one of which is shown in Fig. 2 (b). The generalization agrees well with our intuitive concept of a pinning, abstracting e.g. from the actual number of intermediate squares on the line passed by the rook. Fig. 4 plots the error $\epsilon(C_i^Q)$ of C_i^Q, in dependence of the training size i.

A general merit of knowledge-based methods such as EBG is their low training complexity, as compared to inductive techniques, where often thousands of instances must be supplied. This is also confirmed by our data: e.g., 90% of all won-3-ply states can be recognized by learning from 6 examples.

However, the required training size grows nearly exponentially with the admissible error. For plausibility, assume that every instance leads to a generalization with the same error $\bar{\epsilon}_Q$, and that all these generalizations are statistically independent. Then we should expect the error after having presented a training set of size n to be approximately proportional to $(\bar{\epsilon}_Q)^n$: a fixed number of additional examples reduces the error by a constant factor. In fact, a least square fit explains our experimental data quite neatly (with correlation between 0.96 and 0.99). Its results are shown in the fifth column of Table 1.

Note that an informed teacher could achieve the same accuracy with fewer examples, since he is able to draw examples deliberately rather than randomly as in our experiments. Ideally, training examples should be chosen to illustrate different concepts so that their overlap is minimized. Then, the training size for exact identification is supposed to be of order $1/(1 - \bar{\epsilon}_Q)$, e.g., about a dozen for a search depth of five plies.

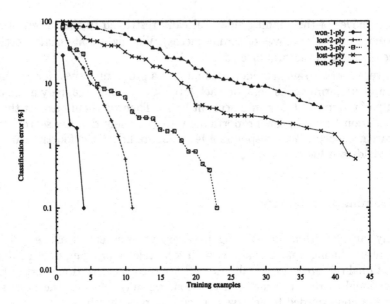

Fig. 4. Training complexity

4.3 Utility for Classification

The utility of a program C has to be judged with respect to the overall task of *classifying* examples as being positive or negative instances of the target concept Q, rather than of merely *recognizing* the positive ones. The effort of a proof attempt crucially depends on whether it succeeds or fails. We have defined $t_Q^+(C)$ above to be the average execution time required to finish a successful proof for a randomly chosen *positive* example of Q using C; similarly, let $t_Q^-(C)$ be the average time until the attempt for a random *negative* example fails. We measured $t_Q^-(C)$ using another test set of 1000 legal (white-to-move resp. black-to-move) *krkn* positions not satisfying Q. Proving a concept won-N-ply can be finished as soon as one successful move at the root has been discovered, whereas in the case of failure, all of them are explored. It turned out that $t_Q^-(C)$ is generally larger (on the average, twice) than $t_Q^+(C)$. The opposite is true for concepts lost-N-ply.

We may estimate the average time $t_Q(D)$ to classify instances w.r.t. Q solely by the original domain theory D as $h_Q \cdot t_Q^+(D) + (1 - h_Q) \cdot t_Q^-(D)$. Suppose that a derived program C is added at the beginning of D; it succeeds in a fraction $h_Q \cdot (1 - \epsilon(C))$ of all cases. Positive examples which are misclassified by C occur with relative frequency $h_Q \cdot \epsilon(C)$; otherwise, the average total classification time is composed of the average failure time of C and that of D. Define

$$
\begin{aligned}
t_Q(C \cup D) := \quad & h_Q(1 - \epsilon(C)) \cdot t_Q^+(C) + (1 - h_Q(1 - \epsilon(C))) \cdot t_Q^-(C) \\
& + h_Q \epsilon(C) \cdot t_Q^+(D) \qquad + (1 - h_Q) \cdot t_Q^-(D).
\end{aligned} \qquad (*)
$$

The *utility* of C can then be read off $t_Q^{rel}(C)$, defined as the ratio $t_Q(C \cup D)/t_Q(D)$ of the execution times with resp. without its addition: $t_Q^{rel}(C) < 1$ indicates an improvement, $t_Q^{rel}(C) > 1$ an overall delay.

In [Schr96], multiple examples are treated such that, as an upper bound for the relative execution time, $t_Q^{rel}(C) \leq 2$ holds. In the limit, the derived program approximates the original domain theory, so that essentially the same steps are carried out at most twice (in the case of negative examples). On the other hand, the assumption $\epsilon(C) = t_Q^+(C) = t_Q^-(C) = 0$ in (∗) (i.e., the learned program classifies all positives examples correctly and does not consume any time) yields a lower bound which is independent of the presented training examples and the form of the derived programs. We have $t_Q^{rel}(C) \geq t_{Q,min}^{rel}$ with $1/t_{Q,min}^{rel} = 1 + h_Q/(1 - h_Q) \cdot (t_Q^+(D)/t_Q^-(D))$. Informally, the usefulness of EBG grows with the probability of the target concept, and with the effort of recognizing positive instances using the domain theory, as opposed to the rejection of negative ones. In our case, we obtain the values shown in the sixth column of Table 1.

These bounds already explain the the ranges of actually observed relative execution times, depending on the number of training examples (seventh column). The overall improvement is only minor, in general performance even degrades up to 123 % in the worst case. Since positive examples are quite infrequent, their accelerated recognition can hardly outweigh the necessary delay for negative ones. Similarly as in other domains where EBG is applied, we have to face the utility problem.

However, as an alternative to the usual scheme, we might sacrifice completeness by discarding the original domain theory. Taking each example not successfully recognized by C (possibly erroneously) as a negative one results in *approximate* classification. In this case, $t_Q(C)$ can be estimated by dropping the third and fourth terms from (∗). Accuracy can be gradually traded for performance: using more training examples reduces the error rate of a derived program, but at the same time increases the average execution time when it is applied. In this way, we arrive at Fig. 5.

E.g., for the concept lost-4-ply, 17.5% of the execution time used by the original domain theory are sufficient if we agree on a misclassification of 0.6% of the positive instances. The greater the search depth N, the more can be gained. Spending an additional constant amount of computation time (by adjusting the training size) roughly reduces the error rate by a constant factor. Denote the average error reduction gained for one additional percent of the time used by the original domain theory as $\epsilon_Q(t + \Delta t)/\epsilon_Q(t)$; a least square fit yields, with correlation between 0.93 and 0.98, the values of the eighth column of Table 1.

In game playing, reasoning under time bounds is an important issue; such constraints are usually imposed by tournament conditions. We could store an ordered sequence of programs for approximate classification (whose first element is the original domain theory itself), along with execution time estimates; then, decide on-line which one of them to use, based on the actually available time. Informally, such a behavior results in selectively exploring deeper parts of the search tree at interesting points while occasionally "overlooking" unlikely variants, as opposed to directly adjusting the global search depth of the unaltered original program in response to time resources. It appears to be appropriate both from the viewpoints of efficiency and cognitive adequacy.

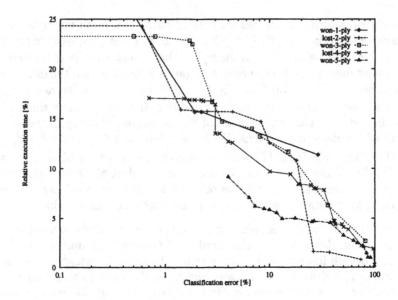

Fig. 5. Performance – accuracy trade-off

5 Conclusion and Discussion

By comparison with humans, Explanation-Based Learning appears to be well-suited for game playing. However, previous approaches failed to provide a universal and provably correct method. We point out that a serious handicap was the fact that the expressive means of Negation as Failure is not considered by the traditional procedure for EBG of [KCMcC87], but that it is nonetheless necessary for a declarative and natural formalization of game tree search. This problem can now be remedied on the basis of the extension proposed in [Schr96].

From a methodical viewpoint, the domain of endgames allows for a more precise and detailed quantitative evaluation than those domains for which similar studies were reported earlier. This work describes the main results of an application and large-scale experimental evaluation of EBG for the chess endgame king-rook vs. king-knight; such an inquiry has not been undertaken before.

A significant speedup can be achieved for recognizing positive examples; the impact of learning strongly grows with the search depth. The number of training examples necessary to achieve a given level of accuracy is strikingly small. Nevertheless, in the overall *classification* task the utility problem occurs, mainly due to the low proportion of the target concepts. Hence, our observations suggest to focus on *approximate* classification instead by discarding the original domain theory. In this case, we can implement *reasoning under time constraints* and nearly continuously trade accuracy for performance by adjusting the training size.

Obviously, our results are only valid with respect to our fixed chess program and for the Prolog selection rule; the influence of different designs of the domain theory and of different inference strategies was not examined.

Quinlan [Qu83] pointed out that most of the effort in *krkn* classification lies in the task of *feature construction*, i.e., finding easily computable attributes of states significant for their outcome. To this end, he applied inductive methods to semi-automatically extract them from a complete endgame database. Interestingly, some of the reported features are very similar to generalizations derived by EBG (such as the shown example of a "pinning"). We believe that combining EBG and similarity-based methods for this task warrants further studies.

References

[Cla78] Clark, K.L., *Negation as Failure*, in: Gallaire, H., and Minker, J. (eds.), Logic and Data Bases, Plenum Press, NY, (1978), pp 293-322

[FiNi71] Fikes, R. E., and Nilsson, N. J., *STRIPS: a New Approach to the Application of Theorem Proving to Problem Solving*, Artificial Intelligence 2(3-4), pp 189 -208

[FlaDi86] Flann, N.S., and Dietterich, T.G., *Selecting Appropriate Representations for Learning from Examples*, AAAI-86, (1986), pp 460-466

[FlaDi89] Flann, N.S., and Dietterich, T.G., *A Study of Explanation-Based Methods for Inductive Learning*, Machine Learning 4, Kluwer Academic Publishers, Boston, (1989), pp 187-226

[GoKe87] Gorlick, M.M., and Kesselman, C.F., *Timing Prolog Programs Without Clocks*, Symp. on Logic Programming, IEEE Computer Society, (1987), pp 426-432

[KCMcC87] Kedar-Cabelli, S.T., and McCarty, L.T., *Explanation-Based Generalization as Theorem Proving*, Proc. of the Fourth International Workshop on Machine Learning, Irvine, (1987)

[Kel88] Keller, R. M., *Defining Operationality for Explanation-Based Learning*, Artificial Intelligence 35, (1988), pp 227-241

[Min84] Minton, S., *Constraint-Based Generalization: Learning Game-Playing Plans from Single Examples*, AAAI-84, (1984), pp 251-254

[Mi90] Minton, S., *Quantitative Results Concerning the Utility of Explanation-Based Learning*, Artificial Intelligence 42, Elsevier Publishers, (1990), pp 363–391

[MKKC86] Mitchell, T., Keller, R., and Kedar-Cabelli, S., *Explanation-Based Generalization: A Unifying View*, Machine Learning 1:1, (1986), pp 47-80

[Pu94] Puget, J.-F., *Explicit Representation of Concept Negation*, Machine Learning 14, Kluwer Academic Publishers, Boston, (1994), pp 233–247

[Qu83] Quinlan, J. R., *Learning Efficient Classification Procedures and their Application to Chess End Games*, in: Michalski, et al. (eds.), Machine Learning: An Artificial Intelligence Approach, San Mateo, CA, Morgan Kaufmann, (1983), pp 463–482

[Schr96] Schrödl, S., *Explanation-Based Generalization for Negation as Failure and Multiple Examples*, ECAI-96, Budapest, Hungary, John Wiley & Sons, (1996), pp 448-452 (1986)

[SiPu88] Siqueira, J. L., and Puget, J. F., *Explanation-Based Generalization of Failures*, Proc. of ECAI-88, Munich, (1988), pp 339–344

[Ta89] Tadepalli, P., *Lazy Explanation-Based Learning: A Solution to The Intractable Theory Problem*, IJCAI-89, Detroit MI, (1989), 694-700

[Wa75] Waldinger, R., *Achieving Several Goals Simultaneously*, in: Elcock, E. W., and Michie, D. (eds.), Machine Intelligence 8, Ellis Horwood, Chichester, England, pp 94-138

[YSUB90] Yee, R.C., Saxena, S., Utgoff, P.E., Barto, A.G., *Explaining Temporal Differences to Create Useful Concepts for Evaluating States*, AAAI-90, (1990), pp 882-888

Scope Classification:
An Instance-Based Learning Algorithm
with a Rule-Based Characterisation

Nicolas Lachiche[1] and Pierre Marquis[2]

[1] LORIA, B.P. 239, 54506 Vandœuvre-lès-Nancy Cedex, France- e-mail:
lachiche@loria.fr* * *
[2] CRIL/Université d'Artois, Rue de l'Université, S.P. 16,
62307 Lens Cedex, France - e-mail: marquis@cril.univ-artois.fr

Abstract. *Scope classification* is a new instance-based learning (IBL)
technique with a rule-based characterisation. Within the scope approach,
the classification of an object o is based on the examples that are closer to
o than every example labelled with another class. In contrast to standard
distance-based IBL classifiers, scope classification relies on partial pre-
orderings $\leq_o$ between examples, indexed by objects. Interestingly, the
notion of closeness to o that is used characterises the classes predicted
by all the rules that cover o and are relevant and consistent for the
training set. Accordingly, scope classification is an IBL technique with
a rule-based characterisation. Since rules do not have to be explicitly
generated, the scope approach applies to classification problems where
the number of rules prevents them from being exhaustively computed.

1 Introduction

In this paper, we are interested in supervised learning. Given a *training set T*
and a set of *objects o* to be classified, our goal is to derive a classifier that best
approximates in the best way the *target function*, i.e., the function that maps
every object to its right class. Because only the classes $class(e)$ of the training
examples e (also called instances) are known, this classifier must be *induced* from
examples. This requires some additional knowledge, that typically has the form
of a *similarity assumption*. Such an assumption states that "every object belongs
to the class of its nearest neighbours in the training set" or "every object shares
the properties relevant to class membership that every example exhibits".

Instance-based learning (IBL) is based on a straightforward interpretation
of the similarity assumption. In the simplest case, every object o is classified
according to its nearest instance, according to some similarity measure or to
some distance measure. The k-nearest neighbours of o can also be used; in this
case, the class of o is computed as the majority class of its k nearest neighbours
from T.

---

* * * Currently at Department of Computer Science, University of Bristol, Merchant Ven-
turers Building, Woodland Road, Bristol BS8 1UB, United Kingdom

Another approach to learning a classifier from examples is *rule-based classification*. A rule $c \rightarrow (y = v_y)$ is said to *classify* (to cover, or to be satisfied by) an object o if $o \models c$, i.e., c is a logical consequence of o. A rule $r_1 = c_1 \rightarrow (y = v_y)$ is said at least as *general* as a rule $r_2 = c_2 \rightarrow (y = v_y)$ if and only if $c_2 \models c_1$. Given a training set T, a rule $r = c \rightarrow (y = v_y)$ is *consistent* for T if and only if for every example e of T, if r classifies e then $class(e) = v_y$. A rule r is *relevant* for T if and only if r is satisfied by at least one example from T.

The number of relevant and consistent rules for a training set can be huge (exponential in the number of attributes). As a consequence, many rule induction algorithms only generate some of these rules, typically the most discriminating ones. Because the most discriminating rules are not always sufficient to approximate the target function in a satisfying way, SE-Learn [Rymon, 1993] completes them with the second most discriminating ones, and so on, until all the (most general) relevant and consistent rules for the training set are generated. [Rymon, 1996b] shows that SE-Learn is more robust to noise than decision trees.

In the following, a new approach to learning from examples, called *scope classification*, is introduced. The scope approach is a point where IBL and rule-based techniques meet. Roughly, the scope algorithm classifies every object o according to the examples of T that are "closer" to o than any example labelled with another class. Since every object can be classified by comparing it to the stored instances (no rules have to be generated), the scope approach is instance-based. However, quite unconventionally, the scope approach:

- relies on partial pre-orderings $\leq_o$ between examples, indexed by objects. In particular, the number of neighbours of o that are kept is not fixed in the scope approach.
- has a rule-based characterisation: the notion of closeness to o that is used characterises the classes predicted by all the relevant and consistent classification rules for T that cover o.

The scope approach achieves an interesting trade-off between accuracy and efficiency. First, scope classification usually considers more neighbours than standard k-nearest neighbours. This makes it less sensitive to noise than these techniques. The price to be paid is a higher but still tractable time complexity (quadratic in the number of examples in the worst case). Second, since every relevant and consistent rule for T covering o is associated with a neighbour of o w.r.t. T in the scope approach, scope classification can prove more accurate than techniques where only a few classification rules are induced. Since rules do not have to be explicitly generated, it can be practical in situations where the number of rules that are relevant and consistent for T prevents them from being exhaustively computed.

The rest of this paper is organised as follows. The scope approach to classification is presented in Section 2. Its performance is compared with standard IBL and rule-based algorithms on many standard benchmarks from many domains in Section 3. Somer related research is discussed in section 4. The conclusions of our study are drawn in Section 5.

2 Scope Classification

In this section, the rule-based characterisation of the scope approach to classification is formally established. The scope algorithm is then presented and its efficiency is analysed. Finally, we show how the logical biases considered in the scope approach can be relaxed to allow it to deal with real-world (noisy) data.

2.1 Basics of the scope approach

Let us introduce the basic definitions of scope classification through an example. Let us consider a set of patients who suffer or not from a disease (y). Each individual is described by its sex s (Man or Woman), weight w in kilos and appetite a (Good, Average, Little).

Patient	s	w	a	y
e_1	M	70	G	T
e_2	W	55	A	F
e_3	M	50	L	T

Given a patient o described by $(s = M) \wedge (w = 75) \wedge (a = A)$, the aim of the classifier is to help the physician to detect whether o suffers or not from disease y. In this case, the classifier has to suggest a class for o given o and the training set $T = \{e_1, e_2, e_3\}$.

We are interested in the relevant and consistent rules for T covering o. Let R be such a rule. If R is relevant for T, then there exists at least one example e_R that satisfies R. Let us assume that $e_R = e_1$. Let us consider $R(o, e_1)$ the most specific rule covering o and e_1.

Definition 1. Let $C(o_1, o_2)$ be the least general generalisation of o_1 and o_2, i.e., $C(o_1, o_2)$ denotes the smallest hyper-rectangle containing the objects. $C(o_1, o_2)$ is defined as the conjunction of conditions (selectors) $C_i(o_1, o_2)$ on each attribute i:

- if the value of attribute i is missing in o_1 or in o_2 then $C_i(o_1, o_2) = True$,
- if i is nominal, if $v_i^{o_1} = v_i^{o_2}$ then $C_i(o_1, o_2) = (a = v_i^{o_1})$ else $C_i(o_1, o_2) = True$,
- if i is numerical or ordered, $C_i(o_1, o_2) = [min(v_i^{o_1}, v_i^{o_2}), max(v_i^{o_1}, v_i^{o_2})]$.

where attribute i is valued $v_i^{o_1}$ in o_1 and $v_i^{o_2}$ in o_2.

Let o be an object and e be an example labelled with $class(e)$. The most specific rule covering o and e is:

$$R(o, e) = C(o, e) \rightarrow (y = class(e))$$

For instance, $C(o, e_1) = (s = M) \wedge (w \in [70; 75]) \wedge (a \in [A; G])$.

By definition, every rule $R = c \rightarrow (y = class(e_1))$ covering o and e_1 is more general than $R(o, e_1)$. Hence, if R is consistent for T then $R(o, e_1)$ is consistent for T. To check whether $R(o, e_1)$ is consistent for T, we just have to check whether no example labelled with another class satisfies $C(o, e_1)$. In order to state it formally, let us define a partial pre-ordering $\leq_o$ between objects:

Definition 2. For every object o, let $\leq_o$ denote the partial pre-ordering defined by, for every o_1 and o_2, o_1 is closer to o than o_2, denoted $o_1 \leq_o o_2$, if and only if o_1 satisfies $C(o, o_2)$, i.e., $o_1 \models C(o, o_2)$.

The rule $R(o, e)$ is consistent for T if and only if no example labelled with a class different from $class(e)$ is closer to o than e according to $\leq_o$. Formally, let us define the neighbours of o w.r.t. T as:

Definition 3. Let e be an example of T and o be an object. Let $CE(e, T)$ denote the set of examples e' of T s.t. $class(e') \neq class(e)$. e is a neighbour of o w.r.t. T, denoted $e \in cons(T, \leq_o)$, if and only if $\forall e' \in CE(e, T), e' \not\leq_o e$.

Stepping back to our example, e_2 does not satisfy $C(o, e_1)$, so $e_2 \not\leq_o e_1$. Since $CE(e_1, T) = \{e_2\}$, e_1 is a neighbour of o w.r.t. T; in other words, the rule $R(o, e_1)$ is consistent and (obviously) relevant for T.

Let us emphasise that e is not required to be closer to o than all examples labelled with a class different from $class(e)$ to belong to $cons(T, \leq_o)$. What is needed is that no "counter-example" ce is closer to o than e. This means that either e is closer to o than ce, or that e and ce are not comparable w.r.t. $\leq_o$, that is the most frequent case. For instance, e_1 is not closer to o than e_2, but e_2 is not closer to o than e_1 (e_1 and e_2 are not comparable).

Let us also stress the fact that the number of neighbours of an object o that are considered in the scope approach is not fixed. This contrasts with the k-nearest neighbours techniques. Moreover, the notion of neighbourhood within scope classification is less restrictive than the ones considered within standard distance-based approaches. For example, if e is as close as possible to o w.r.t. Hamming distance (or w.r.t Minkowski distance $L_q(e_1, e_2) = \sqrt[q]{\Sigma_a(v_a^{e_1} - v_a^{e_2})^q}$), then it belongs to $cons(T, \leq_o)$ but the converse is not necessarily true. Roughly, attributes are considered as *incomparable dimensions* in the scope approach while they are only viewed as *numbers* that can be added and averaged in distance-based approaches. Results on every "dimensions" are dealt with not numerically as in [Demiroz and Guvenir, 1997], but logically.

2.2 The rule-based characterisation of the scope approach

As an immediate consequence of the definition of $cons(T, \leq_o)$, each time an example labelled with v_y belongs to $cons(T, \leq_o)$, a relevant and consistent rule for T labelling o with class v_y exists. Furthermore, the converse is true as well. Thus, the scope approach has a rule-based characterisation:

Theorem 4. *Let T be a set of examples and o be an object. There exists a consistent and relevant rule $c \to (y = v_y)$ for T that covers o if and only if there exists e in $cons(T, \leq_o)$ such that $class(e) = v_y$, and $C(o, e) \models c$.*

Based on this theorem, the scope algorithm prevents relevant and consistent rules from being generated by computing $cons(T, \leq_o)$ instead. Accordingly, scope classification requires no learning phase and no special types of abstractions (like decision trees, rules) have to be derived. However, rules can be easily derived, on a as-needed basis: For every e in $cons(T, \leq_o)$, the rule $R(o, e) = (C(o, e) \rightarrow (y = class(e)))$ is a relevant and consistent rule for T.

In our running example, e_1 is a neighbour of o w.r.t. T. If required, the rule $(s = M) \wedge (w \in [70; 75]) \wedge (a \in [A; G]) \rightarrow (y = T)$ can be generated.

2.3 The scope algorithm

A naive algorithm for generating $cons(T, \leq_o)$ consists in checking for every e whether no example from another class is closer to o than e. This algorithm requires $O(d \times |T|^2)$ comparisons between values of attributes, where d is the number of attributes[1]. A more efficient algorithm can take advantage of the "divide and conquer" paradigm and computes $cons(E_1 \cup E_2, \leq_o)$ as $cons(cons(E_1, \leq_o) \cup cons(E_2, \leq_o), \leq_o)$. Unfortunately, the former set is only a proper subset of the latter in the general case. Hence, each element resulting from the "divide and conquer" search must be compared with the examples of T labelled with other classes.

$cons(T, \leq_o)$ may contain examples labelled with different classes. It could easily be used to return a probability distribution over all classes. Since we are interested in predicting one class only, a *resolution criterion* must be used in the general case. Many criteria can be considered, including user-defined criteria that may incorporate some domain knowledge into classification. When no domain knowledge is available, *simple majority voting* is used: $class(o)$ is computed as the class value occurring the most frequently in $cons(T, \leq_o)$; *quadratic majority voting* is a variant where each example e is weighted by the square length of $C(o, e)$.

Analytically, the space complexity of the search of $cons(T, \leq_o)$ is in $\Theta(d \times |T|)$ in every case. Its time complexity is in $O(d \times C(|T|))$, where $C(|T|)$ is the number of comparisons w.r.t. $\leq_o$ that are performed. In the worst case, $C(|T|) = \Theta(2 * |T|^2)$. Such a quadratic time complexity (in the worst case) is higher than the time complexity of the simplest distance-based IBL techniques ($O(d \times |T|)$). In the best case, $C(T)$ is linear in the number of examples of T. Since a part of the algorithm is based on the "divide and conquer" paradigm, this time complexity is expected to be in $O(d \times |T| \times log_2(|T|))$. We checked it empirically on several benchmarks and we also observed that the worst case situation occurred only rarely.

2.4 Tuning consistency, generality and relevance

Dealing with real data requires the logical basements of scope classification to be relaxed. A tuning of consistency and a tuning of generality inspired from [Sebag, 1996] are presented and a tuning of relevance is introduced.

Actually, a rule that covers a few counter-examples must not be systematically dropped. Hence, the consistency requirement must be relaxed in order for a rule to accept at most ϵ counter-examples.

---

[1] For any set E, $|E|$ denotes its cardinality.

Definition 5. Let $NI(e,T)$ be the number of examples ce s.t. $class(ce) \neq class(e)$ and ce is closer to o than e:

$$NI(e,T) = |\{ce \in CE(e,T)|ce \leq_o e\}|$$

An example e is an ϵ-neighbour of o w.r.t. T if and only if $NI(e,T) \leq \epsilon \times |T|$.

Some attributes may be of no interest in some part of the universe, thus forgetting some of them (at most M) can prove valuable.

Definition 6. An object o_1 is closer to an object o than an object o_2 except on (at most) M attributes, denoted $o_1 \leq_o^M o_2$, if and only if $|\{attribute\ i|(i = v_i^{o_1}) \not\models C_i(o,o_2)\}| < M$. An example e is an M-neighbour of o w.r.t. T, denoted $e \in M - cons(T,\leq_o)$, if and only if $e \in cons(T,\leq_o^M)$.

The relevance requirement can also be strengthened in order to only consider rules satisfied by at least γ examples.

Definition 7. Let $NC(e,T)$ be the number of examples f s.t. $class(f) = class(e)$ and f is closer to o than e:

$$NC(e,T) = |\{f \in T|class(f) = class(e) \text{ and } f \leq_o e\}|$$

An example e is an γ-neighbour of o w.r.t. T if and only if $NC(e,T) > \gamma \times |T|$.

These three parameters can be incorporated all together within the scope approach (the notion of neighbour becomes the notion of (ϵ, M, γ)-neighbour).[2] Their values and the resolution criterion are automatically assessed; we keep the values and criterion for which the accuracy of the corresponding classifier measured by a 10-fold cross-validation on a randomly chosen subset S of T[3] is maximal. Values of ϵ and γ range from 0% to 30% using an increment of 5% and M ranges from 0 to the number of attributes d. Simple and quadratic majority voting are considered as resolution criteria. This is analogous to the wrapper method of [Kohavi and John, 1995]. However, while parameters ϵ, M and γ and the resolution criterion should depend on the distribution of the training set, we assume they depend on the domain only. Thus they are only computed once for a given domain: they are not re-assessed when different Ts are considered over the same domain.

3   An Empirical Evaluation

The performance of scope classification has been compared to some usual instance-based and rule-based classifiers, in the empirical framework described below. Both accuracy and execution time have been considered.

---

[2] Note that the relation $\leq_o^M$ is no longer a pre-ordering since transitivity is lost. However this does not question the correctness of the scope algorithm.
[3] $|S| = 0.1 \times |T|$ whenever $|T| \geq 100$, $0.9 \times |T|$ otherwise.

3.1 The empirical framework

Experiments have been carried out to compare scope classification with some of the most famous rule-based or instance-based approaches to classification. Thus, PEBLS 3.0 [Cost and Salzberg, 1993], a state-of-the art IBL system has been used. Three rule-based learning algorithms have been considered: two of them generate only some rules, CN2 [Clark and Niblett, 1989] and C4.5 [Quinlan, 1993], while the third one, SE-Learn [Rymon, 1996a], builds up all relevant and consistent rules for the training set when possible. We also compare our approach empirically with RISE [Domingos, 1996], an approach unifying rule-based and instance-based learning. The default classifier (always choosing the most frequent class) has also been included in the study as a baseline.

While Kohavi and John [Kohavi and John, 1995] showed that an automatic assignment of parameters could entail a better accuracy (with the drawback of a longer training time), none of those programs includes it. We simply used the latest versions distributed by their authors, using default values except when some other values are known to give better results. In particular, the exemplar weighting "used_correct" as described in [Cost and Salzberg, 1993], with ten trials, was used for PEBLS. Default values of the latest version of CN2 (6.1) were used. C4.5 was used with rules generation and windowing (growing ten trees, the default), requiring a minimum of four examples (instead of two) in the two branches of a test, and using a confidence level of 37.5% (instead of 25%) for rule pruning. Simple majority voting has been chosen as a resolution criterion for both SE-trees. SE-Learn has been run without pruning and has also been run with significance-based statistical pruning at the $p < 0.05$ level.

We have compared the classification accuracies obtained by the classification techniques described above on many domains. The domains datasets used in our experiments have been drawn from the UCI repository [Merz and Murphy, 1996]: audiology (AD), annealing (AN), credit (CE), pima diabetes (DI), echocardiogram (EC), glass (GL), heart disease (Cleveland HDc, Hungarian HDh, Switzerland HDs and V.A. medical center HDv databases), hepatitis (HE), horse colic (HO), iris (IR), labor negotiation (LA), lung cancer (LC), liver disease (LD), contact lenses (LE), LED (LI), post-operative (PO), DNA promoters (PR), solar flares (common SFc, moderate SFm and severe SFx), soybean (SO), splice junctions (SP),voting records (VO), wine (WI) and zoology (ZO).

3.2 Accuracy and execution time

Accuracy is measured by 10-fold cross-validation. Table 1 reports accuracy and standard deviation measured for each dataset, and the confidence level in the hypothesis H_1 = "the difference of accuracy between this classifier and scope classification is significant" using a one-tailed paired t test.

Results of table 1 are summarized on table 2 according to five measures that can be used to compare classifiers:

- **Number of wins.** It counts the number of datasets where scope classification achieves higher accuracy than the other algorithm and those where the

Table 1. Average accuracies and standard deviations. Superscripts denote confidence level: 1 is 99.5%, 2 is 99%, 3 is 97.5%, 4 is 95%, 5 is 90% and 6 is below 90%. - stands for datasets where SE-Learn has been interrupted (more than one CPU day or too much memory was required).

Dom	SCOPE	RISE	PEBLS	C4.5	CN2	SE	SE 0.05	Default
AD	66.5±10.5	80.0±11.1[1]	71.8±0.1[1]	70.3±10.4[5]	77.0±12.1[1]	-	-	18.0±9.8[1]
AN	94.2±2.7	98.4±1.6[1]	99.2±0.0[1]	93.2±1.7[6]	85.7±3.7[1]	-	-	76.2±4.0[1]
CE	86.2±4.9	82.2±5.0[1]	83.3±0.1[3]	83.7±5.1[2]	82.6±4.7[1]	86.3±4.5[6]	89.0±5.1[3]	55.5±4.7[1]
DI	74.7±4.7	70.3±3.4[3]	73.8±0.0[6]	72.9±4.6[6]	73.8±3.1[6]	72.7±4.3[6]	75.9±2.4[6]	65.1±5.6[1]
EC	69.3±13.0	62.7±11.9[6]	63.7±0.2[6]	68.0±12.4[6]	70.1±10.1[6]	67.8±11.5[6]	68.5±13.5[6]	67.1±14.7[4]
GL	74.3±13.7	72.0±7.6[6]	69.7±0.1[4]	63.3±7.0[2]	62.1±13.1[1]	71.4±10.6[6]	58.2±10.5[1]	30.3±13.9[1]
HDc	83.8±4.5	79.2±6.5[1]	80.1±0.1[5]	74.9±3.8[1]	77.2±6.1[3]	82.8±5.6[6]	88.7±5.3[1]	54.0±7.7[1]
HDh	82.9±4.4	76.4±8.0[2]	77.3±0.1[1]	78.7±5.0[1]	75.1±6.3[1]	81.6±7.0[6]	86.6±6.7[2]	64.1±10.1[1]
HDs	93.5±3.3	92.6±4.7[6]	90.9±0.1[5]	90.0±2.0[5]	92.6±2.6[6]	93.5±3.5[6]	82.1±19.0[4]	93.5±3.4[2]
HDv	75.9±11.4	71.4±9.0[5]	64.2±0.1[1]	75.2±12.9[6]	74.8±11.1[6]	75.3±12.7[6]	79.0±13.2[6]	74.4±11.2[5]
HE	78.7±13.3	76.9±14.6[6]	82.4±0.1[6]	81.6±10.1[6]	81.2±11.1[6]	-	-	79.4±14.3[6]
HO	82.1±6.1	82.6±6.0[6]	82.5±0.0[6]	84.3±5.3[6]	82.1±6.5[6]	-	-	63.1±8.1[1]
IR	94.7±5.8	95.3±7.1[6]	95.5±0.1[6]	95.8±5.5[6]	94.0±5.8[6]	96.0±5.6[6]	90.6±7.2[3]	21.3±5.1[1]
LA	87.3±14.4	87.3±23.0[6]	86.8±0.2[6]	78.4±10.8[5]	78.7±11.4[5]	89.0±20.5[6]	83.0±33.3[6]	64.3±29.4[1]
LC	48.3±28.1	43.3±32.8[6]	42.3±0.2[6]	59.0±21.1[6]	44.2±16.7[6]	-	-	40.8±15.0[6]
LD	75.8±8.1	75.8±4.9[6]	71.4±0.1[5]	74.8±5.6[6]	78.2±6.0[6]	78.5±8.5[6]	81.5±7.8[3]	74.7±8.8[6]
LE	70.0±26.7	78.3±29.5[6]	72.0±0.3[6]	87.7±19.0[4]	70.0±28.1[6]	70.0±28.1[6]	93.3±21.1[3]	63.3±27.0[6]
LI	59.0±15.8	55.0±13.5[5]	51.6±0.1[5]	55.7±8.5[6]	63.0±14.2[6]	67.1±23.2[6]	60.4±17.4[6]	18.0±14.0[1]
PO	71.1±11.3	63.3±21.6[6]	57.0±0.2[1]	67.9±11.0[4]	63.3±14.9[4]	63.8±14.1[1]	26.7±14.1[1]	71.1±11.9[1]
PR	82.0±14.4	84.0±8.6[6]	87.5±0.1[5]	84.3±9.7[6]	70.8±7.7[3]	-	-	37.7±5.9[1]
SFc	88.9±3.2	89.2±3.4[6]	83.0±0.0[1]	87.9±3.4[1]	88.8±3.4[6]	86.8±4.4[4]	88.4±8.3[6]	88.8±3.4[6]
SFm	90.1±5.9	89.1±5.8[5]	83.5±0.1[1]	88.4±6.1[3]	89.1±6.8[6]	89.1±6.7[6]	92.2±6.2[5]	90.1±6.2[6]
SFx	97.8±2.4	97.8±2.5[3]	96.2±0.0[1]	97.8±2.5[3]	97.5±2.8[6]	97.4±3.0[6]	47.1±35.6[1]	97.8±2.5[3]
SO	100.0±0.0	100.0±0.0[6]	100.0±0.0[6]	96.8±7.4[6]	97.5±7.9[6]	100.0±0.0[6]	100.0±0.0[6]	37.5±26.4[1]
SP	95.3±1.5	92.7±1.3[1]	94.0±0.0[3]	93.7±1.4[1]	91.2±2.0[1]	-	-	51.9±2.4[1]
VO	93.6±4.2	95.9±3.2[4]	94.8±0.0[5]	95.1±3.1[6]	94.7±3.3[6]	-	-	61.4±7.0[1]
WI	95.5±4.3	98.9±2.4[4]	97.7±0.0[4]	94.9±3.7[6]	92.7±4.6[6]	98.8±3.7[3]	96.5±4.1[6]	39.8±10.1[1]
ZO	94.0±9.2	96.0±7.0[6]	95.5±0.1[6]	88.6±14.0[3]	90.0±15.6[5]	95.0±9.7[6]	95.8±6.8[6]	40.4±16.0[1]

converse happens (draws are not counted either way). For instance, scope algorithm performed better than RISE in 14 datasets and worse in 10.

- **Number of significant wins.** It only counts a dataset when the confidence level in the difference of accuracy is greater than 95%.
- **Wilcoxon test.** This is a non-parametric approach to paired t test. We give the confidence level in hypothesis H_1.
- **Average.** It reports the average accuracy over all domains.
- **Ranks.** For each dataset, accuracies are ranked and are given values from 0 (the worst one) to 1 (the best one) in a uniform way. The global rank is averaged over all domains.

Experiments show that SE-Learn has a better accuracy than scope classification which has a better accuracy than RISE. These three algorithms have better accuracies than PEBLS, C4.5, CN2 and the default classifier.

We have also compared the efficiencies of both approaches. Results are summarized on table 3. In all the experiments, the execution time is the time required by each technique to complete the 10-fold cross-validation from scratch. Thus, for the scope approach, it is the time required to assess the parameters plus the time required to classify the ten test sets (parameters are only assessed once for the ten test sets). For the other approaches, the execution time is the learning time plus the classification time.

Table 2. Comparison of accuracies according to five measures.

Measure	SCOPE	RISE	PEBLS	C4.5	CN2	SE	SE 0.05	Default
No. wins	-	14-10	17-10	18-8	19-7	10-7	6-11	23-1
No. signif. wins	-	5-4	9-3	9-1	8-1	2-1	3-6	18-0
Wilcoxon test	-	80	98	92.5	99.5	<80	80	100
Average	82.3	81.7	80.3	81.6	79.9	83.1	83.9	58.6
Rank	0.67	0.58	0.47	0.55	0.47	0.69	0.75	0.20

Table 3. Comparison of execution times according to three measures.

Measure	SCOPE	RISE	PEBLS	C4.5	CN2	SE	SE 0.05
No. wins	-	19-9	3-25	11-17	6-22	10-10	2-18
Wilcoxon test	-	95.5	100	89	100	<80	99.9
Rank	0.34	0.21	0.79	0.52	0.59	0.41	0.67

We used the following measures:

- **Number of wins.** It counts the number of datasets where scope classification had a smaller execution time than the other algorithm and those where the converse happens (draws are not counted either way).
- **Wilcoxon test.** It is the confidence level in hypothesis H_1 = "the difference of execution time between this classifier and scope classification is significant".
- **Ranks.** For each dataset, execution times are ranked and are given values from 0 (the worst one) to 1 (the best one) in a uniform way. The global rank is averaged over all domains.

We can observe that the execution time of scope classification measured during this evaluation is on average smaller than the one of RISE, but greater than those of PEBLS, C4.5 and CN2. On some benchmarks, the execution time of SE-Learn without pruning is similar to the one of scope classification, and with pruning, it is quite better. However, all the relevant and consistent rules for T must be considered in SE-Learn. Since their number is exponential in the number of attributes d in the worst case, the time required by SE-Learn on a classification task can be much higher than those of the other approaches. For example, SE-Learn had to be interrupted in 8 cases out of 28, namely whenever the number of attributes exceeds 16 (unless the number of examples N was very small).

4   Related Research

In this section, the scope approach is shown to closely relate to approaches where the logical biases of relevance and consistency are considered, in particular the disjunctive version space approach [Sebag, 1996] and the SE-Learn framework [Rymon, 1996a]. Differences between the scope approach and previous approaches combining IBL and rule-based learning are emphasized.

4.1 The disjunctive version space approach

The disjunctive version space ($DiVS$ for short) of T is the disjunction of the version spaces $H(e)$ for every example $e \in T$. The version space $H(e)$ of e is the conjunction of the hypotheses $D(e, ce)$ that discriminate e from its counter-examples $ce \in CE(e, T)$. $D(e, ce)$ is the disjunction of the maximally discriminant selectors $SEL_i(e, ce)$ for each attribute i.

In $DiVS$, an example e is a (ϵ, M)-neighbour of an object o w.r.t. T if and only if

$$|\{ce \in CE(e, T)||\{i|v_i^o \in SEL_i(e, ce)\}| \not> M\}| \leq \epsilon \times |T|.$$

Stepping back to the patient example, $H(e_1) = D(e_1, e_2) = (w > 55) \vee (a > A)$. This hypothesis is clearly different from the left-hand sides of rules considered in scope classification: $C(o, e_1) = (s = M) \wedge (w \in [70; 75]) \wedge (a \in [A; G])$. Whereas the M parameter seems different, the (ϵ, M)-neighbourhoods of an object coincide in both approaches:

Theorem 8. Let o be an object and e an example from T.
$o \in (\epsilon, M) - H(e)$ if and only if $e \in (\epsilon, M) - cons(T, \leq_o)$.

Thus, for the same resolution criterion and parameters ϵ and M, scope classification and the $DiVS$ approach lead to the same neighbourhood. The generality parameter M can be considered from at least two points of view. In scope classification, a counter-example ce may satisfy a rule $R(o, e)$ except on at most M attributes (i.e., $ce \leq_o^M e$). In $DiVS$, an object o must satisfy at least M selectors $D(e, ce)$ discriminating ce from e.

A parameter similar to γ could be used in $DiVS$, but since the hypotheses considered in $DiVS$ (a version space) and in the scope classification (a rule) differ, the neighbourhoods are no longer equivalent. For instance, if we consider the following example in $\mathbb{R}^2$: $o(0; 0)$ an object, $e_1(1; 1)$ and $e_2(-1; 1)$ two positive examples, and $ce_1(1; 2)$ and $ce_2(2, -1)$ two negative examples then $e_2 \in H(e_1)$ but $e_2 \notin C(o, e_1)$. Thus an example is more likely to be kept in $DiVS$ than in the scope classification. Finally, since it combines IBL with rule-based learning, scope classification allows for extensions that cannot be envisioned in the current version of $DiVS$; for instance, examples could be easily generalized into rules in a learning phase within the scope approach.

4.2 SE-Learn

SE-Learn is a rule-based approach based on the same logical biases of relevance and consistency used in the scope approach. It generates all the (most general) relevant and consistent rules for T. If no statistical bias (including the resolution criterion) were used, scope classification and SE-Learn would be closely related, according to Theorem 4. Indeed, for every object o, there exists a (most general) relevant and consistent rule R for T that covers o iff there exists an example e in T s.t. $e \in cons(T, \leq_o)$ and the class value of e is the class value of the right-hand side of R. But there is no quantitative side in Theorem 4. Thus, the number of most general rules that are relevant and consistent for T and cover an object o may easily differ from the number of neighbours of o w.r.t. T in the scope approach. Accordingly, equipped with the same resolution criterion, the two approaches do not give rise to the same classifiers. Moreover, the other statistical bias used in both approaches (parameters ϵ, M, γ in scope classification and statistical pruning p in SE-Learn) do not coincide. Finally, scope classification is an IBL technique while SE-Learn is a rule-based one. As mentioned in Section 3.2, the computational complexity of SE-Learn makes it impractical for problems with many attributes and examples.

4.3 Other related works

Several approaches combine instance-based and rule-based learning, including NGE [Salzberg, 1991], BNGE [Wettschereck and Dietterich, 1995] and RISE [Domingos, 1996]. These approaches generalize the examples from the training set into rules in a learning phase, then classify every object according to its closest rule (w.r.t. some distance). Thus, the rules used to classify an object o do not depend on the object itself (they are fixed during the learning phase). In any case, only one rule is elected to classify o; for instance, the most specific rule among the closest to o [Salzberg, 1991], or the one with the best Laplace accuracy [Domingos, 1996].

Clearly enough, these approaches are very different from scope classification. First, they use rules as instances, while no rules have to be generated within the scope approach (no learning phase is mandatory). Second, they are distance-based while scope classification is not. Third, all the examples e of the training set s.t. $R(o, e)$ is consistent for T are considered in scope classification when o is to be classified. Such rules $R(o, e)$ are different from those considered in the approaches mentioned above in the general case. In particular, they depend on o (every $R(o, e)$ must cover o). Finally, the resolution criteria used in all these approaches differ.

5 Conclusion

The scope approach is an IBL technique with a rule-based characterization. Since it is a bottom-up approach, continuous attributes do not need to be discretized within scope classification. Since the scope algorithm does not focus on a fixed number of neighbours, it appears empirically more accurate than PEBLS where the number of neighbours is constrained. Since every rule associated with a neighbour is implicitly considered in the scope approach, it appears empirically as more accurate than techniques where only a few classification rules are induced, in particular decision trees (C4.5) and CN2. While the whole set of (most general) relevant and consistent rules for T is often too huge to be computed explicitly, the scope approach does not require this set to be generated. Hence it can be practical in many situations where SE-Learn is not.

Acknowledgements

The authors would like to thank Michèle Sebag and anonymous reviewers for their numerous suggestions of improvements, Ron Rymon and Bob Schrag for providing them with the SE-Learn program and for their help and comments. Thanks also to the authors of CN2, PEBLS, C4.5 and RISE systems, and to datasets providers for the UCI repository. The first author is currently supported by the Esprit Long Term Research Project 20237 (ILP2). The second author is supported in part by a "contrat d'objectif de la région Nord/Pas-de-Calais".

References

[Clark and Niblett, 1989] Peter Clark and Tim Niblett. The CN2 induction algorithm. *Machine Learning*, 3(4):261–283, 1989.

[Cost and Salzberg, 1993] Scott Cost and Steven Salzberg. A weighted nearest neighbor algorithm for learning with symbolic features. *Machine Learning*, 10:57–78, 1993.

[Demiroz and Guvenir, 1997] Gulsen Demiroz and H. Altay Guvenir. Classification by voting feature intervals. In *Proc. of the Ninth European Conference on Machine Learning*, pages 85–92, Prague, Czech Republic, 1997. LNAI 1224, Springer-Verlag.

[Domingos, 1996] Pedro Domingos. Unifying instance-based and rule-based induction. *Machine Learning*, 24:141–168, 1996.

[Kohavi and John, 1995] Ron Kohavi and George H. John. Automatic parameter selection by minimizing estimated error. In *Proc. of the Twelfth International Conference on Machine Learning*, 1995. Morgan Kaufmann.

[Merz and Murphy, 1996] C.J. Merz and P.M. Murphy. UCI repository of machine learning databases. http://www.ics.uci.edu/~mlearn/MLRepository.html, 1996.

[Quinlan, 1993] John Ross Quinlan. *C4.5 : Programs for machine learning*. Series in machine learning. Morgan Kaufmann, 1993.

[Rymon, 1993] Ron Rymon. An SE-tree based characterization of the induction problem. In *Proc. of the Tenth International Conference on Machine Learning*, pages 268–275, 1993.

[Rymon, 1996a] Ron Rymon. SE-Learn home page. http://www.isp.pitt.edu/~rymon/SE-Learn.html, 1996.

[Rymon, 1996b] Ron Rymon. SE-trees outperform decision trees in noisy domains. In *Proc. of the Second International Conference on Knowledge Discovery in Databases*, pages 331–334, 1996. AAAI Press.

[Salzberg, 1991] Steven Salzberg. A nearest hyperrectangle learning method. *Machine Learning*, 6:251–276, 1991.

[Sebag, 1996] Michèle Sebag. Delaying the choice of bias: A disjunctive version space approach. In *Proc. of the Thirteenth International Conference on Machine Learning*, pages 444–452, 1996. Morgan Kaufmann.

[Wettschereck and Dietterich, 1995] Dietrich Wettschereck and Thomas G. Dietterich. An experimental comparison of the nearest-neighbor and nearest-hyperrectangle algorithms. *Machine Learning*, 19:5–27, 1995.

Error-Correcting Output Codes
for Local Learners

Francesco Ricci[1] and David W. Aha[2]

[1] Istituto per la Ricerca Scientifica e Tecnologica
38050 Povo (TN), Italy
[2] Navy Center for Applied Research in Artificial Intelligence
Naval Research Laboratory, Code 5510
Washington, DC 20375 USA

Abstract. Error-correcting output codes (ECOCs) represent classes with
a set of output bits, where each bit encodes a binary classification task
corresponding to a unique partition of the classes. Algorithms that use
ECOCs learn the function corresponding to each bit, and combine them
to generate class predictions. ECOCs can reduce both variance and bias
errors for multiclass classification tasks when the errors made at the output bits are not correlated. They work well with algorithms that eagerly
induce *global* classifiers (e.g., C4.5) but do not assist simple *local* classifiers (e.g., nearest neighbor), which yield correlated predictions across
the output bits. We show that the output bit predictions of local learners can be decorrelated by selecting different features for each bit. We
present promising empirical results for this combination of ECOCs, nearest neighbor, and feature selection.

1 Introduction

Error-correcting output codes (ECOCs) can help distinguish classes in classification tasks with $m > 2$ classes by encoding error-correcting capabilities in their
output representation. This can increase the classification accuracy of *global*
learning algorithms [Dietterich and Bakiri, 1995] (e.g., C4.5 [Quinlan, 1993],
backpropagation [Rumelhart *et al.*, 1986]).

However, ECOCs do not benefit *local* learning algorithms [Kong and Dietterich, 1995; Bottou and Vapnik, 1992], which predict classifications for a query q
based only on information from examples local (i.e., nearby) to q. In Section 1.2,
we explain that this limitation occurs because a local learner's predictions are
correlated across the output bits.

This paper presents a method that allows ECOCs to work well with local
learning algorithms; it uses a feature selection algorithm to reduce the correlation
of a local learner's decision boundaries across output bits.

1.1 Error-correcting output codes

Table 1 exemplifies how ECOC encodings differ from two popular output encoding strategies. In each of these output representations, each class $c_i \in C$ is

Table 1. Example Output Representations

Class	Output Representation		
Name	Atomic	Distributed	
		One-Per-Class	ECOC
Earthling	1	100	00000
Martian	2	010	11100
Italian	3	001	00111

assigned a unique *codeword* $s_i = (s_{i1}, \ldots, s_{il})$ of l codeletters (e.g., [Dietterich and Bakiri, 1995]).

The most popular *atomic* strategy sets $l = 1$; it uses a single codeletter to represent class labels. Learning algorithms that use this approach (e.g., C4.5 [Quinlan, 1993]) induce a single concept description that distinguishes all class boundaries.

Conversely, distributed output code strategies set $l > 1$, where each codeletter s_{ij} typically has a binary value (i.e., they are bit strings). This strategy defines l binary functions f_j on the training set, where $f_j(x) = 1$ if x is in class c_i and $s_{ij} = 1$, and $f_j(x) = 0$ otherwise. f_j is also called the j-th *output bit* function; it is defined only by the j-th column of s_{ij} and provides a binary partition of the classes. For a given class c_i and output bit f_j, either f_j maps all examples in c_i to 1 or maps all of them to 0. Each output bit function corresponds to a different learning task. Given a query q, classifiers using distributed output representations generate predictions $\hat{f}_j(q)$ ($1 \leq j \leq l$) for each output bit, and predict the class c_i whose codeword $(s_{i1}, \ldots, s_{il})$ has minimal (e.g., Hamming) distance from the predicted codeword $(\hat{f}_1(q), \ldots, \hat{f}_l(q))$.

Two types of distributed output representations are *one-per-class* and *error-correcting*. In one-per-class each bit function separates the examples in one class from the remaining examples (i.e., exactly one output bit in a one-per-class codeword has value 1; all others have value 0). Learning algorithms that use one-per-class encodings induce a separate concept description per class [Quinlan, 1993; Aha, 1992], where positive instances of a class c_i are negative instances for all other classes $c_j (i \neq j)$.

The Hamming distance between all one-per-class codewords is 2, which means that even one incorrectly predicted output bit can cause a misclassification. In contrast, ECOCs encode error-correcting capabilities: they are not restricted to having exactly as many classes as output bits, their codewords can have multiple output bits with value 1, and each class's codeword differs, in Hamming distance, from all other class codewords by (at least) a pre-determined amount h. This gives ECOCs an *error-correcting* capability of $\lfloor \frac{h-1}{2} \rfloor$. For example, $h = 3$ for the three ECOC codewords shown in Table 1. Thus, even if one bit's value is incorrectly predicted for a query q the correct class still has the minimum Hamming distance to q, and will thus be predicted.

Dietterich and Bakiri [1995] compared these three output representations on several multiclass tasks. They designed ECOC codewords, which typically require a large number of output bits, to maximize both *row separation* of the matrix s_{ij} (i.e., Hamming distance between codewords) and *column separation* (i.e., Hamming distance between two columns of s_{ij}, and between any one column and the complement of another). This ensures that the *errors* of the output bit predictions are uncorrelated. They reported that ECOCs often significantly increased the classification accuracies for C4.5 [Quinlan, 1993] and networks trained by backpropagation [Rumelhart et al., 1986], although training ECOCs is slow because they must learn l concepts (i.e., one per output bit).

Kong and Dietterich [1995] showed that ECOCs work well with global learning algorithms on multiclass classification tasks because they can reduce both the *variance* and *bias* components of the output bit errors. Variance results from random variation and noise in the training set and from any random behaviors of the learning algorithm itself. ECOCs reduce variance through a voting process [Perrone and Cooper, 1993]: because Hamming distance determines the "winning" prediction (i.e., closest codeword), each output bit prediction corresponds to a vote for classes whose codewords match the predicted value.

Bias instead refers to an algorithm's systematic errors. These can also be reduced by voting, but only when the individual predictions are uncorrelated, such as by averaging the contributions of *different* prediction algorithms (e.g., [Zhang et al., 1992]). Alternatively, the same algorithm can be used multiple times, but it must vote on different subproblems (i.e., using different class decision boundaries) that cause the algorithm to generate different bias errors. When output bits have good column separation, global algorithms like C4.5 can induce different class boundary hypotheses for different output bits.

1.2 Problem and proposed solution

Suppose that a query q is in class i but a classifier CL (without using ECOCs) misclassifies it as k. Suppose also that CL_{ecoc} uses error-correcting output codes. Assume further that s_{ij} and s_{kj} $(j = 1, \ldots, l)$ are the two encodings of classes i and k, respectively. CL_{ecoc} can "correct" CL prediction errors for q if and only if it assigns to q the codeword $(\hat{f}_1(q), \ldots, \hat{f}_l(q))$ and there are more j such that $\hat{f}_j(q) = s_{ij}$ than $\hat{f}_j(q) = s_{kj}$ (i.e., for any class k in $1 \leq k \leq m$).

When CL is a local classifier (e.g., nearest neighbor) q's predicted bit value $\hat{f}_j(q)$ will always be the same as the bit value of its nearest neighbor q'. Therefore if the nearest neighbor misclassifies q then its ECOC variant will also misclassify q. Thus *extending nearest neighbor with ECOCs will not modify its class predictions*. More generally, this holds for other distributed output representations, including one-per-class. Kong and Dietterich have shown that a global classifier (e.g., C4.5) can avoid this problem. That is, $C4.5_{ecoc}$ can predict $\hat{f}_j(q) = s_{ij}$ for some j and $\hat{f}_j(q) = s_{kj}$ for some other j.

Figure 1 exemplifies how ECOCs assist global but not local classifiers. It shows two output bit partitions for three classes c_i $(1 \leq i \leq 3)$ in a two-dimensional

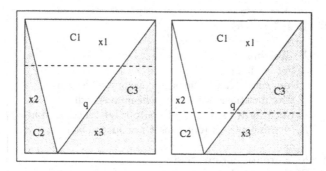

Fig. 1. Class Boundaries (solid lines), Class Groupings (shadings), and a Global Learner's Partition Boundary Hypotheses (dashed lines) for Two Output Bits

continuous space, where each class has a single training instance x_i. The solid lines define the class boundaries, the shadings define each bit's class partition,[3] and the dotted lines show the partition boundary hypotheses that might be induced by a global learner, where the predicted class of each rectangle is the class of its enclosed instances. Thus, the first hypothesis is wrong on q while the second is correct. Therefore, the second bit function can help *correct* the first error, where the underlying assumption is that the majority of hypotheses (bit functions) will correctly predict a query's partition. In contrast, nearest neighbor, when making each bit function hypothesis, will always identify x_3 as q's closest neighbor, and predict x_3's partition.

In this paper, we present empirical evidence that ECOCs can substantially improve the accuracies of the nearest neighbor classifier by incorporating an appropriate feature selection algorithm. Bit-specific decision boundaries can be obtained for nearest neighbor by applying feature selection independently for each bit, which yields a different distance function for each bit. This in turn allows a different nearest neighbor to be selected for each bit's prediction, which decorrelates the output bit errors. The bias/variance decomposition of the error (Section 4) reveals that this accuracy improvement is obtained by drastically reducing bias at the cost of moderately increasing variance.

2 Local Learning with ECOCs

To work well, ECOCs require that the errors for each of the output bits be uncorrelated. Therefore, we extended IB1 [Aha *et al.*, 1991], an implementation of nearest neighbor, to use different features when computing distances for each output bit. Figure 2 summarizes the training algorithm scheme for this extension, named $IB1_{cdwd}$. Using different codeword generation procedures (e.g., atomic, one-per-class, or ecoc), $IB1_{cdwd}$ yields different classifiers. Section 2.1 defines its algorithms for creating ECOC codewords and Section 2.2 describes how it selects features.

---

[3] The grey area denotes the set of examples that the output bit function maps to 1.

```
IB1_cdwd(X, C, l, n)
───────────────────────────────────────────
X: Training set
C: Set of classes
l: Number of bit functions (i.e., codeword length)
n: Max iterations allowed in schemata search
S: Codewords (f_j is the j-th output bit function from S)
F: Feature subsets (one subset per output bit)
───────────────────────────────────────────
1. S := create_codewords(C, l)
2. FOR j = 1 to l DO:
3.     F_j := race-schemata(X, f_j, n)
4. RETURN {S, F}
```

Fig. 2. $IB1_{cdwd}$: An Abstraction of IB1 for Alternative Output Representations

2.1 Generating ECOC codewords

The first step in $IB1_{cdwd}$ inputs C, the set of classes, and l, the number of output bits per codeword. The function *create_codewords* generates the set of codewords S, one for each of the m classes $c_i \in C$. We describe in the following how to generate ECOC codewords. Atomic and one-per-class codewords are generated as explained in Section 1.1.

Algorithms for generating ECOC codewords should maximize both row and column separation. For classification tasks where $m \leq 7$, *create_codewords* uses the *exhaustive codes* technique [Dieterich and Bakiri, 1995]. It creates all $2^{m-1} - 1$ possible codewords that are both column and row separated. The resulting codewords have Hamming distance $h = 2^{m-2}$.

When $m > 7$, *create_codewords* employs a variant of Dieterich and Bakiri's [1995] randomized hill climbing algorithm. Our variant extends the original algorithm to search more efficiently: it searches in directions that either increase row or column separation, or assist in escaping from local maxima. It initially generates m boolean codewords of length l, drawn randomly according to a uniform distribution. It then iteratively modifies these codewords, yielding the set of codewords with maximal row and column separation. During each iteration, it selects the two most similar codewords (rows) and the two bit partitions (columns) that are most similar or most dissimilar. However, the columns are selected *only* if the intersection of these rows and columns (a 2×2 boolean matrix a_{ij}) has either of the following properties:

1. If the columns have small Hamming distance, then either the two rows or the two columns of a_{ij} must be equal (i.e., $a_{11} = a_{12}$ and $a_{21} = a_{22}$ or $a_{11} = a_{21}$ and $a_{12} = a_{22}$).
2. If the columns have large Hamming distance, then the two columns of a_{ij} must differ (i.e., $a_{11} \neq a_{12}$ and $a_{21} \neq a_{22}$).

Some of these four values (a_{ij}) are then changed as follows. If all four are equal, then the values on one of the two diagonals are inverted, which increases the

```
race-schemata(X, f_j, n):
────────────────────────────────────────
f_j: An output bit function
M: Error statistics matrix (l × 2)
p: Schemata bit string of length d (initially all ⋆'s)
q: Schemata bit string of length d (instantiates p)
e: Prediction error (boolean)
────────────────────────────────────────
1.   FOR i ← 1 TO l DO:
2.      M := initialize(p)
3.      DO (k ← 1 TO n):
4.         x := random-select(X)
5.         q := select-constrained-string(p)
6.         e := compute-error(IB1,x, f_j, q)
7.         M := update-matching-statistics(M, q, e)
8.      UNTIL winner(M) or (k = n)
9.      p := update-winning-feature(p, M)
10.  RETURN features selected in p
```

Fig. 3. The Race-Schemata Algorithm for Feature Selection (see Figure 2 for additional documentation)

separation of these rows and columns by two. Otherwise, one of these four values, randomly selected, is inverted. This does not always increase total separation, but it helps to escape from local maximum by exchanging row with column separation (or vice versa). The search process is stopped after a pre-determined maximum number of codeword changes has occurred.

2.2 Selecting features

After creating the codewords, $IB1_{cdwd}$ calls *race-schemata* (Figure 3), which inputs the training set X, a bit function f_j, and the max iteration number n. It returns the subset of features selected by a variant of the schemata racing algorithm [Maron and Moore, 1997] (see [Ricci and Aha, 1997b]). *Race-schemata* searches over the space of schemata strings $p \in P$ of length d, the number of features, whose characters are 0's (feature is not selected), 1's (selected), or ⋆'s (selected with probability 50%). Step 2 begins one race for each (remaining) ⋆ in the schemata p, resetting each feature's error statistics for both 0 and 1. For instance, the first time d races start, and in each race schemata of type "⋆···⋆0⋆···⋆" compete against "⋆···⋆1⋆···⋆", with 0 and 1 in the same position. The interior loop (steps 3–8) iterates until the next race winner is found or n iterations are reached. Each iteration randomly selects a training instance x, selects a binary string q (without ⋆'s) that matches the 0's and 1's currently in p (i.e., it matches at least one of the schemata being raced), computes IB1's error on x for bit function f_j using the features selected in q, and updates the error statistics for all the schemata being raced that match q. The error of a schemata is computed by averaging the error of matching samples. If a "winning" feature is found (i.e. it is highly unlikely that the error of the other schemata is significantly less) then the interior loop terminates and p is updated by fixing the winner's bit value, changing it from $\star$ to either 0 or 1 (see [Ricci and Aha, 1997b] for more details). *Race-schemata* returns the features whose values in p are 1 (i.e., a selected subset of features).

3 Evaluation

We empirically evaluated our hypothesis that ECOCs can increase IB1's accuracies, when coupled with a feature selection algorithm, in situations where feature selection yields different features for each output bit. Thus, we focused on two independent variables in our experiments: the output representation for IB1 and whether it employed feature selection.

We compared three instances of $IB1_{cdwd}$ using the three output encodings described in Section 1.1. Their names are $IB1_{atomic}$, $IB1_{opc}$, and $IB1_{ecoc}$ for the atomic, one-per-class, and ECOC output representations, respectively. Figure 2 applies to all three algorithms except that create_codewords does not modify the single-codeletter codewords for $IB1_{atomic}$ and generates only simple one-per-class codewords for $IB1_{opc}$ (e.g., $10\ldots0, 01\ldots0, \ldots, 00\ldots1$). However, as explained in Section 1.2, distributed output representations will not modify IB1's classification behavior when feature selection is not performed. Thus, rather than reporting results for all six combinations of independent values (i.e., three output representations, either with or without feature selection), we report the results for only four of these combinations: the atomic output representation without feature selection plus all three output representations when using feature selection.

3.1 Data Sets

We selected seven data sets (Table 2) from the UCI Repository [Merz and Murphy, 1996] that have only numeric or boolean features, no missing values, and at least four classes. Even if ECOCs are applicable to general data sets, we avoided those with symbolic features because they often require distinct weighting metrics (e.g., [Stanfill and Waltz, 1986]), which complicates isolating the effects of feature selection. Data sets with fewer than four classes do not greatly benefit from ECOCs. We also used three additional proprietary data sets concerning cloud classification. We will use abbreviations for the data set names.

We conducted a ten-fold cross validation on the data sets with the following exceptions: we used only the usual single training and test set for IS due to its large size, we used only five folds for VO due to its structure, and we inverted the training and test sets for SE due to its ease.

Table 2. Selected Data Sets (C=Classes, d=dimensionality)

	Glass	Clouds98	Clouds99	Clouds204	Isolet	Letter	Satellite	Vowel	Segmentation	Zoo
Code	GL	CL98	CL99	CL204	IS	LE	SA	VO	SE	ZO
Size	214	69	321	500	7797	20000	6435	990	2310	101
|C|	6	4	7	10	26	26	6	11	7	7
d	9	98	99	204	617	16	4	10	19	16

Table 3. Average Percent Accuracies and Standard Deviations

Data Set	No Feature Selection	With Feature Selection		
	$IB1_{atomic}$	$IB1_{atomic}$	$IB1_{opc}$	$IB1_{ecoc}$
GL	68.3±11.9	69.1±11.5	**67.2±8.3**	73.8±7.8
CL98	64.0±15.1	65.7±18.1	65.5±13.4	65.5±11.6
CL99	**53.9±9.3**	58.5±9.3	**48.6±8.3**	59.8±8.4
CL204	**60.6±7.9**	**57.8±6.7**	*46.0±5.1*	73.8±4.6
IS	84.6	84.0	24.4	90.4
LE	**83.4±2.3**	83.5±2.2	**83.5±2.1**	84.9±3.2
SA	**80.7±1.3**	**80.5±2.7**	*79.7±1.7*	82.2±1.6
VO	57.7±8.0	57.7±8.0	57.7±8.0	57.8±8.1
SE	96.8±1.1	96.8±1.1	96.8±1.1	96.9±1.1
ZO	94.5±6.4	92.7±8.4	94.5±6.4	94.5±6.4

boldface: significantly lower 1-tailed t-test accuracies than $IB1_{ecoc}$ ($p < 0.05$)
italics: significantly lower 1-tailed t-test accuracies than $IB1_{atomic}$ with no feature selection ($p < 0.05$)

3.2 Empirical comparison

Table 3 summarizes the results of our experiment. Our primary finding is that, *when feature selection is useful and when different features are selected for different bit functions, ECOCs can significantly improve the accuracy of the local learner IB1.*

Feature selection was not always appropriate; it increased accuracy on only four data sets, and never significantly increased accuracy. $IB1_{ecoc}$ performed well, "repairing" $IB1_{atomic}$'s accuracy whenever it was reduced by feature selection. $IB1_{ecoc}$'s accuracies were always significantly higher or not significantly different than the other algorithms' accuracies.

We hypothesized that ECOC representations increase accuracy for high-dimensional data sets where different feature subsets are useful for learning different output bits (CL98, CL99, CL204, IS, SA). Thus, we examined whether the modified racing schemata algorithm selected different features for different bit functions. We define *Selected* as the average number of features selected per output bit function, and *ComInPairs* as the average number of features in common selected for a given pair of bit functions. The ratio of *Selected* to *ComInPairs* is a rough measure of the variability of the features selected among different bit functions.

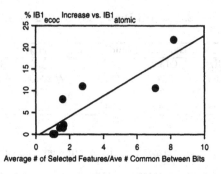

Fig. 4. Correlation Between Variances in the Feature Selection Per Bit and Average ECOC Accuracy Increases Versus $IB1_{atomic}$ Without Feature Selection

Figure 4 plots, for each data set, the ratio of Selected to ComInPairs against the percentage accuracy improvement obtained by $IB1_{ecoc}$ when compared with $IB1_{atomic}$ (without feature selection). The correlation of these variables is fairly high (0.87), suggesting a linear relationship: ECOC accuracy gains tend to increase with increasing diversity among the features selected per output bit. The line in Figure 4 is the linear regression equation computed from these values.

4 Bias, Variance, and Error Decomposition

This section first reviews Breiman's [1996] definitions for bias and variance (i.e., for classification tasks) and then presents the error decomposition for some of the data sets.

A classification problem is completely described by k real deterministic functions $P(Y = i|X = x)$, where X describes the input parameters and Y the output classes. The minimum misclassification rate is obtained using the Bayes optimal classifier:

$$Y_B(x) = \arg\max_i P(Y = i|X = x) \qquad (1)$$

Given a finite training set $T = \{(x_i, y_i) : i = 1, \ldots, m\}$ the classifier induced by a supervised learner depends on T, which we denote as $\hat{Y}(x|T)$. The *aggregate* classifier $Y_A(x)$ can be defined as:

$$Y_A(x) = \arg\max_i P(\hat{Y}(x|T) = i) \qquad (2)$$

The predictions of the Bayes optimal classifier and aggregate classifier differ when $P(\hat{Y}(x|T) = i) \neq P(Y = i|X = x)$. Breiman defines a classifier to be unbiased at x if $Y_A(x) = Y_B(x)$. Let $\mathcal{U}$ be the set of instances at which $\hat{Y}$ is unbiased and $\mathcal{B}$ its complement. The bias, variance, and error decomposition are defined as follows:

$$Bias(\hat{Y}) = P(\hat{Y}(x) \neq Y(x), x \in \mathcal{B}) - P(Y_B(x) \neq Y(x), x \in \mathcal{B}) \qquad (3)$$

$$Var(\hat{Y}) = P(\hat{Y}(x) \neq Y(x), x \in \mathcal{U}) - P(Y_B(x) \neq Y(x), x \in \mathcal{U}) \qquad (4)$$

Table 4. Bias and Variance Decomposition of the Error for Archived Data

algo	Glass	Clouds98	Clouds99	Clouds204	Zoo
IB1	0.318	0.390	0.432	0.385	0.034
Bias	0.302	0.374	0.408	0.371	0.027
Variance	0.016	0.016	0.024	0.013	0.007
$IB1_{atomic}$	0.287	0.349	0.422	0.392	0.038
Bias	0.178	0.286	0.335	0.297	0.031
Variance	0.109	0.063	0.087	0.096	0.007
$IB1_{opc}$	0.313	0.403	0.481	0.566	0.047
Bias	0.232	0.347	0.390	0.418	0.039
Variance	0.080	0.056	0.091	0.148	0.008
$IB1_{ecoc}$	0.234	0.364	0.374	0.268	0.028
Bias	0.177	0.294	0.333	0.209	0.022
Variance	0.057	0.070	0.041	0.058	0.006

$$Er(\hat{Y}) = Er(Y_B) + Bias(\hat{Y}) + Var(\hat{Y}) \qquad (5)$$

To estimate bias and variance, we randomly split the data into 100 partitions, with 90% of the data used for training and 10% for testing. We used the relative frequency that each instance x was classified as i to estimate $P(\hat{Y}(x|T) = i)$. The bias set $\mathcal{B}$ and its complement $\mathcal{U}$ can be obtained based on these estimates. Given that each instance is unique in each of our data sets, we assumed, as did Kohavi and Wolpert [1996], that the Bayes optimal error rate is zero for each data set tested (see also [Ricci and Aha, 1997a]). The results of the experiments conducted on some of the data sets are shown in Table 4.

From these results we conclude that *ECOCs drastically reduce the bias component of the error at the cost of moderately increasing the variance.* Bias is always reduced, from a minimum of 18% (Clouds99) to a maximum of 44% (Clouds204). Conversely the decrease in the total error obtained by $IB1_{ecoc}$ is moderated by an increase in variance (i.e., $IB1_{ecoc}$'s variance was at least twice $IB1_{atomic}$'s variance for each data set).

5 Discussion

In addition to the research reported by Dietterich and his colleagues, this research was inspired by Aha and Bankert [1997], who reported promising ECOC results for one data set using a k-nearest neighbor variant coupled with a forward sequential feature selection algorithm. This paper extends their work, exploring whether feature selection can decorrelate output bit errors sufficiently for nearest neighbor to work well with ECOCs. We found similar behavior with $k > 1$ in other experiments (not reported here).

Previous research on ECOCs did not stress feature selection, which is crucial for some tasks. Due to their low training costs, nearest neighbor classifiers are excellent for use with expensive feature selection approaches [Aha and Bankert, 1997]. Perhaps the most effective feature selectors are those that guide search using feedback from the classifier itself. This is expensive because it requires evaluating the classifier on many feature subsets, which is a good motivation for using an inexpensive classifier such as nearest neighbor. Thus, our contributions are useful for multiclass classification tasks where (1) feature selection is needed and (2) obtaining high predictive accuracy is a priority.

Although they can increase accuracy on some tasks, ECOCs have limitations. For example, the arbitrarily-generated class partitions corresponding to each output bit have no meaningful interpretation. Additional research could explore whether ECOCs can work well with meaningful (e.g., pre-determined) class partitions. Also, training ECOCs is slow because they must induce one classifier per output bit, and they typically require using many more output bits than classes to perform well. Feature selection compounds this problem, which is why we selected a fast feature selector. However, because feature selection algorithms that incorporate classifier feedback are computationally expensive, alternative methods should be considered when speed is important. Finally, $IB1_{ecoc}$ tended to work best with larger training sets, higher dimensional spaces, and when feature selection is appropriate.

6   Summary and Future Work

We investigated the hypothesis that ECOCs can increase the classification accuracies of local learning algorithms (e.g., nearest neighbor) when used in conjunction with a feature selection algorithm. If feature selection yields different features for each output bit, then their errors will be decorrelated because different class partition hypotheses will be generated for each output bit. This is the same reason why global algorithms increase accuracy when integrated with ECOCs.

Our empirical results provide evidence for our hypothesis. We also hypothesized conditions under which this combination of algorithms will perform well, and presented evidence suggesting that it works well for tasks that require feature selection and where different features are selected for each output bit. In some cases, the accuracy improvements were dramatic.

Future research topics include using different distance metrics for different bit functions, using alternative feature selection algorithms, and investigating whether similar benefits can be obtained using feature weighting rather than feature selection algorithms.

Acknowledgements

This work was supported by IRST and the Office of Naval Research. Thanks to Diana Gordon and Ken De Jong for their feedback on earlier versions of this paper, and to Paul Tag and Rich Bankert for the cloud data sets.

References

[Aha and Bankert, 1997] D. W. Aha and R. L. Bankert. Cloud classification using error-correcting output codes. *Artificial Intelligence Applications: Natural Science, Agriculture, and Environmental Science*, 11:13–28, 1997.

[Aha et al., 1991] D. W. Aha, D. Kibler, and M. K. Albert. Instance-based learning algorithms. *Machine Learning*, 6:37–66, 1991.

[Aha, 1992] D. W. Aha. Tolerating noisy, irrelevant, and novel attributes in instance-based learning algorithms. *International Journal of Man-Machine Studies*, 36:267–287, 1992.

[Bottou and Vapnik, 1992] L. Bottou and V. Vapnik. Local learning algorithms. *Neural Computation*, 4:888–900, 1992.

[Breiman, 1996] L. Breiman. Bias, variance, and arcing classifiers. Technical Report 460, University of California, Berkeley, April 1996.

[Dietterich and Bakiri, 1995] T. G. Dietterich and G. Bakiri. Solving multiclass learning problems via error-correcting output codes. *Journal of Artificial Intelligence Research*, 2:263–286, 1995.

[Kohavi and Wolpert, 1996] R. Kohavi and D. H. Wolpert. Bias plus variance decomposition for zero-one loss function. In *Proceeding of the Thirteenth International Conference on Machine Learning*, pages 275–283, Bari, Italy, 1996. Morgan Kaufmann.

[Kong and Dietterich, 1995] E. B. Kong and T. G Dietterich. Error-correcting output coding corrects bias and variance. In *Proceedings of the Twelfth International Conference on Machine Learning*, pages 313–321, Tahoe City, CA, 1995. Morgan Kaufmann.

[Maron and Moore, 1997] O. Maron and A. W. Moore. The racing algorithm: Model selection for lazy learners. *Artificial Intelligence Review*, pages 193–225, 1997.

[Merz and Murphy, 1996] C. Merz and P. M. Murphy. UCI repository of machine learning databases. [http://www.ics.uci.edu/~mlearn/MLRepository.html], 1996.

[Perrone and Cooper, 1993] M. P. Perrone and L. N. Cooper. When networks disagree: Ensemble methods for hybrid neural networks. In R. J. Mammone, editor, *Neural Networks for Speech and Image Processing*. Chapman and Hall, Philadelphia, PA, 1993.

[Quinlan, 1993] J.R. Quinlan. *C4.5: Programs for Machine Learning*. Morgan Kaufmann, San Mateo, CA, 1993.

[Ricci and Aha, 1997a] F. Ricci and D. W. Aha. Bias, variance, and error correcting output codes for local learners. Technical Report 9711-10, IRST, 1997.

[Ricci and Aha, 1997b] F. Ricci and D. W. Aha. Extending local learners with error-correcting output codes. Technical Report 9701-08, IRST, 1997.

[Rumelhart et al., 1986] D. E. Rumelhart, G. E. Hinton, and R. J. Williams. Learning internal representations by error propagation. In D. E. Rumelhart and J. L. McClelland, editors, *Parallel Distributed Processing: Explorations in the Microstructures of Cognition*. MIT Press, Cambridge, MA, 1986.

[Stanfill and Waltz, 1986] C. Stanfill and D. Waltz. Toward memory-based reasoning. *Communication of ACM*, 29:1213–1229, 1986.

[Zhang et al., 1992] X. Zhang, J. Mesirov, and D. Waltz. Hybrid system for protein structure prediction. *Journal of Molecular Biology*, 225:1049–1063, 1992.

Recursive Lazy Learning for Modeling and Control

Gianluca Bontempi, Mauro Birattari, and Hugues Bersini

Iridia - CP 194/6
Université Libre de Bruxelles
50, av. Franklin Roosevelt
1050 Bruxelles - Belgium
email: {gbonte,mbiro,bersini}@ulb.ac.be
http://iridia.ulb.ac.be

Abstract. This paper presents a local method for modeling and control of non-linear dynamical systems from input-output data. The proposed methodology couples a local model identification inspired by the lazy learning technique, with a control strategy based on linear optimal control theory. The local modeling procedure uses a query-based approach to select the best model configuration by assessing and comparing different alternatives. A new recursive technique for local model identification and validation is presented, together with an enhanced statistical method for model selection. The control method combines the linearization provided by the local learning techniques with optimal linear control theory, to control non-linear systems in configurations which are far from equilibrium. Simulations of the identification of a non-linear benchmark model and of the control of a complex non-linear system (the bioreactor) are presented. The experimental results show that the approach can obtain better performance than neural networks in identification and control, even using smaller training data sets.

1 Introduction

In this paper we present a local method to model and control an unknown dynamical system from input-output data. The idea of local approximators as alternative to global models originated in non-parametric statistics [13,11] to be later rediscovered and developed in the machine learning field [1,8]. Recent work on lazy learning (also known as memory-based or instance-based learning) gave a new impetus to the adoption of local techniques for modeling [3] and control problem [4].

Our approach extends the idea of local learning in several directions. First, we propose a model identification methodology based on the use of an iterative optimization procedure to select the best local model among a set of different candidates. Modeling a non-linear mapping using observations, requires the data analyst to make several choices involving the set of relevant variables and observations, the model structure, the learning algorithm, and the validation protocol. Our method defers all of these decisions until a prediction or a local description is requested (query-based approach). In classical methods the many options of a local model are designed according to heuristic criteria and a priori assumptions. Here we propose an automatic procedure which searches for the optimal local model configuration, by returning for each candidate model its parameters and a statistical description of its generalization properties. As a result, a different model tuning is performed locally for each query. This idea is already presented as *local tuning* in Atkeson *et al.* [3] but no reference to any existing application is given. To the authors' knowledge, this is the first work where this approach is used to this larger extent.

The second contribution of the paper is the introduction of a new algorithm to estimate in a recursive way the model performance in cross-validation. Myers [21] introduced the PRESS statistic which is a simple, well-founded, and economical way to perform leave-one-out cross validation [12] and to assess the performance in generalization of local linear models. Here we propose a technique based on recursive least squares methods to compute the PRESS in an incremental way. Moreover, a powerful and well-founded statistical test is used to compare the performance of two alternative candidates on the basis of their cross-validation error sampling distributions.

The third contribution of the paper is a non-linear control design technique, which extensively uses analysis and design tools imported from linear control. The idea of employing linear techniques in a non-linear setting is not new in the control literature but recently had a renewed popularity thanks to methods for combining multiple estimators and controllers in different operating regimes of the system [20]. Gain scheduling [23], fuzzy inference systems [26], and local model networks [17] are well-known examples of control techniques for non-linear systems inspired by linear control. However, two strong assumptions underlie linearization control methods: an analytical description of the locus of equilibrium points is available, and the system is supposed to evolve in a sufficiently restricted neighborhood of the desired regime. Here we propose an indirect control method for performing finite-time horizon control which requires only input-output data from the observed system behavior. The approach is an example of differential dynamic programming algorithm [16,2] where the gradient computation is performed by the lazy algorithm. The controller is designed with optimal control techniques parameterized with the values returned by the linear local estimator. We show that a combination of a local estimator with a time varying optimal control can take into account the non-linearity of a system over a wider range than conventional linearized quadratic regulators (LQR).

2 Local modeling as an optimization problem

Modeling from data involves integrating human insight with learning techniques. In many real cases, the analyst faces a situation where a set of data is available, and an accurate prediction is required. Often, information about the order, the structure, or the set of relevant variables is missing or not reliable. The process of learning consists of a trial and error procedure during which the model is properly tuned on the available data. In the lazy learning approach, the estimation of the value of the unknown function is solved giving the whole attention to the region surrounding the point where the estimation is required. The classical non-adaptive memory-based procedure essentially consists of these steps:

1. for each query point x_q, define a set of neighbors, each weighted according to some relevance criterion (e.g. the distance)
2. choose a regression function f in a restricted family of parametric functions
3. compute the regression value $f(x_q)$.

The data analyst who adopts a local regression approach, has to make a set of decisions related to the model (e.g. the number of neighbors, the weight function, the parametric family, the fitting criterion to estimate the parameters). We extend the classical approach with a method that automatically selects the adequate configuration. To do this, we simply import tools and techniques from the field of linear statistical analysis. The most important of these tools is the PRESS statistic [21], which is a simple, well-founded and economical way to perform *leave-one-out* cross-validation [12] and therefore to assess the generalization performance of local linear models. Due to its short computation time which allows its intensive use, it is the key element of our approach to modeling data. In fact, if PRESS can assign a quantitative performance to each linear model, alternative models with different configurations can be tested and compared in order to select the best one. This same selection strategy is used to select the training subset among the neighbors, as well as various structural aspects like the features to consider and the degree of the polynomial used as a local approximator [6]. The general ideas of the approach can be summarized in the following way.

1. The task of learning an input-output mapping is decomposed in a series of linear estimation problems
2. Each single estimation is treated as an optimization problem in the space of alternative model configurations
3. The estimation ability of each alternative model is assessed by the cross-validation performance computed using the PRESS statistic.

The core operation of the algorithm consists in assessing and comparing local models having different configurations. Each assessment requires the PRESS computation and a comparison with the other candidate models. In order to make these operations more effective we propose two innovative algorithms in the lazy learning method:

1. a recursive algorithm for the parametric estimation and the cross-validation of each local model. This method avoids having to restart each model evaluation from scratch and noticeably decreases the computational cost
2. a more rigorous statistical test to compare the performance of two alternative candidate models. The test does not consider only the average values of the cross-validation errors but also their sampling distributions.

2.1 The PRESS statistic and the recursive method

To illustrate the local regression procedure, we will first define some notation. Let us consider an unknown input-output mapping $f \colon \mathbb{R}^d \to \mathbb{R}$ of which we are given a set of N samples $\{(x_1, y_1), (x_2, y_2), \ldots, (x_N, y_N)\}$. These examples can be collected in an input matrix X of dimensionality $[N \times d]$, and in an output vector y of dimensionality $[N \times 1]$.

Given a specific query point x_q, the prediction of the value $y_q = f(x_q)$ is computed as follows. First, for each sample (x_i, y_i), a weight w_i is computed as a function of the distance $d(x_i, x_q)$ from the query point x_q to the point x_i. Each row of X and y is then multiplied by the corresponding weight creating the variables $Z = WX$ and $v = Wy$, with W diagonal matrix having diagonal elements $W_{ii} = w_i$. Finally, a local model is fitted solving the equation $(Z^T Z)\beta = Z^T v$ and the prediction of the value $f(x_q)$ is obtained by evaluating the model at the query point $\hat{y}_q = x_q^T (Z^T Z)^{-1} Z^T v$.

An important aspect of local learning is that along with the prediction and with the model parameters, an assessment of the performance can be easily computed. We will focus on the *leave-one-out* cross-validation procedure [12], which returns a reliable estimation of the prediction error in x_q. We define the i-th *leave-one-out* error $e^{cv}(i)$ as the difference between y_i and the prediction given by the local model centered at x_q and fitted using all the examples available except the i-th. Hence, an estimation of the prediction error in x_q is given by the average of the errors $e^{cv}(i)$ each weighted according to the respective distance $d(x_i, x_q)$. When considering a local linear model, the *leave-one-out* cross-validation can be performed without recalculating the regression parameter for each excluded example thanks to the local version of the PRESS statistic [3]:

$$\text{MSE}^{cv}(x_q) = \frac{1}{\sum_i w_i^2} \sum_i \left(w_i\, e^{cv}(i) \right)^2. \tag{1}$$

In our modeling procedure the performance of a model in cross-validation is the criterion adopted to choose the best local model configuration. One of the most important parameters to be tuned in a local model configuration is the size of the region surrounding x_q in which the function f can be conveniently approximated by a linear local model. Such a parameter can be defined by the number of training examples which fall into the region of linearity. Consequently the task of identifying the region of linearity can be reduced to the task of finding, among the examples available, the number n of neighbors of x_q to be used in the local regression fit. Thus, we consider different models, each fitted on a different number of examples, and we use the *leave-one-out* cross-validation to compare them and to select the one for which the predicted error is smaller.

To make the procedure faster, and to avoid repeating for each model the parameter and the PRESS computation, we adopt an incremental approach based on recursive linear techniques. Recursive algorithms have been developed for model identification and adaptive control [15] to identify a linear model when data are not available from the beginning but are observed sequentially. Here we employ these methods to obtain the parameters of the model fitted on n nearest neighbors by updating the parameters of the model with $n - 1$ examples. Also, the *leave-one-out* errors $e^{cv}(i)$ are obtained exploiting partial results from the least square method and do not require additional computational overhead. Once adopted as the weighting kernel the indicator function which assigns $w_i = 1$ to the examples used to fit the model, the recursive lazy algorithm is described by the following equations:

$$\begin{cases} P(n+1) = P(n) - \dfrac{P(n)x(n+1)x(n+1)^T P(n)}{1 + x(n+1)^T P(n)x(n+1)} \\ \gamma(n+1) = P(n+1)x(n+1) \\ e(n+1) = y(n+1) - x(n+1)^T \beta(n) \\ \beta(n+1) = \beta(n) + \gamma(n+1)e(n+1) \end{cases} \qquad (2)$$

$$e_{n+1}^{cv}(i) = \frac{y(i) - x(i)^T \beta(n+1)}{1 + x(i)^T P(n+1)x(i)}$$

where, $(x(n+1), y(n+1))$ is the $n+1$-th nearest neighbor of the query point, $P(n)$ is the recursive approximation of the matrix $(Z^T Z)^{-1}$, $\beta(n)$ denotes the optimal least squares parameters of the model fitted on the n nearest neighbors, and $e_n^{cv}(i)$, with $1 \leq i \leq n$, is the vector E_n^{cv} of *leave-one-out* errors. Once this vector is available, the formula (1) is easily computed. This value is a weighted average of the cross-validated errors and is the simplest statistic that can be used to describe the performance of the model defined by n neighbors. However, the problem of assessing the right dimension of the linearity region using a finite number of samples affected by noise requires a more powerful statistical procedure. In the following section, we will discuss in detail the method used in our model selection procedure.

2.2 The statistical test for model selection

The recursive method described in the previous section returns for each size n of the neighborhood a vector E_n^{cv} of *leave-one-out* errors. In order to select the best model, our procedure consists in increasing the number of neighbors considered when identifying the local model, until the model performance deteriorates and a departure from the region of local linearity is detected. This requires a statistical test to evaluate when the enlarged model is significantly worse than those already considered. In terms of hypothesis testing, we formulate the null hypothesis H_0 that E_n^{cv} and E_{n+1}^{cv} belong to the same distribution. To evaluate this hypothesis we use a permutation test [24] which does not require any assumptions about normality, homogeneity of variance, or about the shape of the underlying distribution. We adopt a paired version of the permutation algorithm because of the correlation between the two error vectors.

In simple words, the procedure consists in computing for each pair of errors the difference $d_i = e_n^{cv}(i) - e_{n+1}^{cv}(i)$, and computing the value $D = \sum d_i$ which is assumed to be an instance of the random variable D^*. The sampling distribution of D^* is found by a randomization procedure [10], a computer-intensive statistical method to derive the sampling distribution of a statistic by simulating the process of sample extraction. In the permutation test, this is done by creating a high number of pseudo-samples D^b, with $b = 1, \ldots, B$, derived from the actual sample D by substituting randomly a difference d_i with $-d_i$. Once the sampling distribution of D^* is generated, a one-tailed test determines whether the null hypothesis has to be rejected.

The randomization test shows one of the main advantage of a local modeling procedure: with low computational effort it is possible to return along with the prediction and the linear local parameters also a statistical description of the uncertainty affecting these results. This property can result useful both for prediction and for control problems.

3 Lazy learning optimal control

Although non-linearity characterizes most real control problems, methods for analysis and control design are considerably more powerful and theoretically founded for linear systems than for non-linear ones. Here we propose a hybrid architecture for the indirect control of non linear discrete time plants from their observed input-output behavior. This approach combines the local learning identification procedure described in the previous section with control techniques borrowed from conventional linear optimal control

Consider a class of discrete time dynamic systems whose equations of motion can be expressed in the form

$$y(k) = f\big(y(k-1),\ldots,y(k-ny),u(k-d),\ldots,u(k-d-nu),$$
$$e(k-1),\ldots,e(k-ne)\big) + e(k), \quad (3)$$

where $y(k)$ is the system output, $u(k)$ the input, $e(k)$ is a zero-mean disturbance term, d is the relative degree and $f(\cdot)$ is some non linear function. This model is known as the NARMAX model [18]. Let us assume we have no physical description of the function f but a set of pairs $[u(k), y(k)]$ from the observed input-output behavior. Defining the information vector

$$\varphi(k-1) = \big[y(k-1),\ldots,y(k-ny),u(k-d),\ldots,u(k-d-nu),$$
$$e(k-1),\ldots,e(k-ne)\big], \quad (4)$$

the system (3) can be written in the input-output form $y(k) = f\big(\varphi(k-1)\big) + e(k)$.

Consider the optimal control problem of a non linear system over a finite horizon time. Using a quadratic cost function, the solution to an optimal control problem is the control sequence U that minimizes

$$J = \frac{1}{2}y(t_f)^T P(t_f)y(t_f) + \frac{1}{2}\sum_k \left| y(k)^T u(k)^T \right| \begin{vmatrix} Q_k & M_k \\ M_k^T & R_k \end{vmatrix} \left| y(k)u(k) \right| \quad (5)$$

with Q_k, M_k, R_k, P_f weighting terms designed a priori. While analytic results are not available for a generic non linear configuration, optimal control theory [25] provides the solution for the linear case. Hence, we will now present the non linear problem in a linear time varying setting.

Consider the trajectory of the dynamical system once forced by an input sequence $U = [u(1), u(2), \ldots, u(t_f)]$. Assume that the system can be linearized about each state of the trajectory. Neglecting the residual errors due to the first order Taylor series approximation, the behavior of the linear system along a generic trajectory is the behavior of a linear time varying system whose state equations can be written in the form

$$
\begin{aligned}
y(k+1) &= A\big(\varphi(k)\big)y(k) + B\big(\varphi(k)\big)u(k) + K\big(\varphi(k)\big) \\
&= A_k y(k) + B_k u(k) + K_k
\end{aligned}
\tag{6}
$$

with A_k, B_k, K_k parameters of the system linearized about the query point $\varphi(k)$. K_k is an offset term that equals zero in equilibrium points. This term requires a slight modification in the linear controller formulation. However, in order to simplify the notation, in the following we will neglect the constant term.

Optimal control theory provides the solution for the linear time varying system (6). At each time step the optimal control action is

$$
u(k) = -(R_k + B_k^T P_{k+1} B_k)^{-1}(M_k^T + B_k^T P_{k+1} A_k)y(k)
\tag{7}
$$

where Pk is the solution to the backward Riccati equation.

$$
\begin{aligned}
P_k ={}& Q_k + A_k^T P_{k+1} A_k \\
&- (M_k + A_k^T P_{k+1} B_k)(R_k + B_k^T P_{k+1} B_k)^{-1}(M_k^T + B_k^T P_{k+1} A_k)
\end{aligned}
\tag{8}
$$

having as final condition

$$
P(t_f) = P_f
\tag{9}
$$

The piecewise-constant optimal solution is obtained by solving the Euler-Lagrange equations, the three necessary and sufficient conditions for optimality when the final time is fixed.

$$
0 = \frac{\partial H_k}{\partial u_k} = y_k^T M_k + u_k^T R_k + \lambda_{k+1}^T B_k
\tag{10}
$$

$$
\lambda_k^T = \frac{\partial H_k}{\partial y_k} = y_k^T Q_k + u_k^T M_k^T + \lambda_{k+1}^T A_k
\tag{11}
$$

$$
\lambda_f^T = y_f^T P_f
\tag{12}
$$

with $\lambda_k = P_k y_k$ adjoint term in the augmented cost function (Hamiltonian)

$$
H_k = J + \lambda_{k+1}^T \big(A_k y(k) + B_k u(k)\big)
\tag{13}
$$

The Euler-Lagrange equations do not hold for non linear systems. Anyway, if the system can be represented in the form (6), formula (10) can be used to compute the derivative of the cost function (5) with respect to a control sequence U. This is the idea of differential dynamic programming algorithms [16] which require at each time k the matrices A_k, B_k, linearizations of the system dynamics along the trajectory forced by the input sequence.

As discussed in Section 2, our modeling procedure performs system linearization with minimum effort, no a priori knowledge and only a reduced amount of
data. Hence, we propose an algorithm for non linear optimal control, formulated as a gradient based optimization problem and based on the local system
linearization.

The algorithm searches for the sequence of input actions

$$U^{opt} = arg \min_{U^i} J(U^i) \qquad (14)$$

that minimizes the finite-horizon cost function (5) along the future t_f steps. The
cost function $J(U^i)$ for a generic sequence U^i is computed simulating forward
for t_f steps the model identified by the local learning method. The gradient of
$J(U^i)$ with respect to U^i is returned by (10).

These are the basic operations of the optimization procedure executed each
time a control action is required:

1. forward simulation of the lazy model forced by a finite control sequence U^i
   of dimension t_f
2. linearization of the simulated system about the resulting trajectory
3. computation of the resulting finite cost function $J(U^i)$
4. computation of the gradient of the cost function with respect to simulated
   sequence
5. updating of the sequence with a gradient based algorithm.

Once the search algorithm returns the optimal solution U^{opt}, the first action
of the sequence is applied to the real system (receding horizon control strategy [9]). Let us remark how the lazy learning model has a twofold role in the
algorithm: (i) at step 1 it behaves as an approximator which predicts the behavior of the system once forced with a generic input sequence (ii) at step 2 it
returns a linear approximation to the system dynamics.

Atkeson et al. [4] and Tanaka [27] applied infinite-time LQR regulator to non
linear systems linearized with lazy learning and neuro-fuzzy models. The drawback of these approaches is that an equilibrium point or a reference trajectory
is required. Also, they make the strong assumption that the state of the system
will remain indefinitely in a neighborhood of the linearization point. As discussed
above, the advantage of the proposed approach is that these requirements do not
need to be satisfied. First, lazy learning is able to linearize a system in points
far from equilibrium. Secondly, the time varying approach makes possible the
use of a linear control strategy even though the system operates within different
linear regimes.

Remark: we make the assumption that the parameters returned by the local models are a real description of the local behavior (certainty equivalence
principle). This is a restricting assumption which requires a sufficient degree of
accuracy in the approximation. However, we see in the optimal control theory
a possible solution to this limitation. In fact, stochastic optimal control theory
provides a formal solution to the problem of parameter uncertainty in control
systems (dual control [14]). Further, our modeling procedure can return at no

additional cost a statistical description of the estimated parameters (see Section 2.2). Hence, future work will focus on the extension of the technique to the stochastic control case.

4   Experiments

4.1   The identification of a non-linear discrete time system

The approach has been applied to the identification of a complex non-linear benchmark proposed by Narendra and Li [22]. The discrete time equations of the system are:

$$
\begin{cases}
x_1(k+1) &= \left(\dfrac{x_1(k)}{1+x_1^2(k)} + 1\right) \sin\big(x_2(k)\big) \\[2mm]
x_2(k+1) &= x_2(k)\cos\big(x_2(k)\big) + x_1(k)\,e^{-\frac{x_1^2(k)+x_2^2(k)}{8}} \\[2mm]
&\quad + \dfrac{u^3(k)}{1+u^2(k)+0.5\cos\big(x_1(k)+x_2(k)\big)}
\end{cases}
\tag{15}
$$

$$
y(k) = \frac{x_1(k)}{1+0.5\sin\big(x_2(k)\big)} + \frac{x_2(k)}{1+0.5\sin\big(x_1(k)\big)}
$$

where (x_1, x_2) is the non observable state and only the input u and the output y are accessible. We model the non observable system in the input-output form $y(k+1) = f\big(y(k), y(k-1), y(k-2), y(k-3), u(k)\big)$. We use an initial empty database which is updated all along the identification. We perform the identification for 1500 time steps with a test input $u(k) = \sin\left(\frac{2\pi k}{10}\right) + \sin\left(\frac{2\pi k}{25}\right)$. The plot in Fig. 1a shows the model and the system output in the last 200 points, while the plot in Fig. 1b shows the identification error.

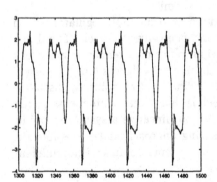 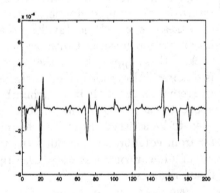

Fig. 1. Non linear system identification results: a) system (solid) and model (dotted) outputs,   b) identification error

We obtain a good performance in modeling this complex non observable system. The experiment reproduces exactly the one proposed in Narendra and

Li [22], with the sole difference that in our case we used a data set of 1500 points instead of the 500,000 used in the cited paper. Unfortunately, Narendra and Li do not report any quantitative index of the neural network (4-layer feed-forward) performance and present only a plot of the results. Anyway, a qualitative comparison between Fig. 11.5 in their article and Fig. 1 of this paper, shows clearly how our method outperforms Narendra's neural identification, even using much less data.

4.2 The control of the bioreactor

Consider, as second example, the bioreactor system [19], a challenging benchmark in control for its non linearity and because small changes in parameters value can cause instability. The bioreactor is a tank containing water, nutrients, and biological cells. Nutrients and cells are introduced into the tank where the cells mix with the nutrients. The state of this process is characterized by the number of cells (c_1) and the amount of nutrients (c_2). Bioreactor equations of motion are the following:

$$\begin{cases} \frac{dc_1}{dt} = -c_1 u + c_1(1 - c_2)\,e^{\frac{c_2}{\gamma}} \\ \frac{dc_2}{dt} = -c_2 u + c_1(1 - c_2)\,e^{\frac{c_2}{\gamma}}\left(\frac{1+\beta}{1+\beta-c_2}\right) \end{cases} \qquad (16)$$

with $\beta = 0.02$ and $\gamma = 0.48$. In our experiment the goal was to stabilize the multi-variable system about the unstable state $(c_1^*, c_2^*) = (0.2107, 0.726)$ by performing a control action each 0.5 seconds.

We use the control algorithm described in Section 3. The system is modeled in the input-output form (3) having the orders $ny = 2, nu = 1, ne = 0, d = 1$. The horizon of the control algorithm is fixed to $t_f = 5$. The initial state conditions are set by to the random initialization procedure defined in [19]. We initialize the lazy learning database with a set of 1000 points collected by preliminarly exciting the system with a random uniform input. The database is then updated on-line each time a new input-output pairs is returned by the simulated system. The plot in Fig. 2a shows the output of the two controlled state variables, while the plot in Fig. 2b shows the control action.

We have better results than Bersini and Gorrini [7] who used an optimal neuro-controller (MLP network with ten neurons in the hidden layer) trained with a much higher number of samples (10,000), and applied control actions at a higher frequency (each 0.01 seconds).

Both identification and control examples show that, by using local techniques, it is possible to deal with complex systems on a wide non-linear range, with no a priori knowledge about the underlying dynamics and using less data than global estimators.

5 Conclusions and future developments

Local modeling techniques are a powerful technique for learning from limited amount of data by providing at the same time an useful insight on the local

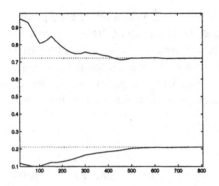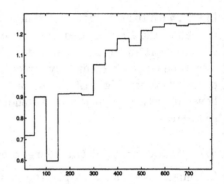

Fig. 2. Control results: a) controlled variables (solid) and references (dotted), b) control action.

behavior of the system being modeled. Furthermore, together with the required prediction and/or parametric description, they return a statistical distribution of the uncertainty affecting this information. We proposed an innovative algorithm to improve the performance of local modeling techniques which is a based on a recursive version of the cross-validation and a statistical model selection. In control literature, local controllers have generally a restricted range of operating conditions. Here, we proposed a controller, which although making extensive use of local techniques, works on an extended range of operating conditions. These characteristics makes of it a promising tool for intelligent control systems, inspired to traditional engineering methods but able to deal with complex non linear systems. Successful applications of the method to simulated identification and control problems were presented. Future developments will concern the combination of the local modeling technique with other certainty equivalence controllers (e.g. minimum variance controller, pole placement) and the extension of the method to stochastic dual control.

Acknowledgments Gianluca Bontempi was supported by the European Union TMR Grant FMBICT960692. Mauro Birattari was supported by the F.I.R.S.T. program of the Région Wallonne, Belgium.

References

1. D.W. Aha. Incremental, instance-based learning of independent and graded concept descriptions. In *Sixth International Machine Learning Workshop*, pages 387–391, San Mateo, CA, 1989. Morgan Kaufmann.
2. C. G. Atkeson. Using local optimizers to speed up global optimization in dynamic programming. In J. D. Cowan, G. Tesauro, and J. Alspector, editors, *Advances in Neural Information Processing Systems 6*, pages 663–670. Morgan Kaufmann, 1994.
3. C.G. Atkeson, A.W. Moore, and S. Schaal. Locally weighted learning. *Artificial Intelligence Review*, 11(1–5):11–73, 1997.
4. C.G. Atkeson, A.W. Moore, and S. Schaal. Locally weighted learning for control. *Artificial Intelligence Review*, 11(1–5):75–113, 1997.

303

5. J.K. Benedetti. On the non parametric estimation of regression functions. *Journal of the Royal Statistical Society, Series B*, (39):248–253, 1977.
6. H. Bersini, M. Birattari, and G. Bontempi. Adaptive memory-based regression methods. In *Proceedings of the 1998 IEEE International Joint Conference on Neural Networks*, 1998. to appear.
7. H. Bersini and V. Gorrini. A simplification of the back-propagation-through-time algorithm for optimal neurocontrol. *IEEE Trans. on Neural Networks*, 8(2):437–441, 1997.
8. L. Bottou and V.N. Vapnik. Local learning algorithms. *Neural Computation*, 4(6):888–900, 1992.
9. D.W. Clarke. *Advances in Model-Based Predictive Control*. Oxford University Press, 1994.
10. P.R. Cohen. *Empirical Methods for Artificial Intelligence*. The MIT Press, Cambridge, MA, 1995.
11. B. V. Dasarathy. *Nearest neighbor (NN) norms : NN pattern classification techniques*. IEEE Computer Society Press, 1991.
12. B. Efron and R.J. Tibshirani. *An Introduction to the Bootstrap*. Chapman and Hall, New York, NY, 1993.
13. V.A. Epanechnikov. Non parametric estimation of a multivariate probability density. *Theory of Probability and Its Applications*, (14):153–158, 1969.
14. A.A. Fel'dbaum. *Optimal control systems*. Academic Press, New York, NY, 1965.
15. G.C. Goodwin and K. S. Sin. *Adaptive Filtering Prediction and Control*. Prentice-Hall, 1984.
16. D. Jacobson and D. Mayne. *Differential Dynamic Programming*. Elsevier Sci. Publ., New York, 1970.
17. T.A. Johansen and B.A. Foss. Constructing narmax models using armax models. *International Journal of Control*, 58:1125–1153, 1993.
18. I.J. Leontaritis and S.A. Billings. Input-output parametric models for non-linear systems. *International Journal of Control*, 41(2):303–344, 1985.
19. W.T. MillerIII, R.S. Sutton, and P.J. Werbos, editors. *Neural Networks for Control*. The MIT Press, 1990.
20. R. Murray-Smith and T.A. Johansen, editors. *Multiple Model Approaches to Modelling and Control*. Taylor and Francis, 1997.
21. R.H. Myers. *Classical and Modern Regression with Applications*. PWS-KENT, Boston, MA, 1990.
22. K.S. Narendra and S.M. Li. Neural networks in control systems. In M.C. Mozer Paul Smolensky and D.E. Rumelhart, editors, *Mathematical Perspectives on Neural Networks*, chapter 11, pages 347–394. Lawrence Erlbaum Associates, 1996.
23. J.S. Shamma and M. Athans. Gain scheduling: Potential hazards and possible remedies. *IEEE Control Systems Magazine*, pages 101–107, June 1992.
24. S. Siegel and Jr. N.J. Castellan. *Non Parametric Statistics for the Behavioral Sciences*. McGraw-Hill International, 2nd edition, 1988.
25. R.F. Stengel. *Stochastic optimal control: theory and application*. John Wiley and Sons, New York, NY, 1986.
26. T. Takagi and M. Sugeno. Fuzzy identification of systems and its applications to modeling and control. *IEEE Transactions on System, Man and Cybernetics*, 15(1):116–132, 1985.
27. K. Tanaka. Stability and stabilizability of fuzzy-neural-linear control systems. *IEEE Transactions on Fuzzy Systems*, 3(4):438–447, November 1995.

Using Lattice-Based Framework as a Tool for Feature Extraction*

Engelbert Mephu Nguifo and Patrick Njiwoua

C.R.I.L, I.U.T de Lens, Université d'Artois,
Rue de l'Université SP-16, 62307 Lens Cedex, FRANCE.

Abstract. Feature transformation (FT) is one of the way to preprocess data in order to improve classification efficiency. Different FT approaches was intensively studied this past years. These approaches wish to give to a learner only those attributes that are relevant to the target concept. This paper presents a process that extracts a set of new numerical features from the original set of boolean features through the use of an empirical mapping function. This mapping is based on the use of an entropical function to learn knowledge over the Galois semi-lattice construction of the initial set of objects. One advantage here is the reduction of effect of possible irrelevant features. This process allows to design an Instance-based Learning system, IGLUE which uses the Mahanalobis measure. A comparison is done with other ML systems, in terms of classification accuracy and running time on some real-world and artificial datasets.

1 Introduction

Learning to classify objects is one of the most studied areas in machine learning (ML). The most well-known ML system is ID3 [Qui86], which is a decision tree-based system. It plays an increasingly important role in ML. Meanwhile important works was done in order to illustrate the efficiency of preprocessing data in the area of statistics, pattern recognition as well as ML. ML systems use data analysis methods towards the search space to outperform both accuracy and complexity of their learning algorithm. These systems generally focus on transformation of original features [AG96],[KS96].

In this paper, we develop a novel constructive method for feature extraction that uses ML techniques to generate new relevant features. Our approach allows to translate initial binary attributes to continuous-valued ones. This translation takes into account only relevant attributes. This feature extraction is achieved for different purposes:

- It is necessary to reduce the effect of irrelevant attributes, by focusing our attention to the way objects are defined in the whole initial context. That is, the

---

* Financial support for this work has been made available by the Ganymede project of the Contrat de Plan Etat Nord-Pas-de-Calais. The authors thank M. Rouxel for English proofreading and the anonymous reviewers for helpful comments. An extended version of this paper can be found at http://www.lifl.fr/~mephu-ng.

definition of an object should be analyzed, not separately, but by considering other examples descriptions.

• In the literature, there are different kinds of discretization methods that allow to transform continuous-valued features into binary or nominal ones. Conversely we propose here a method to achieve the opposite process.

Many Instance-based learners have been developped. They have demonstrated excellent classification accuracy over a large range of domains. Instance-based learners classify an instance by comparing it to a set of pre-classified examples. There is a fundamental assumption that similar instances have similar classifications. The main difficulty is the choice of a distance metric to define *similar instance*, and of a classification function to define *similar classification*. Another difficulty arises from the lack of an integrated theoretical background. To reduce such limitations, IBL systems use a preprocess mechanism on initial data in order to select relevant features. This paper presents a new algorithm for feature extraction that has been integrated in an ML technique to design the IBL system called IGLUE [NMN97]. The feature extraction algorithm consists of two steps (see Fig.1).

First, it builds a join-semi-lattice of the initial context of objects and binary features. To do this, it uses the entropy function to select relevant nodes during the top-down lattice construction. To reduce lattice complexity, only relevant nodes at the top level are taken into account.

Second, all the initial examples are redescribed by the way they are concerned with each relevant node of the semi-lattice. The redescription transforms only relevant initial binary features into new numerical attributes, depending on how examples could appear or not in the relevant nodes. More precisely, we generate a new continuous-valued feature which corresponds to one of the remaining original features. The new feature value for an example is the number of relevant nodes containing both the example and the corresponding binary feature. Consequently, IGLUE applies a 1-nearest neighbor principle to classify unseen examples with the Mahanalobis distance between the redescriptions of unseen examples and training examples.

Experimental comparisons reported in this paper show the effectiveness of IGLUE. Section 2 describes the feature extraction and classification algorithms and Sect. 3 shows experimental comparison on different well-known data sets.

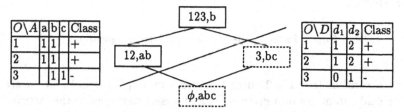

$O \backslash A$	a	b	c	Class
1	1	1		+
2	1	1		+
3		1	1	-

123,b

12,ab

3,bc

ϕ,abc

$O \backslash D$	d_1	d_2	Class
1	1	2	+
2	1	2	+
3	0	1	-

Fig. 1. An initial matrix context, the sup-semi Galois lattice constructed by IGLUE and the continuous-valued features obtained after the redescription process.

2 Feature extraction algorithm

This section describes the feature extraction algorithm which consists of two steps. The first step consists in building the join-semi-lattice of the initial context, and selecting the relevant nodes. The second step generates new continuous-valued attributes and redescribes the training set of examples with these new features. Finally the classification process is described.

2.1 Join-semi-lattice algorithm

The algorithm used here to generate the join-semi-lattice is somehow identical to that of LEGAL [MN94]. However their differ by the heuristics used. While LEGAL selects relevant nodes by using two user-specified learning parameters which are respectively the minimum and maximum required numbers of positive and negative instances inside a node, our method uses the entropy function to select relevant nodes at the h-first levels of the join-semi-lattice. This function has one advantage over the empirical process of LEGAL, since it allows to select all significant nodes even if they contain few training instances.

Algorithm(O, A, I, h, λ)

Begin
1 $F \longleftarrow (O, \phi)$, $L_2 \longleftarrow (O, \phi)$, $P_2 \longleftarrow \phi$.
2 **While** $\exists (O_k, A_k) \in F$
3   Remove (O_k, A_k) from F
4   Construct C_k, the set of sub-nodes of (O_k, A_k)
5   **For each** node $(O_{k_i}, A_{k_i}) \in C_k$
6   **If** $Level(O_{k_i}, A_{k_i}) < h$ **Then**
7   **If** $Entrop(O_{k_i}, A_{k_i}) \leq \lambda$ **Then**
8   **If** $(O_{k_i}, A_{k_i}) \notin L_2$ **Then**
9   **Begin**
10             $P_2 \longleftarrow P_2 \bigcup A_{k_i}$
11             $Insert(O_{k_i}, A_{k_i}, L_2)$
12   **End**
13   **Else**
14   add an edge from (O_k, A_k) to (O_{k_i}, A_{k_i}) in L_2
15 **Endfor**
16 **EndWhile**
17 **Return**(P_2, L_2)
End

Fig. 2. Pseudo-code of Join-semi lattice algorithm

The algorithm (see Fig.2) uses two procedures (*Construct* and *Insert*) to construct all sub-nodes of a given node and, insert new ones in the lattice. The procedure $Level(O_1, A_1)$ restitutes the level of a node inside the lattice. The maximum level, h, of the join-semi-lattice is an input parameter. The procedure $Entrop(O_1, A_1)$ consists in using the entropy function to evaluate the relevance of the node (O_1, A_1). Let $p_1 = |O_1 \bigcap O^+|$ and $n_1 = |O_1 \bigcap O^-|$:

$$Entrop(O_1, A_1) = -\frac{p_1}{p_1+n_1} \cdot log_2(\frac{p_1}{p_1+n_1}) - \frac{n_1}{p_1+n_1} \cdot log_2(\frac{n_1}{p_1+n_1}).$$

A node (O_1, A_1) is *relevant* or *pertinent* if $Entrop(O_1, A_1) \leq \lambda$. Its associate regularity is also pertinent. λ could be an input parameter or settled by the system.

2.2 Feature generation

Here we describe the process to generate new continuous-valued features. We use the set of relevant nodes of the join-semi-lattice for this purpose. Let A^* be the set of attributes of A which appears in at least one relevant node. If an attribute a_i never appears in one of the lattice nodes, then it is not relevant[2]. All training examples are redescribed by the way they interact with the set of relevant nodes. We associate to each attribute a_k of A^*, a new feature, d_k which is defined by the relation J. Let D be the set of those new features, $d_1, \cdots, d_m$, where m is the number of attributes of A^*. Let $P_i \subseteq P$ be the set of relevant regularities which hold for the example o_i.

For an example o_i and a new feature $d_k \in D$, we define a new relation J between O and D, where $J(o_i, d_k)$ is the number of appearances of attribute a_k in all regularities $r \in P_i$, and thus, $0 \leq J(o_i, d_k) \leq |P|$. This relation is then extended to examples of the test set or unseen examples.

Each feature d_k is a quantitative variable and has a correspondence a_k in A^*. The number of new features is less equal to the number of original binary features ($|A^*| \leq |A|$, thus $|D| \leq |A|$). It is important to have a strong dependency between new features and the set of built regularities due to their future use for learning purpose (see Fig.1).

2.3 Classification algorithm

Literature reports extensive studies on nearest neighbor (NN) algorithms for learning from examples. These methods often work as well as other sophisticated ML techniques [Sal91]. Among different similarity measures proposed in the literature, we choose to implement the Mahanalobis distance [QS82] in a 1-NN technique to build the IGLUE system: $s(o_i, o_j) = \sum_{1 \leq k \leq m} \frac{|d_{ik} - d_{jk}|}{\sqrt{d_{ik} + d_{jk}}}$.

• An unseen example o_x is a *positive instance* if its most similar training example is a positive one.

• Otherwise o_x is a *negative instance*.

3 Experimental results

In this section, we present preliminary experiments designed to test our feature extraction algorithm over the new system IGLUE. We report a practical

---

[2] In Fig.1, as the initial feature c doesn't appear in the built semi-lattice, c is an irrelevant attribute. The new generated features d_1 and d_2 respectively correspond to features a and b.

comparison in terms of complexity and prediction accuracy between LEGAL, IGLUE, C4.5 (unpruned version) and K^*. We assembled some data sets from the classification-learning problems available in the UC/Irvine Repository [MM96]. Time and space performances comparison have been carried out using the same domain that was used for prediction tests. The discretization process applied here, for LEGAL and IGLUE, consists of creating a new attribute for each original feature value. C4.5 and K^* are tested with their default parameters values within the Waikato Environment for Knowledge Analysis, WEKA [Zhe96].

For each data set of the Monk's problems, training and testing sets are given. We apply a five cross-validation method on the three other data sets to measure the accuracy of the three systems. In the case of data set with more than two classes, each class was recognized against the others. A batch process has to choose for each system the parameters values which give quite good results on the learning set. These values are then used for test. The different system codes are executed on a Pentium 166 machine with $32M_o$ of RAM.

IGLUE is really faster than LEGAL on all problems, although it is based on a more complex approach that combines different learning strategies. This is a consequence of the level threshold used when building the semi-lattice. When the level threshold increases, the time of IGLUE slightly increases but not exponentially as the theoretical complexity may indicate. This is due to the fact that the lattice construction also depends on the content of the binary table.

Results of classification accuracy obtained on the previous data sets are summarized in Table 1. This table shows that in all the problems except the small soybean, all lattice-based systems could be superior to other systems in terms of prediction accuracy. There is a significant result in the case of the Monks-2 problem. Among the two lattice-based systems, the performance of IGLUE is generally higher than that of LEGAL with a major difference in the two problems: Monks-2 and Breast-Cancer. Since lonely examples are not generally taken into account when LEGAL builds the semi-lattice, including entropy function when generating new features allows to avoid such limitation. Increasing the lattice level leads the system build additional nodes that really encapsulate the behavior of examples descriptions.

When dealing with data where there is a little correlation between examples (this is the case in Monks-2) symbolic ML systems fails to learn. The best results reported in the literature for this problem are that of neural network methods. However varying the level of our semi-lattice (h=3), IGLUE was able by varying the level threshold to obtain significant results that are comparable to neural network techniques. Although taking into account special cases do not guarantee better results, in practice this may be significant as it is the case with the Monks-2 data set.

4 Conclusion

We have presented a new model for generating continuous-valued features from originally binary features. This model is based on the use of entropy function over the Galois lattice framework to induce new features. This framework is the *concisely* largest search space when constructing regularities among examples. This model is a means of preprocessing data before using an appropriated ML system which should deal with continuous-valued features.

For analyzing the efficiency of our model, an IBL system, IGLUE, has been developed. IGLUE works with all the training set of examples which could be huge in practice. Ongoing research is dealing with this problem in order to select pertinent examples in the training set for the classification process. Our intention is to demonstrate the potential of Galois Lattice in Concept Learning.

Table 1. Accuracy results.

Data	Monks1	Monks2	Monks3	Breast C. W. S.	Soybean	Votes
LEGAL	100	75.6	**97.3**	79.0	96.9	95.7
IGLUE (h=1)	89.2	78.7	**97.3**	97.7	94.2	97.7
IGLUE (h=2)	100	73.4	**97.3**	**98.0**	94.2	**98.6**
IGLUE (h=3)	99.3	**91.0**	96.1	**98.2**	94.2	**98.6**
C4.5	97.4	67.8	93.9	92.1	96.6	90.6
K*	89.7	58.9	85.7	95.1	100	92.0

References

[AG96] A. Akkus and H. Güvenir. K Nearest Neighbor Classification on Feature Projections. In *Proceedings of the Thirteenth International Conference (ICML' 96)*, pages 12–19, Bari, Italy, July 3-6 1996.

[KS96] D. Koller and M. Sahami. Toward Optimal Feature Selection. In *Proceedings of the Thirteenth International Conference (ICML' 96)*, pages 284–292, Bari, Italy, July 3-6 1996.

[MM96] C.J. Merz and P.M. Murphy. Uci repository of machine learning databases, http://www.ics.uci.edu/~mlearn/mlrepository.html, 1996.

[MN94] E. Mephu Nguifo. Galois Lattice: A framework for Concept Learning. Design, Evaluation and Refinement. In *Proc. of the sixth International Conf. on Tools with Artificial Intelligence*, pages 461–467, New Orleans, Louisiana, LA, November 6-9 1994. IEEE Press.

[NMN97] P. Njiwoua and E. Mephu Nguifo. IGLUE: An Instance-based Learning System over Lattice Theory. In *Proceedings of ICTAI'97*, pages 75–76, Newport Beach, California, 3-8 November 1997.

[QS82] J. Quinqueton and J. Sallatin. Expansion and compression on binary data to build feature data. In *Proc. of Intl. Conf. on Pattern Recognition*, 1982.

[Qui86] J. Quinlan. Induction of Decisions Trees. In *Machine Learning*, volume 1, pages 81–106. T.M. Mitchell & al. eds., 1986.

[Sal91] S. Salzberg. Distance metrics for instance-based learning. In *Proc. of 6th Intl. Symp. Methodologies for Intelligent Systems*, pages 399–408, 1991.

[Zhe96] Z. Zheng. Effects of Different Types of New Attributes on Constructive Induction. In *Proceedings of 8th Intl. Conf. on Tools with AI, TAI-96*, pages 254–257, 1996.

Determining Property Relevance in Concept Formation by Computing Correlation Between Properties

João José Furtado Vasco

UNIFOR – Universidade de Fortaleza

Centro de Ciências Tecnológicas – Departamento de Computação

Av. Washington Soares 1321

Fortaleza - CE Brazil

vasco@ufc.br

Abstract. We propose a method to incrementally compute and use, during the concept formation, the relevance of a concept property. This relevance is computed through the account of the property correlation with other ones and it is used by the concept quality function in order to improve predictive accuracy. The proposed approach is analyzed concerning both the prediction power of the generated concepts and the time and space complexity of the concept formation algorithm.

1. Introduction

The general aim of concept formation is to construct, based on entity descriptions (observations), a (usually hierarchical) categorization of entities. Each category is provided with a definition, called a concept, which summarizes its elements. Further aim is to use concepts to categorize new entities and to make predictions concerning unknown values of attributes of these entities. Therefore, quality of a concept can be measured in terms of its ability to make *good* predictions about unknown values of attributes (the prediction power). Unlike supervised systems, in which concept quality is measured from the capacity in discovering a value for a single property, in concept formation, the quality of a concept is measured by its capacity in allowing prediction of values for several attributes.

An important aspect that must be considered in concept formation concerns the relevance (sometimes called salience) of particular attributes/values (or properties). Cognitive psychology [Seifert 89] and machine learning [Stepp 86], [Decaestecker 93] researchers have pointed out the necessity to determine how much a certain property is relevant within a concept.

In this paper, we propose a method to compute the relevance of a concept property based on the correlation between properties of the entities covered by the concept. We describe our approach using a COBWEB-based algorithm, called FORMVIEW, which can generate several hierarchies of categories describing different perspectives [Vasco 97]. In a multi-perspective context, the relevance of a property is crucial because it determines the hierarchical organization of categories. Since FORMVIEW uses a probabilistic representation, correlation between properties is computed from conditional probabilities. However, the proposed approach is generic and can be employed in algorithms, which may use other representations.

2. Concept Formation Systems

Concept formation (CF, for short) [Fisher 87] recognize regularities among a set of non-preclassified entities and induce a concept hierarchy that summarizes these entities. A CF algorithm is reduced to a search, in the space of the all possible concept hierarchies, for that one that covers the observed entities and optimizes an evaluation function measuring a quality criterion. In concept formation entities are treated one after another as soon as they are observed and the classification of new entities is made by their adequacy for the existing conceptual categories.

Typically concept representation is probabilistic, in which concepts have a set of attributes and all possible values for them. Each concept has the probability that an observation is classified into the concept and each value of a concept attribute has associated a *predictability* and a *predictiveness* [Fisher 87]. The predictability is the conditional probability that an observation x has value v for an attribute a, given that x is a member of a category C, or $P(a=v|C)$. The predictiveness is the conditional probability that x is member of C given that x has value v for a or $P(C|a=v)$.

3. Concept Formation Taking into Account a Property Relevance

3.1 Using the relevance of a property in concept formation

FORMVIEW's category quality (UCF) is defined as the increase in the expected number of properties that can be correctly predicted given knowledge of a category over the expected number of correct predictions without such knowledge. FORMVIEW, in addition, takes into account the relevance of the properties. We consider that the increase in the expected number of properties to be predicted from a category depends on the relevance of its properties. Formally, UCF is :

$$UCF\ (C) = \left(\sum_{i=1}^{p} \Delta(p_i) P(p_i|C) P(C|p_i) - P(C) P(p_i)^2 \right) \quad (1)$$

Where $\Delta(p_i)$ = (the relevance of the category property $p_i + P(p_i)$).

To compute a property relevance, FORMVIEW uses a strategy that relies on attribute dependence (or attribute correlation) in the way that was defined by Fisher [Fisher 87]. Formally, the dependence of an attribute A_m on other n attributes A_i can be defined as :

$$Mdep\ (A_m, A_i) = \frac{\left(\sum_{i}^{n} \sum_{ji} P(A_i = V_{iji}) \sum_{jm} \left[P(A_m = V_{mi}|A_i = V_{iji})^2 - P(A_m = V_{mjm})^2 \right] \right)}{n} \quad (2)$$

Where V_{iji} signifies the j_ith value of attribute A_i and $A_i \neq A_m$.

In fact, this function measures the average increase in the ability to guess a value of A_m given the value of a second attribute A_j. We consider that this strategy accounts for the relationship between attribute dependence and the ability to correctly infer an attribute's value using a probabilistic concept hierarchy. We can thus determine those attributes that depend on others and, as a consequence, those that influence the prediction of others. By an *influent attribute*, we mean that, if we know its value, it allows a *good* prediction about the value of others. We have thus defined the total influence *Tinfl* of an attribute A_k on others A_m , $m=1,...,n$, as the following:

$$T infl(A_k) = \frac{\sum_{m=1}^{n} M\, dep (A_m, A_k)}{n} \quad \text{where } A_k \neq A_m. \tag{3}$$

Attribute dependence gives a measure to ponder attribute relevance, which, in this context, means how much an attribute correlates with others.

3.2 Computing property relevance for each concept

In formula 2, we have defined the probability of predicting a property p given another property p' ; $P(p|p')$. Actually, for each concept C within a hierarchy, we have $P(p|p'$ and $C)$. The acquisition of this probability is problematic, since it cannot be computed only from the *predictability* and *predictiveness* stored by FORMVIEW. Instead of keeping all the 2x2-property correlation, which would take too much space, or of computing such a correlation for each new observation, which would be computationally expensive, we have defined a procedure that implements a tradeoff between time and space requirements.

Our procedure consists of maintaining two triangular arrays which keep the 2x2-property correlation : *T-root* and *T-son*. These arrays keep such a correlation for all the observations already seen. T-root is updated once for each new observation. It allows computing the relevance of the root's properties. T-son accompanies side by side the path followed by the observation during its categorization. It is updated at each hierarchical level until the observation arrives at the leaves.

Two procedures are responsible for updating the frequency of a property correlation: *UpdateArray* and *RefineTson*. In *UpdateArray*, the frequency of a property correlation is computed for all the concept properties. The procedure *RefineTson* refines *T-son* each time FORMVIEM descends the concept hierarchy. This refinement consists of updating *T-son* in order to let it only with the account of the existing correlation between the properties of observations covered by the current root concept. For each concept, *T-son's* actualization is based on the following strategy: if the quantity of observations covered by a concept is greater than the total of its *brothers* (children of the concept's father), *T-son* is updated from those observations which are covered by these later. Otherwise, *T-son* only stores the property correlation from observations covered by a concept.

Finally, the procedure *ComputeRelevance* computes the relevance of a property using the conditional probability that an entity has a property given that another property is known. These properties are computed from the frequency of a property correlation represented in *T-son*.

4. Performance Task

In our process of evaluation of FORMVIEW, we pay attention to the prediction power of a hierarchy generated by it. The basic idea is to submit a set of «questions» (normally, incomplete observations) to the system, whose answer is based on the generated representation. The quality of the representation is measured according to its capacity to give «good» answers (i.e. to infer values for attributes).

We have used three test domains taken from UCI machine-learning dataset : two animal classification domains (ZOO domains) and the Pittsburgh's bridges domain. The results obtained in the tests were useful to show more clearly the contribution of the use of predictive influence as a heuristic to compute the relevance of a property. Indeed, hierarchies generated from this heuristic have a better prediction power than those generated by other systems. It is due to the fact that concepts are organized around properties having a strong predictive influence. Thus, when one infers the value of a property, he/she increases the probability to infer values for other properties influenced by the first one. Figure 1 and Figure 2 illustrate tests done in the ZOO domains. Tests done in the Pittsburgh domain can be viewed in [Vasco 97].

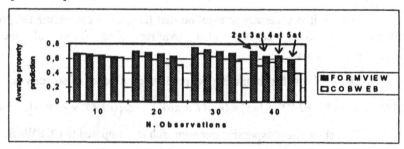

Fig. 1 Prediction of several attributes : ZOO Physiologic

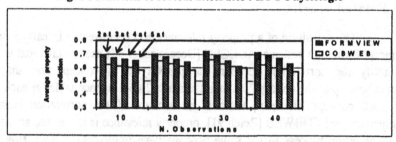

Fig. 2 Prediction of several attributes : ZOO Pet

5. Complexity

To examine the time and space complexity required by FORMVIEW's approach, we consider n the number of categorized entities and L the average branch factor of the concept tree. The cost of the procedure for computing property relevance is bound to the cost of updating $T\text{-}root$ and $T\text{-}son$. It should be reminded that, FORMVIEW stores the 2x2-correlation for each concept property, in these arrays.

First, we determine the necessary space to stock these correlations. Let *cell* be the unit where the frequency of correlation between two properties will be kept. In each array that maintains the frequency of correlation between properties, for n observations, which have in average $nbAT$, attributes with in average nbV values, we need $\sum_{i=1}^{nbATxnbV} i$ cells, that is to say, $O(nbAT \times nbV)^2$ cells.

As for the time complexity, we have the cost to update *T-root* and *T-son*. when a new observation is categorized. The cost of *T-root*'s update is the same as that required in space. *T-son's* updating is more expensive than that of *T-root* because it must be done to each level of the hierarchy (on average time $\log_L^n$). For each level, only the frequencies of correlation between observation properties covered by the current node must be represented. Thus, *T-son* must be actualized m times ($m<n$), where m represents the minimum between the number of observations which are not covered by the current node and the number of observations covered by the current node. In the worst case, we have m = n/2, which would make the geometric progression (n/2, n/4, n/8,..., 1) for all the depth of the tree. The cost of *T-son* actualization is thus the order: $O\left(2^{n/2} \times (nbAT \times nbV)^2\right)$.

Finally, it is necessary to mention that the cost of computing the predictive influence for every concept also requires time effort of the order $O(nbAT \times nbV)^2$.

The total cost for computing the predictive influence of property is:

$$O\left(2^{n/2} \times (nbAT \times nbV)^2 + \log_L^n \times (nbAT \times nbV)^2\right) - O\left((nbAT \times nbV)^2 \left(2^{n/2} + \log_L^n\right)\right)$$

This shows how expensive our approach is, compared to COBWEB.

6. Related Work

The definition of a property relevance has been treated in early incremental concept formation systems. ADECLU [Decaestecker 93] uses a statistical measure to quantify the correlation between the property of a concept and the variable "membership of the concept". It maintains a 2x2-contingence table for each property of each concept. However, there is no account of the correlation between the properties. In ECOBWEB [Reich 91], property relevance is taken into account in the categorization process in the same way we have implemented here. However, the information of which properties are relevant is given by the user. Cluster/CA [Stepp 86] equally uses the information about property relevance defined by the user in the GDN (Goal Dependence Network). Early versions of FORMVIEW also follow this same idea [Vasco 96]. The non-incremental system WITT [Hanson 89] computes the correlation between properties to create categories. It keeps for each (concept, property) pair a contingence table. Such a table contains the frequency of simultaneous occurrence of property pairs. For A attributes, WITT keeps for each concept A(A-1)/2 contingence tables. This is a tough requirement in terms of space.

7. Conclusion and Future Research

We have defined a method to compute and use the relevance of a property in concept formation systems. The first results obtained with the use of property relevance are encouraging. They shown us that, FORMVIEW's approach can provide representations it generates with better prediction power than those generated from systems that do not take into account the relevance of properties. However, additional tests are necessary, mainly with regards to evaluate the performance of FORMVIEW with more data. Moreover, these tests will be useful to analyze, if the gains in accuracy compensates the computational costs required by the method. In order to analyze the generality of the proposed method, future research consists of the application of this method to systems which use different representations.

References

[Decaestecker 93] Decaestecker, C. : Apprentissage et outils statistiques en classification conceptuelle incrémentale. *Revue d'Intelligence Artificielle*, v 7, n. 1, 1993.

[Fisher 87] Fisher, D.H.: *Knowledge Acquisition via Incremental Conceptual Learning*. Machine Learning, vol 2, numero 2, 1987.

[Fisher 91] Fisher, D., Pazzani, M., Langley, P.: *Concept Formation: Knowledge and Experience in Unsupervised Learning*. Morgan Kaufmann, 1991.

[Hanson 89] Hanson, S., Bauer, M. : Conceptual Clustering, Categorization, and Polymorphy. *Machine Learning*, v. 3, pp : 343-372, 1989.

[Reich 91] Reich, Y., Fenves, S. : The Formation and Use of Abstract Concepts in Design. In [Fisher 91].

[Seifert 89] Seifert, C.: *A Retrieval Model Using Feature Selection*. Proc. of the 6th Int. Workshop on ML. Morgan Kaufmann. 1989.

[Stepp 86] Stepp, R., Michalski, R.: *Conceptual Clustering: Inventing goal-oriented classifications of structured objects*. In Michalski, R., Carbonnel, J., Mitchell, T. (Eds), *Machine Learning, An Intelligence Approach*. Vol II. Morgan Kaufmann, CA. 1986.

[Vasco 96] Vasco, J.J.F., Faucher, C., Chouraqui, E.: *A Knowledge Acquisition Tool for Multi-perspective Concept Formation*. In proc. of European Knowledge Acquisition Workshop - EKAW-96. Shadbolt, Shreiber and O'Hara (Eds). Springer Verlag; 1996.

[Vasco 97] Vasco, J.J.F., Formation de concepts dans le contexte des langages de schémas. Thèse de doctorat. Université d'Aix Marseille III, IUSPIM/DIAM, 1997.

A Buffering Strategy to Avoid Ordering Effects in Clustering

Luis Talavera[1] and Josep Roure[2]

[1] Universitat Politècnica de Catalunya
Departament de Llenguatges i Sistemes Informàtics
Campus Nord, Mòdul C6, Jordi Girona 1-3
08034 Barcelona, Catalonia, Spain
talavera@lsi.upc.es
[2] Escola Universitària Politècnica de Mataró
Departament d'Informàtica de Gestió
Avda. Puig i Cadafalch 101-111
08303 Mataró, Catalonia, Spain
roure@eupmt.upc.es

Abstract. It is widely reported in the literature that incremental clustering systems suffer from instance ordering effects and that under some orderings, extremely poor clusterings may be obtained. In this paper we present a new strategy aimed to mitigate these effects, the Not-Yet strategy which has a general and open formulation and it is not coupled to any particular system. Results suggest that the strategy improves the clustering quality and also that performance is limited by its limited foresight. We also show that, when combined with other strategies, the Not-Yet strategy may help the system to get high quality clusterings.

1 Introduction

Ideally, intelligent agents should possess the ability of adapting their behavior to the environment over time through learning. Thus, learning methods should be able of updating a knowledge base in a continual basis as new experience is gained. Particularly, if an agent performing a *clustering* task [5] should be able of using its learned knowledge to carry out some performance task at any stage of learning, the conceptual scheme should evolve as every new instance is observed without simultaneously processing previous instances. This sort of clustering is often referred to as *incremental clustering*. As noted by Langley [8], there can be several interpretations of incremental learning. In the remainder of this paper, we will assume that a clustering method is incremental if inputs one instance at a time, does not reprocess previous instances and maintains only one conceptual structure in memory.

Incremental clustering, as defined above, has to rely on some sort of hill climbing strategy which triggers small modifications of the knowledge base as new instances are observed. This way of incorporating single instances into the cluster structure makes incremental systems to be sensitive to instance order, as widely reported in the clustering literature [4, 6, 7, 8, 9].

```
Let I be an instance and P be a partition
Let E be the expected utility/confidence of adding I to P
Let α be the Not-Yet threshold value
if E ≥ α then add(P,I)
    else add_NY_buffer(I)
endif
```

Table 1. Not-Yet control strategy

We say that incremental clustering algorithms exhibit ordering effects when they may yield different cluster structures when the same instances are presented in different orders. In some cases, they even can produce very poor quality clusterings. The problem lies in that a hill climbing strategy may narrow too much the search through the clustering space in a manner that initial observations may lead to a clustering scheme which does not reflect the real structure in the domain. In the worst case, the system might never be able of reaching a good clustering despite of gaining new experience.

2 The Not-Yet strategy

Since our goal is to (at least partially) solve the instance ordering problem while maintaining the incremental nature of clustering systems, we propose a solution to be applied during the clustering process. We refer to it as the *Not-Yet* strategy and it has a general and open definition. The strategy states that the incorporation of instances will be deferred if they are in either one of the following two cases, a) we do not expect the utility of the resulting clustering after incorporating the instance to be improved, and b) we do not have confidence enough about how the instance should be included in the existing clustering. The Not-Yet strategy assumes the existence of a buffer which stores instances that have not been incorporated into the clustering and some criterion to decide the moment in which the buffer is cleared.

In Table 1 an algorithmic formulation of the Not-Yet control strategy is shown. We introduce a parameter, α, which constraints the amount of utility or confidence required for an instance in order to be incorporated into a clustering. If we assume E to be always positive, when α is 0, the Not-Yet control strategy simply reduces to the original clustering algorithm, which becomes a particular case of a more general strategy. Although a system using the proposed strategy should perform better, it must be noted that the Not-Yet has a limited foresight, so it may perform roughly the same in the worst case.

Complexity when using our strategy will vary from system to system depending on the cost of effectively incorporating an instance and computing the expected utility or confidence of adding the instance. However, most clustering systems use some quality function to decide the best choice when an instance

Let I be an instance and P be a partition
Let $M1,M2$ be the best and second best CQF
Let α be the Not-Yet threshold value
if $(1 - M2/M1) \geq \alpha$ then add(P,I)
  else add_NY_buffer(I)
endif

Table 2. Implementation of the Not-Yet control strategy for the experiments.

is observed, so it is likely that this function is a good candidate to measure the amount of utility/confidence. If this is the case, complexity is augmented by a constant factor. This factor is dependent on the times every instance is considered for incorporation into the cluster structure.

3 Experiments

In order to empirically evaluate the Not-Yet strategy we conducted several experiments using four well-known datasets of the UCI repository. Since the clustering task is an unsupervised learning task, we have treated labels just as another attribute. In the experiments we assume a general model of hierarchical incremental clustering using two basic operators, one for creating a new class and another to incorporate an instance to an existing class. A concept hierarchy grows incrementally as new instances are observed after applying one of these operators according to the value of some *cluster quality function* (*CQF*). This is a typical model of incremental clustering using a hill climbing strategy which estimates the goodness of applying the available operators and chooses the best option, without reconsider any decision made. Particularly, this model corresponds to the one used in the COBWEB system [3]. The measure of *category utility* used in this system is also used in the experiments as the *CQF*. We used a COBWEB-like clustering strategy because it is simple, well-known and it has been applied (or augmented) in several learning systems [1, 7].

As stated before, we embed the basic control procedure into another one implementing the Not-Yet strategy. The buffer is cleared at the end of the clustering process and, therefore, an unlimited size is assumed. The strategy does not incorporate an instance to a cluster structure if there is not evidence enough to decide between the available operators. As shown in Table 2, for each instance, a ratio between the second best *CQF* and the best one is computed. We consider that an operator does not yield a significant better clustering than others if the confidence is below the α threshold, which is in the [0,1] range. In addition, instances in the buffer were randomized before reprocessing.

Experiments were performed on both random and worst case orderings. Table 3 shows the results obtained with both orderings using several values of the α parameter for the Not-Yet strategy. The zero value for this parameter corre-

	α	Basic CQF Rand.	Worst	Buffered inst. Rand.	Worst	Augmented CQF Rand.	Worst	Buffered inst. Rand.	Worst
soyb. small	0.0	1.49 (0.14)	0.91 (0.11)	0.00	0.00	1.62 (0.01)	1.12 (0.19)	0.00	0.00
	0.05	1.52 (0.12)	0.99 (0.13)	0.03	0.46	1.61 (0.03)	1.42 (0.17)	0.21	0.37
	0.10	1.49 (0.15)	1.02 (0.17)	0.11	0.80	1.60 (0.05)	1.52 (0.10)	0.52	0.80
	0.15	1.48 (0.15)	1.04 (0.12)	0.40	0.88	1.60 (0.04)	1.58 (0.05)	0.69	0.89
	0.20	1.46 (0.12)	1.10 (0.11)	0.81	0.90	1.61 (0.04)	1.58 (0.06)	0.83	0.90
	0.25	1.48 (0.13)	1.12 (0.11)	0.93	0.91	1.61 (0.03)	1.59 (0.05)	0.93	0.93
soyb. large	0.0	1.00 (0.10)	0.63 (0.14)	0.00	0.00	1.17 (0.02)	0.95 (0.14)	0.00	0.00
	0.05	1.03 (0.09)	0.65 (0.14)	0.02	0.06	1.16 (0.03)	1.06 (0.11)	0.22	0.40
	0.10	1.05 (0.10)	0.72 (0.10)	0.09	0.81	1.16 (0.03)	1.13 (0.07)	0.52	0.74
	0.15	1.07 (0.10)	0.73 (0.08)	0.31	0.96	1.16 (0.03)	1.16 (0.03)	0.82	0.96
	0.20	1.05 (0.11)	0.76 (0.08)	0.75	0.98	1.17 (0.02)	1.16 (0.03)	0.90	0.98
	0.25	1.01 (0.11)	0.77 (0.09)	0.92	0.99	1.16 (0.03)	1.16 (0.03)	0.96	0.99
house	0.0	1.29 (0.28)	0.85 (0.19)	0.00	0.00	1.61 (0.00)	1.43 (0.12)	0.00	0.00
	0.05	1.33 (0.26)	0.82 (0.17)	0.00	0.01	1.61 (0.00)	1.50 (0.11)	0.01	0.30
	0.10	1.35 (0.25)	0.84 (0.15)	0.01	0.09	1.60 (0.05)	1.53 (0.10)	0.06	0.48
	0.15	1.34 (0.25)	0.83 (0.16)	0.08	0.72	1.60 (0.04)	1.58 (0.07)	0.17	0.80
	0.20	1.37 (0.25)	0.83 (0.13)	0.29	0.98	1.61 (0.01)	1.60 (0.01)	0.38	0.93
	0.25	1.35 (0.27)	0.85 (0.13)	0.64	0.98	1.61 (0.00)	1.60 (0.01)	0.66	0.99
zoo	0.0	1.05 (0.12)	0.67 (0.17)	0.00	0.00	1.17 (0.03)	0.95 (0.14)	0.00	0.00
	0.05	1.06 (0.12)	0.67 (0.14)	0.02	0.10	1.17 (0.03)	1.05 (0.10)	0.13	0.39
	0.10	1.05 (0.13)	0.73 (0.11)	0.06	0.54	1.17 (0.03)	1.10 (0.08)	0.30	0.67
	0.15	1.03 (0.15)	0.77 (0.12)	0.19	0.87	1.16 (0.03)	1.15 (0.05)	0.53	0.87
	0.20	1.00 (0.17)	0.76 (0.08)	0.45	0.92	1.17 (0.03)	1.16 (0.03)	0.70	0.93
	0.25	1.03 (0.17)	0.78 (0.09)	0.78	0.93	1.16 (0.03)	1.16 (0.03)	0.83	0.94

Table 3. Clustering results. Averages and standard deviations over 50 trials

sponds to the original algorithm without buffering any instance. Although we are using a hierarchical clustering method, the CQF is given only for the top level, which is expected to score highest [4]

Results demonstrate that instance ordering has a critical effect in cluster quality. The quality of discovered clusterings consistently drops in a 35-40% when bad orderings are used, being far from the optimal values found in the literature [4]. The Not-Yet strategy modestly improves results in the random case, but note that the good performance of the original clustering procedure on random orderings lets little room for improvement. With bad orderings, the strategy improves the poor scores obtained with the basic algorithm up to a 20%. However, results are still far from the ones obtained with random orderings. Table 3 shows that the number of buffered instances increases as the α value does, and also that this increment is faster with bad orderings. This demonstrates the ability of the Not-Yet strategy for detecting bad instance orders.

In our second experiment, we augmented the basic clustering procedure by adding the *merge* and *split* operators used in COBWEB. Briefly, the merge operator modifies a hierarchy by combining two existing clusters while the split operator breaks existing clusters into smaller ones. Split and merge operators provide a sort of backtracking to the clustering system. However, due to the fact that they are only triggered by new observations, their impact is still limited.

Again, there is almost no chance to improve the results obtained with random orderings. However, our strategy allows the system to reach high quality clusterings under bad instance orderings. These results suggest that combination of several strategies may yield better results than their isolate application.

In both experiments, the most important improvements are obtained at the expense of maintaining a big Not-Yet buffer, i.e., with high α values. It may appear counterintuitive with the idea of incremental learning to maintain a buffer of about the 90% of the instances in the dataset. A solution could be to limit the Not-Yet buffer in a way that it would be cleared several times during learning. It is not clear how this limitation would affect performance and further experiments should be made.

4   Related work

Several works have approached the ordering problem in incremental clustering, although this research has mainly benefited from two particular approaches. Lebowitz first introduced the idea of *deferred commitment* within the framework of his UNIMEM conceptual clustering system [9]. Our proposal extends Lebowitz's work by decoupling the buffering strategy from any particular system. Also, we have introduced the α parameter, that allows to see the original algorithm as a particular case of the new control strategy. We think that this formulation should help in applying the strategy to any existing algorithm without any major changes.

The second related work is the application of this strategy to the LINNEO$^+$ clustering system [2, 10]. This work contains the basic ideas proposed here, but again the application is tuned for an specific system and the problems studied are deeply related to a particular clustering strategy.

Also, we have to mention relevant Fisher's work on iterative optimization of clusterings [4]. This work explores several methods for iteratively improving clustering quality, showing that among these methods some exhibit an optimum performance. But recall that these methods operate by reprocessing the whole dataset and violate the constraints stated for incremental clustering.

5   Conclusions and future work

A new buffering strategy has been proposed to deal with ordering effects. We think that the formulation of the strategy is open in the sense that it is not coupled with any particular evaluation function or algorithm. Since the strategy is applied during the clustering process, its impact over the entire conceptual structure is limited as the experiments have shown. Nevertheless, in the worst case ordering, the Not-Yet strategy consistently improved the quality of obtained clustering, specially when combined with additional operators. It is difficult to assess the quality of this improvement beyond the simple quantitative analysis in terms of the CQF. For some applications it can suppose an important improvement in terms of understandability or performance while for others it may be imperceptible. These benefits are obtained at the expense of maintaining a large Not-Yet buffer. Since an incremental system has to be able of using the acquired knowledge for some performance task at any learning stage, we have to assume that the system has also to be able of quickly incorporate the buffered instances before actuating. If this was not possible, the system should carry out the performance task with the partial knowledge structure learned so far. Future work will study the Not-Yet performance limiting the buffer size. In practice, buffer size will be limited by the amount of instances that the system can manage in a reasonable amount of time before entering in 'performance mode' and this time will be dependent on the particular application.

We plan to extend this work by considering a number of different, probably more complex, buffering strategies. Extensions studying the order of instances in the buffer, the criterion to reprocess instances or the number of times instances may be reprocessed appear to be promising topics for further research.

Acknowledgments. We thank the anonymous referees for their insightful comments which helped to improve the quality and understandability of the paper.

References

1. J. R. Anderson and M. Matessa. Explorations of an incremental, bayesian algorithm for categorization. *Machine Learning*, (9):275–308, 1992.
2. J. Béjar. *Adquisición automática de conocimiento en dominios poco estructurados*. PhD thesis, Facultat d'Informàtica de Barcelona, UPC, 1995.
3. D. H. Fisher. Knowledge acquisition via incremental conceptual clustering. *Machine Learning*, (2):139–172, 1987.
4. D. H. Fisher. Optimization and simplification of hierarchical clusterings. *Journal of Artificial Intelligence Research*, (4):147–180, 1995.
5. D. H. Fisher and P. Langley. Conceptual clustering and its relation to numerical taxonomy. In W. A. Gale, editor, *Artificial Intelligence and Statistics*. Addison-Wesley, Reading,MA, 1986.
6. D. H. Fisher, L. Xu, and N. Zard. Ordering effects in clustering. In *Proceedings of the Ninth International Conference on Machine Learning*, pages 163–168, 1992.
7. J. H. Gennari, P. Langley, and D. Fisher. Models of incremental concept formation. *Artificial Intelligence*, (40):11–61, 1989.
8. P. Langley. Order effects in incremental learning. In P. Reimann and H. Spada, editors, *Learning in humans and machines: Towards an Interdisciplinary Learning Science*. Pergamon, 1995.
9. M. Lebowitz. Deferred commitment in unimem: waiting to learn. In *Proceedings of the Fifth International Conference on Machine Learning*, pages 80–86, 1988.
10. J. Roure. Study of methods and heuristics to improve the fuzzy classifications of LINNEO+. Master's thesis, Facultat d'Informática de Barcelona, UPC, 1994.

Coevolutionary, Distributed Search for Inducing Concept Descriptions

C. Anglano, A. Giordana, G. Lo Bello, L. Saitta

Dipartimento di Informatica, Università di Torino,

C.so Svizzera 185, 10149 Torino, Italy

e-mail:{mino,attilio,lobello,saitta}@di.unito.it

Abstract. This paper presents a highly parallel genetic algorithm, designed for concept induction in propositional and first order logics. The parallel architecture is an adaptation for set covering problems, of the diffusion model developed for optimization.

The algorithm exhibits other two important methodological novelties related to Evolutionary Computation. First, it combines niches and species formation with coevolution, in order to learn multimodal concepts. This is done by integrating the Universal Suffrage selection operator with the coevolution model recently proposed in the literature. Second, it makes use of a new set of genetic operators, which maintain diversity in the population.

The experimental comparison with previous systems, not using coevolution and based on traditional genetic operators, shows a substantial improvement in the effectiveness of the genetic search.

Keywords: Concept Learning, Parallel Genetic Algorithms, Coevolution.

1 Introduction

In the recent literature, Genetic Algorithms (GAs) emerged as valuable search tools in the field of concept induction [2, 8, 6, 3]. The feature that looks particularly attractive for this task is the exploration power, potentially greater than that of traditional search methods.

This paper describes a GA-based inductive learner, oriented to acquire concepts described in First Order Logic. Its architecture relies on a computational model characterized by the absence of global memory, which extends the diffusion model previously developed for GAs. The underlying distributed architecture allows a natural introduction of coevolution. Coevolution has been defined by [7, 10] and refers to the possibility of guiding evolving populations through a global feed-back.

Our starting point is the theory of niches and species formation, which already proved to be effective in learning disjunctive concept definitions. A disjunctive concept definition consists of a set of conjunctive logical formulas, each one capturing a different modality of the target concept. As niches and species formation is a way of addressing multi-modal search problems, disjunctive concept induction naturally fits in this framework. Several recent algorithms, such as COGIN [6] and REGAL [3], exploit this idea, even though they adopt different methods for promoting species formation.

As discussed in [3], methods only based on species formation may require very large populations when small species are required to survive in the presence of very large ones. For this reason, REGAL adopts a long term control strategy resembling to coevolution, in order to reduce the pressure among the species. Here, we propose a new method which combines the Universal Suffrage selection operator with an explicit coevolutionary strategy similar to the one proposed by [10].

Moreover, this paper presents another substantial novelty, with respect to REGAL and other GAs designed for concept induction tasks, which consists of a new set of genetic operators, which explicitly aim at preserving the diversity in the population. Preserving diversity reduces premature convergence and increases the effectiveness of the genetic search.

As it will be shown in Section 7, the new algorithm, while preserving (or even increasing) the accuracy of REGAL, shows a substantial reduction in the complexity of the genetic search.

2 Learning Concepts with Genetic Algorithms

The task of learning concept definitions from examples can be stated as follows: given a learning set $E = E^+ \cup E^-$, consisting of positive and negative examples of a target concept ω, and a logical language L, the task consists in finding a logical formula $\Phi \in L$, which is true of all the positive examples E^+ and false of all the negative ones E^-. If such a Φ is found, the definition $\Phi \to \omega$ holds. Depending on the case, the logical language L can be a propositional or a First Order one. Independently of the order of L, the general structure of a concept definition Φ is a disjunction $\Phi = \phi_1 \vee \phi_2 \vee \ldots \vee \phi_n$ of conjunctive definitions $\phi_1, \phi_2, \ldots, \phi_n$, each one representing a different modality of the concept ω. In the following we will assume that L is a VL_{21} language like to the one used by Induce [9] and by REGAL [3].

As previously mentioned, an appealing method to exploit GAs in Machine Learning consists in combining species and niches formation [5] with coevolution [10]. Several examples can be found in [10] for learning behavioral strategies. In the following we will consider a two-level architecture, whose lower level is a distributed GA, which searches for conjunctive descriptions by promoting the formation of species in the populations. The upper level applies a coevolutive strategy that performs two tasks: on one hand, it continuously updates a disjunctive description, combining together individuals chosen from the different species evolved at the first level; on the other hand, it interacts with the lower level with the aim of favoring the evolution of those species that better go together in the current disjunctive description. The system REGAL [3] is a first example of how such an architecture can be implemented.

However, the way niching and coevolution are integrated in REGAL and in other systems like Samuel [10] is not very suitable to exploit large network computers. In fact, these systems are still based on the network (or island) model described by Goldberg [4], where niches tend to be identified with single computational nodes. Therefore, the available parallelism is limited by the number of emerging species. In order to overcome this limitation, we designed a different computational model, where the notion of global mating pool has been abandoned. As described in Figure 1, the architecture of the resulting system, G-NET, encompasses three kind of nodes: 1) Genetic nodes (*G-nodes*), where individuals mate and reproduce, 2) Evaluation nodes (*E-nodes*), where individuals are evaluated, and 3) a Supervisor node, which coordinates the computation of the G-nodes according to the coevolutive strategy.

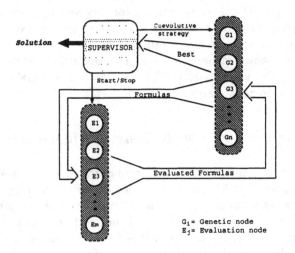

Fig. 1. Parallel Architecture

In G-NET, positive concept instances are considered elementary niches, and each G-node computes an elitist GA, which evolves a micro-population settled on a specific niche. In other words, each G-node searches for the "best" formula covering the positive learning instances associated with it. The same elementary niche can be assigned to many G-nodes at the same time, so that the number of actually active G-nodes depends only upon the available resources and not upon the problem. The Supervisor decides when and how many active copies of a niche must exist.

Upon receiving an individual, an E-node evaluates it on the learning set, computes a fitness value and sends it back (together with the computed information) to the set of G-nodes (broadcast communication), activating thus new genetic cycles. When a G-node finds a solution which is better than the ones it already has, according to a local fitness function f_L, it sends it to the Supervisor as a candidate for assembling the global disjunctive description. Periodically, the Supervisor resumes and actuates the coevolutive strategy: first, it assembles a global disjunctive solution, out of the locally best solutions it received from the

G-nodes, trying to optimize a global fitness function f_G. Afterwards, it gives a feed-back to the G-nodes, in order to guide the genetic search towards solutions that better integrate each other in a global disjunctive description. This coevolutive strategy consists of two components, which act independently. The first component controls the amount of search that has to be done on different niches, and determines the number of G-nodes assigned to each niche. Those niches, which developed solutions "weak" in a global context, are given more processors in order to increase the chance of improving their local solutions. The second component supplies a corrective term to the local fitness function, which allows the genetic search to be explicitly guided towards local solutions which contribute to increase the quality of the global solution. To this aim, the Supervisor broadcasts the current disjunctive description to G-nodes.

The separation of the genetic cycle from the evaluation process simply aims at increasing the explicit parallelism available.

3 The Fitness

In G-NET, two different fitness functions f_G and f_L are used in order to evaluate global (disjunctive) and local (conjunctive) concept descriptions, respectively. The function f_G is a combination of three different terms, correspondings to three different features of a concept description, namely: completeness (v), consistency (w) and syntactic simplicity (z), which are three standard criteria used in machine learning since [9].

In order to introduce the analytic form of f_G we need to introduce some basic definitions. The symbol M^+ shall denote the cardinality of E^+, i.e the number of positive training instances, and M^- shall denote the cardinality of E^-, i.e the number of negative training instances. Let φ be a inductive (disjunctive or conjunctive) hypothesis; $m^+(\varphi)$ and $m^-(\varphi)$ shall denote the number of positive and negative instances covered by φ, respectively. For the sake of simplicity we will write m^+, m^-, and so on, being the argument φ evident from the context.

The completeness is evaluated as $v = m^+/M^+$, whereas the consistency is evaluated as an exponential function $w = e^{-m^-}$ of the covered negative examples. The syntactic simplicity is evaluated as the ratio $z = m^+/(N_a + m^+)$, being N_a the number of conditions occurring in a formula. In practice z tries to capture the information compression represented by the syntactic form with respect to its extension on the learning set. As long as N_a decreases, z increases approaching to 1.

The analytic form for the global fitness f_G is then defined by the expression:

$$f_G(\Phi) = (1 + Av(\Phi) + Bz(\Phi))w(\Phi)^C \tag{1}$$

where A, B and C are user tunable constants, which allow the different components to be weighted.

The local fitness f_L for an hypothesis ϕ adds a corrective term to expression (1), in order to account for how much ϕ contributes to improve (worsen) the current global concept description. Let Φ be the disjunctive concept description currently elaborated by the Supervisor and broadcast to the G-nodes. Let, moreover, ϕ be a conjunctive hypothesis in a G-node. The fitness $f_L(\phi)$ is evaluated as:

$$f_L(\phi) = (1 + Av(\phi) + Bz(\phi))w(\phi)^C + (f_G(\Phi') - f_G(\Phi)) \qquad (2)$$

being Φ' the formula obtained by adding ϕ to Φ and eliminating all redundant disjuncts but ϕ.

4 The Genetic Nodes

Conjunctive solutions (individuals) are represented as bitstrings of fixed length as in REGAL [3]. In the bitstring every bit represents a logical condition; if the bit is "1", the condition occurs in the formula, if it is "0", it does not. This correspondence can always be established, provided that a limit is imposed on the maximum complexity of a conjunctive formula.

Every G-node executes a genetic algorithm aimed at finding the formula that better covers the concept instance it has been assigned to. As described in Figure 2, the basic architecture is quite simple, in order to have a light weight computational object, which can easily be dynamically allocated on a network computer; the architecture comprises the program encoding the genetic cycle, a small memory containing the local population, an input port receiving the individuals sent by the E-nodes, and an output port sending the new individuals to the E-nodes. As the local population is kept small (from 5 to 40 individuals) a non-standard replacement policy (similar to that described in [1]) is used, in order to enforce diversity: all the individuals in the same node are required to be different, so that a richer genetic information is present in the population.

The individuals arriving at the input gate of a G-node are all those evaluated by the E-nodes; then, they may or may not cover the specific instance e assigned to it. Even though the goal of the G-node is to find formulas covering e, individuals not covering e can nevertheless carry information useful to find better generalizations for the individuals which actually cover e. Therefore, individuals both covering and not covering e are allowed to enter the population, but a policy is adopted which does not allow the individuals not covering e take over the other ones.

A G-node repeats the following cyclic procedure, until stopped by the supervisor:

Cellular Genetic Algorithm

1. Select two individuals from the local population with probability proportional to their fitness
2. Generate two new individuals φ_1 and φ_2 by applying the genetic operators
3. Broadcast copies of φ_1 and φ_2
4. **While** the network is ready **do**
   (a) Receive some individuals ψ from the network according to rule (3) (see below)

(b) Replace ψ in the local population by playing a tournament step for each one of them

5. Go to step 1

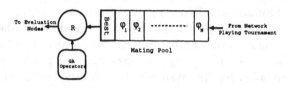

To Evaluation Nodes

R

Best | φ_1 | φ_2 | ・・・・・・・・・ | φ_N

From Network Playing Tournament

GA Operators

Mating Pool

Fig. 2. G-node architecture.

Proportionate selection is used, whereas replacement is made using the tournament policy, adapted to the local need, as it will be explained in the following. First of all, every individual arriving from the network is subject to a probabilistic filter which can accept or refuse it.

> **if** φ *belongs to the local population* **then** *reject* φ (3)
> **else if** φ *matches the learning event* e
> **then** *accept* φ *with probability* p_{cv}
> **else** *accept* φ *with probability* p_{uc}

In (3), $p_{cv} \in [0,1]$ is a user defined parameter, whereas, p_{uc} is computed as $p_{cv}(1-\nu)^6$ being ν the proportion of individuals non covering e in the population. In this way the pressure of the individuals not covering e is automatically limited. Each individual that goes through the filter competes for entering the population by playing a tournament: an opponent is randomly selected and the victory is assigned with probability proportional to the respective fitnesses.

An elitist strategy is used so that in each G-node the currently best solution cannot be replaced by a worse individual. This is obtained by avoiding to choose the best solution as opponent in a tournament. Periodically, all G-nodes send a copy of the best found individuals to the supervisor, which reacts reassigning the examples to the G-nodes.

5 The Genetic Operators

Being conjunctive formulas encoded into fixed length bitstrings, the reproduction operators are straightforward to implement, and borrow many ideas from the Genetic Algorithm theory [4]. In particular, the reproduction operators are: a task specific crossover, a task specific mutation, and the seeding operator [3], used for initializing the population when this last is empty. All operators are implemented in such a way that they always produce offsprings different from the parents.

The *crossover* is a combination of the *two point crossover* with a variant of the *uniform crossover* [11], modified in order to perform either generalization or specialization of the hypotheses. More specifically, the crossover operator can be activated in three different modalities: exchanging, specializing and generalizing, which are stochastically selected depending on the consistency and completeness of the selected chromosomes. Given a pair of chromosomes φ_1, φ_2, the modality to use is decided in two steps. At the first step it is decided whether to apply the exchanging modality, with probability p_{ec}, or to proceed through the second step, with probability $1 - p_{ec}$, being p_{ec} a user definable parameter. Afterwards, if the second step is entered, the system independently decides whether to apply generalization or specialization to each one of the parents. Let φ_i be one of the parents; the probability $p_{gc}(\varphi_i)$, of using generalization, and $p_{sc}(\varphi_i) = 1 - p_{gc}(\varphi_i)$, of using specialization, are computed according to the rule:

$$p_{gc}(\varphi_i) = (m^-(\varphi_i)/(m^+(\varphi) + m^-(\varphi)))^\alpha \qquad (4)$$

being α a user defined parameter. Afterwards, if the same modality has been chosen for both parents, the crossover will be applied with this modality. Otherwise, if the modalities are discordant, the exchanging modality will be used.

In this way, the generalizing modality tends to be used when the parents are both consistent, the specializing modality when the parents are both inconsistents, and the exchanging modality when one is consistent and the other is inconsistent. The first decision step guarantees that an assigned percentage of pure information exchange takes place in any case.

In order to guarantee the actual exchange of information, the crossover algorithm first construct an index $I = \{i_1, i_2, \ldots, i_n\}$ of pointers to the positions in the bitstring where the corresponding bits in the two parents have different value. Afterwards, if the generalization/specialization has been chosen, two temporary offsprings ψ_1 and ψ_2, identical to φ_1 and φ_2, respectively, are created.

Then, for every element $i_j \in I$ the following procedure is repeated:

- **if** generalizing modality has been chosen **then** with probability p_u replace in ψ_1 and ψ_2 the value of the bit $b(i_j)$ with the logical *or* of the corresponding bits in the parents.
- **if** specializing modality has been chosen **then** with probability p_u (a-priori assigned) replace in ψ_1 and ψ_2 the value of the bit $b(i_j)$ with the logical *and* of the corresponding bits in the parents.

If, after applying this stochastic procedure, no bit has been changed, one bit chosen at random in I is generalized/specialized.

When the exchanging modality is chosen, the classical two-point crossover is applied, with the difference that, in order to guarantee an information exchange, the two crossover points are chosen on the index vector I instead of on the whole chromosome.

The *mutation* operator adopts a strategy similar to the one described so far for crossover, and tries to generalize or to specialize an individual, depending on its consistency or inconsistency. Also the mutation operator may have three modalities, namely seeding, generalizing and specializing, which are selected with probability p_{seed}, p_{gm} and p_{sm}, respectively. The seeding probability p_{seed} is given a priori, whereas the probabilities p_{gm} for generalizing mutation and p_{sm} for specializing mutation are computed with the rule:

$$p_{sm} = (1 - p_{seed})(m^-/(m^- + m^+))^\alpha, \quad p_{gm} = 1 - p_{seed} - p_{sm} \qquad (5)$$

If the specializing mutation is chosen, the mutation is applied as follows: let n_1 be the number of bits set to "1" in the bitstring; then, the mutation operator turns to "0" a fraction γ of them, which is obtained by randomly selecting a real number in the interval $[0, \beta_m n_1]$, being $\beta_m \in [0, 1]$ a user defined parameter. The bits to be set at "1" are selected in an analogous way, when the generalizing mutation is chosen.

It is easy to recognize that specializing and generalizing mutations are nothing else than the dropping condition and adding condition operators defined in [2].

In the genetic loop executed by each G-node, two individuals are selected at each iteration with probability proportional to their fitness f_L. If the population is empty, a new individual will be created using the seeding operator. Otherwise, if the two selected individuals φ_1 and φ_2 are genetically different, crossover is applied. On the contrary, if the same individual is selected two times, two new offsprings will be created using mutation.

The nice aspect of this strategy is that it automatically adapts to the composition of the population. When the population in a node is dominated by an individual that has a fitness much higher than the others (and, then, it is frequently selected for reproduction with itself), the genetic search turns into a stochastic hill climbing.

6 The Coevolutive Strategy

The medium-term control strategy actuated by the Supervisor node is based on a coevolutive approach. It basically goes through a cycle, which has a period measured in terms of the number of iterations performed by the G-nodes, in which it receives the best solution found by each one of the G-nodes, elaborates the current disjunctive concept description Φ, and then gives a feedback to the G-nodes which enforces a coevolutionary model.

At the moment, the algorithm used for working out a disjunctive description is very simple and is based on a hill climbing optimization strategy. At first, all conjunctive solutions collected from the G-nodes are included into a redundant disjunctive description Φ'. Then, Φ' is optimized, by eliminating the disjuncts which are not necessary. This is done by repeating the following cycle until Φ' reaches a final form Φ, which cannot be optimized further:

1. Search the disjunct ϕ such that $f_G(\Phi' - \phi)$ shows the greatest improvement.
2. Set $\Phi' = \Phi' - \phi$

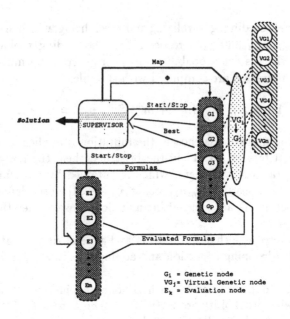

Fig. 3. The medium term coevolutive strategy

The first component of the co-evolutive control strategy on the G-nodes' activity is reminiscent of the techniques used in Operating Systems for multiplexing the Cpu among the processes in execution. According to the model in Section 2, every positive example in the learning set is associated to a local learning task performed by one or more processes executed by the G-nodes. For distinguishing G-nodes from the elementary learning tasks, we will denote the latter as VG-nodes (Virtual Genetic nodes); more specifically, VG_i ($1 \leq i \leq |E_i^+|$) will denote the learning task associated to the example $e_i \in E^+$.

The Supervisor keeps track of the solution state of every VG-node VG_i, i.e. the best solution found for it, a selection (possibly empty) of the individuals found in the populations evolved by the G-nodes associated to it, and other information, such as the number c_i of computational events, related to task VG_i, occurred during the past computation. The kernel of the co-evolutive control strategy is the method used for accounting the events related to every task. As soon as formulas covering many examples will begin to develop, we will find spontaneously born clusters of G-nodes which elect the same formula as current best individual in their population. This can be interpreted as a form of implicit cooperation which led to the generation of a formula representative of the work of all of them. Therefore, the Supervisor attributes to a VG-node VG_i all the events produced by the G-nodes sharing the best formula attributed to VG_i.

When, at the end of a cycle, the control strategy is actuated, the VG-nodes are reassigned to G-nodes. The criterion for the reassignment is that of balancing the work spent for every task VG_i on the basis of the number c_i of computational events. Let C be the maximum value for c_i ($1 \leq i \leq |E^+|$); the Supervisor computes for every VG_i the amount $g_i = C - c_i$ of computational events necessary to balance the computational cost for it. Afterwards, the VG-nodes are stochastically assigned to G-nodes with probability proportional to g_i divided by the fitness $f_{L_i}^{(best)}$ of the currently best formula covering VG_i. Then the G-nodes are initialized with the information saved in the corresponding VG-nodes and restart.

The effect of this strategy is that of focusing the computational resources on the VG-nodes covered by formulas having a low fitness or a low ratio m^+/M^+. In fact, the VG-nodes falling in these cases will have either a low value for $f_i^{(best)}$ or a high value for g_i, because they will accumulate the computational events with few other VG-nodes.

The second component of the co-evolutive strategy reduces to broadcasting the current disjunctive description Φ to all G-nodes, so that they can update the local fitness f_L for the individuals in the local populations.

7 Experimental Evaluation

In order to have a comparison with REGAL, which can be considered the source of inspiration of the current system, we will report a benchmark on the *Mushrooms* dataset and on *Thousand Trains* dataset, used in [3].

A first comparison shows the benefits of using the co-evolutive control strategy illustrated in Section 6 and the new reproduction operators described in Section 5. A second comparison is with REGAL and shows how our system can obtain solutions of at least the same quality as REGAL with a smaller computational cost.

For the Mushrooms dataset the task consists in discriminating between *edible* and *poisonous* mushrooms. The dataset consists of 8124 instances, 1208 of edible mushrooms and 3196 of poisonous ones. Each instance is described by a vector of 22 discrete, multi-valued attributes. By defining a condition for each one of the attribute values, a global set of 126 constraints is obtained, which leads to bitstrings of 126 bits for encoding the individuals. Randomly selected sets of 4000 instances (2000 edible + 2000 poisonous) have been used as learning sets, while the remaining 4124 instances have been used for testing. The system can always found a perfect definition for both classes, covering all the examples and no counterexamples on the test set, as also REGAL and other induction algorithms can do.

The Thousand Trains dataset represents an artificial learning problem in First Order Logic obtained by extending the well known *Trains Going East or Going West* problem proposed by Michalski in order to illustrate Induce' learning capabilities [9]. In this case 500 examples of trains going east and 500 trains going west have been generated using a stochastic generator. A detailed description can be found in [3].

The parameter, which has been used by the previous Genetic Algorithms to evaluate the quality of the found solution, has been the complexity of the final disjunctive solution, measured as the total number of conditions present in it. In the machine learning literature, simple solutions are considered preferable among a set with the same performances.

In Figure 4 we report the evolution of the complexity for the Mushrooms dataset, in terms of the number of genetic cycles executed by all the G-nodes, globally. The curves labeled as "cv", "ncv", and "rough" correspond respectively to using the complete operator set and the coevolutive strategy, disactivating the co-evolutive strategy, and using random assignment and using REGAL' reproduction operators.

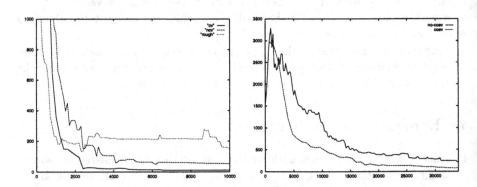

Fig. 4. Mushroom dataset: Complexity of the solution vs. the genetic cycles.

Fig. 5. Thousand Trains dataset: complexity of the solution vs. the genetic cycles.

Here it is possible to appreciate the effect of the co-evolution and of the new reproduction operators, separately. When the co-evolution was disactivated, the G-nodes were assigned to VG-nodes using an equal probability.

An analogous comparison which illustrates the benefit of co-evolution on the Thousand Trains dataset is reported in Figure 5, where the curves labelled as "coev" and "no-coev" correspond to using the co-evolution strategy and disactivating it, respectively. In both experiments the same default setting for $A = B = C = \alpha = 1$ in the fitness function and the same number (400) of G-nodes have been used. It is worth noting that these parameters are not critical, and very similar results have been obtained with quite different settings.

A comparison between REGAL and G-NET on the task of finding a definition for the concept of *poisonous mushroom* is reported in Table 1. We notice that G-NET can reach a complexity smaller than REGAL with a smaller computational cost. We believe that this improvement is substantially due to the use of the mutation operator.

8   Conclusion

A new distributed model for a Genetic Algorithm designed for concept induction from examples has been presented. The algorithm presents several important novelties. A first novelty is represented by the fine-grained distributed mating

333

Table 1. Comparison between G-Net and REGAL

System	G-Net		REGAL	
	avg	min	avg	min
Complexity	11	11	21.40	13
Cost	12423	11738	31130	23900

pool, which eliminates every notion of common memory in the system so that it is easy to exploit distributed computational resources such as Connection Machines and Network Computers. Other novelties are represented by the coevolutive strategy inspired by the model proposed by [10], and by the new set of genetic operators.

The new algorithm has been evaluated on non trivial induction tasks obtaining good results. Therefore, the new architecture seems to be a promising one for facing computing intensive induction problems emerging in data mining applications.

References

1. AUGIER, S., VENTURINI, G., AND KODRATOFF, Y. Learning First Order Logic Rules with a Genetic Algorithm. In *Proc. of the First International Conference on Knowledge Discovery and Data Mining* (1995).
2. DEJONG, K., SPEARS, W., AND GORDON, F. Using genetic algorithms for concept learning. *Machine Learning Journal, 13* (1993), 161–188.
3. GIORDANA, A., AND NERI, F. Search-intensive concept induction. *Evolutionary Computation Journal* (1996), Winter, 1995.
4. GOLDBERG, D. *Genetic Algorithms*. Addison-Wesley, Reading, MA, 1989.
5. GOLDBERG, D., AND RICHARDSON, J. Genetic algorithms with sharing for multimodal function optimization. In *Int. Conf. on Genetic Algorithms* (Cambridge, MA, 1987), Morgan Kaufmann, pp. 41–49.
6. GREENE, D., AND SMITH, S. Competition-based induction of decision models from examples. *Machine Learning Journal, 13* (1993), 229–258.
7. HUSBANDS, P., AND MILL, F. Co-evolving parasites improve simulated evolution as an optimization procedure. In *4th Int. Conf. on Genetic Algorithms* (Fairfax, VA, 1991), Morgan Kaufmann, pp. 264–270.
8. JANIKOW, C. A knowledge intensive genetic algorithm for supervised learning. *Machine Learning Journal, 13* (1993), 198–228.
9. MICHALSKI, R. A theory and methodology of inductive learning. In *Machine Learning: An AI Approach* (Los Altos, CA, 1983), J. C. R. Michalski and T. Mitchell, Eds., Morgan Kaufmann, pp. 83–134.
10. POTTER, M., DEJONG, K., AND GREFENSTETTE, J. A coevolutionary approach to learning sequential decision rules. In *Int. Conf. on Genetic Algorithms* (Pittsburgh, PA, 1995), Morgan Kaufmann, pp. 366–372.
11. SYSWERDA, G. Uniform crossover in genetic algorithms. In *3th Int. Conf. on Genetic Algorithms* (Fairfax, VA, 1989), Morgan Kaufmann, pp. 2–9.

Continuous Mimetic Evolution

Antoine Ducoulombier[1] and Michèle Sebag[2,1]

(1) LRI, CNRS URA 410	(2) LMS, CNRS URA 317
Université d'Orsay	Ecole Polytechnique
91405 Orsay Cedex	91128 Palaiseau Cedex
Antoine.Ducoulombier@lri.fr	Michele.Sebag@polytechnique.fr

Abstract. There exists no memory of biologic evolution besides the individuals themselves. Indeed, the biologic milieu can change and a previously unfit action or individual can come to be more fit; it would be most dangerous to rely on the memory of the past. This contrasts with artificial evolution most often considering a fixed milieu: the generation of an unfit individual previously explored is only a waste of time. This paper aims at constructing a memory of evolution, and using it to avoid such fruitless explorations. A new evolution scheme, called *mimetic evolution*, gradually constructs two models along evolution, respectively memorizing the best and the worst individuals of the past generations. Standard crossover and mutation are replaced by *mimetic mutation*: individuals are attracted or repelled by these models. Mimetic evolution is extended from binary to continuous search spaces. Results of experiments on large-sized problems are detailed and discussed.

1 Introduction

Biologic evolution takes place in a changing environment. Being able to repeat previously unsuccessful experiments is therefore vital. This could explain why Nature does not involve anything like an explicit memory: all the knowledge gathered by evolution is actually implicit and dispatched among the individuals.

Conversely, artificial evolution most often tackles optimization problems and considers *fixed* fitness landscapes. The history of evolution should thus provide reliable information; unfortunately, exploiting the list of all previously generated individuals gets soon intractable as evolution goes on. This paper focuses on constructing a tractable memory of evolution, and using it to guide the further evolution steps. This memory is explicit, in contrast with the implicit memory represented by the current population; and it is collective, i.e. accessible to all individuals, in contrast with the local memory carried by the individuals (e.g. the mutation step sizes [Sch81]).

Many works devoted to the control of evolution ultimately rely on some explicit collective memory of evolution. The memorization process can acquire numerical information; this is the case for the reward-based mechanism proposed by Davis to adjust the operator rates [Dav89], the adjustment of penalty factors in SAT problems [ER96] or the construction of discrete gradients [HOG95], among others. The memorization process can also acquire symbolic information, represented as rules [RS96] or beliefs [Rey94].

Memory-based heuristics can control most steps of evolution: e.g. selection via penalty factors [ER96], operator rates [Dav89], operator effects [HOG95, RS96]... Memory can even be used to "remove genetics from the standard genetic algorithm" [Bal95]: the *Population Based Incremental Learning* (PBIL) algorithm memorizes the best individual of previous populations, and uses this memory to generate the next population from scratch.

Evolution by Inhibition symmetrically memorizes the worst individuals in each generation; this memory is used to modify the current population. The underlying metaphor is that of the *Loser*, virtual individual summarizing the past unfit individuals: offspring aim at be farther away from the loser, than their parents [SSR97].

This paper continues a previous work devoted to *Mimetic Evolution*, which combines PBIL and evolution by inhibition [PDR+97]. Mimetic evolution memorizes the best and the worst individuals previously met by evolution within two "models", the *Winner* and the *Loser*. Mimetic evolution is (remotely) inspired by the social evolution of individuals: any individual imitates, rejects, or ignores independently each one of the models. Practically, these models are used to evolve the genetic material via a single operator termed *social mutation*; social mutation is parameterized by the desired behavior of the individuals with respect to the models, so-called "social strategy". A range of social strategies has been defined, among which the *Entrepreneur* (which imitates the winner and ignores the loser); the *Conformist* (which imitates the winner and rejects the loser); the *Phobic* (which rejects the loser and ignores the winner; this behavior reproduces the Evolution by Inhibition scheme [SSR97])... Last, the *Ignorant* strategy (which ignores both models) serves as reference to check the relevance of the models.

In this paper, all cited schemes (PBIL, evolution by inhibition and mimetic evolution) are extended from binary to continuous search spaces. The interest of this extension is twofold. First, it allows evolution to directly consider the search space ($\mathbb{R}^N$) in many cases (e.g. most engineering optimization problems are numerical); and indeed, the discretization of the search space can hinder evolution [B95]. Second, it incidentally settles the main drawback of binary mimetic evolution, namely the adjustment of the mutation rate (metaphorically, the strength of the social pressure).

This paper is organized as follows. Section 2 first reviews some related work, and describes how the use of virtual individuals, imaginary individuals or models, can support evolution. Binary mimetic evolution is then briefly recalled, in order for this paper to be self-contained; and continuous mimetic evolution is detailed (section 3). Section 4 presents and discusses experiments on several large-sized problems in continuous search spaces. We last conclude and detail some perspectives of research.

2 State of the art

A major question in the field of artificial evolution is that of the respective roles of crossover and mutation. Though the question concerns both binary and continuous search spaces, only the binary case will be considered in this section.

Crossover traditionally relies on the Building Block hypothesis [Hol75, Gol89]. But a growing body of evidence suggests that crossover is efficient because it operates large step mutations. In particular, T. Jones has studied the macro-mutation operator defined as crossing over a parent with a random individual[1]. Macro-mutation obviously does not allow the offspring to combine the building blocks of their two parents; still, macro-mutation happens to outperform standard crossover on benchmark problems [Jon95].

More generally, standard crossover actually behaves like a biased mutation operator. The bias depends on the population and controls both the strength and the direction of the mutation. The "mutation rate" of standard crossover, e.g. the Hamming distance between parents and offspring, depends on average on the diversity of the population; and the "mutation direction" of standard crossover (which genes are modified) also depends on the population.

On the other hand, binary mutation primarily aims at preserving the genetic diversity of the population. This can be done as well through crossover with specific individuals, deliberately maintained in the population to prevent the loss of genetic diversity. For instance, the Surrogate GA [Eva97] maintains imaginary individuals such as the complementary of the best current individual, or all-0 and all-1 individuals; crossover alone thus becomes sufficient to ensure the genetic diversity of the population, and mutation is no longer needed. Another possibility is to deliberately introduce genotypic diversity by embedding the search space Ω into $\{0,1\} \times \Omega$ and identifying the individuals 0ω and $1\bar{\omega}$, as done in Dual Genetic Algorithms [PA94].

Evolution can also be supported by virtual individuals, i.e. individuals belonging neither to the population nor to the search space. This is the case in the PBIL algorithm, where the best individuals (elements of $\{0,1\}^N$) in the previous populations are memorized within an element of $[0,1]^N$. This vector noted $\mathcal{M}$ provides an alternative to crossover and mutation, in that it allows PBIL to generate the current population from scratch: for each individual X and each bit i, value X_i is randomly selected such that $P(X_i = 1) = \mathcal{M}_i$ (where A_i denotes as usual the i-th component of A). $\mathcal{M}$ is initialized to $(0.5, 0.5, ..., 0.5)$ and it is updated from the best individual X_{max} at each generation, by relaxation :

$$\mathcal{M} := (1 - \alpha)\mathcal{M} + \alpha X_{max}$$

where α in $[0,1]$) is the relaxation factor, which corresponds to the fading of the memory. The main advantage of PBIL is its simplicity: it does not involve any modification of the genetic material. The only information transmitted from one

---

[1] Note that this macro-mutation fairly resembles standard crossover on large populations during the first generations of evolution.

generation to another is related to the best individual; still, it is not necessarily sufficient to reconstruct this best individual. This might hinder the exploitation of narrow highly fit regions, such as encountered in the Long Path problem [HG95]. Practically, one sees that even if $\mathcal{M}$ has very little difference with an individual on the path, the population constructed from $\mathcal{M}$ might not overlap the path [SS96].

Evolution by Inhibition involves the opposite memory, that is, the memory of the worst individuals in the previous populations. This memory noted $\mathcal{L}$ (for *Loser*) is also an element of $[0, 1]^N$, constructed by relaxation :

$$\mathcal{L} := (1 - \alpha)\mathcal{L} + \alpha X_{min}$$

where X_{min} denotes the average of half the worst offspring, and α is the relaxation factor. In contrast with PBIL which uses $\mathcal{M}$ to generate a new population, $\mathcal{L}$ is actually used to evolve the current population via a specific operator termed *flee-mutation*. Flee-mutation replaces both mutation and crossover; for each individual X, it selects and flips the bits most similar to those of the loser (minimizing $|X_i - \mathcal{L}_i|$). The offspring thus is farther away from the loser, than the parent was. Metaphorically, the goal of this evolutionary scheme is: Be different from the Loser ! And incidentally, this reduces the chance for exploring again low fit regions.

The potential of evolution by inhibitions is demonstrated for appropriate settings of the flee-mutation rate (number of bits mutated): EBI then significantly outperforms PBIL [SSR97], which itself outperforms most standard discrete optimization algorithms [Bal95]. But the adjustment of the flee-mutation rate remains an open question.

3 Mimetic evolution

Mimetic evolution melts PBIL and evolution by inhibition: besides the Loser constructed by EBI, it uses the memory of best individuals constructed by PBIL, or *Winner*, to guide evolution. This section briefly recalls how mimetic evolution was implemented in binary search spaces (more detail is found in [PDR+97]), and details how it extends to continuous search spaces.

3.1 Binary mimetic evolution

Two elements of $[0, 1]^N$, thereafter called *models*, are gradually constructed by relaxation from the population. These models, the winner $\mathcal{W}$ and the loser $\mathcal{L}$, respectively reflect the best and the worst individuals encountered by evolution so far (Table 1).

Let us first examine how $\mathcal{W}$ can help evolving individual X. Given the most fit individuals of the population (X, Y and Z), some possible causes for being fit are ($bit_2 = 1$), or ($bit_3 = 1$), or ($bit_5 = 1$) (a majority of the most fit individuals has those bits set to this value). Thus, one might want for instance to flip bit_2 and let bit_3 unchanged in X; this amounts to making X more similar to $d\mathcal{W}$, which goes to W in the limit. Metaphorically, X thus "imitates" the winner W. Practically, the bits mutated in X are selected by a tournament of bits, as those maximizing $|X_i - W_i|$; this draws the offspring closer to W than X was.

	1	2	3	4	5	Fitness
X	0	0	1	0	0	Fit
Y	1	1	1	1	1	Fit
Z	0	1	1	0	1	Fit
dW	0.33	0.66	1	0.33	0.66	
S	0	0	0	1	0	Unfit
T	1	0	1	1	1	Unfit
U	1	0	0	1	1	Unfit
$d\mathcal{L}$	0.66	0	0.33	1	0.66	

$$W := (1 - \alpha_w)W + \alpha_w dW$$

$$\mathcal{L} := (1 - \alpha_l)\mathcal{L} + \alpha_l d\mathcal{L}$$

Table 1. *Individuals and virtual individuals*

This mechanism is refined by taking advantage of the loser too. For instance, according to dW, it might be a good idea to mutate bit 5; but $d\mathcal{L}$ suggests that ($bit_5 = 1$) is not a factor of high fitness. This leads to select the bits to mutate, so that the offspring "imitates" W and "rejects" $\mathcal{L}$.

Practically, a new operator termed *social mutation* is defined. In each individual X, social mutation modifies a user-supplied number M of bits; these bits are selected by tournament as those maximizing $|X_i - W_i| - |X_i - \mathcal{L}_i|$; the bits mutated thus depend on X and on the models.

However, there is no reason why one could only imitate the winner and reject the loser. A straightforward generalization is to define a pair (δ_W, δ_L) in $\mathbb{R}^2$, and to select the bits to mutate as those maximizing :

$$\delta_W |X_i - W_i| + \delta_L |X_i - \mathcal{L}_i|$$

One sees that X imitates model $\mathcal{M}$ ($= W$ or $\mathcal{L}$) if $\delta_M > 0$, rejects $\mathcal{M}$ if $\delta_M < 0$, and ignores $\mathcal{M}$ if $\delta_M = 0$. Social mutation finally gets parameterized by the pair (δ_W, δ_L), termed *social strategy*. Some of these strategies have been given metaphorical names for the sake of convenience; obviously, other metaphors could have been imagined. We distinguish mainly:

- The *conformist*, that imitates the winner and rejects the loser;
- The *phobic*, that rejects the loser and ignores the winner;
- The *ignorant*, that ignores both the loser and the winner.

One notices that the social strategy is unchanged if δ_W and δ_L are multiplied by a positive coefficient. Social strategies can then be represented as angles. This angle gives the preferred direction of the individuals, in the changing system of coordinates given by the winner and the loser. Figure 1 shows the possible

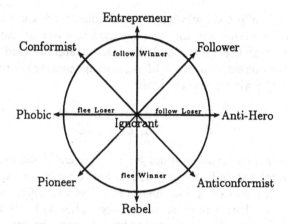

Figure 1. Mimetic Strategies

directions, with angle 0 corresponding to rejecting the loser, and angle $\pi/2$ to following the winner.

The main weakness of binary mimetic evolution is the adjustment of the social mutation rate, that is the number of bits to mutate in each individual. The difficulties encountered have been discussed in [SSR97, PDR+97].

3.2 Continuous social mutation

Mutation offers rather different difficulties depending on whether the search space is binary or continuous.

In a continuous search space, mutation usually proceeds by adding a gaussian perturbation $N(0, \sigma_i)$ to each component X_i of an individual X. The question is how much each gene should be modified, that is, how to set σ_i. To the best of our knowledge, the most efficient answer so far is given by self-adaptive mutation, stemmed from the Evolution Strategy scheme [Sch81, BS93]: the genotypic material of the individual is enhanced with the vector of step sizes $(\sigma_1, \ldots, \sigma_N)$, and evolution then adjusts "for free" the σ_i. Practically, σ_i first undergoes a gaussian mutation with a fixed variance depending on the size of the problem (the recommended values of the parameters are indicated below; see [Sch81] for more detail). The modified σ_i is then used to modify X_i :

$$\tau_{glob} := \tau N(0,1) \qquad \qquad \tau \approx \frac{1}{\sqrt{2N}}$$
$$for\ i = 1..N$$
$$\sigma_i := \sigma_i * exp(\tau_{glob} + \eta_{loc} N(0,1)) \qquad \eta_{loc} \approx \frac{1}{\sqrt{2\sqrt{N}}}$$
$$X_i := X_i + N(0, \sigma_i)$$

Evolution thereby hopefully favors individuals having both accurate phenotypes (i.e. with high performance) and accurate step sizes.

The extension of social mutation to continuous search spaces mostly requires to define how the winner and the loser are used to guide the mutation. Indeed, the computation of the winner and the loser straightforwardly extends from binary to continuous search space, with α_w and α_l denoting the relaxation factors of respectively the winner and the loser:

$$\mathcal{W} := (1 - \alpha_w)\mathcal{W} + \alpha_w\ d\mathcal{W}$$
$$\mathcal{L} := (1 - \alpha_l)\mathcal{L} + \alpha_l\ d\mathcal{L}$$

where $d\mathcal{W}$ and $d\mathcal{L}$ respectively stand for the average of the best (resp. worse) offspring. The relaxation factors α_w and α_l are equal in the experiments.

We investigate two evolution operators. The first one, termed *Fixed social mutation*, involves a fixed social strategy (δ_W, δ_L). If we consider the bi-dimensional space including the individual at hand, the winner and the loser, a social strategy defines a direction in this 2D space (Figure 2). For a given mutation step size, this direction defines a target offspring. The fixed social mutation is built from a standard self-adaptive gaussian mutation, and biased so as to produce an offspring closer to the target offspring, than the parent.

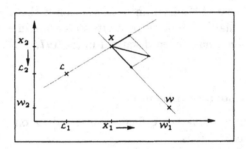

Figure 2. Fixed social mutation in $\mathbb{R}^2$, for a Conformist strategy.

More precisely the sign of the gaussian perturbation is determined so as to move the offspring in the desired direction:

$$X_i := X_i + sign(\delta_L(X_i - \mathcal{L}_i) + \delta_W(X_i - \mathcal{W}_i)) \times |N(0, \sigma_i)|$$

where $sign(A)$ is 1 if A is positive, -1 otherwise.
This evolution scheme is much dependent on the user-supplied strategy: the only degree of freedom is provided by the fact that the system of reference given by the winner and the loser evolves itself. Still it will be hard to recover from a bad social strategy.

A second evolution operator is termed self-adaptive social mutation, as it self-adapts the social strategy of the individuals. The self adaptation of the social strategy parallels that of the mutation step size in self-adaptive mutation.

More precisely, the individual is enhanced with the description of its personal strategy, given as two positive or negative scalars δ_W and δ_L. Evolution thus adjusts for free the social strategy most suited to each individual [2].

The self-adapted social strategy again determines a target offspring with:

$$X_i := X_i + \delta_L(X_i - \mathcal{L}_i) + \delta_W(X_i - \mathcal{W}_i)$$

This extends naturally to self adaptive *vectorial* social mutation where δ_W and δ_L are vectors.

3.3 Continuous PBIL

To the best of our knowledge, there has been only one other attempt to extend PBIL to continuous search space so far [STMS97]. This extension is based on uniform sampling of the domains of the genes, and the PBIL mechanism is used to gradually restrict the domains explored. Let $[Min_i, Max_i]$ be the initial domain of the i-th gene, and let Moy_i denote the half sum of Min_i and Max_i. When generating an individual, one first decides whether X_i should belong to $[Min_i, Moy_i]$ or $[Moy_i, Max_i]$, with:

$$Proba(X_i > Moy_i) = \mathcal{W}_i$$

One then draws X_i with uniform probability in the selected half interval. When $\mathcal{W}_i$ reaches a given threshold (.1 or .9), the domain $[Min_i, Max_i]$ shrinks accordingly (being respectively replaced with $[Min_i, Moy_i]$ or $[Moy_i, Max_i]$). One disadvantage of this procedure is that the search space can only shrink: there is no way to recover from a bad previous choice.

The approach investigated here relies on the natural extension of the computation of $\mathcal{W}$, from the two best individuals X^1_{max} and X^2_{max} and the worst individual X_{min}, as employed in [Bal95] to decrease the odds of premature convergence of $\mathcal{W}$. One finally has:

$$\mathcal{W} := (1 - \alpha)\mathcal{W} + \alpha(X^1_{max} + X^2_{max} - X_{min})$$

$\mathcal{W}$ thus gives the "center" of the region to be sampled in the next population. The sampling involves independent gaussian distributions for each gene i, centered on $\mathcal{W}_i$, and we investigate three mechanisms for determining the variance σ_i of the distributions.

The first one, termed *Constant PBIL*, explores a fixed region centered on $\mathcal{W}$, with $\sigma_i = .1$.

The second one, termed *Adaptive PBIL*, computes σ_i as the variance on gene i

---

[2] Incidentally, this scheme is more satisfactory from the point of view of social modeling (but indeed social modeling is far beyond the scope of this paper), as it constructs populations combining various types of social strategies. It would be most interesting to get, as a by-product of evolution, the social strategy most adapted to the last explored regions of the fitness landscape.

of the best half of the population.

The third one, *Self-Adaptive PBIL*, self adapts the variance σ_i per individual as follows. One considers a standard $(\mu + \lambda)$ evolution strategy, where an off-spring is generated from $\mathcal{W}$ and the variance σ_i of the parent at hand. Here, ES evolves the behavior of the individual with respect to model $\mathcal{W}$, so that the set of behaviors retained is most susceptible to improve $\mathcal{W}$.

4 Experimental Validation

4.1 Problems

The experiments consider the same functions as [Bal95].

$$y_1 = x_1 \qquad y_i = x_i + y_{i-1}, \; i \geq 2 \qquad F_1 = \frac{100}{10^{-5} + \Sigma_i |y_i|}$$

$$y_1 = x_1 \qquad y_i = x_i + sin(y_{i-1}), \; i \geq 2 \qquad F_2 = \frac{100}{10^{-5} + \Sigma_i |y_i|}$$

$$F_3 = \frac{100}{10^{-5} + \Sigma_i |.024 \times (i+1) - x_i|}$$

Functions F_1, F_2 and F_3 are defined on $[-2, 56, 2.56[^{100}$.

4.2 Experimental setting

The evolution scheme is a (10+50)-ES: 10 parents produce 50 offspring and the 10 best individuals among parents plus offspring are retained in the next population. A run is allowed 200,000 evaluations; all results are averaged on 20 independent runs. The relaxation factors α_w and α_l are both set to .01.

The results obtained are represented in polar coordinates (ρ, θ), where θ stands for the social strategy (see section 3.1) and ρ denotes the average best performance obtained for this strategy (each point on the circle thus represents $4,000,000$ evaluations). The unit circle serves as reference: it corresponds to the *ignorant* strategy, that is, a standard (10+50)-ES.

The results of adaptive social mutation and continuous PBIL are also indicated.

4.3 Continuous results and Discussion

In a continuous search space, the ignorant strategy coincides with a standard ES; no wonder that it gets good results, and is hard to be caught up.

The bad performance of fixed mimetic evolution can partly be blamed on what follows. The direction of evolution of the individuals is given in the changing system of coordinates defined by the winner and the loser — and this direction does not change for non-adaptive social mutation. Still, the loser $\mathcal{L}$ changes

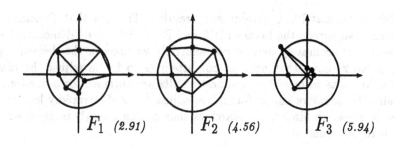

F_1 *(2.91)* F_2 *(4.56)* F_3 *(5.94)*

Figure 3. Fixed continuous social strategies on F_1, F_2 and F_3. The reference circle represents the performance of the ignorant (given in parenthesis)

faster than the winner $\mathcal{W}$ as $\alpha_w = \alpha_l$ and the best individuals of the population vary less than the worst individuals. But following an invariant direction defined with respect to both a fixed and a changing reference point can result in satellizing the individual around the fixed reference point; this also holds for vectorial social strategy.

Additional experiments show that setting $\alpha_w \ll \alpha_l$ actually improves the performance of fixed mimetic evolution for some strategies, though it still does not catch up the ignorant strategy.

	F_1	F_2	F_3
Reference (Ignorant)	2.91	4.56	5.94
CME with Self Adaptation of δ_W, δ_L	1.18	2.57	3.40
CME with Self Adaptation of $\overrightarrow{\delta_W}, \overrightarrow{\delta_L}$	0.07	0.87	0.87
Constant-PBIL	3.13	3.55	13.69
Adaptive-PBIL	1.09	2.31	6.20
Self-Adaptive-PBIL	1.34	1.85	2.69

Table 2. Continuous Mimetic Evolution (CME) and PBIL

The adaptive social mutation encounters other problems. Let us first consider the scalar case. The social strategy (δ_L, δ_W) controls both the direction of mutation, and the mutation step size (section 3.2). Coefficients δ_L and δ_W must therefore be unbounded and can be both positive and negative (to explore all directions of the bi-dimensional space defined by the winner and the loser). Still, the update of δ_L and δ_W, copied from the self-adaptive mutation, primarily aims at exploring $\mathbb{R}^+$ rather than $\mathbb{R}$. The bad performance of adaptive social mutation is thus explained by the fact that the social strategy is not adjusted with sufficient flexibility. Same holds when δ_L and δ_W are vectors rather than scalars. Further research is concerned with designing other mechanisms to evolve the social strategy with more flexibility.

The continuous PBIL obtains good results. The fact that *Constant PBIL* happens to supersede the binary PBIL and ES, satisfactorily demonstrates that the winner is accurately determined and duly wanders in the desired regions. Still, Table 2 shows that none of our attempts so far to adjust the range of exploration, was successful as the best results are obtained for a fixed σ_i. Empirically, the adaptive and self-adaptive adjustments of σ_i rapidly lead to small values of σ_i, which hinders the search as they can only slowly increase when the models rapidly change.

5 Conclusion

This paper investigates how the memory of evolution can support and speed up evolution. Given the fact that the exhaustive history of evolution cannot be tractably exploited after the first generations, the individuals previously met by evolution are packed in form of *models*. The PBIL algorithm [BC95] and Evolution by Inhibitions [SSR97] demonstrated how evolution can respectively take advantage of the model memorizing the best and the worst individuals. A major drawback of these approaches is that evolution easily gets stuck, as individuals only observe one model and adopt a single predetermined behavior (imitation or avoidance) with respect to this model.

Mimetic evolution combines these schemes and uses both models to evolve the current population in binary search spaces [PDR+97]. As one can combine *ad libitum* the influence (basically attractive, repulsive or indifferent) of each model, an individual is offered a rich variety of directions of evolution, metaphorically the "social strategies" of evolution. And indeed, the use of two models avoids some deadlocks of evolution, for the influence of one model acts as a perturbation with respect to the influence of the other one: it gets more difficult to get stuck.

Still, the extension of mimetic evolution to continuous search spaces presented in this paper, shows the limits of the memory mechanism proposed so far. In particular, we clearly need an indicator telling when a model gets stuck, so that to modify the social strategy of an individual regarding this model. Moreover, the continuous mimetic machinery mixes up two different notions, namely the recommended direction of evolution in the changing system of coordinates defined by the models, and the social pressure, namely how far should an individual go in this direction.

Further research is concerned with implementing two kinds of memory, updated at different speed rates. The comparison would hopefully allow one to detect that the models get irrelevant or ineffective to the current stage of evolution: the model gets stuck if the fast recent memory is closer and closer to the slow antique one. Obviously, such a mechanism could take a clue from the long term *versus* short term memories of human beings.

References

B95.   T. Bäck. *Evolutionary Algorithms in theory and practice*. New-York:Oxford University Press, 1995.

BC95.   S. Baluja and R. Caruana. Removing the genetics from the standard genetic algorithms. In A. Prieditis and S. Russel, editors, *Proc. of ICML95*, pages 38–46. Morgan Kaufmann, 1995.

Bal95.   S. Baluja. An empirical comparizon of seven iterative and evolutionary function optimization heuristics. Technical Report CMU-CS-95-193, Carnegie Mellon University, 1995.

BS93.   T. Bäck and H.-P. Schwefel. An overview of evolutionary algorithms for parameter optimization. *Evolutionary Computation*, 1(1):1–23, 1993.

Dav89.   L. Davis. Adapting operator probabilities in genetic algorithms. In J. D. Schaffer, editor, *Proc. of the 3rd ICGA*, pages 61-69. M. Kaufmann, 1989.

ER96.   A.E. Eiben and Z. Ruttkay. Self-adaptivity for constraint satisfaction: Learning penalty functions. In T. Fukuda, editor, *Proc. of the 3rd IEEE ICEC*, pages 258–261. IEEE Service Center, 1996.

Eva97.   I.K. Evans. Enhancing recombination with the complementary surrogate genetic algorithm. In T. Bäck, Z. Michalewicz, and X. Yao, editors, *Proc. of the Fourth IEEE ICEC*, pages 97–102. IEEE Press, 1997.

Gol89.   D. E. Goldberg. *Genetic algorithms in search, optimization and machine learning*. Addison Wesley, 1989.

HG95.   J. Horn and D.E. Goldberg. Genetic algorithms difficulty and the modality of fitness landscapes. In L. D. Whitley and M. D. Vose, editors, *Foundations of Genetic Algorithms 3*, pages 243–269. Morgan Kaufmann, 1995.

HOG95.   N. Hansen, A. Ostermeier, and A. Gawelczyk. On the adaptation of arbitrary normal mutation distributions in evolution strategies: The generating set adaptation. In L. J. Eshelman, editor, *Proc. of the 6th ICGA*, pages 57–64. Morgan Kaufmann, 1995.

Hol75.   J. H. Holland. *Adaptation in natural and artificial systems*. University of Michigan Press, Ann Arbor, 1975.

Jon95.   T. Jones. Crossover, macromutation and population-based search. In L. J. Eshelman, editor, *Proc. of the 6th ICGA*, pages 73–80. Morgan Kaufmann, 1995.

PA94.   P.Collard and J.P. Aurand. Dual ga: An efficient genetic algorithm. In *Proc. of ECAI*, pages 487–491. Amsterdam, Wiley and sons, August 1994.

PDR+97.   M. Peyral, A. Ducoulombier, C. Ravisé, M. Schoenauer, and M. Sebag. Mimetic evolution. In *Artificial Evolution'97*. To appear, Springer-Verlag.

Rey94.   R.G. Reynolds. An introduction to cultural algorithms. In *Proc. of the 3rd Annual Conference on EP*, pages 131–139. World Scientific, 1994.

RS96.   C. Ravisé and M. Sebag. An advanced evolution should not repeat its past errors. In L. Saitta, editor, *Proc. of the 13th ICML*, pages 400–408, 1996.

Sch81.   H.-P. Schwefel. *Numerical Optimization of Computer Models*. John Wiley & Sons, New-York, 1981. 1995 – 2nd edition.

SS96.   M. Sebag and M. Schoenauer. Mutation by imitation in boolean evolution strategies. In H.-M. Voigt, W. Ebeling, I. Rechenberg, and H.-P. Schwefel, editors, *Proc. of the 4th Conference on PPSN*, pages 356–365. Springer-Verlag, LNCS 1141, 1996.

SSR97.   M. Sebag, M. Schoenauer, and C. Ravisé. Toward civilized evolution: Developing inhibitions. In Th. Bäeck, editor, *Proc. of the 7th ICGA*. Morgan Kaufmann, 1997.

STMS97.   I. Servet, L. Trave-Massuyes, and D. Stern. Telephone network traffic overloading diagnosis and evolutionary computation technique. In *Artificial Evolution'97*. To appear, Springer-Verlag.

A Host-Parasite Genetic Algorithm for Asymmetric Tasks

Björn Olsson

Dept. of Computer Science, University of Skövde, Box 408, 541 28 Skövde, Sweden
Phone: +46-500-464716, Fax: +46-500-464725, Email: bjorne@ida.his.se

Abstract. We present a formalisation of host-parasite coevolution in Evolutionary Computation [2]. The aim is to gain a better understanding of host-parasite Genetic Algorithms (GAs) [3]. We discuss Rosin's [10] competetive theory of games, and show how it relates to host-parasite GAs. We then propose a new host-parasite optimisation algorithm based on this formalisation. The new algorithm takes into account the asymmetry of the two tasks: evolving hosts and evolving parasites. By self-adaptation the algorithm can find a suitable balance between the amount of resources spent on these two tasks. Our results show that this makes it possible to evolve optimal solutions by testing fewer candidates.

Keywords: Evolutionary Computation, Genetic Algorithms, Coevolution.

1 Introduction

A number of authors have investigated the use of coevolution as a method of improving current methods in Evolutionary Computation. Examples include cooperative coevolution [8] and competetive coevolution [9] - both of which have been used to design improved Genetic Algorithms (GAs). This paper focuses on host-parasite coevolution, which has previously been addressed in [4], [7], and [5]. A host-parasite GA uses two populations - a "host" and a "parasite" population - to represent candidate solutions and test cases. The central idea is to allow the test cases to coevolve with the candidate solutions, so that the algorithm self-adapts the set of test cases to be as challenging as possible at all stages of the optimisation process. Ideally, this results in a coevolutionary "arms-race" of continuous improvements in both populations.

The host-parasite relationship has obvious similarities with other coevolutionary relationships, such as predator-prey relationships, which have also been the subject of research in Evolutionary Computation [1]. In fact, host-parasite algorithms are often so similar to competetive algorithms, that no explicit distinction is usually made between them in the literature. The algorithms in [9], for example, share many of the properties of host-parasite algorithms, i.e. they use two separate populations where individuals from each population are fitness evaluated by being tested on members of the other population. However, most of the application examples in Rosin's work are tasks which are largely or completely symmetrical, i.e. the two populations are facing very similar tasks. In game playing, for example, the tasks for the two players are either identical or very similar. This means that the competetive GA is best designed so that both populations are evolved in a very similar manner.

We argue that a central distinction between competetive and host-parasite algorithms is that the latter are applied to tasks which are asymmetrical. In the original work on host-parasite algorithms in [4], hosts evolved sorting networks whereas parasites evolved input sequences to be used as test cases. These two tasks are very different, and it seems natural to treat them as two distinct tasks. In this paper we will develop a host-parasite algorithm which explicitly takes the asymmetry of the two tasks into account, and we will show that this makes it possible for the algorithm to self-adapt the amount of effort spent on each.

2 Formalization of host-parasite coevolution

In this section we will develop a formalisation of host-parasite coevolution. This formalisation is based in part on the competetive theory of games in [10], but is is adapted and extended to be applied to host-parasite GAs. We will evolve a set H of host individuals, each representing a candidate solution to a problem. The population H will represent a subset of the possible candidate solutions $\mathcal{H}$. The exact size of $\mathcal{H}$ will depend on the problem (as well as on the chosen representation for candidate solutions), but for all problems of interest our population of hosts will just represent a small fraction of $\mathcal{H}$.

Simultaneously with evolving H, we will evolve a set P of parasites, which represent test cases. Again, P will represent a subset of the full set of possible test cases $\mathcal{P}$. In most cases, P will contain a small fraction of $\mathcal{P}$, but this may not be a necessary requirement for host-parasite algorithms to be advantageous. Our only restriction on the size of P is that it contains a finite number of test cases. We will use the test cases in P for fitness testing, so that the fitness of a host $h \in H$ is equal to the number of test cases in P that it solves. Conversely, the fitness of a parasite $p \in P$ will be equal to the number of candidate solutions in H that fails to solve p.

For any problem that we apply our approach to, we will assume that there is at least one perfect host individual in $\mathcal{H}$, i.e. a host which is able to solve every test case in $\mathcal{P}$. The goal for our optimisation algorithm will be to find such an individual by evolving the two populations H and P. It is important to realize that under the assumption that $\mathcal{H}$ contains a perfect host, the corresponding will not be true of $\mathcal{P}$, i.e. there will not be any test case which is not solvable by any host. Thus, the tasks of evolving H and P are done under different conditions, and this must be taken into consideration in the design of the algorithm. Unlike in many game playing tasks, the learning tasks we apply our algorithms to can be described as asymmetrical.

For formalisation purposes, we now introduce the following definitions, which will later be useful for describing and discussing our algorithms. We let $h \succ p$ denote the fact that the host h solves the test case p. Similarly, we use $H \succ p$ to denote that the set H of hosts solves the test case p, i.e. $\exists h((h \in H) \land (h \succ p))$. We will use $h \succ P$ to denote that h solves every test case in P, i.e. $\forall p((p \in P) \rightarrow (h \succ p))$. Given these definitions, the interpretation of $H \succ P$, will be $\exists h((h \in H) \land \forall p((p \in P) \rightarrow (h \succ p)))$.

Given this formal language, we observe that the fact that a perfect host exists in the space of possible hosts, can be denoted $\mathcal{H} \succ \mathcal{P}$. We also note that the goal for our optimisation algorithm is to evolve the populations until $H \succ \mathcal{P}$.

In order to understand the host-parasite GAs, we first describe an abstract optimisation process where a perfect host is found in a number of steps. This process starts with two empty sets of host and parasite individuals $H = P = \{\}$. We then alternately apply some search algorithm to H and P. In each step we add a host to H which solves all test cases in the current P, so that H contains a host that is perfect w.r.t. P. We then add a parasite to P, so that H no longer contains any host that is perfect w.r.t. P. This can be implemented by using the following algorithm:

```
let t = 0
let Ht = Pt = {}
repeat
    find a host ht, such that ht ≻ Pt
    let Ht+1 = Ht ∪ ht
    find a parasite pt, such that pt ≻ Ht+1
    let Pt+1 = Pt ∪ pt
    let t = t + 1
until (H ≻ P)
```

Note that this algorithm is guaranteed to find a perfect host in a finite number of steps. For every iteration, we add a host that solves every test case found so far. We then add a new parasite, such that every host fails to solve at least one of the members of the new set of parasites. This new parasite must have found a flaw in the most recently added host. When, in the next iteration, we add another host which solves the full set of current test cases, this new host will necessarily be an improvement on the previously added host. In other words, this algorithm is guaranteed to make continuous improvements, and by a bootstrap process will reach $H \succ P$ in a finite number of steps. The process forms a transitive chain of host and parasite pairs leading ultimately to an optimal host. The length of this chain can be referred to as l. We will later be concerned with the expected value of l, when discussing the time complexity of our algorithms. Of great interest, of course, is the relationship between l and the size of $\mathcal{H}$.

In order to develop host-parasite GAs, we need to consider in detail the method to be used in order to find h_t and p_t in each iteration. In our case, we use a GA to evolve these individuals. This raises a number of issues which will be addressed in the following sections.

3 An "asymmetric" host-parasite Genetic Algorithm

In order to guarantee that the algorithm will find $H \succ \mathcal{P}$, it is crucial that no individual is ever lost or deleted from H or P. More formally, the algorithm must ensure that

$$\forall h((h \in H_i) \wedge (j > i) \rightarrow (h \in H_j)) \tag{1}$$

and that the same condition holds for P. This is problematic since a GA does not guarantee that an individual which has been found in one generation will remain in all subsequent generations of the run. This is also true of the host-parasite algorithms studied in [4], [5] and [6]. To solve this problem, we will first design an algorithm where Condition 1 is guaranteed. We then relax this requirement in an algorithm where Condition 1 is likely to hold, but not guaranteed. In exchange for this uncertainty, we will improve the time complexity.

We now introduce a distinction between the evolvable populations H^e, P^e and the static populations H^s, P^s. Our GA will apply reproduction to evolvable populations, while static populations will serve only as fitness tests. More specifically, we will evolve H^e using the members of P^e and P^s as fitness cases, until $H^e \succ P^e \cup P^s$, i.e. until H^e contains at least one host h that solves all current test cases. We will add h to the current H^s, and then evolve P^e using H^e and H^s as fitness cases. Evolution of P^e will continue until every host in H^e and H^s fails to solve at least one of the test cases in P^e. We will then find the parasite $p \in P^e$ which h (i.e. the most recent addition to H^s) fails to solve, and add it to P^s. The process of alternately evolving H^e and P^e will continue until $H^e \succ \mathcal{P}$.

The following algorithm implements these ideas:

```
let t = 0
initialize random H_t^e and P_t^e
H_t^s = P_t^s = {}
while (¬(H_t^e ∧ ≻ P)) do
    repeat
        evaluate and reproduce H_t^e using P_t^e ∪ P_t^s as fitness cases.
    until (∃h_t((h_t ∈ H_t^e) ∧ (h_t ≻ (Pe_t ∪ P_t^s))))
    repeat
        evaluate and reproduce P_t^e using H_t^e ∪ H_t^s as fitness cases.
    until (¬((H_t^e ∪ H_t^s) ≻ P_t^e))
    find p_t, such that ((p_t ∈ P_t^e) ∧ ¬(h_t ≻ p_t))
    let H_{t+1}^s = H_t^s ∪ h_t
    let P_{t+1}^s = P_t^s ∪ p_t
    let H_{t+1}^e = H_t^e
    let P_{t+1}^e = P_t^e
    let t = t + 1
done
```

For implementation purposes we must address the question of the population sizes of H^s and P^s. As noted earlier, the algorithm will form a transitive chain leading from the first host in H^s to the final perfect host. The sum of the population sizes of H^s and P^s in the final time step will be equal to l. Since H^s and P^s are used in fitness testing, it is crucial that we either reduce the expected value of l or the population sizes of H^s and P^s, while still ensuring that the algorithm will find a transitive chain to $h \succ \mathcal{H}$. Unfortunately, it is generally not possible to delete any individual from H^s or P^s without running a risk of losing the transitivity property. To see this, consider the extreme case of limiting population sizes of H^s and P^s to 1. In this case, every new member that we add to H^s replaces the previous member. It is easy to see that problems may arise given two hosts h_1, h_2 and two parasites p_1, p_2, such that $h_i \succ p_j$ iff $i = j$. The algorithm may alternate between h_1 and h_2 as members of H^s (while alternating between p_2 and p_1 as members of P^s). Similar examples can be found for greater population sizes.

In our implementation we treat H^s and P^s as queues where elements are added to the queue at one end and deleted at the other. We hypothesise that the element that has been in the queue for the longest time will be the one least crucial for maintaining the transitivity property.

4 Results

For ease of reference we will call our new algorithm AHPGA, for "Asymmetric Host-Parasite GA". AHPGA takes into account the asymmetry of the two tasks of evolving hosts and parasites, effectively treating these as two separate tasks. If one of the tasks proves more difficult than the other, AHPGA may be able to self-adapt the amount of effort spent on each task, so that a suitable balance is found. We will compare AHPGA with the Simple Host-Parasite GA, SHPGA, which was shown in [6] to give improved results over "standard" GAs.

In the first runs we used the 6 and 7-input sorting networks tasks, for ease of comparison with previous results in [6]. In table 1 and figure 1 we compare the results of AHPGA and SHPGA. For all runs, we used a population size of

30 for both the host and parasite populations. For AHPGA this means that the population sizes of H^e and P^e were fixed at 30 individuals. The static populations H^s and P^s were initially empty, and limited to contain a maximum of 30 individuals. In none of the runs was this upper limit of 30 reached, i.e. no individual was ever discarded from H^s or P^s. All runs were terminated when $3*10^5$ (6-input) or $3*10^6$ (7-input) individuals had been evaluated. It is important to realize that SHPGA evaluates and reproduces both populations in each generation, whereas one of the populations is static in AHPGA. This means that SHPGA evaluates up to twice as many individuals per generation as AHPGA.

	Converged runs		Evaluated solutions	
	6-input	7-input	6-input	7-input
AHPGA	49	50	$4.2*10^4$	$7.7*10^5$
SHPGA	48	3	$6.9*10^4$	$10.0*10^5$

Table 1. Statistics of likelihood and speed of convergence.

As table 1 shows, the average number of evaluated individuals before convergence in AHPGA is less than two thirds of the number in SHPGA. We also found that the fraction of generations during which the parasite population was evolving in AHPGA was only 0.02 for the 6-input task and 0.03 for the 7-input task. This illustrates in a striking way the asymmetru of the tasks - it is obviously very easy to evolve a test case p which the current best host is unable to solve, but very difficult to evolve a host which solves p, since 97-98% of all generations were used to evolve hosts. For the 6-input task it took on average less than 4 generations to evolve p, whereas it took on average 218 generations to evolve a host which solved p. For 7-input, the figures were 10 vs 535 generations.

By taking into account the asymmetry of the two tasks - evolving good solutions and evolving good test cases - AHPGA seems to find solutions by spending more time on the harder of the two tasks and less time on the easier task. Achieving such a balance is impossible in SHPGA, since it does not take the asymmetry of the tasks into account. Keeping in mind that AHPGA only spends 2-3% of all generations on evolving parasites, we realise that a very large proportion of the parasites generated in SHPGA are redundant.

5 Discussion and Conclusions

Our experimental results are quite preliminary since they are only from a single example application. The algorithm must be tested on a large number of examples before definitive conclusions can be made. It should also be kept in mind that there are both observed and potential problems with AHPGA in its current form. While the number of evaluated individuals before convergence is lower in AHPGA than in SHPGA, the number of applications of the fitness function is larger. While AHPGA evaluates 30 individuals per generation (with the population sizes we used) it uses at least as many calls of the fitness function as SHPGA (which evaluates 60 individuals per generations). The reason is that every call of the fitness function in SHPGA gives information on two individuals - one host and one parasite - whereas a fitness function call in AHPGA only gives information about the individual from the currently evolving population.

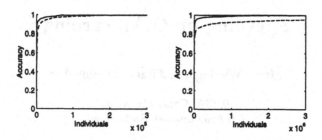

Fig. 1. Average accuracy for best host so far versus number of evaluated individuals for 50 runs on the 6 and 7-input sorting networks design task using AHPGA (solid line) and SHPGA (dashed line).

This work gives us more insight into the dynamics of a host-parasite optimisation process. It shows that the two populations face tasks that are very different, and may best be treated as two separate optimisation tasks. It exposes the often hidden assumption of symmetry behind competetive algorithms and shows that it may be unfortunate to apply this assumption when attacking tasks that are largely asymmetric. We may not yet have found the ideal way of taking asymmetry into account, but AHPGA shows that there are potential advantages of doing so. In other words, we see AHPGA as a starting point for improved host-parasite GAs, better suited to solve inherently asymmetric tasks.

References

1. D. Cliff and G.F. Miller. Co-evolution of pursuit and evasion ii: Simulation methods and results. In *From Animals to Animats 4: Proc. of the 4th Intern. Conf. on Simulation of Adaptive Behavior (SAB96)*, 1996.
2. D.B. Fogel. *Evolutionary Computation: Toward a New Philosophy of Machine Intelligence.* IEEE Press, 1995.
3. D.E. Goldberg. *Genetic Algorithms in Search, Optimization, and Machine Learning.* Addison-Wesley, 1989.
4. D. Hillis. Co-evolving parasites improve simulated evolution as an optimization procedure. In *Proceedings of the 2nd Conf. on Artificial Life*, 1992.
5. B. Olsson. Optimization using a host-parasite model with variable-size distributed populations. In *Proceedings of the 1996 IEEE 3rd International Conference on Evolutionary Computation.* IEEE Press, 1996.
6. B. Olsson. Evaluation of a simple host-parasite genetic algorithm. In *Proc. of the 7th Annual Conf. on Evolutionary Programming*, 1997.
7. J. Paredis. Steps towards co-evolutionary classification networks. In *Proc. the 4th Conference on Artifical Life*, 1994.
8. M.A. Potter. *The Design and Analysis of a Computational Model of Cooperative Coevolution.* PhD thesis, George Mason University, 1997.
9. C.D. Rosin. *Coevolutionary Search Among Adversaries.* PhD thesis, University of California, San Diego, 1997.
10. C.D. Rosin and R.K. Belew. A competetive approach to game learning. In *Proc. of the 9th Annual ACM Conf. on Computational Learning Theory*, 1996.

Speeding up Q(λ)-learning

Marco Wiering and Jürgen Schmidhuber

IDSIA, Corso Elvezia 36
CH-6900-Lugano, Switzerland

Abstract. Q(λ)-learning uses TD(λ)-methods to accelerate Q-learning. The worst case complexity for a single update step of previous online Q(λ) implementations based on lookup-tables is bounded by the size of the state/action space. Our faster algorithm's worst case complexity is bounded by the number of actions. The algorithm is based on the observation that Q-value updates may be postponed until they are needed.

Keywords: Reinforcement learning, Q-learning, TD(λ), online Q(λ), lazy learning

1 Introduction

Q(λ)-learning (Watkins, 1989; Peng and Williams, 1996) is an important reinforcement learning (RL) method. It combines Q-learning (Watkins, 1989; Watkins and Dayan, 1992) and TD(λ) (Sutton, 1988; Tesauro, 1992). Q(λ) is widely used — it is generally believed to outperform simple one-step Q-learning, since it uses *single* experiences to update evaluations of *multiple* state/action pairs (SAPs) that have occurred in the past.

Online vs. offline. We distinguish *online* RL and *offline* RL. Online RL updates modifiable parameters after each visit of a state. Offline RL delays updates until after a trial is finished, that is, until a goal has been found or a time limit has been reached. Without explicit trial boundaries offline RL does not make sense at all. But even where applicable, offline RL tends to get outperformed by online RL which uses experience earlier and therefore more efficiently (Rummery and Niranjan, 1994). Online RL's advantage can be huge. For instance, online methods that punish actions (to prevent repetitive selection of identical actions) can discover certain environments' goal states in polynomial time (Koenig and Simmons, 1996), while offline RL requires exponential time (Whitehead, 1992).

Previous Q(λ) implementations. To speed up Q-learning, Watkins (1989) suggested combining it with TD(λ) learning. Typical *online* Q(λ) implementations (Peng and Williams, 1996) based on lookup-tables or other local approximators such as CMACS (Albus 1975; Sutton, 1996) or self-organizing maps (Kohonen, 1988), however, are unnecessarily time-consuming. Their update complexity depends on the values of λ and discount factor γ, and is proportional to the number of SAPs (state/action pairs) which occurred. The latter is bounded by the size of state/action space (and by the trial length which may be proportional to this).

Lin's *offline* Q(λ) (1993) creates an action-replay set of experiences after each trial. Cichosz' *semi-online* method (1995) combines Lin's offline method and online learning. It needs fewer updates than Peng and Williams' online Q(λ), but postpones Q-updates until several subsequent experiences are available. Hence actions executed before the next Q-update are less informed than they could be. This may result in performance loss. For instance, suppose that the same state is visited twice in a row. If some hazardous action's Q-value does not reflect negative experience collected after the first visit then it may get selected again with higher probability than wanted.

The novel method. Previous methods either are not truly online and thus require more experiences, or their updates are less efficient than they could be and thus require more computation time. Our Q(λ) variant is truly online and more efficient than others because its update complexity does not depend on the number of states[1]. It uses "lazy learning" (introduced in memory-based learning, e.g., Atkeson, Moore and Schaal 1996) to postpone updates until they are needed.

Outline. Section 2 reviews Q(λ) and describes Peng and William's Q(λ)-algorithm (PW). Section 3 presents our more efficient algorithm. Section 4 presents a practical comparison on 100×100 mazes. Section 5 concludes.

2 Q(λ)-Learning

We consider discrete Markov decision processes, using time steps $t = 1, 2, 3, \ldots$, a discrete set of states $S = \{S_1, S_2, S_3, \ldots, S_n\}$ and a discrete set of actions A. s_t denotes the state at time t, and $a_t = \Pi(s_t)$ the action, where Π represents the learner's policy mapping states to actions. The transition function P with elements $P_{ij}^a = P(s_{t+1} = j | s_t = i, a_t = a)$ for $i, j \in S$ and $a \in A$ defines the transition probability to the next state s_{t+1} given s_t and a_t. A reward function R defines the scalar reward signal $R(i, a, j) \in I\!R$ for making the transition to state j given state i and action a. r_t denotes the reward at time t. A discount factor $\gamma \in [0, 1]$ discounts later against immediate rewards. The controller's goal is to select actions which maximize the expected long-term cumulative discounted reinforcement, given an initial state selected according to a probability distribution over possible initial states.

Reinforcement Learning. To achieve this goal an action evaluation function or Q-function is learned. The optimal Q-value of SAP (i, a) satisfies

$$Q^*(i, a) = \sum_j P_{ij}^a (R(i, a, j) + \gamma V^*(j)), \tag{1}$$

where $V^*(j) = \max_a Q^*(j, a)$. To learn this Q-function, RL algorithms repeatedly do: (1) Select action a_t given state s_t. (2) Collect reward r_t and observe successor state s_{t+1}. (3) Update the Q-function using the latest experience (s_t, a_t, r_t, s_{t+1}).

---

[1] The method can also be used for speeding up tabular TD(λ).

Q-learning. Given (s_t, a_t, r_t, s_{t+1}), standard one-step Q-learning updates just a single Q-value $Q(s_t, a_t)$ as follows (Watkins, 1989):

$$Q(s_t, a_t) \leftarrow Q(s_t, a_t) + \alpha_k(s_t, a_t)e'_t,$$

where e'_t is the temporal difference or TD(0)-error given by:

$$e'_t = (r_t + \gamma V(s_{t+1}) - Q(s_t, a_t)),$$

where the value function $V(s)$ is defined as $V(s) = \max_a Q(s, a)$ (evaluated at time-step t), and $\alpha_k(s_t, a_t)$ is the learning rate for the kth update of SAP (s_t, a_t).

Learning rate adaptation. The learning rate $\alpha_k(s, a)$ for the kth update of SAP (s, a) should decrease over time to satisfy two conditions for stochastic iterative algorithms (Watkins and Dayan, 1992; Bertsekas and Tsitsiklis, 1996):

1. $\sum_{k=1}^{\infty} \alpha_k(s, a) = \infty$, and 2. $\sum_{k=1}^{\infty} \alpha_k^2(s, a) < \infty$.

They hold for $\alpha_k(s, a) = \frac{1}{k^\beta}$, where $\frac{1}{2} < \beta \leq 1$.

Q(λ)-learning. Q(λ) uses TD(λ)-methods (Sutton, 1988) to accelerate Q-learning. First note that Q-learning's update at time $t + 1$ may change $V(s_{t+1})$ in the definition of e'_t. Following (Peng and Williams, 1996) we define the TD(0)-error of $V(s_{t+1})$ as

$$e_{t+1} = (r_{t+1} + \gamma V(s_{t+2}) - V(s_{t+1}))$$

Q(λ) uses a factor $\lambda \in [0, 1]$ to discount TD-errors of future time steps:

$$Q(s_t, a_t) \leftarrow Q(s_t, a_t) + \alpha_k(s_t, a_t)e_t^\lambda,$$

where the TD(λ)-error e_t^λ is defined as

$$e_t^\lambda = e'_t + \sum_{i=1}^{\infty} (\gamma\lambda)^i e_{t+i}$$

Eligibility traces. The updates above cannot be made as long as TD errors of future time steps are not known. We can compute them incrementally, however, by using eligibility traces (Barto et al., 1983; Sutton 1988). In what follows, $\eta^t(s, a)$ will denote the indicator function which returns 1 if (s, a) occurred at time t, and 0 otherwise. Omitting the learning rate for simplicity, the increment of $Q(s, a)$ for the complete trial is:

$$\Delta Q(s, a) = \lim_{k \to \infty} \sum_{t=1}^{k} e_t^\lambda \eta^t(s, a)$$

$$= \lim_{k \to \infty} \sum_{t=1}^{k} [e'_t \eta^t(s, a) + \sum_{i=t+1}^{k} (\gamma\lambda)^{i-t} e_i \eta^t(s, a)]$$

$$= \lim_{k \to \infty} \sum_{t=1}^{k} [e'_t \eta^t(s, a) + \sum_{i=1}^{t-1} (\gamma\lambda)^{t-i} e_t \eta^i(s, a)]$$

$$= \lim_{k \to \infty} \sum_{t=1}^{k} [e'_t \eta^t(s, a) + e_t \sum_{i=1}^{t-1} (\gamma\lambda)^{t-i} \eta^i(s, a)] \qquad (2)$$

To simplify this we use an eligibility trace $l_t(s,a)$ for each SAP (s,a):

$$l_t(s,a) = \sum_{i=1}^{t-1}(\gamma\lambda)^{t-i}\eta^i(s,a) = \gamma\lambda(l_{t-1}(s,a) + \eta^{t-1}(s,a))$$

Then the online update at time t becomes:

$$\forall(s,a) \in S \times A \ do: \ Q(s,a) \leftarrow Q(s,a) + \alpha_k(s_t,a_t)[e'_t\eta^t(s,a) + e_t l_t(s,a)]$$

Online Q(λ). We will focus on Peng and Williams' algorithm (PW) (1996), although there are other possible variants, e.g, (Rummery and Niranjan, 1994). PW uses a list H of SAPs that have occurred at least once. SAPs with eligibility traces below $\epsilon \geq 0$ are removed from H. Boolean variables $visited(s,a)$ are used to make sure no two SAPs in H are identical.

PW's Q(λ)-update(s_t,a_t,r_t,s_{t+1}) :

1) $e'_t \leftarrow (r_t + \gamma V(s_{t+1}) - Q(s_t,a_t))$
2) $e_t \leftarrow (r_t + \gamma V(s_{t+1}) - V(s_t))$
3) For each SAP $(s,a) \in H$ Do :
    3a) $l(s,a) \leftarrow \gamma\lambda l(s,a)$
    3b) $Q(s,a) \leftarrow Q(s,a) + \alpha_k(s_t,a_t)e_t l(s,a)$
    3c) If $(l(s,a) < \epsilon)$
        3c-1) $H \leftarrow H \setminus (s,a)$
        3c-2) $visited(s,a) \leftarrow 0$
4) $Q(s_t,a_t) \leftarrow Q(s_t,a_t) + \alpha_k(s_t,a_t)e'_t$
5) $l(s_t,a_t) \leftarrow l(s_t,a_t) + 1$
6) If $(visited(s_t,a_t) = 0)$
    6a) $visited(s_t,a_t) \leftarrow 1$
    6b) $H \leftarrow H \cup (s_t,a_t)$

Comments. 1. The SARSA algorithm (Rummery and Niranjan, 1994) replaces the right hand side in lines (1) and (2) by $(r_t + \gamma Q(s_{t+1},a_{t+1}) - Q(s_t,a_t))$.
2. For "replacing eligibility traces" (Singh and Sutton, 1996), step 5 should be: $\forall a : l(s_t,a) \leftarrow 0; \ l(s_t,a_t) \leftarrow 1$.
3. Representing H by a doubly linked list and using direct pointers from each SAP to its position in H, the functions operating on H (deleting and adding elements — see lines (3c-1) and (6b)) cost $O(1)$.

Complexity. Deleting SAPs from H (step 3c-1) once their traces fall below a certain threshold may significantly speed up the algorithm. If $\gamma\lambda$ is sufficiently small, then this will keep the number of updates per time step manageable. For large $\gamma\lambda$ PW does not work that well: it needs a sweep (sequence of SAP updates) after each time step, and the update cost for such sweeps grows with $\gamma\lambda$. Let us consider worst-case behavior, which means that each SAP occurs just once (if SAPs reoccur then the history list will grow at a slower rate). At the start of the trial the number of updates increases linearly until at some time step t some SAPs get deleted from H. This will happen as soon as $t \geq \frac{\log \epsilon}{\log(\gamma\lambda)}$. Since the number of updates is bounded from above by the number of SAPs, the total update complexity increases towards $O(|S||A|)$ per update for $\gamma\lambda \to 1$.

3   Fast Q(λ)-Learning

The main contribution of this paper is an efficient, fully online algorithm with time complexity $O(|A|)$ per update. The algorithm is designed for $\lambda\gamma > 0$ — otherwise we use simple Q-learning.

Main principle. The algorithm is based on the observation that the only Q-values needed at any given time are those for the possible actions given the current state. Hence, using "lazy learning", we can postpone updating Q-values until they are needed. Suppose some SAP (s, a) occurs at steps $t_1, t_2, t_3, \ldots$ Let us abbreviate $\eta^t = \eta^t(s, a)$, $\phi = \gamma\lambda$. First we unfold terms of expression (2):

$$\sum_{t=1}^{k}[e_t'\eta^t + e_t\sum_{i=1}^{t-1}\phi^{t-i}\eta^i] =$$

$$\sum_{t=1}^{t_1}[e_t'\eta^t + e_t\sum_{i=1}^{t-1}\phi^{t-i}\eta^i] + \sum_{t=t_1+1}^{t_2}[e_t'\eta^t + e_t\sum_{i=1}^{t-1}\phi^{t-i}\eta^i] + \sum_{t=t_2+1}^{t_3}[e_t'\eta^t + e_t\sum_{i=1}^{t-1}\phi^{t-i}\eta^i] + \ldots$$

Since η^t is 1 only for $t = t_1, t_2, t_3, \ldots$ and 0 otherwise, we can rewrite this as

$$e_{t_1}' + e_{t_2}' + \sum_{t=t_1+1}^{t_2} e_t\phi^{t-t_1} + e_{t_3}' + \sum_{t=t_2+1}^{t_3} e_t(\phi^{t-t_1} + \phi^{t-t_2}) + \ldots =$$

$$e_{t_1}' + e_{t_2}' + \frac{1}{\phi^{t_1}}\sum_{t=t_1+1}^{t_2} e_t\phi^t + e_{t_3}' + (\frac{1}{\phi^{t_1}} + \frac{1}{\phi^{t_2}})\sum_{t=t_2+1}^{t_3} e_t\phi^t + \ldots =$$

$$e_{t_1}' + e_{t_2}' + \frac{1}{\phi^{t_1}}(\sum_{t=1}^{t_2} e_t\phi^t - \sum_{t=1}^{t_1} e_t\phi^t) + e_{t_3}' + (\frac{1}{\phi^{t_1}} + \frac{1}{\phi^{t_2}})(\sum_{t=1}^{t_3} e_t\phi^t - \sum_{t=1}^{t_2} e_t\phi^t) + \ldots$$

Defining $\Delta_t = \sum_{i=1}^{t} e_i\phi^i$, this becomes

$$e_{t_1}' + e_{t_2}' + \frac{1}{\phi^{t_1}}(\Delta_{t_2} - \Delta_{t_1}) + e_{t_3}' + (\frac{1}{\phi^{t_1}} + \frac{1}{\phi^{t_2}})(\Delta_{t_3} - \Delta_{t_2}) + \ldots \qquad (3)$$

This will allow for constructing an efficient online Q(λ) algorithm. We define a local trace $l_t'(s, a) = \sum_{i=1}^{t} \frac{\eta^i(s,a)}{\phi^i}$, and use (3) to write down the total update of $Q(s, a)$ during a trial:

$$\Delta Q(s, a) = \lim_{k \to \infty} \sum_{t=1}^{k} e_t'\eta^t(s, a) + l_t'(s, a)(\Delta_{t+1} - \Delta_t) \qquad (4)$$

To exploit this we introduce a global variable Δ keeping track of the cumulative TD(λ) error since the start of the trial. As long as SAP (s, a) does not occur we postpone updating $Q(s, a)$. In the update below we need to subtract that part of Δ which has already been used (see equations 3 and 4). We use for each SAP (s, a) a local variable $\delta(s, a)$ which records the value of Δ at the moment of the last update, and a local trace variable $l'(s, a)$. Then, once $Q(s, a)$

needs to be known, we update $Q(s,a)$ by adding $l'(s,a)(\Delta - \delta(s,a))$. Figure 1 illustrates that the algorithm substitutes the varying eligibility trace $l(s,a)$ by multiplying a global trace ϕ^t by the local trace $l'(s,a)$. The value of ϕ^t changes all the time, but $l'(s,a)$ does not in intervals during which (s,a) does not occur.

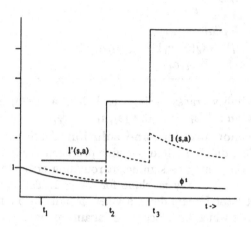

Fig. 1. *SAP* (s,a) *occurs at times* $t_1, t_2, t_3, \ldots$. *The standard eligibility trace* $l(s,a)$ *equals the product of* ϕ^t *and* $l'(s,a)$.

Algorithm overview. The algorithm relies on two procedures: the *Local Update* procedure calculates exact Q-values once they are required; the *Global Update* procedure updates the global variables and the current Q-value. Initially we set the global variables $\phi^0 \leftarrow 1.0$ and $\Delta \leftarrow 0$. We also initialize the local variables $\delta(s,a) \leftarrow 0$ and $l'(s,a) \leftarrow 0$ for all SAPs.

Local updates. Q-values for all actions possible in a given state are updated before an action is selected and before a particular V-value is calculated. For each SAP (s,a) a variable $\delta(s,a)$ tracks changes since the last update:

Local Update(s_t, a_t) :

1) $Q(s_t, a_t) \leftarrow Q(s_t, a_t) + \alpha_k(s_t, a_t)(\Delta - \delta(s_t, a_t))l'(s_t, a_t)$
2) $\delta(s_t, a_t) \leftarrow \Delta$

The global update procedure. After each executed action we invoke the procedure *Global Update*, which consists of three basic steps: (1) To calculate $V(s_{t+1})$ (which may have changed due to the most recent experience), it calls *Local Update* for the possible next SAPs. (2) It updates the global variables ϕ^t and Δ. (3) It updates (s_t, a_t)'s Q-value and trace variable and stores the current Δ value (in *Local Update*).

Global Update(s_t, a_t, r_t, s_{t+1}) :

1) $\forall a \in A$ Do

    1a) *Local Update*(s_{t+1}, a)

2) $e'_t \leftarrow (r_t + \gamma V(s_{t+1}) - Q(s_t, a_t))$

3) $e_t \leftarrow (r_t + \gamma V(s_{t+1}) - V(s_t))$

4) $\phi^t \leftarrow \gamma \lambda \phi^{t-1}$

5) $\Delta \leftarrow \Delta + e_t \phi^t$

6) *Local Update*(s_t, a_t)

7) $Q(s_t, a_t) \leftarrow Q(s_t, a_t) + \alpha_k(s_t, a_t)e'_t$

8) $l'(s_t, a_t) \leftarrow l'(s_t, a_t) + \frac{1}{\phi^t}$

For "replacing eligibility traces" (Singh and Sutton, 1996), step 8 should be changed as follows: $\forall a : l'(s_t, a) \leftarrow 0; l'(s_t, a_t) \leftarrow \frac{1}{\phi^t}$.

Machine precision problem and solution. Adding $e_t \phi^t$ to Δ in line 5 may create a problem due to limited machine precision: for large absolute values of Δ and small ϕ^t there may be significant rounding errors. More importantly, line 8 will quickly overflow any machine for $\gamma \lambda < 1$. The following addendum to the procedure *Global Update* detects when ϕ^t falls below machine precision ϵ_m, updates all SAPs which have occurred (again we make use of a list H), and removes SAPs with $l'(s, a) < \epsilon_m$ from H. Finally, Δ and ϕ^t are reset to their initial values.

Global Update : addendum

9) If $(visited(s_t, a_t) = 0)$

    9a) $H \leftarrow H \cup (s_t, a_t)$

    9b) $visited(s_t, a_t) \leftarrow 1$

10) If $(\phi^t < \epsilon_m)$

    10a) Do $\forall (s, a) \in H$

        10a-1) *Local Update*(s, a)

        10a-2) $l'(s, a) \leftarrow l'(s, a)\phi^t$

        10a-3) If $(l'(s, a) < \epsilon_m)$

            10a-3-1) $H \leftarrow H \setminus (s, a)$

            10a-3-2) $visited(s, a) \leftarrow 0$

        10a-4) $\delta(s, a) \leftarrow 0$

    10b) $\Delta \leftarrow 0$

    10c) $\phi^t \leftarrow 1.0$

Comments. Recall that *Local Update* sets $\delta(s, a) \leftarrow \Delta$, and update steps depend on $\Delta - \delta(s, a)$. Thus, after having updated all SAPs in H, we can set $\Delta \leftarrow 0$ and $\delta(s, a) \leftarrow 0$. Furthermore, we can simply set $l'(s, a) \leftarrow l'(s, a)\phi^t$ and $\phi^t \leftarrow 1.0$ without affecting the expression $l'(s, a)\phi^t$ used in future updates — this just rescales the variables. Note that if $\gamma \lambda = 1$, then no sweeps through the history list will be necessary.

Complexity. The algorithm's most expensive part are the calls of *Local Update*, whose total cost is $O(|A|)$. This is not bad: even simple Q-learning's action selection procedure costs $O(|A|)$ if, say, the Boltzmann rule (Thrun, 1992; Caironi and Dorigo, 1994) is used. Concerning the occasional complete sweep through SAPs still in history list H: during each sweep the traces of SAPs in H are multiplied by $l < e_m$. SAPs are deleted from H once their trace falls below e_m. In the worst case one sweep per n time steps updates $2n$ SAPs and costs $O(1)$ on average. This means that there is an additional computational burden at certain time steps, but since this happens infrequently our method's total average update complexity stays $O(|A|)$.

Comparison to PW. Figure 2 illustrates the difference between theoretical worst-case behaviors of both methods for $|A| = 5$, $|S| = 1000$, and $\gamma = 1$. We plot updates per time step for $\lambda \in \{0.7, 0.9.0.99\}$. The accuracy parameter ϵ (used in PW) is set to 10^{-6} (in practice less precise values may be used, but this will not change matters much). ϵ_m is set to 10^{-16}. The spikes in the plot for fast $Q(\lambda)$ reflect occasional full sweeps through the history list due to limited machine precision (the corresponding average number of updates, however, is very close to the value indicated by the horizontal solid line — as explained above, the spikes hardly affect the average). No sweep is necessary in fast $Q(0.99)$'s plot during the shown interval. Fast Q needs on average a total of 13 update steps: 5 in choose-action, 5 for calculating $V(s_{t+1})$, 1 for updating the chosen action, and 2 for taking into account the full sweeps.

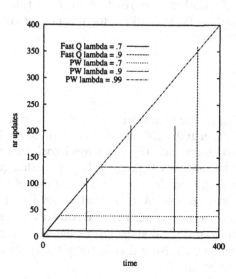

Fig. 2. *Number of updates plotted against time: a worst case analysis for our method and Peng and Williams' (PW) for different values of λ.*

Multiple Trials. We have described a single-trial version of our algorithm. One might be tempted to think that in case of multiple trials all SAPs in the history list need to be updated and all eligibility traces reset after each trial. This is not necessary — we may use cross-trial learning as follows:

We introduce Δ^M variables, where index M stands for the Mth trial. Let N denote the current trial number, and let variable $visited(s, a)$ represent the trial number of the most recent occurrence of SAP (s, a). Now we slightly change *Local Update*:

Local Update(s_t, a_t) :
1) $M \leftarrow visited(s_t, a_t)$
2) $Q(s_t, a_t) \leftarrow Q(s_t, a_t) + \alpha_k(s_t, a_t)(\Delta^M - \delta(s_t, a_t))l'(s_t, a_t)$
3) $\delta(s_t, a_t) \leftarrow \Delta^N$
4) If $(M < N)$
    4a) $l'(s_t, a_t) \leftarrow 0$
    4b) $visited(s_t, a_t) \leftarrow N$

Thus we update $Q(s, a)$ using the value Δ^M of the most recent trial M during which SAP (s, a) occurred and the corresponding values of $\delta(s_t, a_t)$ and $l'(s_t, a_t)$ (computed during the same trial). In case SAP (s, a) has not occurred during the current trial we reset the eligibility trace and set $visited(s, a)$ to the current trial number. In *Global Update* we need to change lines 5 and 10b by adding trial subscripts to Δ, and we need to change line 9b in which we have to set $visited(s_t, a_t) \leftarrow N$. At trial end we reset ϕ^t to $\phi^0 = 1.0$, increment the trial counter N, and set $\Delta^N \leftarrow 0$. This allows for postponing certain updates until after the current trial's end.

4 Experiments

To evaluate competing training methods in practice we created a set of 20 different randomly initialized 100×100 mazes, each with about 20% blocked fields. All mazes share a fixed start state (S) and a fixed goal state (G) (we discarded mazes that could not be solved by Dijkstra's shortest path algorithm). See figure 3 for an example. In each field the agent can select one of the four actions: *go north, go east, go south, go west*. Actions that would lead into a blocked field are not executed. Once the agent finds the goal state it receives a reward of 1000 and is reset to the start state. All steps are punished by a reward of -1. The discount factor γ is set to 0.99. Note that initially the agent has no information about the environment at all.

Experimental set-up. To select actions we used the *max-random* selection rule, which selects an action with maximal Q-value with probability P_{max} and a random action with probability $1 - P_{max}$. A single run on one of the twenty mazes consisted of 5,000,000 steps. During each run we linearly increased P_{max} from 0.5 (start) until 1.0 (end). Every 10,000 steps the learner's performance was monitored by computing its cumulative reward so far. The optimal performance is about $41,500 = 41.5K$ reward points (this corresponds to 194-step paths).

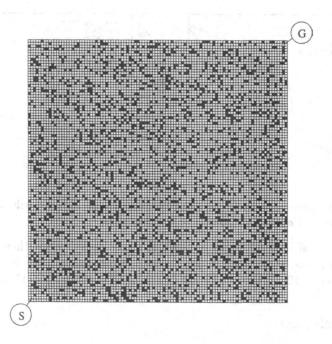

Fig. 3. *A* 100 × 100 *maze used in the experiments. Black states denote blocked field. The agent's aim is to find the shortest path from start S to goal G.*

To show how learning performance depends on λ we set up multiple experiments with different values for λ and β (used for annealing the learning rate). β must theoretically exceed 0.5 but may be lower in practice. If λ is large and β too small, however, then the Q-function will tend to diverge.

Parameters. We always chose the lowest beta (and hence the largest learning rate) such that the Q-function did not diverge. Final parameter choices were: Q(0) and Q(0.5) with $\beta = 0$, Q(0.7) with $\beta = 0.01$, Q(0.9) with $\beta = 0.2$, Q(0.95) with $\beta = 0.3$. Q(0.99) with $\beta = 0.4$. PW's trace cutoff ϵ was set to 0.001. Larger values scored less well; lower ones costed more time. Machine precision ϵ_m was set to 10^{-16}. Time costs were computed by measuring cpu-time (including action selection and almost neglectable simulator time) on a 50 MHz SPARC station.

Results. Learning performance for fast Q(λ) is plotted in Figure 1(A) (results with PW's Q(λ) are very similar). We observe that larger values of λ increase performance much faster than smaller values, although the final performances are best for standard Q-learning and $Q(0.95)$. Figure 1(B), however, shows that fast Q(λ) is not much more time-consuming than standard Q-learning, whereas PW's Q(λ) consumes a lot of CPU time for large λ.

Table 1 shows more detailed results. It shows that Q(0.95) led to the largest cumulative reward which indicates that its learning speed is fastest. Note that for this best value $\lambda = 0.95$, fast Q(λ) was more than four times faster than PW's Q(λ).

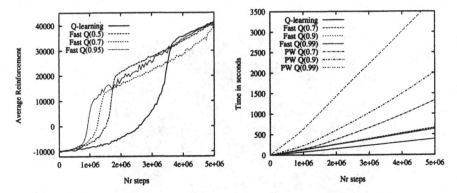

Fig. 4. *(A) Learning performance of Q(λ)-learning with different values for λ. (B) CPU time plotted against the number of learning steps.*

PW's cut-off method works only when traces decay, which they did due to the chosen λ and γ parameters. For λγ = 1 (worst case), however, PW would consume about 100(!) hours whereas our method needs around 11 minutes.

5 Conclusion

While other Q(λ) approaches are either offline, inexact, or may suffer from average update complexity depending on the size of the state/action space, ours is fully online Q(λ) with average update complexity linear in the number of actions. Efficiently dealing with eligibility traces makes fast Q(λ) applicable to larger scale RL problems.

Acknowledgments

Thanks for helpful comments to Nic Schraudolph and an anonymous reviewer.

Table 1. *Average results for different online Q(λ) methods on twenty 100 × 100 mazes. Final performance is the cumulative reward during the final 20,000 steps. Total performance is the cumulative reward during a simulation. Time is measured in cpu seconds.*

System	Final performance	Total performance	Time
Q-learning	41.5K ± 0.5K	4.5M ± 0.3M	390 ± 20
Fast Q(0.5)	41.2K ± 0.7K	8.9M ± 0.2M	660 ± 33
Fast Q(0.7)	39.6K ± 1.4K	7.9M ± 0.3M	660 ± 29
Fast Q(0.9)	40.9K ± 1.0K	9.2M ± 0.3M	640 ± 32
Fast Q(0.95)	41.5K ± 0.5K	9.8M ± 0.2M	610 ± 32
Fast Q(0.99)	40.0K ± 1.1K	8.3M ± 0.4M	630 ± 39
PW Q(0.5)	41.3K ± 0.8K	8.9M ± 0.3M	1300 ± 57
PW Q(0.7)	40.0K ± 0.7K	7.9M ± 0.3M	1330 ± 38
PW Q(0.9)	41.2K ± 0.7K	9.4M ± 0.3M	2030 ± 130
PW Q(0.95)	41.2K ± 0.9K	9.7M ± 0.3M	2700 ± 94
PW Q(0.99)	39.8K ± 1.4K	8.2M ± 0.4M	3810 ± 140

References

[Albus, 1975] Albus, J. S. (1975). A new approach to manipulator control: The cerebellar model articulation controller (CMAC). *Dynamic Systems, Measurement and Control*, pages 220–227.

[Atkeson et al., 1997] Atkeson, C. G., Schaal, S., and Moore, A. W. (1997). Locally weighted learning. *Artificial Intelligence Review*, 11:11–73.

[Barto et al., 1983] Barto, A. G., Sutton, R. S., and Anderson, C. W. (1983). Neuronlike adaptive elements that can solve difficult learning control problems. *IEEE Transactions on Systems, Man, and Cybernetics*, SMC-13:834–846.

[Bertsekas and Tsitsiklis, 1996] Bertsekas, D. P. and Tsitsiklis, J. N. (1996). *Neurodynamic Programming*. Athena Scientific, Belmont, MA.

[Caironi and Dorigo, 1994] Caironi, P. V. C. and Dorigo, M. (1994). Training Q-agents. Technical Report IRIDIA-94-14, Université Libre de Bruxelles.

[Cichosz, 1995] Cichosz, P. (1995). Truncating temporal differences: On the efficient implementation of TD(λ) for reinforcement learning. *Journal on Artificial Intelligence*, 2:287–318.

[Koenig and Simmons, 1996] Koenig, S. and Simmons, R. G. (1996). The effect of representation and knowledge on goal-directed exploration with reinforcement learning algorithms. *Machine Learning*, 22:228–250.

[Kohonen, 1988] Kohonen, T. (1988). *Self-Organization and Associative Memory*. Springer, second edition.

[Lin, 1993] Lin, L. (1993). *Reinforcement Learning for Robots Using Neural Networks*. PhD thesis, Carnegie Mellon University, Pittsburgh.

[Peng and Williams, 1996] Peng, J. and Williams, R. (1996). Incremental multi-step Q-learning. *Machine Learning*, 22:283–290.

[Rummery and Niranjan, 1994] Rummery, G. and Niranjan, M. (1994). On-line Q-learning using connectionist sytems. Technical Report CUED/F-INFENG-TR 166, Cambridge University, UK.

[Singh and Sutton, 1996] Singh, S. and Sutton, R. (1996). Reinforcement learning with replacing eligibility traces. *Machine Learning*, 22:123–158.

[Sutton, 1988] Sutton, R. S. (1988). Learning to predict by the methods of temporal differences. *Machine Learning*, 3:9–44.

[Sutton, 1996] Sutton, R. S. (1996). Generalization in reinforcement learning: Successful examples using sparse coarse coding. In D. S. Touretzky, M. C. M. and Hasselmo, M. E., editors, *Advances in Neural Information Processing Systems 8*, pages 1038–1045. MIT Press, Cambridge MA.

[Tesauro, 1992] Tesauro, G. (1992). Practical issues in temporal difference learning. In Lippman, D. S., Moody, J. E., and Touretzky, D. S., editors, *Advances in Neural Information Processing Systems 4*, pages 259–266. San Mateo, CA: Morgan Kaufmann.

[Thrun, 1992] Thrun, S. (1992). Efficient exploration in reinforcement learning. Technical Report CMU-CS-92-102, Carnegie-Mellon University.

[Watkins, 1989] Watkins, C. J. C. H. (1989). *Learning from Delayed Rewards*. PhD thesis, University of Cambridge, England.

[Watkins and Dayan, 1992] Watkins, C. J. C. H. and Dayan, P. (1992). Q-learning. *Machine Learning*, 8:279–292.

[Whitehead, 1992] Whitehead, S. (1992). *Reinforcement Learning for the adaptive control of perception and action*. PhD thesis, University of Rochester.

Q-Learning and Redundancy Reduction in Classifier Systems with Internal State

Antonella Giani, Andrea Sticca, Fabrizio Baiardi, Antonina Starita

Università di Pisa, Dip. di Informatica
Corso Italia 40 56125 Pisa, Italy

Abstract. The Q-Credit Assignment (QCA) is a method, based on Q-learning, for allocating credit to rules in Classifier Systems with internal state. It is more powerful than other proposed methods, because it correctly evaluates shared rules, but it has a large computational cost, due to the Multi-Layer Perceptron (MLP) that stores the evaluation function. We present a method for reducing this cost by reducing redundancy in the input space of the MLP through feature extraction. The experimental results show that the QCA with Redundancy Reduction (QCA-RR) preserves the advantages of the QCA while it significantly reduces both the learning time and the evaluation time after learning.

1 Introduction

Classifier Systems (CSs) [4, 1] are adaptive Reinforcement Learning (RL) systems whose behavior is driven by a set of condition/action rules. This paper addresses credit assignment in CSs that use a message list (ML) as internal state (IS-CSs). While stimulus-response CSs [9] can only solve Markovian Decision Tasks (MDTs), internal messages allow IS-CSs to solve non-Markovian tasks as well. The Q-Credit Assignment (QCA) [2, 3] is a method, based on Q-learning [8], for allocating credit in IS-CSs. It is more powerful than other proposed methods, because it correctly evaluates rules whose application may have different outcomes depending on the context. However, the QCA has a large computational cost, due to the Multi-Layer Perceptron (MLP) [6] that stores the evaluation function. To reduce this cost, we introduce the Q-Credit Assignment with Redundancy Reduction (QCA-RR), that reduces the size of the MLP by reducing redundancy in its input space, through feature extraction.

2 Q-Credit Assignment

The behavior of a CS emerges from the cooperation of several simple rules. Sharing rules among distinct situations allows both compact knowledge representation and generalisation [1, 3]. Commonly used credit assignment methods, such as the Bucket Brigade algorithm [4], allocate a single credit measure to individual rules. This makes them fail in evaluating shared rules whose activation may result in different outcomes depending on the context. The QCA [2, 3] has been devised to overcome this problem. It is based on Q-learning [8], a well known on-line RL algorithm to solve MDTs. Q-learning incrementally estimates the return $Q(x, a)$ of doing an action a in state x, $Q(x, a) = r + \gamma \max_b Q(y, b)$, where r is the immediate reinforcement and γ is the discount factor. The QCA learns Q values of (state,action) pairs (x, a), where x is the contents of the ML and a is a message specified by the action part of a rule that matches x or a part of it[1]. In this way, the QCA estimates the return of activating a rule by taking into account the whole contents of the ML, and it can correctly evaluate rules that have distinct outcomes in different situations. The Q function is approximated through a MLP with one hidden layer and one linear output unit. Given a (state,action) pair, i.e. a ML configuration $\{m_1, \ldots, m_n\}$ and a candidate message m, the corresponding input pattern is the string $m_1, \cdots, m_n, m$. The MLP is trained with the back-propagation algorithm [6] to reduce the Temporal Difference error between two successive evaluations of each pattern.

3 Improving the QCA by reducing redundancy

The main drawback of the QCA is its large computational cost. The evaluation and learning times depend on the number of satisfied rules at each cycle, as well as on the size of the MLP, which grows with the size of the ML and with the length of the messages. A IS-CS assumes that internal messages are as long as detector (input) and effector (output) messages. However, the information to be stored not always needs the same number of bits for each kind of message. Thus, messages may include unuseful or redundant information. A proper feature extraction process can reduce the size of the input patterns and, as a consequence, the size of the MLP, with minimal loss of information.

3.1 Principal component analysis via Hebbian learning

Feature extraction is the process whereby a p-dimensional data space is mapped onto a m-dimensional feature space, $m < p$, so that the data set is represented by a reduced number of features. Given a p-dimensional zero-mean random vector $\mathbf{x}$, let $\mathbf{u}_1, \ldots, \mathbf{u}_p$ be the normalised eigenvectors of the correlation matrix $\mathbf{R} = E[\mathbf{x}\mathbf{x}^T]$, and let $\lambda_1, \ldots, \lambda_p$ be the associated eigenvalues. Principal Component Analysis (PCA) [5] states that, if $\lambda_1, \ldots, \lambda_m$ are the largest m eigenvalues of $\mathbf{R}$, the matrix $\mathbf{U} = [\mathbf{u}_1, \ldots, \mathbf{u}_m]$ maps $\mathbf{x}$ onto a m-dimensional feature vector $\mathbf{y} = \mathbf{x}^T \mathbf{U}$ with a loss of information which is optimal in the mean-square error sense. The $y_i = \mathbf{x}^T \mathbf{u}_i$ are called *principal components*. Sanger [7] shows that a generalised Hebbian algorithm (GHA) can be used to train a feed-forward neural network with p inputs and a single layer of m linear output units, so that the output unit j computes the j-th principal component of the input distribution. This means that the network performs PCA of size m directly on the input patterns, without computing the eigenvectors and the eigenvalues of R.

---

[1] The QCA uses Q-learning to solve a high-level decision task including both the ML and the original task faced by the CS. The high-level task can be modelled as MDT, even if the original task is non-Markovian, provided that the IS-CS owns the rules to store the appropriate information. For a more complete discussion, see [3]

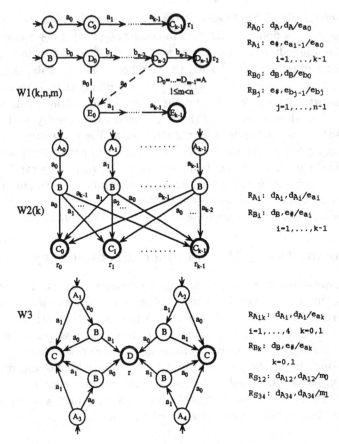

Fig. 1. NMFSW worlds and sets of rules used for the experiments. Initial states have a short entering arrow, whereas final states are double circled.

3.2 QCA with redundancy reduction: QCA-RR

The Q-Credit Assignment with Redundancy Reduction (QCA-RR) reduces the number of connections of the MLP by reducing the dimension of the evaluated data space. The p-dimensional (state,action) patterns are pre-processed by an unsupervised neural network with p inputs and m outputs, $m < p$, which computes the m principal components of each pattern, as described in Sect. 3.1. A preliminar exploration phase is needed to determine the training set of the unsupervised network. During the exploration, no learning is performed and the competition among rules is randomly solved. The length of this phase should be tuned accordingly to the difficulty of the task, so that a meaningful sample of the patterns is examined. After exploration, the unsupervised network is trained with the GHA until it converges to a principal component extractor. Then, the MLP can start estimating the Q function on the m-dimensional feature space of the (state,action) space.

4 Experimental Results

The QCA-RR has been tested in Non-Markovian Finite State World (NMFSW) [3], an abstract domain that can model non-Markovian tasks. A world is modelled as an absorbing Markov process, defined by a set of labelled states, a set of actions, and a state-transition probability matrix. Each state may be paired with a reward, detected as reinforcement by the agent. The label of a state is the information that the agent detects about that state. If distinct states have the same label, the world is non-Markovian. The experiments only concern credit assignment. Any execution is run with a fixed set of rules, which includes both rules leading to a reward and wrong ones. The QCA and the QCA-RR are compared in several worlds, with sets of rules that present an increasing amount of rule sharing. The performance measure, P, is the ratio of the reward obtained in a trial to the possible maximum ($0 \leq P \leq 1$), where a trial is a step sequence from an initial state to a final one. P is plotted versus the number of trials and is averaged on the last n trials. The plotted values are averaged on 3 executions, starting with a different seed of the random number generator. Probability values based on the Boltzmann distribution, with decreasing exploration parameter (temperature) T_b, are used to solve both conflicts on effectors and competitions on the ML. Figure 1 shows three different (classes of) worlds, and the corresponding set of rules. When the agent enters a final state, it gets the associated reward, if any, and it is randomly reset to one initial state. d_X is the condition satisfied in any state labelled as 'X', e_a is the effector message that specifies the external action a, and $e_\#$ is a general condition that matches any effector message. In $W1(k,n,m)$, the states $D_0,\ldots,D_{m-1}$ ($1 \leq m < n$) are detected as 'A', so that the rule R_{A_0} can be applied in $m+1$ different situations. When a message e_{b_i} has been posted at the previous step, R_{A_0} leads to zero reward, otherwise it leads to reward r_1 ($r_1/2 > r_2$). In $W2(k)$, each one of the k rules R_{B_i} can be applied in k different situations, with different outcomes: when a state 'B' is detected, if the previous state was 'A_j', then R_{B_i} leads to the state 'C_h' with reward r_h, where $h = (k - j + i) \bmod k$, $0 \leq i, j < k$. In $W3$, when a state 'B' is detected, the most rewarding action depends on the previous state. While a ML of size 2 is sufficient to solve the tasks in $W1(k,n,m)$ and in $W2(k)$, a ML of size 3 is needed in $W3$. Figures. 2(a), 2(b), and 2(c) show the performance of the CS, using QCA and QCA-RR, in the worlds $W1(3,4,3)$, $W2(4)$ and $W3$, respectively. For each graph, the value of following parameters is specified: the length l of messages, the ML size, the discount factor γ, and the initial value of the exploration parameter T_b. The learning rates are $\eta = 0.01$ for the MLP and $\beta = 0.001$ for the self-organising network (SON). The QCA-RR, like the QCA, learns correct evaluations (fluctuations in the performance are due to stochastic competitions among messages). In addition, dimensionality reduction of the input space makes the task easier for the MLP, so that it needs a lower number of trials to get a large performance. This is also shown in Table 1, which compares the learning times of the QCA and the QCA-RR, measured in number of trials across the task. Learning time is defined as the time taken by the CS to reach and maintain a high performance level ($P > 0.95$). To highlight the improvement

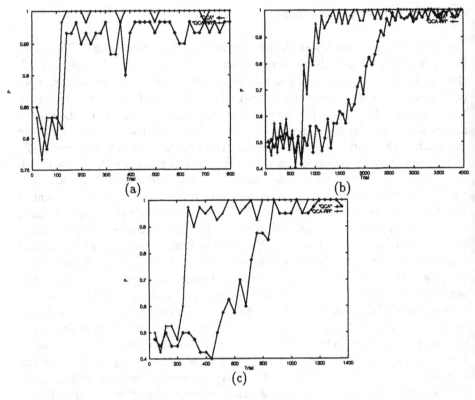

(a)

(b)

(c)

Fig. 2. QCA and QCA-RR performances in $W1(3,4,3)$ ($l = 14$, ML size=2, $\gamma = 0.6$, $T_b = 100$), in $W2(4)$ ($l = 14$, ML size=2, $\gamma = 0.7$ in QCA, $\gamma = 0.4$ in QCA-RR, $T_b = 150$), and in $W3$ ($l = 10$, ML size=3, $\gamma = 0.35$, $T_b = 100$).

in execution time, the table also reports the relative CPU time of the QCA-RR, measured with respect to the QCA, taken as 1. Relative CPU time is given both for learning time, which includes the time taken by the SON to converge, and for evaluation time. To measure the evaluation time, we stopped learning after the CS had reached a high stable performance. Then we measured the CPU time the CS takes to perform a fixed number of trials across the task. The improvement in evaluation time shows that the pre-processing overhead of the QCA-RR is fully balanced by the improvement obtained by reducing the size of the MLP. Table 1 also shows the data compression rate, i.e. the dimensionality reduction rate performed by the SON, and the number of weights of the neural networks for each analysed task.

5 Conclusions

We propose a solution to reduce the large computational cost of the QCA through feature extraction. The experimental results in tasks of increasing com-

Table 1. Comparison of QCA and QCA-RR in three worlds.

	$W1(3,4,3)$		$W2(4)$		$W3$	
	QCA	QCA-RR	QCA	QCA-RR	QCA	QCA-RR
Learning time (trials)	160	120	960	450	2640	840
Learning time (CPU)	1	.667	1	.607	1	.307
Evaluation time (CPU)	1	.500	1	.750	1	.555
# weights SON	–	756	–	880	–	840
# weights MLP	2025	381	1849	553	2025	463
# weights tot	2025	1137	1849	1433	2025	1303
Data compression	57%		52%		45%	

plexity show that the QCA-RR, like the QCA, correctly evaluates rules whose activation may have different outcomes depending on the context. In addition, feature extraction dramatically reduces the number of weights of the MLP, thereby reducing both learning time and evaluation time after learning. In particular, the pre-processing overhead of the QCA-RR is fully balanced by the reduction of the size of the MLP. Feature extraction also reduces the difficulty of the task to be learned by the MLP, so that a CS using the QCA-RR reaches a high stable performance in a lower number of trials with respect to a CS using the QCA.

References

1. L. B. Booker, D. E. Goldberg, and J. H. Holland. Classifier systems and genetic algorithms. In J. G. Carbonell, editor, *Machine learning: paradigms and methods.* MIT Press, 1990.
2. A. Giani, F. Baiardi, and A. Starita. Q-learning in evolutionary rule based systems. In *Proceedings of the 3rd Parallel Problem Solving from Nature/ International Conference on Evolutionary Computing*, LNCS 866. Springer-Verlag, 1994.
3. A. Giani, F. Baiardi, and A. Starita. Using Q-learning in classifier systems with internal state and rule sharing. Submitted for pubblication, 1997.
4. J. H. Holland. Escaping brittleness: The possibilities of general-purpose learning algorithm applied to parallel rule-based systems. In R. S. Michalski, J. G. Carbonell, and T. M. Mitchell, editors, *Machine learning: An artificial inteligence approach*, volume 2. Morgan Kaufmann, 1986.
5. M. Loéve. *Probability Theory.* Van Nostrand, New York, 1963.
6. D. E. Rumelhart, G. E. Hinton, and R. J. Williams. Learning internal representation by error propagation. In D. E. Rumelhart and J. McClelland, editors, *Parallel Distributed Processing*, volume 1. MIT Press, 1986.
7. T. D. Sanger. Optimal unsupervised learning in a single-layer linear feedforward neural network. *Neural Networks*, 12:459–473, 1989.
8. C. J. C. H. Watkins. *Learning with delayed rewards.* PhD thesis, University of Cambridge, England, 1989.
9. S. W. Wilson. ZCS: A zeroth order classifier system. *Evolutionary Computation*, 2(1):1–18, 1994.

Composing Functions to Speed up Reinforcement Learning in a Changing World

Chris Drummond

Department of Computer Science, University of Ottawa
Ottawa, Ontario, Canada, K1N 6N5
cdrummon@csi.uottawa.ca

Abstract. This paper presents a system that transfers the results of prior learning to speed up reinforcement learning in a changing world. Often, even when the change to the world is relatively small an extensive relearning effort is required. The new system exploits strong features in the multi-dimensional function produced by reinforcement learning. The features generate a partitioning of the state space. The partition is represented as a graph. This is used to index and compose functions stored in a case base to form a close approximation to the solution of the new task. The experimental results investigate one important example of a changing world, a new goal position. In this situation, there is close to a two orders of magnitude increase in learning rate over using a basic reinforcement learning algorithm.

1 Introduction

The aim of this work is to maximise the transfer of learning from previous tasks to the current one. At the base of the system is a standard reinforcement learning algorithm. One advantage of reinforcement learning is that it learns even when the information available is very limited. It requires only knowledge of its present state and infrequent numerical rewards to learn the actions necessary to bring a system to some desired goal state. As often occurs in achieving this level of generality, the learning rate is slow. It is important therefore to exploit the results of prior learning to speed up the process while maintaining the robustness of the general learning method.

This work uses syntactic methods of composition much like in symbolic planning, but the novelty arises in that the components of this composition are continuous functions. The functions needed for composition are either learnt individually or extracted from more complex functions associated with compound tasks. The efficacy of this approach is due to the composition occurring at a sufficiently abstract level where much of the uncertainty has been removed. Each function acts much like a funnel operator [1], so although individual actions may be highly uncertain the overall result is largely predictable.

The central intuition of this work is that there are strong features in the multi-dimensional function learnt using reinforcement learning. The important aspect of these features, for the purposes of this paper, is that they largely dictate the shape of this function. A popular technique in object recognition, the snake [12], is used to locate and characterise these features. The snake is then converted into a discrete graph. The graph and its constituent subgraphs act as an index into a case base of previously learnt functions. When a new task is being learnt planning occurs at the graphical level. The relevant cases are determined by graph matching and then a transform is applied to adapt the retrieved function to the new task. The new function is used to initialise the lower level learning process, which may further refine the function to better fit the new task. Thus the planning stage need not be exact. It need only be accurate enough to produce a significant speed-up in the learning process, averaged over many learning episodes.

The rest of the paper begins with section 2 giving a very high level discussion of the approach taken. The intent is to appeal to the intuitions of the reader, with section 3 giving a more in depth discussion of the techniques used. Section 4 presents experiments demonstrating a substantial increase in learning rate. Subsequent sections deal with limitations, future work and related research.

2 An Overview

The experimental testbed used is this paper is a simulated robot environment of different configurations of interconnected rooms. The robot must learn to navigate efficiently through these rooms to reach a specified goal from any start location. Figure 1 shows one example with the goal in the top right corner. The robot's actions are small steps in any of eight directions. Here the location, or state, is simply the robot's x and y coordinates. The thin lines of figure 1 are the walls of the rooms, the thick lines the boundary of the state space.

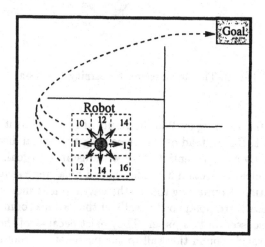

Fig. 1. Robot Navigating Through a Series of Rooms

372

If each action is independent, the task becomes one of learning the best action in any state. The best overall action would be one that takes the robot immediately to the goal. But this is only possible in states close to the goal. Suppose the robot is in a particular state and that the number of steps to goal from each of its neighbouring states is known, indicated by the numbers in figure 1. Then a one step look ahead procedure would try each step and select the one that reaches the neighbouring state with the shortest distance to goal. In figure 1 the robot would move to the state 10 steps from goal. If this process is repeated the robot will take the shortest path to goal. In practice we must, of course, learn such values. This can be done using some type of reinforcement learning [18, 14] which progressively improves estimates of the distance to goal from each state until they converge to the correct values. This paper is not primarily concerned with learning in a radically new environment, the system incorporates a reinforcement learning algorithm for that purpose. This paper rather addresses the transfer of learning between closely related tasks. The principal example for the purposes of this discussion and the experiments of section 4 is the transfer that occurs when the goal position is changed.

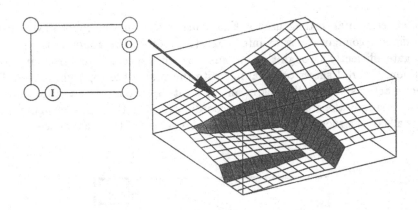

Fig. 2. The Reinforcement Learning Function

The function shown in figure 2 is the result of reinforcement learning on the problem of figure 1. But instead of it representing the actual distance to goal, it represents essentially an exponential decay with distance to goal. The reasons for this will be made clear in section 3.1. The shaded areas represent discontinuities in the learnt function. Comparing this to the environment shown in figure 1 it is apparent that these correspond to the walls of the various rooms. These are the *strong features* discussed in this paper. They exist because of the extra distance for the robot to travel around the wall to the inside of the room on the path to the goal. These features are visually readily apparent to a human, so it seems intuitive to use vision processing techniques to locate them.

An edge detection technique called a snake is used to locate these features. The snake produces a rectangle locating the boundary of each room. The doorways to the room occur where the differential of the function is at a local minimum. The direction of the differential with respect to that of the discontinuity determines if it is an entrance or an exit. From this information a plane graph, with an (x, y) coordinate for each node, is constructed. Figure 2 shows one such example, for the room at the top left corner of the state space. Nodes corresponding to the doorways are labelled "I" or "O" for in and out respectively.

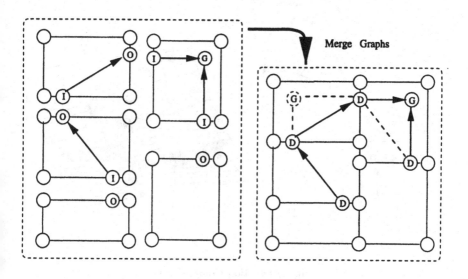

Fig. 3. Graphical Representation

The left hand side of figure 3 shows plane graphs for all the rooms. The node representing the goal is labelled "G". A directed edge is added from "In" to "Out" or "In" to "G" as appropriate. Associated with this edge is a number representing the distance between the nodes. This is determined from the value of the function at the points of the doorways. Each individual graph is then merged with its neighbour to produce a graph for the whole problem, the right hand side of figure 3. The doorway nodes have been relabelled to "D". The composite graph represents the whole function. Each individual subgraph represents a particular part of the function. This information is stored in a case base. Each subgraph is an index, the corresponding part of the function is the case.

Now suppose, the goal is moved from the top right corner to the top left. Reinforcement learning in its most basic form would be required to learn the new function from scratch. In this work if the goal is moved, once the new goal position is known the node representing the goal can be relocated. The new goal position is shown as the dashed circle in figure 3. The edges connecting the doorways and the goal are changed to account for the new goal position.

The dashed lines representing the new edges replace the solid lines in the same subgraph. To produce a new function, the idea is to regress backwards from the goal along these edges. For each edge, the small subgraph containing the edge is extracted. The extracted subgraph is used to index the case base of functions. The retrieved function is transformed and added to the appropriate region of the state space to form the new function.

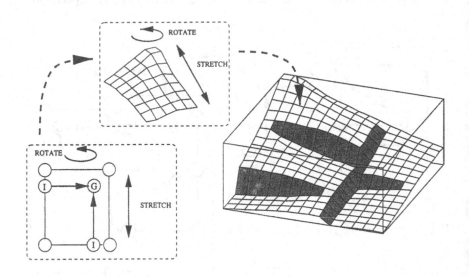

Fig. 4. Function Composition

In this example some of the existing subgraphs match the new configuration. The two that are changed are the one originally containing the goal and the one now containing the goal. It may be possible to exchange these two, using an appropriate transform. But if there are many more cases in the case base other graphs may better match the new task. In this example, the best match for the subgraph containing the new goal is the subgraph for the goal in the original problem. To fit this to the new task the plane graph is rotated and stretched slightly in the new x direction by changing the coordinates of its nodes, see figure 4. Then this same transformation is applied to the function. A case obtained when solving another task is used for the room containing the original goal. The other three rooms use the functions from the original problem, though their heights must be changed. This is simply a multiplication by a value representing the distance to goal from the "O" doorway. Because the matching of the subgraphs allows some error and asymmetric scaling may be used the resulting function may not be exact. But as the experiments will demonstrate, the function is often very close and further reinforcement learning will quickly correct any error.

3 Details of The Techniques Used

This section will discuss in more detail the techniques used. These include: reinforcement learning to produce the initial function, snakes to extract the features producing the graph and the transformation and composition of the subgraphs and their corresponding functions to fit the new task.

3.1 Reinforcement Learning

Reinforcement learning works by progressively improving estimates of the distance to goal from each state. This estimate is updated by the best local action, one moving the robot to the new state with the smallest estimated distance. Early in the learning process only states close to the goal are likely to have accurate estimates of true distance. Each time an action is taken, the estimate of the new state is used to update the estimate of the old state. Eventually this process will propagate back accurate estimates from the goal to all other states.

Rather than directly recording the distance to goal, this paper uses the more usual representation of reinforcement learning, the expected discounted reward for each state $E[\sum_{t=1}^{\infty} \gamma^t r_t]$. The influence of rewards, r_t, are reduced progressively the farther into the future they occur by using a γ less than one. In this work, the only reward is for reaching the goal. So the farther the state is from the goal the smaller the value. This forms a function over the state space, as shown in figure 2. The use of an expectation here allows the actions to be stochastic, so when the robot takes a step in a particular direction from a particular state, the state reached is not always the same.

To do the reinforcement learning this research uses the Q-learning algorithm [18]. This algorithm assumes the world is a discrete Markov process thus both states and actions actions are discrete. For each action a in each state s, Q-learning maintains a rolling average of the immediate reward r plus the maximum value of any action a' in the next state s', see equation 1. The function discussed in previous paragraphs and shown in the figures represents this maximum value. The action selected in each state is usually the one with the highest score. But to encourage exploration of the state space this paper uses an ϵ greedy policy [13] which chooses a random action a fraction ϵ of the time.

$$Q_{s,a}^{t+1} = (1 - \alpha)Q_{s,a}^t + \alpha(r + \gamma max_{a'}Q_{s',a'}^t)$$ (1)

Watkins and Dayan [18] proved that this will converge to the optimal value with certain constraints on the reward and the learning rate α. The optimal solution is to take the action with the greatest value in any state. Thus in this robot problem, a greedy algorithm will take the shortest path to the goal once learning is complete. The extension to continuous spaces can be done using function approximation. The simplest method, and the one used here, is to divide the state dimensions into intervals. Each resulting cell then represents the average Q-value of taking a particular action from somewhere within a region of the state space. In many applications this method is successful but there exists no general proof of its convergence.

3.2 Feature Extraction

Feature extraction uses a vision processing technique called a snake. The right hand side plot of figure 5 is the magnitude of the gradient vector of the function in figure 2. This is the absolute value of the largest gradient in any direction, it forms hills corresponding to the steep slopes of the function. To locate the features a curve is found that lies along the ridge of the hills. On the left hand side of figure 5 the dashed lines are contours for one of the rooms as indicated, the system adds a gradient around the rooms to represent the state space boundary.

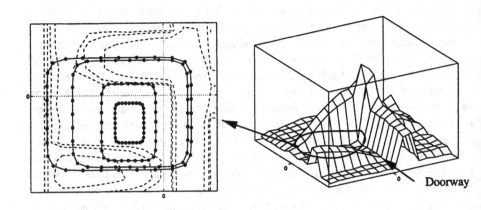

Fig. 5. Fitting the Snake

The dark lines in figure 5 are the snake. Starting from the initial position, the smallest rectangle, the snake is expanded by a ballooning force [2] until it reaches the base of the hills. Now to simplify the exposition, we can imagine that the snake consists of a number of individual hill climbers spread out along the line representing the snake, indicated by the small circles. But instead of being allowed to climb independently their movement relative to each other is constrained, in this instance to maintain a rectangular shape. This prevents individual points getting trapped in local maxima and collecting at the hills' apices. When the snake reaches the top of the ridge, the largest rectangle in figure 5, it will tend to oscillate around an equilibrium position. By limiting the step size the process can be brought into a stationary state. A more detailed mathematical treatment of this approach is given in [2]. Looking at the gradient plot, the doorways are regions with a small differential between the ridges. The position of the doorways can be determined from the magnitude of the gradient along the snake. Taking the corner points of the rectangle and the position of the doorways, a plane graph is produced. The rectangle delimits a region of the state space, and therefore of the learnt function. This becomes a case in the case base, the corresponding graph its index.

3.3 Transformation and Composition

This section discusses the transformation and composition of individual subgraphs and their corresponding functions to form a solution to the new task. The system finds all subgraphs in the case base isomorphic to a subgraph extracted using the snake and all possible isomorphic mappings between their nodes, using a labelling algorithm [6]. Associated with each node of a subgraph is an (x, y) coordinate. A similarity transform is applied to each of the isomorphic subgraphs to minimise the squared distance between the coordinates of the mapped nodes. The transform permits translation, rotation and independent scaling in each dimension. The subgraph selected is a compromise between the best fit and the least scaling, particularly asymmetric scaling. The corresponding function from the case base is then modified using the same transform.

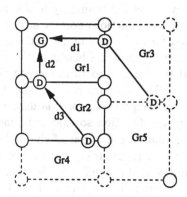

Fig. 6. Using Dijkstra's Algorithm

Function composition uses Dijkstra's algorithm [3] to traverse the edges between doorway nodes. Figure 6 shows the composite graph for the new task. To begin the process, the subgraph which contains the goal is selected and the best matching isomorphic subgraph is found. The edge lengths in the composite graph are then updated using the scaled length of the corresponding edge in the matching subgraph, d1 and d2 in figure 6. As d2 is less than d1, the next subgraph selected, Gr2, is the one sharing the doorway node with the edge of length d2. The best matching isomorphic subgraph is found and the edge length updated, d3. The shortest path is again determined, as d1 is less than d2 + d3 subgraph Gr3 is selected. The process is repeated until all subgraphs have been updated. At each stage when a subgraph is matched, the corresponding transformed function is added to the new function in the appropriate region.

Here there is one path to the goal from each room. If a doorway was added to the lower left corner of room 5, the graph on the left of figure 7 would result. There are now two possible paths, lengths d4 and d5. If the distance across room

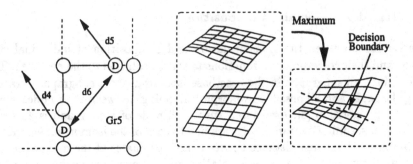

Fig. 7. Combining Two Functions

5, d6, is greater than the absolute difference between d4 and d5, the choice of path will be determined by a decision boundary in this room. This is produced by taking the maximum of two functions one for each path, see figure 7. This principle could be repeated for additional paths to the goal from this room.

When a scaling transform is used the height of the retrieved function must be adjusted. Imagine that to fit a new room the length of the function must be doubled in each dimension. The distance between the doorways will therefore double. As the function is an exponential in this distance the height must be squared, after normalising the function so that it is one at the out doorway. In general, the height is raised to the power of the scale factor. When scaling is symmetric the result is exact, assuming distance is a linear metric. With asymmetric scaling it is not. But if the difference is relatively small it is a useful approximation to use the average of the two scale factors. The height is also adjusted when the retrieved function is added to the function for the whole state space. We need to abut individual functions so that the result is smooth at the doorways. Starting with a normalised function, as it is an exponential the function is multiplied by the exponential of accumulated distance to the goal.

4   Experiments

The experiments investigate the time taken to correct the learnt function when the goal is relocated. The basic Q-learning algorithm is used ($\alpha = 0.1, \epsilon = 0.1, \gamma = 0.8, r = 1.0$ at the goal) with a discrete function approximator as discussed in section 3.1. There are 9 different room configurations, the number of rooms varying from 3 to 5, and four different goal positions. Each room has 1 or 2 doorways and 1 or 2 paths to the goal. The state space is a unit square. A step is ± 0.0625 plus a random value between ± 0.03125 along one or both dimensions, giving the eight possible actions . To initialise the case base, a function is learnt for each of these configurations with the goal always in the top right corner.

The basic Q-learning algorithm is then rerun on each room configuration with the goal in the top right corner. After 300,000 steps the goal position

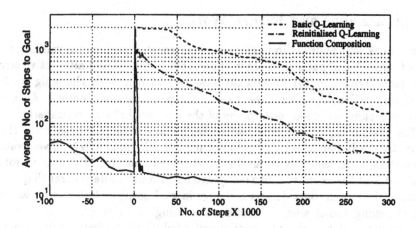

Fig. 8. Learning Curves: Steps to Goal

is moved to one of the three remaining corners of the state space. Learning continues for a further 300,000 steps. At fixed intervals, learning is stopped and the average number of steps to reach the goal is recorded. The average is across 64 different start positions distributed uniformly throughout the state space. The maximum number of steps for each start location is limited to 2000. The curves in figure 8 are the average for three new goal positions for each of the nine room configurations. Zero on the x axis is where the goal is moved.

The basic Q-learning algorithm, the top curve of figure 8, performs poorly. When the goal is moved the existing function pushes the robot towards the old goal position. This is particularly apparent when the room configuration is the one of section 2. If the new goal is at lower left hand corner of the state space, the minimum of the existing function, the learning algorithm has to "flatten" it completely before a new one can be learnt. Here the limit of 2000 steps to the goal was exceeded for the majority of start positions even after 300,000 steps.

A variant of the basic algorithm reinitialises the function to 0.75 everywhere on detecting the relocation of the goal, it being no longer at the maximum of the existing function. This reinitialised Q-learning, the middle curve, performed better and all the start locations took under 2000 steps to the goal after 200,000 steps. Room configurations with a single path to goal, such as the example of section 2, still took the most time. After the function is reinitialised the likelihood of random actions successfully navigating the rooms to the goal is small and this seriously slows the learning process.

The function composition system, the lowest curve, performed by far the best. It first detects when the goal is moved, locates its new position and composes the new function. The number of paths has no impact on learning. It reached the same average steps to goal as the reinitialised Q-learning at about 5000 steps and as the basic Q-learning at about 3000 steps. This is an increase in learning rate of between times 60 and 100.

5 Limitations and Future Work

Future work will address limitations in the present experimental validation. A more thorough comparison to other approaches is needed. An alternative straw man such Dyna-Q+ [14], specifically designed to deal with changing worlds, would unquestionably reduce the speed-up experimentally obtained. Also, experiments using a random positioning of the goal would be more realistic.

The system exploits symmetries in the domain. What happens when these symmetries only partially hold or do not hold at all remains to be investigated. The system at present only works for rectangular rooms, but the snake is not so restricted and this work should readily extend to much more general shapes. In addition, the system only detects a change in goal position. Other changes such as the opening and closing of doors are also being investigated.

Previous work by this author [4] investigated using the features discussed in this paper to recognise if a similar task had been solved previously. Functions stored in a case base were then used to initialise and thus speed up the initial learning process. These two ideas will combined in future work. When a new task is being learnt, the system will progressively build up a solution by function composition, as different features become apparent.

6 Related Work

The most strongly related work is that investigating macro actions in reinforcement learning. Precup and Sutton [9] propose a possible semantics for macro actions within the framework of normal reinforcement learning. Singh [11] uses policies learnt to solve low level problems as primitives for reinforcement learning at a higher level. The work presented here gives one way macro actions can be extracted from the systems interaction with its environment without external help. Thrun's research [16] identifies macro actions used in multiple tasks. But unlike the research presented here, no mapping of such actions to new tasks is proposed. Mahadevan and Connell [7] use reinforcement learning in behaviour based robot control. Although in a much simpler domain, the work presented here does not require rewards for individual macro actions. Rather the macro actions are identified and extracted from the solution of a compound task.

Previous work that combines instance based or case based learning with reinforcement learning has principally addressed the economical representation of the state space. Peng [8] and Tadepalli [15] use learnt instances combined with linear regression over a set of neighbouring points. Sheppard and Salzberg [10] also use learnt instances but they are carefully selected by a genetic algorithm. Unlike this other research, in the work presented here the case is not an example of the value function during learning. Rather it is a function representing a macro action and the principle should be complementary to these other approaches.

This work is also related to case based planning [5, 17], firstly through the general connection of reinforcement learning and planning. But it is analogous in other ways. When there is a small change in the world, a composite plan is modified by using sub-plans, extracted from other composite plans.

7 Conclusions

This paper described a system that transfers prior learning to significantly speed up reinforcement learning in a changing world. Features extracted from the learnt function are use to index and compose functions from a case base to produce a close approximation to the solution of a new task. The experiments demonstrated that the system can rapidly respond to the situation when the goal is relocated.

Acknowledgements The author would like to thank Rob Holte for all his help. This work was supported by NSERC and Ontario Government scholarships.

References

1. A. D. Christiansen. Learning to predict in uncertain continuous tasks. *ICML* pp 72–81, 1992.
2. L. D. Cohen and Isaac Cohen. Finite element methods for active contour models and balloons for 2-d and 3-d images. *PAMI* 15(11):1131–1147, Nov 1993.
3. E. W. Dijkstra. A note on two problems in connection with graphs. *Numer. Math.* 1:269–271, 1959.
4. C. Drummond. Using a case-base of surfaces to speed-up reinforcement learning. *LNAI* volume 1266, pp 435–444, 1997.
5. K. J. Hammond. Case-based planning: A framework for planning from experience. *Journal of Cognitive Science* 14(3):85–443, July 1990.
6. A. MacDonald. Graphs: Notes on symetries, imbeddings, decompositions. Elec. Eng. Dept. TR-92-10-AJM, Brunel University, Uxbridge, Middx, U. K., Oct 1992.
7. S. Mahadevan and J. Connell. Automatic programming of behavior-based robots using reinforcement learning. *Artificial Intelligence* 55:311–365, 1992.
8. J. Peng. Efficient memory-based dynamic programming. *ICML* pp 438–439 1995.
9. D. Precup and R. S. Sutton. Multi-time models for temporally abstract planning. *NIPS* 10 1997.
10. J. W. Sheppard and S. L. Salzberg. A teaching strategy for memory-based control. *Artificial Intelligence Review* 11:343–370, 1997.
11. S. P. Singh. Reinforcement learning with a hierarchy of abstract models. *AAAI* pp 202–207, 1992.
12. P. Suetens, P. Fua, and A. Hanson. Computational strategies for object recognition. *Computing surveys* 4(1):5–61, 1992.
13. R. S. Sutton. Generalization in reinforcement learning: Successful examples using sparse coarse coding. *NIPS* 8 pp 1038–1044, 1996.
14. R. S. Sutton. Integrated architectures for learning, planning, and reacting based on approximating dynamic programming. *ICML* pp 216–224, 1990.
15. P. Tadepalli and D. Ok. Scaling up average reward reinforcement learning by approximating learning by approximating. *ICML* pp 471–479, 1996.
16. S. Thrun and A. Schwartz. Finding structure in reinforcement learning. *NIPS* 7 pp 385–392 1994.
17. M. M. Veloso and J. G. Carbonell. Derivational analogy in prodigy: Automating case acquisition, storage and utilization. *Machine Learning*, 10(3):249–278, 1993.
18. C. J. C. H. Watkins and P. Dayan. Technical note: Q-learning. *Machine Learning*, 8(3-4):279–292, May 1992.

Theoretical Results on Reinforcement Learning with Temporally Abstract Options

Doina Precup[1], Richard S. Sutton[1], and Satinder Singh[2]

[1] Department of Computer Science
University of Massachusetts
Amherst, MA 01003-4610
http://www.cs.umass.edu/{~dprecup|~rich}

[2] Department of Computer Science
University of Colorado
Boulder, CO 80309-0430
http://www.cs.colorado.edu/~baveja

Abstract. We present new theoretical results on planning within the framework of temporally abstract reinforcement learning (Precup & Sutton, 1997; Sutton, 1995). Temporal abstraction is a key step in any decision making system that involves planning and prediction. In temporally abstract reinforcement learning, the agent is allowed to choose among "options", whole courses of action that may be temporally extended, stochastic, and contingent on previous events. Examples of options include closed-loop policies such as picking up an object, as well as primitive actions such as joint torques. Knowledge about the consequences of options is represented by special structures called multi-time models. In this paper we focus on the theory of planning with multi-time models. We define new Bellman equations that are satisfied for sets of multi-time models. As a consequence, multi-time models can be used interchangeably with models of primitive actions in a variety of well-known planning methods including value iteration, policy improvement and policy iteration.

1 Introduction

Model-based reinforcement learning offers a possible solution to the problem of integrating planning with real-time learning and decision-making [20]. However, conventional model-based reinforcement learning uses one-step models [11, 13, 18], that cannot represent common-sense, higher-level actions, such as picking an object or traveling to a specified location.

Several researchers have proposed extending reinforcement learning to a higher level by treating entire closed-loop policies as actions [3–6, 9, 10, 12, 17]. In order to use such actions in planning, an agent needs the ability to create and handle models at a variety of different, interrelated levels of temporal abstraction. Sutton [19] introduced an approach to modeling at different time scales, based on prior work by Singh [17], Dayan [2] and by Sutton and Pinette [21]. This approach enables models of the environment at different temporal scales to be intermixed, producing temporally abstract models. In previous work [14], we generalized this approach from the prediction case, to the full control case. In this paper, we summarize the framework of temporally abstract reinforcement learning and present new theoretical results on planning with general *options* and temporally abstract models of options.

Options are similar to AI's classical "macro operators" [7, 8, 16], in that they can take control for some period of time, determining the actions during that time, and in that one can choose among options much as one originally chose among primitive actions. However, classical macro operators are only a fixed sequence of actions, whereas options incorporate a general (possibly non-Markov) closed-loop policy and completion criterion. These generalizations are required when the environment is stochastic and uncertain with general goals, as in reinforcement learning and Markov decision processes (MDP).

The predictive knowledge needed in order to plan using options can be represented through *multi-time models* [14]. Such models summarize several time scales and have the ability to predict events that can happen at various unknown moments. In this paper, we focus on the theoretical properties of multi-time models. We show formally that such models can be used interchangeably with models of primitive actions in a variety of well-known dynamic programming methods, while preserving the same guarantees of convergence to correct solutions. The benefit of using such temporally extended models is a significant improvement in the convergence rates of these algorithms.

2 Reinforcement Learning (MDP) Framework

First we briefly summarize the mathematical framework of the reinforcement learning problem that we use in the paper. In this framework, a learning *agent* interacts with an *environment* at some discrete, lowest-level time scale $t = 0, 1, 2, \ldots$. At each time step, the agent perceives the state of the environment, s_t, and on that basis chooses a primitive action, a_t. In response to each primitive action, a_t, the environment produces one step later a numerical reward, r_{t+1}, and a next state, s_{t+1}.

The agent's objective is to learn a policy π, which is a mapping from states to probabilities of taking each action, that maximizes the expected discounted future reward from each state s:

$$V^\pi(s) = E\left\{r_1 + \gamma r_2 + \gamma^2 r_3 + \cdots \mid s_0 = s, \pi\right\},$$

where $\gamma \in [0, 1)$ is a *discount-rate* parameter. The quantity $V^\pi(s)$ is called the *value* of state s under policy π, and V^π is called the value function for policy π. The optimal value of a state is denoted

$$V^*(s) = \max_\pi V^\pi(s)$$

The environment is henceforth assumed to be a stationary, finite Markov decision process. We assume that the states are discrete and form a finite set, $s_t \in \{1, 2, \ldots, n\}$. The latter assumption is a temporary theoretical convenience; it is not a limitation of the ideas we present.

3 Options

In order to achieve faster planning, the agent should be able to predict what happens if it follows a certain course of action over a period of time. By a "course of action" we mean any way of behaving, i.e. any way of mapping representations of states to primitive actions. An option is a way of choosing actions that is initiated, takes control for some period of time, and then eventually ends. Options are defined by three elements:

- the set of states $\mathcal{I}$ in which the option applies
- a decision rule μ which specifies what actions are executed by the option
- a completion function β which specifies the probability of completing the option on every time step.

μ is of a slightly more general form than the policies used in conventional reinforcement learning. The first generalization is based on the observation that primitive actions qualify as options: they are initiated in a state, take control for a while (one time step), and then end. Therefore, we allow μ to choose among options, rather than only among primitive actions.

The conventional reinforcement learning setting also requires that a policy's decision probabilities at time t should be a function only of the current state s_t. This type of policy is called *Markov*. For the policy of a option, μ, we relax this assumption, and we allow the probabilities of selecting a sub-option to depend on all the states and actions from time t_0, when the option began executing, up through the current time, t. We call policies of this more general class *semi-Markov*.

The completion function β can also be semi-Markov. This property enables us to describe various kinds of completion. Perhaps the simplest case is that of a option that completes after some fixed number of time steps (e.g. after 1 step, as in the case of primitive actions, or after n steps, as in the case of a classical macro operator consisting of a sequence of n actions). A slightly more general case is that in which the option completes during a certain time period, e.g. 10 to 15 time steps later. In this case, the completion function β should specify the probability of completion for each of these time steps. The case which is probably the most useful in practice is the completion of a option with the occurrence of a critical state, often a state that we think of as a subgoal. For instance, the option `pick-up-the-object` could complete when the object is in the hand. This event occurs at a very specific moment in time, but this moment is indefinite, not known in advance. In this case, the completion function depends on the state history of the system, rather than explicitly on time. Lastly, if β is always 0, the option does not complete. This is the case of usual policies used in reinforcement learning.

Options are typically executed in a *call-and-return* fashion. Each option o can be viewed as a "subroutine" which calls sub-options, according to its internal decision rule. When a sub-option o' is selected, it takes control of the action choices until it completes. Upon completion, o' transfers the control back to o. o also inherits the current time t' and the current state $s_{t'}$, and has to decide if it should terminate or pick a new sub-option.

Two options, a and b, can be *composed* to yield a new option, denoted ab, that first follows a until it terminates and then follows b until it terminates, also terminating the composed option ab.

4 Models of Options

Planning in reinforcement learning refers to the use of models of the effects of actions to compute value functions, particularly V^*. We use the term *model* for any structure that generates predictions based on the representation of the state of the system and on the course of action that the system is following.

In order to plan at the level of options, we need to have a knowledge representation form that predicts their consequences. The *multi-time model* of a option characterizes the states that result upon the option's completion and the truncated return received along the way when the option is executed in various states [14]. Let p be an n-vector and r a scalar. The pair p, r is an *accurate prediction* for the execution of semi-Markov option o in state s if and only if

$$r = E\left\{r_{t+1} + \gamma r_{t+2} + \cdots + \gamma^{T-1} r_T \mid s_t = s, o\right\} \tag{1}$$

and

$$\mathbf{p} = E\left\{\gamma^T \mathbf{s}_T \mid s_t = s, o\right\}, \tag{2}$$

where T is the random variable denoting the time at which o terminates when executed in $s_t = s$, and $\mathbf{s}_T$ denotes the unit basis n-vector corresponding to s_T. p is called the *state prediction vector* and o is called the *reward prediction* for state s and option o.

We will use the notation "·", as in $\mathbf{x} \cdot \mathbf{y}$, to represents the inner or dot product between vectors. We will refer to the i-th element of a vector $\mathbf{x}$ as $x(i)$. The transpose of a vector $\mathbf{x}$ will be denoted by $\mathbf{x}^T$.

The predictions corresponding to the states $s \notin \mathcal{I}$ are always 0. If the option never terminates, the reward prediction r is equal to the value function of the internal policy of the option, and the elements of p are all 0.

The state prediction vectors for the same option in all the states are often grouped as the rows of an $n \times n$ *state prediction matrix*, $\mathbf{P}$, and the reward predictions are often grouped as the components of an n-component *reward prediction vector*, $\mathbf{r}$. $\mathbf{r}, \mathbf{P}$ form the *accurate model* of the option.

A key theoretical result refers to the way in which the model of a composed option can be obtained from the models of its components.

Theorem 1 (Composition or Sequencing). *Given an accurate prediction $r_a, \mathbf{p}_a$ for some option a applied in state s and an accurate model $\mathbf{r}_b, \mathbf{P}_b$ for some option b, the prediction:*

$$g = r_a + \mathbf{p}_a \cdot \mathbf{r}_b \quad \text{and} \quad \mathbf{p} = \mathbf{p}_a{}^T \mathbf{P}_b \tag{3}$$

is an accurate prediction for the composed option ab when it is executed in s.

Proof. Let k be the random variable denoting the time at which a completes, and T be the random variable denoting the time at which ab completes. Then we have:

$$r = E\{r_{t+1} + \cdots + \gamma^{T-1} r_T \mid s_t = s, ab\}$$

$$= E\{r_{t+1} + \cdots + \gamma^{k-1} r_k \mid s_t = s, a\} + E\{\gamma^k r_{k+1} + \cdots + \gamma^{T-1} r_T \mid s_t = s, ab\}$$

$$= r_a + \sum_{i=1}^{\infty} P\{k = i \mid s_t = s, a\} \gamma^i \sum_{s'} P\{s_k = s' \mid s_t = s, k = i\}$$

$$E\{r_{k+1} + \cdots + \gamma^{T-k-1}r_T \,|\, s_k = s', b\}$$

$$= r_a + \sum_{s'}\sum_{i=1}^{\infty} P\{k = i \mid s_t = s, a\}\gamma^i P\{s_k = s' \mid s_t = s, k = i\}r_b(s')$$

$$= r_a + \sum_{s'} p_a(s')r_b(s')$$

$$= r_a + \mathbf{p}_a \cdot \mathbf{r}_b$$

The equation for p follows similarly. □

A simple combination of models can also be used to predict the effect of probabilistic choice among options:

Theorem 2 (Averaging or Choice). *Let* r_i, p_i *be a set of accurate predictions for the options* o_i *executed in state* s, *and let* $w_i > 0$ *be a set of numbers such that* $\sum_i w_i = 1$. *Then the prediction defined by:*

$$r = \sum_i w_i r_i \quad \text{and} \quad \mathbf{p} = \sum_i w_i \mathbf{p}_i \qquad (4)$$

is accurate for the option o, *which chooses in state* s *among sub-options* o_i *with probabilities* w_i *and then follows the chosen* o_i *until completion.*

Proof. Based on the definition of o, $r = \sum_i w_i E\{r_{t+1} + \cdots + \gamma^{T-1}r_T \,|\, s_t = s, o_i\} = \sum_i w_i r_i$ The equation for p follows similarly. □

These results represent the basis for developing the theory of planning at the level of options. The options map the low-level MDP in a higher-level *semi-Markov decision process (SMDP)* [15], which we can solve using dynamic programming methods. We will now go into the details of this mapping.

5 Planning with Models of Options

In this section, we extend the theoretical results of dynamic programming for the case in which the agent is allowed to use an arbitrary set of options, $\mathcal{O}$. If $\mathcal{O}$ is exactly the set of primitive actions, then our results degenerate to the conventional case. We assume, for the sake of simplicity, that for any state s, the set of options that apply in s, denoted $\mathcal{O}_s$, is always non-empty. However, the theory that we present extends, with some additional complexity, to the case in which no options apply in certain states.

Given a set of options $\mathcal{O}$, we define a policy π to be a mapping that, for any state s specifies the probability of taking each option from $\mathcal{O}_s$. The value of π is defined similarly to the conventional case, as the expected discounted reward if the policy is applied starting in s:

$$V^\pi(s) = E\left\{r_{t+1} + \gamma r_{t+2} + \cdots \,\middle|\, s_t = s, \pi\right\}. \qquad (5)$$

The *optimal value function, given the set* $\mathcal{O}$, can be defined as

$$V_{\mathcal{O}}^*(s) = \sup_{\pi \in \Pi_{\mathcal{O}}} V^\pi(s), \qquad (6)$$

for all s, where $\Pi_\mathcal{O}$ is the set of policies that can be defined using the options from $\mathcal{O}$. The value functions are sometimes represented as n-vectors, $\mathbf{V}^\pi$ and $\mathbf{V}^*_\mathcal{O}$ with each component representing the value of a different state.

The value function of any Markov policy $\pi \in \Pi_\mathcal{O}$ satisfies the Bellman evaluation equations:

$$V^\pi(s) = \sum_{o\in\mathcal{O}_s} \pi(s,o)(r_o + \mathbf{p}_o \cdot \mathbf{V}^\pi), \qquad \text{for all } s \in S, \tag{7}$$

where $\pi(s,o)$ is the probability of choosing option o in state s when acting according to π and $r_o, \mathbf{p}_o$ is the accurate prediction for sub-option o in state s. We will show that, similarly to the conventional case, $\mathbf{V}^\pi$ is the unique solution to this system of equations.

Similarly, the optimal value function given a set of options $\mathcal{O}$ satisfies the Bellman optimality equations:

$$V^*_\mathcal{O}(s) = \max_{o\in\mathcal{O}_s}(r_o + \mathbf{p}_o \cdot \mathbf{V}^*_\mathcal{O}), \qquad \text{for all } s \in S, \tag{8}$$

As in the conventional case, $\mathbf{V}^*_\mathcal{O}$ is the unique solution of this set of equations, and there exists at least one deterministic Markov policy $\pi^*_\mathcal{O} \in \Pi_\mathcal{O}$ that is optimal, i.e., for which $\mathbf{V}^{\pi^*_\mathcal{O}} = \mathbf{V}^*_\mathcal{O}$

We will now present in detail the proofs leading to these theoretical results. The practical consequence is that all the usual update rules used in reinforcement learning can be used to compute $\mathbf{V}^\pi$ and $\mathbf{V}^*_\mathcal{O}$ when the agent makes choices among options. We focus first on the Bellman policy evaluation equations.

Theorem 3 (Value Functions for Composed Policies). *Let π be a policy that, when starting in state s, follows option o and, when the option completes, follows policy π'. Then*

$$V^\pi(s) = r_o + \mathbf{p}_o \cdot \mathbf{V}^{\pi'}. \tag{9}$$

Proof. According to the theorem statement, $\pi = o\pi'$. The conclusion follows immediately from the composition theorem. $\square$

Theorem 4 (Bellman Policy Evaluation Equation). *The value function of any Markov policy satisfies the Bellman policy evaluation equations (7).*

Proof. Using the averaging rule and the fact that π is Markov, we have:

$$V^\pi(s) = \sum_{o\in\mathcal{O}_s} \pi(s,o)V^{o\pi}(s)$$

We can expand $v^{o\pi}(s)$ using (9), to obtain the desired result (7). $\square$

We now prove that the Bellman evaluation equations have a unique solution, and that this solution can be computed using the well-known algorithm of *policy evaluation with successive approximations*: start with arbitrary initial values $V_0(s)$ for all states and iterate for all s: $V_{k+1}(s) \leftarrow r_{\pi(s)} + \mathbf{p}_{\pi(s)} \cdot \mathbf{V}_k$, where $\pi(s)$ is the option suggested by π in state s.

Proof. For any option o and any starting state s, there exists a constant ϵ_o such that $\| \mathbf{p}_o \|_1 \leq \epsilon_o < 1$, where $\| \cdot \|_1$ denotes the $l_1 - norm$ of a vector: $\| \mathbf{x} \|_1 = \sum_i x(i)$. The value of ϵ_o depends on γ and on the expected duration of o when started in s. For any option o, we show that the operator $T_o(\mathbf{V}) = r_o + \mathbf{p}_o \cdot \mathbf{V}$ is a contraction with constant ϵ_o. For arbitrary vectors $\mathbf{V}$ and $\mathbf{V}'$, we have:

$$T_o(\mathbf{V}) - T_o(\mathbf{V}') = \sum_{s'} p_o(s')(V(s') - V'(s')) \leq \sum_{s'} p_o(s') \| \mathbf{V} - \mathbf{V}' \|_\infty,$$

where $\| \cdot \|_\infty$ denotes the $l_\infty - norm$ of a vector: $\| \mathbf{x} \|_\infty = \max_i x(i)$. Therefore, $T_o(\mathbf{V}) - T_o(\mathbf{V}') \leq \epsilon_o \| \mathbf{V} - \mathbf{V}' \|_\infty$ The result follows from the contraction mapping theorem [1]. $\quad\square$

So far we have established that the value functions of Markov option policies have similar properties with the Markov policies that use only primitive actions. Now we establish similar results for the optimal value function that can be obtained when planning with a set of options.

Theorem 5 (Bellman Optimality Equation). *For any set of options $\mathcal{O}$, the optimal value function $\mathbf{V}_{\mathcal{O}}^*$ satisfies the Bellman optimality equations (8).*

Proof. Let π be an arbitrary policy which, at time step 0, in state $s_0 = s$, chooses among the available options with probabilities w_o.

$$V^\pi(s) = \sum_{o \in \mathcal{O}_s} w_o(r_o + \sum_{s'} p_o(s') W_\pi(s'))$$

where $W_\pi(s')$ is the expected discounted return from state s' on. Since $p_o(s') \geq 0, \forall s'$, using the definition of $V_{\mathcal{O}}^*(s')$, we have:

$$V^\pi(s) \leq \sum_{o \in \mathcal{O}_s} w_o(r_o + \mathbf{p}_o \cdot \mathbf{V}_{\mathcal{O}}^*) \leq \max_{o \in \mathcal{O}_s}(r_o + \mathbf{p}_o \cdot \mathbf{V}_{\mathcal{O}}^*)$$

Since π is arbitrary, due to the definition of $V_{\mathcal{O}}^*(s)$,

$$V_{\mathcal{O}}^*(s) \leq \max_{o \in \mathcal{O}_s}(r_o + \mathbf{p}_o \cdot \mathbf{V}_{\mathcal{O}}^*).$$

On the other hand, let $o_0 = \arg\max_{o \in \mathcal{O}_s}(r_o + \mathbf{p}_o \cdot \mathbf{V}_{\mathcal{O}}^*)$. Let π be the policy that chooses o_0 at time step 0 and, after o_0 ends, in state s', switches to a policy $\pi_{s'}$ such that $v^{\pi_{s'}}(s') \geq V_{\mathcal{O}}^*(s') - \epsilon$. $\pi_{s'}$ exists because of the way in which $V_{\mathcal{O}}^*$ was defined. From (9), we have:

$$V^\pi(s) = r_{o_0} + \sum_{s'} p_{o_0}(s') v^{\pi_{s'}}(s') \geq r_{o_0} + \sum_{s'} p_{o_0}(s')(V_{\mathcal{O}}^*(s') - \epsilon) \geq r_{o_0} + \mathbf{p}_{o_0} \cdot \mathbf{V}_{\mathcal{O}}^* - \epsilon$$

Since $V_{\mathcal{O}}^*(s) \geq v^\pi(s)$, we have:

$$V_{\mathcal{O}}^*(s) \geq \max_{o \in \mathcal{O}_s}(r_o + \mathbf{p}_o \cdot \mathbf{V}_{\mathcal{O}}^*) - \epsilon$$

Since ϵ is arbitrary, it follows that

$$V_{\mathcal{O}}^*(s) = \max_{o \in \mathcal{O}_s}(r_o + \mathbf{p}_o \cdot \mathbf{V}_{\mathcal{O}}^*) \quad\square$$

The following step is to show that the solution of the Bellman optimality equations (8) is bounded and unique, and that it can be computed through a *value iteration algorithm*: start with arbitrary initial values $V_0(s)$ and iterate the update: $V_{k+1}(s) \leftarrow \max_{o \in O_s} r_o + p_o \cdot V_k, \forall s$.

Proof. For any set of actions O let us consider the operator T_O which, in any state s, performs the following transformation: $T_{O_s}(V) = \max_{o \in O_s} (r_o + p_o \cdot V)$ Let V and V' be two arbitrary vectors. Then we have:

$$T_{O_s}(V) = \max_{o \in O_s} (r_o + p_o(V' + V - V')) = \max_{o \in O_s} (T_o(V') + p_o \cdot (V - V'))$$

$$\leq T_{O_s}(V') + \max_{o \in O_s} \sum_{s'} p_o(s') \| V - V' \|_\infty = T_{O_s}(V') + \epsilon_{O_s} \| V - V' \|_\infty,$$

where $\epsilon_{O_s} = \max_{o \in O_s} \epsilon_o$. Similarly,

$$T_{O_s}(V') \leq T_{O_s}(V) + \epsilon_{O_s} \| V - V' \|_\infty$$

Therefore, $\forall s$,

$$\| T_O(V) - T_O(V') \|_\infty \leq \epsilon_O \| V - V' \|_\infty,$$

where $\epsilon_O = \max_s \epsilon_{O_s}$. Therefore T_O is a contraction with constant ϵ_O. The results follow from the contraction mapping theorem [1].

So far we have shown that the optimal value function V_O^* is the unique bounded solution of the Bellman optimality equations. Now we will show that this value function can be achieved by a deterministic Markov policy:

Theorem 6 (Value Achievement). *The policy* π_O^* *defined as*

$$\pi_O^*(s) = \arg\max_{o \in O_s} r_o + p_o \cdot V_O^*$$

achieves V_O^*

Proof. For any arbitrary state s, we have:

$$0 \leq V_O^*(s) - V^{\pi_O^*}(s) = p_{\pi_O^*(s)} \cdot (V_O^* - V^{\pi_O^*}) \leq \epsilon_{O_s} \| V_O^* - V^{\pi_O^*} \|_\infty.$$

Since $\epsilon_O < 1$, $V_O^*(s) = V^{\pi_O^*}(s)$. □

In order to find the optimal policy given a set of options, one can simply compute V_O^* and then use it to pick actions greedily. Another popular planning method for computing optimal policies is *policy iteration*, which alternates steps of policy evaluation and policy improvement. We have already investigated policy evaluation, so we turn now to policy improvement:

Theorem 7 (Policy Improvement Theorem). *For any Markov policy* π *defined using options from a set* O, *let* π' *be a new policy which, for some state* s, *chooses greedily among the available options, and then follows* π

$$\pi'(s) = \arg\max_{o \in O_s} r_o + p_o \cdot V^\pi,$$

Then $V^{\pi'}(s) \geq V^\pi(s)$.

Proof. Let o_0 be the option chosen by π in state s. Then, from (7),

$$V^\pi(s) = r_{o_0} + \mathbf{p}_{o_0} \cdot \mathbf{V}^\pi \leq \max_{o \in \mathcal{O}_s} r_o + \mathbf{p}_o \cdot \mathbf{V}^\pi = V^{\pi'}(s). \square$$

Given a set of options $\mathcal{O}$ such that $\mathcal{O}_s$ is finite for all s, the policy iteration algorithm, which interleaves policy evaluation and policy improvement, converges to $\pi^*_\mathcal{O}$ in a finite number of steps.

The final result relates the models of options to the optimal value function of the environment, V^*.

Theorem 8. *If $r_o, \mathbf{p}_o$ is an accurate prediction for some option b in state s, then*

$$r_o + \mathbf{p}_o \cdot \mathbf{V}^* \leq V^*(s)$$

We say that accurate models are non-overpromising, *i.e. they never promise more that the agent can actually achieve.*

Proof. Assume that the agent can use o and all the primitive actions in the environment. Let $\pi = o\pi^*$, where π^* is the optimal policy of the environment. Then we have:

$$V^*(s) \geq V^\pi(s) = r_o + \mathbf{p}_o \cdot \mathbf{V}^* \quad \square$$

6 Illustrations

The theoretical results presented so far show that accurate models of options can be used in all the planning algorithms typically employed for solving MDPs, with the same guarantees of convergence to correct plans as in the case of primitive actions. We will now illustrate the speedup that can be obtained when using these methods in two simple gridworld learning tasks.

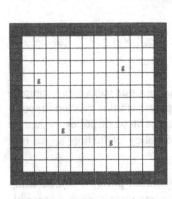 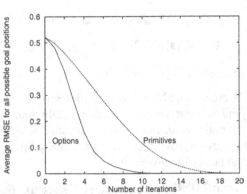

Fig. 1. Empty gridworld task. Options allow the error in the value function estimation to decrease more quickly

The first task is depicted on the left panel of figure 1. The cells of the grid correspond to the states of the environment. From any state the agent can perform one of four primitive actions, up, down, left or right. With probability 2/3, the actions cause the agent to move one cell in the corresponding direction (unless this would take the agent into a wall, in which case it stays in the same state). With probability 1/3, the agent moves instead in one of the other three directions (unless this takes it into a wall, of course). There is no penalty for bumping into walls. In addition to these primitive actions, the agent can use four additional higher-level options, to travel to each of the marked locations. These locations have been chosen randomly inside the environment. Accurate models for all the options are also available. Both the options and their models have been learned during a prior random walk in the environment, using Q-learning [22] and the β-model learning algorithm [19].

The agent is repeatedly given new goal positions and it needs to compute optimal paths to these positions as quickly as possible. In this experiment, we considered all possible goal positions. In each case, the value of the goal state is 1, there are no rewards along the way, and the discounting factor is $\gamma = 0.9$. We performed planning according to the standard value iteration method, where the starting values are $V_0(s) = 0$ for all the states except the goal state, for which $V_0(goal) = 1$. In the first experiment, the agent was only allowed to use primitive actions, while in the second case, it used both the primitive actions and the higher-level options.

The right panel in figure 1 shows the average root mean squared error in the estimate of the optimal value function over the whole environment. The average is computed over all possible positions of the goal state. The use of higher-level options introduces a significant speedup in convergence, even though the options have been chosen arbitrarily. Note that an iteration using all the options is slightly more expensive than an iteration using only primitive actions. This aspect can be improved by using more sophisticated methods of ordering the options before doing the update. However, such methods are beyond the scope of this paper.

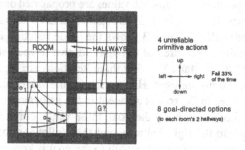

Fig. 2. Example Task. The natural options are to move from room to room

In order to analyze in more detail the effect of options, let us consider a second environment. In this case, the gridworld has four "rooms". The basic dynamics of the environment are the same as in the previous case. For each state in a room, two higher-level options are available, which can take the agent to each of the hallways adjacent to the room. Each of these options has two outcome states: the target hallway, which corresponds to a successful outcome, and the state adjacent to the other hallway, which corresponds to failure (the agent has wandered out of the room). The completion function β is therefore 0 for all the states except these outcome states, where it is 1. The policy π underlying the option is the optimal policy for reaching the target hallway.

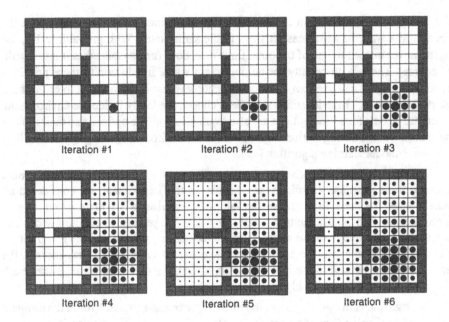

Fig. 3. Value iteration using primitive actions and higher-level options

The goal state can have an arbitrary position in any of the rooms, but for this illustration let us suppose that the goal is two steps down from the right hallway. The value of the goal state is 1, there are no rewards along the way, and the discounting factor is $\gamma = 0.9$. We performed planning again, according to the standard value iteration method, with the same setting as in the previous task.

When using only primitive actions, the values are propagated one step on each iteration. After six iterations, for instance, only the states that are within six steps of the goal are attributed non-zero values. Figure 3 shows the value function after each iteration, using all available options. The area of the circle drawn in each state is proportional to the value attributed to the state. The first three iterations are identical to the case in which only primitive actions are used. However, once the values are propagated to the first hallway, all the states in the rooms adjacent to the hallway receive values as well. For the states in the room containing the goal, these values correspond to performing the option of getting into the right hallway, and then following the optimal primitive actions to get to the goal. At this point, a path to the goal is known from each state in the right half of the environment, even if the path is not optimal for all the states. After six iterations, an optimal policy is known for all the states in the environment.

7 Discussion

Planning with multi-time models converges to correct solutions significantly faster than planning at the level of primitive actions. There are two intuitive reasons that justify this result. First, the temporal abstraction achieved by the models enables the agent to reason at a higher level. Second, the knowledge captured in the models only depends only on the MDP underlying the environment and on the option itself. The options and multi-time models can therefore be seen as an efficient means of transferring knowledge across different reinforcement learning tasks, as long as the dynamics of the environment are preserved.

Theoretical results similar to the ones presented in this paper are also available for planning in optimal stopping tasks [1], as well as for a different regime of executing options, which allows early termination. Further research will be devoted to integrating temporal and state abstraction, and to the issue of discovering useful options.

Acknowledgments

The authors thank Amy McGovern, Andy Fagg, Leo Zelevinsky, Manfred Huber and Ron Parr for helpful discussions and comments contributing to this paper. This research was supported in part by NSF grant ECS-9511805 to Andrew G. Barto and Richard S. Sutton, and by AFOSR grant AFOSR-F49620-96-1-0254 to Andrew G. Barto and Richard S. Sutton. Satinder Singh was supported by NSF grant IIS-9711753. Doina Precup also acknowledges the support of the Fulbright foundation.

References

1. Dimitri P. Bertsekas. *Dynamic Programming: Deterministic and Stochastic Models.* Prentice Hall, Englewood Cliffs, NJ, 1987.
2. Peter Dayan. Improving generalization for temporal difference learning: The successor representation. *Neural Computation*, 5:613–624, 1993.
3. Peter Dayan and Geoff E. Hinton. Feudal reinforcement learning. In *Advances in Neural Information Processing Systems*, volume 5, pages 271–278, Cambridge, MA, 1993. MIT Press.
4. Thomas G. Dietterich. Hierarchical reinforecement learning with maxq value function decomposition. Technical report, Computer Science Department, Oregon State University, 1997.
5. Manfred Huber and Roderic A. Grupen. Learning to coordinate controllers - reinforcement learning on a control basis. In *Proceedings of the Fifteenth International Joint Conference on Artificial Intelligence, IJCAI-97*, San Francisco, CA, 1997. Morgan Kaufmann.
6. Leslie P. Kaelbling. Hierarchical learning in stochastic domains: Preliminary results. In *Proceedings of the Tenth International Conference on Machine Learning ICML'93*, pages 167–173, San Mateo, CA, 1993. Morgan Kaufmann.
7. Richard E. Korf. *Learning to Solve Problems by Searching for Macro-Operators.* Pitman Publishing Ltd, London, 1985.
8. John E. Laird, Paul S. Rosenbloom, and Allan Newell. Chunking in SOAR: The anatomy of a general learning mechanism. *Machine Learning*, 1:11–46, 1986.
9. Sridhar Mahadevan and Jonathan Connell. Automatic programming of behavior-based robots using reinforcement learning. *Artificial Intelligence*, 55(2-3):311–365, 1992.
10. Amy McGovern, Richard S. Sutton, and Andrew H. Fagg. Roles of macro-actions in accelerating reinforcement learning. In *Grace Hopper Celebration of Women in Computing*, pages 13–18, 1997.
11. Andrew W. Moore and Chris G. Atkeson. Prioritized sweeping: Reinforcement learning with less data and less real time. *Machine Learning*, 13:103–130, 1993.
12. Ronald Parr and Stuart Russell. Reinforcement learning with hierarchies of machines. In *Advances in Neural Information Processing Systems*, volume 10, Cambridge, MA, 1998. MIT Press.
13. Jing Peng and John Williams. Efficient learning and planning within the Dyna framework. *Adaptive Behavior*, 4:323–334, 1993.
14. Doina Precup and Richard S. Sutton. Multi-Time models for temporally abstract planning. In *Advances in Neural Information Processing Systems*, volume 10, Cambridge, MA, 1998. MIT Press.
15. Martin L. Puterman. *Markov Decision Processes.* Wiley-Interscience, New York, NY, 1994.
16. Earl D. Sacerdoti. *A Structure for Plans and Behavior.* Elsevier, North-Holland, NY, 1977.
17. Satinder P. Singh. Scaling reinforcement learning by learning variable temporal resolution models. In *Proceedings of the Ninth International Conference on Machine Learning ICML'92*, pages 202–207, San Mateo, CA, 1992. Morgan Kaufmann.
18. Richard S. Sutton. Integrating architectures for learning, planning, and reacting based on approximating dynamic programming. In *Proceedings of the Seventh International Conference on Machine Learning ICML'90*, pages 216–224, San Mateo, CA, 1990. Morgan Kaufmann.
19. Richard S. Sutton. TD models: Modeling the world as a mixture of time scales. In *Proceedings of the Twelfth International Conference on Machine Learning ICML'95*, pages 531–539, San Mateo, CA, 1995. Morgan Kaufmann.
20. Richard S. Sutton and Andrew G. Barto. *Reinforcement Learning. An Introduction.* MIT Press, Cambridge, MA, 1998.
21. Richard S. Sutton and Brian Pinette. The learning of world models by connectionist networks. In *Proceedings of the Seventh Annual Conference of the Cognitive Science Society*, pages 54–64, 1985.
22. Christopher J. C. H. Watkins. *Learning with Delayed Rewards.* PhD thesis, Cambridge University, 1989.

A General Convergence Method for Reinforcement Learning in the Continuous Case

Rémi Munos

CEMAGREF, LISC, Parc de Tourvoie
BP 121, 92185 Antony Cedex, FRANCE
E-mail: Remi.Munos@cemagref.fr

Abstract. In this paper, we propose a general method for designing convergent Reinforcement Learning algorithms in the case of continuous state-space and time variables. The method is based on the discretization of the continuous process by convergent approximation schemes: the Hamilton-Jacobi-Bellman equation is replaced by a Dynamic Programming (DP) equation for some Markovian Decision Process (MDP).

If the data of the MDP were known, we could compute the value of the DP equation by using some DP updating rules. However, in the Reinforcement Learning (RL) approach, the state dynamics as well as the reinforcement functions are a priori unknown, leading impossible to use DP rules.

Here we prove a general convergence theorem which states that if the values updated by some RL algorithm are close enough (in the sense that they satisfy a "weak" contraction property) to those of the DP, then they converge to the value function of the continuous process. The method is very general and is illustrated with a model-based algorithm built from a finite-difference approximation scheme.

1 Introduction

This paper proposes a convergence result for Reinforcement Learning (RL) algorithms in the case of continuous state-space and time variables. RL uses the method of Dynamic Programming (DP) which defines the optimal feed-back control by approximating the *value function*, which is the best future cumulative reinforcement as a function of initial state.

A classical approach in optimal control for computing the value function consists in using approximation schemes (deduced from finite-element or finite-difference methods) which replace the continuous process by a discrete one (see [KD92]) for some given resolution. We obtain a finite Markovian Decision Process (MDP) whose DP equation may be computed by classical value iteration DP rules, knowing that (in the discounted case) the convergence of this method is guaranteed by some "strong" contraction property satisfied by the updated values.

However, in the RL approach, the state dynamics as well as the reinforcement functions are considered (at least partially) unknown from the system. Thus the values of the DP updating rule are unknown and the "strong" contraction property is no more valid.

This paper states that if this contraction property is weakened, we still have the convergence of the method as the resolution of the discretization tends to zero and the number of iterations tends to infinity. *This result allows approximation while keeping the convergence.* The theorem is very general and may apply for a wide class of RL algorithms such as model-based or model-free algorithms, with some "on-line" or "off-line" updating rule, for deterministic or stochastic state dynamics. We propose an example of model-based algorithm in the deterministic case whose values satisfy the "weak" contraction property, thus insuring its convergence.

Section 2 proposes the formalism for optimal control problems in the continuous case. The method of DP is described : the value function is introduced and the Hamilton-Jacobi-Bellman (HJB) equation is stated. A finite-difference approximation scheme is detailed and a theorem of convergence for the scheme is stated. *Section 3* is concerned with RL algorithms. The general theorem is stated and its proof is given. Then an example of model-based algorithm built from a finite-difference scheme is described and the proof that the computed values satisfy the "weak" contraction property is given in *appendix A*.

2 The Optimal Control Formalism

We illustrate our method in the particular case of *deterministic* controlled systems with *infinite time horizon* and *discounted reinforcement*. A study of the stochastic case may be found in [MB97].

Let $x(t) \in \bar{O}$ be the state of the system with O an open and bounded subset of $\mathbb{R}^d$. The evolution of the system (its *state dynamics f*) depends on the *current state* $x(t)$ and *control* $u(t)$; it is defined by a controlled differential equation :

$$\frac{d}{dt}x(t) = f(x(t), u(t)) \tag{1}$$

where the control $u(t)$ is a bounded, Lebesgue measurable function with values in a compact U. From any initial state x, the choice of a control $u(t)$ leads to a unique *trajectory* $x(t)$. Let τ be the *exit time* of $x(t)$ from $\bar{O}$ (with the convention that if $x(t)$ always stays in $\bar{O}$, then $\tau = \infty$). Then, we define the discounted reinforcement functional of state x, control $u(.)$:

$$J(x; u(.)) = \int_0^\tau \gamma^t r(x(t), u(t)) dt + \gamma^\tau R(x(\tau))$$

Where $r(x, u)$ is the *running reinforcement* and $R(x)$ the *boundary reinforcement*. γ is the *discount factor* $(0 \leq \gamma < 1)$.

The **objective of the control problem** is to find the optimal control (which can be expressed here as a feed-back law $u^*(x)$) that optimizes the reinforcement functional for any state x.

2.1 The Method of Dynamic Programming (DP)

The DP method computes the optimal control by introducing the *value function*, maximal value of the functional as a function of initial state x :

$$V(x) = \sup_{u(.)} J(x; u(.)) \tag{2}$$

Following the DP principle, we prove that the value function satisfies a first-order nonlinear partial differential equation called the *Hamilton-Jacobi-Bellman* equation (see [FS93] for a survey) (in the stochastic case, it is of a second order).

Theorem 1 : Hamilton-Jacobi-Bellman. *If V is differentiable at $x \in O$, let $DV(x)$ be the gradient of V at x, then the following HJB equation holds at x.*

$$V(x)\ln\gamma + \sup_{u\in U}[DV(x).f(x,u) + r(x,u)] = 0$$

Hypotheses 1 In the following, we assume that :
- f and r are bounded with M_f (respectively M_r) and Lipschitzian :
$|f(x,u) - f(y,u)| \le L_f \|x-y\|_1$ (resp. $|r(x,u) - r(y,u)| \le L_r \|x-y\|_1$),
with the norm $\|x\|_1 = \sum_{i=1}^{d} |x_i|$.
- R is Lipschitzian : $|R(x) - R(y)| \le L_R \|x-y\|_1$.
- The boundary ∂O is C^2.

Besides, we consider the following hypothesis concerning the state dynamics around the boundary, and we state a result of continuity for V (see [Bar94]).

Hypothesis 2 For all $x \in \partial O$, let $\vec{n}(x)$ be the outward normal of O at x, we assume that :
- If $\exists u \in U$, s.t. $f(x,u).\vec{n}(x) \le 0$ then $\exists v \in U$, s.t. $f(x,v)\vec{n}(x) < 0$.
- If $\exists u \in U$, s.t. $f(x,u).\vec{n}(x) \ge 0$ then $\exists v \in U$, s.t. $f(x,v)\vec{n}(x) > 0$.

Theorem 2 : Continuity. *Suppose that these hypotheses hold, then the value function is continuous in O.*

2.2 Approximation Schemes

In order to approximate the value function, we use the numerical schemes (for example based on finite-element (FE) or finite-differences (FD) methods) of Kushner [KD92], which replace the continuous problem by a discrete one. The HJB equation is discretized, for some resolution δ, by a DP equation for some MDP, whose value is V^δ. We state that the value V^δ of the approximation scheme converges to the value function V of the continuous process as the discretisation step δ tends to 0. As an illustration, we describe here the FD method.

Description of a FD scheme : Let $e_1, e_2, ..., e_d$ be a basis for $\mathbb{R}^d$. The state dynamics is : $f = (f_1, ..., f_d)$. Let the positive and negative parts of f_i be : $f_i^+ = \max(f_i, 0)$, $f_i^- = \max(-f_i, 0)$.

For any discretization step δ, we consider the lattice $\delta\mathbb{Z}^d = \left\{ \delta. \sum_{i=1}^d j_i e_i \right\}$ where $j_1, ..., j_d$ are any integers, and define :

- the **discretized state space** : $\Sigma^\delta = \delta\mathbb{Z}^d \cap O$ (see figure 1), and
- its **frontier** $\partial\Sigma^\delta = \{\xi \in \delta\mathbb{Z}^d \setminus \Sigma^\delta$, such that at least one adjacent points $\xi \pm \delta e_i \in O\}$

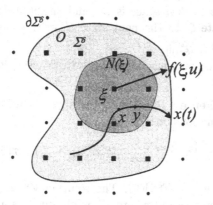

Fig. 1. The discretized state space Σ^δ (the square dots) and its frontier $\partial\Sigma^\delta$ (the round dots). A trajectory $x(t)$ crosses the neighbourhood $N(\xi)$ (in dark grey) of vertex ξ. Let 2 points of the trajectory $x = x(t_0)$ and $y = x(t_0 + \tau)$ be such that the control u is kept constant during $t \in [t_0, t_0 + \tau]$. Then we make the model $\widetilde{f}(\xi, u) = \frac{y-x}{\tau}$ of the state dynamics $f(\xi, u)$.

We approximate the control space U by some finite control spaces $U^\delta \subset U$ such that for $\delta \leq \delta'$ we have $U^{\delta'} \subset U^\delta$ and besides, $\overline{\cup_\delta U^\delta} = U$.

The FD approximation consists in discretizing the HJB equation by :

$$V^\delta(\xi) \ln \gamma + \sup_{u \in U^\delta} \left\{ \sum_{i=1}^d \left[f_i^+(\xi, u).\Delta_i^+ V^\delta(\xi) + f_i^-(\xi, u).\Delta_i^- V^\delta(\xi) \right] + r(\xi, u) \right\} = 0$$

(3)

where the gradient $DV(\xi)$ is replaced by the forward and backward difference quotients of V at ξ in direction $i = 1..d$:

$$\Delta_i^+ V(\xi) = \frac{1}{\delta} \left[V(\xi + \delta e_i) - V(\xi) \right]$$

$$\Delta_i^- V(\xi) = \frac{1}{\delta} \left[V(\xi - \delta e_i) - V(\xi) \right]$$

Knowing that $(\Delta t \ln \gamma)$ is an approximation of $(\gamma^{\Delta t} - 1)$ as Δt tends to 0, we obtain from (3) the following equivalent equation: for $\xi \in \Sigma^\delta$,

$$V^\delta(\xi) = \sup_{u \in U^\delta} \left\{ \gamma^{\tau(\xi, u)} \sum_{\xi'} p(\xi, \xi', u).V^\delta(\xi_i) + \tau(\xi, u)r(\xi, u) \right\} \qquad (4)$$

$$\text{with}: \tau(\xi, u) = \frac{\delta}{||f(\xi, u)||_1} \text{ and }: p(\xi, \xi', u) = \frac{f_i^\pm(\xi, u)}{||f(\xi, u)||_1} \text{ for } \xi' = \xi \pm \delta e_i \quad (5)$$
$$= 0 \text{ otherwise.}$$

This equation is a DP equation for a finite MDP (see [FS93]) whose *state space* is $\Sigma^\delta \cup \partial\Sigma^\delta$. Its *control space* is U^δ and the *probabilities of transition* $p(\xi, \xi', u)$ from the state ξ, to the next state ξ' with some control u are the normalized coordinates $\frac{|f_i(\xi, u)|}{||f(\xi, u)||_1}$.

Besides, we have the boundary condition $V^\delta(\xi) = R(\xi)$ for $\xi \in \partial\Sigma^\delta$.

Resolution of the scheme : By defining the approximation scheme F^δ, operator on the space of functions on Σ^δ :

$$F^\delta[W](\xi) = \sup_{u \in U^\delta} \left\{ \gamma^{\tau(\xi, u)} \sum_{\xi'} p(\xi, \xi', u).W(\xi_i) + \tau(\xi, u)r(\xi, u) \right\}, \qquad (6)$$

equation (4) becomes $V^\delta = F^\delta[V^\delta]$. The solution V^δ may be computed by some DP value iteration method where V^δ is obtained as a limit of successive iterations:

$$V_{n+1}^\delta \leftarrow F^\delta[V_n^\delta]. \qquad (7)$$

For any initial V_0^δ, we compute $V_1^\delta \leftarrow F^\delta[V_0^\delta]$, then $V_2^\delta \leftarrow F^\delta[V_1^\delta]$, and so on. Thank to the discounted factor γ, such updated values satisfy the following "strong" contraction property (with some $\lambda = 1 - \frac{\delta}{2M_f} \ln \frac{1}{\gamma}$):

$$\left\| V_{n+1}^\delta - V^\delta \right\|_{\Sigma^\delta \cup \partial\Sigma^\delta} \leq \lambda. \left\| V_n^\delta - V^\delta \right\|_{\Sigma^\delta \cup \partial\Sigma^\delta} \qquad (8)$$

(with $||.||_\Xi$ denoting $\sup_{\xi \in \Xi} |.|$), from which we deduce that for any given discretisation step δ, the constant $\lambda < 1$ thus the values V_n^δ converge to V^δ as n tends to infinity.

Convergence of the scheme The following theorem, whose proof uses the general convergence result of Barles (see [BS91] and [Bar94]) and the strong comparison result between sub- and super- viscosity solution (see [FS93]) of HJB equations, insures that V^δ is a convergent approximation of V.

Theorem 3 : Convergence of the scheme. *Let us assume that the hypotheses 1 and 2 hold, then V^δ converges to V as δ tends to 0 :*

$$\lim_{\substack{\delta \downarrow 0 \\ \xi \to x}} V^\delta(\xi) = V(x) \text{ uniformly on any compact } \Omega \subset O$$

Figure 2 summarizes the two previous results of convergence, which are : for any distretization step δ, the values V_n^δ computed by the DP updating rule (7) tend to the value V^δ of the DP equation (4) as n tends to infinity, and from the convergence of the scheme (theorem 3), V^δ tends to the value function V of the continuous process as δ tends to zero.

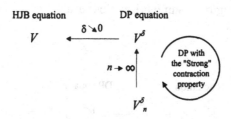

Fig. 2. The HJB equation is discretized, for some resolution δ, into a DP equation whose solution is V^δ. The convergence of the scheme insures that $V^\delta \to V$ as $V \to 0$. Thanks to the "strong" contraction property, the iterated values V_n^δ tend to V^δ as $n \to \infty$.

3 Reinforcement Learning

RL is a constructive and iterative process, based on experience, that intends to estimate the value function by successive approximations. Thus, **in the RL approach, we have the constraint that the state dynamics f and the reinforcement functions r, R are a priori unknown from the system.**

Thus the probabilities of transition $p(\xi, \xi', u)$ and the time $\tau(\xi, u)$ are unknown and have to be approximated. We deduce that the strong contraction property (8) cannot hold any more. However, we prove that if some weaker contraction property does hold, then we can obtain the convergence as well. The following section states the general convergence theorem for RL algorithms provided that the updated values satisfy some **"weak" contraction property**. *The statement of such "good approximations" satisfying this property is the basis for designing convergent algorithms.*

3.1 A general Theorem of Convergence

Theorem 4 : Convergence of RL algorithms. *Suppose that the values V_n^δ updated with some algorithm satisfy the following* **"weak" contraction property** *with respect to a solution V^δ of a convergent approximation scheme (such as (6)):*

$$\left\| V_{n+1}^\delta - V^\delta \right\|_{\Sigma^\delta} \leq (1 - k_1.\delta).\left\| V_n^\delta - V^\delta \right\|_{\Sigma^\delta} + e(\delta)\delta \tag{9}$$

$$\left\| V_{n+1}^\delta - V^\delta \right\|_{\partial \Sigma^\delta} \leq k_2.\delta \tag{10}$$

for some positive constants k_1, k_2 and some fonction $e(\delta) \searrow 0$ as $\delta \searrow 0$. Then for all $\varepsilon > 0$, there exists Δ and N, such that $\forall \delta \leq \Delta, \forall n \geq N$,

$$\sup_{\Sigma^\delta \cap \Omega} \left\| V_n^\delta - V \right\| \leq \varepsilon \text{ on any compact } \Omega \subset O.$$

Remark. Here, one cannot expect any more that for a given δ the values V_n^δ converge to V^δ. However the theorem states that the convergence occurs as $\delta \searrow 0$ and $n \to \infty$. Figure 3 summerizes this result.

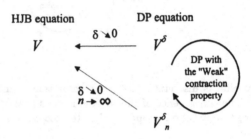

Fig. 3. When the "strong" contraction property property does not hold any more, one cannot expect that the computed values V_n^δ tend to V^δ. However, the theorem states that, thanks to the "weak" contraction property, the values V_n^δ tend to the value function V as $n \to \infty$ and $\delta \searrow 0$.

Proof of theorem 4. Let us denote $E_n^\delta = \left\| V_n^\delta - V^\delta \right\|_{\Sigma^\delta \cup \partial \Sigma^\delta}$. Let $\Omega \subset O$ be any compact. For any $\varepsilon > 0$, let us choose $\varepsilon_1 > 0$ and $\varepsilon_2 > 0$ such that $\varepsilon_1 + \varepsilon_2 = \varepsilon$. From the convergence of the scheme, theorem 3 states that there exists Δ_1 such that for all $\delta \leq \Delta_1, \sup_{x \in \Omega} |V^\delta(x) - V(x)| \leq \varepsilon_1$. The idea is to prove that there exists Δ_2, for $\delta \leq \Delta_2$, there exists N, for all $n \geq N$,

$$E_n^\delta \leq \varepsilon_2. \tag{11}$$

Then we will obtain that for any $\delta \leq \Delta = \min\{\Delta_1, \Delta_2\}$, for all $n \geq N$,

$$\sup_{\xi \in \Omega \cap \Sigma^\delta} |V_n^\delta(\xi) - V(\xi)| \leq \sup_{x \in \Omega} |V^\delta(x) - V(x)| + \sup_{\xi \in \Sigma^\delta \cup \partial \Sigma^\delta} |V_n^\delta(\xi) - V^\delta(\xi)|$$

$$\leq \varepsilon_1 + \varepsilon_2 = \varepsilon$$

A sufficient condition for (11) : Suppose that there exists a positive constant α such that the following conditions hold true:

$$\text{If } E_n^\delta > \varepsilon_2 \text{ then } \left\| V_{n+1}^\delta - V^\delta \right\|_{\Sigma^\delta} \leq E_n^\delta - \alpha \tag{12}$$

$$\text{If } E_n^\delta \leq \varepsilon_2 \text{ then } \left\| V_{n+1}^\delta - V^\delta \right\|_{\Sigma^\delta} \leq \varepsilon_2 \tag{13}$$

then we deduce that there exits N such that for $n \geq N$, $\left\|V_{n+1}^{\delta} - V^{\delta}\right\|_{\Sigma^{\delta}} \leq \varepsilon_2$.
Besides, from the property (10), for $\delta \leq \frac{\varepsilon_2}{k_2}$, $\left\|V_{n+1}^{\delta} - V^{\delta}\right\|_{\partial \Sigma^{\delta}} \leq \varepsilon_2$, thus $E_n^{\delta} \leq \varepsilon_2$.

Proof of the sufficient condition:

Let us prove that for all $\varepsilon_2 > 0$, there exists Δ_2 such that for all $\delta \leq \Delta_2$, conditions (12) and (13) are satisfied. For any $\varepsilon_2 > 0$, from the convergence of $e(\delta)$ to 0 as $\delta \downarrow 0$, there exists Δ_2 such that for $\delta \leq \Delta_2$ the following condition hold:

$$e(\delta) - k_1.\frac{\varepsilon_2}{2} \leq 0 \tag{14}$$

First, suppose that $E_n^{\delta} > \varepsilon_2$, then from (9),

$$\left\|V_{n+1}^{\delta} - V^{\delta}\right\|_{\Sigma^{\delta}} \leq (1 - k_1.\delta)E_n^{\delta} + e(\delta).\delta \leq E_n^{\delta} - k_1.\delta.\varepsilon_2 + e(\delta).\delta.$$

and from (14), $\left\|V_{n+1}^{\delta} - V^{\delta}\right\|_{\Sigma^{\delta}} \leq E_n^{\delta} - k_1.\delta.\frac{\varepsilon_2}{2} + e(\delta).\delta - k_1.\delta.\frac{\varepsilon_2}{2} \leq E_n^{\delta} - k_1.\delta.\frac{\varepsilon_2}{2}$.
Thus condition (12) hold true for $\alpha = k_1.\delta.\frac{\varepsilon_2}{2}$.

Now suppose that $E_n^{\delta} \leq \varepsilon_2$, then from (9),

$$\left\|V_{n+1}^{\delta} - V^{\delta}\right\|_{\Sigma^{\delta}} \leq (1 - k_1.\delta)\frac{\varepsilon_2}{2} + \frac{\varepsilon_2}{2} + e(\delta)\delta - k_1.\delta\frac{\varepsilon_2}{2} \leq \frac{\varepsilon_2}{2} + \frac{\varepsilon_2}{2} = \varepsilon_2$$

and condition (13) is true. Thus conditions (12) and (13) are true and for $\delta \leq \Delta = \min\{\Delta_1, \Delta_2, \frac{\varepsilon_2}{k_2}\}$, for all $n \geq N$, we have:

$$\sup_{\xi \in \Omega \cap \Sigma^{\delta}} |V_n^{\delta}(\xi) - V(\xi)| \leq \sup_{x \in \Omega} |V^{\delta}(x) - V(x)| + \sup_{\xi \in \Sigma^{\delta} \cup \partial \Sigma^{\delta}} |V_n^{\delta}(\xi) - V^{\delta}(\xi)|$$

$$\leq \varepsilon_1 + \varepsilon_2 = \varepsilon \quad \blacksquare$$

This theorem provides a general method for designing convergent RL algorithms. It may apply to model-free (see [Mun96] or [Mun97]) or model-based algorithms, with on-line or off-line (for example synchronous, Gauss-Seidel, asynchronous) DP updating methods, and for deterministic or stochastic dynamics.

3.2 An Example of Model-Based Algorithm

The idea is to build a model of the state dynamics f and of the reinforcement function r at the vertices ξ of the discretization from samples of trajectories going through their neighbourhood. Then, from this model, we define the approximated transition probabilities which are used, instead of the exact ones $p(\xi, \xi', u)$, in the updating rule (7).

In the following, we assume that the state dynamics f is bounded from below (there exists m_f such that $\|f\|_1 \geq m_f$).

- **Estimation for** $\xi \in \Sigma^{\delta}$: For any vertex $\xi \in \Sigma^{\delta}$, any control $u \in U^{\delta}$, we build a model $\tilde{f}$ and $\tilde{r}$, approximations of f and r from trajectories $x(t)$ going through the neighbourhood of ξ: we consider some states $x = x(t_0)$ and $y = x(t_0 + \tau)$ such that:
  - $x \in N(\xi)$ *neighbourhood* of ξ (whose diameter is inferior to $k_N.\delta$ for some positive constant k_N).

- the control u is kept constant for $t \in [t_0, t_0 + \tau]$,
- the time τ satisfies, for two positive constantes k_1 et k_2, the relation:

$$k_1 \delta \leq \tau \leq k_2 \delta. \tag{15}$$

See figure 1. Then we make the following model for state ξ and control u:

$$\widetilde{f}(\xi, u) = \frac{y - x}{\tau}$$

$$\widetilde{r}(\xi, u) = r(x, u)$$

Then we compute the approximated probabilities $\widetilde{p}(\xi, \xi', u)$ and time $\widetilde{\tau}(\xi, u)$ by using in the equations (5) the model $\widetilde{f}$ instead of f and obtain the following updating rule based on (7):

$$V_{n+1}^{\delta}(\xi) \leftarrow \gamma^{\widetilde{\tau}(\xi, u)} \cdot \sum_{\xi'} \widetilde{p}(\xi, \xi', u) . V_n^{\delta}(\xi') + \widetilde{\tau}(\xi, u) . \widetilde{r}(\xi, u) \tag{16}$$

which can be used as an "off-line" (synchronous, Gauss-Seidel, asynchronous) or "on-line" (for example by updating $V_n^{\delta}(\xi)$ as soon as a trajectory leaves the neighbourhood of ξ) updating DP method (see [BBS95]).

- **Estimation for $\xi \in \partial \Sigma^{\delta}$** : As soon as a trajectory $x(t)$ exits from the state space at $y \in \partial O$, we consider the states $\xi \in \partial \Sigma^{\delta}$ whose respective neighbourhoods $N(\xi)$ contain y and we update their value with:

$$V_{n+1}^{\delta}(\xi) \leftarrow R(y) \tag{17}$$

The following theorem states that the algorithm consisting in updating regularly all the states $\xi \in \Sigma^{\delta}$ with rule (16) and all states $\xi \in \partial \Sigma^{\delta}$ (at least once each) with (17) satisfies the "weak" contraction property (9) and (10) thus defines a convergent algorithm. The proof is given in *appendix A*.

Theorem 5. Convergence of the model-based, FD algorithm. *The updating rules (16) and (17) satisfy the "weak" contraction property (9) and (10) with respect to the convergent approximation scheme (6), thus the theorem 4 applies and the model-based FD algorithm is convergent.*

4 Conclusion

We proposed a framework for designing RL algorithms and proving their convergence. The method is very general since the only required property is the "weak" contraction property with respect to some convergent approximation scheme. The choice of such a numerical scheme is free and may come from any discretization method such as finite difference or finite element method, using a constant or a variable resolution. As an illustration, we proposed a very simple model-based algorithm build from a finite-difference approximation scheme and proved its convergence.

A Convergence of the Model-Based FD Algorithm

A.1 Some Majorations

Comparison of the times $\tau(\xi, u)$ and $\tilde{\tau}(\xi, u)$.
From the Lipschitz property of f, we have the following Taylor majoration:

$$\|y - x - f(x,u).\tau\|_1 \leq \tfrac{1}{2} L_f.\tau^2$$

Since the neighbourhood of ξ is of a diameter inferior to $k_N.\delta$, we have:

$$\|f(x,u) - f(\xi,u)\|_1 \leq L_f.\|x - \xi\|_1 \leq L_f k_N \delta.$$

But $\|y - x - f(\xi,u).\tau\|_1 = \|y - x - f(x,u).\tau + \tau[f(x,u) - f(\xi,u)]\|_1$, thus from (15), we have: $\|y - x - f(\xi,u).\tau\|_1 \leq \left(\tfrac{k_2}{2} + k_N\right) L_f k_2 \delta^2$. And because the state dynamics f is bounded from below by m_f and that $\tau \geq k_1\delta$, we have $\|y - x\|_1 \geq k_1 m_f \delta$, thus:

$$|\tau(\xi,u) - \tilde{\tau}(\xi,u)| \leq k_\tau \delta^2 \tag{18}$$

with: $k_\tau = \frac{(\frac{k_2}{2} + k_N) L_f k_2}{k_1 m_f^2}$. We deduce, by using a property of the exponential function that:

$$\left|\gamma^{\tau(\xi,u)} - \gamma^{\tilde{\tau}(\xi,u)}\right| \leq k_\tau \ln\frac{1}{\gamma}.\delta^2 \tag{19}$$

Comparison of the probabilities $p(\xi, \xi', v)$ and $\tilde{p}(\xi, \xi', v)$.
For $\xi' \neq \xi \pm \delta e_i$, $\tilde{p}(\xi, \xi', v) = p(\xi, \xi', v) = 0$ and for $\xi' = \xi \pm \delta e_i$, we have:

$$\left|\frac{\tilde{f}_i^\pm(\xi,u)}{\|\tilde{f}(\xi,u)\|_1} - \frac{f_i^\pm(\xi,u)}{\|f(\xi,u)\|_1}\right| \leq \frac{\left|\|\tilde{f}(\xi,u)\|_1 - \|f(\xi,u)\|_1\right| + \left|f_i^\pm(\xi,u) - \tilde{f}_i^\pm(\xi,u)\right|}{\|f(\xi,u)\|_1}$$

From what precedes, $\left\|\tilde{f}(\xi,u) - f(\xi,u)\right\|_1 \leq \left(\tfrac{k_2}{2} + k_N\right) L_f \delta$ and we deduce:

$$|\tilde{p}(\xi,\xi',v) - p(\xi,\xi',v)| \leq \frac{L_f}{m_f}(k_2 + 2k_N)\delta \tag{20}$$

A.2 Convergence of the Model-Based FD Algorithm

The value $V_n^\delta(\xi)$ is updated with:

$$V_{n+1}^\delta(\xi) \leftarrow \sup_{u \in U^\delta} \left\{ \gamma^{\tilde{\tau}(\xi,u)}.\sum_{\xi'} \tilde{p}(\xi,\xi',u).V_n^\delta(\xi') + \tilde{\tau}(\xi,u).\tilde{r}(\xi,u) \right\}$$

and its difference to the value V^δ of the scheme, is:

$$V^\delta(\xi) - V_{n+1}^\delta(\xi) = \sup_{u \in U^\delta} \left\{ \sum_{\xi'} \left[\gamma^{\tau(\xi,u)} p(\xi,\xi',u).V^\delta(\xi') - \gamma^{\tilde{\tau}(\xi,u)} \tilde{p}(\xi,\xi',u).V_n^\delta(\xi') \right] \right.$$
$$\left. + \tau(\xi,u).r(\xi,u) - \tilde{\tau}(\xi,u).\tilde{r}(\xi,u) \right\}$$

$$V^\delta(\xi) - V^\delta_{n+1}(\xi) = \sup_{u \in U^\delta} \left\{ \gamma^{\tau(\xi,u)} \sum_{\xi'} [p(\xi,\xi',u) - \widetilde{p}(\xi,\xi',u)] V^\delta(\xi') \right.$$

$$+ \left[\gamma^{\tau(\xi,u)} - \gamma^{\widetilde{\tau}(\xi,u)} \right] \sum_{\xi'} \widetilde{p}(\xi,\xi',u).V^\delta(\xi')$$

$$+ \gamma^{\widetilde{\tau}(\xi,u)} \sum_{\xi'} \widetilde{p}(\xi,\xi',u). \left[V^\delta(\xi') - V^\delta_n(\xi') \right]$$

$$+ \widetilde{\tau}(\xi,u) \left[r(\xi,u) - \widetilde{r}(\xi,u) \right] + \left[\tau(\xi,u) - \widetilde{\tau}(\xi,u) \right] r(\xi,u) \Big\}$$

And from (19), (18) and the Lipschtz property of r, we deduce:

$$\left| V^\delta(\xi) - V^\delta_{n+1}(\xi) \right| \leq \sup_{u \in U^\delta} \left\{ \gamma^{\tau(\xi,u)} . \left| \sum_{\xi'} [p(\xi,\xi',u) - \widetilde{p}(\xi,\xi',u)] V^\delta(\xi') \right| \right.$$

$$\left. + \gamma^{\widetilde{\tau}(\xi,u)} \sum_{\xi'} \widetilde{p}(\xi,\xi',u). \left| V^\delta(\xi') - V^\delta_n(\xi') \right| \right\} \qquad (21)$$

$$+ k_\tau \ln \frac{1}{\gamma} . M_{V^\delta} . \delta^2 + \frac{k_2 L_r}{k_1 m_f} \delta^2 + k_\tau M_r \delta^2 .$$

Majoration of $\sum_{\xi'} [p(\xi,\xi',u) - \widetilde{p}(\xi,\xi',u)] V^\delta(\xi')$:

We have: $V^\delta(\xi') = V^\delta(\xi) + \left[V^\delta(\xi') - V^\delta(\xi) \right]$. But from the properties of the probabilities $p(\xi,\xi',u)$ and $\widetilde{p}(\xi,\xi',u)$, we deduce:

$$\sum_{\xi'} [p(\xi,\xi',u) - \widetilde{p}(\xi,\xi',u)] V^\delta(\xi') = \sum_{\xi'} [p(\xi,\xi',u) - \widetilde{p}(\xi,\xi',u)] \left[V^\delta(\xi') - V^\delta(\xi) \right]$$

$$(22)$$

Moreover, $|V^\delta(\xi') - V^\delta(\xi)| \leq |V^\delta(\xi') - V(\xi')| + |V(\xi') - V(\xi)| + |V(\xi) - V^\delta(\xi)|$. From the theorem 3, the approximation error $\sup_\Omega |V^\delta - V|$ of the scheme tends to 0 as $\delta \downarrow 0$ for any compact $\Omega \subset O$ and thanks to the continuity of V (theorem 2), $\sup_{\substack{z \in \Omega \\ \|h\| \leq \delta}} |V(z) - V(z+h)|$ tends to 0 as $\delta \downarrow 0$.

We deduce: $|V^\delta(\xi') - V^\delta(\xi)| \leq \varepsilon(\delta)$,

with $\varepsilon(\delta) = 2\sup_{z \in \Omega} |V^\delta(z) - V(z)| + \sup_{\substack{z \in \Omega \\ \|h\| \leq \delta}} |V(z) - V(z+h)|$, which

tends to 0 as $\delta \downarrow 0$. From (22) and (20), we obtain:

$$\left| \sum_{\xi'} [p(\xi,\xi',u) - \widetilde{p}(\xi,\xi',u)] V^\delta(\xi') \right| \leq \frac{L_f}{m_f} (k_2 + 2k_N) \delta . \varepsilon(\delta) \qquad (23)$$

The "weak" contraction property (9) and (10) holds :

– Suppose that $\xi \in \Sigma^\delta$: from the property of the exponential function $\gamma^{\Delta t} \leq 1 - \frac{\Delta t}{2} \ln \frac{1}{\gamma}$ for Δt small enough, we deduce: $\gamma^{\widetilde{\tau}(\xi,u)} \leq 1 - \frac{\widetilde{\tau}(\xi,u)}{2} \ln \frac{1}{\gamma}$, thus $\gamma^{\widetilde{\tau}(\xi,u)} \leq 1 - \frac{\delta}{2M_f} \ln \frac{1}{\gamma}$ for small δ, and from (21) and (23) we deduce that:

$$\left| V^\delta_{n+1}(\xi) - V^\delta(\xi) \right| \leq (1 - k.\delta) E^\delta_n + e(\delta).\delta$$

$$\text{with}: k = \frac{1}{2M_f} \ln \frac{1}{\gamma}$$

$$\text{and}: e(\delta) = \frac{L_f}{m_f}(k_2 + 2k_N)\varepsilon(\delta) + k_\tau \ln \frac{1}{\gamma}.M_{V^\delta}.\delta + \frac{k_2 L_\tau}{k_1 m_f}\delta + k_\tau M_r \delta$$

Since $\varepsilon(\delta) \downarrow 0$ as $\delta \downarrow 0$, $e(\delta)$ also tends to 0 and the property (9) holds.
- Now suppose that $\xi \in \partial\Sigma^\delta$: from the Lipschitz property of R,

$$\left|V_{n+1}^\delta(\xi) - V^\delta(\xi)\right| = |R(y) - R(\xi)| \le L_R.\,\|y - \xi\| \le L_R.k_N.\delta$$

and the property (10) holds.

Thus the theorem 4 applies and the model-based FD algorithm is convergent. ∎

References

[Bar94] Guy Barles. *Solutions de viscosité des équations de Hamilton-Jacobi*, volume 17 of *Mathématiques et Applications*. Springer-Verlag, 1994.

[BBS95] Andrew G. Barto, Steven J. Bradtke, and Satinder P. Singh. Learning to act using real-time dynamic programming. *Artificial Intelligence*, (72):81–138, 1995.

[BS91] Guy Barles and P.E. Souganidis. Convergence of approximation schemes for fully nonlinear second order equations. *Asymptotic Analysis*, 4:271–283, 1991.

[FS93] Wendell H. Fleming and H. Mete Soner. *Controlled Markov Processes and Viscosity Solutions*. Applications of Mathematics. Springer-Verlag, 1993.

[KD92] Harold J. Kushner and Dupuis. *Numerical Methods for Stochastic Control Problems in Continuous Time*. Applications of Mathematics. Springer-Verlag, 1992.

[MB97] Rémi Munos and Paul Bourgine. Reinforcement learning for continuous stochastic control problems. *Neural Information Processing Systems*, 1997.

[Mun96] Rémi Munos. A convergent reinforcement learning algorithm in the continuous case : the finite-element reinforcement learning. *International Conference on Machine Learning*, 1996.

[Mun97] Rémi Munos. A convergent reinforcement learning algorithm in the continuous case based on a finite difference method. *International Joint Conference on Artificial Intelligence*, 1997.

Interpretable Neural Networks with BP-SOM

Ton Weijters[1], Antal van den Bosch[2], and Jaap van den Herik[3]

[1] Information Technology, Eindhoven University of Technology, The Netherlands
[2] ILK / Computational Linguistics, Tilburg University, The Netherlands
[3] Department of Computer Science, Universiteit Maastricht, The Netherlands

Abstract. Interpretation of models induced by artificial neural networks is often a difficult task. In this paper we focus on a relatively novel neural network architecture and learning algorithm, BP-SOM, that offers possibilities to overcome this difficulty. It is shown that networks trained with BP-SOM show interesting regularities, in that hidden-unit activations become restricted to discrete values, and that the SOM part can be exploited for automatic rule extraction.

1 Introduction

Nowadays artificial neural networks (ANNs) are successfully used in industry and commerce. However, the interpretation of ANNs is still an obstacle: "For ANNs to gain a even wider degree of user acceptance and to enhance their overall utility as learning and generalization tools, it is highly desirable if not essential that an *explanation capability* becomes an integral part of the functionality of a trained ANN."[ADT1995]. BP-SOM is an relatively novel neural network architecture and learning algorithm which overcomes the obstacle mentioned during the learning of classification tasks.

In earlier publications [Wei95, WVV97, WVVP97] experimental results were reported in which the generalization performances of BP-SOM were compared to two other learning algorithms for multi-layer feed-forward networks (MFNs), viz. BP and BPWD (BP augmented with *weight decay* [Hin86]). In this paper, we concentrate on interpreting two aspects of the typical knowledge representation of BP-SOM: (i) hidden-unit activations tend to end up oscillating between a limited number of discrete values, and (ii) the SOM can be seen as an organizer of the instances of the task at hand, dividing them into a limited number of subsets that are homogeneous with respect to their class labelling. Furthermore, we illustrate how dividing the learning material into a limited number of homogeneous subsets can be exploited for automatic rule extraction.

2 BP-SOM

Below we give a brief characterisation of the functioning of BP-SOM. For details we refer to [Wei95, WVV97, WVVP97]. The aim of the BP-SOM learning algorithm is to establish a cooperation between BP-learning and SOM-learning in order to find adequate hidden-layer representations for learning classification tasks. To achieve this aim, the traditional MFN architecture [RHW86] is combined with SOMs [Koh89]: each hidden layer of the MFN is associated with one SOM (see Figure 1). During training of the weights in the MFN, the corresponding SOM is trained on the hidden-unit activation patterns.

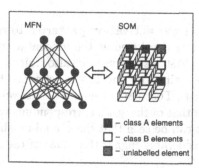

Fig. 1. An example BP-SOM network.

After a number of training cycles of BP-SOM learning, each SOM develops, to a certain extent, self-organisation, and translates this self-organisation into classification information, i.e., each SOM element is provided with a class label (one of the output classes of the task). For example, let the BP-SOM network displayed in Figure 1 be trained on a classification task which maps instances to either output class A or B. We can visually distinguish areas in the SOM: areas containing elements labelled with class A and class B, and areas containing unlabelled elements (no winning class could be found).

The self-organisation of the SOM is used as an addition to the standard BP learning rule [RHW86]. Classification and reliability information from the SOMs is included when updating the connection weights of the MFN (for more details, cf. [Wei95,WVV97, WVVP97]).

3 Knowledge representations in BP-SOM

In this section, knowledge representations of BP-SOM are compared to two related learning algorithms for MFNs, viz. BP [RWH86] and BPWD [Hin86] by training the three algorithms on the parity-12 classification task, i.e., to determine whether a bit string of 0's and 1's of length 12 contains an even number of 1's. The training set contains 1,000 instances selected at random (without replacement) out of the set of 4,096 possible bit strings. The test set and the validation set contain 100 other instances each.

For all experiments reported we have used a fixed set of parameters for the learning algorithms. The BP learning rate is set to 0.15 and the momentum to 0.4. In all SOMs a decreasing interaction strength from 0.15 to 0.05, and a decreasing neighbourhood-updating context from a square with maximally 9 units to only 1 unit (the winner) is used [Koh89].

The hidden layer of the MFN in all three algorithms contains 20 hidden units (the optimal number for a BP trained network), and the SOM in BP-SOM contained 7×7 elements. The algorithms are run with 10 different random weight initialisations. If we compare the average incorrectly-processed test instances of BP, BPWD, and BP-SOM, we see that BP-SOM performs significantly better (6.2%) than BP (27.4%) and BPWD (22.4%).

Clustering of hidden-layer activation patterns To visualise the differences among the representations developed at the hidden layers of the MFNs trained with BP, BPWD, and BP-SOM, respectively, we also trained SOMs with the hidden-layer activations of the trained BP and BPWD networks. Figure 2 visualises the class labelling of the SOMs. The SOM of the BP-SOM network is much more organised and clustered than that of the SOMs corresponding with the BP-trained and BPWD-trained MFNs. It can be seen that the overall reliability of the SOM of the BP-SOM network is considerably higher than that of the SOM of the BP-trained and BPWD-trained MFNs.

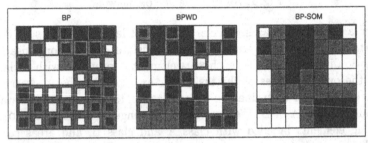

Fig. 2. Graphic representation of a 7×7 SOM: associated with a BP-trained MFN (left), with a BPWD-trained MFN (middle), and with a BP-SOM network (right). White squares represent class 'even'; black squares represent class 'odd'. The width of a square represents the reliability of the element; a square of maximal size represents a reliability of 100%.

Simplified hidden-unit activations When analysing the hidden-unit activations in BP-SOM networks, we observe two effects. Hidden-unit activations tend to culminate either (i) in having one stable activity with a very low variance or (ii) in oscillating between a limited number of approximately discrete values. This clearly contrasts with hidden unit activations in MFNs trained with BP, which usually display a high variance.

To illustrate the first effect, Figure 3 displays the standard deviation of the 20 hidden-unit activations of an MFN trained with BP (left), and MFN trained with BPWD (middle) and a BP-SOM network (right), each of them trained on the parity-12 task (1,000 instances). The standard deviations of ten out of twenty units in the BP-SOM network are equal to 0.01 or lower.

Whenever a unit has a stable activation with a low standard deviation for all training instances, it is redundant in the input-output mapping, and the unit can be pruned from the network. Using a stability threshold parameter s of 0.01 (units with a standard deviation below 0.01 are pruned), we found that BP-SOM

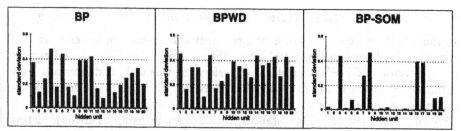

Fig. 3. Standard deviations of the activations of the 20 hidden units of a BP-trained MFN (left), a BPWD-trained MFN (middle), and a BP-SOM network (right), trained on the parity-12 task (1,000 instances).

was able to prune 12 out of 20 hidden units (averaged over 10 experiments), without loss of generalisation accuracy. With the same setting of s, trained on the same tasks, no hidden units could be pruned with BP, nor with BPWD.

To illustrate the second effect, viz. the oscillating of hidden-unit activations between a limited number of discrete values, one typical experiment with an MFN trained with BP-SOM on the parity-12 task is chosen as a sample. In this experiment, 12 out of the 20 hidden units were pruned, while the accuracy of the trained MFN on test material was still acceptable (classification error 0.59%). Figure 4 displays the activations of the first hidden unit of the BP-SOM-trained MFN (displayed on the y-axis), measured for each of the 4096 possible instances (displayed on the x-axis). The instances are grouped on the basis of their respective SOM clustering: we collected for each labelled SOM element all associated instances.

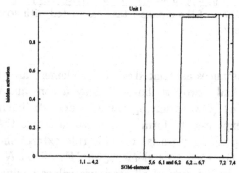

Fig. 4. Activations of the first hidden unit of a BP-SOM network, trained on the parity-12 task, on all 4096 possible instances. The x-axis orders the instances according to their clustering on SOM elements, indicated by the co-ordinates of the elements (e.g., 1,1 indicates SOM element (1,1)).

It can be seen from Figure 4 that the hidden unit ends up oscillating between a discrete number of values, depending on the SOM element on which instances are clustered. The activation values oscillate (approximately) between 0.0, 0.1, and 1.0. The same oscillating phenomenon is present in the activations of the other seven hidden units.

4 Automatic rule extraction based on SOM clustering

In this section we focus on automatic rule extraction based on the clustering of the SOM of a BP-SOM network trained on the monks-1 tasks [Thr91], and give an interpretation of BP-SOM's method of performing this task. Instances are characterised by six attributes $a1 \ldots a6$ which have two, three, or four discrete possible values. An instance is mapped to a class '1' if and only if $(a1 = a2)or(a5 = 1)$. The training set contains 124 instances; all 432 possible instances are used as test material. We used MFNs with one hidden layer of 5 units, 5×5-sized SOMs, and the same experimental settings as described earlier. We found that this network was able to arrive at 100% correct classifications of all instances. After training we collected for each labelled SOM element all associated training instances. Table 1 lists some instances associated with the SOM element at SOM co-ordinates (1,1).

a1	a2	a3	a4	a5	a6	Class
1 2 3	1 2 3	1 2	1 2 3	1 2 3 4	1 2	
1 0 0	1 0 0	0 1	0 1 0	1 0 0 0	0 1	1
1 0 0	1 0 0	0 1	0 1 0	1 0 0 0	1 0	1
1 0 0	1 0 0	0 1	0 1 0	0 1 0 0	1 0	1
1 0 0	1 0 0	0 1	0 1 0	0 1 0 0	0 1	1
1 0 0	1 0 0	0 1	0 1 0	0 0 1 0	1 0	1
1 0 0	1 0 0	0 1	1 0 0	0 0 0 1	0 1	1
1 0 0	1 0 0	0 1	1 0 0	0 0 0 1	1 0	1
...	...	...	...	...	...	...
1 0 0	1 0 0	1 0	0 0 1	0 0 0 1	0 1	1
1 0 0	1 0 0	1 0	0 0 1	0 1 0 0	0 1	1
1 0 0	1 0 0	1 0	0 0 1	0 1 0 0	1 0	1
1 0 0	1 0 0	1 0	0 1 0	0 0 1 1	1 0	1
1 0 0	1 0 0	1 0	0 1 0	0 0 0 1	0 1	1
1 0 0	1 0 0	1 0	0 0 1	1 0 0 0	1 0	1
1 0 0	1 0 0	1 0	0 0 1	1 0 0 0	0 1	1

Table 1. List of instances of the monks-1 task associated with SOM element (1,1) of a trained BP-SOM network.

The subset of instances associated with this element are all classified as '1'. More interestingly, only two attributes display a constant value in the subset, viz. attributes $a1$ (always having value 1) and $a2$ (having value 1). This regularity can be exploited to form a rule, which states that if $a1 = 1$ and $a2 = 1$, the corresponding class is '1'. This rule extraction procedure is formalised as follows. For each SOM element, an $IF \ldots THEN$ rule is extracted; it is composed of a conjunction of all attribute values having a constant value throughout the instance subset associated (they are concatenated on the left-hand side of the rule), and of the classification of the instances (on the right-hand side). This procedure, when applied to SOM element (1,1), leads to the rule IF $(a1 = 1)$ & $(a2 = 1)$ $THEN$ class= 1. Application of this procedure to all labelled SOM elements results in the rules listed in Table 2. The rules are arranged on the basis of the number of (in)equalities in them. Applying these rules results in a 100% correct classification.

SOM element	rule	coverage	reliability
(1,1)	IF (a1=1 and a2=1) THEN class=1	48	100
(1,5)	IF (a1=2 and a2=3 and a5=1) THEN class=1	12	100
(4,5)	IF (a1=3 and a2=2 and a5=1) THEN class=1	12	100
(5,3)	IF (a1=2 and a2=3 and a5 $\neq$ 1) THEN class=0	36	100
(5,5)	IF (a1=3 and a2=3 and a5 $\neq$ 1) THEN class=0	36	100
(1,4)	IF (a1 $\neq$ 2 and a2 $\neq$ 3 and a5=1) THEN class=1	24	100
(2,5)	IF (a1 $\neq$ 1 and a2 $\neq$ 1 and a5=1) THEN class=1	24	100
(1,3)	IF (a1 $\neq$ 3 and a2 $\neq$ 2 and a5=1) THEN class=1	24	100
(3,1),(3,2)	IF (a1 $\neq$ 2 and a2 $\neq$ 3 and a5 $\neq$ 1) THEN class=0	72	100
(3,4),(3,5)	IF (a1 $\neq$ 1 and a2 $\neq$ 1 and a5 $\neq$ 1) THEN class=0	72	100
(5,1)	IF (a1 $\neq$ 3 and a2 $\neq$ 2 and a5 $\neq$ 1) THEN class=0	72	100
	Totals	433	100

Table 2. The eleven different IF − THEN-rules extracted from the monks-1 training instances matching the same SOM-elements.

5 Conclusions

By letting BP and SOM learning cooperate, BP-SOM can arrive at interpretable MFNs in which both hidden unit activations and SOM clustering display more structure and organisation than with BP. BP-SOM constitutes a basis for automatic rule extraction by means of its ability to structure the data in relevant, task-specific instance subsets. It does so automatically, without the need for postprocessing discretisation or normalisation methods.

References

[ADT95] Andrews, R., Diederich, J., and Tickle, A. B. (1995). A Survey And Critique of Techniques for Extracting Rules from Trained Artificial Neural Networks. *Knowledge Based System*, 8:6, 373–389.

[Hin86] Hinton, G. E. (1986). Learning distributed representations of concepts. In *Proceedings of the Eighth Annual Conference of the Cognitive Science Society*, 1–12. Hillsdale, NJ: Erlbaum.

[Koh89] Kohonen, T. (1989). *Self-organisation and Associative Memory*. Berlin: Springer Verlag.

[RHW86] Rumelhart, D. E., Hinton, G. E., and Williams, R. J. (1986). Learning internal representations by error propagation. In D. E. Rumelhart and J. L. McClelland (Eds.), *Parallel Distributed Processing*, Vol. 1: Foundations (pp. 318–362). Cambridge, MA: The MIT Press.

[Thr91] Thrun, S. B., et. al (1991). *The MONK's Problems: a performance comparison of different learning algorithms*. Technical Report CMU-CS-91-197, Carnegie Mellon University.

[Wei95] Weijters, A. (1995). The BP-SOM architecture and learning rule. *Neural Processing Letters*, 2, 13–16.

[WVV97] Weijters, A., Van den Bosch, A., Van den Herik, H. J. (1997). Behavioural Aspects of Combining Backpropagation Learning and Self-organizing Maps. *Connection Science*, 9, 235–252.

[WVVP97] Weijters, A., Van den Herik, H. J., Van den Bosch, A., and Postma, E. O. (1997). Avoiding overfitting with BP-SOM. *Proceedings of the Fifteenth International Joint Conference on Artificial Intelligence*, IJCAI'97, San Francisco, Morgan Kaufmann, 1140–1145.

Convergence Rate of Minimization Learning for Neural Networks

Marghny H. Mohamed, Teruya Minamoto, and Koichi Niijima

Kyushu University, Department of Informatics, Fukuoka, Kasuka 816, Japan,
Phone:+81-92-583-7635, Fax: +81-92-583-7635,
e-mail: mohamed@i.kyushu-u.ac.jp

Abstract. In this paper, we present the convergence rate of the error in a neural network which was learnt by a constructive method. The constructive mechanism is used to learn the neural network by adding hidden units to this neural network. The main idea of this work is to find the eigenvalues of the transformation matrix concerning the error before and after adding hidden units in the neural network. By using the eigenvalues, we show the relation between the convergence rate in neural networks without and with thresholds in the output layer.

1 Introduction

The size of a hidden layer in multilayer neural networks is one of the most important considerations when solving actual problems using the networks. There are many methods to reduce the structure of the networks such as destructive, constructive, and genetic algorithms (Weymaere and Martens, 1994).

Destructive or pruning methods start from a fairly large network and remove unimportant connections or units (Hassibi and Stork, 1993). Constructive or growth methods start from a small network and dynamically grow the network (Giles, Chen, Sun, Chen, Lee and Goudreau, 1995; Niijima et al., 1997). Constructive learning algorithms were used to handle multi-category classification with convergence to zero classification errors (Parekh et al., 1995). The advantage in using this method is that it can automatically find the size and the topology of the neural network without specifying them before training.

In the paper (Niijima et al., 1997), we proposed a learning algorithm which is carried out by mininmizing the erreor function to determine the topology of the neural network. This paper describes the convergence rate of our method. This analysis is carried out by finding the transformation matrix concerning the error before and after adding hidden units in the neural network. The key idea is to find the eigenvalues of this matrix. We consider two types of neural network without and with thresholds in the output layer.

413

2 Convergence Rate in a Neural Network without Thresholds in the Output Layer

We consider a neural network which consists of an input layer with $n+1$ nodes, a hidden layer with h units, and an output layer with l units:

$$y_i = g\left(\sum_{j=1}^{h} w_{ij} f\left(\sum_{k=1}^{n+1} v_{jk} x_k\right)\right), \quad i = 1, 2, \ldots, l, \tag{1}$$

where x_k indicates the k-th input value, y_i the i-th output value, v_{jk} a weight connecting the k-th input node with the j-th hidden unit, and w_{ij} a weight between the j-th hidden unit and the i-th output unit. The functions $f(t)$ and $g(t)$ are given by $f(t) = (1 - \exp(-t))/(1 + \exp(-t))$ and $g(t) = 1/(1 + \exp(-t))$, respectively. We write (1) as $y = g(Wf(Vx))$, where we set $x = {}^t(x_1, x_2, \ldots, x_n, x_{n+1})$ with $x_{n+1} = -1$, $y = {}^t(y_1, y_2, \ldots, y_l)$, $V = (v_{jk})$ and $W = (w_{ij})$. This network is shown in Fig.1 (a). Let $(x^\nu, y^\nu), \nu = 1, 2, \ldots, m$, be training data for the network. We define an output error between the outputs of the network for the inputs x^ν and the relevant outputs y^ν by

$$J(V, W) = \sum_{\nu=1}^{m} \|g^{-1}(y^\nu) - Wf(Vx^\nu)\|^2, \tag{2}$$

where $g^{-1}(y^\nu) = {}^t(g^{-1}(y_1^\nu), g^{-1}(y_2^\nu), \ldots, g^{-1}(y_l^\nu))$ with the inverse function $g^{-1}(s)$ of $s = g(t)$, and $\|\cdot\|$ stands for the Euclidean norm. To determine V and W, we need to minimize the error function (2).

The paper (Niijima et al., 1997) presents a technique for determining the weights V and W successively by adding one unit to the hidden layer of this network. Let $\mathbf{v}$ denote a connection weight vector between the $(h+1)$-th hidden unit and the input layer, and let $\mathbf{w}$ be a weight vector connecting the $(h+1)$-th hidden unit with the output layer. The neural network after adding the $(h+1)$-th hidden unit is shown in Fig.1 (b). We denote the weight matrices $(V, \mathbf{v})$ and $(W, \mathbf{w})$ by $\widetilde{V}$ and $\widetilde{W}$, respectively. Then a new error function can be written as

$$J(\widetilde{V}, \widetilde{W}) = \sum_{\nu=1}^{m} \|g^{-1}(y^\nu) - \widetilde{W}f(\widetilde{V}x^\nu)\|^2.$$

We describe how to determine the added weight vector $\mathbf{w}$. Since

$$\widetilde{W}f(\widetilde{V}x^\nu) = Wf(Vx^\nu) + \mathbf{w}f(\mathbf{v}x^\nu),$$

the error function can be written as follows:

$$J(\widetilde{V}, \widetilde{W}) = J(V, W) - 2\langle d, \mathbf{w}\rangle + a\|\mathbf{w}\|^2 \tag{3}$$

in which d and a denote $d = \sum_{\nu=1}^{m} f(\mathbf{v}x^\nu)c^\nu$ and $a = \sum_{\nu=1}^{m} f^2(\mathbf{v}x^\nu)$, where $c^\nu = g^{-1}(y^\nu) - Wf(Vx^\nu)$ and the symbol $\langle\cdot,\cdot\rangle$ indicates an inner product in R^l.

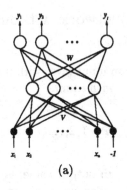 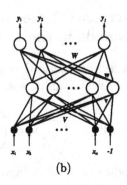

(a)   (b)

Fig. 1. (a) Neural network without thresholds in its output layer. (b) Neural network after adding one unit in the hidden layer in (a)

When the vector $\mathbf{v}$ is fixed, the vector $\mathbf{w}$ which minimizes the error function (3) is given by $\mathbf{w} = d/a$. So the error after adding a hidden unit can be expressed as

$$\tilde{c}^\nu = c^\nu - \frac{d}{a}f(\mathbf{v}x^\nu).$$

Furthermore, let ${}^t\widetilde{C_i} = (c_i^1, c_i^2, \ldots, c_i^m)$, ${}^tC_i = (c_i^1, c_i^2, \ldots, c_i^m)$ and ${}^tS = (s_1, s_2, \ldots, s_m)$ with $s_\nu = f(\mathbf{v}x^\nu)$ and so we can get

$$ {}^t\widetilde{C_i} = {}^tC_i\left(E_m - \frac{1}{a}S\,{}^tS\right) = {}^tC_i\Gamma_1(\mathbf{v}),$$

where $\Gamma_1(\mathbf{v}) = E_m - S\,{}^tS/a$ and E_m is the unit matrix. The matrix $\Gamma_1(\mathbf{v})$ is symmetric and has various remarkable characterizations as in the following theorem.

Theorem 1. *The matrix $\Gamma_1(\mathbf{v})$ satisfies $0 \le \langle \Gamma_1(\mathbf{v})U, U \rangle \le \|U\|^2$ and the eigenvalues λ_j of this matrix are given by*

$$\lambda_1 = 1, \quad \lambda_2 = 1, \ldots, \lambda_{m-1} = 1, \quad \lambda_m = 0.$$

The proof can be found in (Mohamed, et al., 1997). These eigenvalues mean that the convergence rate of errors before and after adding hidden units is not depending on the connection weights $\mathbf{v}$ between the hidden layer and input layer.

3 Convergence Rate in a Neural Network with Thresholds in the Output Layer

We consider the network with thresholds $\theta_i, i = 1, 2 \ldots, l$, in its output layer as shown in Fig.2 (c). In this case, we can write

$$y_i = g\left(\sum_{j=1}^h w_{ij} f\left(\sum_{k=1}^{n+1} v_{jk}x_k\right) - \theta_i\right), \quad i = 1, 2, \ldots, l$$

whose simple form is $y = g(Wf(Vx) - \theta)$, where $\theta = (\theta_1, \theta_2, \ldots, \theta_l)$. The error function related to the present network takes the following form

$$J(V, W, \theta) = \sum_{\nu=1}^{m} \|g^{-1}(y^\nu) - Wf(Vx^\nu) + \theta\|^2.$$

We add one unit to the hidden layer and represent new weight vectors again by **v** and **w**. By adding one hidden unit, the threshold vector θ must be changed. We denote a new threshold by $\tilde{\theta}$ and write as $\tilde{\theta} = \theta + \Delta\theta$. The network after adding one hidden unit is shown in Fig.2 (d). The error function related to this network can be expressed as

$$J(\tilde{V}, \tilde{W}, \tilde{\theta}) = \sum_{\nu=1}^{m} \|g^{-1}(y^\nu) - \tilde{W}f(\tilde{V}x^\nu) + \tilde{\theta}\|^2,$$

where we have used again the symbols $\tilde{V} = (V, \mathbf{v})$ and $\tilde{W} = (W, \mathbf{w})$.

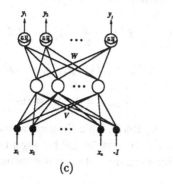
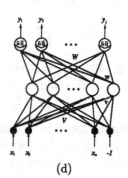

(c) (d)

Fig. 2. (c) Neural network with thresholds in its output layer. (d) Neural network after adding one unit in the hidden layer in (c)

The same procedure as in the previous section will be applied in order to determine **w** and $\Delta\theta$ so that $J(\tilde{V}, \tilde{W}, \tilde{\theta})$ is minimum. Since $\tilde{W}f(\tilde{V}x^\nu) = Wf(Vx^\nu) + \mathbf{w}f(\mathbf{v}x^\nu)$ and $\tilde{\theta} = \theta + \Delta\theta$, we can decompose the error function $J(\tilde{V}, \tilde{W}, \tilde{\theta})$ as

$$J(\tilde{V}, \tilde{W}, \tilde{\theta}) = J(V, W, \theta) - 2\sum_{\nu=1}^{m} f(\mathbf{v}x^\nu)\langle q^\nu + \Delta\theta, \mathbf{w}\rangle$$

$$+ \sum_{\nu=1}^{m} f^2(\mathbf{v}x^\nu)\|\mathbf{w}\|^2 + 2\sum_{\nu=1}^{m}\langle\Delta\theta, q^\nu\rangle + \sum_{\nu=1}^{m}\|\Delta\theta\|^2,$$

where

$$q^\nu = g^{-1}(y^\nu) - Wf(Vx^\nu) + \theta .$$

By minimizing this error function, we can easily determine **w** and $\Delta\theta$ as

$$\mathbf{w} = \frac{md_1 - a_2 d_2}{b}, \quad \Delta\theta = \frac{a_2 d_1 - a_1 d_2}{b}, \tag{4}$$

416

where $a_1 = \sum_{\nu=1}^{m} f^2(\mathbf{v}x^{\nu})$, $a_2 = \sum_{\nu=1}^{m} f(\mathbf{v}x^{\nu})$, $d_1 = \sum_{\nu=1}^{m} f(\mathbf{v}x^{\nu})q^{\nu}$, $d_2 = \sum_{\nu=1}^{m} q^{\nu}$, and $b = ma_1 - a_2^2$. Now we consider the convergence rate of the error as in the previous section. Since

$$\widetilde{q}^{\nu} = q^{\nu} - \mathbf{w}f(\mathbf{v}x^{\nu}) + \Delta\theta,$$

we can write the error at the i-th component in the output layer as

$$\widetilde{q}_i^{\nu} = q_i^{\nu} - \mathbf{w}_i f(\mathbf{v}x^{\nu}) + \Delta\theta_i. \tag{5}$$

From (4), the i-th component of $\mathbf{w}$ and $\Delta\theta$ can be written as

$$\mathbf{w}_i = {}^t Q_i \left[\frac{m}{b}S - \frac{a_2}{b}\mathbf{1}\right], \quad \Delta\theta_i = {}^t Q_i \left[\frac{a_2}{b}S - \frac{a_1}{b}\mathbf{1}\right],$$

where ${}^t\widetilde{Q}_i = (\widetilde{q}_i^1, \widetilde{q}_i^2, \ldots, \widetilde{q}_i^m)$, ${}^t Q_i = (q_i^1, q_i^2, \ldots, q_i^m)$, ${}^t S = (s_1, s_2, \ldots, s_m)$, and ${}^t\mathbf{1} = (1,1,\ldots,1)$ with $s_{\nu} = f(\mathbf{v}x^{\nu})$. Hence, we have by (5),

$${}^t\widetilde{Q}_i = {}^t Q_i [E_m - \frac{m}{b}S\,{}^tS + \frac{a_2}{b}\mathbf{1}\,{}^tS + \frac{a_2}{b}S\,{}^t\mathbf{1} - \frac{a_1}{b}\mathbf{1}\,{}^t\mathbf{1}] = {}^t Q_i \Gamma_2(\mathbf{v}).$$

Theorem 2. *The matrix $\Gamma_2(\mathbf{v})$ satisfies $-\|U\|^2 \le \langle \Gamma_2(\mathbf{v})U, U\rangle \le \|U\|^2$ and the eigenvalues λ_j of this matrix are given by*
$$\lambda_1 = 1, \quad \lambda_2 = 1, \ldots, \lambda_{m-2} = 1, \quad \lambda_{m-1} = 0, \quad \lambda_m = 0.$$

The proof can be found in (Mohamed, et al., 1997). This theorem show that the error after determining the weight $\mathbf{w}$ and the correction $\Delta\theta$ between the hidden unit and output layer converges and its convergence rate is not depending on $\mathbf{v}$.

4 Simulations

Based on the proposed algorithm (Niijima, et al., 1997), we constructed a neural network without and with thresholds for 40 pictures, part of them are illustrated below. A summary of the number of hidden units generated for each pattern with 30% added noise appears in Tab.1 and 2 for the network without and with thresholds, respectively. From these results we see that the network with thresholds performs better than without thresholds.

Fig. 3. Part of the memorized patterns

Table 1. Simulation results for the neural network in Sect.2

6	10	2	5	9	4	7	3	7	9	8	2	7	5	5	3	5	6	10	7
x^1	x^2	x^3	x^4	x^5	x^6	x^7	x^8	x^9	x^{10}	x^{11}	x^{12}	x^{13}	x^{14}	x^{15}	x^{16}	x^{17}	x^{18}	x^{19}	x^{20}
6	8	7	5	4	7	5	6	10	5	5	7	4	10	3	5	8	8	5	4
x^{21}	x^{22}	x^{23}	x^{24}	x^{25}	x^{26}	x^{27}	x^{28}	x^{29}	x^{30}	x^{31}	x^{32}	x^{33}	x^{34}	x^{35}	x^{36}	x^{37}	x^{38}	x^{39}	x^{40}

Table 2. Simulation results for the neural network in Sect.3

6	10	4	7	6	3	6	3	8	8	5	4	5	5	1	4	5	4	8	3
x^1	x^2	x^3	x^4	x^5	x^6	x^7	x^8	x^9	x^{10}	x^{11}	x^{12}	x^{13}	x^{14}	x^{15}	x^{16}	x^{17}	x^{18}	x^{19}	x^{20}
4	4	7	6	4	3	5	4	6	5	2	7	4	10	3	5	6	9	2	7
x^{21}	x^{22}	x^{23}	x^{24}	x^{25}	x^{26}	x^{27}	x^{28}	x^{29}	x^{30}	x^{31}	x^{32}	x^{33}	x^{34}	x^{35}	x^{36}	x^{37}	x^{38}	x^{39}	x^{40}

5 Conclusion

In this paper, we presented a novel approach to extract the convergence rate for neural networks which were learnt by a constructive method. This approach is carried out by finding the eigenvalues of the transformation matrix concerning the error before and after adding hidden units. The results show that this error is convergent in both networks without and with thresholds in the output layer, and not depending on the connection weights between the hidden layer and input layer. Moreover, the performance of the network with thresholds is better than that without thresholds in its output layer.

References

[1] Giles, C.J., Chen, D., Sun, G., Chen, H., Lee, Y., and Goudreau, M.W.: Constructive learning of recurrent neural networks: Limitations of recurrent cascade correlation and a simple solution. IEEE Trans. Neural Networks. 6(1)(1995) 829–836
[2] Hassibi, B., Stork, D. G.: Second order derivatives for network pruning: Optimal brain surgeon. In S.J. Hanson, J.D.Cowan, C.L. Giles (Eds.). Advances in Neural Information Processing Systems. 5(1993) 164–171, San Mateo, CA: Morgan Kaufmann
[3] Mohamed, H.M., Minamoto, T., and Niijima, K.: Convergence rate of minimization learning for neural networks. DOI Technical Report, DOI-TR-141, Kyushu University, (1997)
[4] Niijima, K., Yamada, M., Mohamed,H.M., Akanuma, T., Minamoto, T., and Ohkubo, A.: Minimization learning of neural networks by adding hidden units. Research Reports on Information Science and Electrical Engineering of Kyushu University. 2(2)(1997) 173–178
[5] Parekh, R., Yang, J., Honavar, V.: Constructive Neural Networks Learning Algorithms for Multi-Category Pattern Classification. Technical Report TR95-15, AI Research Group, Dept. of Computer Science, Iowa State University
[6] Weymaere, N., and Martens, J.: On the initialization and optimization of multilayer perceptrons. IEEE Trans. Neural Networks. 5(5)(1994) 738-751

Author Index

Springer
and the
environment

At Springer we firmly believe that an
international science publisher has a
special obligation to the environment,
and our corporate policies consistently
reflect this conviction.
We also expect our business partners –
paper mills, printers, packaging
manufacturers, etc. – to commit
themselves to using materials and
production processes that do not harm
the environment. The paper in this
book is made from low- or no-chlorine
pulp and is acid free, in conformance
with international standards for paper
permanency.

Springer

Lecture Notes in Artificial Intelligence (LNAI)

Lecture Notes in Computer Science